"All the main churches of the UK have 'mission' high on t'   ˙ at the
moment—mostly in the sense of 'missional church'   ˙hael
W. Stroope's findings that 'mission' is a late us˙   ˙d
premodern Christian literature—will ce˙
much is invested in mission, this in-˙   ˙ discourse and rhetoric is essential reac
Kirsteen Kim, professor of theology and v   ˙iversity, UK

"In conference after conference, in conversa   ˙ation, the question ine-
vitably surfaces: *Should we abandon the wo.*   . ˙ This is the question that
Michael Stroope asks in this volume. His answ   ˙s affirmative. Perhaps the word
'mission' has run its course, and in its place we should substitute the phrase 'pilgrim
witness to the kingdom.' Not everyone will agree, and not everyone will fully accept
the new language that he proposes. Nevertheless, Michael Stroope has taken the risk
of a frank discussion and a fresh proposal. This work should provoke a lively and
creative debate, one that will no doubt transcend the present impasse."
Stephen Bevans, Catholic Theological Union

Transcending

THE ECLIPSE OF A

MODERN TRADITION

MICHAEL W. STROOPE

IVP Academic

An imprint of InterVarsity Press
Downers Grove, Illinois

InterVarsity Press
P.O. Box 1400, Downers Grove, IL 60515-1426
ivpress.com
email@ivpress.com

InterVarsity Press® is the book-publishing division of InterVarsity Christian Fellowship/USA®, a movement of students and faculty active on campus at hundreds of universities, colleges, and schools of nursing in the United States of America, and a member movement of the International Fellowship of Evangelical Students. For information about local and regional activities, visit intervarsity.org.

All Scripture quotations, unless otherwise indicated, are taken from the New American Standard Bible®, copyright 1960, 1962, 1963, 1968, 1971, 1972, 1973, 1975, 1977, 1995 by The Lockman Foundation. Used by permission.

While any stories in this book are true, some names and identifying information may have been changed to protect the privacy of individuals.

Cover design: David Fassett
Interior design: Dan van Loon

ISBN 978-0-8308-5167-6 (print)
ISBN 978-0-8308-8225-0 (digital)

Printed in the United States of America ♾

Library of Congress Cataloging-in-Publication Data

Names: Stroope, Michael W., author.
Title: Transcending mission : the eclipse of a modern tradition / Michael W.
  Stroope.
Description: Downers Grove : InterVarsity Press, 2017. | Includes index.
Identifiers: LCCN 2016046968 (print) | LCCN 2016056722 (ebook) | ISBN
  9780830851676 (pbk. : alk. paper) | ISBN 9780830882250 (eBook)
Subjects: LCSH: Missions.
Classification: LCC BV2061.3 .S774 2017 (print) | LCC BV2061.3 (ebook) | DDC
  266--dc23
LC record available at https://lccn.loc.gov/2016046968

P	23	22	21	20	19	18	17	16	15	14	13	12	11	10	9	8	7	6	5	4	3	2	1
Y	34	33	32	31	30	29	28	27	26	25	24	23	22	21	20	19	18	17					

To students past and present

For Lilias, Silas, Micah, Violet, and Ian

Contents

Abbreviations

AIL   *The Autobiography of St. Ignatius Loyola.* Translated by Joseph F. O'Callaghan. New York: Fordham University Press, 1992.

CSJ   *The Constitutions of the Society of Jesus.* Translated by George E. Ganss. St. Louis: Institute of Jesuit Sources, 1970.

HCM   Stephen Neill. *A History of Christian Missions.* 2nd ed. London: Penguin Books, 1986.

HEC   K. S. Latourette. *A History of the Expansion of Christianity.* 7 vols. Grand Rapids: Zondervan, 1970

RM   *Re-thinking Missions: A Laymen's Inquiry After One Hundred Years.* Edited by William Ernest Hocking. New York: Harper & Brothers, 1932.

SE   George E. Ganss, SJ. *The Spiritual Exercises of Saint Ignatius. A Translation and Commentary.* Chicago: Loyola University Press, 1992.

SJ   *The Spiritual Journal of St. Ignatius Loyola, 1544–1545.* Translated by William J. Young. Woodstock, MA: Woodstock College Press, 1958.

TM   David Bosch. *Transforming Mission: Paradigm Shifts in Theology of Mission.* Maryknoll, NY: Orbis Books, 2011.

WMC   *World Missionary Conference, 1910.* 9 vols. Edinburgh: Oliphant, Anderson & Ferrier, 1910.

Acknowledgments

THIS BOOK EXISTS because of the support and assistance of many institutions and individuals. Chief among the institutions are Baylor University and George W. Truett Theological Seminary, Waco, Texas. Through a generous research grant and a sabbatical leave from the university, I was able to concentrate time and effort for initial research and writing. However, more than financial support and leave from class responsibilities, I am thankful for the remarkable support of colleagues and administrators at both the seminary and university. It is rare in any endeavor of life to find the level of collegiality that exists at Truett Seminary. Research and writing can be productive and done with joy when strife and egos are not constant distractions. I am especially grateful to Dennis Tucker, David Garland, Terry York, and Todd Still, for their personal encouragement and for the nurturing and learning community at Truett Seminary. In addition, I have benefited from the competency and responsiveness of the staff at Baylor's Moody Memorial Library. I am amazed at the dogged determination with which its staff tracked down materials and the speed at which these made their way to my desk. Without the assistance and resources, encouragement, and support of Baylor University and Truett Seminary this book would not have been possible.

This book represents a long journey with colleagues, students, and friends. Conversations about church and mission at kitchen tables, in airport lounges, in classrooms, and at endless meetings, always over coffee, have formed my thinking and prompted me to reflect and write. This group of fellow travelers is considerable, and thus it is impossible to acknowledge everyone. But from this crowd, I must mention the debt I owe to Holly and Matt Sprink, Katie and Baxter Bentley, Ashley and Ben Mangrum, Stephanie and Aaron Glenn, Robin and Don Martin, Sherri and Ben Booz, Megan and Marty Pike, Robin and Lee Fox, Stephanie and Aaron Beazley, Myra and Richard Harbin, Cindy and Dennis Wiles, Ashley and Jayson Berryhill, Jessie and Chris Fillingham, Kari and Josh Kulak, James Hampton, Swami Muktanand, Sam Say,

Rebecca Hernandez, Ellen Price, Kristen Donnelly, Angie French, Joell
Beagle, Leah Grundset Davis, Karen Hatley, Sharyl Loeung, Andy Thomas,
Mike Smith, Cara Jane Brister, Scott Bertrand, Brett Gibson, Scott Shelton,
Sagar Bhukiya, Monica and Clint Followel, Jacob Overby, Jessica Moses,
Kwame Acheampong, Curt Kruschwitz, Joe Bumbulis, Lucas Land, Mike
Mantooth, Kathryn Seay, Jamie McCallum, Chad Mustain, Celina Varela, Eli
Jackson, Tim Ivey, Brett Spivey, Dustin Kunz, Zachariah Seanor, Xiuli Zhang,
Joben David, Erica Whitaker, Luke Stehr, Scott Day, Rachel Tate, Elizabeth
Andrasi, Mary Carpenter, Matt Snowden, and Andy Arterbury. Along with
love and encouragement, I am grateful to these friends for their probing
questions and provocative lives. As many of the conclusions of this book
have formed around lively discussions in room 236 at Truett Seminary, I
offer it as a summa of sorts for the students who have been at those tables—
and for those who are still to come.

Friends at Cottonwood Baptist Church, Dublin, Texas, have reaffirmed
again and again my belief in the church as a community of pilgrim witnesses. Through the faith and obedience of these fellow congregants, I have
seen firsthand a faithful intersection of the people of God and witness to
the world. I am grateful to my pastor and friend, Mike Fritscher, as well as
Craig Scoffield and the leadership of Cottonwood. Iron has sharpened iron,
as we have shared life, worshiped, and experienced God's grace and
goodness together.

I have benefited from frequent and stimulating conversations with Sam
and Chris, my son and son-in-law, and Elizabeth and Jessica, my daughter
and daughter-in-law. All four are fearless when it comes to asking questions
and equally courageous in following where the questions lead. They have
helped me to clear the clutter that clouds the hardest of issues. Hopefully I
have helped them in some small way to clarify their questions and not just
add more clutter.

I am especially thankful to Jessica Stroope, Josh Kulak, Lucy Jordan, Elizabeth Andrasi, and Ben Mangrum, who read drafts in part or whole. In-
sights and suggestions from these friends have helped to make this a much
better and more readable book. And I greatly appreciate the willingness of
Dan Reid, senior editor at IVP Academic, to risk along with me on this
controversial topic. With keen editorial skill and theological insight, Dan

has offered careful guidance and encouragement along the way. While these good people have saved me from scores of errors and misstatements, the remaining oversights and inaccuracies are solely mine.

I am grateful to my parents, Frances and Dale Stroope, who have encouraged me at every stage of life to explore faith and pursue questions, and I am thankful for Sam, Elizabeth, and Anna, my adult children, who challenge me every day to believe and hope when both at times seem impossible.

Above all, I am deeply grateful for Kay, who has been my companion on this journey from the beginning. Through ups and downs, joys and disappointments, parties and meetings, floods and fires, Europe and Asia, she has been more than just present and supportive but an earnest and ready sojourner. After untold miles and countless new beginnings, she remains to this day a believing and loving fellow traveler and friend.

Prologue

WHY A BOOK ABOUT the language of mission? Isn't *doing* mission much more important than *talking* about the way we *talk* about mission? A book about the language of mission is important because our talk about mission determines *who we are* and *what we do*. Language forms identity as words shape and express belief and ideals, choices and purpose. Notions conveyed in words and phrases provide the framework on which life decisions are made and efforts are expended. Because mission language forms particular ideals and notions that shape identity and purpose, that determines why and how we act, an exploration into the origin and use of these words is more than semantic quibbling. And more to the point, mission is important because it is the language that determines our stance toward the world and the means through which we respond to surrounding realities.[1]

My encounter with mission language as a young person included images of exotic places and heroic figures. These came to me by way of vivid stories and colorful pictures presented by visiting missionaries. The church I attended believed in mission and thus educated its children and youth with stories of mission adventures, and it promoted the offerings of the denominational mission effort. My early vision of mission can be summarized in two statements: "Mission is going to people in faraway places to rescue them from eternal damnation" and "Mission is a calling that only a few can receive." Both statements provided a clear and simple way to understand my place in the world and a basis on which to act out my faith.

What I did not realize in my youth was that the rhetoric of mission was highly ambiguous. With time, mission as an uncomplicated, singular notion

---

[1] As the reader will note, I have chosen to use *mission* as a lexeme, a lexical unit of meaning. I have made this choice in order to be consistent throughout the discussion. Other inflectional forms and grammatical variants (missions, *missio*, and missional) are included when necessary, but they are little more than derivatives of the singular form of the term. The intent is not to preference *mission* over *missions, missional,* or *missio* but to focus attention on the linguistic phenomenon and the historical use of mission language.

became more and more puzzling. First, seminary studies muddied my idea of mission. I went to seminary to become a missionary, so I read books and articles on mission. My received beliefs regarding mission were challenged by competing images and accounts of what mission meant and how it operated. Even more difficult to reconcile were the passages within history where representatives of mission conquered, coerced, and destroyed in the name of Christianity. And yet, because mission was an ultimate duty and offered me a positive identity and a constructive understanding of reality, its ideals remained intact and continued without serious critique. For sure, mission had its detractors, but these, I was told, were from outside the church or on its fringe, and thus their critiques could be dismissed as negative assessments originating from its enemies. During seminary studies and afterwards, I remained mission enthused and even became a missionary in my mid-twenties. Yet, these early questions never really disappeared.

The second assault on my received notion of mission came during missionary service in Sri Lanka. This island nation had a long history of mission work, first by the Portuguese, then the Dutch and British, but most recently by a wider array of foreign Christians. Remnants of all of these efforts existed in communal pockets and mirrored the progressive colonial conquest of the island. Portuguese Catholics were mainly along the southern coastline. Dutch Reform churches were on the coast but also further inland. Anglican, Methodist, and Baptist churches, as well as the Salvation Army, the remnants of British rule, occupied every section of the country. Yet after centuries of mission work, the church looked and sounded foreign and remained divided along the identities of the various colonial powers. Only in the late arrivals, the Assemblies of God and Pentecostals, was the colonial legacy and sectarianism less evident. Mission had bequeathed to insular communities imported brands of Christianity.

My assignment was to work with the Sri Lanka Baptist Sangamaya (Convention), the bequest of British Baptists, with the intent to steer them more toward American Southern Baptist ways. The Buddhist religion was the main competition, but so were the Catholics, Anglicans, Methodists, Lutherans, and Assemblies of God. The mission was to evangelize Sri Lankans and plant churches that would look like Southern Baptist churches. Mission, as received in my youth and seminary education, collided headlong with the mission legacy of colonialism. The mission past was not dead and gone but was alive and well in Sri Lanka and continued to shape the church's interactions and identity. In addition to the burden of history, social ills and ethnic conflicts also confronted my mission-oriented understanding of reality. Was mission only evangelism that resulted in churches, or did it include humanitarian and social activities? Missionaries from other organizations defined mission broadly enough to include a wide range of activities, such as relief and development, educational, and agricultural concerns. Though these missionaries were considered liberal, and their nonevangelistic approach was seen as part of the reason that Sri Lanka remained predominantly Buddhist, we shared the language of mission, and everyone identified as a missionary. When Lutheran missionaries spoke of mission, its meaning was different from how it was used by the Assemblies of God missionaries working in the same city. And the Sri Lankans understood mission from an entirely different perspective. Mission was the sending of persons from England and America to their country, and thus, as those on the receiving end, mission shaped *who they were* and *what they did.*

Even though the colonial mission legacy raised perplexing questions and doubts, I carried on as a missionary in Sri Lanka and did mission-type activities. I remained committed to mission but was no longer as certain of its meaning. Continuing as a missionary meant embracing the ambiguity of mission. After my first term in Sri Lanka, I began doctoral studies in the United States. My intention was to explore how best to evangelize Sri Lankans, so my topic of study was to be developing ways to understand and approach Theravada Buddhists. However, after discovering Karl Barth and the language of *missio Dei,* I changed my focus and completed a dissertation on Karl Barth's doctrine of God.[2] The language of *missio Dei* reframed mission as activity initiated and sustained by God, and thus it created for me a measure of distinction or sacredness for mission. *Missio Dei,* in effect, gave me a way to address my growing confusion. This discovery did not resolve the mounting questions, but it allowed me to talk with some comfort and theological reason about mission.

---

[2]Michael W. Stroope, "Eschatological Mission: Its Reality and Possibility in the Theology of Karl Barth and Its Influence on Contemporary Mission Theology" (PhD diss., Southwestern Baptist Theological Seminary, 1986).

A few years after I completed my doctoral studies, David Bosch's *Trans-forming Mission* made its appearance (1991). I read Bosch, and my small difficulty with mission became a demanding problem. Along with a helpful critique of the modern, Enlightenment paradigm of mission, Bosch offers a clear and substantial connection between expansion of the European co-lonial powers and the advance of the church. I remember being jolted as I read for the first time his section on "missionary wars."[3] He charts the de-velopment of war theory from Augustine to Pope Gregory VII that even-tually led to the acceptance of the idea that "aggressive war for the sake of the expansion of Christianity was both justified and practiced."[4] Bosch then extends this argument into the next section to assert that "colonialism and missions, as a matter of course, were interdependent; the right to have col-onies carried with it the duty to Christianize the colonized."[5] The right to colonize granted to Spain and Portugal by Pope Alexander VI, exercised in various forms and levels of coercion, was an extension of the warring men-tality detailed in Bosch's previous section on the Crusades. His reasoning was simple and convincing, and it was confusing. This was not the mission of my upbringing, nor was it my mission in Sri Lanka. And yet, it was the mission legacy. My doctoral studies had helped me to separate mission as presented in the New Testament, commanded by Jesus, and enacted by Paul from this other mission, and now Bosch was tying them back together. I reassured myself that the "missionary wars" were something different, the result of Constantine, popes, Crusaders, Spain, and Portugal. Mission, as commanded by Jesus in Matthew 28:19-20 and enacted by the apostle Paul, had been co-opted for other causes and then corrupted. With both hands, I held firmly onto Jesus and Paul as expressions of true and biblical mission.

In my initial reading of *Transforming Mission*, three sentences in the section on colonization had escaped my notice. In a subsequent reading, what was left of my received notion of mission came unhinged. In the midst of his discussion on the interdependence of colonialism and mission, Bosch mentions that the terms *mission* and *missionary* came into use during this

---

[3]David J. Bosch, *Transforming Mission: Paradigm Shifts in Theology of Mission* (Maryknoll, NY: Orbis Books, 2011), 227-31. Hereafter cited as *TM*.
[4]Ibid., 229.
[5]Ibid., 232-33.

period as the assignment and designation of "ecclesiastical agents." "The new word 'mission,'" he concludes, "is historically linked indissolubly with the colonial era and with the idea of a magisterial commissioning."[6] Astonishing! Bosch up to this point generously and consistently employs *mission* and *missionary* in his discussions of Matthew, Luke, Acts, and Paul, and in descriptions of the early church, monks, and monasteries. And he continues to use both terms from this point until the end of the book. He admits to being anachronistic, and then attempts to redeem mission. In his efforts to transform mission, Bosch leaves mission rhetoric untouched, with only a brief admission of misplacing it in the chronology. By doing so, Bosch does not transform mission but compounds the confusion, perpetuates a problem. His admission does little to solve its rhetorical difficulty or clarify its meaning. His emphasis on *missio Dei* appears to add clarity and to identify which questions we should be asking, but in the end, such an emphasis does little to resolve the difficulties with the source and meaning of mission.

My growing dissonance and Bosch's admission has sent me on a quest. Because mission is more than a casual topic for polite church discussion or an academic subject to be dispassionately critiqued, but a matter of identity and how we frame reality, the question of its origin and meaning requires a thorough investigation. For many of us, formation from childhood to young adulthood has centered in mission—think, for example, about the mission education programs that were commonplace in many churches—and thus it has given us personal and vocational identity and purpose. As such, mission is more than a concept or idea but a central theme of life. Its examination is crucial, lest we find ourselves living for ideas that are less than clear and even unbiblical. Might we have wrongly identified ourselves or misunderstood our encounter with the world? Might we be pursuing wrong ends? At the center of this quest are questions of mission's use and aim, origin and meaning. Is *mission* even biblical? If so, then what does it mean? If not, when did the church begin using mission language, and why? And what baggage might mission bring into its Christian use from those extrabiblical sources?

This book appears at the end of years of personal and professional dissonance and questioning. It is like arriving at a vantage point along a winding

---

[6]Ibid., 233. Bosch alludes to the same in his introduction (1).

trail from which I am looking back and reviewing the path that led me to where I now stand. And from this vantage point, I am also looking for the trail ahead and where it might lead. Writing has given me the gifts of perspective and alternative vision. Where I began this process is not where I ended, nor was I aware of how much it would change my language, identity, and actions. My hope is for a similar change of perspective for those who read these pages, especially my students, to whom I dedicate this book. I also offer it to my grandchildren—Lilias, Silas, Micah, Violet, and Ian—as a vantage point, with the hope that they will, in their day, engage the world in a fresh and faithful manner.

Introduction

The Enigma of Mission

Missions mean the extensive realization of God's redemptive
purpose in Christ by means of human messengers.

W. O. Carver, *Missions in the Plan of the Ages*

It is falling now; it will still be falling when all these things
shall have sunk down the afternoon of history, and the
twilight of tradition, and been swallowed up in the thick
night of oblivion. Has everything a purpose and a mission?

Tom Sawyer on the formation of stalagmites in McDougal's cave,
in Mark Twain, *The Adventures of Tom Sawyer*

Find Your Mission

Cover of *Fast Company* magazine, November 2014

Mission is ubiquitous. Mission is enigmatic. In everyday speech,
popular and academic books, tweets, and blogs, *mission* is a rather common
word with seemingly obvious and straightforward meaning. Yet, on closer
inspection, the meaning of *mission* is not so ordinary or straightforward.
In its many specialized and technical uses, mission is complex and
often bewildering.

Mission operates chiefly as noun and adjective and only occasionally as
verb. As a noun, *mission* has a wide variety of meanings: action, organization,
task or duty, building, delegated groups of people, and vocation. Its meaning

as verb is narrow and defined, specifying action performed for a task.[1] And as an adjective, it modifies and qualifies structures, places, and activities. Rather than a shallow and clear stream, mission is a wide and deep river. Because it has so many sources, mission is a confluence of varying ideas, interests, and movements. The result is a dense term that causes a great deal of confusion and hides a host of currents in its depths.

The oldest and most common use of *mission* is as a political or diplomatic term. The national and political interests of one country or territory are represented to another country or territory through its diplomatic mission. Representatives of a mission travel from one country to another to communicate ideals, negotiate agreements, and protest actions. As part of a diplomatic agenda, the ambassador of one country takes up residence in another and establishes an embassy, consulate, or mission. For example, as a result of treaties negotiated between the governments of the United States and Morocco, a diplomatic mission was undertaken and an embassy opened in Tangier, Morocco, in 1787. As a diplomatic term, *mission* connotes representation and the presence of a representative.

In contemporary life, the use of *mission* is everywhere. Companies and organizations, from IBM and General Electric to the Girl Scouts, Starbucks, and the United States Marines, employ the term to describe who they are and what they do. Proctor and Gamble, the manufacturing and services company, states that their mission is "to provide products of superior quality and value that improve the lives of consumers all over the world. This mission is one of the cornerstones of the company's success."[2] Proctor and Gamble informs the consumer that as a company they do not move dirt, put out fires, or provide rooms for travelers. Instead, their service—their mission—includes the manufacturing of "products of superior quality and value," and through these products (toothpaste, deodorant, soap) they intend to "improve the lives of consumers all over the world." The same use

---

[1]In rare cases, one finds the verb form *missioning*. See Trevor J. Burke, "The Holy Spirit as the Controlling Dynamic in Paul's Role as Missionary to the Thessalonians," in *Paul as Missionary: Identity, Activity, Theology, and Practice*, ed. Trevor J. Burke and Brian S. Rosner, Library of New Testament Studies 420 (London: T&T Clark, 2011), 153; Paul Barnett, *Paul: Missionary of Jesus*, vol. 2 of *After Jesus* (Grand Rapids: Eerdmans, 2008), 83.

[2]"P&G Worldwide Site: The Power of Purpose," www.pg.com/en_US/company/purpose_people /index.shtml.

of mission is illustrated in the title of a book written by the founders of Honest Tea, *Mission in a Bottle: The Honest Guide to Doing Business Differently—and Succeeding.* Their book on the company's history details the development of a unique plan of marketing and how Honest Tea became a successful business by selling something as ordinary as tea.[3] Mission, for them, is more than a product. Mission is a way of operating their company and their path to success. Mission is an essential component of a serious business plan.

The world of personal development offers yet another context and meaning for mission. Stephen Covey, Denis Waitley, and other motivation experts stress the necessity of successful persons having a mission, expressed in a personal mission statement.[4] Seminars, workshops, and self-help books promote the importance of defining this statement. More than referring to organizations, companies, or group endeavors, mission is personal and individualized. It is internalized and experienced. Mission describes the way one frames existence and provides motivation for success. Mission is a thing of the mind. It is psychological.

Since the middle of the twentieth century, many people associate mission with the National Aeronautics and Space Administration (NASA) and its designation of particular space endeavors. NASA lists some 131 current and former missions—missions to Mars, Juno's mission to Jupiter, the Apollo missions, and the mission of the Rosetta orbiter to Comet 67P.[5] The aim of NASA's Kepler mission is to discover new planetary systems and planets within those systems. Mission engineers and mission administrators direct this and other missions from a place called "mission control." Mission is a term that describes what NASA docs in general and is a designation for its particular projects. Mission is exploration and endeavor.

For most of us, *mission* is a common word used in a rather routine manner. In many settings and conversations, it is the default term to express vocation, purpose, or a particular task. The educated and uneducated alike use these

---

[3]Seth Goldman, Barry Nalebuff, and Choi Soonyoon, *Mission in a Bottle: The Story of Honest Tea* (New York: Crown Business, 2013).
[4]Stephen R. Covey, *The Seven Habits of Highly Effective People: Restoring the Character Ethic* (New York: Simon and Schuster, 1989); Denis Waitley, *Empires of the Mind: Lessons to Lead and Succeed in a Knowledge-Based World* (London: N. Brealey, 1995).
[5]See "NASA Missions A-Z," www.nasa.gov/missions/index.html.

commonsense meanings, whether in sports and business conversations, in everyday and academic settings, and religious as well as nonreligious. Even in religious circles, this plain, commonsense use of *mission* is found in church and seminary discourse, in popular and theological books, among liberals and fundamentalists, laity and clergy. It is familiar language, and thus the meaning of the word is broad and expansive. *Mission* fits in almost every situation, plays well in every crowd, and is present in every arena of life. No one group or type of people can lay claim to the term. It is everywhere and used by everyone. Mission is everyday speech.

In contrast to these routine uses of *mission*, some within modern Christianity employ the term in a specialized sense. This use of mission differs from that of the Girl Scouts, IBM, the Marines, Stephen Covey, and everyday speech. *Mission*, in this narrow Christian sense, refers to a definite set of ideas, processes, activities, identities, organizations, strategies, and documents that relate to the advance of Christianity. In this particular Christian use, *mission* connotes specialization (certain ideas and activities), utility (processes, systems, and organizations), and viewpoint (a way of interpreting the world and the human dilemma). Thus, *mission* is rhetoric that describes specific Christian ideals and actions unique to its encounter with the world.

A MURKY RIVER

As is evident, mission is a broad river in which there is space for many usages and meanings. And yet, even when restricted to its specialized Christian use, the waters do not become clearer. In fact, the waters become murkier. For all its specialization as a Christian term, *mission* does not have a uniform or fixed definition even within its narrower Christian use and is quite elastic in its meaning. David Bosch muses that we have reached the point where "almost anybody using the concept of mission has to explain how it is understood if serious confusion is to be avoided."[6] James Scherer's assessment is that "discourse about mission is hampered by a growing lack of preciseness about what any given speaker means when speaking of mission."[7]

---

[6]David J. Bosch, "Theological Education in Missionary Perspective," *Missiology* 10, no. 1 (January 1982): 13.
[7]Quoted in Jan A. B. Jongeneel, *Philosophy, Science, and Theology of Mission in the 19th and 20th Centuries*, Studien Zur Interkulturellen Geschichte Des Christentums, 92 (Frankfurt am Main: Peter Lang, 1995), 60.

For most Christians, mission is simply the effort, through various actions, to address the human condition, proselytize others, and spread the Christian faith. Money is raised for mission efforts, young people go on short-term mission trips, preachers urge young people to take up the mission vocation, and established churches start mission churches across town. *Mission* is a staple of Christian speech. In this uncritical, generic sense, *mission* can refer to a variety of activities and emphases, large and small, corporate and personal. But for a narrow group of religious professionals, mission is seen as a specialty, or some would even say a science, with its own community of practitioners and scholars who use insider technical language and conduct specialized discussions.[8] Missionaries and missiologists discuss and debate mission strategies, missionary methods, mission theology and motives, and myriad other topics that fall within "missiology." And yet, even among these specialists, the meaning of mission is varied and contested.[9]

For some practitioners and specialists, mission is narrowly defined as "evangelism that results in churches," and thus mission is restricted to the conversion of non-Christians to the faith and to preaching, evangelism, and church planting. *Mission*, for this group, emphasizes proclamation to the near exclusion of other activities or emphases.[10] For example, Andreas

---

[8]An emphasis on the scientific nature of mission is evident in the titles of J. H. Bavinck, *An Introduction to the Science of Missions*, trans. David Hugh Freeman (Philadelphia: Presbyterian and Reformed, 1960); and Carine Dujardin and Claude Prudhomme, eds., *Mission & Science, Missiology Revised, 1850-1940* (Leuven: Leuven University Press, 2015). See also Rufus Anderson, *Foreign Missions: Their Relations and Claims* (New York: Charles Scribner, 1869), xi.

[9]The variety of meanings for *mission* within missiology is noted in Stanley H. Skreslet, *Comprehending Mission: The Questions, Methods, Themes, Problems, and Prospects of Missiology*, American Society of Missiology Series 49 (Maryknoll, NY: Orbis Books, 2012), 17; William David Taylor, ed., *Global Missiology for the 21st Century: The Iguassu Dialogue* (Grand Rapids: Baker Academic, 2000); Jongeneel, *Philosophy, Science, and Theology of Mission*, 15-41. Vincent J. Donovan, *Christianity Rediscovered: An Epistle from the Masai*, 3rd ed. (London: SCM Press, 2001), notes, "The word 'mission' is used in different ways, so many different ways today, that it has almost lost its meaning." He explains that the appropriation of mission for all kinds of work has resulted "in a complete distortion of the word, emptying it of all its meaning" (75, 77).

[10]See Stanley E. Porter, "The Content and Message of Paul's Missionary Teaching," in *Christian Mission: Old Testament Foundations and New Testament Developments*, ed. Stanley E. Porter and Cynthia Long Westfall, McMaster New Testament Studies Series (Eugene, OR: Pickwick, 2010), 135; Robert L. Plummer, *Paul's Understanding of the Church's Mission: Did the Apostle Paul Expect the Early Christian Community to Evangelize?*, Paternoster Biblical Monographs (Exeter, UK: Paternoster, 2006), 1-2. Zane G. Pratt, M. David Sills, and Jeff K. Walters, *Introduction to Global Missions* (Nashville: B&H, 2014), assert, "The heart of Christian missions is evangelism—proclaiming the gospel publicly and privately with a view toward persuading men and women to

J. Köstenberger and Peter Thomas O'Brien maintain that mission is solely "a conscious, deliberate, organized and extensive effort to convert others to one's religion by way of evangelization or proselytization."[11] David Filbeck in a similar manner defines mission as "the express purpose and goal of winning the lost to belief in Jesus Christ as Lord and Savior and establishing God's Kingdom, Christ's Church, to be a light or witness for God."[12] For those of this perspective, medical, educational, agricultural, or other humanitarian efforts, while good and necessary, are not mission and thus are excluded from or are auxiliary to its definition. The concern in part is to maintain an undiluted understanding of the term, but more than clarity, they fear that evangelism and church planting might lose their place of importance and thus be neglected. Donald McGavran, for example, expresses the fear that the commitment to evangelism is being "crowded out" by the more urgent cries of humanitarian needs.[13] Thus, McGavran, Arthur Johnson, and others offer strong protests against attempts to broaden mission beyond evangelism. They characterize efforts to expand the term as the weakening or demise of mission.[14]

At the other extreme are those who employ mission as the alternative or counterpoint to evangelism, and thus, in some cases, mission is everything but evangelism. Mission, for this group, includes a long list of concerns and

---

reject their idols and put their faith in Christ for salvation. . . . Missions revolves around church planting" (207).

[11] Andreas J. Köstenberger and Peter Thomas O'Brien, *Salvation to the Ends of the Earth: A Biblical Theology of Mission*, New Studies in Biblical Theology 11 (Downers Grove, IL: InterVarsity Press, 2001), 254.

[12] David Filbeck, *Yes, God of the Gentiles, Too: The Missionary Message of the Old Testament*, A BGC Monograph (Wheaton, IL: Billy Graham Center, Wheaton College, 1994), 11. See also Peter Beyerhaus, "Mission, Humanization, and the Kingdom," in *Crucial Issues in Missions Tomorrow*, ed. Donald A. McGavran (Chicago: Moody Press, 1972), 54-76.

[13] Donald A. McGavran, "Crisis of Identity for Some Missionary Societies," in McGavran, *Crucial Issues in Missions Tomorrow*, 192-99. A similar sentiment is found in Eckhard J. Schnabel, "Evangelism and the Mission of the Church," in *God and the Faithfulnss of Paul: A Critical Examination of the Pauline Theology of N. T. Wright*, ed. Christoph Heilig, J. Thomas Hewitt, and Michael F. Bird (Tübingen: Mohr Siebeck, 2016), 701-4.

[14] Arthur Johnston, *The Battle for World Evangelism* (Wheaton, IL: Tyndale House, 1978); McGavran, "Crisis of Identity for Some Missionary Societies," 189-90; James A. Scherer, *Gospel, Church & Kingdom: Comparative Studies in World Mission Theology* (Eugene, OR: Wipf & Stock, 2004), 37. See also Zane Pratt, "The Heart of the Task," in *Discovering the Mission of God: Best Missional Practices of the 21st Century*, ed. Mike Barnett and Robin Martin (Downers Grove, IL: InterVarsity Press, 2012), 130-43. See Bavinck's critique of the "comprehensive approach," in *Introduction to the Science of Missions*, 90-120.

activities, with evangelism and proclamation, if mentioned, named as only secondary emphases. Thus, mission means anything and everything the church does, from discipleship to eldercare, building homes through Habitat for Humanity to disaster relief in cooperation with the Red Cross. Describing *mission* as the action of God in world history or as "Jubilee proclamation" captures this wide and inclusive sense of the term.[15] The focus is on God's liberating acts in world history through a myriad of forms and many agents. Such action may or may not include human participation and may even exclude the church. For those within mainline strands of Protestantism, particularly in the World Council of Churches (WCC), mission can include political and social action, peace making and reconciliation—even revolutionary activities and movements unrelated to the church or Christianity.[16] Sprinkled throughout official statements of WCC assemblies and related documents are statements in which mission encompasses the breadth and depth of the human experience in its social, political, personal, and ecological dimensions. The WCC consultation at Lucknow (1952) states that the church fulfills its missionary task as it forms its corporate life into "a witness to social justice and political freedom."[17] Evanston (1954) calls for churches "to realize more fully that they have a duty to society as part of their mission in the world."[18] The WCC statement "Towards Common Witness" (1997) declares, "Mission in Christ's way is *holistic*, for the whole person and the totality of life are inseparable in God's plan of salvation accomplished in Jesus Christ."[19] A similar statement from the WCC consultation at Athens (2005) emphasizes that "the church's mission in the power of the Spirit is to work for reconciliation and healing in the context of brokenness."[20] Salvation, conferred through mission efforts, means the improvement of the common

---

[15]Mortimer Arias, "Mission and Liberation, The Jubilee: A Paradigm for Mission Today," *International Review of Mission* 73 (January 1984): 44, maintains that "in the perspective of the reign of God and following the paradigm of the Jubilee, mission is, in the first place, the proclamation of liberation, the announcement of the Lord's Year of Liberation."

[16]Ibid., 46.

[17]World Council of Churches, *Statements of the World Council of Churches on Social Questions*, 2nd ed. (Geneva: Department on Church and Society, Division of Studies, 1956), 43.

[18]Ibid., 48.

[19]World Council of Churches and World Conference on Mission and Evangelism, *"You Are the Light of the World": Statements on Mission by the World Council of Churches 1980-2005* (Geneva: WCC Publications, 2005), 46. Emphasis is in the statement.

[20]Ibid., 114.

life, redemption of societal structures, and humanization of systems that alienate and destroy.[21] Evangelicals, such as John Stott and Samuel Escobar, also have broadened the definition of mission to include more than proclamation and conversion. Stott asserts that mission is "a comprehensive word, embracing everything which God sends his people into the world to do. It therefore includes evangelism and social responsibility, since both are authentic expressions of the love which longs to serve man in his need."[22] Escobar insists that in order to avoid a "dualistic spiritualization" that is so prevalent among evangelicals, mission must be defined as relating "to every area of human need." Mission must be holistic.[23] Christopher Wright expands mission to include creation care and combating HIV/AIDS.[24] These, for Wright, are not auxiliary or tangential concerns but central to mission. Wright's definition of mission thus includes compassion toward and care for the whole of creation *and* a call to conversion, addressing both disease *and* planting churches. This more inclusive definition of mission of Stott, Escobar, and Wright has, on the one hand, been vigorously opposed by more conservative detractors and, on the

---

[21]See Arne Sovik's commentary on the theme from the Bangkok Assembly (1982), *Salvation Today* (Minneapolis: Augsburg, 1973).

[22]John R. W. Stott, *Christian Mission in the Modern World* (Downers Grove, IL: InterVarsity Press, 1975), 35. David J. Bosch, *Witness to the World: The Christian Mission in Theological Perspective* (Atlanta: John Knox, 1980), 11, offers a similar definition. Lesslie Newbigin, *The Open Secret: An Introduction to the Theology of Mission*, rev. ed. (Grand Rapids: Eerdmans, 1995), argues that the "logic of gospel" draws the Christian witness into the "work of education, healing the sick, feeding the hungry, helping the helpless" (91-92). In a similar manner, Dean Flemming, *Recovering the Full Mission of God: A Biblical Perspective on Being, Doing and Telling* (Downers Grove, IL: IVP Academic, 2013), seeks to strike a balanced perspective between mission as proclamation and acts of compassion. Flemming asks, "How should the verbal and nonverbal dimensions of our mission as God's people connect?" (14). A critique of the wider definition of mission by Stott, Flemming, and others is voiced by Johnston, *Battle for World Evangelism*, 300-306.

[23]Samuel Escobar, "Evangelical Missiology: Peering into the Future at the Turn of the Century," in *Global Missiology for the 21st Century: The Iguassu Dialogue*, ed. William D. Taylor (Grand Rapids: Baker Academic, 2000), 105. Cf. Howard Peskett and Vinoth Ramachandra, *The Message of Mission: The Glory of Christ in All Time and Space*, The Bible Speaks Today (Downers Grove, IL: InterVarsity Press, 2003), 13. For commentary on the language and intent of the statements on social ethics in the 1974 Lausanne Covenant, see Klaus Bockmühl, *Evangelicals and Social Ethics: A Commentary on Article 5 of the Lausanne Covenant*, trans. David T. Priestley, Outreach and Identity: Evangelical Theological Monographs, no. 4 (Downers Grove, IL: InterVarsity Press, 1979).

[24]Christopher J. H. Wright, *The Mission of God: Unlocking the Bible's Grand Narrative* (Downers Grove, IL: IVP Academic, 2006), 412-20, 433-39.

other hand, been critiqued by those within mainline Christianity as not going far enough.

Then there are those Christians, usually of the younger generation, who do not care for the church's mission language at all and refuse to use it. And, given the glut of meanings and usages, who can blame them? Their objection is most often based either on a lack of emotional connection with mission as evidenced in previous generations or seeing mission as belonging to an era that has long since passed. For the better informed of these, the history of conquest and subjugation associated with mission is disturbing, and thus they react against it. Mission, for them, means colonialization and Western imperialism. Mission is tainted language freighted with unsavory images of an oppressive past or void of emotional content and motivation. For these, mission is antiquated and unfortunate verbiage.

The converging streams of mission use and meaning make for highly imprecise, complex, and capricious language. *Mission* elicits exacting definitions from many, who in turn divide into opposing factions, and for others, it is meaningless. In short, the term contradicts, creates confusion, and can be divisive language.

CONTESTED MEANINGS

When the church declares that it has a mission, or says it is part of God's mission, those outside the church, as well as many within, are unsure of what is meant. Even more perplexing is when those in the church describe themselves as "mission-minded," or as having "a heart for mission," or as "loving missions." More than enigmatic, *mission* can sound nonsensical and strange. Definitions and uses of *mission* are not just unsettled but contested, not just unclear but confusing, and thus they are the subject of ongoing (and often contentious) debate.[25] David Bosch is correct when he claims that mission is neither self-evident nor clear. In both its specialized Christian expression

---

[25]A. Scott Moreau, "Mission and Missions," in *Evangelical Dictionary of World Missions,* ed. A. Scott Moreau (Grand Rapids: Baker Books, 2000), 636-38. The difficulty with the imprecise nature of mission is pointed out by Andreas J. Köstenberger, *The Missions of Jesus and the Disciples According to the Fourth Gospel: With Implications for the Fourth Gospel's Purpose and the Mission of the Contemporary Church* (Grand Rapids: Eerdmans, 1998), 1-4, 37-41; and John M. Hull, *Towards the Prophetic Church: A Study of Christian Mission* (London: SCM Press, 2014), 235. Martin Goodman, *Mission and Conversion: Proselytizing in the Religious History of the Roman Empire* (Oxford: Clarendon, 1994), adds, "The study of mission is complicated by the variety of uses of

and its everyday use, among the initiated and the uninitiated, mission is a contradiction that both opposes and defies itself.

The problem with *mission* is not that there are so many meanings; the problem is the word itself. *Mission is the problem.* The term is a difficulty rather than an aid to understanding—an inadequate rather than a suitable medium of ideas and intents. One might quip, "What's the worry, its only semantics?"[26] But that is the worry: it is semantics. Words more than represent reality; words, as spoken by a speaker, heard by a listener, per a particular situation, *form* reality. Speech creates conceptual frameworks for what exists, and while use and context determine how we view and interact with others in the act of speaking, words themselves are an integral part in shaping that reality. A word is a premise from which conclusions flow and from which action is taken. Because *mission* exists in the mind, long before what we mean by the word is touched or seen in the real world, our usage of the term forms mental constructs of events, activities, and persons. Because mission is imprecise and contested, our encounter with the world becomes amorphous and confused. Or mission conveys, either for those who speak the word or those who hear it, latent assumptions that cast relationships, actions, and the gospel message in a particular light. Or even worse, mission becomes co-opted by whatever ideology or cause wishes to promote its agenda.

To illustrate the breadth of meaning in the word, and thus the extent of its problem, I differentiate below seven possible meanings of *mission* and provide statements representative of each. As can be seen, the meaning of mission varies, and how each of these is expressed differs per the context and speaker.

M1 Mission as general, common task of representation or personal assignment
  a) *Elizabeth has made it her mission to make sure all the children in the area are able to attend school.*
  b) *The mission of the soldiers is to take control of the tower.*

---

the word 'mission' itself in modern scholarship" (3). Goodman complicates the meaning of *mission* further by differentiating the various types of mission in the ancient world (4-7).

[26] As M. David Sills, *Changing World, Unchanging Mission: Responding to Global Challenges* (Downers Grove, IL: InterVarsity Press, 2015), advises, "Do not get bogged down in the difference between terms like *missio Dei* (mission of God), mission of the church and all the missions efforts of the church. The greater question for now is, What has Christ commissioned his church to do in this world until he come?" (13).

M2 Mission as specified aim or goal of a corporate entity

a) *The mission of our company is to provide products of superior quality and value that improve the lives of consumers all over the world.*

b) *The mission of International Justice Mission is to combat human trafficking.*

M3 Mission as specific and personal life purpose or calling

a) *My mission in life is to raise three children and provide hospitality for those who enter my home.*

b) *God called me to mission work in Japan when I was ten years old.*

M4 Mission as evangelism and church planting

a) *Mission means proclamation of the gospel to those who have never heard.*

b) *Mission is evangelism that results in new converts and churches.*

M5 Mission as the ministry of the church in all its forms

a) *The ministries of the church contribute to the accomplishment of its overall mission.*

b) *The mission of Shady Oaks Baptist Church is to make disciples through all of its activities.*

M6 Mission as structures or entities related to the expansion of Christianity

a) *Mission San Juan Capistrano was established in 1776 by Spanish Catholics of the Franciscan order.*

b) *A mission was established across the border as a base for Christian witness in the surrounding area.*

M7 Mission as the activity of God in the world, often with little to no reference to the church

a) *God's mission is much larger and often different from the work of the church.*

b) *Mission is the function of the kingdom of God in world history.*

While there are undoubtedly more definitions and examples, these seven represent the broadest and most common uses of *mission*. Since the phonological or written form of the term is the same in each example, ambiguity and overlap at the level of the actual meaning are not only probable but highly likely. For example, the first three usages (M1–M3) occur in both secular and religious contexts and can mean something quite different in each. A secular use of M3 communicates that whatever one is doing gives purpose and meaning to life. On the other hand, a religious use of M3 refers to a unique, definite call to a divine undertaking requiring specialized preparation and deep devotion. Not only is it necessary to determine whether the context is religious or secular in order to understand what is being communicated, but also one must know the specifics of the context. Ambiguity is just as likely when these words are used exclusively in a religious setting. For example, a speaker may mean the third sense of *mission* (life purpose) as he talks to a congregation, but the congregants hear the fourth sense (evangelism and church planting). The speaker wants his hearers to consider God's personal call to participate in redemptive activities wherever they live and through whatever they do professionally (M3), but they hear that the speaker wants them to become professional evangelists and church planters in a foreign country (M4).

Because hearers have their own hierarchy of meanings for mission, they default to meaning in a particular sense, though someone may use *mission* in an entirely different way. Many evangelicals, for example, often consider M4 and M5 more important or of higher value, so these hearers will automatically hear those meanings. For some, the fourth sense of the term (evangelism and church planting) is the only true mission, and they will hear it as such, unless clearly and definitely specified. But even when specified, the hearer may not be able to hear anything but *mission* in the fourth sense. Or, for those less religious, mission will always be M1, or mission may be a distorted caricature of M4, void of any compassion and highly self-serving.

As is evident, the sense of the word *mission*, in all its usages, is prone to murkiness rather than clarity. The word is a confluence of contested meanings. Stephen Neill's quip "If everything is mission, nothing is mission" sounds truer today than when first spoken in 1959.[27] Instead, he might remark today that *because* no one thing is mission, anything and everything is mission. Adapting John Macquarrie's words in reference to theological language, one could say, "The jungle of *mission* verbiage stands badly in need of some cleaning up."[28]

---

[27]Stephen Neill, *Creative Tension* (London: Edinburgh House, 1959), 81.
[28]John Macquarrie, *Twentieth-Century Religious Thought*, 316, cited in Garth L. Hallett, *Theology Within the Bounds of Language: A Methodological Tour* (Albany: State University of New York Press, 2011), 222.

RECENT HISTORY OF *MISSION*

The various senses of mission have not always been in circulation. In fact, many of these semantic nuances developed as a result of attempts to bring clarity to the term during the later half of the twentieth century. Scholars during that era frequently made a distinction between the singular form *mission* and the plural *missions*.[29] Michael Goheen, for instance, describes the mission-missions distinction as either differentiating between the total calling of the church and explicit crosscultural witness, or as a way of highlighting the mission of God over against the activities of the church. He identifies the first of these distinctions, the ecclesial distinction, with Lesslie Newbigin.[30] For Newbigin, "the entire Church is called to *mission*," but *missions* is reserved for those "activities directed to the task of bringing into existence an authentic witness to Christ in situations (whether defined geographically, ethnically, culturally, or otherwise) where such witness is absent."[31] In the midst of a wide variety of definitions, Newbigin's ecclesial distinction in the singular mission is meant to ensure a place for the plural missions, as the crosscultural missionary endeavor. For Newbigin, the singular-plural distinction provides linguistic space for the crosscultural category of the church's witness.

The same singular-plural distinction is made by Bosch and others, but for a different reason. For these, the boundary between mission and missions establishes a line between divine and human activities.[32] Their differentiation is in large measure an effort to "rescue" mission from its more unsavory

---

[29]See Avery Willis, *The Biblical Basis of Missions* (Nashville: Convention, 1986), 11; Carlos F. Cardoza-Orlandi, *Mission: An Essential Guide* (Nashville: Abingdon), 13-15; M. Thomas Starkes, *The Foundation for Missions* (Nashville: Broadman, 1981), 20; R. Pierce Beaver, *From Missions to Mission: Protestant World Mission Today and Tomorrow* (New York: Association, 1964).

[30]Michael W. Goheen, *Introducing Christian Mission Today: Scripture, History, and Issues* (Downers Grove, IL: InterVarsity Press, 2014), 85.

[31]Lesslie Newbigin, "The Future of Missions and Missionaries," *Review & Expositor* 74, no. 2 (March 1, 1977): 216. See also Newbigin, *One Body, One Gospel, One World: The Christian Mission Today* (London: Wm. Carling, 1958), 43.

[32]See *TM*, 10; Gailyn Van Rheenen, *Missions: Biblical Foundations & Contemporary Strategies* (Grand Rapids: Zondervan, 1996), 20; Carlos F. Cardoza-Orlandi and Justo L. González, *To All Nations from All Nations: A History of the Christian Missionary Movement* (Nashville: Abingdon, 2013), 5. Scott Sunquist, *Understanding Christian Mission: Participation in Suffering and Glory* (Grand Rapids: Baker Academic, 2013), distinguishes his use of *missions* to be when he refers to "particular mission societies and organizations" (7).

associations with colonial, nationalistic, and ecclesial expressions. In this way, one might view *missions* as suspect, while *mission* remains above the taint of humanity. *Mission* is divine activity, but *missions* includes human and ecclesial activity. In a similar manner, others offer a specific variation of this distinction through capitalized and lowercased forms of *mission*. The capitalized *Mission* refers to divine activity, whereas lowercased *mission* is reserved for human endeavors.[33]

The question that the mission-missions distinction raises is this: Where does one draw the line between the two terms—that is to say, between ecclesial and evangelistic activity, between divine and human endeavors? In many cases, the line is either quite fuzzy or tends to creep in one direction or another. For example, William Larkin uses both *mission* and *missions*, and while he makes a distinction between the two, he also confuses the two. He defines mission as divine activity but includes in it the enterprise of *sending*, which at some level involves those who are sent. In his use of the singular, he does not differentiate between *mission* as a theological term and *mission* as an operational term—a conflation that mixes every possibility of mission.[34] Larkin thus rolls divine activity and human endeavor together into mission (singular).[35] He tries to differentiate meanings with the mission-missions distinction, and yet in the end confuses the two and creates a mixture of the divine and human activities that is even more problematic. One is left asking, In what way does the twelve disciples' mission approximate Jesus' mission? Are the two one and the same? This problem surfaces when Larkin later says he aims to promote contemporary mission activities "for the completion of the church's universal mission [singular] in this generation." In this way, the mission endeavors of the contemporary

---

[33]R. K. Orchard, *Missions in a Time of Testing: Thought and Practice in Contemporary Missions* (Philadelphia: Westminster, 1964) makes an even finer distinction: "I use 'Mission' with a capital to denote the divine Mission in Jesus Christ, 'mission' with a small 'm' to denote a general way the activities of Christians in response to their being sent into human societies, and 'missions' in the plural to denote the organizations for mission and their activities" (15).

[34]William J. Larkin Jr., "Introduction," in *Mission in the New Testament: An Evangelical Approach*, ed. William J. Larkin Jr. and Joel F. Williams, American Society of Missiology Series 27 (Maryknoll, NY: Orbis Books, 1988), 3.

[35]Larkin uses mission in a similar manner in his contributions on Luke and Acts in the same volume, "Mission in Luke" and "Mission in Acts," in Larkin and Williams, *Mission in the New Testament*, 152-86.

church are equated with those of Jesus. But isn't that the very distinction meant in the mission-missions dichotomy?

In an earlier version of this problem, George Peters uses missions to refer to "the sending forth of authorized persons beyond borders of the New Testament church and her immediate gospel influence to proclaim the gospel of Jesus Christ." At the same time, he defines mission as the "total biblical assignment of the church of Jesus Christ."[36] There does not seem to be a difference between the two—mission and missions merge into all the church *does*. The distinction between the two is nonexistent, as they are combined in Peters's ecclesiocentric view of mission. Thomas Starkes likewise makes the mission-missions distinction, and yet he adds the curious phrase, "The doing of missions is God's favorite work."[37] For Starkes, God's activity is not just mission but is included in missions. The intent of Larkin, Peters, Starkes, and others is to acknowledge divine activity as distinct and, at the same time, relate human activity to the divine mission. However, in their attempts at greater precision, the mission-missions distinction itself is blurred and indistinct.

And yet, the alternative of drawing a solid line between mission and missions without any overlap between divine and human activity is unrealistic. In this distinction, mission, as divine activity, is totally other than missions, as an operation of humans and the church. A problem of another kind emerges when divine mission has no reference point in human activity or secular history. It becomes abstract and even more nebulous. Absent of ecclesial or human expression, mission becomes an unrealized ideal without definite form. In the end, mission becomes one or the other, either human or divine, but with no point of connection. Within this distinction, what the church does in missions has no reference point in God's mission.

However, for those who deny the distinction and use only *mission* in the singular, the inverse problem occurs: the wholesale integration of the divine and the ecclesial. For example, Dean Flemming maintains that mission "begins with God. It flows out of the boundless love of the triune God, whose purpose is to bring fullness and restoration to all of creation, especially people created in God's image." Flemming does not stop here with "mission"

---

[36]George W. Peters, *A Biblical Theology of Missions* (Chicago: Moody Press, 1972), 11.
[37]Starkes, *Foundation for Missions*, 21.

as "divine mission," but also insists "the mission of God's people, then, is no more and no less than a participation in the full mission of God." Thus, mission refers to "God's comprehensive purpose of the whole of creation and all that God has called and sent the church to do in connection with that purpose."[38] Mission represents both human and divine activity—mission is everything.

The aim of the mission-missions distinction, as expressed by Bosch, Starkes, Newbigin, and others, is to guard against making mission a strictly mundane or ecclesial function and to elevate it to the status of divine activity. Yet the manner in which this distinction has been used more often than not compounds the confusion, if only by conflating the opposing senses it purports to highlight. While the ecclesial and theological distinctions of *mission* and *missions* are helpful in a limited sense, the basic problem of the term remains. Whether singular or plural, referring to divine or ecclesial activity, *mission* is still ambiguous.

These versions of the mission-missions distinction pale in comparison to an especially influential use of mission that originates in the twentieth century and is still gaining momentum—that is, the idea of *missio Dei* or the mission of God.[39] Originating conceptually in an address by Karl Barth at the Brandenburg Mission Conference in 1932 and subsequently formulated and articulated by Karl Hartenstein, *missio Dei* first took root in ecumenical circles but now can be found in the language of church leaders and practitioners across all traditions. In most cases, proponents of *missio Dei* equate

---

[38]Flemming, *Recovering the Full Mission of God*, 17.

[39]For an account of the history of *missio Dei* and those who promoted its use, see *TM*, 398-402. Accounts and interpretations of the development of *missio Dei* are quite varied. See J. Andrew Kirk, *What Is Mission? Theological Explorations* (London: Darton, Longman & Todd, 1999), 25-30; Georg F. Vicedom, *Missio Dei: Einführung in Eine Theologie Der Mission* (München: Chr. Kaiser Verlag, 1958); Wilbert R. Shenk, "The Relevance of a Messianic Missiology for Mission Today," in *The Transfiguration of Mission: Biblical, Theological & Historical Foundations*, ed. Wilbert R. Shenk, Institute of Mennonite Studies, Missionary Studies 12 (Scottdale, PA: Herald, 1993), 17-18; Johannes Nissen, *New Testament and Mission: Historical and Hermeneutical Perspectives*, 2nd ed. (Frankfurt am Main: Lang, 2002), 17; Pratt, Sills, and Walters, *Introduction to Global Missions*, 69-74; Winston Crawley, *Biblical Light for the Global Task: The Bible and Mission Strategy* (Nashville: Convention, 1989), 16, 31-33, 45. For a historical and theological critique of the various ways in which *missio Dei* has found expression for modern interpreters, see John G. Flett, *The Witness of God: The Trinity, Missio Dei, Karl Barth, and the Nature of Christian Community* (Grand Rapids: Eerdmans, 2010), 4-10; Lesslie Newbigin, "Recent Thinking on Christian Beliefs, 8: Mission and Missions," *The Expository Times* 88, no. 9 (1977): 260-64.

it with the singular form of mission, thereby aiming to distinguish the contemporary practice of mission from that of the eternal mission of the triune God.[40] For some, *missio Dei* refers to divine essence (this is who God is in himself), and for others it signifies divine operation (this is what God does among humanity). Thus, one could say the who and what of God is *missio Dei*, and the who and what of the church is *missio ecclesia*.

While *missio Dei* has been helpful in differentiating theological from ecclesiological activities and providing unique language for the discussion, the problems inherent in the mission-missions distinction still persist. What is meant by the mission of God? Is there a difference between the mission of God and the action of God? Does *missio Dei* refer to God's special or particular activity among non-Christian people, God's activity of planting churches, or God as he sends missionaries, or does it refer to all of his actions in all of his creation in all places? By linking God with mission, the ambiguity of meaning and use already existing in the term compounds. Likewise, the joining of God with mission raises questions regarding the nature of God's activity. Might the language of *missio Dei* reduce or restrict divine activities, as these are placed alongside or are identified with church and agency kinds of mission actions? It appears that mission language in this case limits rather than heightens divine activity, reduces rather than expands.

This abiding trouble appears, for instance, in J. Jayakiran Sebastian's question: "Can we make the claim that mission is *of* God?"[41] In other words, does God, via *missio*, share some essential nature with the church, with humanity? While the claim that mission is "an attribute of God" may be popular consensus, can one with certainty say this of God or of mission?[42]

---

[40]*TM*, 10. Cf. Walter Kaiser, *Mission in the Old Testament: Israel as a Light to the Nations* (Grand Rapids: Baker Books, 2000), 11; R. Geoffrey Harris, *Mission in the Gospels* (London: Epworth, 2004), x-xii, 153-54, 225-28. Christopher Wright, *Mission of God*, defines mission in a way that mirrors *missio Dei* without the reference to the Latin. "Our mission (if it is biblically informed and validated) means our committed participation as God's people, at God's invitation and command, in God's own mission within the history of God's world for the redemption of God's creation" (22-23).

[41]J. Jayakiran Sebastian, "Interrogating Missio Dei: From the Mission of God Towards Appreciating Our Mission to God in India Today," in *Mission and Postmodernities*, ed. Rolv Olsen, Regnum Edinburgh 2010 Series (Eugene, OR: Wipf & Stock, 2012), 206-7, 220.

[42]*TM*, 400. In a similar manner, Ross Hastings, *Missional God, Missional Church: Hope for the Re-evangelizing the West* (Downers Grove, IL: IVP Academic, 2012), 246-65, presents a biblical and theological case for missional as an attribute of God.

Might we be refusing to come to terms with or covering up the difficulties of mission by giving it divine origin and character? L. A. Hoedemaker claims *missio Dei* is "an artifcial device" in which a "current concept (mission) is linked retrospectively with a dogmatic term (*missio*)"; thus "the linking of two heterogeneous notions of *missio* is confusing."[43] Rather than adding clarity to mission, *missio Dei* appears to be a theological veil, a way to justify talk about ourselves with talk about God.

What's more, when we consider how *missio Dei* informs not just our theological concepts but also our practices, it is undeniable that mission remains *missio ecclesia*, and church activity morphs into *missio Dei*. The distinction made in theory becomes blurred in speech and practice. *Missio Dei*, when operationalized, becomes an endorsement for a host of ecclesial endeavors. *Missio Dei* now is the latest branding for a variety of causes and practices, the headliner for youth events and national women's conferences, and a way of validating particular strategies.[44] The stamp of *missio Dei* becomes certainty and proof of divine approval. As a popular cliché, one finds rampant, uncritical conflation of divine and human activities and programs. But also in scholarly writings, *missio Dei* has become an under-explained and overworked phrase. For example, Michael Gorman assumes that the meaning and history of *missio Dei* is clear and evident, and thus he does not see the need to explain its use. He simply asserts that *missio Dei* is "what God is up to in the world . . . in a word, salvation."[45] As an inexact, and thus vague, concept, *missio Dei* is a wide gate through which almost any concern, issue, or cause can traffic—ecclesiology, ecology, ecumenics, liberation, justice. While the Latinized patina has breathed new life into mission, it also has created even murkier waters. *Missio Dei* is everywhere and means everything.

---

[43]L. A. Hoedemaker, "The People of God and the Ends of the Earth," in *Missiology: An Ecumenical Introduction*, ed. A. Camps, L. A. Hoedemaker, M. R. Spindler, and F. J. Verstraelen, Texts and Contexts of Global Christianity (Grand Rapids: Eerdmans, 1995), 162-63. Bert Hoedemaker, "Mission Beyond Modernity," in *Christian Mission in Western Society: Precedents, Perspectives, Prospects*, ed. Simon Barrow and Graeme Smith (London: CBTI, 2001), offers a smiliar critique, noting that "*missio dei* thinking retains a measure of modern containment" (230).

[44]Per the title, *Discovering the Mission of God: Best Missional Practices for the 21st Century*, ed. Michael Barnett and Robin Martin (Downers Grove, IL: InterVarsity Press, 2012).

[45]Michael J. Gorman, *Becoming the Gospel: Paul, Participation, and Mission* (Grand Rapids: Eerdmans, 2015), 11, 21-49.

A more recent addition to the rhetoric of mission has been the intro-duction of the adjective *missional*. First used by missiologists as a technical term, *missional* was popularized by the 1998 publication of *The Missional Church*.[46] Missional has since become the adjective of choice. Rather than speaking of a missionary church or a missionary endeavor, these are now referred to as missional church or missional endeavor. The new word offers alternative language for the problems associated with *missionary*, and this aversion, in fact, is the principle reason for the adjec-tive's surging popularity.[47] Missional, according to Darrell Guder, at-tempts "to move the discussion beyond too narrow definitions of mission as merely one among the various programs of the church, and to find ways to think about the church's calling and practice today in light of the fact of the multicultural global church."[48] In addition to being alternative language, the advent of *missional* signals a shift in emphasis to mission as integral to the very nature of the church, and thus, according to Mark Laing, "the church is missional wherever it is located."[49] With the neol-ogism of *missional*, mission becomes more than evangelism, social action, or foreign enterprise. The term denotes *who* the church is and *what* the church does. Missional represents "the merger of ecclesiology and missiology into one discipline."[50]

G. E. Dames is even more pointed in his assessment of *missional*. The term, according to Dames, "refers to the shift from a cultural church to a church that reflects and engages actively with the immediate community," and thus the term signals a shift from evangelism in an international setting or among people of other faith traditions to an idealized state to which the

---

[46]Darrell L. Guder et al., *Missional Church: A Vision for the Sending of the Church in North America* (Grand Rapids: Eerdmans, 1998). Prior to the publication of *Missional Church*, *missional* is used, for example, by Francis M. DuBose, *God Who Sends: A Fresh Quest for Biblical Mission* (Nashville: Broadman, 1983), 13.

[47]Darrell L. Guder, *Called to Witness: Doing Missional Theology* (Grand Rapids: Eerdmans, 2015), 11.

[48]Ibid., 65.

[49]Mark T. B. Laing, "Missio Dei: Some Implications for the Church," *Missiology* 37, no. 1 (January 2009): 91.

[50]Guder, *Called to Witness*, 187. This all-inclusive description of mission and church is similar to F. Hahn's definition of mission as "the church's service, made possible by the coming of Christ and the dawning of the eschatological event of salvation, and founded in Jesus' commission," *Mission in the New Testament*, trans. Frank Clarke (London: SCM Press, 1965), 173.

church in North America is to aspire.[51] In his examination of "contemporary images of mission," Donald Messer similarly states that *mission* and *missional* are no longer "synonymous with 'foreign missions.' Mission means the Christian church and its ministers, lay and clergy, discerning and responding to God's loving and liberating initiatives in the world."[52] Missional transforms mission into a barometer of church life—a measurement of the church's nature and essence, its activities and health. *Missional*, therefore, chiefly refers to all that the church does, when it does these well.

While *missional* began as an attempt to reframe ecclesiology for the North American church, it has turned into the new way of talking about mission in all its forms. In the words of Alan J. Roxburgh, "the word 'missional' seems to have traveled the remarkable path of going from obscurity to banality in only one decade."[53] Kevin DeYoung and Greg Gilbert characterize missional as "a big trunk that can smuggle a great deal of unwanted baggage."[54] Missional has spread beyond the activity of the church and ecclesiastical well-being to include almost anything—*missional* vision, *missional* communities, *missional* language, *missional* era, *missional* trip, and *missional* growth.[55]

This kind of pervasive, and undefined, use of *missional* is found in Michael Gorman's scholarly discussion of Paul and participation in the gospel. *Missional* is the adjective that describes anything associated with the

---

[51]G. E. Dames, "New Frontiers for Mission in a Post-Modern Era: Creating Missional Communities," *Missionalia* 35, no. 1 (April 2007): 36.

[52]Donald E. Messer, *A Conspiracy of Goodness: Contemporary Images of Christian Mission* (Nashville: Abingdon, 1992), 17-18.

[53]Cited in Craig Van Gelder and Dwight J. Zscheile, *The Missional Church in Perspective: Mapping Trends and Shaping the Conversation*, The Missional Network (Grand Rapids: Baker Academic, 2011), 1. Darrell Guder, "Theological Formation for Missional Practice," in *Walk Humbly with the Lord: Church and Mission Engaging Plurality*, ed. Viggo Mortensen and Andreas Østerlund Nielsen (Grand Rapids: Eerdmans, 2010), admits that the word "has become a buzzword, a cliche, a term that can mean almost anything" (307). Cf. Flemming, *Recovering the Full Mission of God*, 17-18; Sunquist, *Understanding Christian Mission*, 8-9.

[54]Kevin DeYoung and Greg Gilbert, *What Is the Mission of the Church? Making Sense of Social Justice, Shalom, and the Great Commission* (Wheaton, IL: Crossway, 2011), 21.

[55]See such titles as Alan J. Roxburgh and Fred Romanuk, *The Missional Leader: Equipping Your Church to Reach a Changing World* (San Francisco: Jossey-Bass, 2006); Mark Russell, *The Missional Entrepreneur: Principles and Practices for Business as Mission* (Birmingham, AL: New Hope, 2010); Brian Kirk, *Missional Youth Ministry: Moving from Gathering Teenagers to Scattering Disciples* (Grand Rapids: Zondervan, 2011); Roger Helland, *Missional Spirituality: Embodying God's Love from the Inside Out* (Downers Grove, IL: InterVarsity Press, 2011); Helen Lee, *The Missional Mom: Living with Purpose at Home and in the World* (Chicago: Moody, 2011); Bob Hopkins and Freddy Hedley, *Coaching for Missional Leadership* (ACPI, 2008).

missio Dei, and thus it is the vehicle by which Gorman brings a host of concerns into the mission arena: *missional* people, *missional* theology, *missional* theologians, *missional* communities, *missional* perspective, *missional* framework, *missional* significance, *missional* life, *missional* participation, *missional* theosis, *missional* Christology, and *missional* God.[56] Gorman also goes the next step and turns *missional*, the adjective, into *missionally*, an adverb. Thus, he asserts that an adequate understanding of gospel means that Paul is to be read "missionally" by way of a "missional hermeneutic."[57] The same tendency is found in Darrell Guder. In his attempt to rescue mission from its neglect and misuse, he recasts much of traditional Christian vocabulary via a program of "missional reclamation."[58] In this reclamation, all things Christian are qualified as missional: *missional* theology, *missional* theologian, *missional* calling, *missional* nature, *missional* priority, *missional* practice, *missional* outline, *missional* conversion, *missional* authority, *missional* purpose, *missional* community, *missional* ecclesiology, *missional* mandate, *missional* connectedness, *missional* ecumenism, *missional* thrust. Guder's overqualification of emphases and compounding of meanings is especially evident with his use of "missional witness," which appears to be tautological and unnecessary.[59] In its short history, *missional* has become an inexact, wide-ranging term that colors everything with a mission hue.

In the new missional language, mission evolves into a descriptive term that parses Christianity into mission and nonmission categories. What distinguishes a particular theologian as just a theologian and another a missional theologian, one community as only a community and another a missional community, is often asserted rather than explained. The adjectival excess of *missional* tends to conflate meaning and produces redundancy. As well as being an inexact and meaningless cliché, *missional* tends to read as an emblem for real, evangelical, or orthodox Christianity. As such, it is the least helpful of mission-related terms.[60]

---

[56]Gorman, *Becoming the Gospel*, uses *missional* and *missionally* fifty-seven times in his introduction (1-20).

[57]Ibid., 50-51. Dean Flemming, *Why Mission? Reframing New Testament Theology* (Nashville: Abingdon, 2015), xxi, and Guder, *Called to Witness*, 87, employ the adverb *missionally* to describe a way of reading Scripture.

[58]Guder, *Called to Witness*, 49.

[59]Ibid., 75, 103, 110.

[60]Craig Van Gelder and Dwight J. Zscheile in *The Missional Church in Perspective* attempt to explain the various meanings and uses for *missional* and extend the conversation regarding

The confusion grows even greater with the rhetoric of *missionary*. Is *missionary* a religious professional, or anyone who takes up the title and its associated activities? Is it a term to describe all Christians or just some? Can *missionary* be used as a nonreligious as well as a religious term?

In its modern technical sense, a missionary is an agent sent by an ecclesial or religious body to evangelize others.[61] But when employed as an adjective, *missionary* modifies all kinds of nouns in order to give these a mission character, hue, or designation. So, calling becomes *missionary* calling, a church is a *missionary* church, work becomes *missionary* work, and lands become *missionary* lands.[62] As an adjective, *missionary* can modify anything, including secular ideas: the salesman pursues his goals with *missionary* zeal, the *missionary* fervor of a politician seeking votes. *Missionary* indiscriminately communicates zeal or enthusiasm for any task or cause. For those outside the church, *missionary* zeal is synonymous with any fanatical, puritanical, narrow-minded, passionate crusader, or bigot. Such a caricature can be seen in contemporary movies and literature, and even in the language of business and politics. One only has to think of Barbara Kingsolver's main character, Nathan Price, in *The Poisonwood Bible*, or Abner Hale in James Michener's *Hawaii*.[63]

---

its biblical and theological basis. Hastings, *Missional God, Missional Church*, argues that "despite its semantic ambivalence, I deem it important to persist with the term *missional* for the simple reason that the majority of Western churches still need awakening to this core identity" (35).

[61]Dennis Othel Brotherton, "An Examination of Selected Pauline Passages Concerning the Vocational Missionary: An Interpretive Basis for Critiquing Contemporary Missiological Thoughts" (PhD diss., Southwestern Baptist Theological Seminary, 1986), notes that prior to the modern era titles such as *apostolos, euangelistēs, kēryx, prophētēs, episcopus, diaconus, archiepiscopum,* and *frater* were in use, but not *missionary* (35-36).

[62]Bavinck, *Introduction to the Science of Missions*, 48. Christopher Dawson, *Religion and the Rise of Western Culture* (New York: Sheed & Ward, 1950), writes of Christianity as "a missionary movement," with a "missionary character" (12).

[63]Barbara Kingsolver, *The Poisonwood Bible* (New York: HarperCollins, 1998); James Michener, *Hawaii* (repr., New York: Random House, 2002). Similar characterizations are found in *The Missionary* (1982), starring Michael Palin and Maggie Smith. The film is a parody on an African missionary who returns to England to work with prostitutes. For examples of *missionary* in business and politics, see Emily S. Rosenberg, *Financial Missionaries to the World: The Politics and Culture of Dollar Diplomacy (1900–1930)*, American Encounters / Global Interactions (Durham, NC: Duke University Press, 2004); Antonio Giustozzi and Artemy Kalinovsky, *Missionaries of Modernity: Advisory Missions and the Struggle for Hegemony, from the 1940s to Afghanistan* (London: Hurst, 2016).

QUESTIONING MISSION

For many Christians, mission language is emotionally charged and thus gives definition to how they feel about their place in the world and how to view those who are different. More than semantics or academic enquiry, mission, for them, means a call to a life commitment, an appeal to sacrifice resources for the cause of Christ, or the essence of true church, real faith. To critique the term raises uncomfortable questions about personal identity and life purpose. For others, mission is simply a given that has always been and will continue, and thus they see questioning mission as an unproductive waste of time. The meaning of mission, for them, is obvious. Or even if its meaning is cloudy, mission is something to do and not a topic of speculation. Trying to get at its meaning only distracts from doing mission work. For sure, to view mission as the problem—to critique its viability—and to suggest a shift in terminology represents a minority position. And yet, I am not alone in these questions.

Scholars and practitioners of mission are sounding an alarm, or they acknowledge something is amiss. David Smith, former lecturer in mission and world Christianity at the International Christian College in Glasgow, traces the demise of Western, modern mission and concludes that it "has lost its credibility and can no longer survive," unless there is a drastic and fundamental change.[64] Wilbert Shenk, professor of mission history and contemporary culture at Fuller Seminary, states that "re-visioning" must take place in the "Christendom assumptions and habits of mind" that continue to "determine the conceptual framework," especially for those who participate in the global mission.[65] Lesslie Newbigin contends, "There is need for penitence on the side of 'missions.' The whole modern mission movement is full of the marks of man's greatness and misery." While much good has been accomplished and generosity extended, "the missionary movement of the past two centuries, has been profoundly infected by cultural and economic domination, by paternalism, by all the elements which have brought colonialism into disrepute in so many parts of the world."[66] Newbigin and

---

[64]David Smith, *Mission After Christendom* (London: Darton, Longman and Todd, 2003), 4.
[65]Wilbert R. Shenk, *Write the Vision: The Church Renewed* (Valley Forge, PA: Trinity Press International, 1995), 52. See also Shenk, "Relevance of a Messianic Missiology for Mission Today," 26-28.
[66]Newbigin, *One Body, One Gospel, One World,* 14.

Bosch attribute the contemporary crisis in mission to "a fundamental paradigm shift, not only in mission or theology, but in the experience of the whole world." The ensuing crisis, according to Bosch, is due to "an inadequate foundation for mission and ambiguous missionary motives and aims" that "lead to an unsatisfactory missionary practice."[67] Bosch likewise suggests, "The harsh realities of today compel us to reconceive and reformulate the church's mission, to do this boldly and imaginatively, yet also in continuity with the best of what mission has been in the past decades and centuries."[68] Beyond these singular voices, scholars from different traditions and contexts convened at Columbia Theological Seminary in 2000 and made the same point:

> Unevenly but decisively, the long sojourn of the Christian religion as the established cultus of the Western world has almost spent itself. Although pockets of "Christendom" persist, and the temptation to religious hegemony and triumphalism is perennial, the process of Christian disestablishment seems likely to continue throughout the present century and beyond. . . . Mission, under these circumstances, must be profoundly reconsidered. Christians may no longer entertain the "Christianization" of the world as a faithful expression of Christ's mandate.[69]

Reasons for the crisis in mission are offered from various directions. Orlando Costas identifies mission's association with the free-enterprise system and capitalist ideology as the chief problem for the modern missionary movement. The solution, according to Costas, is to "unmask the secret alliance between the world missionary movement and the internationalist capitalist enterprise, repossessing the liberating character of mission."[70] Lesslie Newbigin's critique of the mission enterprise shaped by the colonial era is that this "traditional picture of the missionary enterprise . . . of the lonely pioneer going out from the secure citadel of Christendom into the world of heathendom . . . must be redrawn."[71]

---

[67]TM, 4-5. See also Bosch, *Witness to the World*, 2-3; Newbigin, *One Body, One Gospel, One World*, 8-13.

[68]TM, 8. A similar sentiment is seen in the title of R. K. Orchard's book: *Mission in a Time of Testing*.

[69]Walter Brueggemann, *Hope for the World* (Louisville: Westminster John Knox, 2001), 14-15.

[70]Orlando E. Costas, *Christ Outside the Gate: Mission Beyond Christendom* (Maryknoll, NY: Orbis Books, 1982), 69.

[71]Lesslie Newbigin, *A Word in Season: Perspectives on Christian World Missions* (Grand Rapids: Eerdmans, 1994), 12.

But he also insists that something even more fundamental must take place—"the way forward for 'missions' must begin with repentance."[72] James Scherer enumerates similar dynamics that have eroded or undermined mission and states that the present task "is to rebuild the foundations and to lay the groundwork for a new era of mission."[73] Scott Bessenecker takes up these themes and judges the whole of Western Protestant mission as "born of a corporate, culturally white, middle class paradigm," and as such in need of "refreshed forms of mission."[74] His critique is not so much of "the *content* of Western mission" but "the *container* of Western mission."[75] The problem with mission, at least in its Western expression, is its focus and dependence on money. For Bessenecker, the difficulty lies in the Western church's refusal to abandon its "Christian-Industrial Complex," and the answer is for the church to "rediscover," "refresh," "reorient," "reform," and "reenvision" its mission.[76] Michael Herbst simply asserts that mission is a "diseased word" that needs to be "rehabilitated."[77]

Smith, Hall, Shenk, Bosch, Costas, Newbigin, Scherer, Bessenecker, Herbst, and others signal that there is a problem and advocate for the reconsideration, refreshment, rehabilitation, and reformulation of mission.[78] Their many proposals and plans for rediscovery and rehabilitation represent responsible and constructive responses to an urgent need. Yet, in order to reconceive the church's encounter with the world, something more than rehabilitation, reformulation, or even repentance must take place. The rhetorical practices that frame "what mission has been" must be honestly and courageously examined.

---

[72]Newbigin, *One Body, One Gospel, One World*, 15.

[73]Scherer, *Gospel, Church & Kingdom*, 35.

[74]Scott A. Bessenecker, *Overturning Tables: Freeing Missions from the Christian-Industrial Complex* (Downers Grove, IL: InterVarsity Press, 2014), 43, 185.

[75]Ibid., 37, emphasis by Bessenecker.

[76]Ibid., 41, 43, 66, 113, 160, 185. Bessenecker employs all of these words to describe what he believes is needed in regard to mission. Bert Hoedemaker, *Secularization and Mission: A Theological Essay* (Harrisburg, PA: Trinity Press International, 1998), hopes for "the possibility of a missionary revival in the context of modern Western culture itself" (41).

[77]Michael Herbst, "Plural Mission and Missionary Plural in a Post-Socialist Context: Using the Example of a Post-'Volkskirche,' East German Region," in *Mission and Postmodernities*, ed. Rolv Olsen, Regnum Edinburgh 2010 Series (Eugene, OR: Wipf & Stock, 2012), 40.

[78]The question of the validity and purpose of mission is not new. See, for example, R. E. Welsh, *Challenge to Christian Missions: Missionary Questions and the Modern Mind* (New York: Young People's Missionary Movement, 1908). D. T. Niles, *Upon the Earth: The Mission of God and the Missionary Enterprise of the Churches* (New York: McGraw-Hill, 1962), in the mid-twentieth century, called for the "re-minting of the word 'missionary'" (39).

Hendrik Kraemer, missionary statesman of the last century, declares, "We do not stand at the end of mission." Rather, he contends, "we stand at the definite end of a specific period or era of mission, and the sooner we see this and accept this with all our heart, the better. We are called to a new 'pioneer task' which will be more demanding and less romantic than the heroic deeds of the past missionary era."[79] Kraemer suggests that the chief problem does not reside with forces outside the Christian faith, or between different confessions or practices, but within mission itself. Along with Kraemer, a host of missionaries, pastors, scholars, and friends of the church, many of whom have spent entire lives as active witnesses to the faith, are warning of collapse and call for a "more demanding" task—one that goes beyond simply revising mission. This rising tide of discontent suggests that if we do not respond to the tensions within mission language—if we neglect the "pioneer task"—we will soon find ourselves sitting under the heap of worn and antiquated rhetoric without a voice. While many have done the hard work of rehabilitation and sought to offer earnest answers, mission itself remains the problem, and thus an entirely different approach is needed.[80] A more fundamental form of questioning is necessary.

Mission, birthed and developed in the modern age, is itself inadequate language for the church in the current age. Rather than rehabilitating or redeeming mission, we have to move beyond its rhetoric, its practice, and its view of the world. The task is one of *transcending* mission. Even if the language and activity of mission were necessary and appropriate for a former age, we must look to what the Spirit is doing now and listen to his directives for what might be fresh expressions of the church's witness and service. The current situation is dire and thus calls for more than a vindication of mission language, or a renewed emphasis on mission, or a deeper commitment to mission, or better strategies and methodology, or more funding in the name of mission. Instead, we must do the hard work of reimaging witness, service, and love in conceptual and linguistic frameworks that allow for creativity and freedom. To state the problem in its most fundamental terms: it is not

---

[79]Kraemer, cited in *TM*, 8.
[80]Donald Messer, *Conspiracy of Goodness*, is one of those who shares the criticisms of past and present missionary activities but seeks to overcome these difficulties and "revitalize the missional dimension of all ministries" (21-22).

that mission *has* a problem, mission *is* the problem.[81] While some, such as Andrew Kirk, insist that "mission is here to stay," an attempt must be made to move beyond this murky language—to transcend its clutter and confusion.[82] The rhetorical problem of modern mission is a barrier to faithful witness to Jesus Christ.

Rhetorical Shifts

I agree with David Bosch's assessment that "the solution to the problem . . . does not lie in a simple return to an earlier missionary consciousness and practice. Clinging to yesterday's images provides solace, but little else."[83] And yet, such a new vision requires another kind of paradigm shift within the framework of mission. Rather than marking, as Bosch does, the various shifts in an understanding of mission by means of historical paradigms, my approach is to demonstrate that there are in reality two shifts rather than Bosch's six and that the shifts are rhetorical rather than historical. More specifically, the shift to the rhetoric of mission and missionary in the sixteenth century gave rise to and formed what became known as modern mission. This has been the defining shift. And in the early twenty-first century, a second shift is taking place as the rhetoric of modern mission is being displaced by different language. Between these two shifts, the meaning of mission *compounded*, and an aggregation of meaning occurred in order to accommodate a variety of agendas and to support a particular version of church history. In order to establish and sustain the term and its growing meanings, the language of mission and missionary was continually justified and historicized. Mission had to be read into the biblical and historical narratives anachronistically in order to create continuity between

---

[81] A sentiment attributed to Walter Freytag, "Strukturwandel der weslichen Missionen," in *Reden und Aufsätze* I (Theologische Bücherei 13.1, 1961), 111: "Damals hatte de Mission Probleme, heute ist sie selbst zum Problem geworden." Freytag's words are cited often by those assessing mission: Carl Braaten, *The Flaming Center: A Theology of the Christian Mission* (Philadelphia: Fortress, 1977), 87n16; Hahn, *Mission in the New Testament*, 167n3; Douglas Webster, *Yes to Mission* (New York: Seabury, 1966), 10.

[82] Kirk, *What Is Mission?*, 24. David Bosch, *Witness to the World*, expresses something of the same sentiment: "Mission is a permanent aspect of the life of the Church as long as the Church is, in some way or another, standing in a relationship to the world. Mission is the traditional and scriptural symbol that gives an answer to the question about the dynamic and functional relationship of the Church to the world" (10). Cf. Lesslie Newbigin's chapter, "The Enduring Validity of Cross-Cultural Mission," in *Word in Season*, 113-20; Newbigin, *One Body, One Gospel, One World*, 41-42.

[83] *TM*, 7.

mission past and mission present. The more demanding task today calls for us to do more than justify, revise, promote, and bolster mission. Rather, the pioneering task is to acknowledge the habits of language and thought that developed around mission beginning in the sixteenth century and to foster new rhetorical expressions for the church's encounter with the world.

The problem of mission language is a complicated one, with multiple dimensions, each related to and indicative of the other. Just as a physican who hears the complaints from a patient with a headache, fever, and neck pain must probe beyond symptoms for the possibility of a more serious condition, such as meningitis or dengue fever, our investigation into mission must do more than treat the symptoms of murky or confusing language. Ubiquitous, enigmatic language is indicative of a more serious, graver diagnosis. Our study must do more than just deal with the complaints of such language and propose yet another revision. Rather, we must press beyond symptoms to an examination of the source and suppositions of mission. Thus, what follows is a multifaceted investigation into the language of mission. Part one of this investigation (chapters one to four) is an assessment of the various methods and means through which modern interpreters have justified and historicized mission. Chapter one details the place of mission in Christian Scripture. The chief questions are whether *mission* and *missionary* are biblical terms and how various methods and means of interpretation have been influenced by the need to justify mission. Chapter two explores the use of *mission* in the Old and New Testaments, Jesus, and Paul in order to demonstrate how methods of interpretation permit interpreters to read Scripture as mission. Chapter three moves beyond the Scriptures and the early church to the use of *mission* and *missionary* in the historical accounts of the church's expansion. In this chapter, I rehearse how the writings of early historians and the lives of historical figures have been presented as mission. In the last chapter of this first section, I offer an overall critique of mission language. And yet, while the scriptural and historical justifications for mission described in this initial examination are problematic and in need of comment and critique, this is not the critical, more serious problem. These are only symptoms.

In part two (chapters five to eight), I probe beyond symptoms to what I suspect to be the graver diagnosis—mission's origins and its modern use.

From within attitudes and events that gave rise to the expansion of Spain and Portugal, mission emerged, and from within the colonial expansion of the church, mission developed into a modern tradition. The Crusades provided framework, and the colonial expansion of Western powers offered opportunity for the innovation of modern mission. The assumptions and aims of these political and cultural forces gave rise to the notions of conquest and occupation that exist within mission language.

Part three (chapters nine and ten) offers an analysis of modern mission. Protestants developed mission language into its ultimate expression as the modern mission movement. The growing importance of mission rhetoric in the nineteenth and twentieth centuries prompted the creation of mission as a modern tradition and thus the mounting efforts to justify mission. The grave concerns of Christendom assumptions and modern aims inherent in mission language have been minimized or dismissed in continual efforts to justify and revise mission.

As with the diagnosis of any threatening disease, treatment of the cause and not just the symptoms is essential to recovery and health. In the final stage of my investigation, I offer an epilogue, in which I identify language that could serve as rhetoric for the church's encounter with the world and suggest a conceptual framework for this encounter.

The overall intent of this study is an appraisal of the long and enigmatic course of mission rhetoric. My concern is not merely to dismiss mission language, nor to damage the church's witness and service to the world. Nor do I believe it is possible or even wise to abandon mission language altogether. Rather, the aim is to identify the source and severity of the mission problem and offer language that I feel more appropriately expresses the church's being and activity for the time in which we live. More than an exercise in discrediting interpreters and historians, this book aims to strengthen and fortify the witness and life of the church, not to minimize or destroy it. Nor is my aim to denigrate or ridicule the sacrifice and devotion of those who have crossed cultures throughout the years and have given witness to Jesus Christ, or to discount the fact that Christianity has expanded throughout the world. However, we no longer live in "the Great Century" of missionary expansion. We live on this side of two world wars and in the new realities of increasing pluralism, heightened secularism, and vibrant localized expressions of Christian faith. Because language frames and represents our understanding of reality, which in turn forms our response to the real world, the way we identify ourselves in the present world situation and how we act toward others must be carefully considered. Failure to assess mission's formation of our lives and ministries is to misidentify who we *are* and what we are to *do*. Put simply, because of the power and effect of mission language, we must probe beyond its surface, do more than rehabiltate it once again. Our pioneering task is to transcend mission and to discover fresh impulse and renewed vision for witness to the gospel of Jesus Christ.

I

Justifying
mis·sion

Mission, as a foundational term, is sustained by way of biblical and historical evidence. As these methods and means of justification shape the witness and service of the church, it is essential that the use of *mission* in these narratives be examined in order to determine whether mission language has sure biblical footing and is historically appropriate. Chapters one and two explore the biblical justifications of mission. Chapters three and four provide similar analysis for the historical accounts of the early church and beyond. The aim is to investigate the routes taken by interpreters and historians in making the case for mission and to ask whether these are warranted and valid. This first part of our investigation lays the groundwork for a focused diagnosis of mission language, which follows in parts two and three.

1

Partisans and Apologists

Christian missions are as old as Christianity itself.
The missionary idea, indeed, is much older.

GUSTAV WARNECK, *OUTLINE OF A HISTORY OF PROTESTANT MISSIONS*

Mission is what the Bible is all about; we could
as meaningfully talk of the missional basis of
the Bible as of the biblical basis of mission.

CHRISTOPHER J. H. WRIGHT, *THE MISSION OF GOD*

From cover to cover the Bible is a missionary
book, so much so that, as someone has expressed
it, one cannot cut out its missionary significance
without completely destroying the book.

ROBERT H. GLOVER, *THE BIBLE BASIS OF MISSIONS*

THE CLAIMS FOR MISSION by Gustav Warneck, Christopher Wright, and Robert Glover are quite grand. Robert Horton goes further, claiming that "the gospel not only contains the missionary idea, but it is the missionary idea and nothing else."[1] Walter Kaiser likewise asserts, "Missions cannot be an afterthought for the Old Testament: it is the heart and core of

---

[1]Robert F. Horton, *The Bible, A Missionary Book* (1908), cited in Jan A. B. Jongeneel, *Philosophy, Science, and Theology of Mission in the 19th and 20th Centuries*, Studien Zur Interkulturellen Geschichte Des Christentums 92 (Frankfurt am Main: Peter Lang, 1995), 124.

the plan of God."[2] Are assertions that mission is the core of God's plan, as old as Scripture, and what the Bible and the gospel are about justifiable? Is mission the heart and core of God's plan? Is Christian mission as old as Christianity itself? These interpreters maintain that mission stretches back to the beginnings of Christianity and even into divine purposes. Are these the isolated claims of a few on the margin, or are these representative of mainstream Christianity?[3]

Douglas Webster makes a bold statement of another sort. He claims that "if any subject needs demythologizing, that subject is mission. The myths which surround it are not to be found in the Scriptures but in people's mind."[4] Webster argues that many of the biblical claims for mission are fanciful assertions without a shred of biblical evidence, and they exist only as created myths. He suggests that a "reassessment" of the biblical concept of mission is in order.

The aim of this chapter is to join Webster and others in examining the claims for mission language and determine to what extent mission as an interpretive framework can be substantiated. The central and crucial questions include the following: Are mission and the words derived from mission, such as *missionary* and *missional*, found in Scripture? How do interpreters of the Bible treat these terms? In what ways are these terms nuanced or employed by different interpreters from the earliest generations of Christians? And must *mission* and *missionary* be "biblical terms" to justify their use today?

Our beginning point is to state the obvious. *Mission* and *missionary* are extrabiblical language. And yet, many within the church assume that both words can be found throughout the pages of the Bible. While some Christians might not be entirely sure as to whether these terms are in the Old Testament, they insist they are definitely in the New Testament. *Mission* and

---

[2]Walter Kaiser, *Mission in the Old Testament: Israel as a Light to the Nations* (Grand Rapids: Baker Books, 2000), 38.

[3]Arthur Glasser makes the same kinds of claims—"The whole Bible, both Old and New Testaments, is a missionary book," *Announcing the Kingdom: The Story of God's Mission in the Bible* (Grand Rapids: Baker Academic, 2003), 17. Joel Williams, "The Missionary Message of the New Testament," in *Discovering the Mission of God: Best Missional Practices of the 21st Century*, ed. Mike Barnett and Robin Martin (Downers Grove, IL: InterVarsity Press, 2012), declares that "the New Testament is a Missionary book" (47).

[4]Douglas Webster, *Yes to Mission* (New York: Seabury, 1966), 20.

missionary, they believe, are among the words spoken by Jesus, and if not him, then certainly by the apostle Paul and the early church. And yet, the majority of translators through the history of the church have not employed either word in their translations of the Old or New Testaments, nor have they attributed them to the sayings of Jesus and Paul.[5] *Mission* and *missionary* are not biblical language but religious terminology. So, in answer to the first of our questions above, we can say *mission* and *missionary* are not strictly biblical terms. But a quick, definitive answer does not completely settle the matter. There are attendant questions that a critic of the rhetoric of mission must address: Do corresponding, word-for-word sources for mission exist that warrant its use in modern translations? Can present-day translators and interpreters of Scripture justify in some manner the use of mission as a concept? Do the earliest traditions of the church argue for the use of mission terminology? If so, then by what means or under what conditions can mission and missionary be used? Who defends the use of mission and for what ends? We begin with the last of these questions.

Activists and Defenders

Interpreters who endorse the use of *mission* and *missionary* can be divided into two groups. I characterize the first of these as Partisans. Partisans are activists for mission. They read and apply Scripture with a view to promote mission endeavors. In churches, conferences, and publications, Partisans speak and write of *mission* and *missionary* with the assumption that both words—or at least the meaning of both words—are evident throughout the Bible. The aim of the Partisan is to convince and move people toward commitment to or support of contemporary mission activities and missionaries. They proclaim *mission* and *missionary* as biblical without qualifying statements or accompanying evidence. Their argument is usually based on an

---

[5]A fact explicitly affirmed by a host of interpreters from a variety of perspectives: Francis M. DuBose, *God Who Sends: A Fresh Quest for Biblical Mission* (Nashville: Broadman, 1983), 15; Paul Kollman, "At the Origins of Mission and Missiology: A Study in the Dynamics of Religious Language," *Journal of the American Academy of Religion* 79, no. 2 (June 2011): 425-58; L. Nemer, "Mission and Missions," *New Catholic Encyclopedia* (Washington, DC: Catholic University of America Press, 2003), 683; Ferdinand Hahn, *Mission in the New Testament*, trans. Frank Clarke (London: SCM Press, 1965), 16n1; E. Weiner, "Mission," in *The Oxford English Dictionary* (Oxford: Oxford University Press, 2004); Winston Crawley, *Biblical Light for the Global Task: The Bible and Mission Strategy* (Nashville: Convention, 1989), 9; *TM*, 1.

uncritical, and at times naive, reading of these terms into Scripture. Partisans leave the impression that Jesus and Paul speak of *mission* and *missionary*, and thus both words are in the Bible to be literally seen and understood. Moreover, these preachers, writers, and conference speakers rush past matters of terminology and passionately proclaim that Scripture offers a foundation for mission and proof for the existence of New Testament missionaries. Their concern is not to nuance terms or discern the meaning of words but to justify missionary work and supply ample motivation for Christians to join the "mission cause." Thus, their interpretations are often romanticized, sentimental versions of mission.[6] Rarely is the basis from which they make their plea critically examined. They are not trying to justify the rhetoric of mission and missionary but employ it to move others to commitment and participation.

And yet, similar partisan readings of Scripture can be found among a few within academic circles. In scholarly literature, *mission* and *missionary* are often depicted as biblical without critical assessment and argument. These scholars either assume a biblical pedigree for mission, or they use the term in a broad, commonsense manner, letting the reader insert his or her own assumptions. In this way, *mission* is used in a nontechnical manner but still used for the purpose of interpreting Scripture and promoting the mission endeavor. As a partisan interpretive device, mission describes an all-encompassing and boundless phenomenon. With such a broad use of mission, the Partisan is able to locate mission within a number of emphases, activities, and people within the biblical text and then from these promote the modern mission cause.

The chief aim of the Partisan is to construct a biblical foundation for both the idea and activity of mission. While this may be viewed as acceptable and necessary, the problem arises when these interpreters uncritically assume the meaning of mission as legitimate and coherent, or when scholars fail to acknowledge that mission is an interpretive rather than a biblical category. The obvious difficulty is that such an unexamined practice with so many unchecked

---

[6]Eckhard J. Schnabel, *Early Christian Mission,* vol. 1, *Jesus and the Twelve* (Downers Grove, IL: InterVarsity Press, 2004), xxiii, 7; and Christopher J. H. Wright, *The Mission of God: Unlocking the Bible's Grand Narrative* (Downers Grove, IL: IVP Academic, 2006), 21-22, are among those who critique such a romanticized, sentimental, and partisan approach to mission.

inferences opens the door for Partisans to interpret Scripture from mission's wide range of meanings, each with a host of freighted assumptions.[7]

Apologists are the second group of interpreters. They recognize the obvious absence of *mission* in Scripture and seek to establish justification for the term. These interpreters acknowledge that the use of *mission* and *missionary* cannot be assumed, so they mount a defense of their use. Unlike Partisans, Apologists do not rush past terminology without giving some definition to their use or making a case for *mission* and *missionary*. Eckhard Schnabel, Andreas Köstenberger, Andrew Kirk, Christopher Wright, and David Bosch are among those representative of this group. They address the absence of *mission* and justify their use of this language in various methods and by different means. While Partisans may refer to these same methods and means, justification of mission is chiefly the concern of Apologists.

METHODS AND MEANS

The use of mission as an interpretive category is justified by way of three methods. Partisans and Apologists either construct a biblical foundation for mission, interpret the whole of Scripture via a missional hermeneutic, or identify mission themes. Partisans justify mission chiefly via a biblical foundation, while Apologists may use all three methods but mainly develop a mixture of missional hermeneutics and mission themes. Alongside these methods, Apologists argue for the language of mission by means of a lexical trail or by establishing mission through a semantic field.

Biblical foundation for mission. The most common method by which Partisans and some Apologists justify mission is through a biblical foundation.[8] The tack is to build a "foundationalist" case for mission by assembling biblical texts into an argument, with the majority of emphasis on New

---

[7]This tendency is generally acknowledged by numerous scholars. See, for example, Schnabel, *Early Christian Mission*, 1:xxiv.

[8]As witnessed in Donald Senior and Carroll Stuhlmueller's title, *Biblical Foundations for Mission* (Maryknoll, NY: Orbis Books, 1983). See also Avery Willis, *The Biblical Basis of Missions* (Nashville: Convention, 1986); part one, "Biblical Foundation of Mission," in George W. Peters, *A Biblical Theology of Missions* (Chicago: Moody, 1972); Robert Hall Glover, *The Bible Basis of Missions* (Chicago: Moody, 1946); Zane G. Pratt, M. David Sills, and Jeff K. Walters, *Introduction to Global Missions* (Nashville: B&H, 2014), 37-66; M. Thomas Starkes, *The Foundation for Missions* (Nashville: Broadman, 1981); and J. H. Bavinck's first section, "The Foundation of Missions," in *An Introduction to the Science of Missions*, trans. David Hugh Freeman (Philadelphia: Presbyterian and Reformed, 1960), 10-76.

Testament passages, especially the commissioning words of Jesus. As a result, "Mission texts" are carefully arranged into a sustained argument to bolster the need for deeper and bolder mission commitment and effort. The line of argument usually begins with a broad foundation of God's work and purpose in creation and the disobedience of Adam and Eve. The fall of humanity establishes the need for the "call" of Abram and the election of Israel to be a blessing to the nations and thus the basis for mission. So, Abram's call and Israel's election are identified as "mission."[9] Some go as far as naming Abraham as the "first missionary."[10] Some similarly identify God's call to Jonah as a "missionary call" and thus as instructive for today's missionaries.[11] For others, these are only pre- or protomission, while a true foundation for mission is located in the New Testament.[12]

The primary aim of the "foundationalist" approach is to build a case for mission commitment and participation. For example, Avery Willis expresses the hope that a biblical basis for mission will result in his readers "making world missions the overriding purpose of [their] life."[13] Likewise, after a quick overview of Old Testament Scriptures in order to establish that Jesus came to fulfill the mission of God, Bryan Beyer asserts, "The Bible calls everyone everywhere to participate in the mission of God."[14] Following an extended argument for the biblical foundation for and dynamics of mission, George Peters similarly concludes that because mission is inherent in the nature of Christianity, the church that neglects mission "deprives herself of the most intimate relationship with her Lord, fails to identify herself with the primary purpose of God, robs her membership of the deepest experiences of the Holy Spirit, and denies the world the greatest blessings the Lord in grace has provided. She ceases to be truly Christian."[15] For these interpreters an inquiry into Scripture should lead the reader to

---

[9]Glasser, *Announcing the Kingdom*, 7-179.

[10]David W. Shenk, *God's Call to Mission* (Scottdale, PA: Herald, 1994), 29.

[11]Pratt, Sills, and Walters, *Introduction to Global Missions*, 6-7.

[12]See Ferris L. McDaniel, "Mission in the Old Testament," in *Mission in the New Testament: An Evangelical Approach*, ed. William J. Larkin Jr. and Joel F. Williams, American Society of Missiology Series 27 (Maryknoll, NY: Orbis Books, 1998), 20; *TM*, 17.

[13]Willis, *Biblical Basis of Missions*, 7.

[14]Bryan E. Beyer, "Jesus Christ—The Living Word—and the Mission of God," in Barnett and Martin, *Discovering the Mission of God*, 126.

[15]Peters, *Biblical Theology of Missions*, 350.

make a decision for "mission." Call to mission and promotion of mission are the reasons they construct a foundation for mission and are where they conclude their argument.

The foundation for mission in the New Testament does not rest ultimately on broad arguments but in a singular manner on Jesus. In the sending of the Son by the Father, one finds mission. The justification for contemporary mission then develops from the specific sending of Jesus to include the apostles and the early church and extends to the present day. Some interpreters describe the link between Jesus' sending and the sending of contemporary missionaries as "the incarnational model of mission."[16] Followers of Christ are to approximate the same *sentness* of Jesus. Whether through a careful arrangement of "mission texts" or the sending of Jesus, "mission" provides the connection and a biblical basis for what God does throughout the ages and what we are to do today. The thread that ties all kinds of activity and emphasis into a compelling foundation is the *sentness* inherent in "mission." The basis and argument of this approach relies on mission as its interpretive device.

Mission as biblical foundation is problematic in a number of ways. First, it is a misuse of Scripture. The task of constructing a foundation becomes a matter of collecting texts from here and there to argue the case for mission, without careful regard for matters of history and context. Scripture becomes utility for mission. Christopher Wright's critique is that this approach tends toward proof texting. He argues that in doing this "we have already decided what we want to prove (that our missionary practice is biblical), and our collection of texts simply ratifies our preconception."[17] As such, a biblical foundation approach for mission begins with the end—that is, mission— and constructs a set of texts that will point to this end. This approach assumes that mission is necessary and thus only needs to be biblically demonstrated as such. Partisans and Apologists assert that "mission" represents divine intent, and so Scripture must fit this assumption. But to place, for

---

[16]See John R. W. Stott, *Christian Mission in the Modern World* (Downers Grove, IL: InterVarsity Press, 1975), 23-25. For a critique of Stott and the "incarnational model," see Andreas J. Köstenberger, *The Missions of Jesus and the Disciples According to the Fourth Gospel: With Implications for the Fourth Gospel's Purpose and the Mission of the Contemporary Church* (Grand Rapids: Eerdmans, 1998), 212-17.

[17]Wright, *Mission of God*, 36.

example, the Abraham narrative alongside other "mission texts" from across
Scripture disregards the significance of Genesis 12:1-3 in the development of
Israel's understanding of Yahweh and ignores the richness of the historical
setting of the passage.[18] The foundationalist approach accentuates mission
at the expense of the historical and contextual phenomena. The result is the
neglect and misuse of rich biblical narratives.

Second, a biblical-foundation-of-mission approach is problematic because of its direction. Rather than beginning with the text and moving to
contemporary life and practice, it often seeks to construct a foundation for
what already *is*—that is to say, "mission" as practiced by mission organizations and mission professionals.[19] From *outside* the text, mission, as exemplified in ideals, practices, and organizations, comes *to* the text and asks the
text to give it substance and credibility. Johannes Nissen correctly asserts
that missionaries and mission promoters "tend far too easily to read back
into the Bible aspects of the missionary enterprise in which they are involved
today."[20] And yet, it is impossible to do otherwise when one's intention is to
establish a biblical foundation for anything in which there is vested interest,
or where conviction and commitment already exist. In the end, the Bible
becomes utility for mission: its contemporary promotion, funding,
recruitment, and strategies.

Such an approach is problematic not only because it fails to situate the
text in relation to its historical contexts and because of its direction, but also
because it treats the Bible as a source book to justify contemporary mission

---

[18]Rather than reducing the Abraham narrative to "a high and lofty missionary teaching" (Kaiser,
Mission in the Old Testament, 20), critical and reputable scholars offer commentary on the historical and social dynamics of Gen 12:1-3 without any mention of "mission." Their interpretations
highlight the establishment of covenant with Abraham and the election of Israel.

[19]David J. Bosch, "The Why and How of a True Biblical Foundation for Mission," in *Zending Op
Weg Naar de Toekomst: Essays Aangeboden Aan Prof. Dr. J. Verkuyl* (Kampen: J. H. Kok, 1978),
observes, "It has become customary, in writing on the 'theology of mission,' to begin with a
chapter on the 'biblical foundation of mission.' The argument seems to be that we already know
what 'mission' is and that, once we have established the validity of mission, we may proceed to
the exposition of mission theory and methodology" (33, cited in Michael D. Barram, "The Bible,
Mission, and Social Location: Toward a Missional Hermeneutic," *Interpretation* 61, no. 1 [January
2007]: 47n11).

[20]Johannes Nissen, *New Testament and Mission: Historical and Hermeneutical Perspectives*, 2nd ed.
(Frankfurt am Main: Lang, 2002), 13. In a similar fashion, Christopher Little warns against
employing Paul to represent a particular perspective in *Mission in the Way of Paul: Biblical Mission for the Church in the Twenty-First Century*, Studies in Biblical Literature 80 (New York: Peter
Lang, 2005), 77-78.

concepts, organizational entities, and strategies rather than as divine revelation.[21] One of the aims of the foundationalist approach is to extract from the biblical account what mission is to look like today. In order to assert that mission exists in Scripture, one has to locate intents, actions, methods, and structures of mission preaching, mission teams, and missionaries within Scripture. Constructing a basis for mission practices minimizes the Bible as revelation of who God is and as a record of divine activity in the world. The Bible becomes a manual for how to go about a human endeavor. The primary purpose of Scripture is not to provide a foundation for human causes and activities, whether these are social programs, governmental actions, or religious practices. In fact, Scripture witnesses to the fact that God often opposes human striving and activity rather than approving them.

In the end, attempts to justify mission by way of a biblical foundation make mission improbable. The foundation argument becomes a kind of litmus test for who is really Christian or orthodox and who is not. If mission is the core, as old as Scripture, and what the Bible is all about, then it is reasonable to assume that the person or group that is nonmissionary or less than enthusiastic about mission is in some measure less than Christian or not as committed. If mission is thoroughly biblical or absolutely necessary, then the unenthused are less than Bible-believing Christians. To oppose mission or to show indifference to the term means one is "out of harmony with God."[22] In their attempt to establish mission as central or essential, Partisans and Apologists turn mission into sacred language or the test for true and orthodox Christianity, and thereby exclude many from the cause they seek to justify and promote. The case for mission is not made, except for those already convinced, and for others it is just another partisan cause.

Missional hermeneutic. Many who write about the intersection of mission and Scripture have shifted from a foundationalist approach to reading the Bible with a missional hermeneutic.[23] Francis DuBose maintains

---

[21]See Bavinck's section, "The Missionary Approach," in *Introduction to the Science of Missions*, 78-152.

[22]Glover, *Bible Basis of Missions*, 30.

[23]Examples of this shift include Christopher Wright, *Mission of God*, 29-69; George R. Hunsberger, "Proposals for a Missional Hermeneutic: Mapping a Conversation," *Missiology* 39, no. 3 (July 2011): 309-21; David Filbeck, *Yes, God of the Gentiles, Too: The Missionary Message of the Old Testament*, A BGC Monograph (Wheaton, IL: Billy Graham Center, Wheaton College, 1994), 17-20; Darrell L. Guder et al., *Missional Church: A Vision for the Sending of the Church in North*

that the problem in defining mission is hermeneutical and that a clear system of hermeneutics is the only response to the "proof-texting method" of a foundationalist approach.[24] In the shift to a missional hermeneutic, interpreters read the whole of Scripture through the lens of "mission" rather than in particular, selected texts. In a missional hermeneutic, mission becomes the door of access into Scripture's meaning. Yet, this shift has been more than an update of foundationalist methodology; it is an entirely different approach to the use and meaning of mission.

The terminology of *missional hermeneutic* is a recent development, and its exact meaning is still evolving.[25] Francis DuBose uses the terminology as early as 1982 as a way to read Scripture, and James Brownson and others have further developed its use since 1992.[26] George Hunsberger's helpful article "Proposals for a Missional Hermeneutic: Mapping Conversation" traces the rise and evolution of such terminology and outlines its varied emphases. He groups these emphases in the current development of missional hermeneutics within four streams: the missional direction of the story, the missional purpose of the writings, the missional locationedness of the reader, and the missional engagement with cultures.[27] While these streams reveal "sharp differences emerging between the various proposals," Hunsberger contends they are not in competition, nor are they "mutually exclusive." Instead, "each depends on and begs for the other accents."[28] As Hunsberger explains, these streams converge, and "a certain kind of synergy begins to exhibit itself, and that is what makes this ongoing conversation promising."[29] Hunsberger's aim is to illustrate points of connection between

---

America (Grand Rapids: Eerdmans, 1998), 90-120; Barram, "Bible, Mission, and Social Location"; James V. Brownson, "Speaking the Truth in Love: Elements of a Missional Hermeneutic," in *The Church Between Gospel and Culture: The Emerging Mission in North America*, ed. George R. Hunsberger and Craig Van Gelder (Grand Rapids: Eerdmans, 1996), 228-59.

[24]DuBose, *God Who Sends*, 22.

[25]See Hunsberger, "Proposals for a Missional Hermeneutic."

[26]DuBose, *God Who Sends*; Hunsberger, "Proposals for a Missional Hermeneutic," 320n6.

[27]Hunsberger, "Proposals for a Missional Hermeneutic," 310-18. Michael J. Gorman, *Becoming the Gospel: Paul, Participation, and Mission* (Grand Rapids: Eerdmans, 2015), 54-55, provides a summary of each of these "streams."

[28]Hunsberger, "Proposals for a Missional Hermeneutic," 309, 318. Dean Flemming, "Revelation and the *Missio Dei*: Toward a Missional Reading of the Apocalypse," *Journal of Theological Interpretation* 6, no. 2 (2012), concurs that "no consensus has yet emerged as to what [a missional hermeneutic] entails" (162).

[29]Hunsberger, "Proposals for a Missional Hermeneutic," 318-19.

various emphases and to demonstrate how together these form an overall "robust missional hermeneutic." At the same time, he admits that these streams run in different directions, and indeed their definitions and approaches for a missional hermeneutic vary.

Illustrative of the diverse approaches to a missional hermeneutic, Michael Barram defines "missional hermeneutic" as "an approach to biblical texts that privileges the missiological 'location' of the Christian community in the world as a hermeneutical key."[30] This privileging of "missiological 'location,'" in Barram's opinion, is necessary for the "health and vitality of the faith community." What Barram suggests is that the church will be weak and sickly unless one's hermeneutical approach privileges social location. He does this by identifying the early Christian community in terms of its participation in "mission," which he describes as rooted in "the nature, character, and purposes of God."[31] Thus, for Barram, a missional hermeneutic "will self-consciously, intentionally, and persistently bring the biblical text a range of focused, critical, and 'located' questions regarding the church's purpose in order to discern the faith community's calling and task within the *missio Dei*."[32] Identifying the location of the early Christians in "God's mission" is the interpretive lens.

Christopher Wright represents yet another stream of the missional hermeneutic. "The whole canon of Scripture is a missional phenomenon," so according to Wright, "*the whole Bible renders to us the story of God's mission through God's people in their engagement with God's world for the sake of the whole of God's creation.*"[33] Rather than taking "the human activities of mission" as his starting point, Wright anchors his hermeneutic in the grand narrative of God's "purposeful, sovereign intentionality."[34] "The church was made for mission—God's mission," and thus, a missional hermeneutic "begins there—with the mission of God—and traces the flow of all other dimensions of mission as they affect human history from that

---

[30]Barram, "Bible, Mission, and Social Location," 42-43.

[31]Ibid.

[32]Ibid., 58.

[33]Wright, *Mission of God*, 48, 51. Wright's emphasis. H. D. Beeby, *Canon and Mission* (Harrisburg, PA: Trinity Press International, 1999), makes the same point: "The more we reclaim the Bible as a whole, the more we see the canonical scriptures as providing a missionary mandate, a mission critique, and a missionary objective" (29).

[34]Wright, *Mission of God*, 531.

center and starting point."[35] Wright suggests that discovery of this narrative is accomplished through reading Scripture with a "hermeneutical
map" that is "mission."

Central to Barram and Wright's missional hermeneutic is their definition
of *mission*. According to Barram, location is not confined to an understanding of mission as crosscultural witness or evangelism. Rather, mission
is before and above all else located in and defined by the *missio Dei*. Thus,
since mission is "the activity of God as revealed in Scripture as a whole," the
church's "missional vocation" must be more than "a set of strategies for rescuing as many sinners as possible from eternal perdition."[36] Instead, mission
is comprehensive, encompassing all of creation and all of God's activity
within the created order. Wright likewise nuances *mission*. He uses the term
in a "more general sense of a long-term purpose or goal."[37] Mission simply
depicts God as active and purposeful in all history and creation. Michael
Gorman treats mission and *missio Dei* in a similar manner. Both have to do
with what "God is up to in the world," particularly salvation in its various
expressions, and thus can include "love, peace/reconciliation, justice" as dimensions of the "missional God."[38] Mission defined as a comprehensive
concept allows Barram, Wright, and Gorman to uncouple their hermeneutic
from a narrow "missionary" definition of *mission*. And yet, in uncoupling
mission from a more operational meaning, what has happened? If *mission*
or *missional* refers merely to general purpose or goal, then in what way is a
missional hermeneutic unique or definitive, or even necessary? Wright's
emphasis on covenant, election, and redemption as ultimate concerns of
divine purpose is helpful, but is a missional hermeneutic the necessary lens
or hermeneutic for these emphases and his conclusions? He could have just
as easily employed other descriptors, such as *coherent, holistic,* or

---

[35]Ibid., 62.

[36]Barram, "Bible, Mission, and Social Location," 44.

[37]Wright, *Mission of God*, 23. Dean Flemming, *Why Mission? Reframing New Testament Theology*
(Nashville: Abingdon, 2015), follows Barram and Wright in defining mission "from a broad
perspective" and thus as "anchored in God's sweeping project to bring about salvation in every
dimension" (xviii). Flemming, "Revelation and the *Missio Dei*," concludes his missional reading
of John's Apocalypse with the judgment that "mission in Revelation is comprehensive" (177).

[38]Gorman, *Becoming the Gospel*, 11, 17, 23. For an extensive argument for a comprehensive mission
interpretation of Paul, see Michael D. Barram, *Mission and Moral Reflection in Paul*, Studies in
Biblical Literature 75 (New York: Peter Lang, 2006).

comprehensive, each with the same result, that is unless his aim is to link divine activity with the particular human endeavor of mission. Christian mission as enacted by missionaries and the mission activity of the church eventually makes its way into these ultimate concerns. As much as Wright tries to distance *mission* from *missionary*, missional hermeneutic as general, divine intention becomes specific actions of missionaries.[39] Gorman, on the other hand, connects human participation directly to divine mission, in order to assert, "*All Christian praxis is inherently missional*," and thus interpretation must lead to the question of how "we discern *our* role in the divine mission (the *missio Dei*) in *our* situation today."[40] Therefore, in the comprehensive language of "mission," Barram, Wright, and Gorman not only conflate divine and human activity but also inflect Scripture with mission and missionary.

David Filbeck is less nuanced and more direct in his claim that mission is "the missing dimension" or emphasis that readers must rediscover "in order to adequately explain the message of the Old Testament for our age."[41] His claim, as he explores and applies the mission dimension to the Old Testament, is that it "gives structure to the whole Bible" in "a way that no other theological theme can hope to match."[42] Unlike Wright, Barram, and Gorman, Filbeck does not hesitate to blatantly use *mission* or *missionary* in their contemporary senses. He asserts, "The missionary message of the Old Testament may be termed the missionary hermeneutic, or more simply the hermeneutic, of the Old Testament."[43] He exhorts readers to approach the Old Testament by way of "a missionary interpretation" and "a missionary dimension," so that interpreters may see "the missionary message" and "missionary understanding" through "the missionary structure" of the Old Testament.

Richard Bauckham frames his hermeneutical approach in a slightly different manner. Rather than mission location or mission narrative, his

---

[39]Wright, *Mission of God*, 106, 501, 502, 504-5.
[40]Gorman, *Becoming the Gospel*, 40, 50. Gorman's emphasis. Flemming, *Why Mission?*, defines mission in a manner similar to Wright and Gorman and likewise connects the broad, divine purposes of the mission of God directly to the missionary endeavor (see 48).
[41]Filbeck, *Yes, God of the Gentiles, Too*, 8, 9.
[42]Ibid., 10.
[43]Ibid., 19.

concern is "how to read the Bible in a way that takes seriously its missionary direction."[44] The Bible's missionary direction, he maintains, is best seen in the movement from the particular to the universal. This movement is the framework of a particular story "towards the universal realization of God's kingdom in all creation." "In the narrative work of the Bible," Bauckham contends, "the people of God is also given its identity in this movement from the particular to the universal, an identity whose God-given dynamic we commonly sum up in the word 'mission.'"[45] Bauckham maintains that the kingdom of God is the main theme of the Bible, but mission is the hermeneutical window through which we are able to interpret this theme of direction. Through mission, the narrative of particular stories moves in a variety of ways toward the kingdom of the one God.

Writing from a Caribbean-Latino perspective, Carlos Cardoza-Orlandi claims that the purpose of a missional hermeneutic "is to discover in the biblical text the distinct perspectives of God's mission and God's peoples' participation (or lack thereof) in order to help us discern and continue to participate in the mission of God in our days."[46] In other words, a missional hermeneutic should lead to participation in God's mission that expresses itself in a variety of ways. This kind of hermeneutic is not built on "a literal reading or a traditional interpretation of the passage, but rather the *missional perspective with which the text is read.*"[47] Mission means translatability, so a key component for Cardoza-Orlandi is the inclusion of voices from other faith traditions. A missional reading of the text is an enriched reading.

Shawn B. Redford offers yet another version of the missional-hermeneutical approach. In response to what he considers to be a secularized hermeneutical process (the historical-critical hermeneutic methodology), as well as "a very basic missiological hermeneutic" employed by some scholars, Redford offers a "biblically informed missional hermeneutics" that focuses on intertextual interpretations that reveal mission

---

[44]Richard Bauckham, *Bible and Mission: Christian Witness in a Postmodern World* (Grand Rapids: Baker Academic, 2003), 11.

[45]Ibid., 13.

[46]Carlos F. Cardoza-Orlandi, *Mission: An Essential Guide* (Nashville: Abingdon, 2002), 54.

[47]Ibid., 64. Cardoza-Orlandi's emphasis.

interpretations within Scripture.[48] According to Redford, these are instances in which biblical figures interpret existing scriptural promises as mission and are thus examples of where "the people of God 'got it,' meaning that they put aside their own misconceived theologial and missiological baggage and understood God's missional concerns. The real crux is to discover what made the difference in their renewed understanding of Scripture that ultimately improved their mission practice."[49] For example, when Peter and Paul interpret the Old Testament by way of a "missional hermeneutic," they discover God's "missional concerns" as expressed in the Old Testament and then make "missional application." The problem, Redford maintains, is that "the genuine mission activity in Scripture is drowned out by a hurricane of contemporary 'theological' force, . . . leaving Christians and non-Christians with the perception that Scripture has little to say in terms of mission."[50] In order to privilege the intertextual approach, Redford focuses on the emotional and psychological background of biblical characters and their responses to scriptural promises and activities, and thereby he is able to identify the transformation of their understanding and practice. The overall aim is to detect where these missional interpretations produced a "missional breakthrough" and then identify how their "missional insight" should guide the interpretation of the biblical witness, as well as current mission practice.[51] Redford reasons that since biblical figures, such as Jesus, Paul, and Peter, "consistently make use of missional hermeneutic in their own interpretation of the Old Testament . . . Scripture itself demonstrates an underlying and expanding missional hermeneutic."[52]

Redford's particular form of missional hermeneutics raises several questions. First, what makes an intertextual hermeneutic missional? The criteria by which some intertextual hermeneutics are classified as missional and others as nonmissional are not identified. Or should we assume that all examples of intertextual hermeneutic are ultimately missional? He simply

---

[48]Shawn B. Redford, *Missiological Hermeneutics: Biblical Interpretation for the Global Church,* American Society of Missiology Monograph Series 11 (Eugene, OR: Pickwick, 2012), 1, 3, 8.
[49]Ibid., 10.
[50]Ibid., 292.
[51]Ibid., 10, 84.
[52]Ibid., 68.

says that they are "missional" rather than offering distinguishing characteristics for a missional intertextual interpretation. Related to this is a second question. What does Redford mean by *mission* and *missional*? He assumes mission language without clarification of what is meant. A definition of *mission* is supplied in the glossary at the back of his book but not in the discussion. In this definition, he repeats Stephen Neill's understanding of mission with its emphasis on the church crossing barriers, proclamation in word and deed, and the coming of the kingdom of God in Jesus Christ. Redford adds that mission does not have to be crosscultural but can occur "within one's own cultural context by indigenous workers."[53] Thus, in Redford's missional hermeneutics, *mission* can be read as either narrow or broad, domestic or international. Third, and most importantly, is Redford justified in generalizing from what he labels as a missional intertextual interpretation to all of Scripture? For him, mission discovered in identifiable intertextual interpretations means that all of Scripture is missional. This hermeneutical leap results in a totalization of *mission* and *missional*. Not only do biblical figures, such as Joseph, Peter, and Paul, have a "missional hermeneutic," but Abraham's witness is "missional witness"; Jacob's life has "missional impact" and a "missionary calling"; Melchizedek provides "a very powerful missional contrast" and has a "missional role"; Joseph has a "missional vision" and reflects "a larger missional fulfillment"; Daniel, Shadrach, Meshach, and Abednego are "examples of missionary witness"; and the early church is a "missional community."[54] Likewise, God's intent, concerns, providence, promises, response, agenda, plan, vision, efforts, and heart are "missional," as he enacts his "providential missionary activity."[55]

As these various streams illustrate, *missional hermeneutic* should be read as plural—hermeneutics, conceived and applied in different ways. Nevertheless, whether the focus is location, narrative, direction, inclusion, or intertextuality, this "hermeneutic of diversity," according to James Brownson, is biblically and theologically grounded.[56] He cites evidence for this grounding in the particular election of both Israel and the church. This

---

[53]Ibid., 325-26.
[54]Ibid., 25, 26, 27, 30, 31, 37n32, 58, 69.
[55]Ibid., 9, 10, 41, 43, 45, 50, 52, 54, 64, 66, 70.
[56]Brownson, "Speaking the Truth in Love," 13.

election, he claims, entails God's universal, salvific purposes, which Brownson understands in terms of the multicultural dynamism of God's activity and concern for the whole world. Brownson uses *mission* because it expresses a vision of "God who enters deeply into the everyday particularity of each cultural setting," while also maintaining that God "invites us to widen our vision to a vast human community."[57] And yet, these evidential pieces could serve not just a missional hermeneutic but any number of hermeneutical agendas. One might ask, what makes Brownson's hermeneutical posture distinctively missional? Justifications for labeling this approach as *mission* or *missional* are never explored by Brownson except to assert that the early church has "a specifically missionary character."[58] Brownson's construction of a missional hermeneutic as an "interpretative matrix" could have easily been designated as a coherent, centered, or holistic hermeneutic rather than missional.[59] The point is that the categorization is not only extrabiblical (i.e., the language and its implications are imposed on Scripture), but it is a privileging of one type of descriptive terminology when other types appear to be just as suitable. Given the recent rhetorical history of the language of mission, traced in later chapters, the idea of a *missional* hermeneutic is more than an arbitrary preference: it is a historically contingent "interpretative matrix" and a modern addition to Christian history and thought. Therefore, one must ask if a *missional* hermeneutic is necessary or appropriate, as it appears to be an imposition of foreign notions on the sacred texts being interpreted.

Christopher Wright insists that rather than creating a bias, "a missional hermeneutic of the whole Bible" subsumes other hermeneutics and offers a way to read the Bible's "coherent story with a universal claim" amid so many particular stories and claims.[60] Wright argues that mission is uniquely qualified, because it integrates and provides coherence and wholeness to Scripture. A "missiological reading of biblical theology," according to Wright, allows the interpreter "to identify some of the underlying themes that are woven all through the Bible's grand narrative."[61] Wright's rationale is that

---

[57]Ibid., 238, 239.
[58]Ibid., 233.
[59]Ibid., 246-57.
[60]Wright, *Mission of God*, 41, 44, 47.
[61]Ibid., 17, 18.

"the Bible is itself a 'missional' phenomenon," and therefore it is necessary to read Scripture through this particular hermeneutical lens in order to make sense of its narrative.[62] Wright's attempt to provide a comprehensive framework to the biblical narrative is certainly worthwhile and needed, and yet, is mission the necessary, or best, "hermeneutical map"?

While far better than a biblical foundation for mission, a missional hermeneutic is suspect in its own way. The idea of a missional hermeneutic admits a bias toward or privileging of mission in the interpretive process. One is saying, in effect, "I have a prejudiced starting point. I am reading Scripture from a prior understanding that anticipates a certain outcome." And yet, admitting such a bias does not automatically justify one's hermeneutic or the privileging of mission language. The fact that one admits a hermeneutical starting point, in other words, does not make that particular hermeneutical approach right, correct, or legitimate. Part of the process of exegesis is to identify and inspect the lenses through which we read the text. To privilege a particular hermeneutic is to deny that others exist or to question their validity. Graham Stanton warns of the interpreter who allows "his own personal bias or prejudice or his pre-understanding to dominate the text." While this cannot be avoided in some measure, our pre-understanding "must be no more than a door through which the text is approached. The text is prior: the interpreter stands before it humbly and prays that through the scholarly methods and the question with which he comes to the text, God's word will be heard afresh."[63] In order to do this, one must avoid biases, not add more. Those who advocate for a missional hermeneutic claim that rather than obscuring the text or coating it with unnecessary bias, their approach actually facilitates faithfulness to the text and provides a serious response to the contemporary world. Brownson champions a missional hermeneutic, because it "places the question of the relationship between Christianity and diverse cultures at the very top of the interpretative agenda."[64] But by doing this, advocates of a missional

---

[62]Ibid., 22.

[63]Graham N. Stanton, "Presuppositions in New Testament Criticism," in *New Testament Interpretation: Essays on Principles and Methods*, ed. I. Howard Marshall (Exeter, UK: Paternoster, 1985), 69.

[64]Brownson, "Speaking the Truth in Love," 233. Brownson expands these arguments in James V. Brownson, *Speaking the Truth in Love: New Testament Resources for a Missional Hermeneutic*, Christian Mission and Modern Culture (Harrisburg, PA: Trinity Press International, 1998).

hermeneutic assume that the relationship between Christianity and culture is the chief issue for interpretation and thus privileges it. And yet, is culture the one issue above all other issues?

The chief criticism of a missional hermeneutic is that it places secondary and even foreign conditions on divine revelation. The hermeneutical lens of mission unnecessarily qualifies activities, institutions, and attitudes as mission and missionary. Read through the hermeneutical lens of mission, preaching becomes *missionary preaching*, work becomes *missionary work*, method becomes *missionary method*, activity becomes *missionary activity*, and experience becomes *missionary experience*. This particular reading of Scripture provides a filter that guarantees a specific missionary interpretation. Once the whole of Scripture passes through the filter of a missional hermeneutic, every piece looks like mission. As in the case of the biblical foundation for mission, a missional hermeneutic tends to totalize mission. And such totalization leads to distortion. If the lens itself is blurred or monocular, the interpretation is myopic and will foster areas of blindness. What if, as I attempt to demonstrate in chapters five to eight, the lens itself is cloudy or marred? What if the development and historical meaning of mission makes the missional lens problematic? Or what if there is more to everything in Scripture than just mission? Through the hermeneutical lens of mission, Wright claims that events, actions, and emphases obtain "missional relevance," "missional significance," "missional thrust," and "missional perspective."[65] But must biblical events be "missional" in order to have relevance and significance, or to be a worthy perspective? When mission equals significance or relevance, then covenant automatically must be interpreted as "missional covenant," love becomes "missional love," motivation turns into "missional motivation," and blessing and election are identified as missional.[66] In the end, the rich, biblical language of covenant, love, blessing, and election becomes less than relevant, is categorized as inadequate, and is in need of a qualifying adjective.

What should guide the interpreter in his or her hermeneutical approach to Scripture? Possibly one place to look for guidance is the canonization of the New Testament. The long process by which the limits of the New

---

[65]Wright, *Mission of God*, 103, 106, 122, 126, 132, 177.
[66]Ibid., 129, 177, 179, 211. See also Flemming, *Why Mission?*, 58.

Testament canon were set is a window into how the faith and practice of the church was measured and approved. Canonization reveals criteria for inclusion and exclusion, standards and framework for interpretation. Thus, was a "missional reading" among the standard by which the early church determined the authenticity or worthiness of books? Or to ask the question another way, is there a "canonical basis" for mission? H. D. Beeby believes this is the case and thus asks, "If mission requires a canonical basis, does the canon in some ways demand a missionary hermeneutic if it is more fully to release it riches so that treasures both old and new might emerge?"[67] He probes further—"Is it possible that among the *raison d'être* of the canon concepts and of the specific canons we can find cause to say that they were called into being for a missionary purpose?"[68] Beeby's answer to both questions is yes, and the means for discovery of this missionary purpose is a missionary hermeneutic. He does not deny the place of other hermeneutical approaches, but the missionary motivation of the missionary hermeneutic should have "a normative function."[69] Beeby's assertion is that missionary demands and concerns prioritized some books over others and guided in the formation of the canon. And while "mission" is cited as a contributing factor in the formation of the canon by Beeby and other commentators, there is no evidence that the modern rhetoric or conception of "mission" played a role for the ancient church in forming the canon.[70] Rather, the canon came into being as the measurement, boundary, or norm for faith and practice—the church's *rule of faith*. Critieria for the books that became authoritative included a range of concerns: authorship, inspiration, and ecclesial use.[71] Mission, as either an idea or hermeneutic, was not identified by the church fathers or early historians in deliberations concerning the

---

[67]Beeby, *Canon and Mission*, 100-101.

[68]Ibid., 103.

[69]Ibid., 113. Beeby admits that one of the weaknesses in his approach is the absence of a definition of *mission*. While he sketches the parameters of a missionary hermeneutic, he leaves the question of which mission (Roman Catholic, charismatic, Orthodox, or Reformed) unanswered.

[70]See Lee Martin McDonald, *Formation of the Bible: The Story of the Church's Canon* (Peabody, MA: Hendrickson, 2012), 90, 104; Michael J. Kruger, *The Question of Canon: Challenging the Status Quo in the New Testament Debate* (Downers Grove, IL: IVP Academic, 2013), 76.

[71]Bruce M. Metzger, *The Canon of the New Testament: Its Origin, Development, and Significance* (Oxford: Clarendon, 1987), 251-57.

formation of the canon.[72] Indeed, the early church viewed Jesus Christ as the canon or standard for Scripture. He, above all other measurements, is the authoritative center, the norming standard for Scripture.

An overriding concern for many Apologists is that a missional hermeneutic is necessary because mission has been neglected or slighted.[73] It is feared that unless one's reading of Scripture is in some way tilted toward mission, mission will not be given its proper place. But what if mission has been neglected because, in fact, it does not have a prominent place in canonization, location, intertextual interpretation, and language of the text? What if "mission" must be used as a lens in order to appear in the text in the first place? Or what if it is given too much of a place? The case may be that when mission is privileged as a priori via a missional hermeneutic, other emphases, clearly evident in the text, are slighted and do not receive adequate attention and proper place.

While the shift to a missional hermeneutic offers Apologists a more defensible justification for mission, the question of the priority of this particular lens of interpretation and its language remains. In a missional hermeneutic, the meaning and use of *mission* becomes murkier and even more confusing, especially for those not versed in the amended definitions of mission. Those utilizing a missional hermeneutic argue for a biased reading of the biblical text that guarantees a "mission interpretation," based on a specialized use of mission. In the end, justifying mission by way of a missional hermeneutic is a form of revision, rehabilitation, or reformulation of mission and skirts the central problems of mission language—its history, use, and meaning.

Mission themes. In an attempt to rescue mission from the absolutizing tendencies of establishing a biblical foundation or a missional hermeneutic, some have instead identified missionary themes—emphases, motifs, aspects, or ideas—across Scripture. Through these, interpreters highlight "mission

---

[72]Craig G. Bartholomew, *Introducing Biblical Hermeneutics: A Comprehensive Framework for Hearing God in Scripture* (Grand Rapids: Baker Academic, 2015), 5-16.

[73]Redford, *Missiological Hermeneutics*, 1-2, 8-10. Michael W. Goheen, *Introducing Christian Mission Today: Scripture, History, and Issues* (Downers Grove, IL: InterVarsity Press, 2014), contends, "Happily, a missional hermeneutic is developing today that attends to the central importance of mission in interpreting Scripture. Moreover, in the past the universalization of an Enlightenment methodology has masked the local character of a Western hermeneutical approach to Scripture suppressing other contextual approaches and marginalizing mission" (27-28).

intent" or "mission consciousness" within Scripture, often acknowledging that themes or motifs appear within certain books of the Bible and not others.[74] This approach is quite different from a foundationalist approach, as it offers "mission" as a frame of reference that guides the reading both of the Old and New Testaments, but it is only slightly different from a missional hermeneutic. As such, this method is a bit more modest in its claims.

An example of the mission theme method is found in Walter Kaiser, who claims that "the Bible actually begins with the theme of missions in the Book of Genesis and maintains that driving passion throughout the entire Old Testament and on into the New Testament."[75] Repeatedly, Kaiser places "the theme of missions" into the events in the life of Israel and the early church. "This theme of a mission to the whole world," he says, "forms one giant envelope (a figure of speech called an *inclusio*) framing the whole Bible, from Genesis to Revelation."[76] Thus, for Kaiser, the mission theme is the key to faithful interpretation of all Scripture. The mission theme does not operate alongside other themes but is paramount, defining Scripture from beginning to end. The idea of "theme" is so comprehensive that it seems to function for Kaiser as another word for hermeneutic.

Senior and Stuhlmueller, in a more modest manner, guide the reader through the Old and New Testaments in order to identify the "missionary impulse" or "missionary thrust" in the Prophets, historical accounts, Gospels, and Epistles.[77] With each chapter or new topic, they ask "the

---

[74]See William J. Larkin Jr., "Mission in Acts," in Larkin and Williams, *Mission in the New Testament: An Evangelical Approach*, 178-80; Joel F. Williams, "Conclusion," in Lark and Williams, *Mission in the New Testament: An Evangelical Approach*, 241-44; Williams, "The Missionary Message of the New Testament," 47; Stephen G. Wilson, *The Gentiles and the Gentile Mission in Luke–Acts* (Cambridge: Cambridge University Press, 1973), 1, 54-55, 57, 193, 239, 242, 245; Glover, *Bible Basis of Missions*, 29; Starkes, *Foundation for Missions*, 28-34, 49; Henry Cornell Goerner, *Thus It Is Written: The Missionary Motif in the Scriptures* (Nashville: Broadman, 1944); John Quinlan, "A Missionary Reflection From St. John," in *A New Missionary Era*, ed. Padraig Flanagan (Maryknoll, NY: Orbis Books, 1979), 120-22; Donald E. Messer, *A Conspiracy of Goodness: Contemporary Images of Christian Mission* (Nashville: Abingdon, 1992), 34-44; Andreas J. Köstenberger and Peter Thomas O'Brien, *Salvation to the Ends of the Earth: A Biblical Theology of Mission*, New Studies in Biblical Theology 11 (Downers Grove, IL: InterVarsity Press, 2001), 20.
[75]Kaiser, *Mission in the Old Testament*, 7.
[76]Ibid.
[77]Senior and Stuhlmueller, *Biblical Foundations for Mission*, 142, 205.

mission question" and respond with a particular "missionary thrust."[78] For example, in their discussion concerning the relationship of Jesus' purpose and that of the early church in Luke–Acts, Senior and Stuhlmueller note, "Here is where the mission question comes to the fore."[79] Harnack likewise reads the New Testament with the intent of finding "missionary zeal," "missionary impulse," "missionary function," "missionary force," and "missionary influence."[80] Geoffrey Harris leads the reader to "perceive aspects of the Church's mission in the later part of the first century by reading between the lines of the Gospel accounts."[81] His method can be seen as he repeatedly highlights mission patterns, themes, ideas, flavors, phases, concerns, aspects, motifs, and signs.[82] The method of Eckhard Schnabel in his massive two-volume study of the historical and social conditions of the early Christian mission is to identify the "missionary dimension" and the "missionary intention that is linked with specific action."[83] These dimensions and intentions frame a thematic approach through which Schnabel is able to emphasize the transmission of the universal message and to identify the activities of agents who communicate this message. With this perspective as his compass, Schnabel locates a missionary dimension and intention in all kinds of activity.[84] Schnabel defends his methods of interpretation by maintaining that these dimensions and intentions are true to the "missionary

---

[78]For Senior and Stuhlmueller, "the mission question is intrinsic to the Bible" (ibid., 3). At the outset of sections and discussions, they remind the reader that the question of mission or the mission question is the central concern. See, for example, 161, 177, 211, 233, 235, 238, 275, 280, 297, 309, 318, 320.

[79]Ibid., 256.

[80]Adolf Harnack, *The Mission and Expansion of Christianity in the First Three Centuries* (New York: Harper, 1962), 9, 441, 511, 512.

[81]R. Geoffrey Harris, *Mission in the Gospels* (London: Epworth, 2004), xii.

[82]Harris's extensive use of these words in *Mission in the Gospels* points to his method: patterns (43, 75, 93, 111, 133, 142, 160, 171, 172, 181), themes (47, 48, 62, 68, 74, 75, 83, 110, 139, 140, 154, 158, 183), ideas (53), flavor (57), phases (57, 123, 134), concern (70), aspects (108, 110, 112, 201, 232), motifs (112), and sign (79).

[83]Eckhard J. Schnabel, *Early Christian Mission*, vol. 1, *Jesus and the Twelve* (Downers Grove, IL: InterVarsity Press, 2004), 10. For the language of "missionary intentions," see also Stanley E. Porter and Cynthia Long Westfall, "A Cord of Three Strands: Mission in Acts," in *Christian Mission: Old Testament Foundations and New Testament Developments*, ed. Stanley E. Porter and Cynthia Long Westfall, McMaster New Testament Studies Series (Eugene, OR: Pickwick, 2010), 123.

[84]See, for example, Schnabel, *Early Christian Mission*, 1:13.

idea," because they are accompanied by "missionary praxis," identified
specifically as going and witnessing.[85]

Borrowing language from Thomas Kuhn, David Bosch turns missionary
theme into "missionary paradigm." Paradigm, in Bosch's approach, signifies
a shift or change in perspective, as well as a static characterization of person's ideas or of a historical period. For example, he chronicles the historical
shift from the missionary paradigm of primitive Christianity to that of the
Eastern church.[86] In a similar manner, Bosch highlights "elements which are
unique to the Matthean paradigm of mission," as well as Lukan and Pauline
missionary paradigms.[87] These collectively make up the "Apocalyptic Paradigm," the primal or the first of six subsequent historical mission paradigms. The notion of "paradigm" becomes Bosch's interpretive device for
emphasizing singular issues as mission, as well as larger themes and whole
periods of history.

With a slightly different twist, M. R. Spindler characterizes mission as a
theological theme. Spindler appeals to Scripture to justify mission not on
the basis of language but as "a natural and self-evident activity" of Scripture.
For him, this natural and self-evident basis is supernatural and thus theological.[88] His concern lies in two directions: "fundamentalists," who offer a
simplified biblical foundation for mission, and "modernists," who employ
mission without reference to the Bible. In navigating between these two
extremes, he insists, "a biblical grounding of mission is not just one among
several ways to justify mission, but the justification par excellence."[89] This
assertion sets in motion his construction of a framework of various theological topics to justify the essence and methods of mission. Rather than
grounding mission in a foundation or via a hermeneutic, Spindler locates
mission in the themes of sending, discipleship, deliverance, witness,

---

[85]See ibid., 1:1-12, 59, 90, 91.

[86]*TM*, 185-94. Bosch uses the language of *dimension* rather than *paradigm* in his earlier work,
David J. Bosch, *Witness to the World: The Christian Mission in Theological Perspective* (Atlanta:
John Knox, 1980), 98.

[87]*TM*, 81, 114, 172.

[88]M. R. Spindler, "The Biblical Grounding and Orientation of Mission," in *Missiology: An Ecumenical Introduction, Texts and Contexts of Global Christianity*, ed. A. Camps et al. (Grand Rapids:
Eerdmans, 1995), 124.

[89]Ibid.

salvation history, and eschatology.[90] Mission, he maintains, is not complete in any one of these, but its grounding lies partially in all. His theology of mission has a polemical undertone that critiques the modern understanding and use of the term. According to Spindler, the modern view of mission is too natural, while he alternatively grounds mission in the transcendent activity of God.[91] Spindler's assessment is that many practitioners misuse the Bible to offer a contrived justification for established missionary practice and methods. He insists that mission must "be seen as arising from something fundamental, from the basic movement of God's people toward the world."[92] Spindler's critique of other approaches is helpful, and yet, like Harris, Schnabel, and Bosch, Spindler's overall aim is to perpetuate the idea of mission itself. While he offers a more robust theological justification of mission, mission is still a priori, and thus it is still the prevailing category. The constant for these Apologists is the language of mission, and thus the semantic problem remains.

In each of these three methods, justifying mission via an interpretive matrix, as theological a priori, or in a governing theme, there is a common problem. Whether constructing a foundation, employing a missional hermeneutic, or focusing on mission themes, each dodges the linguistic conflation and the historical contingencies of the language of "mission." N. T. Wright, in his exposition of the aims and intentions of the apostle Paul, notes our tendency to "squash [these] into something smaller." He has in mind specifically the "normal modern western meanings of words like 'mission' and 'evangelism.'" He notes that there has been

> a good deal of discussion as to what these words mean, and no agreement is in sight. Both words are labels which different groups stick on different activities which for whatever reason they believe they ought to undertake (or, in the case of some relativists, believe they ought not to undertake). The meanings shift with the activities.[93]

---

[90]Nissen offers a similar theological framework using trinitarian and incarnational categories. He does this in order to locate mission in the Gospel of John; *New Testament and Mission*, 89-93.

[91]Spindler, "Biblical Grounding and Orientation of Mission," 136.

[92]Ibid., 125. Spindler indicates that he is using "a layered concept of 'biblical grounding'" that navigates between the tensions of those who see the Bible only as a book of doctrine and those who give inadequate attention to doctrine (126).

[93]N. T. Wright, *Paul and the Faithfulness of God* (Minneapolis: Fortress, 2013), 2:1484.

Indeed, the variances in meaning that exist because of the conflation and contingencies of mission do not disappear through argumentation for its place within Scripture. Inherent problems with mission justification only intensify as Apologists attempt to legitimize mission language by way of a lexical trail from ancient words or a semantic field.

Lexical trail. The approach of some Apologists is to trace the route that leads from the biblical languages to the English term *mission.* Such a lexical trail begins with the Greek *apostellein* and *pempein,* and then moves to the Latin *missio,* and finally arrives at mission.[94] The quest is to establish a biblical pedigree for mission through linguistic genealogy. Some create an even longer trail beginning with the Hebrew term *shalakh* (to send), and then move to Greek, Latin, and the modern equivalent.[95] For these interpreters, mission originates from the Hebrew concept of sending, especially in the divine sending of messengers (prophets and angels). Whether the trail begins with the Hebrew or the Greek, the principal aim is to justify mission by way of its biblical lineage.

One interpreter who justifies mission via a lexical trail is Lucien Cerfaux. His premise is that "just as the mission of the Apostles is the mission pattern which will be reproduced countless times until the very end of time, so the advice of our Lord is our pattern too. It is true for all missions and for all apostolates."[96] He makes such a statement on the assumption

---

[94]See Jongeneel, *Philosophy, Science, and Theology of Mission,* 50-51, 58-59; Jacques A. Blocher and Jacques Blandenier, *The Evangelization of the World: A History of Christian Mission* (Pasadena, CA: William Carey Library, 2013), xv; Eckhard J. Schnabel, *Paul the Missionary: Realities, Strategies and Methods* (Downers Grove, IL: IVP Academic, 2008), 22-27. There are Partisans who mount a similar defense of mission: see Willis, *Biblical Basis of Missions,* 11.

[95]See Kaiser, *Mission in the Old Testament,* 11-12; McDaniel, "Mission in the Old Testament," 11-20. Schnabel, *Early Christian Mission,* argues that there is "a semantic gap" between the Hebrew term and *apostello* (1:282-83). See also Schnabel, "'As the Father Has Sent Me, So I Send You' (John 20:21): The Mission of Jesus and the Mission of the Church," *Missionalia* 33, no. 2 (August 2005): 279. Jongeneel, *Philosophy, Science, and Theology of Mission,* indicates that while there is a connection between the Hebrew and Greek terms, "there is no likeness" between the two (120). Francis H. Agnew, "The Origin of the NT Apostle-Concept: A Review of Research," *Journal of Biblical Literature* 105, no. 1 (March 1986): 75-96, provides a detailed account for the arguments for and against the *apostello* and *shalakh* connection, favoring, in the final analysis, a relationship between the two. David Daube, *The New Testament and Rabbinic Judaism,* Jordan Lectures 1952 (London: Athlone, 1956), 352-61, finds reason to label other Hebrew terms (*kanas, qana, sakhar*) as "missionary terms."

[96]Lucien Cerfaux, *Apostle and Apostolate According to the Gospel of St. Matthew,* trans. Donald D. Duggan (New York: Desclee, 1960), 3.

that there is a direct connection between apostolate and missionary, and thus mission must be the pattern for all people at all times. A similar correspondence is made by Jan A. B. Jongeneel: "The Greek noun *apostole* = apostolate, apostleship, (com)mission."[97] Cornell Goerner states without explanation, "The word *apostle* means 'one sent forth,' or 'missionary.'"[98] Seyoon Kim references Paul's use of *apostolē* as "an eschatological herald of the gospel to the Gentiles," and thus proof of Paul's "apostolic commission."[99] By extension, he then asserts that Paul is a "missionary" with "missionary destination" and an "apostolic mission."[100] Likewise, Catholic historian Joseph Schmidlin maintains that because *apostle* etymologically means ambassador or messenger, as in the case of Paul and others in the New Testament, this means they are "the first vocational missionaries of Christianity."[101] Thus, Schmidlin finds reason to derive missionary vocation and missionary office from the biblical word *apostle*. Once a lexical trail is established, the interpreter is able by extension to connect mission language to a host of concepts and ideas. In other words, the effort to link *apostolos* and *apostellein* to mission language does not stop with evidence of a trail but turns into a matter of wider interpretation. Persons, activities, institutions, and locations are designated as "missionary" once a trail is established.

While *pempo* and *apostello* are both translated as "send," Apologists focus in the main on *apostello* and its derivatives, *apostolē* and *apostolos*, when establishing a lexical connection.[102] *Apostellein*, the verb form, is

---

[97] Jongeneel, *Philosophy, Science, and Theology of Mission*, 50.

[98] Henry Cornell Goerner, *All Nations in God's Purpose: What the Bible Teaches About Missions* (Nashville: Broadman, 1979), 99. See also Jongeneel, *Philosophy, Science, and Theology of Mission*, 57; Willis, *Biblical Basis of Missions*, 108; Sherwood Eddy, *Pathfinders of the World Missionary Crusade* (New York: Abingdon-Cokesbury, 1945), 13.

[99] Seyoon Kim, "Paul as an Eschatological Herald," in *Paul as Missionary: Identity, Activity, Theology, and Practice*, ed. Trevor J. Burke and Brian S. Rosner, Library of New Testament Studies 420 (London: T&T Clark, 2011), 13-16.

[100] Ibid., 9, 13, 16.

[101] Joseph Schmidlin, *Catholic Mission History*, ed. Matthias Braun (Techny, IL: Mission Press, S. V. D. 1933), 57, 58, 67, 123. For other examples, see Roger Bowen, *So I Send You: A Study Guide to Mission* (London: SPCK, 1996), 38; Webster, *Yes to Mission*, 39; Don Dent, "Apostles Even Now," in Barnett and Martin, *Discovering the Mission of God*, 356; Scott Sunquist, *Understanding Christian Mission: Participation in Suffering and Glory* (Grand Rapids: Baker Academic, 2013), 7, 8.

[102] On the use of *pempo* and *apostello*, see Andreas J. Köstenberger, "The Two Johannine Verbs for Sending: A Study of John's Use of Words with Reference to General Linguistic Theory," in *Linguistics and the New Testament* (Sheffield, UK: Sheffield Academic, 1999), 143.

found 135 times in the New Testament and conveys the idea of sending out or sending forth.[103] This verb usage carries both a general and specified meaning. In its general sense, *apostellein* refers to a wide range of sending of persons and objects: Herod *sends* those who kill male children (Mt 2:16), demons beg to be *sent* into swine (Mt 8:31), a message or word is *sent* forth (Mt 14:35; Mk 3:31; Acts 10:36; 13:15), and workers are *sent* into the vineyard (Mt 20:2). These instances are ordinary and commonplace kinds of sending.

However, the more prevalent use of *apostellein* refers to the sending of an envoy, ambassador, or representative, and thus "sending implies a commission bound up with the person of the one sent."[104] In secular Greek, this representative kind of sending is from a monarch, king, or another authority, and thus the sending carries with it deputation. In the New Testament, we see this type of sending applied to a variety of people and situations: the Twelve/disciples (Mt 10:5, 16; Mk 3:14; 6:7; 11:1; 14:13; Lk 9:2; Jn 17:18); the seventy-two (Lk 10:1); the Son (Mt 10:40; 15:24; Mk 9:37; Lk 4:43; Jn 3:17; 6:57; 17:3; Acts 3:20; 1 Jn 4:9; 4:14); John the Baptist (Mt 11:10; Mk 1:2; Jn 1:6); angels (Mt 13:41; 24:31; Mk 13:27; Lk 1:26; Rev 1:1); the Holy Spirit (Lk 24:49; 1 Pet 1:12); Ananias (Acts 9:17); prophets and wise men (Mt 23:34, 37); Paul (1 Cor 1:17); and servants (Mt 21:34, 36; 22:3, 4; Mk 12:2, 4; Lk 11:17; 20:10). In this use, the sending is for a definite purpose or intent, and the one sent thus carries with him or her authorization of the one who sends. In most New Testament instances of the verb, the authorization or authority is divine in origin and not from another human being.[105]

The noun form *apostolē* occurs only four times (Acts 1:24-25; Rom 1:5; 1 Cor 9:2; Gal 2:8). Translators have rendered the term with consistency as "apostolate" and "apostolic ministry" or "the ministry which an apostle

---

[103]Jongeneel, *Philosophy, Science, and Theology of Mission*, 50; Karl Heinrich Rengstorf, "ἀποστέλλω," ed. Gerhard Kittel, *Theological Dictionary of the New Testament* (Grand Rapids: Eerdmans, 1964), 1:398, 403.

[104]Rengstorf, "ἀποστέλλω," 398. Rengstorf contrasts the NT use of ἀποστέλλω and πέμπω (403-4) and concludes that "when πέμπειν is used in the NT the emphasis is on the sending as such, whereas when ἀπέστελλειν is used it rests on the commission linked with it, no matter whether the one who sends or the one which is sent claims prior interest" (404). He highlights the peculiar use of these words in the Gospel of John. Rengstorf's differentiation of the two verbs is challenged by Köstenberger, "Two Johannine Verbs for Sending."

[105]Rengstorf indicates this same sense is what is found in the use of *apostellein* in the LXX and Judaism, "ἀποστέλλω," 400-402.

performs."[106] Bavinck translates *apostolē* as "the sending forth."[107] An apostolate has less to do with an office and more with being charged with a message; in other words, the conveying of this message is the chief function of the apostle.[108]

Apostolos is more frequent (seventy-nine times) and specifies one who has been sent.[109] An *apostolos* is a messenger. The one sent is under assignment to represent another and responsible to the one who charges him or her. The one sent therefore fully represents the sender. In its primary New Testament use, *apostolos* denotes one who is sent with authority to bear the gospel message (e.g., of Paul and Barnabas in Acts 14:4). Individuals are named as apostles of Christ (1 Thess 2:6) and apostles of the church (Phil 2:25). Also, Christ himself is referred to as *apostolos* (Heb 3:1).[110]

Translators of Greek to Latin and Greek to English rarely render *apostellein*, *apostello*, *apostolē*, and *apostolos* as "mission" and "missionary." In cases where these have been translated as such, the aim has been intelligibility and relevance and not a literal translation. In Latin translations, *apostolos* has infrequently been translated into corresponding Latin words. Instead, the Greek has been used as loan words (e.g., *apostolus*), especially for ecclesiastical references.[111] In the case of Greek to modern English translations and paraphrased versions of Scripture, translators have seldom

---

[106]Martin Luther, *A Commentary upon the Epistle of Paul to the Galatians* (Connecticut: Salmon S. Miles, 1837), 111; Hans Dieter Betz, *Galatians: A Commentary on Paul's Letter to the Churches in Galatia*, Hermeneia—A Critical and Historical Commentary on the Bible (Philadelphia: Fortress, 1979), 97-98; Adolf von Schlatter, *The Theology of the Apostles: The Development of New Testament Theology*, trans. Andreas J. Köstenberger (Grand Rapids: Baker Book House, 1999), 193-97; John Murray, *The Epistle to the Romans: The English Text with Introduction, Exposition and Notes* (Grand Rapids: Eerdmans, 1968), 12-13. C. K. Barrett, *Acts: A Shorter Commentary* (London: T&T Clark, 2002), renders Acts 1:25 simply as "service consisting of apostleship" (14); and Barclay Newman and Eugene Nida, *A Translator's Handbook on the Acts of the Apostles* (New York: United Bible Societies, 1966), indicate that it is to be understood as "the ministry which an apostle performs" (31).

[107]Bavinck, *Introduction to the Science of Missions*, xvi.

[108]See Rengstorf's discussion, "ἀποστέλλω," 427.

[109]Jongeneel, *Philosophy, Science, and Theology of Mission*, 50.

[110]Rengstorf, "ἀποστέλλω," 422-23.

[111]Ibid., 408. See also Theodore A. Bergren, *A Latin-Greek Index of the Vulgate New Testament: Based on Alfred Schmoller's Handkonkordanz Zum Griechishen Neuen Testament with an Index of Latin Equivalences Characteristic of "African" and "European" Old Latin Versions of the New Testament*, Resources for Biblical Study 26 (Atlanta: Scholars Press, 1991), 13.

rendered the Greek as "mission" and "missionary."[112] When they have done so, these words are used as dynamic or functional equivalents rather than literal or formal translations of Greek words.[113] For example, the Revised Standard Version (1952) renders the words of Paul as reporting that God "who worked through Peter for the mission to the circumcised worked through me also for the Gentiles" (Gal 2:8). The translators offer "mission" as an equivalence of ἀποστολὴν rather than "apostle" (TNIV), "apostleship" (NASB), or "ministry" (J. B. Philips). Thus, mission and missionary are equivalent or interpretive concepts and not direct, literal translations of the Greek sending verbs and nouns. The translators have determined that sending is at the root of the terms, and thus contemporary meanings of *mission* and *missionary* approximate the intent of the New Testament writers.[114] The claim of lexical trail for *mission* as a biblical word is in reality built on equivalence and not literal translation.

The linguistic trail presents several difficulties. The first, and most obvious, problem is that rather than a clear and literal lexical trail from the Greek terms to modern mission, there is, in fact, only a faint footpath of functional equivalence. Contrary to the claims of those who use this approach, a direct linguistic line cannot be drawn from *apostellein, apostello, apostolē,* and *apostolos* to "mission" and "missionary." The validity of the dynamic or functional equivalent rendering of these terms in mission language is not the chief issue here. Rather, the issue is one of assertion of a direct or literal trail from one to the other. The problem with the lexical trail as proof for mission is that it claims too much. Functional equivalence is not formal correspondence, and equivalence does not constitute a lexical trail.

Second, the lexical trail as an approach falls prey to the "root fallacy." James Barr explains that this fallacy occurs when the assumption is made that the "meaning" of any word equals that of its root. The meaning of a root

---

[112]"Mission" is found in the Twentieth Century New Testament (Gal 2:8), the Revised Standard Version (Gal 2:8; Acts 12:25; 2 Cor 11:12), and New International Version (Josh 22:3; 1 Sam 15:18, 20; 21:2, 5; Is 48:15; Acts 12:25). The Living Bible paraphrases most instances of *apostolos* as "missionary": Lk 6:13; Rom 1:1; 1 Cor 1:1; Gal 1:1; 1 Tim 1:1; 2:7; 2 Tim 1:1, 11; 1 Pet 1:1; 2 Pet 1:1.

[113]See Eugene A. Nida and Charles Taber, *The Theory and Practice of Translation* (Leiden: E. J. Brill, 1982), 12-14, 22-32.

[114]Schuyler Brown, "Apostleship in the New Testament as an Historical and Theological Problem," *New Testament Studies* 30, no. 3 (July 1984): 478. Cf. Michael C. Griffths, "Today's Missionary, Yesterday's Apostle," *Evangelical Missions Quarterly* 21, no. 2 (April 1985): 154-65.

does not necessarily convey the same meaning of one of its derived forms.[115] According to Barr, the root fallacy comes from "giving excessive weight to the origin of a word as against its actual semantic value."[116] A word may be related semantically or historically but not have the same meaning as the root from which it evolves. This means that a generalized overemphasis on a declension of words from a root can lead to spurious, misguided connections. Indeed, for mission to be argued from *apostello*, the root, the distinct semantic values of the two words, *apostello* and mission, must be overlooked. Wholesale translation of *apostello* to mission disregards the wide uses, ranging contexts, and variant meanings of the root term. This common error, Grant Osborne explains, "assumes that the root of a term and its cognates carries a basic meaning that is reflected in every subordinate use of the word(s)."[117] With the lexical trail, the basic assumption made by the Apologist is that in "'sending,' there is the idea of mission,"[118] and thus the meaning of mission is within the biblical term, and a connection can in most cases, if not always, be inferred and established.

Such an inference is made by Karl Rengstorf in his article on *apostellein* in the *Theological Dictionary of the New Testament*. He assumes a connection between the root verb and mission without even reference to the Latin *missio*, or without an explanation of the historical and contextual development of terms. He thus ties the root *apostello* directly to the language of "missionary enterprise," "missionary expedition," and the "missionary element."[119] Mission, in this way, crosses the line from rhetorical device to interpretation and quickly becomes an established way of modifying or designating peoples and places with a missionary kind of "sentness." While the interpretation of "sending" as mission may be a convenient way to create continuity between concepts in both Testaments and

---

[115]James Barr, *The Semantics of Biblical Language* (Oxford: Oxford University Press, 1961), 102.

[116]Ibid., 103. Barr adds that the damage with "etymologizing is not that they attempt to make historical statements about the words but that they are worked into arguments in which something seems to depend on these words, and commonly give a spurious twist to the meaning of a word at some crucial point in an argument" (108).

[117]Grant R. Osborne, *The Hermeneutical Spiral: A Comprehensive Introduction to Biblical Interpretation* (Downers Grove, IL: InterVarsity Press, 1991), 66.

[118]DuBose, *God Who Sends*, 24; Howard Peskett and Vinoth Ramachandra, *The Message of Mission: The Glory of Christ in All Time and Space*, The Bible Speaks Today (Downers Grove, IL: InterVarsity Press, 2003), 11.

[119]Rengstorf, "ἀποστέλλω," 400, 412, 418, 420, 422, 431-32, 435.

connect practices of the early church with those of the contemporary church, this kind of generalized association falls prey to the root fallacy, and, as we shall see later, comes with unintended historical references, uses, and meanings.

Third, the lexical trail approach underappreciates the extent to which the various forms of *apostellein* and *pempein* differ in use and meaning across the Gospels and Epistles.[120] In the case of *apostello*, it is obvious in some passages that Paul uses the word to refer to authority equal to that of Peter, while elsewhere he uses the word to assert his claim against those who preach another gospel. Each use has a context that should be appreciated and not ignored. James Barr is certainly correct in the contention that "all lexical treatments which neglect the determinative importance of the syntactical context risk misrepresentation of the facts."[121] He labels such as the "illegitimate totality transfer" of a word's use and meaning. When the meaning of a word is transferred from one place to another, the particularity or textual meanings are often ignored and can be lost. Problems arise "when the 'meaning' of a word . . . is read into a particular case as its sense and implication there."[122] In the case of mission, even if mission's meaning might be assigned to *apostolos* in one syntactical context, the same meaning does not necessarily transfer to the same word in another.

Fourth, while the linguistic trail purports to demonstrate a link between mission and New Testament words, it is in fact only a thirdhand etymological connection. The English word mission is not the Greek word *apostello*, and missionary is not *apostolos*. In order to connect *mission* and *apostle*, the interpreter must turn to Latin, not Greek. Apologists assert that mission and missionary have their roots in the Latin word *mittere*, meaning "to send."[123] And they are correct. "Mission" is the English translation of *mittere*. And yet, while *mittere* is the Latin translation of *apostello* and "mission" is the English translation of *mittere*, and while this points to an etymological connection, there is not necessarily a trail of meaning from *apostello* to

---

[120]See Ernest Best, "The Revelation to Evangelize the Gentiles," *Journal of Theological Studies* 35, no. 1 (April 1984): 20.

[121]James Barr, *Biblical Words for Time*, Studies in Biblical Theology 33 (London: SCM Press, 1962), 160.

[122]Barr, *Semantics of Biblical Language*, 218.

[123]Willis, *Biblical Basis of Missions*, 11; Pratt, Sills, and Walters, *Introduction to Global Missions*, 3.

mittere to mission.[124] Equality of meaning is assumed, because there is similarity in form, sound, and spelling. And yet, though the modern English word looks and sounds like the Latin *mittere* or *missio*, they are not necessarily the same words. One should not assume the similarity between the Latin *mittere* or *missio* and the English "mission" means they are cognates and thus a trail from one to the other. The leap from *mittere* to "mission" was not made in any of the Latin or early English translations. Though the Latin Vulgate renders the Greek verbs *apostellein* and *pempein* as *mittere* (and related forms, such as *mitto, misi,* and *missus*), the trail stops there. The noun form, *apostolos*, was considered unique enough that Jerome and those who followed him transliterated it rather than use a Latin equivalence. The nouns *missionibus* and *missionarius* are nowhere to be found in the Latin Vulgate.[125] And the earliest English translations of the Vulgate do not turn *mittere* into mission or missionary.[126] It is only in the modern era that a connection between *mittere* and mission is made, and only with Apologists does the lexical trail appear. A leap from what was originally meant and preserved in the text as *apostellein, apostolos,* and *apostole* to the modern expressions of mission disregards the fact that translators did not acknowledge the connection, nor did they create a trail. Instead, the lexical trail too easily traces mission from English to Latin to Greek and back again from Greek to Latin to English. In this means of justifying mission, the interpreter disregards the translator, and the translator disagrees with the interpreter.

In the end, justifying mission by means of a linguistic trail is faulty. The alleged trail from biblical words to mission can only be inferred and not literally established. And yet, the greater issue is when a quest to justify mission through sending terms governs one's interpretation of Scripture, other important emphases are denied their place. To base one's argument on

---

[124]For Schnabel, sending implies "intentionality and movement," and thus he is justified in equating "to send" with *mission* (*Paul the Missionary*, 22-23).

[125]Jongencel, *Philosophy, Science, and Theology of Mission*, 58.

[126]Neither word is found in the 1609 Douai Bible, trans. from the Vulgate, *The Holy Bible Translated from the Latin Vulgate: Diligently Compared with the Hebrew, Greek, and Other Editions in Diverse Languages. And First Published by the English College at Douay, Anno 1609. Newly Revised and Corrected, According to the Clementin Edition of the Scriptures. With Annotations for Clearing up the Principal Difficulties of Holy Writ.*, 4 vols. (Edinburgh: J. Moir, 1796). The 1823 translation of the Vulgate does insert *mission* into a section heading for Lk 3 in reference to John the Baptist, "John's mission and preaching." This, of course, is a nineteenth-century English translation, *Translation of the New Testament . . . from the Latin Vulgate* (London, 1823), 148.

a single Greek word and its Latin equivalence, *mittere,* accentuates "sending" over all other dimensions of redemptive history and activity. Such is the weakness of Frances DuBose's approach in *God Who Sends: A Fresh Quest for Biblical Mission.* The mission tail ends up wagging the whole of Scripture. Because of these difficulties, Apologists have shifted away from trying to establish a direct lexical trail from biblical words to mission and moved to a broader, more encompassing means of establishing mission.

Semantic field. A semantic domain or field is a linguistic range that represents an idea or concept. According to Louw and Nida, related meanings, "often regarded as partial synonyms because the ranges of their meaning tend to overlap," are grouped together in a "semantic space."[127] Semantic field theory operates on the assumption that related words, though not synonymous, taken together refer to a general phenomenon. Words and phrases find common meaning and are thus members of a class. For example, bluebonnets and roses are flowers.[128] Flower is the category under which bluebonnets and roses can be grouped. Bluebonnets and roses are in the field of flowers (literally and figuratively). In the same way, Apologists justify mission with the claim that certain activities, people, places, and goals belong to the semantic field of "mission." Because these are members of the class called mission, and thus related to mission, they, in turn, substantiate mission. Justification takes place as the semantic space of mission is populated by terms and phrases.

Andreas Köstenberger provides a clear example of this means of justification in his study of mission in the Gospel of John. He states at the outset that the concern of his study is "a firsthand exploration of the Fourth Gospel's teaching on mission," and thereby to establish the validity of mission.[129] Köstenberger's aim is to authenticate the concept of mission within the field of Johannine language and then make application of the concept to the contemporary church. He does this by establishing a range of words and phrases that refer to the general mission phenomenon. First he

---

[127]Johannes Louw and Eugene Nida, eds., *Greek-English Lexicon of the New Testament, Based on Semantic Domains,* 2nd ed. (New York: United Bible Societies, 1989), x.

[128]F. de Saussure refers to this kind of connection as "associative relations" in *Course in General Linguistics* (London: Duckworth, 1983), 123-25.

[129]Köstenberger, *Missions of Jesus and the Disciples,* 2. He summarizes his rationale for using a semantic field approach on 26-27.

acknowledges the role of sending terminology (*pempo* and *apostello*) within the Gospel of John and then expands his investigation by emphasizing the specific context of various passages and their semantic field. Through these means, he asserts that related words and phrases form a semantic field for "mission." This methodology allows Köstenberger to give attention to the concept of mission rather than the word *mission*, the semantic field rather than sending terminology.

Köstenberger's methodology works in this way: in order to identify words and phrases belonging to semantic domains related to mission, he first establishes a working definition of mission. This definition then provides a basis for establishing the semantic field.[130] Once the field is populated, he revisits his definition and measures this against the semantic field. In this circular manner, mission justifies mission. In both the initial and revisited definitions, mission is assumed and not questioned. In other words, he labors over a definition of the term as it forms a basis for the semantic field and justifies mission by the field without questioning mission, its source, meaning, and assumptions. Both the terminology of mission and the field of mission are assumed, and thus an a priori definition based on contemporary notions of mission commands the field. In the end, Köstenberger's argument is tautological. At several points, he raises questions regarding employing contemporary understandings of mission in interpretation, but does not indicate how this can be prevented, nor does he acknowledge inherent understandings existing already within the term.[131]

Eckhard Schnabel follows Köstenberger in the same approach and does for the whole of the New Testament what Köstenberger attempts for the Gospel of John. Schnabel lists and categorizes terms and phrases throughout the New Testament that he considers to be within the semantic field of mission. Because the field is larger, Schnabel's range of semantic words and phrases representing related concepts and activities is much broader and more extensive than Köstenberger's. Schnabel describes his field as encompassing "the existence and self-understanding, the activity and expansion of the church." His "range of missionary concepts and activities" includes the

---

[130]Ibid., 37–41.
[131]Ibid., 1, 17, 25, 40. The cautions Köstenberger lists on 25 are those of Angelico-Salvatore Di Marco.

following: the subjects of missionary work, addressees of missionary work, place of missionary work, sending and position of missionaries, proclamation by word, content of proclamation, goal of proclamation, proclamation by deed, execution of the missionary task, interpretation of missionary work, effort of missionary work, and misunderstandings.[132] Under each of these categories, New Testament words and phrases are organized according to Schnabel's general understanding of mission. Schnabel explains that though these "are not 'technical terms' for 'mission,'" they do reflect a mission emphasis and demonstrate missionary activity.[133] For example, he classifies ἐκκλησία (assembly, church) under the general heading "Goal of the Proclamation." Because church is the goal of proclamation, and the goal of proclamation is part of the semantic field of mission, "missionary concepts and activities" are substantiated.[134]

Rather than creating a trail of words connecting ancient words with mission language, Köstenberger and Schnabel construct a range of words and phrases that relate to mission as a conceptual field. The semantic field method addresses the problems of the root fallacy and the "illegitimate totality transfer" and thus avoids the pitfalls of the lexical approach. However, the semantic field, as a means of justifying mission, has its own set of problems.

First, the semantic field approach, as employed by Köstenberger and Schnabel, is prejudiced toward affirmative testing or self-justification. In its use for biblical interpretation, a semantic field is not meant solely to create sameness but also to demonstrate incompatibility, nuanced differences between words and phrases. Any discussion regarding mission and its semantic field should include variances and incongruity, as well as shared relationship.[135] Given the fact that the Gospel writers varied in their choice of words and distinctive styles, diversity as well as uniformity should exist and may even be the norm. Assembling words and phrases from across various authors and contexts with variance in word usage and intent under mission categories disregards the potential for incompatibility and nuanced meaning.

---

[132]Schnabel, *Early Christian Mission*, 1:35-37.
[133]Ibid., 1:36.
[134]Ibid., 1:36, 37.
[135]Louw and Nida, *Greek-English Lexicon*, 1:vi, x.

However, the chief problem in this method of justifying mission is the amalgamation or mixing of meanings. What Apologists communicate in the creation of a semantic field is that mission is the sum of all these emphases and activities. When lumped together under one class, nuances and variances of meaning in the various words and phrases are compromised. It appears that the aim of a semantic field approach is to prove the validity of this one term or concept through the weight of as many meanings as possible. In the end, though, the meanings associated with mission compound, and the term becomes even murkier. Such an amalgamation of meanings spreads the meaning of mission across a wide range of words. An expanded collection of words and phrases, and thus compounded meaning, does not clarify mission. Instead, it broadens mission into an undifferentiated ideal. Rather than establishing a foundation for mission, these interpreters construct a broad, thin basis of meaning that is shifting sand.

A semantic field approach poses the same basic problem found in other approaches: the problem of meaning. The strength of this method is that it shifts the emphasis from mission as a word to mission as a concept. And yet, as a concept, mission becomes a general, all-inclusive category of meaning that permits all manner of terms for people, activities, and ideas to be grouped under or associated with it. Such conceptualization of mission does not resolve the issue of meaning. Rather, it amplifies its problems. By definition, a concept is an abstraction, and thus it compounds rather than limits meaning. The murkiness of the term *mission* only becomes more nebulous with the complexity of mission as a concept. Once mission as concept is established via its semantic field, then *mission* the word can be ascribed broadly to all kinds of actions, events, people, and places. The circularity of this process highlights what little foundation is necessary to name something as "mission" or to construct a theology of mission. Apologists take the general and inclusive concept, mission, and translate it into definite events and actions. For example, in order to substantiate the concept of mission, *proclamation* is listed by Schnabel in its semantic field. The logic is that the field qualifies proclamation as mission proclamation, which is to say that including *proclamation* in the semantic field of mission inflects what one means by the specific activity—the selfsame activity is invoked to justify the broader category. Mission describes and justifies mission. That is to say, mission qualifies the terms in its semantic field as mission terms, even as those terms justify the category of mission.

The difficulty with these methods and means is in where they begin. Mission is a priori, and thus, justifying modern mission becomes the aim. Rather than arguing from Scripture to mission, the rhetoric of mission frames the linguistic or conceptual beginning point. The simple fact remains: Partisans and Apologists build a biblical foundation for mission, read Scripture through a mission hermeneutic, and look for mission themes with mission as the beginning point. Therefore, mission must be asserted as a basic assumption by Partisans and argued into existence semantically and theologically by Apologists. Either way, this kind of justification represents a herculean effort to establish a case for the term while minimizing historical and textual meaning.

MEANS AND ENDS

To this point, I have characterized Partisans as those who read mission into Scripture without qualification or explanation and thus blatantly freight their interpretation with assumptions contained in mission language. Apologists, on the other hand, recognize the absence of *mission* and *missionary* in the biblical text and devise ways to construct connective links to mission language by means of a lexical trail or semantic field. For both Partisans and Apologists, the aim is to justify mission. Their efforts are crucial steps in the justification of mission, but these efforts are not the end. Once justified, the task is to mobilize personnel and resources, to interpret Scripture in light of mission, and to construct a mission theology. Thus, the work of a biblical foundation, missional hermeneutic, and mission themes is not disinterested but functions as a means to mobilization, interpretation, and theologizing.

Especially for Partisans, but also for many Apologists, these ends can be seen as justifying their means. Increased funding, more evangelists and church planters, and wider involvement by the church are viewed as critical and worthy ends, and thus these ends provide validation for the means used to get to those ends. Or the health and vitality of the Western church is such an overwhelming need and such a high priority that the goal of discovering its missional nature and missional practices exceeds every other concern. And yet, no matter how worthy or right the ends, means must legitimately lead to those ends, and not vice versa. Once again, the matter is what is a priori.

While mobilization of personnel and resources, and the health and vitality of the Western church, are important considerations, the greater matter is biblical interpretation and its ensuing theology. Once Apologists justify their use of mission, they are then able to apply mission to their interpretation of the text and their formulation of theology. Mission established as a lexical, semantic, or thematic reality allows the interpreter to shape the content of John's writings into "the Johannine theology of mission," the Pauline epistles into "Paul's missionary theology," and the teachings of Jesus into "the mission theology of Jesus."[136] Collectively "an overall New Testament theology of mission" becomes the basis from which one is able to construct an overall "theology of mission."[137] The critical point for theology of any kind is that it provides motivation and shapes practice.[138] In the case of mission theology, motivation for mission activity, the principles of mission work, and the message of missionaries are established by way of questionable methods and means. In other words, where one begins determines the outcome of one's interpretation and theology, and ultimately one's motivation, practice, and message. The interpretive influence of the rhetoric of mission has shaped our modern reading of the Old and New Testaments, our interpretation of the words of Jesus and Paul, and the actions of the early church, as we shall see in the next chapter.

---

[136]Senior and Stuhlmueller, *Biblical Foundations for Mission*, 165, 280-94, 317; *TM*, 141; Dean S. Gilliland, *Pauline Theology & Mission Practice* (Eugene, OR: Wipf and Stock, 1998), 30-31; Little, *Mission in the Way of Paul*, 2, 47-73; Jongeneel, *Philosophy, Science, and Theology of Mission*, 132.

[137]For example, "Towards a Theology of Mission?," in Johannes Blauw, *The Missionary Nature of the Church: A Survey of the Biblical Theology of Mission* (New York: McGraw-Hill, 1962), 104-36. See also Senior and Stuhlmueller, *Biblical Foundations for Mission*, 306, 307, 309; Schnabel, *Early Christian Mission*, 1:15; Robert L. Plummer, *Paul's Understanding of the Church's Mission: Did the Apostle Paul Expect the Early Christian Community to Evangelize?*, Paternoster Biblical Monographs (Exeter, UK: Paternoster, 2006), 4.

[138]Not every theologian feels compelled to develop a "mission theology." For example, Alister E. McGrath, *Christian Theology: An Introduction*, 3rd ed. (Oxford: Blackwell, 2001), constructs his theology on traditional doctrinal categories of God, Trinity, Person of Christ, salvation, human nature, sin, grace, church, sacraments, and last things with hardly a mention of mission, and nothing of missional or *missio Dei*. Likewise, Stanley J. Grenz, *Theology for the Community of God* (Grand Rapids: Eerdmans, 1994), frames theology around God who loves and relates as Trinity. Grenz mentions mission only in terms of the church's outreach in evangelism and service (505-10, 656), but not as a hermeneutic or theme.

Whether one constructs a biblical foundation for mission, employs a missional hermeneutic, or locates mission themes or paradigms and justifies these by means of a lexical trail or a semantic field, the edifice on which Partisans and Apologists make a claim for mission language is tenuous. And while language usage is at the center of this problem, the greater issue is the interpretation and application of Scripture. The murkiness of mission terminology clouds rather than clarifies and hinders rather than assists with a faithful interpretation of Scripture. In the end, mission controls the manner in which we read Scripture.

2

Reading Scripture as Mission

Here we are confronted with the real starting
point of the primitive Christian mission: it lies
in the conduct of Jesus himself. If anyone is to be
called "the primal missionary," he must be.

Martin Hengel, "The Origins of the Christian Mission"

The New Testament is a missionary book. The writers of the
New Testament were actively involved in the missionary
work of the church, and the various books within the New
Testament were written for people who had only recently
believed in Jesus through the efforts of missionaries.

Joel Williams, "The Missionary Message of the New Testament"

Justification of mission leads one to read Scripture as mission.
Though *mission* and *missionary* are not found in the Bible, and though such
language embodies modern interpretations derived from Latinized forms
of Greek words, interpreters of all kinds frame their reading of the Old and
New Testaments in mission language. In this chapter, I pursue two questions:
What is the extent of these "mission interpretations" of Scripture? What
difficulty does this kind of modern interpretation pose?

OLD TESTAMENT AND MISSION

Most interpreters of mission reserve the majority of space and ink for the New Testament and only glance in the direction of the Old Testament as a preface for a study of mission in the New Testament. A minority of interpreters devote considerable effort in developing a mission foundation or exploring mission as a theme in the Old Testament.[1] Of the interpreters who comment on mission in the Old Testament, the following positions represent the range of their approaches.

First, there are those who say mission is completely absent for Israel, and thus it is not found in the Old Testament. They maintain that if mission is to be found in Scripture it begins only with Jesus and the early church. While some of these interpreters find evidence of what they would characterize as a missionary vision or missionary texts within the Old Testament, missionary intent does not translate into missionary praxis, and thus they find it inappropriate to label the actions of Israel as "mission."[2] They maintain that while Israel may have believed in the universal nature of its religion and sensed the need to make God known among the other nations, signs of Israel moving toward the nations to convert others to the worship of God are absent. Schnabel, for example, acknowledges universalistic elements within Israel's faith and identifies hints of salvation for the nations but concludes, "Judaism had neither a missionary theory nor organized missionary activity before the first century A.D. The missionary work of the first Christians cannot be explained with prototypes in the Old Testament or with models of an

---

[1]Examples of those who provide a substantial examination of mission in the Old Testament include Christopher J. H. Wright, *The Mission of God: Unlocking the Bible's Grand Narrative* (Downers Grove, IL: IVP Academic, 2006); Donald Senior and Caroll Stuhlmueller, *Biblical Foundations for Mission* (Maryknoll, NY: Orbis Books, 1983), 9-138; Arthur Glasser, *Announcing the Kingdom: The Story of God's Mission in the Bible* (Grand Rapids: Baker Academic, 2003), 17-179; David Filbeck, *Yes, God of the Gentiles, Too: The Missionary Message of the Old Testament*, A BGC Monograph (Wheaton, IL: Billy Graham Center, Wheaton College, 1994); Walter Kaiser, *Mission in the Old Testament: Israel as a Light to the Nations* (Grand Rapids: Baker Books, 2000). John Dickson positions those who do and do not affirm the presence of mission in the ancient Judaism in *Mission-Commitment in Ancient Judaism and in the Pauline Communities: The Shape, Extent and Background of Early Christian Mission*, Wissenschaftliche Untersuchungen Zum Neuen Testament (Tübingen: Mohr Siebeck, 2003), 11n1.

[2]See Eckhard J. Schnabel, *Early Christian Mission*, vol. 1, *Jesus and the Twelve* (Downers Grove, IL: InterVarsity Press, 2004), 59-60, 90-91, 173; Ferdinand Hahn, *Mission in the New Testament*, trans. Frank Clarke (London: SCM Press, 1965), 20, 24.

early Jewish mission."[3] Scot McKnight likewise adds, "There is no evidence that could lead to the conclusion that Judaism was a 'missionary religion' in the sense of aggressive attempts to convert Gentiles or in the sense of self-identity."[4] Converts to Judaism and the presence of proselytes, according to McKnight, do not prove that Judaism was a "missionary religion."[5] David Bosch, in a rather definitive manner, restricts mission to the New Testament. While the Old Testament might be considered as fundamental to understanding mission in the New Testament, mission itself does not commence until the advent of the church. According to Bosch, "There is, in the Old Testament, no indication of the believers of the old covenant being sent by God to cross geographical, religious, and social frontiers in order to win others to faith in Yahweh."[6]

Christopher Wright takes a mediating position with a no-but-yes interpretation. Because he defines mission in the "more general sense of a long-term purpose or goal," Wright feels at liberty to use mission language throughout his Old Testament discussion. Where he draws the line is with the word *missionary*, since "Israel was not mandated by God to send missionaries to the nations," nor were they condemned for their failure to play a missionary role among the nations. Wright affirms mission as God's general purpose in the Old Testament but does not find sending and evangelization by Israel, as these connote missionary kinds of activities.[7] Dean

---

[3]Schnabel, *Early Christian Mission*, 1:173.

[4]Scot McKnight, *A Light Among the Gentiles: Jewish Missionary Activity in the Second Temple Period* (Minneapolis: Fortress, 1991), 117. A similar assessment is made by W. Paul Bowers, "Paul and Religious Propaganda in the First Century," *Novum Testamentum* 22, no. 4 (October 1980): 321. An opposing opinion is found in Elisabeth Schüssler Fiorenza, "Miracles, Mission, and Apologetics: An Introduction," in *Aspects of Religious Propaganda in Judaism and Early Christianity* (South Bend, IN. University of Notre Dame Press, 1976), 1-25.

[5]McKnight, *Light Among the Gentiles*, 49.

[6]*TM*, 17. In *Witness to the World: The Christian Mission in Theological Perspective* (Atlanta: John Knox, 1980), Bosch concludes "that the Old Testament reflects an 'entirely passive character' [citing F. Hahn] with regard to mission. Indeed, the idea of a going out to evangelize the nations is almost entirely absent from it" (47). See also Stanley H. Skreslet, *Comprehending Mission: The Questions, Methods, Themes, Problems, and Prospects of Missiology*, American Society of Missiology Series 49 (Maryknoll, NY: Orbis Books, 2012), 22.

[7]Wright, *Mission of God*, 23, 24, 502-3. This distinction works for Wright to a point, and then the line becomes blurred. To refer to the mission of Israel in this way is fine, but in other places, he also treats mission in a "missionary" manner. Richard Bauckham, *Bible and Mission: Christian Witness in a Postmodern World* (Grand Rapids: Baker Academic, 2003), takes a similar stance: "The concept of mission itself is scarcely to be found in the Old Testament, but it is also essential

Flemming makes a similar distinction. He omits *missionary* and *missions* from his discussion of the Old Testament, because these words would portray Israel as participating in crosscultural evangelism. But in his use of *mission* (singular) as God's mission, he is also able to declare "the Old Testament breathes mission from beginning to end."[8] And yet, both Wright and Flemming encourage the reader to connect their treatment of mission in the Old Testament to contemporary missionary efforts. Flemming, for all his qualifying of language and insistence that a modern missionary model not be imposed on the Old Testament, moves back and forth between the rhetoric of general, purposeful mission to "God's missionary people," "Israel's missionary outreach," and "Yahweh's 'missionaries.'"[9] Wright, as well, connects his specialized, Old Testament use of mission with familiar New Testament uses of mission: the early Christian mission, the Gentile mission, the missionary task, Paul's missionary journeys, and the "missionary apostles."[10]

For these interpreters, the absence of the rhetoric of *mission* and *missionary* in the Old Testament does not seem to be the stated problem. Rather, their concern is that Israel was not performing modern mission activities or crossing into other cultures like modern missionaries, going to other nations and inviting others into their exclusive faith, so their assessment is that either there is no mission in the Old Testament, or mission is present only as general or divine purpose. Their own use of mission language is not questioned but assumed in their appraisal of the Old Testament.

Second, there are those who see mission and missionaries throughout the Old Testament. Versions of this position can be found in Walter Kaiser, Robert Glover, David Filbeck, and Adolf Harnack. Along with the Old Testament themes of election and covenant, Kaiser asserts that "Israel was to be God's missionaries to the world," and thus his aim is to construct "the case

---

to add that this does not diminish the importance of the Old Testament for the theme of Christian mission" (47).

[8]Dean Flemming, *Recovering the Full Mission of God: A Biblical Perspective on Being, Doing and Telling* (Downers Grove, IL: IVP Academic, 2013), 21.

[9]Ibid., 38, 47, 51. Flemming goes as far as to identify Jonah as "the one explicit Old Testament case in which God sends someone on a 'crosscultural mission'" (47).

[10]Wright, *Mission of God*, 508, 513, 517, 519.

of missions in the Old Testament."[11] At every turn, Kaiser frames the Old Testament as a missionary document. For example, he describes the Davidic covenant of promise and the charter for all humanity given in 2 Samuel 7 as "missions at its highest watermark!"[12] He calls Psalm 67 "a missionary psalm," insists that the whole Bible offers a "missionary vision," refers to "Israel's missionary duty," identifies the Servant figure in Isaiah as "a missionary servant," characterizes Israel's call as "an active missionary call," and argues that Jonah is "a missionary book."[13]

Robert Glover concedes that while mission in its full expression is not seen until the New Testament, "the fact should not be overlooked that the missionary idea is to be found all through the Old Testament."[14] He describes Abraham as "one of a number of Old Testament characters who were striking examples of missionary spirit and effort. In him began a long procession of missionaries which has now covered 4,000 years."[15] Glover asserts that Joseph is "a great missionary," Moses is "a true missionary leader," the book of Esther is "a fascinating missionary narrative" as well as "a thrilling missionary romance," the Prophets are full of "missionary teachings," Jonah is in the final analysis "an obedient and successful missionary," and Daniel is a "great foreign missionary."[16]

Adolf Harnack, in his introductory remarks on New Testament mission, notes that the Jewish religion of the Old Testament "possessed a missionary impulse," "felt missions to be a duty," and "attained so large a measure of success" in its mission.[17] Thus, missionary zeal existed within Judaism and was inherited by Christianity. For Harnack, "Christian mission is a continuation of the Jewish propaganda."[18] Missionary impulse in the Old Testament precedes Christian mission expressed in the New Testament.

---

[11]Kaiser, *Mission in the Old Testament*, 20, 60. Kaiser does acknowledge the sixteenth-century introduction of *missions* (11) but then proceeds to use the plural form throughout his discussion without further qualification.

[12]Ibid., 27.

[13]Ibid., 31, 39, 55, 59, 62-63, 67-70.

[14]Robert Hall Glover, *The Bible Basis of Missions* (Chicago: Moody, 1946), 15.

[15]Ibid., 17.

[16]Ibid., 17-21.

[17]Adolf Harnack, *The Mission and Expansion of Christianity in the First Three Centuries* (New York: Harper, 1962), 9, 10.

[18]Ibid., 15.

For some interpreters in this second approach, the presence of mission in the Old Testament is evident simply because the nations feature prominently in Israel's story. For example, Cornell Goerner argues for a missionary motif or message in the Old Testament in the refrain of "all nations." By means of this motif of the nations, he highlights the "sweepingly universal" features of the story of Abraham, Moses and the exodus, Leviticus, Numbers, Deuteronomy, the Prophets, and the Psalms.[19] The title of Goerner's short book, *All Nations in God's Purpose: What the Bible Teaches About Missions*, places the nations at the center of his justification of mission. H. H. Rowley insists that "the Old Testament is a missionary book," and yet he concedes this is not because Israel saw itself as sending missionaries but because the monotheistic faith of Israel must include a vision of the nations worshiping God.[20] In similar fashion, Mark Boda views the Psalter as "truly a missional collection," because its focus is on the reign of God over all the nations.[21] Boda's point is that an emphasis on divine rule over all the nations, specifically evidenced in the Psalms, translates into mission in the Old Testament and displays "the antiquity and ubiquity of a missional vision for the nations among the people of God."[22] The mission beginning point for Boda is God's universal regard for all nations and Israel's role of blessing all the peoples of the earth. This regard is highlighted in divine actions, such as election, covenant, universality, and blessing. The overall intent is that Yahweh be known not just in Israel or only among a particular people but among all the peoples of the earth. Universal regard for the nations and divine activity toward them are identified by Goerner, Rowley, and Boda as "mission."[23]

---

[19]See Henry Cornell Goerner, *All Nations in God's Purpose: What the Bible Teaches About Missions* (Nashville: Broadman, 1979), 22-68.

[20]H. H. Rowley, *The Missionary Message of the Old Testament* (London: Carey, 1945), 76-77.

[21]Mark J. Boda, " 'Declare His Glory Among the Nations': The Psalter as Missional Collection," in *Christian Mission: Old Testament Foundations and New Testament Developments*, ed. Stanley E. Porter and Cynthia Long Westfall, McMaster New Testament Studies Series (Eugene, OR: Pickwick, 2010), 13-41.

[22]Ibid., 38.

[23]Cf. Carlos F. Cardoza-Orlandi and Justo L. González, *To All Nations from All Nations: A History of the Christian Missionary Movement* (Nashville: Abingdon, 2013), 21-24. See Schnabel's brief survey of Old Testament scholarship on this subject, *Early Christian Mission*, 1:55-57. Johannes Blauw, *The Missionary Nature of the Church: A Survey of the Biblical Theology of Mission* (New York: McGraw-Hill, 1962), likewise names universality as "the *basis* for the missionary message of the Old Testament" (17).

Critics of this second position note that even a cursory reading of the Old Testament shows that Israel does not view itself as the agent of mission and only occasionally and in the broadest sense is it seen as an active and willing partner in the divine plan to make Yahweh known.[24] Yahweh reveals Yahweh, and Israel receives this revelation. Also, critics ask whether universality, either that of Yahweh or of Israel, must be regarded as "mission." While the nations are part of the Old Testament story, and there is divine regard for the nations, do these aspects warrant that "mission" be read into the Old Testament?[25] Can it be that God's intention toward all nations be the Creator's love for his creation or his design for the peoples of the earth? Why define such divine regard as "mission"? In the Old Testament, God's intention is expressed in the language of love, covenant, and election but not mission. To call these "mission" qualifies universal love, covenant, and election to particular kinds of actions—missionary kinds of actions. Is such conditioning of love, covenant, and election necessary?

In the third approach are those who see mission as an Old Testament theological category, and thus, rather than mission consisting of cross-cultural sending, the Old Testament contains theological expressions or models of mission.[26] They use *mission* to describe election, covenant, and God.[27] They reason that mission, as found in the Old Testament, is solely a divine affair. God is a missionary God, and thus it does not really matter what Israel believes about the nations or what they put into practice. God defines mission, God is missionary, and thus mission is found in the Old Testament.[28] Instead of determining whether the Jews operate in active or passive modes of mission, theological concerns define mission. Geoffrey

---

[24]See Senior and Stuhlmueller, *Biblical Foundations for Mission*, 4, 9, 141.

[25]George W. Peters, *A Biblical Theology of Missions* (Chicago: Moody, 1972), attempts to differentiate between mission and universality, and thus he cautions that "universality must not be confused with missions as it is thought of at present" (21).

[26]See James Chukwuma Okoye, *Israel and the Nations: A Mission Theology of the Old Testament*, American Society of Missiology Series 39 (Maryknoll, NY: Orbis Books, 2006).

[27]Avery Willis, *The Biblical Basis of Missions* (Nashville: Convention, 1986), 40-41.

[28]Roger Bowen, *So I Send You: A Study Guide to Mission* (London: SPCK, 1996), 20, 21; Andreas J. Köstenberger and Peter Thomas O'Brien, *Salvation to the Ends of the Earth: A Biblical Theology of Mission*, New Studies in Biblical Theology 11 (Downers Grove, IL: InterVarsity Press, 2001), 52-53; Alan J. Roxburgh, *Joining God, Remaking Church, Changing the World: The New Shape of the Church in Our Time* (New York: Morehouse, 2015), 42-44. Wright, *Mission of God*, uses language that suggests that he approaches the Old Testament in the same manner: "The whole canon of Scripture is a missional phenomenon in the sense that it witnesses to the self-giving

Harris explains, "In the one case, God initiates mission by revealing himself from Zion to all the nations in an eschatological event, which leads to a process of ingathering. . . . In the other case, . . . God sends his Son Jesus out on a mission to the world (John 3:16) and thus, wherever God's people go, Jesus is with them."[29] For Harris, mission is not absent in the Old or New Testament, because it is the theological starting point for both.

Those who critique this third position do so either on the basis of a narrow definition of mission (i.e., as only the sending of human agents), or because mission-language terms are too ordinary or limiting to describe God. For them, mission must involve human agents who believe in God's universality and thus actively bring nonbelievers into the knowledge and worship of God. To employ mission strictly as a theological term is too all-encompassing or indefinite, and thus not real mission. For others, to ascribe to God such a human attribute as "mission" and "missionary" qualifies or conditions the transcendent nature of the divine.[30] Should we narrowly define God as "missionary" and his divine intent as "mission"? In either case, the problem is that too little or too much is made of mission. Difficulty lies in the imprecise nature of the language of mission itself.

In all three positions, the manner in which mission is defined and used determines one's interpretation of the Old Testament. To define mission as human agency restricts its use to what Israel does in response to interactions with peoples surrounding them. Framing one's interpretation within this definition creates the expectation that Israel is to look and act like contemporary expressions of *mission* and *missionary*. By such standards, Israel certainly fails to look missionary. The rhetoric of mission unfairly condemns Israel.

On the other hand, if one's definition includes all of the activity of God, then mission is a transcendent reality and thus as broad as all of human and divine activity. As has already been noted, this totalizes the concept of mission. Mission becomes everything. If the aim is to speak inclusively of who God is and his activities, a number of other words of more suitable biblical pedigree are better choices: *covenant, love,* and *reconciliation.*

---

movement of this God toward his creation and us" (49). Thus, for Wright, mission exists in the Old Testament because "mission belongs to God" (62).

[29]R. Geoffrey Harris, *Mission in the Gospels* (London: Epworth, 2004), 31.

[30]See my discussion of *missio Dei* above.

James Okoye, in his survey of various ideas of mission in the Old Testament, concludes, "Because scholars differ on what constitutes mission in the Old Testament, it is necessary to clarify the sense or senses in which 'mission' is being used in [this] work."[31] I concur with Okoye. Whether the definition is narrow or broad, the fact is that mission imposes restrictions on the activity of God or erects an unfair, anachronistic standard for Israel. Contemporary notions of mission lie outside the bounds of the Old Testament story and presume too much of the text. Behind such approaches lie arguments for contemporary mission theory and practice, or modern mission is placed onto ancient actions and concepts to justify current notions of sending.

When the chasm between ancient Israel and contemporary mission organization and practice goes unacknowledged or is underappreciated, confusion rather than clarity is the result. The divide between then and now cannot so easily be bridged. Nor can it just be dismissed. Divine intent, Israel, surrounding nations, and the context of the Near East must be interpreted for what they are and not used as a foundation for modern mission practice, or manipulated by hermeneutical technique, or reduced to a theme. Mission, as a rhetorical device, improperly controls interpretation and communicates more than the Old Testament text intends.

NEW TESTAMENT AND MISSION

The New Testament, as Glover claims, is "uniquely and preeminently missionary—the greatest missionary volume ever produced."[32] Interpreters often describe the New Testament as a mission story from beginning to end because, as Williams puts it, "Jesus himself is on a mission and because the story ends with Jesus sending his followers on a mission to the nations."[33] Interpreters point to the predominance of *sending* in the Gospels, Acts, and the Epistles as evidence of the mission nature of the New Testament and thus describe the letters of the New Testament as "missionary documents written

---

[31]Okoye, *Israel and the Nations*, 9.
[32]Glover, *Bible Basis of Missions*, 22.
[33]Joel Williams, "The Missionary Message of the New Testament," in *Discovering the Mission of God: Best Missional Practices of the 21st Century*, ed. Mike Barnett and Robin Martin (Downers Grove, IL: InterVarsity Press, 2012), 50.

in the context of missionary advance."[34] As noted in the previous chapter, the idea of sending, expressed in the two verbs *pempein* and *apostellein*, forms the primary argument for these claims.[35]

In the mission approach to the New Testament, interpreters use *mission* as a noun to designate institution, movement, and collective action, and as an adjective to qualify various nouns. Interpreters make reference to "the early Christian mission," "Judean mission," "Gentile mission," "Samaritan mission," "Jerusalem mission," "mission to Israel," "church's mission," "Paul's mission," "Jesus' mission," and "cosmic mission."[36] As a noun, *mission* identifies specific ideas, actions, and people, and it conveys the idea of task, assignment, or organized work that is definitive and historical. The "Samaritan mission," for example, refers to specific actions by Jesus at a particular place and time in history. While such a conceptual description may be a useful device to construct a category of actions and to place these within a period of time, it is an imagined or presumed construct and not actual. There was no such thing as *the* Samaritan mission, as if such a program were the intent of Jesus or the disciples. Rather than the segregation of places, peoples, or times into definitive missions, we read of Jesus crossing social and religious boundaries in every direction at the same time without special descriptors.

---

[34]Zane G. Pratt, M. David Sills, and Jeff K. Walters, *Introduction to Global Missions* (Nashville: B&H, 2014), 42. See Glover, *Bible Basis of Missions*, 22-26.

[35]Glover, *Bible Basis of Missions*, 26. Cf. David J. Bosch, "Reflections on Biblical Models of Mission," in *Landmark Essays in Mission and World Christianity*, American Society of Missiology Series 43 (Maryknoll, NY: Orbis Books, 2009), 4-5.

[36]For example, see Schnabel's title, *Early Christian Mission*, and 1:207; Senior and Stuhlmueller, *Biblical Foundations for Mission*, 141, 157, 174, 270, 271; James C. Miller, "Paul and His Ethnicity: Reframing the Categories," in *Paul as Missionary: Identity, Activity, Theology, and Practice*, ed. Trevor J. Burke and Brian S. Rosner, Library of New Testament Studies 420 (London: T&T Clark, 2011), 44; Don N. Howell Jr., "Mission in Paul's Epistles: Genesis, Pattern, and Dynamics," in *Mission in the New Testament: An Evangelical Approach*, ed. William J. Larkin Jr. and Joel F. Williams, American Society of Missiology Series 27 (Maryknoll, NY: Orbis Books, 1998), 77; Michael Knowles, "Mark, Matthew, and Mission: Faith, Failure, and the Fidelity of Jesus," in Porter and Westfall, *Christian Mission*, 64, 65, 67; Paul Barnett, *Paul: Missionary of Jesus*, vol. 2 of *After Jesus* (Grand Rapids: Eerdmans, 2008), 142; Michael F. Bird, *Jesus and the Origins of the Gentile Mission*, Library of Historical Jesus Studies (London: T&T Clark, 2006); Kaiser, *Mission in the Old Testament*, 38; Craig A. Evans, "A Light to the Nations: Isaiah and Mission in Luke," in Porter and Westfall, *Christian Mission*, 103; Seyoon Kim, "Paul as an Eschatological Herald," in Burke and Rosner, *Paul as Missionary*, 19, 20, 22; Hahn, *Mission in the New Testament*, 68, 74; Stanley E. Porter and Cynthia Long Westfall, "A Cord of Three Strands: Mission in Acts," in Porter and Westfall, *Christian Mission*, 117; Harris, *Mission in the Gospels*, 165, 206; William J. Larkin Jr., "Mission in Luke," in Larkin and Williams, *Mission in the New Testament*, 169.

In addition, New Testament interpreters frequently use *missionary* as an adjective to qualify concepts and activities. *Missionary* as an attributive construction colors the noun it modifies. Thus, interpreters refer to *missionary* activity, *missionary* practices, *missionary* work, *missionary* discourse, *missionary* vision, *missionary* commissions, *missionary* spirit, *missionary* character, *missionary* message, *missionary* outreach, *missionary* instructions, *missionary* church, *missionary* movement, *missionary* travels, and *missionary* successes.[37] With this kind of adjectival construction, interpreters are able to characterize specified and unspecified, ordinary and definite concepts and actions as "missionary." Rather than just traveling, the trip is a *missionary* kind of trip. Rather than proclaiming a message, the message being proclaimed is a *missionary* kind of message. Other capable and reputable New Testament scholars, interpreting the same passages, describe these same actions without the necessity of qualifying them as *missionary*.[38] The difference lies in the disposition or hermeneutic lens employed by the interpreter. If one's objective is to find a basis or foundation for mission and missionary, then travel, proclamation, message, work, and activity will be designated as *missionary*. The criteria for designating these concepts and activities as *mission* or *missionary* are unstated and thus often appear to be arbitrary. To qualify concepts and actions as missionary in such a manner limits the scope and intent of preaching, travels, discourse, and work to one category, an ambiguous and unwieldly category. Is it possible, or even necessary, to qualify such actions with this one particular adjective?

Likewise, named individuals and groups of people are given the title of *missionary*. Used as a title, *missionary* designates a role for a person doing a

---

[37]For example, see Schnabel, *Early Christian Mission*, 1:171, 208, 265, 273, 303, 306-10, 315, 323, 330, 348; Senior and Stuhlmueller, *Biblical Foundations for Mission*, 161, 163, 185, 211, 238, 242, 251, 252, 292, 294, 298, 302, 305, 308; Karl Baus, *From the Apostolic Community to Constantine*, Handbook of Church History 1 (Freiburg, West Germany: Herder, 1965), 124; Karl Olav Sandnes, "A Missionary Strategy in 1 Corinthians 9:9-23?," in Burke and Rosner, *Paul as Missionary*, 137, 138; Evans, "Light to the Nations," 101; Best, "Revelation to Evangelize the Gentiles," 7; Williams, "Conclusion," 242; Stanley E. Porter, "The Content and Message of Paul's Missionary Teaching," in Porter and Westfall, *Christian Mission*, 141; Hahn, *Mission in the New Testament*, 120; J. H. Bavinck, *An Introduction to the Science of Missions*, trans. David Hugh Freeman (Philadelphia: Presbyterian and Reformed, 1960), 34.

[38]For example, N. T. Wright, *Jesus and the Victory of God*, Christian Origins and the Question of God 2 (Minneapolis: Fortress, 1996), 244-319, characterizes Jesus' intent as proclamation and summons to his "kingdom story." See also Wright, *Paul and the Faithfulness of God* (Minneapolis: Fortress, 2013), 2:538-69.

specific task or job. Interpreters replace names, such as Mark, John, Matthew, Aquila, Priscilla, and Timothy, as well as groups of people, such as the disciples and the Twelve, with the designation of *missionary* in order to depict their actions as particularly related to mission.[39] In so doing, they give the impression that these individuals and groups of people have a special, designated task or have a vocational and professional designation. Such replacement represents either a high degree of interpretation or blatant suppositions about profession placed onto first-century men and women. Through such depictions, Mark is styled either vocationally as missionary or as having missionary intent as his chief focus. Both presume too much of the biblical account. Mark does not self-describe as a missionary, and he performs a variety of activities, none of which he designates as mission. In the end, such a sweeping categorization of peoples and groups is both anachronistic and reductionistic. One must concede that the disciples' aims, intents, activities, and identities are much larger than what might be conveyed in the term *missionary*.

Confusion grows when *mission* and *missionary* are employed with little or no definition or qualification, and the reader is left to make mission into whatever she wishes—the organizational structure of her denominational agency or a recent mission trip to Haiti. Too easily, we work backward from the denomination or Haiti to Jesus, Paul, and the New Testament, when the aim should be just the opposite. William Larkin, New Testament scholar at Columbia Biblical Seminary and Graduate School of Missions, appears to do just this. In his introduction to a collection of essays on the New Testament, Larkin states that the aim of the volume is to offer "a fresh statement of the biblical foundation of mission," which will "serve as a catalyst for the completion of the church's universal mission in this generation." He then asserts "the New Testament is a missionary document, containing preaching (the Gospels), model mission history (Acts), and letters written primarily by

---

[39]For example, Knowles, "Mark, Matthew, and Mission," 86, 87; Peters, *Biblical Theology of Missions*, 134, 146; Harnack, *Mission and Expansion of Christianity*, 53, 75, 76, 79, 321; Köstenberger and O'Brien, *Salvation to the Ends of the Earth*, 121; I. Howard Marshall, *Beyond the Bible: Moving from Scripture to Theology*, Acadia Studies in Bible and Theology (Grand Rapids: Baker Academic, 2004), 68.

missionaries while on mission."[40] While Larkin decries those who "have tended to read their own established church situation back into the New Testament," it appears that his use of the language of *mission* and *missionaries* does exactly this. Rather than treating the New Testament as "confessional history," Larkin and other interpreters turn it into a "missionary document" meant to pose the question of "missions responsibility."[41] The New Testament documents thus exist as examples of and motivation for the furtherance of modern mission endeavors.[42]

Even more confusing is to convey the notion that actors in the early church or those who wrote the New Testament documents had a "missiology." Michael Knowles refers to "the missiology of Mark" and "Matthew's missiology," contrasting the two as if each had a developed and systemized body of knowledge called "missiology."[43] While the intent may be to say Mark and Matthew were thoughtful as they acted, what is communicated is that Mark and Matthew acted in a studied and scientific manner.[44] Since the academic study of mission was not established until the nineteenth century, and not until 1896, with the appointment of Gustav Warneck (1834–1910) as professor at the University of Halle, was missiology given a place in theological studies, it seems imprudent to say Mark had a missiology. To characterize his thought as missiology is saying too much.[45] Yet more than being

---

[40]William J. Larkin Jr., "Introduction," in Larkin and Williams, *Mission in the New Testament*, 1. Bavinck, *Introduction to the Science of Missions*, makes a similar claim for the book of the Acts of the Apostles. He states that it is "a missions document par excellence. It is obviously rich with data on every phase of missions, including the missionary approach, preaching on the missions field, and the organization of the young churches" (36).

[41]Larkin, "Introduction," 2, 3.

[42]See also Senior and Stuhlmueller, *Biblical Foundations for Mission*, 211.

[43]Knowles, "Mark, Matthew, and Mission," 77, designated also as "Matthean missiology" (78) and "Markan missiology" (88).

[44]Among the many names for missiology, *mission studies* and the *science of mission* are most preferred. See Jan A. B. Jongeneel, *Philosophy, Science, and Theology of Mission in the 19th and 20th Centuries*, Studien Zur Interkulturellen Geschichte Des Christentums 92 (Frankfurt am Main: Peter Lang, 1995), 79-81.

[45]David J. Bosch, "Theological Education in Missionary Perspective," *Missiology* 10, no. 1 (January 1982): 14; Marc Spindler, "The Protestant Mission Study: Emergence and Features," in *Mission & Science, Missiology Revised, 1850–1940*, ed. Carine Dujardin and Claude Prudhomme (Leuven, Belgium: Leuven University Press, 2015), 39-52; and Johannes Verkuyl, *Contemporary Missiology: An Introduction* (Grand Rapids: Eerdmans, 1978), 26, offer a Protestant perspective on the beginnings of missiology, while Andrew V. Seumois, "The Evolution of Mission Theology Among Roman Catholics," in *The Theology of the Christian Mission*, ed. Gerald H. Anderson (Nashville: Abingdon, 1961), 122-34, provides a Catholic version. Jongeneel, *Philosophy, Science, and Theology*

a nineteenth-century addition to theological studies, missiology is an erroneous description of what Mark and Matthew were doing as they wrote
their Gospels. First and foremost, they were offering an account of what they
had witnessed of Jesus' life, death, and resurrection.

When the intent is to employ the New Testament to justify contemporary
mission activities, concepts, and roles, mission becomes a problem; it confuses
rather than clarifies. Whether as a noun, adjective, proper title, or academic
discipline, mission introduces foreign elements into the New Testament and
prejudices interpretation and application. When the assertion is made that
"everything about the New Testament is missionary in character," every emphasis, theme, event, and personality is subsumed under the moniker of
mission.[46] In the end, mission becomes the whole—an all-encompassing notion.

JESUS AND MISSION

While mission might be questionable in other parts of Scripture, surely it
is found in the words and actions of Jesus. Or so it might seem. The assumption is that mission is at the heart of what Jesus said and did. "In the
act of God in Jesus Christ," R. K. Orchard asserts, "mission is inherent."[47]
And yet, while a myriad of Jesus' words, images, and directives point to
witness (Lk 24:48; Jn 5:31), proclamation (Mt 10:7, 26; Mk 13:10; 16:15;
Lk 12:3), and love (Mt 5:44; 22:37; Jn 15:12, 17), mission is not recorded as
among the utterances of Jesus or registered as his intent. If mission is attributed to Jesus, it is as a characterization of his words and actions or used
as an interpretive category. But when speculated as inherently the act of
God, it then assumes a place over all other divine words and categories—
mercy, reconciliation, and love.

Some contend that because the sending of the Son by the Father is the
central truth of the New Testament, mission is central to who Jesus is and
the main theme of Scripture. This is the approach taken by Francis DuBose
in *God Who Sends*. Within the notion of sending, according to DuBose,

---

of Mission, indicates that the term *missiology* was coined by Ludwig J. van Rijckevorsel at the
beginning of the twentieth century (63).

[46]Pratt, Sills, and Walters, *Introduction to Global Missions*, 42-43.

[47]R. K. Orchard, *Missions in a Time of Testing: Thought and Practice in Contemporary Missions*
(Philadelphia: Westminster, 1964), 28. Orchard adds that God's act in Jesus "is missionary in
character, not that it's only missionary in character" (30).

"there is a biblical idea of mission." There is, he contends, "rather universal consensus" in this regard, and sending is "one point on which most everyone seems to agree."[48] And thus, DuBose feels justified in using *sending*, and by extension mission, as the framework through which he interprets Jesus and the whole of Scripture. Just as Jesus is sent from the Father, so the early disciples and church are sent. The Father sends Jesus, and Jesus sends his disciples in the same way (Jn 20:21). But equating Jesus' "sentness" and mission presents several difficulties. First, does Jesus make this connection? Jesus refers to sending—not mission. Jesus refers to the action of sending and not the undertaking of mission. A plain predicate is transformed into a complex concept or belief with all its attending ideas—strategy, organization, and profession. Once a leap is made from sending to mission, the horizon of the present eclipses that of the text.

Second, in such an interpretation, mission overwhelms and then monopolizes other themes and emphases found in Jesus' words. In an effort to justify mission as a concept, the richness and mystery of the incarnation is minimized. Instead, hazy modern concepts of "mission" and "missionary" swamp the incarnation and consign divine sending to human mission, and divine intent to missionary vocation.

Third, Jesus' emphasis is on something beyond the operation of sending, more than the pursuit of "mission." Jesus focuses the disciples' attention on his hands and side, on his wounds (Jn 20:20). He then says, "Peace be with you; as the Father has sent Me, I also send you." Sacrificial suffering is the aim, and sending is a modest means to the grand goal of redemption. When conveyance to this end becomes the emphasis rather than the end itself, the implications of Jesus' death and his victory over sin and death become less than ultimate.

Others view Jesus' boundary-breaking, universal message as the point where his thoughts and actions translate into mission. Ferdinand Hahn posits the essential element of the Old Testament and Jewish presuppositions adopted by Jesus and the early church to be "the universalist understanding of God."[49] Jesus' message of the reign of God is thus the

---

[48]Francis M. DuBose, *God Who Sends: A Fresh Quest for Biblical Mission* (Nashville: Broadman, 1983), 24. The same sending notion is emphasized by Williams, "Missionary Message of the New Testament," 50-52.

[49]Hahn, *Mission in the New Testament*, 18.

seminal root for mission in the New Testament, Paul, and the early church.
It is argued that because universality is mission, Jesus is a missionary. Thus,
mission is universality. Harnack references the "missionary efforts of Jesus"
and Jesus' "Gentile mission" as central to an argument for Jesus' inclusive
message.[50] The reasoning is as follows: the parables, sayings, and encounters of Jesus are saturated with the reign of God over the whole of
humanity. This reign is enacted first in the sending of the Son, then
through the witness of the apostles, and eventually through the church.
And thus, God's reign and the church's witness are evidence of mission.
However, to characterize the cosmic rule and reign of God as "mission"
reduces the entire scope of the biblical narrative to this single theme—and
an anachronistic and troublesome one, at that. If the story is to be simplified or compressed into one word, might the universality of Jesus' action
be better served with more biblical descriptors, such as, for example, love,
covenant, or reconciliation?

The tendency to cloak the sayings and actions of Jesus in mission language is common among interpreters. Regarding Matthew 10, Donald
Senior construes the entire passage as a "mission discourse" and Jesus' dis-
ciples as "missionaries." Principles and instructions Senior draws from
Jesus' words to the disciples are summarized simply as "mission principles"
and "missionary instructions." Among these, he points out that "the scope
and content of the community's mission are the same as that of
Jesus" (Mt 10:7-8); "the missionary can expect opposition and persecution"
(Mt 10:24-25); "the missionary can count on the empowerment of the
Spirit" (Mt 10:19-20); and "the underlying theme of the whole discourse is
the identity of the risen Jesus with his missionaries."[51] Senior's characterization of Jesus' words and instructions as "mission" and his disciples as
"missionaries" disregards the contingencies of the particular, historical situation and the tremendous gap between first-century Palestine and the
modern mission situation. Numerous interpreters use the phrases "mission
of Christ" and "mission of Jesus" to refer in a general manner to the whole
of Jesus' life, death, and resurrection. Perhaps it could be assumed that what
is meant here is simply Jesus' purpose or aim, and yet the stated intent of

---

[50]Harnack, *Mission and Expansion of Christianity*, 36-43.
[51]Senior and Stuhlmueller, *Biblical Foundations for Mission*, 250-51, 277.

many of these interpreters is to promote and mobilize for mission, and thus "the mission of Christ" can easily be read as being in many ways similar to or a type of modern enterprise.[52]

As Partisans and Apologists insert the role or vocation of missionary into Jesus' discourses, they represent Jesus as calling missionaries, instructing missionaries, and commissioning missionaries and thus infer that "missionary" is a fixed title or an established role or office.[53] And yet, what we find in Scripture is that those whom Jesus calls are given a variety of titles. They are named as apostles (Mt 10:1; Mk 3:13-15), disciples (Mt 10:1; Jn 13:22), and the Twelve (Mk 9:35; Lk 9:1), but not "missionaries."[54] Even *apostles*, *disciples*, and *the Twelve* appear to be interchangeable, referring to the same people, so no one title stands apart from the rest or has special meaning. In parallel passages, *apostle* is used in place of *disciple* (compare Lk 17:5 with Mt 17:19; Mk 9:28). Thus, not even *apostle* is a fixed title for a vocation or a designation for a particular group of people; rather, it is a descriptive term to denote that the disciples are among those who are sent.[55] Yet, interpreters portray *missionary* as a fixed title and as an established vocation.

Missionary vocation is asssumed in Larkin's discussion titled "Disciples' Mission," in which he equates Jesus' calling of the disciples "to be 'fishers of men'" with being "sent on mission to bear witness to the kingdom and call others into it."[56] He views Jesus' call to be fishers of men not as a calling to *be* but a command to *go*. Thus, a way of being in the world becomes "the mission." Larkin's interpretation moves mission from merely being sent to the undertaking of a specific plan or program. Schnabel develops the missionary nature of their calling even further by asserting that Mark 1:16-20 is more than a "discipleship narrative." Rather, he equates the call to be "fishers of people" to a call or commission to become vocational missionaries. Thus, the passage is to be read as a narrative that provides "the foundation and

---

[52]Willis, *Biblical Basis of Missions*, 43; Bowen, *So I Send You*, 26; Paul Barnett, *Jesus & the Rise of Early Christianity: A History of New Testament Times* (Downers Grove, IL: InterVarsity Press, 1999), 170.

[53]Schnabel, *Early Christian Mission*, 1:290-305; Peters, *Biblical Theology of Missions*, 135, 178-79; *TM*, 37, 115; Köstenberger and O'Brien, *Salvation to the Ends of the Earth*, 119.

[54]For the use of *apostle* in the Gospels, see Schnabel, *Early Christian Mission*, 1:280-84.

[55]See ibid., 1:281. Cf. Senior and Stuhlmueller, *Biblical Foundations for Mission*, 266.

[56]Larkin, "Mission in Luke," 165.

justification, for their 'profession' as missionaries."[57] He argues that the disciples switch from their previous trades and professions to the profession of missionary. Thus, Jesus' call to the disciples entails something other than obedience (follow me) and action (fish for people). It is a change of vocation. To respond to Jesus' call means the disciples stopped their trade or profession and assume the designation of missionary.[58] Such an inference that Jesus' summons to the Twelve to become fishers of people is a call to change their vocation is not supportable, and that their vocation after this call became missionary is untenable. First, the text does not state this as the case. Second, this interpretation forces Jesus' calling of these fishermen into specialized and modern notions of vocation (the profession of missionary). On the other hand, to read this text as a summons to be a disciple who simply "fishes for people" opens the possibility for people of all kinds of abilities and vocational callings to participate in fishing for people. To read profession into the text limits "fishing" to people who are professionals and construes Jesus' summons in the terms of a profession.

Not only do interpreters characterize Jesus as calling people to be missionaries, but also they portray Jesus as a missionary. Martin Hengel calls Jesus "the primal missionary."[59] Köstenberger and O'Brien state that God "sent his Son Jesus as the missionary *par excellence.*"[60] Robert Glover gives Jesus the title of "God's great world Missionary."[61] And George Peters describes Jesus as one who "shines forth as the ideal Missionary, the Apostle of God."[62] If Jesus is the "primal missionary," the "missionary *par excellence,*" or "the ideal Missionary," then a missionary interpretation of the disciples and the early church must surely follow. If mission is inherent to the person

---

[57]Schnabel, *Early Christian Mission*, 1:273. See also Schnabel, "Mission, Early Non-Pauline," in *Dictionary of the Later New Testament & Its Development*, ed. Ralph Martin and Peter H. Davids (Downers Grove, IL: IVP Academic, 1997), 763.

[58]Schnabel, *Early Christian Mission*, 1:320, calls the seventy-two sent out (Lk 10:1-16) missionaries. David Garland, *Luke*, Zondervan Exegetical Commentary Series on the New Testament (Grand Rapids: Zondervan, 2011), 232-33, identifies the calling to be fishers of men as missionary work, but does not interpret this calling as a change of vocation.

[59]Martin Hengel, "The Origins of the Christian Mission," in *Between Jesus and Paul: Studies in the Earliest History of the Christianity*, trans. John Bowden (Waco, TX: Baylor University Press, 2013), 62. Joseph Schmidlin says that "Jesus Christ was actually the first Christian missionary," in *Catholic Mission History*, ed. Matthias Braun (Techny, IL: Mission Press, S. V. D., 1933), 32. Cf. *TM*, 31.

[60]Köstenberger and O'Brien, *Salvation to the Ends of the Earth*, 147.

[61]Glover, *Bible Basis of Missions*, 13, 24.

[62]Peters, *Biblical Theology of Missions*, 36.

of Jesus Christ, then mission epitomizes God and all of his activity. And to characterize Jesus in this way opens the door for an array of mission interpretations throughout the New Testament.

"Jesus' ministry," Eckhard Schnabel explains, "defined a missionary ministry in the proper sense."[63] Schnabel builds the case for this claim on Jesus' understanding as having been sent by God, and his message and the kinds of activities that he performed as having a missionary intent. And yet, if *missionary* means a vocational designation of one who is part of an explicit program or plan, especially in the term's contemporary expression, or construed as the performance of a modern human endeavor, is it appropriate and helpful to designate Jesus as a missionary or to speak of his mission?[64] In addition to the questions of whether Jesus had such titles, designations, or plans in mind, and whether the early church deduced these from his teachings, there is the issue of language and meaning. For sure, Jesus does not define himself with the term *missionary*, nor does he employ the language of *mission* to describe his actions. *Mission* and *missionary* are at best shapeless shadows of what Jesus reveals of himself and what others confess him to be. The revelation of God in Jesus Christ and the coming of the Spirit are divine categories unparalleled with human identities and actions. To characterize Jesus' ministry and identity as mission and missionary misrepresents the uniqueness of revelation and consigns divine being and act to categories of contemporary vocational identity and organizational structures.

Should we say that Jesus is the first (primal) or even the best of the profession called *missionary*? Jesus is more than a missionary, and his coming is qualitatively different from mission activity. To locate eternal action and divine being in such temporal ideas inappropriately constricts and distorts divine reality and possibility. Can Jesus' eternal existence as God becoming human flesh and living with us, his teachings and actions, death and resurrection be confined to the categories or conceptions of *mission* and *missionary*? The obvious answer is no. When Jesus is identified and described in this way, the chief aim is to validate and perpetuate modern notions by way of analogy. While the incarnation links the divine life and actions with

---

[63]Schnabel, *Early Christian Mission*, 1:207.
[64]Cf. Senior and Stuhlmueller, *Biblical Foundations for Mission*, 142-44, 151.

our lives, is it our prerogative to reduce divine activity to our temporal ideas and institutions—to construct an *analogia missio*?

Schnabel goes as far as to insist "Jesus' mission is inseparably linked with his self-understanding."[65] Much of Schnabel's argument centers on "the obedience and the dependence of the Son on the Father," in being sent by the Father, doing the will of the Father, and bringing glory to the Father.[66] And yet, must obedience and dependence be equated with or construed as mission? An extrapolation of mission from obedience and dependence is an unreasonable and unnecessary leap. Others point to the universal dimension in Jesus' self-designation "Son of Man" as indication of his mission self-understanding.[67] But, once again, must the universality of the Son of Man mean "mission"? The aim of justifying mission forces interpreters to locate ideas and themes within Scripture to which they might tether mission.

Such interpretations of Jesus and mission set the stage to view Paul and the early church as fully vested in mission, complete with missionaries and mission strategies.[68] With the mission premise in place, the step from Jesus the missionary to Paul the missionary is an easy one.[69]

PAUL THE MISSIONARY

For most people, the apostle Paul embodies what moderns mean by "missionary." The majority of interpreters simply characterize Paul as "a missionary" or as "the missionary."[70] Others go beyond a simple missionary designation and add qualifying adjectives: "the greatest missionary of history," "model missionary," "pioneering missionary," "a pioneer church-planting missionary," "the missionary *par excellence*," "the great missionary leader and statesman," "the canonical standard for missionary work," "the

---

[65]Schnabel, *Early Christian Mission*, 1:210.
[66]Ibid., 1:213.
[67]Ibid., 1:212.
[68]See Senior and Stuhlmueller, *Biblical Foundations for Mission*, 157-58.
[69]Cf. ibid., 269.
[70]Larkin, "Mission in Luke," 152; Goerner, *All Nations in God's Purpose*, 122; Richard J. Gibson, "Paul the Missionary, in Priestly Service of the Servant-Christ (Romans 15.16)," in Burke and Rosner, *Paul as Missionary*, 51, 61; I. Howard Marshall, "Luke's Portrait of the Pauline Mission," in *The Gospel to the Nations: Perspectives on Paul's Mission*, ed. Peter Bolt and Mark Thompson (Downers Grove, IL: InterVarsity Press, 2000), 99, 100, 102; Redford, *Missiological Hermeneutics*, 60-61; Johannes Nissen, *New Testament and Mission: Historical and Hermeneutical Perspectives*, 2nd ed. (Frankfurt am Main: Lang, 2002), 99.

most important missionary figure in the early church," and "a colossus in the missionary landscape of the early church."[71] Included in the depiction of Paul as missionary is his "missionary call" and "missionary vocation," and references to his "missionary conviction," "missionary focus," "missionary career," "missionary work," "missionary letters," "missionary ambition," "missionary language," and "missionary sufferings."[72] Paul the apostle and Paul the missionary are synonymous. The only manner in which to interpret his life is to view "Paul's identity, activity, theology and practice as missionary."[73] The argument moves in a circular fashion: mission identifies Paul, Paul defines mission.

However, Paul identifies himself not as a missionary but as an apostle. He says he is one who is sent (Rom 1:1; 11:13; 1 Cor 1:1; 15:9; 2 Cor 1:1; Gal 1:1;

---

[71]Senior and Stuhlmueller, *Biblical Foundations for Mission*, 333; Williams, "Conclusion," 242; Jacques A. Blocher and Jacques Blandenier, *The Evangelization of the World: A History of Christian Mission* (Pasadena, CA: William Carey Library, 2013), 7; C. Peter Wagner, *Acts of the Holy Spirit: A Modern Commentary on the Book of Acts* (Ventura, CA: Regal Books, 2000); Harnack, *Mission and Expansion of Christianity*, 77; Trevor J. Burke and Brian S. Rosner, "Introduction," in Burke and Rosner, *Paul as Missionary*, 1; Howell, "Mission in Paul's Epistles," 63; Dickson, *Mission-Commitment in Ancient Judaism*, 4, 5; Kaiser, *Mission in the Old Testament*, 81; Glover, *Bible Basis of Missions*, 28, 72; Williams, "Missionary Message of the New Testament," 57; Pratt, Sills, and Walters, *Introduction to Global Missions*, 98; M. Thomas Starkes, *The Foundation for Missions* (Nashville: Broadman, 1981), 7, 144. Barnett, *Paul*, claims, "Paul the missionary became the great example for centuries of those who would leave the security and comfort of home for the perils and uncertainty of the itinerant missionary. . . . Paul was and remains the exemplary missionary" (199).

[72]See Glover, *Bible Basis of Missions*, 74, 76, 82, 84, 87, 128; Senior and Stuhlmueller, *Biblical Foundations for Mission*, 165, 184, 193, 194, 298, 308; J. Ayodeji Adewuya, "The Sacrificial-Missiological Function of Paul's Sufferings in the Context of 2 Corinthians," in Burke and Rosner, *Paul as Missionary*, 97; Marshall, "Luke's Portrait of the Pauline Mission," 111; David G. Peterson, "Maturity: The Goal of Mission," in *The Gospel to the Nations: Perspectives on Paul's Mission*, ed. Peter Bolt and Mark Thompson (Downers Grove, IL: InterVarsity Press, 2000), 188, 198; Robert Jewett, *Romans: A Commentary*, Hermeneia—A Critical and Historical Commentary on the Bible (Minneapolis: Fortress, 2007), 109, 111; Goerner, *All Nations in God's Purpose*, 125; Miller, "Paul and His Ethnicity," 37; Dickson, *Mission-Commitment in Ancient Judaism*, 153; Williams, "Missionary Message of the New Testament," 58; Hahn, *Mission in the New Testament*, 95, 97; Glasser, *Announcing the Kingdom*, 293; Barnett, *Paul*, xi, 9, 80, 191; Brian S. Rosner, "The Glory of God in Paul's Missionary Theology and Practice," in Burke and Rosner, *Paul as Missionary*, 168; James W. Thompson, "Paul as Missionary Pastor," in Burke and Rosner, *Paul as Missionary*, 25.

[73]Burke and Rosner, "Introduction," 1. John Dickson, *Mission-Commitment in Ancient Judaism*, in his discussion of Paul's self-conception (86-94), argues that Paul self-identifies as a "missionary." In most cases, justification for calling Paul a missionary is not offered but assumed. We see this tendency in Williams, "Missionary Message of the New Testament," 60. In the case of James Ware, *The Mission of the Church in Paul's Letter to the Philippians in the Context of Ancient Judaism*, Supplements to Novum Testamentum 120 (Leiden, The Netherlands: Brill, 2005), mission is defined by "Paul's own consciousness of mission as this is revealed in his letters" (8).

Eph 1:1; Col 1:1; 1 Tim 1:1; 2 Tim 1:1). His self-designation as apostle is often offered as firm evidence that Paul understood himself as a missionary.[74] For example, while acknowledging there are other meanings and uses of *apostle*, Howell upholds *apostle* and *missionary* as one and the same.[75] Schnabel, as well, concedes other meanings and uses but glosses *missionary* "as the original sense of the word 'apostle.'"[76]

In contrast to these interpretations, a careful reading of various texts shows Paul's use of apostle can be interpreted in a number of ways. The term embodies his appeal to authority, as well as responsibility, as he writes to churches to instruct them in matters of practice, and the term is even used over against those who preach a different gospel (1 Cor 9:1-2). In some instances, he uses the word to assert his authority in matters of belief and practice among the churches. Indeed, along with these uses, Paul refers to himself as an apostle sent by God. But he does not utilize his sentness as an "apostle" as a technical term, or as a professional or vocational designation, especially in the modern sense of the professional or vocational missionary.[77] When Paul self-identifies, it is not as a missionary; not with this one title. Rather, he self-identifies in a variety of ways: apostle (2 Cor 1:1; Gal 1:1), bondservant (Phil 1:1; Tit 1:1), prisoner of Christ Jesus (Eph 3:1; Philem 1), and ambassador (Eph 6:20). No one title or designation is definitive.

Paul's experience and writings, it is maintained, are source material for his "mission theology" or "a missionary theology."[78] Thus, in an attempt to

---

[74]See Howell, "Mission in Paul's Epistles," 64-67; Schnabel, *Early Christian Mission*, 1:11-12. Goerner, *All Nations in God's Purpose*, claims that the literal meaning of "an apostle to the Gentiles" in the Greek means "missionary to the nations" (122).

[75]Howell, "Mission in Paul's Epistles," 65. Cf. Glasser, *Announcing the Kingdom*, 302.

[76]*Early Christian Mission*, 1:11. See also Schnabel, "Mission, Early Non-Pauline," 762. Harnack, *Mission and Expansion of Christianity*, interprets the apostle in the early church as a type of supervising regional bishop or superintendent, "discharging functions for a whole province" (445). This function, according to Harnack, may or may not include missionary activity (440-41).

[77]John Dickson, *Mission-Commitment in Ancient Judaism*, 136-40, suggests that by the time Paul wrote 2 Corinthians *apostle* was a "technical designation." The same kind of technical/professional designation is implied by historian Henry Chadwick, *The Early Church*, The Pelican History of the Church 1 (Harmondsworth, UK: Penguin Books, 1967), 45-46.

[78]See Howell, "Mission in Paul's Epistles," 115; Rosner, "Glory of God"; Stanley E. Porter, "Reconciliation as the Heart of Paul's Missionary Theology," in Burke and Rosner, *Paul as Missionary*, 169-79; Dean S. Gilliland, *Pauline Theology & Mission Practice* (Eugene, OR: Wipf and Stock, 1998), 30-34; Christopher Little, *Mission in the Way of Paul: Biblical Mission for the Church in the Twenty-First Century*, Studies in Biblical Literature 80 (New York: Peter Lang, 2005), 47; Nissen, *New Testament and Mission*, 99, 101.

combine his roles of missionary and theologian, Paul is frequently labeled a "missionary theologian."[79] Senior claims "the theology of mission is practically synonymous with the totality of Paul's awesome reflections on Christian life," and thus mission theology (its questions and themes) becomes the framework for understanding Paul.[80] Senior's argument develops in the following manner: the starting point for the development of Paul's theology is his encounter with Christ on the Damascus road. Ananias goes to Paul and lays hands on him with the Lord's assurance that Paul would bear Jesus' name "before the Gentiles and kings and the sons of Israel" (Acts 9:15). Thus, according to Senior, because "Paul himself explicitly identifies his own missionary vocation with this inaugural Christian experience, we can be justified in our construction of his mission theology from this point."[81] Yet, what is missing is an explicit identification of this encounter as commissioning Paul as a "missionary" and his task as "mission," and the necessity of linking Paul's encounter with a Pauline "mission theology." What is clear is that Paul continued as a leatherworker and supported himself, and thus did not become a full-time religious professional of any kind. He proclaimed the name of Christ to everyone he encountered, never in the name of mission or under the identity of missionary.[82]

Interpreters determine that the groups that traveled and ministered with Paul were his "missionary team," "missionary band," "missionary colleagues," or "subordinate missionaries."[83] Because Paul is assumed to be a missionary, those who accompanied him are missionaries and part of his missionary team.

---

[79]Barnett, *Paul*, 200-202; Gilliland, *Pauline Theology & Mission Practice*, 49.

[80]Senior and Stuhlmueller, *Biblical Foundations for Mission*, 161, 169.

[81]Ibid., 165, 171.

[82]Though Christopher Little, *Mission in the Way of Paul*, uses the rhetoric of *mission* and *missionary*, he concedes that Paul was not a "missionary" based on the fact that he did not serve for "a prolonged period of time in only one locality" (119).

[83]Schnabel, "Mission, Early Non-Pauline," 763; Blocher and Blandenier, *Evangelization of the World*, 7; David Seccombe, "The Story of Jesus and the Missionary Strategy of Paul," in Bolt and Thompson, *Gospel to the Nations*, 122; Barnett, *Jesus & the Rise of Early Christianity*, 389-90. J. G. Davies, *The Early Christian Church*, History of Religion Series (New York: Holt, Rinehart and Winston, 1965), refers to those who worked with or under Paul as "subordinate missionaries" (47), but at the same time insists that "there was no elaborate missionary machinery" (87). Dickson, *Mission-Commitment in Ancient Judaism*, argues, "It is not difficult to imagine that by the time Philippians was written, the phrase 'workers/brothers in the Lord' had become something of a technical expression for missionaries" (149, see also 94, 99, 142, 143, 148). Thus, Dickson views Paul's various coworkers and colleagues as part of the missionary team.

To think of Paul as missionary leads Harnack to name Aquila and Priscilla the "missionary couple."[84] By grouping and designating these men and women as missionaries, the intent is to identify them with Paul's activity and place them in the same "mission cause." But to characterize Paul as having a "missionary organization," as David Seccombe does, presents an erroneous picture of the nature and scope of his work and those who labored with him.[85] In addition to those on the "mission team," others are characterized as "mission supporters," sympathizers who stood with Paul, convinced of his cause and the validity of his apostleship.[86] And yet, the effect is that through such language Paul and his band are subtly transformed into a modern mission team, with accompanying modern assumptions about organization, supporters, and finances. Perhaps unqualified and unmodified words for these coworkers, such as *believers, brothers and sisters, ministers,* or *preachers,* would be clearer and less confusing designations for those who worked alongside or in conjunction with Paul.

The activities of Paul and those associated with him are described as "missionary work," "missionary enterprise," "missionary campaign," "missionary labours," and "missionary ventures" that occur within "the real missionary epoch."[87] More than mere work, enterprise, labors, or ventures, these are specified as "missionary." Paul's proclamation is "missionary preaching" or "missionary address" rather than just preaching or simple address.[88] One wonders

---

[84]Harnack, *Mission and Expansion of Christianity,* 370.

[85]Seccombe, "Story of Jesus and the Missionary Strategy of Paul," 118.

[86]Barnett, *Paul,* 182-86; Dickson, *Mission-Commitment in Ancient Judaism,* 179, 199, 200.

[87]Williams, "Conclusion," 242, 243; Blocher and Blandenier, *Evangelization of the World,* 7, 8; Schnabel, *Early Christian Mission,* 1:7; Baus, *From the Apostolic Community to Constantine,* 100, 102, 104; Trevor J. Burke, "The Holy Spirit as the Controlling Dynamic in Paul's Role as Missionary to the Thessalonians," in Burke and Rosner, *Paul as Missionary,* 142, 156, 157; Rosner, "Glory of God," 159; Seccombe, "Story of Jesus and the Missionary Strategy of Paul," 122; Bavinck, *Introduction to the Science of Missions,* 37; Marshall, "Luke's Portrait of the Pauline Mission," 104-6, 110, 111; Harnack, *Mission and Expansion of Christianity,* 60; Adewuya, "Sacrificial-Missiological Function of Paul's Suffering," 89; Porter, "Reconciliation as the Heart of Paul's Missionary Theology," 169; Robert L. Plummer, *Paul's Understanding of the Church's Mission: Did the Apostle Paul Expect the Early Christian Community to Evangelize?,* Paternoster Biblical Monographs (Exeter, UK: Paternoster, 2006), 2; William J. Larkin Jr., "The First Decades of the Mission of God," in Barnett and Martin, *Discovering the Mission of God,* 196; Porter and Westfall, "Cord of Three Strands," 120; Hahn, *Mission in the New Testament,* 137.

[88]Harnack, *Mission and Expansion of Christianity,* 73, 84-100, 381-87. See also Senior and Stuhlmueller, *Biblical Foundations for Mission,* 185-87; Porter and Westfall, "Cord of Three Strands," 119; Davies, *Early Christian Church,* 47.

what is intended by the adjective *missionary*. Harnack uses the adjective to define some preaching as "missionary preaching" when such preaching is the "crucial message of the faith and the ethical requirements of the gospel," as well as when "all the forces of influences, attraction, and persuasion which the gospel had at its command."[89] Thus, Harnack's designation defines "missionary preaching" as having distinct content and a unique effect. In Harnack's estimation, the church's abandonment of "missionary preaching" is the cause for the loss of Christianity's revolutionary nature and passion. Thus, Harnack's intent is not only to highlight the distinct nature of "missionary preaching" over against other kinds of preaching, but to characterize it as necessary for the church. Senior even indicates that Paul's "missionary preaching" had a unique "mission message," making it doubly distinct.[90] Likewise, Peter's sermon at Pentecost was a "mission sermon."[91] Porter and Westfall differentiate Paul's "missionary speeches" from his "apologetic speeches" and his "farewell speeches." The "missionary speeches" were unique in content and style and thus are characteristic of Paul's "missionary emphasis."[92]

The result of Paul's missionary preaching or propaganda, according to Harnack, was a "missionary church."[93] Harnack does not indicate that *missionary* is descriptive of the church's nature; rather, it is such because it is created by a missionary (Paul) and thus responsible to its founder. In this case, *missionary* is used to denote a type of relationship. *Missionary* frames the relationship of Paul to the churches he establishes in terms of dependency or authority. Mark Thompson characterizes the connection as "churches within [Paul's] missionary orbit."[94] Interpreters' use of *missionary* in this specialized way creates the impression of dependency that possibly runs counter to the relationships Paul actually had with churches he founded.[95]

---

[89]Harnack, *Mission and Expansion of Christianity*, 86.
[90]Senior, *Biblical Foundations for Mission*, 187. Regarding the church's "missionary message," see 248.
[91]Ibid., 274.
[92]Porter and Westfall, "Cord of Three Strands," 127. See also Nissen, *New Testament and Mission*, 60-66.
[93]Harnack, *Mission and Expansion of Christianity*, 466; or for "mission churches," see Barnett, *Paul*, 143. Cf. Gilliland, *Pauline Theology & Mission Practice*, 181-82.
[94]Mark D. Thompson, "The Missionary Apostle and Modern Systematic Affirmation," in Bolt and Thompson, *Gospel to the Nations*, 367, 369.
[95]See Roland Allen, *Missionary Methods: St. Paul's or Ours?* (Grand Rapids: Eerdmans, 1983).

An ongoing debate among interpreters is whether Paul had a "missionary strategy" or "missionary policy," and what exactly were his "missionary methods."[96] The intent in many cases seems to be to prove that Paul had a particular strategy and methodology, and then maintain that these strategies and methods are the ones modern missionaries should employ.[97] In addition to advocating for a particular strategy, some interpreters designate certain methodologies as "missionary" and others as not. This is done in the following manner: methods and strategies connected with Paul are by association qualified as missionary, while those not seen in Paul's activities are described as other than missionary. Thus, Paul becomes a way of approving and disapproving of methods and strategies. Thus, some interpreters do not consider activities that address social needs, while useful and necessary, to be "missionary," because they lack a crosscultural, proclamation, or church-planting dimension. The question of whether Paul had a defined strategy or policy that determined his methodology may be a valid discussion, but to couch the discussion in terms of *missionary* is not helpful. It does not appear that Paul differentiates between methods that are missionary and those that are nonmissionary. He performs a variety of activities, each with vigor and purpose.

The preaching trips that Paul undertook from his home base at Antioch are characterized as "missionary journeys,"[98] "missionary campaigns,"[99] and

---

[96]See Blocher and Blandenier, *Evangelization of the World*, 15-16; Schnabel, "Mission, Early Non-Pauline," 753-55; Porter and Westfall, "Cord of Three Strands," 123; Sandnes, "Missionary Strategy," 128-41; Porter, "Reconciliation as the Heart of Paul's Missionary Theology," 171; Little, *Mission in the Way of Paul*, 91-97; Gilliland, *Pauline Theology & Mission Practice*, 284-91; Pratt, Sills, and Walters, *Introduction to Global Missions*, 63-64; Seccombe, "Story of Jesus and the Missionary Strategy of Paul," 115-29; Nissen, *New Testament and Mission*, 108.

[97]For example, Rufus Anderson, *Foreign Missions: Their Relations and Claims* (New York: Charles Scribner, 1869), makes an appeal to Paul's superior strategy and thus asserts that his "theory of missions is substantially that of the Apostle to the Gentiles" (vii).

[98]For examples of the widespread use of this language, see Howell, "Mission in Paul's Epistles," 63; Blocher and Blandenier, *Evangelization of the World*, 6; Bernard R. Youngman, *Into All the World: The Story of Christianity to 1066 A.D.* (New York: St. Martin's, 1965), 25, 45; Goerner, *All Nations in God's Purpose*, 110, 113; Larkin, "Mission in Acts," 177; Stephen G. Wilson, *The Gentiles and the Gentile Mission in Luke–Acts* (Cambridge: Cambridge University Press, 1973), 263; Dickson, *Mission-Commitment in Ancient Judaism*, 194; Bavinck, *Introduction to the Science of Missions*, 38-39; Baus, *From the Apostolic Community to Constantine*, 104; Rosner, "Glory of God," 161; Barnett, *Paul*, 88, 146; Davies, *Early Christian Church*, 42-44, 52. Porter and Westfall, "Cord of Three Strands," 111, 114, 120-23, refer to these trips as both "missionary journeys" and "mission trips."

[99]Marshall, "Luke's Portrait of the Pauline Mission," 104-6.

"missionary tours,"[100] and the places to which he traveled or wished to travel, such as Arabia and Spain, are "missionary destinations."[101] John Townsend maintains that the designation of missionary journeys was imposed on Acts with the rise of Catholic and Protestant mission societies. He traces the earliest reference to "missionary journey" language to J. A. Bengel's *Gnomon Novi Testamenti* (1742).[102] Following Bengel's lead, the missionary journey pattern became the standard exegetical tradition. Evidence of this can be seen in the language of "missionary journey" that has been inserted as subject headings in modern translations of Acts.

Underlying the discussions of Paul as missionary and the various aspects of his activity are implications of a "Pauline mission," or mission originating from Paul.[103] In establishing Paul as *missionary*, designating his *mission* strategy, and framing his life around *missionary* journeys, *mission* is activity that Paul initiates, executes, and extends. According to Paul Barnett, "Apart from Paul's herculean efforts, it is difficult to imagine how the gospel of Christ would have taken root so comprehensively in the Greco-Roman world."[104] While divine initiative may be in some way tacitly acknowledged, *mission* is named as Paul's unique response to the gospel and his responsibility to humanity. The recurring refrain of "Paul's mission" fills the pages of commentaries and textbooks. "Paul's missionary thrust into the Greco-Roman world" and his "missionary responsibility"[105] dominate. The result is that mission becomes defined as originating from Paul and belonging to Paul.[106] Since Paul is commemorated as the mission prototype, strategist, and hero, mission and Paul define each other.

---

[100]Harnack, *Mission and Expansion of Christianity*, 74; Barnett, *Paul*, 144, 207.

[101]Kim, "Paul as an Eschatological Herald," 13. Schnabel uses the same language to refer to the "missionary travels" of the "Johannine missionaries," in "Mission, Early Non-Pauline," 769.

[102]John T. Townsend, "Missionary Journeys in Acts and European Missionary Societies," *Anglican Theological Review* 68, no. 2 (April 1986): 103.

[103]Bowers, "Paul and Religious Propaganda in the First Century," 317, 323; Dickson, *Mission-Commitment in Ancient Judaism*, 131; Hengel, "Origins of the Christian Mission," 49-54.

[104]Barnett, *Paul*, 6.

[105]Ibid., ix; Dickson, *Mission-Commitment in Ancient Judaism*, 135.

[106]Contrary to Paul as initiator and sustainer of mission, Beverly Gaventa interprets Paul's role in Romans as one of response to God's initiative. "Talk of 'mission' in Romans is not simply talk about what human being do to deliver God's gospel to other human beings or what they do by way of encouraging one another." Rather, Gaventa frames mission as "nothing less than God's own action." Beverly Roberts Gaventa, "The Mission of God in Paul's Letter to the Romans," in Burke and Rosner, *Paul as Missionary*, 75.

EARLY CHURCH

Even as Paul became the founder of a "missionary church," commentators on the book of Acts and early Christianity inflect this history through the paradigm of our modern missionary language. Much has been made of how the early church was "a genuinely missionary church."[107] It is described as a church with a "missionary edge," "missionary temperature," "missionary spirit," "missionary zeal," "missionary work," having a "missionary enterprise," and operated according to "missionary principles."[108] Such sweeping characterizations often eclipse the other realities of the early church, such as its struggle with race, order, and false teachings. It was also known to have bouts of division, laxness, and immorality. And yet, attempts are frequently made to paint a picture of the nascent church solely as a *missionary* entity or as embodying the *mission* ideal. The depiction of the book of Acts as "entirely a missionary story" not only inflates one dimension but also anachronistically misrepresents much that transpires in the early years following Christ.[109] Far from a pristine, monodimensional exemplar of mission, the early church, much like the church today, struggled with its own identity and purpose.

The most pressing problem with conventional readings of the early church is that the concepts of mission and missionary are not developed in the book of Acts, nor do they exist as terminology or ideals toward which the early church aspired. This language distorts the story—a modern misreading. And yet, Harnack depicts the preaching to and the conversion of Greeks by unnamed "adherents of Stephen" as "mission." These men are, according to Harnack, "the first missionaries to the heathen."[110] He also

---

[107]Stephen Neill, *A History of Christian Missions*, 2nd ed. (London: Penguin Books, 1986), 21, 22. Hereafter cited as *HCM*. Cf. Robert Hall Glover, *The Progress of World-Wide Missions* (New York: Harper & Row, 1960), 11, 19; Howard Peskett and Vinoth Ramachandra, *The Message of Mission: The Glory of Christ in All Time and Space*, The Bible Speaks Today (Downers Grove, IL: InterVarsity Press, 2003), 11.

[108]See Senior and Stuhlmueller, *Biblical Foundations for Mission*, 305; Glover, *Bible Basis of Missions*, 25, 39; Baus, *From the Apostolic Community to Constantine*, 82, 97; Eleanor Harvey Tejirian and Reeva Spector Simon, *Conflict, Conquest, and Conversion: Two Thousand Years of Christian Missions in the Middle East* (New York: Columbia University Press, 2012), 3. William Larkin goes as far to say that the early church "is on a missional DNA-driven mission," in "First Decades of the Mission of God," 200.

[109]Pratt, Sills, and Walters, *Introduction to Global Missions*, 61.

[110]Harnack, *Mission and Expansion of Christianity*, 52-53.

describes the founding of the "Gentile Christian communities . . . like that of Rome," as "founded by unknown missionaries." Harnack identifies Prisca in Ephesus as a "distinguished missionary."[111] Barnabas, Silas, Aquila, Apollos, Timothy, Mark, Luke, Titus, Peter, John the Presbyter, Philip, Aristion, and Andrew are classified as part of the "first Christian missionaries."[112] Senior likewise makes the same distinction, referring to "missionaries Mark and Silvanus" in the "Petrine Group."[113] When the scattering of Christians throughout Judea and Samaria takes place following the stoning of Stephen, Harnack says, "they acted as missionaries, i.e., as apostles."[114] And yet, in the final analysis, Harnack concedes, "the great mission of Christianity was in reality accomplished by means of informal missionaries. . . . It is impossible to see in any one class of people inside the church the chief agents of the Christian propaganda."[115] He distinguishes certain offices as nonmissionary (bishop, prophet, teacher, apologist) but with the possibility that any of these might serve a "missionary function."[116] And yet, those in these offices are contrasted with those Harnack deems to be "regular missionaries."[117] John Mark Terry similarly concludes that along with "missionary bishops" and "lay missionaries," there was "a body of full-time missionaries" identified with the "office of missionary."[118]

William Larkin makes a related distinction in describing "the human agents of mission" as including "evangelists and missionaries" in the early church.[119] Larkin also selects various events in the book of Acts as "activity of mission."[120] For him, "the missionary's primary activity" includes actions related to "spiritual salvation," specifically proclamation or preaching, and

---

[111]Ibid., 75, 79.

[112]Ibid., 78-83; Schnabel, "Mission, Early Non-Pauline," 764; Fiorenza, "Miracles, Mission, and Apologetics," 14.

[113]Senior and Stuhlmueller, *Biblical Foundations for Mission*, 298.

[114]Harnack, *Mission and Expansion of Christianity*, 51.

[115]Ibid., 368. Harnack contradicts himself in his discussion of the various titles for believers (disciples, saints, brethren, sisters, confessors, martyrs, Christians) on 399-418. In this section, there is no mention of the title *missionary*.

[116]See ibid., 440-41.

[117]See ibid., 511.

[118]John Mark Terry, "The Ante-Nicene Church on Mission," in Barnett and Martin, *Discovering the Mission of God*, 212-14. See also Pratt, Sills, and Walters, *Introduction to Global Missions*, 99.

[119]Larkin, "Mission in Acts," 177. See also Glover, *Bible Basis of Missions*, 39.

[120]Larkin, "Mission in Acts," 178.

verbal witness.[121] Again, the implication is that other activities—caring for orphans and widows, performing miracles, managing conflict among believers, and teaching new believers how to live and behave—while good and necessary, fall outside the designation of "mission" or "missionary activity." Thus, a distinction is made between activities that are missionary and those that are nonmissionary.

To identify the activities recorded in Acts as a "missionary enterprise" or "missionary expedition" portrays the early church as an established mission organization.[122] To designate Acts as "the first chapter in the history of Christian missions" is more than merely anachronistic but historically inaccurate.[123] To name the church in Philippi a "mission-minded congregation" says little about their nature and in fact overstates their aims.[124] Even without the historical problems of mission language, the falsity of such distinctions demonstrates that missionary designations do not adequately represent the richness and complexity of the early church.

Characterizations of the early church as a *missionary church* with a *missionary spirit* are problematic for several reasons. First, with such characterizations, the assumption is made that these communities were more than churches: they were *missionary* churches. In other words, being the church was not enough. A church had to be or should be a "missionary church." And yet, Paul does not make such a distinction or create this type of gradation among the early Christian communities. The saints at Ephesus and Galatia are known to Paul simply as "church" (Gal 1:2). He even calls those embroiled in all kinds of controversy at Corinth "saints" belonging to the church (2 Cor 1:1-2). Never does he differentiate between mere churches and missionary churches.

What's more, the terminology of *missionary church* often signals the opposite—these churches were in a dependent relationship, belonging to or identifying as Paul's churches. Or, in a related vein, commentators use *missionary church* to suggest that these communities were a type of church-in-waiting,

---

[121]Ibid., 178-79. Contra Senior and Stuhlmueller, *Biblical Foundations for Mission*, 332-39.

[122]Glover, *Bible Basis of Missions*, 33; Baus, *From the Apostolic Community to Constantine*, 98. Cf. Bavinck, *Introduction to the Science of Missions*, 43, 63-65.

[123]Goerner, *All Nations in God's Purpose*, 99. The same claim for "the beginning of the Christian mission" is made by Davies, *Early Christian Church*, 41.

[124]Seccombe, "Story of Jesus and the Missionary Strategy of Paul," 126.

not a complete or mature church. Both possibilities are contrary to Paul's ministry and the tenor of his correspondence with various New Testament communities. Paul writes against the idea of converts or churches belonging to himself or anyone else (1 Cor 1:10-17) and speaks of these churches as having all they need to be the church in their cities and provinces (Rom 1:8; Col 1:3-6). Either way, the Bible does not qualify or define the nascent assemblies of believers as "missionary churches" or "churches of a second order." They are simply known as *ekklēsia,* or assemblies of new believers.

Also, to portray the activities of the early church as a "missionary enterprise" is to say too much. "Enterprise" gives the impression that methods, strategies, and structure were organized and coordinated into a definite schema or plan, which they further designated as missionary. The book of Acts conveys the story of the Spirit's movement, which was at times chaotic and unpredictable rather than systematized and methodical.[125] To say the early church is distinguished and noteworthy because of its missionary spirit may attribute too much to the early church's activity and minimize the work and power of the Holy Spirit. The primary actor in the book of Acts is the Spirit and not a church "deeply imbued with the missionary spirit."[126] In order to substantiate this missionary spirit, interpreters must gloss everything as "missionary." For example, the meeting of leaders in Jerusalem in Acts 15 becomes "the first recorded missionary conference."[127] Such a gloss is part of a modern interpretive frame, not an accurate representation of the patchwork early history of Christianity.

Lauding the early church through missionary language may present an inspiring picture of early believers, but it does not aid us in understanding the dynamics of the faith and witness in their context and at their time. The language of *mission* and *missionary* prejudices our reading of the text so that a clear understanding of motives and intentions is impeded by a retrospective burnishing of Christian history. And while the substitution of *missional* for *missionary* to refer to activities and ideas related to Jesus, Paul, and the early church may sidestep unfavorable caricatures and

---

[125]Hahn, *Mission in the New Testament,* describes the Hellenists witness among Gentiles as "a systematic mission" (165).

[126]Glover, *Bible Basis of Missions,* 39.

[127]Ibid., 67, 101.

stereotypes, this latest mission declension carries many of the same assumptions, aims, and associations.

PROFANE AND SACRED LANGUAGE

Our survey of the Old and New Testaments, Jesus, Paul, and the early church
stresses that (1) interpreters employ *mission* and *missionary* to modify and
qualify concepts, actions, and institutions; (2) there is a tendency to use
mission as a means of interpretation in order to validate contemporary organizations and activities; and, most importantly, (3) mission language and
its concomitant interpretive frames are not the most faithful or helpful renderings of the divine activity as expressed in Scripture. In a few cases,
mission, missionary, and *missionary journey* are set off in quotation marks
to indicate that they are being used with special or technical meaning.
However, interpreters often make this qualification once at the outset of an
article or book and then do not repeat the qualification, nor do they provide
reasons for this technical or special use of *mission* and *missionary*.[128] For
example, in arguing for Jesus' mission being inseparably linked with his
self-understanding, Schnabel notes that Jesus' lifestyle could be described
as "missionary."[129] And while Schnabel uses quotation marks around missionary in this particular instance to denote its specialized use, the
association of the word with modern notions of a particular vocation and
certain ways of living—that is, the missionary lifestyle—is unavoidable. The
fact that the word must be set off with quotation marks highlights the inherent confusion. The suggestion that these words and concepts need to be
considered in a specialized way is indicative of the problem. And yet, the
majority of Partisans and Apologists give no indication that either word is
being used in a specialized or qualified manner.

The alternative to justifying mission through establishing a biblical foundation or developing a mission hermeneutic or identifying missionary
themes is to allow the sending activities of Scripture to be simply what they
are—means to an end. In the case of mission justification, means become

---

[128]See, for example, Bowers, "Paul and Religious Propaganda in the First Century," 317; Bowen,
So I Send You, 1; Marshall, "Luke's Portrait of the Pauline Mission," 101, 102; Schnabel, "Mission,
Early Non-Pauline," 766, 771.

[129]Schnabel, *Early Christian Mission*, 1:217.

an end. *Mission* is exalted to the status of a biblical word as a means for justifying contemporary paradigms and programs. Likewise, when mission is established as a theological concept by way of a "missional hermeneutic" or "mission themes," mission fills the whole horizon. The result is that mission becomes sacred rhetoric and, as such, *mission* does not have to be exact or critically evaluated, because it is holy language. Its meaning can be assumed, because Partisans and Apologists claim that it is biblical and theological. Such language then is beyond being contested, because it represents a kind of orthodoxy. Yet, mission as sacred rhetoric is perilous, because of its imprecision, and because it assumes too much. In the end, it does not elevate or explain but diminishes the place of more theologically rich and biblical concepts, such as covenant, reconciliation, witness, and love. The great themes of Scripture become lost or obscure when the rhetoric of *mission* and *missionary* controls the text. As mission ascends to sacred language, it becomes larger, more important than the text itself. Scripture becomes a means to justify mission.

3

Presenting History as Mission

He admonishes and teaches, saying,
Going therefore teach now all the gentiles,
Baptizing them in the name of the Father
and the Son and the Holy Spirit,
teaching them to observe all things
whatsoever I have commanded to you,
and look, I am with you all days,
as far as the highest perfection of the age.
And again He says, Going therefore into the entire world,
Proclaim the Gospel to every creature.

PATRICK, "CONFESSIO"

[Pope Gregory I] being moved by Divine inspiration, in
the fourteenth year of the same emperor [Maurice], and
about the one hundred and fiftieth after the coming of the
English into Britain, sent the servant of God, Augustine,
and with him divers other monks, who feared the Lord,
to preach the Word of God to the English nation.

THE VENERABLE BEDE, *THE ECCLESIASTICAL HISTORY OF THE ENGLISH PEOPLE*

VARIOUS WORDS have been used throughout history to explain the expansion of Christianity, and *mission* has not always been the word of choice. In fact, it is absent from the language used by early figures of this expansion and its earliest historians. Patrick and the Venerable Bede tell this story in language quite different from that of modern mission historians. Instead of *mission*, these early historians employ the language of *witness, pilgrimage*, and *martyrdom*. Rather than *missionaries*, they name the actors as *bishops, pilgrims, servants*, and *apostles*.

In this chapter, I explore whether *mission* and *missionary* are words or concepts in use by the primitive church, or whether they are rhetoric from the modern era. Have they, as in the case of Scripture, been inserted into the historical record? If, in fact, mission language has been historicized, in what ways have place and substance been created for them within the historical account? Conversely, if the language of mission is absent, is it necessary or helpful to designate people and activities as *missionary* and *mission*?

What will become clear is that *mission* and *missionary* are not the language of historical figures of the ancient church. Mission language has been spliced into their letters and reports, infused into the historical records of their lives, and presented as their activities and words. Mission, as modern mission, was not in the rhetorical palette of early church historians; rather, it has been asserted as their language by those who translate these historians and interpret their meaning. By presenting activities as "mission," historical figures as "missionaries," and history as "mission history," interpreters turn these into historical justification for modern mission.

MISSIONARIES?

Giving key historical figures the title of *missionary* historicizes mission. Because the language of mission can too easily be assigned to premodern persons, it is important to determine whether, in fact, these individuals identify themselves as missionaries and whether their contemporaries designate their activities as mission. The question has two sides: Do medieval individuals see their activities as "mission," and do they self-identify as "missionaries"? Do their contemporaries describe their activities as "mission," and do they name these individuals as "missionaries"? What follows is an investigation into the language of Patrick, Columba, Columban, Gregory the Great, the Nestorians, and Boniface, and the accounts of their eyewitnesses. Other individuals could be included, but these persons are representative of the premodern era and

the ones most often identified by historians as "mission luminaries" and used
repeatedly to historicize mission.[1]

Patrick (ca. 385–460) and the arrival of Christianity in Ireland appear to
be one and the same.[2] The question of whether his story is historical fact and
how much of his life and activity are fabrication continues to be debated.[3]
The facts of his life, for sure, are sparse, and the accounts of his activities vary
widely. Stories of his birth, life at home, years as a slave, return to Britain,
and his activities in Ireland contain ample amounts of legend, and thus these
accounts are considered to be equal parts hagiography and history.[4] The
earliest histories of Patrick's life, such as Muirchú moccu Machthéni's *Vita
Patricii* (Life of Patrick), composed in the seventh century, must not be read
as critical or exacting histories that provide precise accounts of what did and
did not happen. Rather, their purpose is to provide a sympathetic remembrance of Patrick during his lifetime and a commemoration of the beginning
of Irish Christianity.

Muirchú, in *Vita Patricii*, uses a variety of designations to refer to Patrick:
confessor, holy man, saint, bishop, eminent teacher, Christian, and apostolic
man.[5] Throughout *Vita*, biblical imagery and personalities are used as typo-
logical patterns to depict Patrick's life. According to Muirchú, Patrick is like
Jonah, Moses, John the Baptist, and Paul, and is compared to Gideon,
Stephen, and Christ.[6] Muirchú reports Patrick's involvement in a number of
activities, including preaching and teaching. For example, once the local
ruler in Ireland, King Lóiguire, was converted to Christianity, Patrick went
"off teaching all nations and baptising them in the name of the Father and of

---

[1]For a provocative, alternative interpretation of the means of the church's witness, and thus expansion, in the patristic era, see Alan Kreider, *The Patient Ferment of the Early Church: The Improbable
Rise of Christianity in the Roman Empire* (Grand Rapids: Baker Academic, 2016).
[2]For accounts of Patrick's role in the establishment of Christianity in Ireland, see Thomas
O'Loughlin, *Discovering Saint Patrick* (London: Darton, Longman & Todd, 2005); F. F. Bruce, *The
Spreading Flame: The Rise and Progress of Christianity from Its First Beginnings to the Conversion of
the English* (Grand Rapids: Eerdmans, 1958), 371-83.
[3]See O'Loughlin, *Discovering Saint Patrick*, 3-42.
[4]Ibid., 8-14.
[5]Muirchú, "The Vita Patricii by Muirchú," in O'Loughlin, *Discovering Saint Patrick*, 192-229. On
Muirchú's literary style and content, see Ludwig Bieler, "Muirchú's Life of St. Patrick as a Work
of Literature," in *Studies on the Life and Legend of St. Patrick*, ed. Richard Sharpe, Variorum Reprint CS244 (London: Variorum Reprints, 1986), ix, 219-33.
[6]Muirchú, "Vita Patricii by Muirchú," 196, 197, 198.

the Son and of the Holy Spirit."[7] Patrick traveled to the "head of all the churches of the whole world," because he wished "to bring divine Grace to foreign nations by converting them to the Christian faith."[8] In another instance, an old friend, Victoricus, told Patrick that it is "time for him to fish with the evangelical net among the wild and barbarian nations."[9] In addition to baptizing, teaching, and converting, Muirchú reports that Patrick performed miracles and raised the dead.

Epistola ad milites Corotici is Patrick's fierce condemnation of a British warrior named Coroticus. In the midst of his threats against this ruthless man, Patrick accounts for his own life and his desire to teach nonbelievers the way of God. He chronicles his role in the extension of the Christian faith "among barbarian gentiles."[10] This role is fulfilled as a bishop, a sojourner, a refugee, and a slave to Christ.[11] His task is "to proclaim the gospel" and "perform pious acts of pity toward that gentile people [of Ireland]."[12] The language he uses most to describe his sojourn in Ireland is pilgrimage.

Confessio (Declaration) is Patrick's defense of his life and actions. In this work, he describes himself as having the same kinds of roles and tasks described in *Epistola.* This much longer and detailed statement of Patrick's life includes his self-descriptions as sinner, servant, Christian, exile, deacon, and debtor.[13] His proclamation of the gospel is aimed at "all gentiles" and framed in spatial and ethnic language, such as "among many gentiles even as far as the furthest part of land," "among members of a strange race," "as far as the furthest part of land," "every nation which is under every heaven," "to all the gentiles before the end of the world," "all the world," and "going into the entire world."[14]

Vita, Epistola ad milites Corotici, and *Confessio* narrate Patrick's life in the language of slavery, return to Ireland, preaching, and sainthood, but not in

---

[7]Ibid., 213.

[8]Ibid., 198.

[9]Ibid.

[10]Patrick, "Epistola Ad Milites Corotici: Text and Translation," in *The Book of Letters of Saint Patrick the Bishop,* ed. and trans. D. R. Howlett, Liber Epistolarum Sancti Patricii Episcopi (Dublin: Four Courts, 1994), 27.

[11]Ibid., 27, 31.

[12]Ibid., 29, 31.

[13]Patrick, "Confessio: Text and Translation," in Howlett, *Book of Letters of Saint Patrick the Bishop,* 53, 61, 65, 71, 77.

[14]Ibid., 53, 55, 59, 75, 79.

the rhetoric of *mission*. The aim of these texts is to portray Patrick as a saint and an apostle, alongside his saintly predecessors in the Bible. Nowhere do we find the intent expressed by Patrick or those who record his life to name him as a "missionary" or associate him with "mission." Instead, we find biblical illusions and language referring backward to biblical events and figures rather than Patrick launching a trajectory toward the nineteenth century. The language of Old Testament *prophet* and designation of New Testament *apostle* are used because they substantiate the claims for Patrick's sainthood. Mission and missionary are nonexistent as categories for Patrick and Muirchú; such concepts are nowhere to be found, because these categories developed much later—during the modern era. And yet, contrary to Patrick and Muirchú, modern historians name Patrick as "the missionary from Roman Britain,"[15] "the first great missionary to Ireland,"[16] "a model for foreign missionaries,"[17] a "distinguished missionary,"[18] consecrated as a "missionary bishop,"[19] and depict his return to Ireland as a "mission"[20] or as "missionary labour."[21]

---

[15]O'Loughlin, *Discovering Saint Patrick*, 5, 58-59, 71. See also J. D. Douglas, "Patrick," in *Evangelical Dictionary of World Missions*, ed. A. Scott Moreau (Grand Rapids: Eerdmans, 2000), 731.

[16]Robert Hall Glover, *The Bible Basis of Missions* (Chicago: Moody Press, 1946), 26. See also Stephen B. Bevans and Roger Schroeder, *Constants in Context: A Theology of Mission for Today* (Maryknoll, NY: Orbis Books, 2004), 120; or as "the best-known missionary of this period," Zane G. Pratt, M. David Sills, and Jeff K. Walters, *Introduction to Global Missions* (Nashville: B&H, 2014), 102; Philip Freeman, *The World of Saint Patrick* (Oxford: Oxford University Press, 2014), 6.

[17]O'Loughlin, *Discovering Saint Patrick*, 135.

[18]Kenneth Scott Latourette, *A History of the Expansion of Christianity*, vol. 1, *The First Five Centuries* (Grand Rapids: Zondervan, 1970), 216, 221. Hereafter cited as *HEC*.

[19]Newport J. D. White, "St. Patrick: Introduction," in *St. Patrick, His Writings and Life*, trans. Newport J. D. White, Translations of Christian Literature, Series V: Lives of the Celtic Saints (London: Society for Promoting Christian Knowledge, 1920), 13, 14. See also David Lawrence Edwards, *Christianity: The First Two Thousand Years* (Maryknoll, NY: Orbis Books, 1999), 175; Henry Chadwick, *The Early Church*, The Pelican History of the Church 1 (Harmondsworth, UK: Penguin Books, 1967), 255.

[20]See Rufus Anderson, *Foreign Missions: Their Relations and Claims* (New York: Charles Scribner, 1869), 69-74; O'Loughlin, *Discovering Saint Patrick*, 51, 54, 60, 91-92; Benedicta Ward and G. R. Evans, "The Medieval West," in *A World History of Christianity*, ed. Adrian Hastings (Grand Rapids: Eerdmans, 1999), 112; Ian Wood, *The Missionary Life: Saints and the Evangelisation of Europe, 400–1050* (Harlow, UK: Longman, 2001), 8, 27; Peter Robert Lamont Brown, *The Rise of Western Christendom: Triumph and Diversity, AD 200–1000* (Cambridge, MA: Blackwell, 1996), 131-33.

[21]White, "St. Patrick," 20; Bruce, *Spreading Flame*, 376; Carlos F. Cardoza-Orlandi and Justo L. González, *To All Nations from All Nations: A History of the Christian Missionary Movement* (Nashville: Abingdon, 2013); R. A. Fletcher, *The Barbarian Conversion: From Paganism to*

The stated reason historians use the language of mission to describe Patrick varies, as well as the ways they apply mission to his life. For George Stokes, the question is whether Patrick had received "a regular commission from the see of Rome." If commissioned by Rome, then Patrick was a missionary. "Missionary," for Stokes, refers to representation and extension of the Roman church. And yet, Stokes admits, "the writings of St. Patrick himself undoubtedly contain not even the remotest hint of such a mission."[22] Ian Wood, on the other hand, characterizes Patrick as a missionary on the simple fact that he was among pagans and demonstrates sufficient faith necessary for such work. According to Wood, if a Christian is living among and preaching to pagans, then he or she is a missionary. Presence and activity accompanied by "faith, bolstered by prayer and visions," among pagans, give Patrick a missionary quality.[23] Louis Gougaud, Richard Fletcher, and Malcolm Lambert, in like manner, persist in calling Patrick a missionary, link his vocation with the "missionary imperative" he receives, and even enumerate "Patrick's missionary methods."[24] Lambert refers to Patrick as a "missionary" and "missionary priest," identifies his work as "missionary work," and characterizes him as "the first major figure to be impelled by a missionary zeal to reach out to all."[25] Fletcher goes as far in his assessment of Patrick to say that he initiated what was to become a "foreign missionary enterprise."[26] F. F. Bruce describes Patrick's encounters with social structures and political figures as "missionary campaigns."[27] According to Cardoza-Orlandi and González, Patrick initiated "a great missionary movement . . .

Christianity (New York: Henry Holt, 1998), 84; G. F. Maclear, *A History of Christian Missions During the Middle Ages* (Cambridge: Macmillan, 1863), 62, 67, 73. Such language can be seen not just in popular or mission-oriented literature but in specialized, scholarly works as well. For example, the language of *mission* and *missionary* is used throughout David N. Dumville, *Saint Patrick, A.D. 493–1993*, Studies in Celtic History XIII (Woodbridge, Suffolk, UK: Boydell, 1993).

[22] George Thomas Stokes, *Ireland and the Celtic Church: A History of Ireland from St. Patrick to the English Conquest in 1172* (London: Hodder & Stoughton, 1892), 47.

[23] Wood, *Missionary Life*, 27.

[24] Louis Gougaud, *Christianity in Celtic Lands: A History of the Churches of the Celts, Their Origin, Their Development, Influence, and Mutual Relations*, trans. Maud Joynt (London: Sheed & Ward, 1932), 41; Fletcher, *Barbarian Conversion*, 85, 514; Malcolm Lambert, *Christians and Pagans: The Conversion of Britain from Alban to Bede* (New Haven, CT: Yale University Press, 2010), 135-47.

[25] Lambert, *Christians and Pagans*, 139, 140, 147.

[26] Fletcher, *Barbarian Conversion*, 86.

[27] Bruce, *Spreading Flame*, 378.

that would eventually extend throughout most of northern Europe."[28] And
W. H. C. Frend distinguishes Patrick's emphasis and enthusiasm from that
of other "Western missionaries," and thereby creates the impression that
Patrick was one among many in an established class of individuals known
as missionary.[29] These interpreters read mission language into Patrick's activities with the chief aim of historicizing *mission* and *missionary*. Once
these words are inserted into Patrick's account, mission is confirmed as historical and conceptual reality.

The obvious difficulty is that mission as language or concept is not
the language of Patrick or his contemporaries. And because "mission" is
an anachronistic imposition on Patrick's context and language, it reposi-
tions and repurposes Patrick. Rather than a man living in the fifth
century and concerned with the spread of the gospel among the Irish,
Patrick becomes a mission type or "mission everyman" for modern times.
According to Catholic historian Joseph Schmidlin, Patrick's writings
taken together "serve to produce a delineation of the character and spiritual force of the great missionary."[30] In other words, Patrick becomes an
ideal or type that operates across all time and contexts. In restating Patrick's life and ministry in language different from that of *Vita*, *Epistola
ad milites Corotici*, and *Confessio*, Schmidlin, along with others, alters
not only the story but also the person. In a way, they transport Patrick
from the fifth century into the modern era. When the historian sup-
plants the language of those closest to Patrick and the events of his life,
and when modern notions of *mission* and *missionary* are transported
into the narrative, Patrick and his story are obscured. Removed from
context and language, Patrick becomes an insignia for mission ideas
from another time. In the case of Patrick, mission language clutters
rather than clarifies his intent, activities, and life.

Columba (ca. 520–597) landed on I or Hy (Iona) in 563 and established
a monastery on the island. The Gaelic name, *Í Chaluim Cille* (Saint Columba's
Island), confirms Columba's place in history and his association with the

---

[28]Cardoza-Orlandi and González, *To All Nations from All Nations*, 81.
[29]W. H. C. Frend, *The Rise of Christianity* (Philadelphia: Fortress, 1984), 794.
[30]Joseph Schmidlin, *Catholic Mission History*, ed. Matthias Braun (Techny, IL: Mission Press,
    S. V. D., 1933), 145.

island. He traveled to this remote spot while on pilgrimage and established a monastery. The monastery became a staging point from which Columba and other monks made similar pilgrimage to various places and peoples, particularly the Picts.

St. Adomanán, ninth abbot at Iona, from 679 to 704, wrote *Vita Columbae* (Life of St. Columba) approximately a century after Columba's death.[31] Adomanán's purpose in *Vita* is to prove Columba as worthy of sainthood, and thus the account is full of miracles, many of which mirror accounts from the life of Jesus, such as changing water to wine and raising the dead.[32] Columba is described as a saint, pilgrim, abbot, "island soldier," "the man of the Lord," "a true prophet," "blessed man," "holy man," and "venerable man."[33] Above all, Columba is characterized as a pilgrim and his life as a pilgrimage.[34] According to Adomanán, "Columba sailed away from Ireland to Britain, choosing to be a pilgrim for Christ."[35] Richard Sharpe, translator of the 1995 Penguin edition of *Vita Columbae*, notes that the phrase "pilgrimage of Christ" (*deorad Dé*) could be easily rendered as "stranger of God." This designation is likely a legal status given Columba for one of a number of reasons. Sharpe suggests that Columba could have been sent into exile in order to do penance for some sin or political indiscretion, or his designation signifies that he is a holy man with the power to perform miracles.[36] Whatever the reason, Columba is not sent on a "mission," nor is "mission" representative of his motivations; instead, Columba is a pilgrim. Seven times in *Vita Columbae,* Adomanán characterizes Columba's existence as the "life of pilgrimage." Mission and the missionary life are never mentioned as his

---

[31]For the context and factors for Adomanán's *Life of St. Columba*, see Michael MacCraith, "The Legacy of Columba," in *Christian Mission in Western Society: Precedents, Perspectives, Prospects*, ed. Simon Barrow and Graeme Smith (London: CTBI, 2001), 77-81.

[32]Bieler, "Muirchú's Life of St. Patrick as a Work of Literature," describes Adomanán's account "as a collection of individual miraculous events arranged by subject matter—prophecies, miscellaneous, angelic visions" (219).

[33]See Adomanán, *Life of St. Columba*, trans. Richard Sharpe, Penguin Classics (Middlesex, UK: Penguin Books, 1995), 105, 106, 109, 112, 152.

[34]Ibid., 113, 122, 161, 224.

[35]Ibid., 105.

[36]Sharpe, in the introduction, *Life of St. Columba*, 12-14 and 248n17. Lambert, *Christians and Pagans*, agrees that the motivation for Columba's move to Iona was for "a more perfected monastic life" or white martyrdom and not mission (113; see also 149-50). Cf. Brown, *Rise of Western Christendom*, 327.

motivation, task, or vocation.[37] The Venerable Bede's *Ecclesiastical History of the English People*, another principal source for Columba's life written a generation after Adomanán's *Vita*, likewise does not identify Columba as a "missionary" or his activity as "mission."[38]

Contrary to Adomanán and Bede, modern historians often characterize Columba's move to Iona as a "mission," name him a "missionary," and portray the monastery at Iona as a "headquarters for a major missionary movement."[39] Robert Glover, referring to the monastery at Iona, distinguishes Columba as establishing "the most noted missionary school in history."[40] F. F. Bruce characterizes Columba's attempt to evangelize the Pictish king as being "in the tradition of Irish missionary policy."[41] According to Frend, Columba was part of "a missionary movement" that began at Iona and spread throughout the world.[42] And George Stokes similarly reports that "the period of missionary activity begins with Columba, whom we may designate the first Irish missionary, the apostle of pagan Scotland."[43] Such designations and descriptions suggest intentions and plans that Columba himself does not claim and that his contemporaries do not attribute to him.

---

[37]Adomanán, *Life of St. Columba*, 105, 113, 118, 122, 161, 224, 229. Sharpe uses *mission* and *missionary* in his introduction to characterize Columba's life and work (19, 22, 30-32, 38-39, 97), though Adomanán never employs these terms. The fact that Sharpe is given to this language and yet does not translate Adomanán's words as such is ample proof that *mission* and *missionary* do not exist in the Latin text.

[38]The Venerable Bede, *Ecclesiastical History of the English People*, ed. Bertram Colgrave and R. A. B. Myers, Oxford Medieval Texts (Oxford: Clarendon, 1969), 221-25.

[39]Florence R. Scott, "Columba of Iona," in Moreau, *Evangelical Dictionary of World Missions*, 211; Margaret Deanesly, *A History of the Medieval Church, 590–1500* (London: Methuen, 1951), 12; Edwards, *Christianity*, 176; John Finney, *Recovering the Past: Celtic and Roman Mission* (London: Darton, Longman & Todd, 1996), 29. On the other hand, John Smith, *The Life of St. Columba, the Apostle and Patron Saint of the Ancient Scots and Picts, and Joint Patron of the Irish* (Edinburgh: Mundell & Son, 1798), does not use *mission* and *missionary* to describe Columba. Rather, Smith names Columba as an apostle.

[40]Robert Hall Glover, *The Progress of World-Wide Missions* (New York: Harper & Row, 1960), 26. Stephen B. Bevans and Roger Schroeder, *Constants in Context: A Theology of Mission for Today* (Maryknoll, NY: Orbis Books, 2004), picture Columba's Iona as "the headquarters for training and sending out monk-missionaries, particularly among the Picts on the Scottish mainland" (121).

[41]Bruce, *Spreading Flame*, 389.

[42]Frend, *Rise of Christianity*, 877-79.

[43]Stokes, *Ireland and the Celtic Church*, 111. Richard Fletcher, *Barbarian Conversion*, concludes that Columba went among the northern Picts as a pilgrim or to enter exile. "Columba was no more the apostle of Pictland than Ulfila was the apostle of the Goths" (95).

One of the main reasons Columba's story is turned into mission is because of his encounter with the king of the Picts.[44] However, those closest to the events, Adomanán and Bede, depict Columba's exchange with the Picts as something other than "mission" and his role other than "missionary." Adomanán relates a number of miracles among the Picts and recounts Columba's visits with their king, Bridei (Bridius), near the River Ness and his confrontation with the king's wizards.[45] But according to Adomanán, these encounters were incidental and not intentional trips for evangelization. On another occasion, Adomanán reports that Columba moved among the Picts, "preaching the word of life through an interpreter." And yet, Adomanán does not describe these encounters in the language of mission.[46] Rather, he simply reports that Columba preached to the Picts as he encountered them. No authority sent him, nor did he undertake a "mission" at the commission of another. Likewise, Bede's *Ecclesiastical History* places Columba, whom he describes as a priest and abbot, among the northern Picts in 565. Columba's role, according to Bede, was to "preach the word of God" and through preaching turn "them to the faith of Christ by his words and example."[47] It is uncertain whether Columba traveled to Pictland on one or several occasions, and nowhere does Adomanán or Bede report that Columba established a church among the Picts. He is characterized as a wandering pilgrim who preached to those whom he happened to encounter. To interpret these chance meetings and confrontations as mission and to call Columba a missionary moves beyond plain facts and ventures into speculation regarding Columba's motivations and aims.

Some might respond that though the early historians of Columba's life do not use mission language, such terminology represents his intent. Thus, "mission," as a concept or idea, should be ascribed to Columba, and his activities given a category in which to be classified. But as a category, "mission" does not clarify who Columba was or what he did. It clouds his identity and cloaks his activities. Mission inserted into Columba's pilgrimage to Iona

---

[44]See Maclear, *History of Christian Missions During the Middle Ages*, 81, 88-90.

[45]Adomanán, *Life of St. Columba*, 183. See Sharpe's discussion regarding Columba's travel in Pictland in introduction, 30-34, and 332n283.

[46]Ibid., 179.

[47]Bede, *Ecclesiastical History*, ed. Colgrave and Myers, 223. Cf. Adomanán's account of Columba's miraculous deeds and his encounter with King Bridei, *Life of St. Columba*, 181-84.

and his encounter with the Picts only serves to establish a narrative of Christianity's advance via mission means and missionary expansion rather than to report his life and encounters as they actually happened. Placing mission language onto Columba's pilgrim existence and confrontations with those outside his community co-opts events and activities in order to serve a different narrative—one that bears decisively modern contours. Columba's unique activities and personality are swallowed by the larger mission category.

Columban (ca. 543–615), another Irish monk, traveled from the monastery of Bangor with twelve others to Brittany in eastern France, where the group established a monastery at Luxeuil. Though named as a "missionary" by both popular and scholarly historians, Columban only self-describes as a *monk* and a *pilgrim*.[48]

An early history of St. Columban's life, written in approximately 665 by Jonas of Bobbio, a monk from northern Italy, gives a glowing account of St. Columban's exploits and encounters. As in the case of Patrick and Columba, Jonas's account of Columban's life is a litany of miracles and confrontations with demons and powers. And as in the case of Muirchú, Adomanán, and Bede, Jonas never calls any of these acts or encounters *mission*, nor does he name Columban a *missionary*. Rather, Jonas calls Columban "a holy man," a "man of God," "venerable man," and "the servant of God."[49] Columban's activities are described as preaching, performing miracles, journeying on pilgrimage, building monasteries, confronting powerful people, spreading the faith, baptizing, and restoring churches.[50] Jonas's concern is to report the miraculous activity of Columban's life in a manner that gives him the most honor and qualifies him as a saint.

---

[48]*HEC*, 2:40; Ward and Evans, "Medieval West," 113; Wood, *Missionary Life*, 31-35; Bruce, *Spreading Flame*, 390. G. S. M. Walker confronts the issue head-on in his essay "St Columban: Monk or Missionary?," in *The Mission of the Church and the Propagation of the Faith: Papers Read at the Seventh Summer Meeting and the Eight Winter Meeting of the Ecclesiastical History Society*, ed. G. J. Cuming, Studies in Church History 6 (Cambridge: Cambridge University Press, 1970), 39-44. He concludes that Columban "was a missionary through circumstances, a monk by vocation; a contemplative, too frequently driven to action by the vices of the world; a pilgrim, on the road to Paradise" (39-40).

[49]Jonas, *Life of St. Columban*, vol. 2, no. 7, Translations and Reprints from the Original Sources of European History (Felinfach: Llanerch Publishers, 1895), 6, 7, 8, 14, 18, 19.

[50]Ibid., 6, 11, 19-21, 31, 32, 35.

Some scholars consider Columba and Columban to be the first of what they characterize as "missionary monasticism."[51] Echoing Christopher Dawson, David Bosch stresses "the monastery was not only the center of culture and civilization, but also of mission."[52] Bosch concludes that "although the monastic communities were not *intentionally* missionary (in other words, created for the purpose of mission), they were permeated by a missionary *dimension*."[53] And yet, characterization of the monastic movement as missionary, either in intention or dimension, inflates the motives and aims of these monks, and thus misrepresents the essential nature of monasticism and those who took monastic vows. Both Columba and Columban operated out of the Irish tradition of *peregrine* (wandering) and thus were *peregrinatio pro Christo* (wandering for the sake of Christ). Pilgrim-monks roamed as an act of love for God and to express their devotion by way of exile from home and kin. Their purpose was not overt evangelization; rather, the faith went with them as they established outposts for Christianity in the places they went.[54] They did not always travel among pagans but often among peoples who were already Christianized or those in the process of being brought into the sphere of the Roman church, its ecclesiastical structures and hierarchy. Thus, they did not set out on pilgrimage with the expressed purpose of spreading Christianity to new areas. Gilbert Márkus agrees that pilgrimage "was a form of asceticism, not a technique of conversion or evangelical persuasion."[55] For sure, to frame *peregrine*

---

[51]Pratt, Sills, and Walters, *Introduction to Global Missions*, 102-3.

[52]*TM*, 235. See Christopher Dawson, *The Making of Europe: An Introduction to the History of European Unity* (New York: Sheed & Ward, 1932), 154-63. According to Dawson, "The real importance of this movement lies in the impulse that it gave to missionary activity, and it was as missionaries that the Celtic monks made their most important contribution to European culture" (158). See also Dawson, *Religion and the Rise of Western Culture* (New York: Sheed & Ward, 1950), 55-64; Dawson, *The Formation of Christendom* (New York: Sheed & Ward, 1967), 168.

[53]*TM*, 238. Bosch's emphasis.

[54]For discussions of the motivations and dimensions of *peregrini*, see Dale T. Irvin and Scott W. Sunquist, *History of the World Christian Movement*, vol. 1, *Earliest Christianity to 1453* (Maryknoll, NY: Orbis Books, 2001), 343-45; *TM*, 235-41; *HEC*, 2:38-40; Gougaud, *Christianity in Celtic Lands*, 129-31; Henry Mayr-Harting, *The Coming of Christianity to Anglo-Saxon England*, 3rd ed. (University Park: Pennsylvania State University Press, 1991), 91-92.

[55]Gilbert Márkus, "Iona: Monks, Pastors and Missionaries," in *Spes Scotorum, Hope of the Scots: Saint Columba, Iona and Scotland*, ed. Dauvit Broun and Thomas Owen Clancy (Edinburgh: T&T Clark, 1999), 132. Ian Wood, *Missionary Life*, draws a distinction between being a pilgrim and missionary in pagan lands, "not least because the *peregrini* that we know about settled in contexts which were at least officially Christian" (34-35). C. H. Talbot, *The Anglo-Saxon Missionaries in*

as missionary in intention is to misrepresent the original motivation and aim of pilgrimages. And while characterizing the monastic movement as having a "missionary dimension" may offer an example of "authentic evangelization" and even "a genuine concern for others" during the medieval age, it says too much as well.[56] When medieval monasticism is glossed as having a missionary dimension, the identity and activity of Columba and Columban are promptly "missionary" writ large. To characterize these wanderers for Christ as missionaries is to infer too much from their pilgrim motivation and existence.

Gregory I, or Gregory the Great (590–604), is lauded as the greatest pope of the Middle Ages. Gregory became pope after a stint in civil service and life as a monk. His tenure as pope was marked by extensive reforms within the church and the extension of the Roman church into England.[57]

As pontiff, Gregory sent forty monks to England under the leadership of Augustine to establish the Catholic faith among the Anglo-Saxons. Because the people of England were reported as untamed, speaking unknown languages, and living in primitive conditions, Augustine and his band of monks were tempted to abandon Gregory's project before it even began. Augustine's fear and reluctance changed once he discovered an Anglo-Saxon Christian queen and a bishop. With the queen's help, Augustine was able to speak to King Ethelbert about the Christian faith. The king was converted and baptized in 597, and thus Roman Christianity took root in England. Augustine became archbishop of the English people, and Canterbury was established as the seat of the episcopal see. Ethelbert did not force his subjects to receive baptism, but most followed in their king's decision and became Christians.

As with Patrick, Columba, and Columban, modern interpreters load Gregory's initiative and Augustine's endeavors with mission language. Latourette renders the papal initiative of Gregory as the "Roman mission,"

Germany: Being the Lives of SS. Willibrord, Boniface, Sturm, Leoba, and Lebuin, Together with the Hodoeporicon of St. Willibald and a Selection from the Correspondence of St. Boniface, Makers of Christendom (New York: Sheed and Ward, 1954), on the other hand, views *peregrinatio pro Christo* as "voluntary exile for the purpose of spreading the Gospel" (xi).

[56] *TM*, 235.

[57] For details of the life and papacy of Gregory, see J. N. D. Kelly, *The Oxford Dictionary of Popes*, 2nd ed. (New York: Oxford University Press, 2010), 63-65; John Moorhead, *Gregory the Great*, The Early Church Fathers (London: Routledge, 2005), 1-48; F. Homes Dudden, *Gregory the Great: His Place in History and Thought*, 2 vols. (New York: Longmans, Green, 1905).

and those sent by Gregory as "bands of missionaries."[58] Bruce refers to Augustine and companions as a "missionary party" and their work as "missionary operations."[59] Numerous historians proclaim Gregory the Great as the first missionary pope, identify missionary work as his chief accomplishment, and classify efforts toward the Anglo-Saxons as "the Gregorian mission."[60] He sends missionaries, instructs missionaries, has a missionary strategy, and operates from a "missionary policy," all as part of his "English mission."[61] Gregory's initiation of work in Britain, according to Neill, is "a carefully planned and calculated mission," using monks and the monastery in "missionary work among the new nations."[62] Augustine and his party of monks are routinely distinguished as early missionaries of the Roman church. W. H. C. Frend states that the "main stream of Western thought concerning missions" during the medieval period comes from Gregory's initiative, as demonstrated in Gregory's call to "vigorous missionary efforts among the Lombards," "the mission to Ethelbert's kingdom of Kent," and his correspondence with Augustine regarding "effective missionary work."[63] Pope Gregory, according to Schmidlin, had wished "to go to Britain as a missionary" himself and had set out for Britain but was recalled for his post in Rome. Schmidlin also reports that in order to fulfill this call Gregory

---

[58]*HEC*, 2:72. See similar claims in Finney, *Recovering the Past*, 21-26; Frend, *Rise of Christianity*, 887-90.

[59]Bruce, *Spreading Flame*, 397, 398; Cardoza-Orlandi and González, *To All Nations from All Nations*, 86-87.

[60]Mayr-Harting, *Coming of Christianity to Anglo-Saxon England*, 51.

[61]Bernard R. Youngman, *Into All the World: The Story of Christianity to 1066 A.D.* (New York: St. Martin's, 1965), 125; Fletcher, *Barbarian Conversion*, 112-19; Eleanor Harvey Tejirian and Reeva Spector Simon, *Conflict, Conquest, and Conversion: Two Thousand Years of Christian Missions in the Middle East* (New York: Columbia University Press, 2012), 16. Ian Wood, "The Mission of Augustine of Canterbury to the English," *Speculum* 69, no. 1 (January 1994): 1-17, describes Gregory's "papal mission" and the "mission of Augustine to Kent" (10). Wood liberally employs the language of *mission* and *missionary* throughout the article (76 times in 17 pages). In addition to the English mission, Augustine's mission, and missionaries, Wood refers to missionary strategy, missionary work, missionary ideology, missionary saints, and missionary field. Likewise, R. A. Markus, "Gregory the Great and a Papal Missionary Strategy," in Cuming, *Mission of the Church and the Propagation of the Faith*, references Gregory's "missionary strategy," "missionary policy," and "missionary situation" (29, 31, 35, 37).

[62]*HCM*, 58, 59. See also Deanesly, *History of the Medieval Church*, 43-46; Dana Lee Robert, *Christian Mission: How Christianity Became a World Religion* (Chichester, UK: Wiley-Blackwell, 2009), 23, 30.

[63]W. H. C. Frend, "The Missions of the Early Church, 180–700 A. D.," in *Religion Popular and Unpopular in the Early Christian Centuries*, ed. W. H. C. Frend (London: Variorum Reprints, 1976), 18-19.

instructed rectors to purchase young English slaves "to be trained as missionaries for their native land."[64]

Chief among the reasons Gregory rises to missionary prominence for modern interpreters is that his papacy marks the beginning of the Catholic faith in Britain. Schmidlin is representative of those who use Gregory as the turning point in history of the Catholic church, and thus Schmidlin's accounts of Gregory are steeped in language of *mission, missionary,* and *missionary commission.* For Schmidlin, Gregory's actions are overt initiatives in which the Roman church extends its jurisdiction by sending agents into pagan lands. Richard Sullivan underlines the same sentiment when he celebrates "the missionary activity of Gregory the Great, perhaps the first pope to dispatch missionaries from Rome for the purpose of converting pagans." Gregory's efforts, according to Sullivan, "remained a model for successful missionary ventures" throughout the medieval period. For Sullivan, Gregory's papal effort to convert England is explicit "missionary work."[65] Catholic historian Henri Marrou likewise designates Gregory's papacy as the beginning of Christian mission. According to Marrou, prior to Gregory there was no "officially organized mission, directed from above by hierarchical authority." He maintains that the church's mission is nonexistent until 596, "when St. Gregory the Great sent a mission to the Anglo-Saxons."[66] *Mission* for these interpreters means the extension and establishment of the Roman Catholic church by Pope Gregory, the chief agent of the church.

And yet, one searches without success in the three volumes of *The Letters of Gregory the Great* to find language that names the extension and establishment of the Roman church as "mission."[67] While John R. C. Martyn,

[64]Schmidlin, *Catholic Mission History,* 150, 151, 152. The cited source for Schmidlin's claims regarding Gregory and Augustine is Bede's *Ecclesiastical History.* See also Maclear, *History of Christian Missions During the Middle Ages,* 99.

[65]Richard E. Sullivan, *Christian Missionary Activity in the Early Middle Ages,* Variorum Collected Studies Series (Aldershot, UK: Variorum, 1994), 3:48. Sullivan's descriptions of Gregory and Augustine are full of the language of *mission* and *missionary*—missionary party, missionary activity, missionary work, missionary problems, missionary personnel, missionary service, and missionary history.

[66]Jean Daniélou and Henri Marrou, *The First Six Hundred Years,* trans. Vincent Cronin, The Christian Centuries: A New History of the Catholic Church 1 (New York: McGraw-Hill, 1964), 282. Marrou refutes Eusebius's account of mission sentiments prior to Gregory "as an idealized picture of the missionary movement in general" (282).

[67]On the other hand, Maclear, *History of Christian Missions During the Middle Ages,* cites Gregory's letter (Gregory, *The Letters of Gregory the Great,* trans. John R. C. Martyn, Mediaeval Sources in

translator and editor of these volumes, supplies mission language in his introduction and a few footnotes,[68] he does not render any of Gregory's Latin as "mission" or "missionary." Gregory instead refers to himself as a servant of God and uses the language of preaching, teaching, loving neighbors, doing good works, and performing acts of charity. He exhorts others to preach, "bring foreigners to God," "lead pagans to faith," and work toward "the winning of souls."[69] Those he addresses directly or names in his letters are identified as priests, monks, evangelists, abbesses, nuns, messengers, chaplains, clerics, emissaries, patriarchs, abbots, deacons, and subdeacons. None of these he addresses or those he writes about are given a missionary classification.[70] In his correspondence soliciting support for the conversion of England to the Catholic faith, Gregory describes Augustine as a "monk" and "bishop," never a "missionary."[71] Likewise, Augustine's task is depicted in numerous ways but not as *missio* or "mission." Rather than lauding Augustine's efforts as a "missionary triumph," Gregory cautions the bishop and his company of monks that "a weak mind puffs itself up in its pride" and "vainglory," and thus brands them as "weak preachers."[72]

A letter dated July 18, 601, was sent from Pope Gregory to the abbot Mellitus, who in turn shared the contents of the letter with Augustine. The intent of Gregory's letter is to guide Augustine and others in how they should treat existing pagan religious practices and places of worship. Rather than destroying these places of worship, Gregory advises that

> the temples of the idols in that nation ought not to be destroyed; but let the idols that are in them be destroyed; let water be consecrated and sprinkled in the said temples, let altars be erected, and relics be placed there. For if those

Translation 40 [Toronto: Pontifical Institute of Mediaeval Studies, 2004], vi, 58) as confirmation that Ethelbert and Bertha "made application to the Frankish bishops for missionary," when this language is not in the letter at all (98).

[68]For example, Martyn's references to mission and missionary in Gregory, *Letters of Gregory the Great*, 1:47-72, 155n202, 304n74, 308n88, 2:34n62, 404n10, 409n28, 438n138, 524n116, 691n647, 705n714, 3:778n206, 783n227, 802n286.

[69]Ibid., 1:171, 179, 307, 2:307, 354.

[70]*Emissary* and *missionary* should not be confused. An emissary is a clerical papal ambassador to heads of states and other bishops. He carries letters and personal messages from the pope and reports information and messages in return. See ibid., 1:302, 2:371.

[71]Ibid., 2:438, 439, 440, 441, 442, 443, 444, 524, 532, 645, 691, 3:778, 779, 785, 788, 789, 793, 795, 802.

[72]In a letter to Augustine, June 22, 601, ibid., 3:780.

temples are well built, it is requisite that they be converted from the worship of devils to the service of the true God.[73]

These instructions became principled practice for Augustine and aided in the spread of Roman Christianity throughout England. And yet, rather than allowing these instructions to be what they are (local prescriptions for dealing with specific situations), interpreters make them into universally applicable "missionary methods," or an "approach to mission," an example of "missionary accommodation," or "the rule and code of Christian missions."[74]

Outside Gregory's letters and pronouncements, Bede's *Ecclesiastical History* is the most reliable and nearest source to Gregory. Bede calls Gregory the "apostle to the British people" and gives him the title of "a servant of God" who came "to preach the word of God to the English race."[75] Bede notes the significance of the conversion of Ethelbert by Augustine but does not mark this as the start of a "Roman mission." Thus, much like Gregory's own letters, Bede's account suggests that the initiatives of Gregory and Augustine signal the beginning of the Roman church in the British Isles. The language of the primary actors and chroniclers at the scene casts the story as one of papal authority, political conversion, monastic duties, and Catholic dominance. And yet, these dynamics become skewed, or are neglected and even lost, when cast in the language of mission.

Winfrid of Crediton or Boniface (ca. 675–754) is linked to the evangelization of Germany and is best known for confronting pagan practices by felling the Oak of Thor (or Jupiter). For Joseph Schmidlin, Boniface is the pinnacle of "Medieval Mission," and, because his work parallels that of "Paul in antiquity and Francis Xavier in modern times," Boniface is "numbered among the greatest figures of missions and the Church."[76] Stephen Neill calls

---

[73]Ibid., 3:802-3. Cited by Bede, *The Ecclesiastical History of the English People*, trans. A. M. Sellar (Mineola, NY: Dover, 2011), 67.

[74]*HEC*, 2:68; Irvin and Sunquist, *History of the World Christian Movement*, 1:328; *TM*, 463; Montalember, *Monks of the West*, 3:369, cited in Schmidlin, *Catholic Mission History*, 152.

[75]Bede, *Ecclesiastical History* (1969), 69, 123. Cf. Peter Hunter Blair's chapters on Bede's account of Gregory's sending of Augustine to Britain in *The World of Bede* (New York: St. Martin's, 1971), 41-78.

[76]Schmidlin, *Catholic Mission History*, 165, 166.

Boniface "the greatest of all the missionaries of the Dark Ages."[77] Latourette goes even further by naming Boniface "one of the most remarkable missionaries in the entire history of the expansion of Christianity."[78] In another instance, Latourette calls him "the most famous English missionary to the Continent."[79]

For these interpreters, Boniface embodies the missionary ideal. Their grand mission descriptions are meant to identify and promote what a missionary of the medieval period should be and do. In his discussion of the efforts prior to Boniface, Schmidlin laments the ineffective measures to evangelize the German peoples. He cites the reason for the lack of success as the absence of genuine missionaries. The problem was that

> the majority of the earlier representatives of the faith were not so much missionaries in the strict sense of the word as Christian monks and ascetics— pious pilgrims who aimed to exercise influence rather by their example in monastic or eremitic settlements than by systematic conversion. Their work thus lacked organization and continuity; and their activities were individual, isolated, and scattered, so that much missionary effort was expended to little avail and nothing of a permanent nature was effected.[80]

According to Schmidlin and others, Boniface made the crucial difference in that he followed what is deemed to be an established "missionary tradition" that includes "missionary aims," "missionary methods," "missionary tactics," "missionary work," and "missionary strategy" that took him on "missionary journeys." In the "strict sense of the word," he is a true missionary.[81]

---

[77]*HCM*, 64. Herbert Kane describes Boniface in the same manner in *A Global View of Christian Missions from Pentecost to the Present* (Grand Rapids: Baker Book House, 1971), 41. See also E. Randolph Daniel, *The Franciscan Concept of Mission in the High Middle Ages* (Lexington: University Press of Kentucky, 1975), xi; Wood, *Missionary Life*, 58-59.

[78]*HEC*, 2:85. See also Glover, *Progress of World-Wide Missions*, 27; Ward and Evans, "Medieval West," 113; Edwards, *Christianity*, 186.

[79]Kenneth Scott Latourette, *Christianity Through the Ages* (New York: Harper & Row, 1965), 90. See also Frank Barlow, "The English Background," in *The Greatest Englishman: Essays on St. Boniface and the Church at Crediton*, ed. Timothy Reuter (Exeter, UK: Paternoster, 1980), 13, 23; Maclear, *History of Christian Missions During the Middle Ages*, 187-89.

[80]Schmidlin, *Catholic Mission History*, 159.

[81]Ibid., 168, 171n16; Timothy Reuter, "Saint Boniface and Europe," in Reuter, *Greatest Englishman*, 78, 79, 81, 84.

Latourette indicates that Boniface had skills and abilities to follow a number of careers but "preferred, however, to become a missionary."[82] In this way, Latourette frames "missionary" as a vocation or role over against that of monk, priest, or abbot. James Addison gives "missionary" a similar status when he describes a shift in Boniface's direction of life and distinguishes a time "before beginning his independent career as a missionary."[83] Neill lauds Boniface's "missionary efforts" and "missionary methods," and Kane similarly praises his "brilliant missionary career."[84] Latourette describes in detail Boniface's "missionary dreams," references his unique "missionary methods," and details the events of "his Hessian mission."[85] Ian Wood calls him a "missionary bishop" and writes of his "missionary trips to Frisia."[86] Bruce gives Boniface the dubious title of "foreign missionary," Talbot characterizes those with whom he labored as "his missionary band," and Dawson refers to Boniface's "mission field."[87] While David Bosch places Boniface within his discussion of monasticism and thus labels him a "missionary-monk," Boniface distinguishes himself from other monastics, according to Bosch, by responding to an "inward call to mission."[88]

For these interpreters, Boniface parallels the life of the apostle Paul and thus provides a type of missionary connection between the early church and the modern period. Boniface is a medieval Paul. And yet, because Boniface is interpreted through the language of *mission* and *missionary*, he looks and acts more like a modern professional than a man of the seventh century. For many, Boniface is the mission link between the early church and the modern era. But he is titled a *missionary* because of what interpreters deem as *mission*. Historians identify him as a missionary, but this is not how Boniface's contemporaries identify him or how he describes himself. Bishops, monks, abbesses, kings, and queens address Boniface as a servant of God, beloved

---

[82]*HEC*, 2:86.

[83]Ibid., 11.

[84]*HCM*, 64, 66; Kane, *Global View of Christian Missions*, 41. Cf. C. H. Talbot, "St. Boniface and the German Mission," in Cuming, *Mission of the Church and the Propagation of the Faith*, 45-47.

[85]*HEC*, 2:87, 92, 93, 97.

[86]Wood, *Missionary Life*, 59.

[87]Bruce, *Spreading Flame*, 416; Talbot, "St. Boniface and the German Mission," 50; Dawson, *Formation of Christendom*, 178.

[88]*TM*, 240. See also Robert, *Christian Mission*, 24; Pratt, Sills, and Walters, *Introduction to Global Missions*, 103.

brother, fellow priest, prophet, evangelist, archbishop, father, friend, and martyr and describe his task chiefly as preaching.[89] Likewise, Boniface self-describes as "servant of the servants of God" and bishop.[90]

Several modern translations of Boniface's correspondence insert *mission* and *missionary* into the text of his letters when neither word is present in the Latin. For example, for a letter dated May 15, 719, the translator has supplied a heading that names the subject of the letter—"Pope Gregory II entrusts the priest, Boniface, with the mission to the heathen." Likewise, the translated words of Gregory's charge to Boniface are to dedicate himself "ceaselessly to missionary work."[91] The supplied heading and reference to "mission" and "missionary," however, do not appear in the Latin. Gregory uses *praedicationis*, which means to proclaim or announce.[92] The same translation of *praedicationis* is provided for a letter dated December 722. Pope Gregory II commends Boniface to Charles Martel and asks for Martel's support as Boniface "goes forth to undertake this missionary work."[93] Again, in a letter to the Archbishop Nothelm of Canterbury, the translator, Ephraim Emerton, has Boniface asking when "the first missionaries sent by Saint Gregory to the English people arrived" (*praedicatores primi missi a sancto Gregorio ad gentem Anglorum venissent*). A literal translation reads as Boniface asking when "the first preachers sent by Saint Gregory to the English people arrived."[94] In Emerton's modern mind, sending and proclamation equal "missionary."[95] And yet, we must assume that what Pope Gregory and Boniface meant was what was written—proclamation.

---

[89]Boniface, *The English Correspondence of Saint Boniface: Being for the Most Part Letters Exchanged Between the Apostle of the Germans and His English Friends*, trans. Edward Kylie, The Medieval Library (New York: Cooper Square, 1966), 47, 49, 51, 52, 57, 68, 93, 110, 114, 145, 150, 196, 199, 203, 204.

[90]Ibid., 56, 71, 74, 76, 92, 112, 115, 130, 132, 135, 138, 147, 150, 158, 173, 176, 193, 194.

[91]Boniface, *The Letters of Saint Boniface*, trans. Ephraim Emerton, Records of Civilization 31 (New York: Columbia University Press, 1940), 32, 33.

[92]For the Latin text of Boniface's letters, see Boniface, *Die Briefe Des Heiligen Bonifatius Und Lullus*, Monumenta Germaniae Historica (Berlin: Weidmannsche Verlagsbuchhandlung, 1955), 17. The supplied German heading for this letter likewise names the subject as *Heidenmission*.

[93]Boniface, *Letters of Saint Boniface* (trans. Emerton), 45.

[94]Ibid., 63. For the Latin text, see Boniface, *Die Briefe Des Heiligen Bonifatius Und Lullus*, 58.

[95]Emerton, *Letters of Saint Boniface*, opens his introduction with a commentary on "foreign missions" in twentieth century. One of his aims in translating Boniface's correspondence is to make comparison between Boniface's situation and efforts "with the unhappy denominational futilities of modern mission effort" (5).

A more accurate description of Boniface comes to us by way of Willibald, an Anglo-Saxon priest who wrote an account of Boniface's life within a few years of the saint's death. He identifies Boniface as priest, "man of God," "servant of God," bishop, archbishop, "legate of the Roman Church," saint, and martyr.[96] In a passage in which Willibald records a reply Boniface makes to Willibrord, an aging archbishop, he quotes Boniface as describing himself as an "ambassador of the apostolic see to the western lands of the barbarians."[97] As an ambassador, Boniface is simply asserting authority and his right to represent the pope. Boniface distinguishes himself, according to Willibald, by "preaching the gospel," confronting paganism and heresy, teaching the doctrine of the church, and establishing the Catholic faith among the peoples of Germany. While these activities might sound like mission activities to modern ears, Willibald and Boniface do not call them mission. Instead, Willibald describes the progression of events and actions of Boniface's life as a "long pilgrim journey" or "pilgrimage."[98] The typical way Willibald describes Boniface's life is that "he traversed all Frisia, and removed the pagan worship and overthrew the erroneous way of heathenism, and earnestly preached the word of God; and, having destroyed the divinity of the heathen temples, he built churches with great zeal."[99] Willibald's descriptions are not brief but expansive and illustrative of all that Boniface attempted. The temptation is to reduce these rich, expansive descriptions to the shorthand of mission, but such economized language neglects, and even counters, Willibald's firsthand descriptions. While some of Boniface's activity may resonate with our own language of mission, it is inaccurate to equate the two.

The Nestorians are often cited as early missionaries to the East. Chronicling the history of Syriac Christianity, Cardoza-Orlandi and González note, "The most remarkable and far-reaching missionary expansion during this period was the arrival of Nestorian Christianity in China, taken there by

---

[96]George W. Robinson, introduction to Willibald, *The Life of Saint Boniface*, trans. George W. Robinson, Harvard Translations (Cambridge, MA: Harvard University Press, 1916), 17, 24, 25, 27, 30, 44, 53, 54, 74. For an examination of the emphases and tenor of Willibald's *Vita Bonifatii*, see Wood, *Missionary Life*, 61-64.
[97]Willibald, *Life of Saint Boniface*, 55.
[98]See ibid., 48, 78.
[99]Ibid., 80-81.

Alopen, a missionary from Syria."[100] Alopen and those accompanying him, according to John Foster, are "Christian missionaries," and their venture is named as "the Christian mission to China."[101] Bosch also identifies Alopen as a "missionary" and describes the Nestorians as "the major missionary force in non-Roman Asia." Their "imposing missionary activity," according to Bosch, marks them as "missionary through and through" and as early pioneers of the mission legacy. Citing Wolfgang Hage, Bosch asserts that the Nestorian church was "the 'missionary' church par excellence in the overall context of medieval Christianity."[102] Terijan and Simon note the Nestorians' "remarkable Christian missionary expansion to the east" through "an army of dedicated missionaries."[103] Likewise, Schmidlin and Moffett acknowledge the role of Nestorian missionaries and celebrate their reach into the East and their efforts in the midst of foreign rule. Moffett, chronicling in detail the Nestorian story, notes that with these "Persian or Syrian missionaries," we find "the first recorded notice of the missionary entry of the Christian faith into the Chinese empire."[104] Noted by Moffett and other interpreters is the fact that the Nestorians "developed missionary activities of no little importance" and their "Monophysite missionaries" traveled throughout the East.[105]

And yet, earliest records of the Nestorian work in the East do not contain mission language and thus do not report these efforts as "mission," nor are Nestorians identified as "missionaries." The most substantial evidence of Nestorian presence and activity in China is a black limestone stele erected in 781, known as the Nestorian Monument. It records the arrival of "a Bishop

---

[100]Cardoza-Orlandi and González, *To All Nations from All Nations*, 90. See also Charles Henry Robinson, *History of Christian Missions*, International Theological Library (New York: Charles Scribner's Sons, 1915), 164; Deanesly, *History of the Medieval Church*, 6; Maclear, *History of Christian Missions During the Middle Ages*, 369.

[101]John Foster, *The Church of the T'ang Dynasty* (London: Society for Promoting Christian Knowledge, 1939), 21, 23, 33, 39, 43, 44, 47.

[102]*TM*, 209-10. Bosch quotes Wolfgang Hage, *Der Weg nach Asien: Die ostsyrische Missionskirche* (1978). Similar language is used by R. G. Tiedemann, "China and Its Neighbours," in *A World History of Christianity*, ed. Adrian Hastings (Grand Rapids: Eerdmans, 1999), 369-70.

[103]Tejirian and Simon, *Conflict, Conquest, and Conversion*, 20, 21.

[104]Samuel H. Moffett, *A History of Christianity in Asia*, vol. 1, *Beginnings to 1500* (Maryknoll, NY: Orbis Books, 1998), 291.

[105]Schmidlin, *Catholic Mission History*, 115; Dawson, *Making of Europe*, 105. See also Daniélou and Marrou, *First Six Hundred Years*, 1:371.

(Lofty Virtue) named Alopen."[106] Among his activities, "he conveyed the true Scriptures," "he rode through hardship and danger," and brought "scriptures and images from afar."[107] Contrary to Moffett's account, the Persians and Syrians listed on the monument are not identified as "missionaries."[108] Instead, they are called priests, monks, archdeacons, and elders. Buried in mission language are the controversies over the nature of Christ, distinct cultural expressions of Nestorian faith, and motivations behind their far-ranging ventures to the East. What circumstances caused Alopen and others to venture to China? What was the nature of their presentation of the gospel? How did they conduct themselves? But such questions become secondary, or even lost, when the Nestorians are branded as *missionary*. Mission language obscures the history and nature of the Nestorian venture into China.

MISSION HISTORIES?

The earliest histories of Christianity describe the expansion of the faith and the activities of those who preached and evangelized in an array of terms. Mission is not the descriptor of choice. Nor do these histories refer to those who participated in the expansion of the faith as missionaries. Four prominent and representative historians of the early church are evidence of this absence: Eusebius, Rufinus of Aquileia, Prosper of Aquitaine, and the Venerable Bede. These historians and their histories are of interest for a number of reasons, not least of which because they are often cited in making the historical case for mission.

   Eusebius of Caesarea (ca. 260–339) is best known for *The History of the Church from Christ to Constantine.*[109] Divided into ten books, *The History of*

---

[106]John Foster, ed., *The Nestorian Tablet and Hymn: Translations of Chinese Texts from the First Period of the Church in China, 635–C. 900*, Texts for Students 49 (London: Society for Promoting Christian Knowledge, 1939), 9. The monument was discovered outside of Xian, China, in 1623.

[107]Ibid., 9, 10.

[108]Moffett, *History of Christianity in Asia*, asserts that the monument contains "a long list of names of Persian or Syrian missionaries" (1:291).

[109]Eusebius, *The History of the Church from Christ to Constantine*, trans. G. A Williamson (Minneapolis: Augsburg, 1975). In addition to *The History of the Church*, Eusebius wrote *Chronicle*, *Life of Pamphilus*, *Life of Constantine*, *Preparation for the Gospel*, *Theophany*, *Defense of Origen*, *Against Marcellus*, and *Ecclesiastical Theology*. J. G. Davies, *The Early Christian Church*, History of Religion Series (New York: Holt, Rinehart and Winston, 1965), 165, outlines Eusebius's life and works and assesses his contribution as a source for early church history.

the Church chronicles the transition of the church from an outlawed, persecuted community to the church at peace and the establishment of Christianity as the religion of the Roman Empire. Eusebius takes in a wide range of themes: the story of Christ, the fate of the Jews, pagan attacks on the faith, martyrdom, episcopal succession, and the writings of the faithful. In his pursuit of these subjects, he refers to prominent individuals, quotes from their sermons and letters, and provides commentary on events within the early church. Eusebius describes the expansion of Christianity as occurring through a range of activities and events: preaching, teaching, evangelizing, sending, spreading the message, sowing of seed, confessing, witnessing, miracles, and martyrdom.[110] He gives the actors in these activities a variety of titles: apostles, bishops, disciples, evangelists, martyrs, preachers, witnesses, fellow soldiers, ambassadors, and Christians.[111]

One event reported by Eusebius and interpreted by modern historians as an example of early missionary activity is King Abgar's request for Jesus to come to him in order to cure an ailment. Jesus, according to Eusebius, responded to the king by sending one of his disciples, Thaddeus.[112] Contrary to Eusebius's language, modern interpreters translate Jesus' response to Abgar as "mission." For example, Jean Daniélou places Eusebius's account of Thaddeus and King Agbar under the heading of "the Palestine mission," as if this were an established, organized effort or event with programmatic objectives and missionaries.[113]

Another example of a mission interpretation of Eusebius is his account of Pantaenus. Eusebius reports that a "scholar and teacher" of Alexandria named Pantaenus was "appointed to preach the gospel of Christ to the peoples of the East," and thus he traveled "as far as India."[114] Pantaenus's activities and motives remain in the shadows, as there is not enough information to determine

---

[110]Examples of such designations can be seen in *History of the Church*, 38, 66, 68, 107, 195, 204, 208, 300, 311.

[111]Examples of Eusebius's use of these titles can be found in ibid., 31, 62, 66, 73 109, 148, 208, 254, 300, 311.

[112]Ibid., 67-69.

[113]Daniélou and Marrou, *First Six Hundred Years*, 1:46. Compare Daniélou's account with Schmidlin, *Catholic Mission History*, 51; and Irvin and Sunquist, *History of the World Christian Movement*, 1:59-60. See also Doron Mendels, *The Media Revolution of Early Christianity: An Essay on Eusebius's Ecclesiastical History* (Grand Rapids: Eerdmans, 1999), 194-96.

[114]Eusebius, *History of the Church*, 213.

what his intentions were or what he actually did. And yet, modern historians from Harnack to Moffett classify Pantaenus as a "missionary."[115] Citing Eusebius, W. H. C. Frend writes of "Pantaenus' mission to India," and Joseph Schmidlin refers to Pantaenus undertaking as a "missionary journey," classifies his efforts as "missionary work," and describes him as among those who are "vocational missionaries."[116] In similar fashion, Eckhard Schnabel references Eusebius in his claim that Pantaenus was one of several "active Christian missionaries."[117] Jean Daniélou asks,

> Did the Judaeo-Christian mission spread as far as India? Eusebius says that Pantaenus undertook a mission to those parts and found there a *Gospel of Matthew* in Hebrew writing (*HE*, V, 10). May we suppose that Christianity penetrated as far as India by way of Judaeo-Christian missionaries in the first half of the second century? . . . Pantaenus, moreover, was a Judaeo-Christian missionary who came from Egypt.[118]

Daniélou adds much more to what Eusebius actually reports. While interpretation and commentary are appropriate and needed, mission language does not aid in explaining Pantaenus's intent or Eusebius's narrative. On the contrary, it obscures the realities of Pantaenus, the "scholar and teacher." These aspects of his life are absorbed into the language of "missionary." And while even modern notions of Eusebius's descripton of Pantaenus as a scholar and teacher might in themselves prejudice our reading, why add the additional layer of missionary? For sure, if asked, Pantaenus would not have had the conceptual construction of what *missionary* means today to be able to identify with that title. Likewise, Eusebius did not have the vocabulary, category, or reason to call Pantaenus a missionary. But

---

[115]Harnack, *Mission and Expansion of Christianity*, 348, 351; Moffett, *History of Christianity in Asia*, 1:37. The same characterization of Pantaenus is made by Latourette in *HEC*, 1:116. Terry, "Ante-Nicene Church on Mission," cites and interprets Eusebius as saying Pantaenus "left Alexandria and went into Asia as a missionary" (212). Cf. Robin Lane Fox, *Pagans and Christians* (San Francisco: Harper & Row, 1995), 278.

[116]Frend, "Missions of the Early Church," 6; Schmidlin, *Catholic Mission History*, 58, 59, 97. And yet, Schmidlin admits in his introductory section on sources for his mission history that the "Church History of Eusebius contains little data for mission history, and also lacks entirely any general survey of this subject" (21).

[117]Eckhard J. Schnabel, "Mission, Early Non-Pauline," in *Dictionary of the Later New Testament & Its Development,* ed. Ralph Martin and Peter H. Davids (Downers Grove, IL: IVP Academic, 1997), 771.

[118]Daniélou and Marrou, *First Six Hundred Years*, 1:48.

Daniélou's account implies that the stated description of Pantaenus by Eusebius is inadequate and thus adds that "missionary" is how Eusebius intended to describe Panteanus. Reading modern mission rhetoric into the ancient text is more than expanding Eusebius's words; it changes his account of Pantaenus.

When interpreters and translators read mission into Eusebius, two problems surface. First, there is the problem of presumption. When mission language is presented as fact at the outset of a claim, there is no need for argument, definition of terms, or even to make a case. *Mission* and *missionary* are presumed as ancient rhetoric and in use during the time of Eusebius, and thus the events and agents of his account are interpreted as referring to an enterprise called *mission*. For example, from Eusebius's statement "Very many of the uncircumcised had come to faith in Christ" (*History of the Church* 3.35), Karl Baus concludes, "It is clear that the new community, like its predecessor, engaged in missionary activity."[119] Presumption leads to the establishment of mission as fact. Baus presumes the same from Eusebius's description of Dionysius, a bishop in Egypt, and his companions when forced into exile.[120] Baus thus declares that in exile they act as missionaries. Likewise, when Doron Mendels announces that Eusebius "endows the Christian mission with a historical pedigree," presumptive rhetoric settles the claim before it is argued.[121]

The second problem is one of translation. Modern translators of Eusebius insert the language of *mission* and *missionary* into the text when it is not there. The reader then assumes that Greek equivalents of *mission* and *missionary* are Eusebius's actual words. Preference for mission language is especially pronounced in G. A. Williamson's 1965 translation of *History of the Church*. In four places Williamson recaps Eusebius's references to Christ's earthly life and endeavors as "His mission"—"our Saviour and Lord, Jesus the Christ of God, beginning His mission at the age of about thirty," "He began His mission in the high priesthood of Annas," "about the coming of Jesus and how it happened; about His mission and the purpose for which

---

[119]Karl Baus, *From the Apostolic Community to Constantine*, Handbook of Church History 1 (Freiburg, West Germany: Herder, 1965), 205. And yet, Baus admits "there is no indication of a central direction and organization of missionary work" (211).

[120]Ibid., 369-70. Baus uses Eusebius in a similar manner on 372, 375.

[121]Mendels, *Media Revolution of Early Christianity*, 183.

His Father sent Him," and "the story of what Christ had done first of all at
the beginning of His mission."[122] Each of these accounts could be as easily
translated with the language of purpose, aim, or intent, but Williamson
chooses the imprecise and historically conditioned language of mission.
While Williamson may translate Eusebius with a general use of mission, he
communicates to the reader a definite or defined mission. Kirsopp Lake's
1926 translation, on the other hand, renders three of these not as mission but
offers a more descriptive translation. In these cases, Lake translates Christ's
activity as preaching and teaching.[123] There is one instance in which both
Williamson and Lake translate Eusebius's meaning as *mission*. Thaddaeus
requests Abgar to assemble all his citizens to hear "about the coming of Jesus
and how it happened; about His mission and the purpose for which His
Father sent Him."[124] A literal rendering would be that Thaddaeus wants to
preach to them concerning Jesus' being sent or his apostleship (περὶ τῆς
ἀποστολῆς αὐτοῦ).[125] In this case, both Williamson and Lake translate Jesus'
apostleship as mission.

   Besides the references to Jesus' life and ministry, Williamson inserts
mission in two other instances. Williamson translates the title of a historical
work by Philo as *The Mission*.[126] The Greek word Eusebius uses for Philo's
work is Πρέσβεια, meaning "embassy" or "ambassador." Earlier translations
of the same passages by Lake, Deferrari, Lawlor and Oulton, and Cruse
render the title of Philo's work in a more literal sense as *The Embassy*.[127] It
appears that *mission* in this instance means diplomatic representation.

---

[122]Eusebius, *History of the Church*, 61, 69, 132.

[123]Eusebius, *The Ecclesiastical History*, trans. Kirsopp Lake, The Loeb Classical Library (Cambridge,
    MA: Harvard University Press, 1926), 75, 77 (I, X), 251 (III, xxiv).

[124]Mission is used in this instance by Williamson (69) and Lake (95), as well by Lawlor and Oul-
    ton in their 1927 translation, Eusebius, *The Ecclesiastical History and the Martyrs of Palestine*,
    trans. Hugh Jackson Lawlor and John Ernest Leonard Oulton (London: SPCK, 1927), 1:31, and
    in the 1953 translation by Deferrari, Eusebius, *Ecclesiastical History*, trans. Roy J. Deferrari, The
    Fathers of the Church 19 (New York: Fathers of the Church, 1953), 81.

[125]Eusebius, *Ecclesiastical History* (Lake trans.), 94/95 (I, XIII). Lawlor and Oulton, as well as C. F.
    Cruse, also translate this passage as *mission*: Eusebius, *Ecclesiastical History* (Lawlor and Oulton
    trans.), 1:31; Eusebius, *Ecclesiastical History*, trans. Christian Frederick Cruse (Grand Rapids:
    Baker Book House, 1955).

[126]Eusebius, *History of the Church* (Williamson trans.), 78.

[127]Eusebius, *Ecclesiastical History* (Lake trans.), 121 (II, 5); Eusebius, *Ecclesiastical History* (Deferrari
    trans.), 95; Eusebius, *Ecclesiastical History* (Lawlor and Oulton trans.), 1:40; Eusebius, *Ecclesias-
    tical History* (Cruse trans.), 55.

In the same manner, Williamson does more than give a word-for-word translation of Eusebius's account of Pantaenus's travel to India. In reference to Eusebius's statement that a copy of Matthew's Gospel existed prior to Pantaenus's arrival, Williamson specifies that the Gospel was "preserved till the time of Pantaenus' mission."[128] The Greek text offers no reason to insert *mission* into the translation. In fact, Lake's 1926 translation simply says that the Gospel was "preserved until the time mentioned," and Lawlor and Oulton (1927) as "preserved up to the said time."[129] Because travel is involved and Pantaenus's destination is India, Williamson takes the liberty to translate this phrase as *mission*.

When reading Williamson's English translation, the reader assumes that *mission* is Eusebius's term of choice, and thus mission has already become established rhetoric for the early church. To characterize Jesus' life and ministry as mission, to insert *mission* into statements concerning Philo's historical work, and to name Pantaenus a "missionary" in the East appropriate Eusebius to substantiate *mission* as historical rhetoric. One generalizes from the present to the past and falsely imposes the contemporary use of *mission* as Eusebius's intent, when such a concept is not the most accurate rendering of Eusebius's words.

Once *mission* and *missionary* are glossed as Eusebius's words, they become historical fact. They are cited as consensual thinking or tradition of earliest Christianity. Quoting Eusebius at length, G. M. Rae in 1892 regards Pantaenus as "the first historical missionary to India."[130] Though Rae admits that it is not known how long Pantaenus stayed in India, if in fact India is where he went, what he actually did, or whether there was any fruit from his labors, he nonetheless uses *missionary* as Pantaenus's title. This type of historicizing is perpetuated in Samuel Moffett's three-page discussion of Pantaenus under the heading "The Mission of Pantaenus." Moffett reports that Pantaenus was sent as "a missionary to the East" and that "Eusebius gives this account of

---

[128]Eusebius, *History of the Church* (Williamson trans.), 214.

[129]Eusebius, *Ecclesiastical History* (Lake trans.), 462-63 (V, 10); Eusebius, *Ecclesiastical History* (Lawlor and Oulton trans.), 1:156.

[130]George Milne Rae, *The Syrian Church in India* (Edinburgh: W. Blackwood, 1892), 65-67. George Smith, *The Conversion of India: From Pantaenus to the Present Time, A.D. 193–1893* (New York: Fleming H. Revell, 1894), makes the same connection with Eusebius, asserting that Pantaenus is "first missionary to the Brahmans and Buddhists" and establishes a "training school of missionaries" (12-14).

the mission."[131] Likewise, Latourette uses Eusebius to substantiate Pantaenus "as being sent as a missionary" to the East.[132] Because Rae, Moffett, Latourette, and others call Pantaenus a missionary and label his travel to India as mission, it is assumed that this is Eusebius's language as well.[133]

Eusebius is too important for our understanding of the early church to be handled without careful regard for his language, and thus every measure should be made to clarify his meaning. Among these measures is the clearing of unwarranted presumptions and inaccurate translations of his words. Such measures guard against a misuse of Eusebius and his text and a misreading of the history of the early church.

Rufinus of Aquileia (ca. 340–410/411) followed immediately after Eusebius and produced a Latin translation of Eusebius's *History of the Church*. He took liberty with Eusebius's *History* by altering its chronology and paraphrasing sections. Rufinus reduced Eusebius's ten books to nine and then extended the whole by adding two of his own, books ten and eleven. In his extension of Eusebius's *History*, Rufinus writes of bishops and councils, controversies and disputes, doctrine and regulations, and persecution and martyrdom. Because Rufinus's translation and extended history provide the first Latin history of the church, its influence on other writers of his day was considerable.[134]

Rufinus does not use the language of *mission* or *missionary*. He has opportunity to do so in book ten, section nine, as he outlines "the division of the earth which the apostles made by lot for the preaching of God's word," but he does not. In this section Rufinus lists different parts of the known world as assignments for the apostles: Parthia to Thomas, Ethiopia to Matthew, and "Hither India" to Bartholomew.[135] Among the apostles, Rufinus includes Meropius, a philosopher of Tyre, who "decided to go to India."[136] The stated reason is to preach God's word and

---

[131]Moffett, *History of Christianity in Asia*, 1:37.
[132]*HEC*, 1:116.
[133]Irvin and Sunquist, *History of the World Christian Movement*, cite Eusebius as the basis for their claim Pantaenus "went to India as a missionary," and thus he is among "the first Christian missionary evangelists to India" (1:94, 95).
[134]Philip R. Amidon in the introduction to Rufinus, *The Church History of Rufinus of Aquileia, Books 10 and 11*, trans. Philip R. Amidon (New York: Oxford University Press, 1997), xii.
[135]Ibid., 18 (10.9).
[136]Ibid., 19 (10.9).

the identities of those who are sent are philosopher and apostles.[137] In addition to preaching, Rufinus mentions "signs and wonders" (11.8) and exemplary lives being the means by which the gospel is made known to those outside the faith. Rufinus does not convey these activities and actors in mission language, nor does he translate Eusebius's Greek text into Latin *missio* terminology. Rather, he describes the extension of the gospel in other language, such as preaching and miracles, and those who carried the gospel are identified as apostles, saints, and servants.[138] Along with Eusebius, this early historian does not find reason to employ the language of *mission* or *missionary*.

   Prosper of Aquitaine (ca. 390–ca. 455) writes against semi-Pelagianism and for Augustine's views of grace and predestination. His defense of Augustine (354–430) is found in a number of letters and treatises, including *Epistula ad Rufinum* and *Pro Augustino responsiones ad exerpta Genuensuim*.[139] In *De vocatione omnium gentium* (On the calling of all the nations), a two-part essay composed in Rome around 450, Prosper voices support for Augustine's teachings concerning the salvation of infidels. The doctrinal question of *De vocatione* is whether God's gift of grace extends to all humankind. Prosper responds that a general grace is given to all and a special grace to some. His discussion focuses on how this grace becomes effectual for the elect and thus explains the means of grace. Though "every man who is converted to God is first stirred by God's grace," it is in the ministry of the preacher that "the action of the divine power fuses with the sound of a human voice," and grace accomplishes its special work.[140] Prosper refers to this ministry of grace in a variety of ways: preaching, sacrament, "the light of grace," summons, call, gift, witness, signs, sowing of seed, and prayer.[141] Human voices fuse with the divine

---

[137] Amidon, the translator of Rufinus, characterizes this as mission in a footnote to the text (46n18) and later refers to "other missionary work" in 48n21.

[138] Rufinus, *Church History of Rufinus*, 11, 18, 61, 66, 68.

[139] For fuller details of the life and writings of Prosper of Aquitaine, see P. de Letter, "introduction," in Prosper of Aquitaine, *The Call of All Nations*, Ancient Christian Writers: The Works of the Fathers in Translation 14 (Westminster, MD: Newman, 1952), 3-20; Roland J. Teske and Dorothea Weber, "Introduction," in *Prosper of Aquitaine: De Vocatione Omnium Gentium*, Corpus Scriptorum Ecclesiasticorum Latinorum 97 (Wien: Verlag der Österreichischen Akademie der Wissenschaften, 2009), 9-77.

[140] Prosper, *Call of All Nations*, book I, chapter 8 (37, 38).

[141] Ibid., 50, 52, 60, 62, 65, 66, 67, 73, 83, 91, 93, 97, 98, 102, 106, 111, 113, 120, 122.

power in preachers, messengers, ministers, saints, "His people," and apostles to accomplish the work of salvation.[142] *Missionary* is absent from Prosper's list of human voices, and the means of God's grace is not described as mission.

De vocatione is classified as a "missionary work" by interpreters because of Prosper's reference to Palladius, the first bishop for Ireland. This reference provides evidence of early evangelizing efforts among the Irish, prior to Patrick.[143] Morrau, Lambert, Brown, and Maclear are among those who cite Prosper in their evidence of missionary activity in Britain, beginning with Palladius.[144] For these interpreters, the sending of Palladius is depicted as more than the attempt to halt Pelagianism in Britain; it is the "mission of Palladius."[145] Likewise, Palladius's preaching is more than just preaching. According to Richard Fletcher, it is "missionary preaching."[146] Mission language eclipses crucial doctrinal matters and pushes mission as endeavor or task to the forefront.

P. de Letter, translator of *De vocatione*, inserts *mission* twice into the English text. He has Prosper saying of the Divine, "I shall not forsake you in this great mission till the end of the world" (91), and that "the preachers of God's word were discharging their mission" (93). Prosper, in both cases, does not use the Latin *missio* or another word that could be construed as "mission." Rather, it appears Letter employs *mission* in the general sense, in

---

[142]Ibid., 58, 90, 92, 93, 98, 115, 117, 119.

[143]T. M. Charles-Edwards, "Palladius, Prosper, and Leo the Great: Mission and Primatial Authority," in *Saint Patrick, A.D. 493–1993*, ed. David N. Dumville, Studies in Celtic History XIII (Woodbridge, UK: Boydell, 1993), 1-12. Charles-Edwards indicates that *De vocatione* was one of "three works which bear upon the theme of missionary work beyond the frontiers of the Empire" (3).

[144]Daniélou and Marrou, *First Six Hundred Years*, 1:456; Lambert, *Christians and Pagans: The Conversion of Britain from Alban to Bede*, 135; Brown, *Rise of Western Christendom*, 130; Maclear, *History of Christian Missions During the Middle Ages*, 59-60.

[145]Brown, *Rise of Western Christendom*, 130. According to Lambert, Pelagianism was among Prosper's chief concerns. Prosper "referred to the 'British serpent' who 'vomits' a doctrine 'steeped in the venom of the ancient serpent.'" Prosper, *Carmen de ingratis*, quoted by Lambert, *Christians and Pagans*, 45. Because Christian communities were already in existence among the Irish, Robert Markus, "The Papacy, Missions and the Gentes," in *Integration Und Herrschaft: Ethnische Identitäten Und Soziale Organisation Im Frühmittelalter*, ed. Walter Pohl and Max Diesenberger, Forschungen Zur Geschicte Des Mittelalters 3 (Wien: Verlag der Österreichischen Akademie der Wissenschaften, 2002), cautions that we should be "reluctant to see the sending of Palladius to the Irish as a mission to the heathen" (37).

[146]Fletcher, *Barbarian Conversion*, 32.

the same way one would use *task* or *purpose*. In the opening sections of book two, Prosper cites Matthew 28:19-20 and Mark 16:15. In reference to these passages, Letter renders Prosper's summary of Christ's words of exhortation, "I shall not forsake you in this great mission till the end of the world." The Latin text conveys the promise of Christ's presence to the consummation of the age (*qui vos usque ad consummationem saeculi in omni hoc opera non relinquam*) but nothing of mission.[147]

Prosper's *Contra Collatorem* (c. 434) and *Chronica Minora* are labeled as mission works, as interpreters point to them as evidence of "Palladius's mission."[148] Schmidlin cites Prosper as his source for his claim that Palladius's "Irish mission" preceded that of Patrick.[149] Latourette likewise suggests that "the mission of Palladius" may have preceded that of Patrick. The source Latourette cites for this suggestion is Prosper.[150] And Malcolm Lambert references Prosper of Aquitaine in his description of the "papal mission" of deacon Palladius to Ireland. Lambert concludes, "Prosper's language and papal thinking about the duty to move across the Roman frontier to bring the faith to the barbarians show that side by side with the caretaking task was an aspiration to mission."[151]

For Prosper, God is the sole actor in the means of grace. The grace of God makes its way into lives, as it "urges on with exhortations, moves by example, inspires fear from dangers, rouses with miracles, gives understanding, inspires counsel, illumines the heart itself and inspires it with the aspiration of the faith."[152] Human means can only cooperate with God's work of grace. The prayers and good works of the elect, animated by God's grace, are aids to God's work. Never is human-initiated mission or the work of missionaries named as the means of this grace. Interpreting Prosper's meaning as mission and inserting mission into the text muffles Prosper's overriding doctrinal concerns.

---

[147]Prosper, *Call of All Nations*, book 2, chapter 2 (91). For the Latin text, see Prosper, *De Vocatione Omnium Gentium*, 143.
[148]Charles-Edwards, "Palladius, Prosper, and Leo the Great," 5.
[149]Schmidlin, *Catholic Mission History*, 143.
[150]*HEC*, 1:221n278.
[151]Lambert, *Christians and Pagans*, 135.
[152]Prosper, *Call of All Nations*, book 2, chapter 26 (135).

The Venerable Bede (673–735) wrote *Ecclesiastical History of England* (731) to detail the coming of the Christian faith to the British Isles. His account is chiefly the story of the expansion of the Roman church via Canterbury and the establishment of bishops and monasteries throughout Britain, Scotland, Ireland, and various islands. Bede calls the actors in this story bishops, monks, hermits, abbots, priests, pastors, ministers, teachers, confessors, heralds, and martyrs, and characterizes their actions in the establishment of Christianity as preaching, suffering, miracles, evangelistic work, instruction, and righteous living. The aims of these actors and activities, as chronicled by Bede, are the conversion of kings and queens, the building of churches, and the normalization of ecclesiastical structures and practices. Missionaries are not named as actors, and mission is not identified as the means to accomplish these aims. And yet, historians cite mission as Bede's organizing principle and his history as "missionary history."[153] Ian Wood points to the "mission of Palladius to the Irish," "the mission of Augustine," and "mission to the Frisians and Saxons" to substantiate the claim that Bede's *Ecclesiastical History* has a "missionary message."[154] Likewise, Richard Fletcher depicts Paulinus, an Italian priest who travels to the court of King Edwin, as a missionary, and the initiation of Christianity in Northumbria as mission. Fletcher's source for these assertions is Bede.[155] Bede, according to Frank Barlow, chronicles the "missionary work of his compatriot Wilfrid."[156] In an expansive manner, Peter Hunter Blair credits Bede as his source for descriptions of missions to Britain, Ireland, and the continent. Without qualification or proviso, Bede is reputed as reporting the exploits of missionaries in the English/Gregorian, Columban, and Roman missions through their missionary activities.[157] Christopher Dawson names Bede as "a typical representative of the new Christian culture which had been planted in Northumbria" by the Roman and Irish mission efforts, and thus Bede is well placed to give witness to the "life and work of the great Irish

---

[153]Wood, *Missionary Life*, 26, 42. Wood concludes, "Perhaps more than any previous historian since Luke in the Acts of the Apostles, Bede set himself a task where the history that he wished to cover was, to a large extent, missionary history" (43).

[154]Ibid., 43, 45.

[155]Fletcher, *Barbarian Conversion*, 4.

[156]Barlow, "English Background," 25.

[157]Hunter Blair, *World of Bede*, 41-78, 100-113. According to Peter Brown, *Rise of Western Christendom*, "Bede presented the missionaries, bishops, and great holy men of his century as worthy heirs of the Hebrew prophets" (352).

missionary saint, like St. Columba of Iona and Columban of Luxeuil."[158] Malcolm Lambert's assessment is,

> No doubt Acts would have especially interested [Bede] as the story of the spread of the Gospel among the Gentiles; in just the same way as Paul and his companions, a small body of missionaries worked among his pagan predecessors generations before his day. It is their story which he narrates in the *Ecclesiastical History*, his greatest achievement.[159]

Therefore, Lambert is quick to connect Bede with "missionary efforts" and states that Bede's "purpose was to confirm faith through narrating the lives and achievements of Christian missionaries and the kings and aristocrats who aided them."[160]

Though these historians treat Bede's *Ecclesiastical History* as mission history with a missionary message, Bede does not use the language of *mission* or *missionary*. There are several instances where it might appear as though Bede is using mission language, and yet on closer inspection it is clear he does not. In one instance, Bede states that Egbert intends "to bring blessing to many peoples by undertaking the apostolic task [*inito opere apostolico*] of carrying the word of God, through the preaching of the gospel, to some of those nations who had not yet heard it."[161] Bede names Egbert's task as apostolic, because it involves traveling to peoples beyond the British Isles and to those who had yet to hear the gospel. Bede's Latin is *apostolico* and not *missio*. As it appears his aim is to link Egbert in retrospect with the activities of the apostles, mission language seems inappropriate. To the contrary, *mission* would infuse Bede's motives with modern aims and activities.

In a letter that Bede reports to be from Gregory to Etherius, archbishop of Arles (Lyons), Gregory asks that Augustine be favorably received. Some modern English translation renders Augustine's task as "mission." And yet, the Latin original is cause (*causam*) and not mission (*missio*).[162]

---

[158]Dawson, *Formation of Christendom*, 174-74.
[159]Lambert, *Christians and Pagans*, 296.
[160]Ibid., 60.
[161]Bede, *Ecclesiastical History*, ed. Colgrave and Myers, 476-77.
[162]Ibid., 72-73. The 1565 English translation by Stapleton translates this as "cause." See *The History of the Church of Englande* (1565), trans. Thomas Stapleton (Amsterdam: Theatrum Orbis Terratum, 1970), 30.

Likewise, in a volume of Gregory's letters translated by John Martyn, this letter makes no mention of mission but only that Augustine provided help and support.[163]

Another example is the oft-repeated incident in which Gregory the Great, prior to becoming pope, encountered young boys from Britain for sale in a Roman market. This prompted him to ask the bishop of Rome to send "ministers of the word to the Angles in Britain to convert them to Christ." Bede records that Gregory would go himself, but he was unable because of duties in Rome. The Oxford 1969 English translation reports Bede's words as "he was unable to perform this mission."[164] In the Latin text, Bede uses the verb *mitteret,* denoting action rather than a noun. The verb denotes the simple action of sending instead of a formal, planned, or organized mission or even of a general task or purpose. Rendering the verb as a noun and thus turning action into a planned affair or an organized delegation is less than accurate. An earlier translation of the same passage by John Stevens and J. A. Giles (1907) renders *mitteret* as Gregory's inability to go, and Stapleton's 1565 translation simply states he could not obtain permission for his request to go.[165]

In another instance, the 1969 Oxford translation of Bede's account of Willibrord's plan to evangelize the Frisians is rendered as "the missionary task," when the Latin is clearly "evangelize" (*euangelizandi*).[166] Rather than using the rhetoric of modern missions, Stevens and Giles (1907) are much more descriptive in their translation to explain Willibrord's intent as to "undertake the desired work of preaching the Gospel to the Gentiles," and Stapleton (1556) explains the affair as "setting forth of God's word."[167] Once again, the Oxford translation renders "mission" as a translation of Bede's account of Romanus, the bishop of Rochester.[168] Bede explains that

---

[163]Gregory, *Letters of Gregory the Great,* 2:439. Contrary to Bede's claim, the letter is not addressed to Etherius but is from Gregory to Pelagius to Tours and Serenus of Marseilles, bishops of Gaul (July 23, 596).

[164]Bede, *Ecclesiastical History,* ed. Colgrave and Myers, 134-35. See similar renderings by the translator on 330-31, 332-33.

[165]*Bede's Ecclesiastical History of England,* trans. J. A. Giles and John Stevens, Bohn's Antiquarian Library (London: Bell & Sons, 1907), 68; *History of the Church of Englande* (1565), 49.

[166]Bede, *Ecclesiastical History,* ed. Colgrave and Myers, 484-85.

[167]*Bede's Ecclesiastical History* (1907), 251-52; *History of the Church of Englande* (1565), 163.

[168]Bede, *Ecclesiastical History,* ed. Colgrave and Myers, 160-61.

the reason there is no bishop at the church of Rochester is that Romanus drowned in the Italian Sea while on an "appointed mission" to Pope Honorius. As Romanus's trip was to Rome and not to the hinterlands of Ireland or Germany, the Latin *missus* is better translated as merely *sent* or *sending*, as it points to a diplomatic or representative role for Romanus.

Besides the common use of the Latin verb "to send," Bede does use the noun form of *missus* three times. The 1969 Oxford translation consistently renders these as "mission," whereas earlier translations do not. In one instance, the Oxford translation renders Bede's reference to a priest by the name of Peter, the first abbot of the monastery at Canterbury, as being sent on "a mission to Gaul" (*Galliam missus*).[169] Giles's and Stevens's translation states that Peter is being sent as an "Ambassador to France," and Stapleton calls him a "legate unto France."[170] In these earlier translations, Peter is named as an emissary for political representation of the church, as there appears to be no intent to evangelize. In a second instance, Bede's reference to a letter from Abbot Ceolfrith, in which he names Adomanán, an abbot of the monks of Iona and author of *Vita Columbae*, is rendered as "sent by his people on a mission to Aldfrith, king of the Angles" (*cum legationis gratia missus a sua gente uenisset ad Aldfridum regem Anglorum*).[171] Once again, Giles and Stevens translate *missus* as ambassador, and thus Adomanán is an ambassador to Aldfrith, representing political concerns, rather than as a "missionary."[172] And in a third instance, the same reference concerning Adomanán is made in a rather long letter from Abbot Ceolfrith to King Nechtan. The Oxford translation states that Adomanán is being "sent on a mission from his people to King Aldfrith," while both the 1907 and 1565 translations indicate he is being sent as an "ambassador."[173] *Missus* is used by Bede in these instances to convey a sense of political representation or deputation. The Latin text of the Venerable Bede's early history of the expansion of Christianity into England does not give preference to "mission" or

---

[169]Ibid., 114-15.
[170]*Bede's Ecclesiastical History*, 60; *History of the Church of Englande*, 44.
[171]Bede, *Ecclesiastical History*, ed. Colgrave and Myers, 506-7.
[172]*Bede's Ecclesiastical History*, 262. No mention is made of "mission" in Stapleton's translation, *History of the Church of Englande*, 171.
[173]Bede, *Ecclesiastical History* (1969), 550-51; *Bede's Ecclesiastical History*, 287; *History of the Church of Englande*, 188.

"missionary." The presence of *missus* language in Bede evidences its early use in a diplomatic or representative sense but not as language of the modern mission enterprise.

MISSION REALITY?

A careful inspection of the language of historical figures and early historians of the church reveals that *missionary*—as an ecclesiastical title, vocational class, or profession—is nonexistent. Rather, a range of terms describes ecclesial roles and offices. Those who spread the faith are identified as bishops, disciples, saints, monks, nuns, pilgrims, and martyrs. Individuals and groups, both at the center and at the margins of the church, are not defined by mission language. Their activities are expressed in many terms, but mission is not one of them. The closest descriptor that approximates mission or missionary is *apostolic*, but in these cases, the reference is to the office or role similar to that of the twelve disciples and not to a modern vocation. Modern interpreters, in spite of the absence of mission among these early individuals and historians, feel compelled to insert such conceptual language into the historical record. The imprecise vocabulary of mission and its anachronistic rendering of history are the product of something other than a plain reading. Rather, mission is either generalized to express any kind of common purpose or task, or it is historicized in order to promote modern mission endeavors. While the first of these is certainly a problem because of the manner in which generalized language miscommunicates, the promotion of mission as an early church or medieval reality is the bigger problem.

Interpreters claim that historical figures are talking and writing about mission, even if this is not their exact language. They allege that mission is what these premoderns were doing and intended to say. Some interpreters assert that though Patrick and Boniface do not use mission language, we know what they were doing was mission, and they were acting like missionaries. Similarly, even though Eusebius and Bede do not write in mission language, both are describing mission work and missionaries.

And yet, this is precisely the problem. Mission and missionary are unknown ideas or concepts to Patrick and Eusebius, and thus it can only be mission and missionary as moderns conceive these ideas that are read into their ancient worlds. Because language contains assumptions and aims on which realities are constructed, mission language matters. Its assumptions and aims cause the historian to determine that some preaching is mission preaching and other preaching is just preaching, or one person is a missionary and another is just a monk, priest, or trader. *Mission* words are the means by which existing beliefs are voiced and mission as a reality is established. The beliefs and values of the historian, aided by *mission* words, become the vehicles that explain Pantaenus's travel to the East, the Nestorians' activities in China, and Patrick's return to Ireland. The meaning of these events and individuals is construed as mission and missionary realities to which the historian is predisposed.

Rather than the single reality of mission, the shape of the church's expansion from the New Testament era forward comes via a multitude of realities and a variety of descriptors. No one understanding or practice of expansion dominates, nor does one form persist. Diversity rather than sameness, and multiformity rather than uniformity, are the norm. Activity is plural, and the actors are varied.

While mission classification may seem to be appropriate and helpful, mission presents problems similar to those found in attempts to justify mission with Scripture. Renaming preaching, witnessing, evangelizing, and traveling as *mission* alters these realities. Identifying preachers, witnesses, and martyrs as *missionaries* skews identity. Grouping activities, situations, and personalities under the modern classification of mission obscures nuanced causes for actions and the motives of actors. The intent of historians is to harmonize different kinds of forms and actors into one reality. When used as a category or rubric, readers understand mission as all inclusive, comprehensive event or activity, but this kind of compression into mission, a single, aggregating reality, can lead to erroneous conclusions. What is absolutely clear is that the forms and practices and the ways of expansion varied greatly throughout the centuries. Methods, actions, initiatives, dynamics, causes, and results of growth look different per location and agents, and thus they are reported via an array of descriptive terms, processes, and agents. The practice of joining this wide and varied assortment of forms and actors together under a single rubric presents history as the collective dynamic of church expansion known as *mission*.

The categorization of a whole range of events, forms, and actors under mission is not just the practice of a few historians but the majority.[174] The persistent historicizing of mission establishes what seems to be an unassailable rubric or category and gives mission an aura of uncontestable historicity. And yet, a faithful rendering of the past is best done by way of actual activities, such as preaching and witnessing, rather than via a general category or rubric. A close reading of history shows mission to be a constructed reality and not reality in itself. Why and how this happens is the subject of the next chapter.

---

[174]The use of both *mission* and *missionary* is truly universal and ubiquitous. It is impossible to overstate the pervasive use of these terms across different types of histories of the early and medieval church. Among the many examples of historians using *mission* and *missionary*, see Joseph H. Lynch, *Early Christianity: A Brief History* (New York: Oxford University Press, 2010), 24, 37, 223-39; Paul Johnson, *A History of Christianity* (New York: Atheneum, 1976), 40, 41, 44, 134, 169, 181, 182; Chadwick, *Early Church*, 11, 12, 19, 21, 23, 248-49, 256; Marshall W. Baldwin, "Missions to the East in the Thirteenth and Fourteenth Centuries," in *A History of the Crusades*, vol. 5, *The Impact of the Crusades on the Near East*, ed. Norman Zacour and Harry W. Hazard (Madison: The University of Wisconsin Press, 1985), 452-518; James D. Ryan, "Conversion or the Crown of Martyrdom: Conflicting Goals for Fourteenth-Century Missionaries in Central Asia?," in *Medieval Cultures in Contact*, ed. Richard F. Gyug, Fordham Series in Medieval Studies (New York: Fordham University Press, 2003), 19-38; Hilarin Felder, *The Ideals of St. Francis of Assisi*, trans. Berchmans Bittle (New York: Benziger Brothers, 1925); Finney, *Recovering the Past*; Fletcher, *Barbarian Conversion*; Edward Gibbon, *The Triumph of Christendom in the Roman Empire*, ed. J. B. Bury (New York: Harper & Row, 1958), 60; Robert M. Grant, *Augustus to Constantine: The Rise and Triumph of Christianity in the Roman World* (San Francisco: Harper & Row, 1970), 57-58, 254, 255; Jerry H. Bentley, *Old World Encounters: Cross-Cultural Contacts and Exchanges in Pre-Modern Times* (New York: Oxford University Press, 1993), 61; Bruce, *Spreading Flame*, 392, 397; Brown, *Rise of Western Christendom*, 5, 130; Sullivan, *Christian Missionary Activity in the Early Middle Ages*; Frend, *Rise of Christianity*, 54, 88, 126-27, 285-86, 884; Daniélou and Marrou, *First Six Hundred Years*, 1:18, 19, 21.

4

Rhetoric and Trope

The conversion of Britain, as we have indicated, proceeded
chiefly from two sources. One was Rome. From this
centre of the Western Church, on the initiative of
Gregory the Great, came small bands of missionaries.

KENNETH SCOTT LATOURETTE, *A HISTORY OF THE EXPANSION OF CHRISTIANITY*

Britain first re-entered the full tide of European
history when Pope Gregory the Great personally
initiated the mission to England and in 596 dispatched
Augustine and his party of monks to Canterbury.

STEPHEN NEILL, *A HISTORY OF CHRISTIAN MISSIONS*

ACCORDING TO Kenneth Scott Latourette, Stephen C. Neill, and a host of
other historians, the expansion of Christianity from Jerusalem to the ends
of the earth is the story of mission. In their histories, one encounters mission
language in account after account and, in some cases, on every page. The
story of Christianity is saturated with the language of *mission* and *missionary*,
and thus Christian history is presented *as* mission history. On the other
hand, there are those who recount the history of early Christianity with little
or no mention of "mission." The story is told in a manner without reference
to mission activities or mission agents. According to these histories, the
death and resurrection of Jesus propelled groups of people throughout Palestine speaking of Jesus' life and teaching, death, and resurrection. As they

interacted with neighbors, family, and friends, they spoke of their experience in the "Jesus Way." Their interactions expanded the new faith into homes, communities, and societies. Christianity spread, and yet, mission was not identified as the cause, nor were missionaries named as its agents. For them, Christian history was the history of the faith and the church.[1]

The causes for Christianity's expansion can be identified in a number of ways, depending on the historian's assumptions. If one's starting point is the social sciences, expansion takes place through networks of relationships, political and social needs and forces, and by way of the dynamics of such events as migration, famine, and disease.[2] If the intellectual conviction of the historian is tilted more toward the phenomenon of religion, the story is one of a stronger, more vibrant religion displacing waning cultic practices of mystery and civil religions. If the growth and development of Christianity are viewed through the lens of its divergence and splits into language and cultural tendencies, then the ecclesial controversies that issue from these are identified as the fuel for expansion.[3] Or, if one's disposition is more theological, the story centers in the activity of God from eternity, the death and resurrection of Jesus, and the work of the Spirit. Through election and covenant, divine providence is at work in the selection and empowerment of a particular people who are to love and bear witness to the whole of humanity. The Way of Jesus spreads by means of miracles and martyrdom, words of proclamation, and the Spirit's power. So, whether from the viewpoint of social science, religion, ecclesiology, or theology, defining assumptions shape the writing of history, and particular words give voice to these assumptions.

What we know for certain is that the new faith made its way through families, associations, clans, and societies. The "Jesus Way" crossed the boundaries of custom, ethnicity, religion, and language. The astounding effect was that within a few centuries the story based in the teachings and

---

[1]See Andrew F. Walls, "Structural Problems in Mission Studies," *International Bulletin of Missionary Research* 15, no. 4 (October 1991): 146.
[2]The interplay between these dynamics and the expansion of the church has been developed by Rodney Stark, *The Rise of Christianity: How the Obscure, Marginal Jesus Movement Became the Dominant Religious Force in the Western World in a Few Centuries* (San Francisco: HarperSanFrancisco, 1997).
[3]See Diarmaid MacCulloch, *Christianity: The First Three Thousand Years* (New York: Viking, 2009), 2-4.

person of Jesus became the faith of Western civilization. Historians describe this progression with more than just one word—*mission*—but with an array of terms—*evangelism, miracles, expansion, church growth, propagation, conversion,* and *apostolate.* While one person or group may prefer one descriptor over another, no one word is definitive or sacred. All are freighted with assumptions, some with more than others, and each offers its biased construction of history.

CONSTRUCTING HISTORY

Written history of any type is constructed history. What appears as a written historical account can only be a semblance or fragment of actual history. Actual history is the whole of the past, a boundless mixture of political, social, economic, linguistic, cultural, and religious causes and effects. More than a simple narrative of place and people, history is the intertwining of multiple narratives and the jumbling of many forces into a multilayered, multifaceted story. Societal and environmental factors may cause a political crisis in one locale, while the same elements in another place produce stability. In one place, these factors promote decay and decline, and transition and progress in another. Encounters between various groups of people and the clash of a wide range of forces within these societies generate dynamics that make history elaborate and elusive. Any number of vagaries, such as war, famine, trade, or migration, make encounters what they are, and once introduced, the history of each society and the collective history of peoples and places become complex and intricate puzzles of causes and effects. These mixtures are the engines that produce rise and decline, innovation and stagnation, acculturation and differentiation for cultures and societies. In and through this mix is the divine work of God's Spirit. The collective force of these changes produces the wild tapestry of history, most of which cannot be apprehended or recorded. Those who stand at a distance from these events must recognize that the phenomenon they seek to apprehend is in reality a wide-ranging set of activities and actors, social and environmental conditions. The piece that appeals to or stimulates the imagination of a particular historian may not be the most pertinent piece of the puzzle or may be merely an indicator or symptom of other causes. So, even in its most accurate and faithful expression, history, as it is assembled and conveyed by the historian, is constructed reality.

On one hand, the historian reaches into a rich mound of complex data to construct an account. When ample data exists, the historian, according to Will Durant and Ariel Durant, "always oversimplifies, and hastily selects a manageable minority of facts and faces out of a crowd of souls and events whose multitudinous complexity he can never quite embrace or comprehend."[4] The historian selects small fragments from the mound and draws significance for the whole. He must determine whether one event or a certain personality is more significant than another and whether to place these front and center in his account. The massive heap of people, cities, institutions, and events makes selecting and prioritizing doubly difficult. Because facts are ample and the historian must preference some pieces over others, written history is constructed history.

Or, as is often the case, the historian must assemble the story from a meager pool of facts, filling in missing details in a reasoned manner. In the case of the primitive history, the "church's mission," Adolf Harnack confesses, "lies buried in legend; or rather, it has been replaced by a history (which is strongly marked by tendency) of what is alleged to have happened in the course of a few decades throughout every country on the face of the earth."[5] In order to offer a reasonable account, the historian must fill in gaps between the data and what he or she surmises could or should have happened. This means the historian's task includes speculation, conjecture, and guesswork. According to the Durants, "Most of history is guessing, and the rest is prejudice."[6] When the historian has only a meager amount of data, written history must be constructed reality.

"The historical record," laments Hayden White, "is both too full and too sparse," and this presents problems of both excluding and speculating.[7] Whether there are too many facts or too few faces, the historian crafts a

---

[4] Will Durant, *The Age of Faith*, 979, cited in Will Durant and Ariel Durant, *The Lessons of History* (New York: Simon and Schuster, 1968), 12.

[5] Adolf Harnack, *The Mission and Expansion of Christianity in the First Three Centuries* (New York: Harper, 1962), xi.

[6] Will Durant, *Our Oriental Heritage*, 12, cited in Durant and Durant, *Lessons of History*, 12.

[7] Hayden V. White, *Tropics of Discourse: Essays in Cultural Criticism* (Baltimore, MD: Johns Hopkins University Press, 1978), 51.

narrative that is more or less constructed. The construction of history operates not only per the historian's access to data and her ability to analyze that data but also per her interpretation of the data. Facts are not just facts, and history is not just the presentation of facts. Rather, the selection, prioritization, and arrangement of facts by the historian represent a reasoned interpretation of how events occurred and why persons did what they did. Selection, prioritization, and arrangement come via a process of exclusion and inclusion by the historian. The reader never receives history as raw data but as selected facts and thus as an orchestrated interpretation.

The level of speculation or conjecture needed to construct history becomes even greater when comprehension must reach beyond not just time and place but also across language and culture. The span of centuries cloaks circumstances and causes, motives and dynamics. But this is especially true, for example, when a person from Scotland writes a history of India, or an American writes a history of Japan. The language and culture of place and people of the past make intent and reason near impossible to unravel. Time and place, language and culture separate the historian from the actual events and thus limit what he can with veracity state when writing of the past. The gap between then and now is not easily crossed. Facts take the historian only so far, and then imagination must take over in order for a plausible bridge between time and space, language and culture to be constructed for the reader to cross.

The limitations of the historian's time and place, language and culture, are compounded by the fact that the historian, every historian, has a belief structure. While place and time, language and culture define the parameters of the historian's construction, internal beliefs guide in constructing history. This internal guide is defined as mentality, conviction, or worldview. Without it, the historian would be unable to construct the past into any sensible narrative. It is scaffolding on which the historian determines why causes have certain effects, what motivates people to act, and how systems function. And yet, while belief structure facilitates, it also prejudices the construction of history. The historian stands at a distance and in another place, deciphering facts through her own language and culture, at a particular time and place, and yet, more than anything else, her own story, education, values, and beliefs determine the construction of history.

So, reading history is as much about reading the historian as the actual events. Just as the historian is unable to grasp all that occurs in the past, neither is she free from the time and place, language and culture, beliefs and biases that define her. Standards set by the discipline of history and followed by those who write histories offer a measure of assurance that methods of gathering and analyzing data are as scientific and objective as possible, and yet, standards take the historian only so far. The historian by necessity constructs history, a history based on what he believes happened and what he happens to believe.

Mission is not just fact or event but one belief structure among many possible structures that governs how a historian constructs history. As a belief structure, mission determines what events, actions, and persons are selected, organized, and presented in order to give a sensible, constructed history.[8] *Mission* and *missionary* are more than simple terms, neutral concepts, or bare facts—they give voice to and communicate particular beliefs, and as a belief structure, mission constructs reality in a particular way.[9]

OBSCURING HISTORY

Clarity and accuracy in written history are hard enough to achieve without mission language adding its assumptions and aims. In part two of this study, I explore the Christendom assumptions and modern aims inherent in mission language, and attempt to measure the extent to which these formed the modern mission movement. My contention is that not only do these shape modern mission, but they persist in contemporary mission language. When draped in the assumptions and aims of mission language, the voice and identity of ancient peoples can be obscured and even lost. A prime example is the way historians account for the establishment of Christianity in England. Stephen Neill labels Augustine and his band as missionaries and the whole endeavor as "Augustine's mission," and the monks accompanying

---

[8]Latourette (*HEC*, 2:xvi), for example, admits that his seven-volume history is limited by his own presuppositions. He states these beliefs and values at the outset, so the reader knows that these have shaped his interpretation of the data.

[9]Paul Kollman, "At the Origins of Mission and Missiology: A Study in the Dynamics of Religious Language," *Journal of the American Academy of Religion* 79, no. 2 (June 2011): 425-58, highlights the dualism inherent in mission. There exists "the performative capacity of the term *missio*, especially its ability to constitute subjects and objects in discourse, and to lend theological legitimation to such discursive performance" (436).

him as having "missionary zeal."[10] Mission language complicates Augustine and his entourage of monks by infusing their activities and intentions with modern mission convictions and thus dislocating the story of these actors. The near, more accessible, and familiar language of *missionary* dominates the distant and illusive Augustine. While moderns have little idea what a monk does or what might motivate Augustine to travel to England, they have some idea about what missionaries do and how they look.

Neill is certainly not alone in this kind of inflection of the facts. In a similar way, Dale Irvin and Scott Sunquist make Augustine and his fellow monks into a "missionary delegation."[11] Such language molds Pope Gregory and his dispatch of Augustine to the British Isles into a specific kind of specialized endeavor with particular intentions. The rhetoric of mission communicates that Rome is the center of Christianity, from which true faith radiates and crosses into areas of "darkness" via delegations of mission activities and mission agents. Such language makes the historical account look a great deal like modern mechanisms of profession, expansion, and conquest. The rhetoric of mission, shaped by modern beliefs about organization and profession, constructs Pope Gregory and Augustine into peculiar actors, and their activity into specialized forms. In the process, Augustine and Gregory, cloaked in mission garb, reinforce Christendom assumptions of place and promote modern mission aims. Mission does not enlarge or activate our understanding of people's motives and actions—it obscures them.

Examples of obfuscating tendencies of mission are easy to find in written histories. Bernard Youngman, in his narration of the evangelization of Britain in the fifth century, claims that "not all the missionary activity in Britain came from abroad; devout men and women had been at work, missionaries in their own land."[12] Roland Bainton, eminent twentieth-century church historian, in his chapter "The Ministry in the Middle Ages," includes "missionary" as a vocation along with his discussion of monks and priests.[13]

---

[10]*HCM*, 59.

[11]Dale T. Irvin and Scott W. Sunquist, *History of the World Christian Movement*, vol. 1, *Earliest Christianity to 1453* (Maryknoll, NY: Orbis Books, 2001), 327.

[12]Bernard R. Youngman, *Into All the World: The Story of Christianity to 1066 A.D.* (New York: St. Martin's, 1965), 135.

[13]Roland H. Bainton, *Early and Medieval Christianity*, The Collected Papers in Church History (Boston: Beacon, 1962), 49, 50, 60.

Both Youngman and Bainton employ *missionary* to communicate certainty about ancient offices that assumes a great deal and projects definite ministry positions. So, it is assumed that alongside bishop, abbot, pastor, and monk, there is the office of missionary. In addition to preaching, evangelizing, and healing, mission vocation, and activity is asserted. Youngman and Bainton do not explain, qualify, or define mission but dress their histories in its assumptions and aims. Mission language connects the reader to a particular construction of the medieval church history imbued with modern mission.[14] Though *mission* may be a received tradition and may represent conventional, consensus vocabulary, it does not clarify the past. Rather, it tends to restrict and muddle our understanding.

It is the rare historian who acknowledges the problem of mission language and thus qualifies his or her use of mission and missionary. Ian Wood, *The Missionary Life: Saints and the Evangelisation of Europe, 400–1050*, liberally uses the language of *mission* throughout his discussion, only to admit in his conclusion that "there is no classical or medieval Latin word *missionarius*: the category of 'missionary' is not an early medieval one, but rather a modern catch-all, in which religious figures of various kinds have been enshrined."[15] In a similar manner, Peter Brown refers to various missions and missionaries throughout *The Rise of Western Christendom* only to state toward the end of his massive work, "The idea of the 'missionary' seems so normal to us that we have to remember that it was only in this period [the eighth century] that anything like a concept of 'missions' developed in Western Europe." Brown's evidence for this conclusion is not from word usage of early historians and individual Christians. Rather, his interpretation of how Continental European Christians viewed the Christian faith causes him to conclude that Christianity was

---

[14]Gerd Tellenbach, *The Church in Western Europe from the Tenth to the Early Twelfth Century*, trans. Timothy Reuter, Cambridge Medieval Textbooks (Cambridge: Cambridge University Press, 1993), 6-21, offers another example of unqualified and thus confusing use of *mission* and *missionary*. He writes of missionaries, missionary style, missionary work, missionary consciousness, missionary functions, missionary plans, and missionary successes without definition or qualification of these terms.

[15]Ian Wood, *The Missionary Life: Saints and the Evangelisation of Europe, 400–1050* (Harlow, UK: Longman, 2001), 247. Wood goes on to say that the "notions of 'missionary hagiography' and even of 'the missionary' are constructs which may be very useful categories in certain contexts, but they should also be recognised for what they are" (248).

not "missionary" until the eighth century. Christianity shifted from the faith others *could* accept to the faith others *should* accept, and thus Continental Christianity became "missionary." Until this shift, according to Brown, there "was not a missionary drive directed to faraway places."[16] Benjamin Kedar, *Crusade and Mission: European Approaches Toward the Muslims*, uses *mission* and *missionary* throughout, but he notes at the outset of his study, "The term 'mission' and its derivatives appear only in early modern time." He adds that he uses these words because "it would be pedantic to dispense with them."[17] Similarly, Dana Robert, in *Christian Mission: How Christianity Became a World Religion*, uses mission language but, as she comes to her discussion of the Jesuits, notes that they "were the first to use the Latinized word 'mission' to represent the deliberate sending of special agents of the church, 'missionaries,' for the purpose of converting non-Catholics or of reviving lapsed ones."[18] Her qualified use of *mission* adds a measure of understanding but cannot undo the blinkered view she has communicated up to that point.

Raymond Van Dam is less willing to employ the title of *missionary*. His refusal to mislabel certain people as missionary is evidenced in "Hagiography and History: The Life of Gregory Thaumaturgus." Van Dam comments,

> In general histories of the Christian church, references to the episcopal career of Gregory tend to be perfunctory and stereotyped, usually describing him as a "missionary" and then considering his missionary work to have been an important factor in the Christianization of Pontus, especially to the peasants in the rural districts.

> These descriptions of the activities of Gregory Thaumaturgus are rarely shown up as labor-saving devices they have become. On a purely empirical basis alone, the conception of Gregory as a missionary is misguided and anachronistic.[19]

---

[16]Peter Robert Lamont Brown, *The Rise of Western Christendom: Triumph and Diversity, AD 200–1000* (Cambridge, MA: Blackwell, 1996), 414. Brown indicates this was view of Continentals alone, and the situation was different in other places, such as the British Isles.

[17]Benjamin Z. Kedar, *Crusade and Mission: European Approaches Toward the Muslims* (Princeton, NJ: Princeton University Press, 1984), xii.

[18]Dana Lee Robert, *Christian Mission: How Christianity Became a World Religion* (Chichester, UK: Wiley-Blackwell, 2009), 37.

[19]Raymond Van Dam, "Hagiography and History: The Life of Gregory Thaumaturgus," *Classical Antiquity* 1, no. 2 (October 1982): 274. Unlike Van Dam, Karl Baus makes this exact characterization. According to Baus, Gregory Thaumaturgus is a missionary, and "in his activities a

Van Dam explains this misconception is based on notions of preaching across a variety of local dialects, how evangelization actually occurs, and the nature of conversion. He concludes, "Since the process [of evangelization and conversion] happened in a particular society, it must be analyzed in the context of how people lived and thought in that specific society."[20] If Gregory and his context are simply labeled as *missionary*, both are lost. Van Dam's analysis of Gregory Thaumaturgus's life and actions demonstrates how complex and elusive history can be, and thus to use the language of *missionary* for the sake of brevity or convenience often misleads and distorts.

Yet Woods, Brown, Kedar, Robert, and Van Dam are exceptions.[21] The overwhelming and unqualified impression presented by the majority of historians is that mission language belongs to an ancient time and culture, and it exists as part of a belief structure of ancient people. And yet, such a universal and general imposition of mission on events and people endangers the essential narrative of history.

REPURPOSING HISTORY

Historicized *mission* and *missionary* language has the power to relocate events and people in the historical sequence and to repurpose the dynamics of Christianity's expansion. Mission language communicates that there was a defined, organized, and institutionalized enterprise called mission when there was nothing of the sort. To the contrary, historical accounts point to the fact that the expansion of Christianity within the Roman Empire and its eventual reach throughout Europe was fueled by a myriad of forces and was enacted by a host of agents. Mission language aggregates these people and events into a specialized history called "mission history" and a grand

---

well-thought-out missionary plan can be detected"; *From the Apostolic Community to Constantine*, Handbook of Church History I (Freiburg, West Germany: Herder, 1965), 375.

[20]Van Dam, "Hagiography and History," 276. Cf. *HEC*, 1970, 1:89-90, 116; Stephen B. Bevans and Roger Schroeder, *Constants in Context: A Theology of Mission for Today* (Maryknoll, NY: Orbis Books, 2004), 96.

[21]Marios Costambeys, Matthew Innes, and Simon MacLean, *The Carolingian World* (Cambridge: Cambridge University Press, 2011, refrain from using *mission* and *missionary* without qualification or quotation marks. They assert that "by suggesting that non-Christian religion was insubstantial and adaptable we are also undermining the traditional notion of conversion to Christianity (from something else, equally well defined) as a result of 'mission.' Contemporary narrative made much play of the idea of missions to the pagans, thus presenting the development of Christianity as a black-and-white conflict" (102).

narrative communicated as "mission narrative." The intent of both is to advance the notion of "mission."

Mission as history. Adolf Harnack (1851–1930) begins *The Mission and Expansion of Christianity in the First Three Centuries* with the lament that "missionary history has always been neglected" by historians of the church.[22] This neglect, he reasons, is because the facts of the church's mission are hidden or shrouded in legend and thus need to be brought to light. Quite possibly mission has been neglected as a form of history not because it is hidden, but because it is a modern phenomenon. It is only as mission emerges in the modern era that mission history becomes a genre, a literary category.[23] Not until the modern era did mission histories appear, and not until the twentieth century did mission history become a discipline in the academy. In Jan A. B. Jongeneel's description of the rise of mission histories, he notes that the type of history in which mission language figures prominently is recent and modern. It was not until Gustav Warneck (1834–1910) and his *Outline of a History of Protestant Missions from the Reformation to the Present Time* (*Evangelische Missionslehre*, 1897–1903) that history was written with mission as its overall structuring theme.[24] On the Catholic side, Joseph Schmidlin (1876–1944), the first person to occupy a Catholic chair for missionary science at Münster, in 1914, offered his *Catholic Missions History* (*Katholische Missionsgeschichte*, 1925) as a Catholic version of the missionary expansion of the church in response to Warneck's Protestant account. Prior to these two books, the history of the expansion of Christianity existed chiefly in biographies and brief overviews. William Carey, for example, provides an overview of Christian expansion in his *Enquiry* as part of his argument for the "use of means" to spread the gospel, but he does not present

---

[22]Harnack, *Mission and Expansion of Christianity*, xi. Stephen Neill registers a similar complaint in "The History of Missions: An Academic Discipline," in *The Mission of the Church and the Propagation of the Faith: Papers Read at the Seventh Summer Meeting and the Eight Winter Meeting of the Ecclesiastical History Society*, ed. G. J. Cuming, Studies in Church History 6 (Cambridge: Cambridge University Press, 1970), 149-70.

[23]Hubert Jedin views "the history of Missions" as an independent study established after the modern discipline of missiology was born. See Jedin's concise history of its development in "General Introduction to Church History," in *From the Apostolic Community to Constantine*, Handbook of Church History 1 (Freiburg, West Germany: Herder, 1965), 45.

[24]Gustav Warneck, *Outline of a History of Protestant Missions from the Reformation to the Present Time* (New York: Fleming H. Revell, 1901). First published as *Evangelische Missionslehre* in 1882, Warneck's history went through numerous revisions before the last edition at his death in 1910.

his "short review of former undertakings for the conversion of the heathen" as a case for a continuous mission from the early church to the present.[25] It was with Warneck and Schmidlin that mission emerged as an organizing principle that produced modern mission histories. Central to these histories is an effort to create a sustained genealogy for the concept of mission by classifying the works of Eusebius and Bede as "mission histories" and naming these early historians as forerunners of a "missionary historiography."

Mission as history is a modern phenomenon that arose at the height of the expansion of Protestant missionary efforts and resulted from the need to account for the establishment of Protestant churches in new territories. Until the age of expansion, the history of Christianity was known as church or ecclesial history. With the differentiation of Christianity in Europe from the evangelizing efforts in the rest of the world, one history became two: church history and mission history. The *history of the church* is what happened in the historic places of the faith, such as Europe; the *history of mission* is what occured at the margins, such as India and Japan. Church history and mission history, according to Andrew Walls, "do not just represent different periods, but different *kinds* of history."[26] In other words, the function and nature of mission history is different from that of church history. Each serves a purpose, and one may, at times, contravene or contradict the other. What is evident is that mission history emerged as the need grew to defend and promote Western church expansion.

Because mission history arose from the need to provide justification and explanation for patterns of Western church expansion beyond Europe and to create historical continuity for modern efforts to expand the church, this necessitated that mission be established as a historical phenomenon originating at the beginning of the church and continuing to the present. For mission to offer a credible explanation of Western church expansion during the colonial era, it must evidence roots in Scripture and demonstrate its

---

[25]William Carey, *An Enquiry into the Obligations of Christians to Use Means for the Conversion of the Heathens* (London: Carey Kingsgate, 1961), 14-37. Carey does not identify Patrick, Columba, or Boniface as missionaries, nor does he name their activities as mission (32, 33). He does use mission language for the modern era in reference to Capauchins (34), David Brainerd (36), and the Moravians (37).

[26]Walls, "Structural Problems in Mission Studies," 146. See also Eric J. Sharpe, "Reflections on Missionary Historiography," *International Bulletin of Missionary Research* 13, no. 2 (April 1989): 80.

continuity from the earliest days of Christianity. Mission, historized and used in this way, serves the needs of the Western church in framing a Western narrative of church within Christendom and sanctions its expansion into territories beyond its borders.

And yet, this historicized presentation of history aggregates too many traditions, too many dynamics, and varying kinds of actors into a single category in an attempt to provide continuity and an overreaching, encompassing narrative. Mission history totalizes mission as the defining category. When mission history neatly consolidates the expansion of the church into a single history, simply known as Western, Catholic, or Protestant, it neglects other stories, other histories that were already in existence and expanding. Philip Jenkins's *The Lost History of Christianity* illustrates the extent of the story's diversity and extension. He argues that "for most of its history, Christianity was a tricontinental religion, with powerful representation in Europe, Africa, and Asia, and this was true into the fourteenth century."[27] Alongside the medieval church in Europe, there was "the much wealthier and more sophisticated Eastern world centered in Constantinople. But there was, in addition, a third Christian world, a vast and complex realm that stretched deep into Asia."[28] The rise and fall of these Christian worlds, each with their own political, religious, economic, social, and demographic hues and tones, is greater than mission and wider than mission history. Mission tends to refer to expansion in terms of Christendom assumptions (Europe as the true center of the faith) and privileges the history of the European church over other histories. Mission becomes the simplification of a complex, varied story of Christian expansion into the rest of the world. To represent the expansion of Christianity as mission history is to minimize the rich diversity of traditions and stories, dynamics, and forces of expansion.

From its beginnings, Christian history has in fact been not a single, totalizing history but *histories*. Varying histories tied to the traditions of

---

[27]Philip Jenkins, *The Lost History of Christianity: The Thousand-Year Golden Age of the Church in the Middle East, Africa, and Asia—and How It Died* (New York: HarperOne, 2008), 3.
[28]Ibid., 5. The same point is made by Andrew F. Walls, "Eusebius Tries Again: The Task of Reconceiving and Re-Visioning the Study of Christian History," in *Enlarging the Story: Perspectives on Writing World Christian History*, ed. Wilbert R. Shenk (Maryknoll, NY: Orbis Books, 2002), 8-13; and Samuel H. Moffett, *A History of Christianity in Asia*, vol. 1, *Beginnings to 1500* (Maryknoll, NY: Orbis Books, 1998), 1:4-20.

the Western church, Catholic, Protestant, and Orthodox, have chronicled the extension of their particular church, its doctrine and practices, throughout the world. While distinctions between these traditions are nuanced and appreciated by those within the traditions, those on the receiving end view each particular extension as the whole of the Christian tradition. This is reinforced as agents of each tradition preach and teach their tradition as the true narrative of Christian history.[29] For Schmidlin, mission history is the extension of Catholic traditions, practices, and rites, and thus mission history chronicles the triumph of Catholic theology and practice in new places and over other traditions. While church history is the narrative of the European church with its variances and schisms, mission history is the extension and establishment of each particular church as normative for places and people beyond Christendom. Thus, mission history becomes the means of telling the story of a tradition's expansion into new territories.

An increasing number of historians acknowledge the diversity of Christian expansion and insist that history is more than the extension of particular churches within the Western tradition. History, they insist, must account for a wider, more global history.[30] Paul Kollman notes that the trend toward histories with a global or world perspective reflects a number of shifts; among these is an emphasis on those who appropriated the Christian message locally rather than just those who carried it internationally.[31] According to Kwame Bediako, "Absolutisation of the pattern of Christianity's transmission should consequently be avoided and the nature

---

[29]A. Mathias Mundadan, "The Changing Task of Christian History: A View at the Onset of the Third Millennium," in Shenk, *Enlarging the Story: Perspectives on Writing World Christian History*, notes that "the church got so identified with this medieval cultural expression of the gospel that it was even named 'the Christian era,' 'the Christian civilization,' as if no other expression could be considered" (24). Neill, "History of Missions," admits, "Almost all Church history has been presented exclusively from the western point of view" (152).

[30]See Irvin and Sunquist, *History of the World Christian Movement*; Wilbert R. Shenk, "A Global Church Requires a Global History," *Conrad Grebel Review* 15, nos. 1–2 (December 1997): 3-18; David Chidester, *Christianity: A Global History* (San Francisco: HarperSanFrancisco, 2000); Adrian Hastings, ed., *A World History of Christianity* (Grand Rapids: Eerdmans, 1999); William A. Dyrness, "Listening for Fresh Voices in the History of the Church," in *Teaching Global Theologies: Power & Praxis*, ed. Kwok Pui-Lan, Cecilia González-Andrieu, and Dwight N. Hopkins (Waco, TX: Baylor University Press, 2015), 29-43.

[31]Paul Kollman, "After Church History? Writing the History of Christianity from a Global Perspective," *Horizons* 31, no. 2 (2004): 325.

of Christian history itself be re-examined."[32] And yet, mission history, all too often, offers an uncomplicated history that neglects preexisting cultural, linguistic, political, and religious streams of lived experience and understandings. Mission creates the mistaken illusion that Christianity was established exclusively by outside agents and minimizes the role of the cultural insider. Acknowledgment of local expressions of faith affirms the global dimension of church history, and yet mission history often counters and even negates this wider, more diverse story. Mission history tends to perpetuate the notion that local expressions of faith were illegitimate or inept, and thus missionaries were necessary in order to correct or replace existing faith.

Andrew Walls characterizes the new task for the historian and students of Christian history as reconception of the resources for history and re-visioning of the multitude of processes whereby Christianity became established.[33] Central to this task is the necessity of addressing the assumptions inherent in mission language. For example, mission promotes distinct spatial language of *center* and *periphery* and thereby perpetuates a Christendom view of the world. According to Enrique Dussel, mission history is often "an account of the extension of the evangelizing process from the 'centre,' from the standpoint of the dominant culture."[34] Instead, he advocates a reversal of this kind of process. History should be written from the periphery and represent local issues and narratives rather than distant issues and narratives. Dussel describes the new process as an "emancipation" that will take place as a transition is made from "histories of mission" to "histories of church on the periphery," and gives an account for life and religion prior to the "invasions" from the "centre."[35] For historians such as Walls and Dussel, it is no longer appropriate to frame history as a movement from the Western center of Christianity to the "mission field." The language of *mission field*, *center* and *periphery*, *church* and *mission* are telling reminders of the

---

[32]Kwame Bediako, *Jesus and the Gospel in Africa: History and Experience* (Maryknoll, NY: Orbis Books, 2004), 116.

[33]Walls, "Eusebius Tries Again," 3.

[34]Enrique Dussel, "Toward a History of the Church in the World Periphery," in *Towards a History of the Church in the Third World*, ed. Lukas Vischer (Ecumenical Association of Third World Theologians, Geneva, Switzerland: Evangelische Arbeitsstelle Oekumene Schweiz, 1983), 3:112.

[35]Ibid., 125-30.

persistent nature of Christendom assumptions. Dale Irvin concurs, "European historical identity, . . . what is essentially a tribal theological tradition (variously described as 'the West,' 'Western Christianity,' or 'Christendom') has been universalized and thus has become an idol."[36] Bluntly stated, "The history of Western missions is not the history of the churches in Africa."[37] What Western Christians label as "mission history" sounds a great deal like "colonial history" in the ears of Africans, South Asians, and Latin Americans.[38] Mission history as the expansion of the Western church anticipates that real churches, churches that look and sound like churches in the West, will eventually appear all over the world.[39] Successful mission will result in churches in India and Ethiopia adopting the history of churches in London and Dallas.[40] Once they grow up and are no longer "mission churches," they will be folded into Western church history.

Because Christendom assumptions are hard to reverse, mission history remains in place. And yet, in the new age of world Christianity, the emerging global church is challenging the notion of mission history.[41] As non-Western churches come to prominence and write their own histories, mission history becomes less and less important and may disappear altogether. "African and Asian and Latin American Church history," Andrew Walls reminds us, "is not the same as missionary history; in itself, the missionary movement is a

---

[36]Dale T. Irvin, *Christian Histories, Christian Traditioning: Rendering Accounts* (Maryknoll, NY: Orbis Books, 1998), 4.

[37]Ibid., 76.

[38]See Terence Ranger, "New Approaches to the History of Mission Christianity," in *African Historiography: Essays in Honour of Jacob Ade Ajayi*, ed. Toyin Falola (Ikeja, Nigeria: Longman Nigeria, 1993), 181. For an example of these sentiments from Sri Lanka, see Stephen C. Berkwitz, "Hybridity, Parody, and Contempt: Buddhist Responses to Christian Missions in Sri Lanka," in *Cultural Conversions: Unexpected Consequences of Christian Missionary Encounters in the Middle East, Africa, and South Asia*, ed. Heather J. Sharkey (New York: Syracuse University Press, 2013), 99-120.

[39]Andrew Walls, "Eusebius Tries Again," asserts, "If this is the only lens through which we study Christian history, we have bypassed the story of the whole people of God in favor of clan history" (7).

[40]Richard Fletcher's chapter title, "Mission into Church," in *The Barbarian Conversion*, conveys this sentiment. He writes of "mission-station in a hostile environment," which in time is "turned into a church" (451).

[41]Carlos F. Cardoza-Orlandi and Justo L. González, *To All Nations from All Nations: A History of the Christian Missionary Movement* (Nashville: Abingdon, 2013), affirm the waning days of mission history but believe "for some time it will be necessary to discuss and to write the history of missions as if it were a different field" (9).

product of Western Church history."[42] Mission history matters most as it offers prologue for local histories and critiques the exploits of the Western church. Irvin suggests that rather than locating the history of Korean Christianity within the history of Western mission history, one must now "tell the longer narrative of Korean history, in its full religious and cultural formations."[43] I would add that this is well and good, as long as Koreans are writing this history, from a distinctive Korean perspective. As Christendom assumptions continue to collapse, mission as history will become more of a difficulty and less of a viable voice.[44]

Mission as grand narrative. Narrative is the organization of events and actors in such a manner as to convey chronology and development. Within the creases of narrative lies emplotment. As a literary device, plot arranges complex events and personalities into an accessible and comprehensible story. The historian's task is to integrate these pieces into a story of the whole in order to craft a narrative. Thus, narrative constructs events and actors into a coherent whole that makes sense. While history is discovery of the past, it is equally the artistic emplotment of a narrative.[45]

Stephen Neill and K. S. Latourette weave personalities and events into stories of the expansion of Christian faith and tradition in Europe. In their narratives, Western missionaries are the carriers of this tradition to the rest of the world. Emplotment for Neill and Latourette's histories lies in the narration of faith radiating from its origin. In this narrative, they chronicle Christianity's progression from place to place, culture to culture, and language to language. The success of Christianity, according to Neill, is due to the fact that it "alone has succeeded in making itself a universal religion."[46]

---

[42]Andrew F. Walls, "The Eighteenth-Century Protestant Missionary Awakening in Its European Context," in *Christian Missions and the Enlightenment*, ed. Brian Stanley, Studies in the History of Christian Missions (Grand Rapids: Eerdmans, 2001), 23.

[43]Irvin, *Christian Histories, Christian Traditioning*, 133.

[44]Lamin Sanneh, "World Christianity and the New Historiography: History and Global Interconnections," in *Enlarging the Story: Perspectives on Writing World Christian History*, ed. Wilbert R. Shenk (Maryknoll, NY: Orbis Books, 2002), maintains that we cannot "emphasize enough the scale of the crisis we face in the standard historiography of mission and world Christianity" (98).

[45]Regarding whether history is science or literature, see James G. Crossley, "Defining History," in *Writing History, Constructing Religion*, ed. James G. Crossley and Christian Karner (Aldershot, UK: Ashgate, 2005), 13-17.

[46]*HCM*, 4.

The language of "universal religion" communicates a centered and uniform religious system that eventually triumphs, as it moves from a provincial faith to the faith of the empire and eventually to a universal religion. Emplotment, for Neill, is the spread of bishoprics and churches outward in an ever-increasing expansion. Latourette opens his seven-volume history with a similar narrative objective. "Geographically," Latourette asserts, Christianity "has spread more widely than any other religion in all the millenniums of mankind's long history." Because Christianity has penetrated every environment, "the story must include the spread of Christianity into all the people and regions where it has had adherents."[47] Narrative, for Neill and Latourette, functions as it does for any historian, except mission is the narrative.

Mission provides Neill and Latourette with more than a narrative structure for history. Mission *is* narrative. Mission *is* plot. And thus, it is the scheme that forms events and characters into a narrative of breakthroughs and expansion. Stephen Neill's intent is more than just to present "an arid catalogue of dates, events, and names." Such chronicling of massive amounts of data does not produce a narrative. Instead, Neill determines to keep before his eyes "the main lines of Christian advance" in the hopes of "conveying to the reader a sense of movement, not always movement in a straight line of progress, often aberrant, sometimes retarded or diverted, at times seeming to come altogether to a standstill, but always in the end acquiring new impetus and so leading to the point in history at which we now find ourselves."[48] Neill emplots and argues the story of movement as mission. The events and characters Neill selects, the distinct interconnectedness he produces, and the pieces he pursues become a particular expression of movement called "mission," and thus he presents a mission narrative.

The storyline of the advance of mission toward triumph can proceed by way of a number of plot variations. James Addison's *The Medieval Missionary* (1936) appraises various social, moral, and religious forces between the years 500 and 1300. While each of these contributes to the conversion of northern Europe, central to his account of the spread of Christianity is the missionary. With the missionary as the central character, Addison constructs a narrative of the heroic figure that conquers language,

[47] *HEC*, 1:ix.
[48] *HCM*, 9.

culture, and religions. Over and over, Addison brings the missionary to center stage, as he highlights the "education and motives of medieval missionaries," the relationship between "kings and missionaries," and the "missionary message" of the medieval missionary.[49] As actor and agent, the missionary provides a protagonist for the plot and advances the storyline. For Addison, the story of the conversion of northern Europe turns on the missionary. As the missionary acts, Christianity advances and the narrative moves to its conclusion. Among the actors in the narrative Addison constructs is Columba, whom Addison describes as a "missionary organizer" and "ascetic missionary" involved in "foreign missionary work."[50] Columba's expertise of organization and devotion to the task provides plot or force for the narrative. Columba, the missionary, serves as the figure of competence, professionalism, and expertise. The same force is seen in Addison's use of *missionary* as an adjective that distinguishes and elevates activities and qualities to a special status and thus make these plot worthy: missionary career, missionary work, missionary labor, missionary motive, missionary expedition, missionary ardor, missionary leaders, missionary efforts, the missionary cause, missionary journey, missionary role, missionary center, missionary advance, missionary agency, missionary seminary, missionary cause, missionary enthusiasm, missionary progress, missionary preaching, and missionary message.[51] Connected activities and motives with qualities and functions essential to the missionaries and for the mission are the defining elements of the narrative. For Addison, the plot of Christian expansion centers on persons and activities that are named as missionary.

Stephen Bevans and Roger Schroeder, in *Constants in Context: A Theology of Mission for Today* (2004), offer narrative case studies that represent "historical models of mission."[52] Their aim is to demonstrate the constants of the church's one mission narrative throughout various historical contexts.

---

[49]James Thayer Addison, *The Medieval Missionary: A Study of the Conversion of Northern Europe, A.D. 500–1300*, Studies in the World Mission of Christianity 2 (New York: International Missionary Council, 1936), 1-3.

[50]Ibid., 4. See also 44.

[51]Ibid., 8, 9, 12, 13, 15, 18, 20, 25, 30, 32, 42, 44, 47, 53, 54, 55, 59, 70, 75, 82, 88, 89, 91, 93, 97, 99, 101, 104, 106, 107, 129, 132, 136, 140, 141.

[52]Bevans and Schroeder, *Constants in Context*, 73.

Mission and missionaries are central to these models and form the framework from which they interpret history. For Bevans and Schroeder, mission carries the narrative, and missionaries are the agents of Christian expansion encountered in each context. Thus, mission and missionaries are the "constants in context."

All of this may be well and good, as there will be and must be plot to any narrative. A particular plot must be chosen and then preferenced. And yet, mission does more than provide a storyline for historical narratives. Mission is the understructure of style and consciousness and thus a regulating ideology. Histories, according to Hayden White, ultimately represent the ascetic or moral preferences of the historian.[53] The historian takes the "primitive elements" of history and arranges these into stories embedded with their ideology or consciousness. White explains that behind the historian's "modes of emplotment" and "modes of argument" there exists "an irreducible ideological component" that defines or determines the implications to be drawn from history.[54] Hence, White asserts, "Commitment to a particular *form* of knowledge predetermines the *kinds* of generalizations one can make about the present world, the kinds of knowledge one can have of it, and hence the kinds of projects one can legitimately conceive for changing that present or for maintaining it in its present form indefinitely."[55] Emplotment, argumentation, and ideology combine to create a unique "historiographical style" that ultimately produces a particular history.[56] This mixture is what gives a history its specific

---

[53]Hayden V. White, *Metahistory: The Historical Imagination in Nineteenth-Century Europe* (Baltimore: Johns Hopkins University Press, 1973); White, *The Content of the Form: Narrative Discourse and Historical Representation* (Baltimore: Johns Hopkins University Press, 1990). For a critical examination of White's theory and method, see David M. Hammond, "Hayden White: Meaning and Truth in History," *Philosophy & Theology* 8, no. 4 (June 1994): 291-307.

[54]Modes of emplotment, as defined by White, allow us to characterize the historian's processes and operations of structuring story and providing history with meaning. At another level, the historian argues the relationship of events, causes, conditions, and conclusions. The modes of argument (formist, organicist, mechanistic, and contextualist) are White's explanations of the relationship between historical units or entities that provide an answer to the question of what was the point of what happened. Modes of argument are different ways of applying "universal causal laws" in order to explain the relationship of a given sequence of events. Argumentation is what causes one historian to interpret a set of events in a particular way and another historian to come to a different conclusion. See White's discussion of modes of argument in *Metahistory*, 11-21.

[55]Ibid., 21.

[56]Ibid., 29.

style and attributes. Thus, the historian does not just begin with the data, but he or she "must first *prefigure* the field—that is to say, constitute it as an object of mental perception."[57]

As prefigurative act, the historical account is formed in the consciousness of the historian and, once written, becomes poetic expression. White explains that history is "poetic insofar as this is constitutive of the structure that will subsequently be imaged in the verbal model offered by the historian as a representation and explanation of 'what *really* happened' in the past."[58] History as poetic expression means historical consciousness ultimately takes shape in the form of language. Building on ideas from structuralist Claude Lévi-Strauss and Giambattista Vico's notion of "master tropes,"[59] White explains the manner in which language forms "the deep structure of historical imagination."[60] Written history is the linguistic expression of consciousness or vision formed within the imagination. Tropes convey this consciousness via figures of speech and association between concepts, and tropes create "connection between things so that they can be expressed in a language that takes account of the possibility of their being expressed otherwise."[61]

Neill and Latourette employ *mission* as a trope of both an expressed and figurative ideology. As trope, mission represents or symbolizes the "deep structure" of the whole, and thus it is the integrative symbol of their narratives. Events, actions, and actors of mission history are to be read as poetic, prefigurative representations, and thus parts of the mission trope. As trope, mission infuses events and actors with a consciousness that presents history as an ideology. More than a mere subject of historical enquiry, mission as trope guides and constructs the entire narrative.

---

[57] Ibid., 30.
[58] Ibid., 31.
[59] In a rather long footnote, ibid., 31-33, White details these and other influences.
[60] Ibid., 38.
[61] White, *Tropics of Discourse*, uses a fourfold conception of tropes (metaphor, metonymy, synecdoche, and irony) to characterize stylistic expressions of thought that become figurative discourse. In the case of nineteenth-century master historians, White sees tropes as a way to demonstrate the progression, interaction, and reaction within and between their modes of thought. White concludes that "a given historian will be inclined to choose one or another of the different modes of explanation, on the level of argument, emplotment, or ideological implication, in response to the imperatives of the trope which informs the linguistic protocol he has used to prefigure the field of historical occurrence singled out by him for investigation" (2).

The mission narrative is not the sole narrative at the historian's disposal—
it is a choice. Even a casual reading of various histories reveals that mission
is not the only choice, as other compelling tropes exist. Historians from
varied viewpoints have written capable histories of Christianity from vantage
points other than mission. For example, Robert Bartlett in *The Making of
Europe* argues that the plot for the expansion of the faith is Latin Christianity.[62]
The thrust of the faith is unity in and obedience to the Roman see and thus
papal authority. Christianity meant Latin Christianity, and the faith of
Christian peoples (*populus christianus*) defined with increasing coherence
identity for the Western European people. Eventually the line of identity
drawn between Christian and pagan becomes the line between Latin Christianity and everyone else. Rather than mission being the "deep structure" for
the establishment of the Christian faith within Europe and beyond, the story
line is the growing Latin Christian identity both of those in the faith and
those to whom it expanded. To the Irish, Patrick was a Roman Christian—
not a missionary. In the eyes of the pagan Friesians, Boniface was a representative of Rome-centric Christianity—not a missionary. Though they
preached and taught the tenets of the faith, they above all represented the
cultural identity known as "Latin Christian" and a territorial designation
that becomes known as "Christendom" (*Christianitas*). Thus, expansion of
the faith was in an essential way the encounter between heathendom (*pa-
ganismus*) and Christendom, the encounter of "one quasi-ethnic territorial
entity" with others.[63] What mission historians and missiologists have identified as missionaries are for Bartlett diffusers of the Roman *brand* of Christianity over against other brands of Christianity or non-Christian ethnic
identities. "The future cultural shape of Europe," according to Bartlett, "was
determined as one king or people chose Rome, another the Greek Church.
The Russians chose east, the Poles and Magyars west."[64] For Bartlett,
Christian identity is the defining narrative of choice. Yet when the historian
selects ideas or actors and forms the narrative framework on another trope,
history becomes history of another type.

---

[62]Robert Bartlett, *The Making of Europe: Conquest, Colonization and Cultural Change, 950–1350*
(Princeton, NJ: Princeton University Press, 1993), 250-55.
[63]Ibid., 253.
[64]Ibid., 255.

In its assertion as the sole narrative of history, mission claims the role of grand narrative. When driven by ideology in a totalizing manner, objectivity is compromised, and history becomes argument for the mission narrative. It turns into more than a simple narrative but is one that is all encompassing and seeks to justify a specific agenda.[65] Thus, as a grand narrative alongside other grand narratives, the mission narrative competes for dominance. The narrative of mission contends with the narratives of Rome, the medieval Catholic church, Reformation Europe, Western Enlightenment, and American western expansion. Those who write history from the mission narrative tend to view it as the superior narrative that surpasses competing narratives. Dale Irvin warns that narrative, if

> left unexamined, . . . functions as a working mythology (often behind the scenes) shaping methods and content of other theological disciplines such as systematics, preaching, ethics, pastoral care, or biblical studies. Left uncriticized, it functions as a working ideology, reasserting the dominance of the North Atlantic world and European modes of knowledge/power.[66]

The same is true of the mission narrative. It is not immune to the same tendencies. If unexamined and uncriticized, it will function as working mythology/ideology that shapes events and agents into its grand narrative. To contend for its place among other narratives, the mission narrative must assert its dominance over competing narratives.

And yet, the expansion of Christian faith is not one grand narrative. From its beginning, expansion has been a confluence of multifaceted narratives. These chronicle in unique ways the birth of the Christian faith in the Middle East and its rapid establishment in the surrounding cultures and languages.[67] Such a confluence is even seen at Pentecost. We read of "Jews

---

[65]The distinction between grand and master narratives is explored by Allan Megill, "Grand Narrative and the Discipline of History," in *A New Philosophy of History*, ed. Frank Ankersmit and Hans Kellner (Chicago: University of Chicago Press, 1995), 151-73. Jeffrey Cox and Shelton Stromquist, "Introduction: Master Narratives and Social History," in *Contesting the Master Narrative: Essays in Social History*, ed. Jeffrey Cox and Shelton Stromquist (Iowa City: University of Iowa Press, 1998), explain that for Megill "a master narrative is a big story that makes smaller stories intelligible. Because it is a master narrative, it is often partly hidden, lying in the background, to be deployed selectively by the historian. For Megill, a master narrative is more limited than a 'grand narrative,' which is the 'whole story' as told by the objective historian, or by God" (15n33).

[66]Irvin, *Christian Histories, Christian Traditioning*, 88.

[67]See ibid., 107.

living in Jerusalem, devout men from every nation under heaven," gathering as "Parthians and Medes and Elamites, and residents of Mesopotamia, Judea and Cappadocia, Pontus and Asia, Phrygia and Pamphylia, Egypt and the districts of Libya around Cyrene, and visitors from Rome, both Jews and proselytes, Cretans and Arabs" (Acts 2:5, 9-11). The Christian faith, from its beginning, was a diverse narrative. The vitality and rich history of the church in places beyond the Latin West, such as Persia, North Africa, Egypt, Ethiopia, and India, prior to AD 1000 counters the claims that there was one governing plot from which the Christian faith expanded. Christian faith was polycentric from its beginning, and the faith radiated not from one narrative and in one direction, but from many directions and many locales, languages, and expressions. According to Peter Brown, "Europe was only the westernmost variant of a far wider Christian world, whose center of gravity lay, rather, in the eastern Mediterranean and in the Middle East."[68] More than a mission from a central point, the faith was, in fact, a multidirectional movement. Dale Irvin notes that Greco-Roman civilization was not European, and one cannot even speak of Europe as an entity until Charlemagne in the ninth century. "One is even historically hardpressed to locate such a unified civilization called Europe prior to the modern period."[69]

The net result is that the mission narrative located in the expansion of Catholic European Christianity relativizes local expressions of faith to the point that the mission narrative becomes historical Christianity's defining identity. Christianity as "universal religion" or a Roman-centric faith communicates that those who become Christian must find themselves compressed into or formed by this one narrative. And while mission communicates the universalization of Christianity as a religion, the Christian faith itself resists such compression, as it has morphed or translated itself into local languages, identities, and narratives. Mission as grand narrative denigrates localized faith narratives and disregards the vibrant translatability of the Christian faith.

---

[68]Brown, *Rise of Western Christendom*, 2. According to Dale Irvin, *Christian Histories, Christian Traditioning*, "What we see at the beginning of the sixth century of the common era is not a Christendom flowing through the twin streams of Greek and Latin traditions, but Christendom which is already embodied in multiple trajectories of tradition" (115).

[69]Irvin, *Christian Histories, Christian Traditioning*, 119.

Rhetorical Confusion

Mission language enables the construction of a particular kind of history called "mission history" and a single narrative known as the "mission narrative," and yet, to produce this history and narrative, mission must be the defining trope. And yet there are assumptions, constructions, emplotment, and voices foreign to Patrick and Boniface, Bede and Eusebius—presuppositions that invade their letters, sermons, actions, and personal identities. The result is a quagmire of contested narratives and conflicted understandings of history. This confusion creates a number of rhetorical dynamics.

Generalized language. Because *mission* has multiple meanings and uses, it creates problems in comprehension. As illustrated in the introduction, one of the problems with *mission* and *missionary* is the breadth of meanings and uses for both words, and as the present chapter demonstrates, confusion is especially pronounced in mission histories. One wonders whether the mission language of the histories of Youngman and Bainton, for example, refers to call, vocation, profession, church planting, evangelism, development, social concerns, the nature of the local church, the work of the church universal, God's activity in Christ, or God's overall, general purpose. The reader does not know how mission is being used, nor has the reader been instructed in how narrow or wide to read mission. So, the reader's experience, education, prejudices, and preferences ultimately determine how mission is understood. One might exclaim, "Well, that is just the nature of language. Difficulty of meaning cannot be avoided." And another must retort, "Yes, that is the challenge of language. Because words convey meaning, their use must be coherent and clear instead of general and broad." Indeed, precision in word usage and meaning is paramount. Generalization, on the other hand, causes all kinds of confusion.

Ramsey MacMullen identifies generalization as a chief cause of historical distortion. What one knows of a phenomenon, idea, or activity at the current time does not necessarily correspond with what the phenomenon, idea, or activity was for those of another time. Distortion arises when a generalization is made from now to all contexts and for all times. MacMullen insists, "The historical conclusion must be shown to arise out of the minds of the people being studied, not out of generalizing."[70] So, what appears to be Neill's specific use of mission, Gregory's sending of Augustine, is generalized to all contexts and for all times. Generalizing from Gregory to the now and from now to Gregory creates all kinds of distortions.

The rhetoric of mission provides ample opportunity for historians and readers alike to generalize mission in such a way so as "to slip into romantic error."[71] Generalized language crowds a bewildering array of initiatives, activities, and actors into a single category. This relocates and misrepresents the actions and intents of individuals and movements. Mission language becomes a way of absorbing parts into a whole. A telling example of this kind of generalizing absorption is Adrian Hastings's assessment of the period from AD 150 to 500. Beginning with Patrick and ending with Boniface, Hastings's summation is that the "missionary centre of Western Church" is established in the western islands of Britain and Ireland.[72] *Missionary* allows Hastings to offer an inexact, broad conclusion that crowds all manner of activities into a single category and thereby asserts a particular (idealized) narrative about the progress of Western Christianity. Mission as generalized language fails to distinguish between a range of ideas and phenomena, does not offer qualification or specification, but compresses these into a convenient category. As generalized language, mission offers a neat, compressed narrative.

Etic language. Mission language also confuses, because it is etic in orientation and thus asserts an outsider's perspective.[73] An emic orientation, on the other hand, offers an "insider" view from those who are participants in events or presents the perception of immediate eyewitnesses. Because the

---

[70]Ramsay MacMullen, *Christianizing the Roman Empire: (A.D. 100–400)* (New Haven, CT: Yale University Press, 1984), 8. MacMullen concludes the section on his approach to early church history with the admonition that "the adhesion to the church that turned it into a dominant institution is to be traced and understood as much as possible from the ancient evidence, and with the least possible coloring imported from other worlds" (9). Though MacMullen admits that missionaries are not mentioned in the literature of the first four centuries (111), he does what he warns others not to do by importing *mission* and *missionary* into accounts of the growth and expansion of the early church (34, 59, 83, 106).

[71]Brown, *Rise of Western Christendom*, 30.

[72]Adrian Hastings, "150–500," in *A World History of Christianity*, ed. Adrian Hastings (Grand Rapids: Eerdmans, 1999), 64.

[73]My use of *etic* and *emic* is borrowed from the field of linguistics and cultural anthropology in order to contrast perspectives of insiders and outsiders. See Louis J. Luzbetak, *The Church and Cultures: New Perspectives in Missiological Anthropology*, American Society of Missiology Series 12 (Maryknoll, NY: Orbis Books, 1988), 150.

etic perspective is an outsider's look at events, persons, and entities, it can at best be reinterpretation or restatement.

Mission is not the language of insiders, such as Patrick, Columba, Boniface, or Gregory, and thus it is etic. Their emic language is quite different. Because mission language is not emic language, except for moderns, it skews the historical narrative and presents an abridged or anachronistically mediated and thus often erroneous version of the church's expansion. When an attempt is made to compress insider and outsider perspectives into one uncomplicated and uncritical history, the etic will trump the emic. While mission language may facilitate an easier grasp of events and persons by giving the reader an easy-to-grasp linguistic handle, it disregards the emic perspective of actors and eyewitnesses and thus does not offer an insider explanation of events or an accurate identification of persons. A faithful account of why, when, and through whom the church expanded requires a preference for the perspective of those nearest the events. And yet, the emic must be more than acknowledged. It must be heard and preferred. When the historian favors the emic perspective, richer and fuller descriptions of events and people rather than shorthand explanations will follow.

Inflated language. Mission language confuses, because it says more than it should. Mission inflates the intent of actors and the meaning for events beyond their original purpose. Thus, what Eusebius meant by preaching swells when rendered as mission preaching. Columba's encounters with the Picts balloon in meaning when turned into missionary journeys.

Mission language often highlights what should remain hidden and hides what should be brought to light. People and movements that should remain in the shadows are brought to center stage, and characters that could be prominent remain at the margins of the narrative. When mission controls the narrative, outliers and misfits step into the roles of hero and missionary, when quite possibly they are only outliers and misfits. Mission has the power to pull certain kings and queens, diplomats and explorers, to the center, and to push droughts, migrations, plagues, and birthrates to the margins of the story.

In many cases, persons classified as missionary are *pereginantes* (wanders). These are religious individuals outside the mainstream of the convent, monastery, or established ministries of the church who move to the margins for various reasons. They are often considered to be malcontents or oddities in their home societies and thus are exiled or have to flee, transporting faith as they travel. To force them into the mainstream of history may be to misidentify them and distort their unique voice. Protests against civil religion and the Roman church, quests for personal holiness and salvation, forces of plagues and droughts are often underestimated or lost in the language of mission. Structures, organizations, journeys, relationships, and encounters are overrated or misconstrued when encased in the language of mission. To identify Patrick as a "distinguished missionary" and Dominicans as the "first 'missionary society' in history" repurposes who they were and what they contributed, all for the sake of the mission narrative.[74]

Modern rhetoric. As we shall see in the next section, *mission* and *missionary* do not come into use to describe the church's encounter with the world until Ignatius and the Jesuits, and thus both are modern, rhetorical innovations that provide proper and accurate interpretation of events and individuals only when used for the modern era. Only in modern times does *mission* as a description of the expansion of the Christian faith and *missionary* as agents of that expansion appear in sermons, letters, publications, and firsthand accounts. When this shift in rhetoric goes unacknowledged, these words are misplaced in chronology and out of sequence in use and meaning. They become incongruous and thus anachronistic.

Premodern monks, abbots, pilgrims, priests, and popes do not reference mission as their activity, nor do they self-describe as missionaries. So should we put these words in their mouths, impose these foreign words on them, or force their varied activities into the mission category? There does not seem to be ample reason for the use of *mission* and *missionary* in premodern histories. When the shift in rhetoric is not respected and a backward application of mission is made to Scripture, the early church, and medieval history, errors in judgment, interpretation, and application follow.

---

[74]*HEC*, 1:216; Jacques A. Blocher and Jacques Blandenier, *The Evangelization of the World: A History of Christian Mission* (Pasadena, CA: William Carey Library, 2013), 116.

Protest against mission language is more than an exercise in splitting hairs, accusations of imprecise and anachronistic use of words, or a rant about compromise with colonialism. Its importance lies in correctly defining the shifts that have taken place and in recognizing mission language as an important hinge on which these shifts turn. By reading *mission* and *missionary* into the ancient narrative, the shift in rhetoric, as well as changes in how the church-world encounter has occurred, is lost. Without this recognition, we misidentify the forces at work in the ancient context, as well as those of modernity.

TAINTED RHETORIC

The issues of the language of mission identified in these first four chapters are only symptomatic of a more substantial problem. Difficulties with mission as a retrospective, constructed interpretive device are considerable, but they do necessarily in themselves warrant a shift away from mission language. Partisans and Apologists will assert that there is little reason to disqualify mission just because it cannot be found in Scripture or the early history of the church. And I agree. The present-day concepts of mission and missionary, they insist, ably describe the phenomenon and agents found in Scripture and church history. Partisans and Apologists maintain that many words essential to the church and in wide use today cannot be found in Scripture or the early church. And they are correct. The chief example, of course, is *Trinity*. Invented by Tertullian, the actual word *Trinity* (*Trinitas*) is not found in Scripture but becomes the normative term to describe the pattern of divine activity and person found throughout Scripture.[75] Similarly, *mission*, Partisans and Apologists argue, is a distinctive term that emerged as an expression of biblical ideas and a signal of the action of God and the early church. They claim that if *mission* is disqualified as extrabiblical language, then *Trinity* as well must be disqualified.

Yet, while *mission* and *Trinity* might at first glance seem to be an appropriate comparison, they are not. The histories of the two words are quite different. *Trinity* entered Christian vocabulary quite early in Christian

---

[75]See Alister E. McGrath, *Christian Theology: An Introduction*, 3rd ed. (Oxford: Blackwell, 2001), 321-22.

history out of the necessity to describe the complexities of "three persons, one substance," while *mission*, in its current use, emerged much later, at the beginning of the modern era. More important than these chronologies are the circumstances from which mission language develops and the assumptions it bears. The retrospective reading of mission into Scripture and history as described in these first four chapters presents difficulties, but these are not *the* critical problem. These are symptoms that point to a more serious malady. The decisive issue is not an anachronistic reading of mission into Scripture and history but the mentality, worldview, or framework this reading imposes. The assumptions present in trinitarian language have been the subject of theological debate and councils throughout the centuries. And thus, the Trinity has been continually refined and reaffirmed but determined to be helpful, even necessary, for the church. My contention is that mission has been revised and reaffirmed without sufficient examination of its origins and assumptions. My intention in the following chapters is to move beyond the symptoms mission presents to a diagnosis of the source and cause of its problem.

A simple analogy may help to illustrate the mission condition and what I hope to accomplish. If the water that comes from the tap in my house tastes and smells bad, I am going to assume that something is wrong with the water. I will either ask people in my city responsible for water safety to remedy the problem, or I will call a plumber to inspect the pipes in my house. If a city official or a plumber, without inspecting the source of the water or the pipes, simply told me to put an additive in the water or put a filter on the tap to improve the taste and eliminate the smell, I would be less than satisfied. While an additive and a filter may remedy the symptom, I would not be convinced the cause of the taste and smell had been adequately addressed. I would want a full and thorough investigation. Quite possibly, petrol or diesel has made its way into the water system. If the taste is metallic, then quite possibly lead from old pipes is contaminating the water. Or if there is a strong sulfurous smell, there could possibly be chemicals or human waste in the water. My ultimate concern is not how the water looks, smells, or tastes. I want to ensure that my water is not compromised and the health of my family is not at risk. In the pages that follow, I am asking whether mission merely requires revision and rehabilitation (additives and filters), or whether in fact the language is is contaminated and therefore less than fit to drink. While I have hinted at this greater problem several times in the discussion to this point, it is now time to trace the emergence of "mission" as both a conceptual framework and modern tradition, and to explore the difficulties in its origins and development as a modern term.

I I

Innovating
mis·sion

If the language of mission is not found in Scripture or in the language of the early church, then from where is it derived and when does it come into use? How did *mission* and *missionary* become descriptors of the expansion of Christianity? And how did the ideas and beliefs contained in this language shape what became the modern mission movement?

Examination of these questions begins with language that describes the church's interaction with the world beyond Europe and the expansion of Christianity during the Middle Ages. *Exile, sojourner,* and *pilgrim* are among these terms, ancient notions from the days of Israel and the New Testament era. Mission language eventually emerged from pilgrim language, and yet, this happened incrementally as pilgrimage was co-opted and then shaped for political ends and territorial conquest. Our examination of this process begins with Pope Urban II's sermon in a field outside Clermont, France, and culminates with vows by Ignatius of Loyola and his companions in a chapel at the outskirts of Paris.

5

Holy Conquest

Whoever therefore shall carry out this holy pilgrimage
shall make a vow to God, and shall offer himself as a living
sacrifice . . . and he shall display the sign of the cross
of the Lord on his front or on his chest. When, truly, he
wishes to return from there having fulfilled his vow, let
him place the cross between his shoulders; in fact, by
this twofold action they will fulfill that precept of the
Lord which he prescribed himself through the Gospel.

EYEWITNESS REPORT OF POPE URBAN II'S WORDS
AT CLERMONT, NOVEMBER 1095

Inside [Jerusalem], our pilgrims chased after and killed
Saracens right up to the Temple of Solomon, where they
gathered and where they fought furiously against our men
the whole day, until their blood ran throughout the temple.

ANONYMOUS CHRONICLER OF THE SIEGE OF JERUSALEM IN *GESTA FRANCORUM*

THE GENERAL OPINION is that those living in Catholic Europe during
the Middle Ages responded to those outside Christendom in one of two
ways.[1] On one side was Christendom's violent assault on Muslims and Jews,
known as the *Crusades*, and on the other was the expansion of the Christian
religion by way of preaching and charity, known as *mission*. Often these two,

---

[1] I am following Benjamin Kedar in my use of "Catholic Europe"; *Crusade and Mission: European Approaches Toward the Muslims* (Princeton, NJ: Princeton University Press, 1984), xii.

crusade and mission, are characterized as polar opposites, each with a different aim, method, and end, and yet existing alongside each other. However, the language of the age reveals not two approaches expressed in these two terms but a multitude of approaches with a variety of means and outcomes and known by a wide range of terms. Chief among these is the language of *pilgrim* and *pilgrimage*. While pilgrim language traditionally described those who moved voluntarily beyond the bounds of Christendom, it was co-opted by the Latin church to mobilize Catholic Europe to march on Jerusalem. In this shift, pilgrimage evolved from an inward and peaceful disposition of movement and alienation to one that was outward and militant. The aim of this new kind of pilgrimage was the capture of Jerusalem and the establishment of enclaves of Latin Christianity in the Levant. Pilgrimage became the language of utility to propel Catholic Europe toward the world beyond Europe, and it was the soil from which mission eventually emerged. This connection of language is often made in a general manner, but the causes for this connection are not specified. My contention is that an understanding of the evolution and eventual emergence of mission begins with questions regarding how pilgrimage served the crusading endeavor, how the Crusades modified pilgrimage, and what resulted from these changes. This examination begins with a papal summons in 1095.

URBAN'S SUMMONS

In November 1095, Pope Urban II (1042–1099) assembled the council of bishops at the city of Clermont in the French Auvergne. During the assembly, he preached one of the better-known sermons in history, in which he called on bishops and laypeople throughout Catholic Europe to march on the Holy Land.[2] The exact content of his sermon is not known, but eyewitnesses report that his principal message was a summons to liberate Jerusalem from the control of Muslims and to rescue Christians in the East. Urban's grand cause was to take up the cross, battle against the Saracens, and conquer

---

[2]Penny Cole compares and contrasts various versions of Urban's sermon in *The Preaching of the Crusades to the Holy Land, 1095–1270*, Medieval Academy Books 98 (Cambridge, MA: The Medieval Academy of America, 1991), 1-36. J. Riley-Smith, *The Crusades: A Short History* (New Haven, CT: Yale University Press, 1987), 10, names Urban II as the "originator" of the Crusades but emphasizes that all the elements of crusade were already present prior to his sermon, having been established by previous popes.

Jerusalem.[3] According to reports, those present responded with shouts of *Deus lo volt*—"God will it" or "God wants this." Would-be Crusaders then cut pieces from their garments in the shape of a cross and attached these to their shoulders, signifying that they accepted the cause to liberate Jerusalem and were thus following the injunction of Jesus Christ to take up their cross and follow him (Mt 16:24).[4] From Clermont, Urban toured through the south of France, preaching versions of the same sermon as he made his way back to Rome. He also sent letters along the way to promote the battle for Jerusalem. No matter how one interprets motives or causes for Urban's sermon, the intent of his summons is clear even to this day. He called Catholic Europe to a holy war against an enemy two thousand miles away. His sermon initiated what has come to be known as the First Crusade.

A number of forces and factors prompted Urban's call for a crusade. The most obvious and immediate was a plea from Byzantine Emperor, Alexius I Comnenus (1057–1118), to the pope and his subjects to aid in Constantinople's defense against advancing Turks.[5] The second was the idea of liberating the holy places of the East that had been desecrated or destroyed by "the enemies of Christ." Both aims were couched in the language of holy pilgrimage, words that resonated with and gave cause for rulers, knights, clergy, and ordinary people from across France, Germany, Italy, and England to set out for the Holy Land.

The thought of a pilgrimage to liberate Jerusalem so enthused the populace of Catholic Europe that many set out before the official start of the expedition (August 15, 1096). Bands of pilgrims spontaneously gathered with spouses, children, and belongings and made their way toward Constantinople. Estimates of those who answered Urban's summons range from fifty thousand to 136,000, depending on whether the number represents only

---

[3]It is uncertain whether Urban named Jerusalem as the chief objective in this sermon, but it was certainly named in later sermons and communications. See Hans Eberhard Mayer, *The Crusades*, trans. John Gillingham (London: Oxford University Press, 1972), 11.

[4]As reported in Nirmal Dass, ed., *Deeds of the Franks and Other Jerusalem-Bound Pilgrims: The Earliest Chronicle of the First Crusades* (Lanham, MD: Rowman & Littlefield, 2011), 26. This is a translation of *Gesta Francorum et aliorum Hierosolimitanorum* (the *Gesta*), an anonymous chronicle of the First Crusade.

[5]Alexius did not request a massive intrusion of Western power, personnel, and politics into Byzantium but mercenaries to assist his armies. See Mayer, *Crusades*, 8; Frederic Duncalf, "The Councils of Piacenza and Clermont," in *A History of the Crusades*, vol. 1, *The First Hundred Years*, ed. Marshall W. Baldwin (Madison: The University of Wisconsin Press, 1969), 227-28.

fighting men or also includes noncombatants.[6] One chronicler, Guibert, on seeing the response exclaimed that "the whole of Christendom capable of bearing arms" had taken up the cross.[7]

Not only did hordes of Latin Christians take up the symbol of the cross and set out for Jerusalem, but some actually completed the journey. However, many who set out were not present for the assault on Jerusalem, either because they turned back or they died along the way. At several junctions, the crusading pilgrims were at the brink of disaster, near starvation, bickering and fighting among themselves, or in complete chaos.[8] Those who went the distance were spurred by visions, miracles, and the thought of recovering Christian relics. Within four years of Urban's sermon at Clermont, Turkish forces holding Jerusalem were defeated, a patriarch was installed in the Holy City, conducting the Mass in Latin, and European settlements were established in the Levant.[9] During the two centuries that followed, summonses were made again and again for others to take up the cross, more armies assembled and marched across Europe to the East, and many other battles were fought against the "enemies of Christ."

Holy war was Catholic Europe's mode of encounter with those at its margins and beyond. To war against the enemy was Urban's answer to the threats to Catholic Europe's collective political and religious lives. While holy war may have begun as a defensive measure against perceived aggression, it turned into offensive expansion of the language and institutions

---

[6]Riley-Smith, *Crusades: Short History*, 11; Christopher Tyerman, *Fighting for Christendom: Holy War and the Crusades* (Oxford: Oxford University Press, 2004), puts the number somewhere between fifty thousand and seventy thousand (39) and estimates that 80 percent of those who set out did not survive (147). Cf. Malcolm Barber's discussion of numbers in *The Crusader States* (New Haven, CT: Yale University Press, 2012), 5.

[7]Cited in Duncalf, "The First Crusade: Clermont to Constantinople," in Baldwin, *History of the Crusades*, 1:255.

[8]The march from Constantinople to Antioch and beyond is detailed by Steven Runciman, "The First Crusade: Constantinople to Antioch," in Baldwin, *History of the Crusades*, 1:280-307; and Runciman, "The First Crusade: Antioch to Ascalon," in Baldwin, *History of the Crusades*, 1:308-41. Samuel H. Moffett, *A History of Christianity in Asia*, vol. 1, *Beginnings to 1500* (Maryknoll, NY: Orbis Books, 1998), makes the judgment that the Crusaders' success was not due so much to the great Christian faith, conduct, or unity of the Crusaders but "the greater disunity of the Muslim defenders of the Holy Land" (387).

[9]On the establishment and development of Latin states or colonies in Palestine and Syria, see Harold S. Fink, "The Foundation of the Latin States, 1099-1118," in Baldwin, *History of the Crusades*, 1:368-409. Moffett, *History of Christianity in Asia*, describes the attempts of Latin Christianity to assert itself and the fate of the "native Christians" (1:388-91).

of Christendom. While diplomacy and trade, preaching and charity were part of Catholic Europe's response to those near and far, assault was the primary framework for encounters with outsiders and epitomized Catholic Europe in the eleventh and twelfth centuries. More than making war against the Turks and pagans, holy wars asserted identity, established boundaries, and provided means for dealing with non-Christians. As in earlier periods, the rhetoric of *mission* and *missionary* was not in use to describe this encounter and thus did not inform motives, nor did it provide a framework from which people viewed their task or identity. Instead, pilgrim language resounded in Urban's sermon and was the cause to which Catholic Europe responded. The rhetoric was pilgrimage, and the strategic aim was to retake and defend the holy places of Christianity.

Causes and Consequences

An investigation of extensive detail into the reasons or motivations for the First Crusade is not our purpose, but a survey of some of these provides context for pilgrim language.[10] Historians, sociologists, theologians, psychiatrists, and church leaders offer reasons for holy wars that span an array of perspectives. Most acknowledge that there is not just one cause or one result but a range of causes and a mix of consequences.[11] These fall within a number of categories, with plenty of overlap and interplay.

Among political causes, some stress the shifting balance of power between the papacy and secular authorities. Urban's call for Catholic Europe to retake and defend Jerusalem was an assertion of papal preeminence. By uniting factions within Europe in a common cause against an external threat,

---

[10]The aim of this chapter is not to present a new history of the Crusades or to explore all the reasons for crusading. Nor can the purpose be to offer a chronology of events or catalog of even the main personalities. Rather, I intend to examine one aspect among the many motives and its relationship to mission. Among better-known histories of the Crusades are Mayer, *Crusades*; Jonathan Riley-Smith, *The First Crusade and the Idea of Crusading*, The Middle Ages (Philadelphia: University of Pennsylvania Press, 1986); Duncalf, "Clermont to Constantinople," 253-79; Runciman, "Constantinople to Antioch," 280-307; Jonathan Riley-Smith, ed., *The Oxford History of the Crusades* (Oxford: Oxford University Press, 1999); Christopher Tyerman, *God's War: A New History of the Crusades* (Cambridge, MA: Harvard University Press, 2006); Norman Housley, *Fighting for the Cross: Crusading to the Holy Land* (New Haven, CT: Yale University Press, 2008); Thomas Asbridge, *The Crusades: The Authoritative History of the War for the Holy Land* (New York: HarperCollins, 2010).
[11]See Christopher Tyerman's discussion in *The Invention of the Crusades* (Toronto: University of Toronto Press, 1998), 1-6.

Urban was able to marginalize papal opposition and silence detractors. "From its inception," according to Christopher Tyerman, "crusading represented a practical expression of papal ideology, leadership, and power."[12] Holy war was about power, the power of the papacy to act in a unilateral manner to mobilize both subjects and rulers. As a consequence of crusading, papal authority solidified throughout Europe and was extended to heretical groups on the margins of Latin Christianity. Papal authority was asserted even among Christians in the East and, in a manner, among Jews, Muslims, and pagans.

Others highlight the pursuit of peace within the boundaries of Christendom as the reason for the Crusades. An assault on Jerusalem created common cause among the various factions within Europe and galvanized these into a common identity.[13] A summons to war far away assuaged the warring tendencies of kings and knights and thus promoted peace at home. This motivation was demonstrated in the repeated attempts to control fighting and lawlessness through the "Peace of God" and the "Truce of God" initiatives in the years leading up to Urban's sermon.[14] In these and other initiatives, knights and militias were given specific roles in maintaining the peace and warring for the cause of others. This, in effect, demonstrates that able and willing fighting forces were available, but feuds and rivalries needed be redirected toward a sanctioned cause.[15] The consequence of Urban's summons was the uniting of various factions behind the church's war and under papal leadership.

Others identify the provocations of Islam as the chief cause for the First Crusade.[16] The long history of brutality and conquest of Muslim rulers and forces, particularly as they swept through Syria, North Africa, Persia, Egypt, southern Italy, Spain, and the Holy Land, had come to a head and provoked the West to respond. According to this view, the First Crusade was just the next in a long series of wars that had been going on for some time.[17] The

---

[12]Tyerman, *Fighting for Christendom*, 38.
[13]See Riley-Smith, *Crusades: Short History*, 14-15; Riley-Smith, *Idea of Crusading*, 3-4.
[14]See Carl Erdmann, *The Origin of the Idea of Crusade*, trans. Marshall Baldwin and Walter Goffart (Princeton, NJ: Princeton University Press, 1977), 59-94, for a discussion of the rise and influence of these movements.
[15]Duncalf, "Councils of Piacenza and Clermont," 231, 242-43.
[16]Rodney Stark, *God's Battalions: The Case for the Crusades* (New York: HarperOne, 2009).
[17]Paul Johnson, *A History of Christianity* (New York: Atheneum, 1976), 243.

difference was the level of papal involvement and thus the religious fervor that catalyzed the resolve to act. Mounting grievances and provocations required a weighty response, which Urban's sermon supplied.

Among the more religious causes was the threat to orthodoxy and unity of the Latin church. At an earlier time when the unity of the faith was under threat, Augustine of Hippo's just war (*bellum justum*) theory provided justification for the use of force against those considered outside the bounds of orthodoxy.[18] The aim of Augustine's theory had been to maintain unity of belief and practice within the church. In time, force was justified as a defensive act against those who threatened the faith from the outside. Thus, when an enemy outside Europe threatened the church, holy war offered justification for preemptive attacks.[19] Because Muslims occupied holy sites in the East and were disrupting pilgrimages of Christians to these sites, the faith was under siege. The liberation of fellow Christians and restoration of access to Jerusalem fit within *bellum justum* and justified the pope's call to protect the faith from dilution and fracture.[20] A defense of the faith's purity required an assault on those who threatened orthodoxy and unity.[21]

There were also more personal motivations for holy war. An overwhelming concern of medieval men and women was impending punishment for their sins. This was the worry of kings, abbots, and common folks, but especially troubling for those who had been involved in killing and war, such as knights. The church held the power to absolve people from sin and release them from eternal damnation. Thus, as holy war was presented as a means

---

[18] Augustine, *Concerning the City of God Against the Pagans*, trans. Henry Bettenson (London: Penguin Books, 1984), 19.13-15 (pp. 870-75). For summaries of Augustine's *bellum justum*, see Riley-Smith, *Idea of Crusading*, 5-6, 17; Louise Riley-Smith and Jonathan Riley-Smith, *The Crusades: Idea and Reality, 1095–1274*, Documents of Medieval History 4 (London: Edward Arnold, 1981), 4-6; *TM*, 225-29.

[19] Erdmann, *Idea of Crusade*, is a leading proponent of the "holy war" view. The opposing view can be found in Mayer, *Crusades*, 22.

[20] John Gilchrist, "The Papacy and War Against the 'Saracens,' 795–1216," *The International History Review* 10, no. 2 (May 1988): 174-97, takes issue with the thesis that the Augustinian doctrine of just war forms a basis for the Crusades, citing the fact that the term is not used during this period.

[21] Peter Frankopan, *The First Crusade: The Call from the East* (Cambridge, MA: Belknap Press of Harvard University Press, 2012), 8, 11, maintains that while the roots of the First Crusade were political, the initiative came from the East and not the West. Thus, the Emperor Alexius's appeal catalyzed the West: "Alexios I Komnenous puts in motion the chain of events that introduced the Crusades to the world" (206).

of penance for sins, it became a worthwhile and valued endeavor.[22] Urban characterized liberating Jerusalem as an act of merit toward one's salvation. "He called it a *recta oblatio* (a right kind of sacrifice)," as one observer recounted, "and an act of devotion for the participant's soul."[23] At the time of Urban's sermon, the practice of indulgences was widely accepted by the general populace, though it was not completely worked out and codified into canonical laws by church officials until the thirteenth century.[24] But no matter what canonical law prescribed, the common belief among the populace was that indulgence-earning works authorized and approved by Christ's representative on earth could remove the penalty of their sins. As a result, tens of thousands responded to Urban's summons in hope of remission of sin.

Among personal causes, plundering and looting the property of those they defeated was overtly stated as a prospect. In Baldric's version of the pope's sermon, he reports Urban saying, "The possessions of the enemy will be yours, too, since you will make spoil of his treasures."[25] Thus, Urban sanctioned the seizure of land and property belonging to heretics and infidels. This resulted in devastation of property and killing of people along the route to Constantinople and in the Levant. In their wake, Crusaders left mayhem and destruction. They foraged food and supplies as they passed through towns, attacked local authorities, and massacred scores of Jews or forced them to be baptized.[26] The spirit that enthused the liberation of Jerusalem spilt over into settling vendettas, acting on prejudicial hatred, and looting for personal gain.[27] While Urban's summons to take the cross set

---

[22]"Whoever out of devotion along and not for the acquisition of honor or money will journey to Jerusalem to free the church of God, that journey will count for him in place of all penance [*pro omni penitenta*]." "The Councils of Urban II: Decreta Claromontensia," cited in Giles Constable, "The Place of the Crusader in Medieval Society," *Viator* 29 (January 1998): 387.

[23]Riley-Smith, *Idea of Crusading*, 26.

[24]See Tyerman, *Invention of the Crusades*, 35-36.

[25]Quoted in Duncalf, "Councils of Piacenza and Clermont," 244. See also Runciman, "Antioch to Ascalon," 341.

[26]Riley-Smith, *Idea of Crusading*, 49-55; Duncalf, "Clermont to Constantinople," 263-64.

[27]For the idea of vengeance as motivation in the crusades, see Susanna Throop, "Vengeance and the Crusades," in *Crusades*, ed. Benjamin Z. Kedar and Jonathan Riley-Smith, Society for the Study of the Crusades and the Latin East 5 (Hampshire, UK: Ashgate, 2006), 21-38. Throop demonstrates that vengeance was not just a motive for the laity and was not just a phenomenon of the First Crusade but grew more widespread with each crusade.

thousands on the path toward Jerusalem, he seemingly did not sanitize motives or censure bad behavior.

So, crusading was undertaken for a variety of reasons, resulting in a number of consequences, and yet, the catalyst for these causes was the ancient practice of pilgrimage. The language of *pilgrim* and *pilgrimage* touched a nerve within the psyche of Catholic Europeans that motivated them to leave home and family, expend personal resources, and risk their lives. The vision of pilgrimage is clearly present in Urban's sermon and subsequent letters, papal bulls, and reports, as well as the sermons of those who promoted the Crusades. The designation of *pilgrim* and the rhetoric of *pilgrimage* served as utility for a range of causes and provided primary impetus for the crusading movement. Urban summoned people to make pilgrimage to Jerusalem, and as a result, thousands took up the cross and joined a holy pilgrimage to retake the Holy Land.

Ancient Language

While taking up the cross and setting out for Jerusalem as pilgrims captures the essence of the First Crusade, this was not new language for those who heard Urban's sermon at Clermont. Urban capitalized on an existing practice and used ancient language to rally Latin Christians to leave towns and cities, farms and shops, homes and families to cross Europe and venture to the East. Pilgrimage was the vision into which political, religious, and personal motives converged to mobilize thousands of people from all sectors of life and across the social strata. Other factors may have provided supplemental reasons, but pilgrimage fueled the fervor and passion necessary for such an endeavor.[28]

---

[28]It is generally accepted by historians that a connection of some kind existed between the Crusades and pilgrimages, especially the First Crusade. See, for example, Mayer, *Crusades*, 13-15, 29-32; Tyerman, *Invention of the Crusades*, 20-21; Housley, *Fighting for the Cross*, 4; William J. Purkis, *Crusading Spirituality in the Holy Land and Iberia, c.1095–c.1187* (Woodbridge, UK: Boydell, 2008); Ward and Evans, "Medieval West," 138; E. O. Blake, "The Formation of the 'Crusade Idea,'" *Journal of Ecclesiastical History* 21, no. 1 (January 1970): 12; Riley-Smith, *Idea of Crusading*, 22-25; Hans Küng, *Christianity: Essence, History, and Future*, trans. John Bowden (New York: Continuum, 2003), 399; Jean Leclercq, Dom Francois Vandenbroucke, and Louis Bouyer, *The Spirituality of the Middle Ages*, A History of Christian Spirituality (New York: Desclee, 1968), 130-33. Others, such as Erdmann, *Idea of Crusade*, xxxiii, 301, acknowledge the connection but view it as of little consequence. For an opposing view, see Janus M. Jensen, "Peregrinatio Sive Expedito: Why the First Crusade Was Not a Pilgrimage," *Al-Masaq: Islam and the Medieval Mediterranean* 15, no. 2 (September 2003): 119-37. Jensen argues that Urban II did not describe the First Crusade as a pilgrimage and that holy war was viewed as a separate kind

The practice of pilgrimage to the Holy Sepulchre in Jerusalem, as the supreme act of penance for sins, was familiar language—a progenitor—for what became the Crusades.[29] In fact, the term *crusade* was unknown at the time of Urban's sermon. Not until the thirteenth century were wars to conquer Jerusalem described as *crozeia*, *crozea*, or *crozada*, after the most prominent symbol of its fighters, the cross.[30] The English word *crusade* was supplied only in the eighteenth century. Instead, this new venture was described with words of motion or movement, such as *iter* (journey), *iter in terram sanctam* (journey into the Holy Land), *via* (way), *via Dei* (way of God), *via sancti Sepuchri* (the road to the Holy Sepulchre), *expeditio* (expedition), and *generale passagium* (a general passage).[31] Muslims described those who took the cross with a variety of designations, such as *bellatores* (those who fight), *milites* (knight or soldier), *Hierosolymatani* (travelers to Jerusalem), and *Franj* (Franks). But above all, the movement to rescue the church of the East and retake the Holy City was spoken of in terms of a *peregrinatio* (pilgrimage), and those who responded were designated as *peregrini* (pilgrims).[32] The exact words of Pope Urban's sermon have not

---

of penitential act. Joshua Prawer, *The Latin Kingdom of Jerusalem: European Colonialism in the Middle Ages* (London: Weidenfeld and Nicolson, 1973), insists that "the Crusades did not develop organically out of pilgrimages, although the latter contributed to their formation" (192).

[29] The Holy Sepulchre, dating from the fourth century, was a shrine that enclosed traditional sites of Golgotha and Jesus' tomb. The assessment of Asbridge, *Crusades*, is that "this one shrine encapsulated the very essence of Christianity: the Crucifixion, Redemption, and Resurrection" (90-91).

[30] Tyerman, *Fighting for Christendom*, 29.

[31] See Riley-Smith, *Idea of Crusading*, 17, 108; Tyerman, *Invention of the Crusades*, 50-51; Tyerman, *Fighting for Christendom*, 13; Asbridge, *Crusades*, 40.

[32] Fulcher of Chartres, "Deeds of the Franks on Their Pilgrimage to Jerusalem," in *The First Crusade: The Chronicle of Fulcher of Chartres and Other Source Materials*, ed. Edward Peters (Philadelphia: University of Pennsylvania Press, 1971), is a firsthand account of the Crusades that contains pilgrim language throughout: "pilgrimage" (40, 49, 70), "pilgrimage to Jerusalem" (24), "pilgrims" (28, 32, 35, 39, 49, 65). The same language is observed in other early histories of the First Crusade: Dass, *Deeds of the Franks and Other Jerusalem-Bound Pilgrims*, 35, 36, 78, 83, 89, 90, 96, 97, 100, 104; Ralph of Caen, *The Gesta Tancredi of Ralph of Caen: A History of the Normans on the First Crusade*, ed. Bernard S. Bachrach and David Stewart Bachrach, Crusade Texts in Translation 12 (Burlington, VT: Ashgate, 2005), 19, 103, 124, 128. Similarly, Robert the Monk, "Historia Iherosolimitana," in *Robert the Monk's History of the First Crusade*, trans. Carol Sweetenham, Crusade Texts in Translation (Aldershot, Hants, UK: Ashgate, 2005), employs "pilgrim" (81, 82, 91, 92, 96, 97, 98, 103, 159, 162, 186, 187, 212) and "pilgrimage" (81, 82, 83, 92, 93, 97, 103, 186). The use of *pilgrim* and *pilgrimage* language by early Crusaders is mentioned by Jonathan Riley-Smith, *The First Crusaders, 1095-1131* (Cambridge: Cambridge University Press, 1997), 67; Johnson, *History of Christianity*, 400; Erdmann, *Idea of Crusade*, xv; Geoffrey Hindley, *The Crusades: A History of*

survived, but those present report that his call for a holy war was encased in the ancient language of pilgrimage.[33]

The basic meaning of *peregrinus*, dating back to the time of Cicero, carries the idea of being foreign or alien.[34] Thus, those who go on a pilgrimage are strangers who take up a journey to a foreign place.[35] Pilgrims of the religious sort are not mere wanderers or travelers, but they make pilgrimage with the purpose and intent to gain merit through acts of privation and prayers and to worship at sacred sites.

Pilgrimage activity is central to the Judeo-Christian tradition. The Hebrew Scriptures recount Abram setting out from his homeland and family to a new land (Gen 12:1-3) and traveling to a sacred site to make sacrifice (Gen 22). The Israelites sojourn in the Sinai on their way to the Promised Land, and in their Babylonian Exile, they long for their return to Jerusalem. These Jewish roots are background for the Christian tradition of journeying into foreign lands and to sacred places. Luke writes of pilgrimage at the outset of the Christian church, as devout Jewish men and women from various nations traveled to Jerusalem for the Feast of Pentecost (Acts 2:5-11). Peter describes the existence of early Christians as aliens and strangers or sojourners (1 Pet 1:1; 2:11), as does the writer of Hebrews. Those who exhibit faith are "strangers and exiles on the earth" (Heb 11:13). They "are seeking . . . a country of their own. . . . They desire a better country, that is, a heavenly

---

Armed Pilgrimage and Holy War (London: Constable & Robinson, 2003), 1; Mayer, *Crusades*, 15; Jessalynn Bird, "Crusades," in *Encyclopedia of Medieval Pilgrimage* (Leiden: Brill, 2010), 142.

[33] According to Riley-Smith, *Crusades: Idea and Reality*, "The First Crusade certainly was a pilgrimage—the attraction of Jerusalem would have ensured that—and this contributed to its spirituality, but one cannot avoid the impression that in papal eyes it was a pilgrimage for the technical reason that the pope could make use of the duties and the privileges of pilgrims to subordinate the crusaders to the Church" (11). See also J. G. Davies, "Pilgrimage and Crusade Literature," in *Journeys Toward God: Pilgrimage and Crusade*, ed. Barbara N. Sargent-Baur, Studies in Medieval Culture 30 (Kalamazoo, MI: Medieval Institute Publications, 1992), 13-16; Diana Webb, *Pilgrims and Pilgrimages in the Medieval West* (London: I. B. Tauris, 1999), 8. And yet, the connection between pilgrimage and crusade is not mentioned at all by Dee Dyas, "Medieval Patterns of Pilgrimage: A Mirror for Today?," in *Explorations in a Christian Theology of Pilgrimage*, ed. Craig Bartholomew and Fred Hughes (Aldershot, UK: Ashgate, 2004), 92-109.

[34] The earliest examples and types of religious pilgrimage are not found in Christianity but in the religions of India. Thus, pilgrimage is not exclusively Christian but is an essential element in other religious traditions. For the universality of pilgrimages, see Linda Kay Davidson and Maryjane Dunn-Wood, *Pilgrimage in the Middle Ages: A Research Guide*, Garland Medieval Bibliographies 16 (New York: Garland, 1993), 16-21.

[35] Webb, *Pilgrims and Pilgrimages*, 7.

one" (Heb 11:14, 16).[36] The biblical image of sojourner or pilgrim encouraged early Christians to move beyond the bounds of the familiar and become strangers, to set out for new places and encounter the world. Some of their sojourns were forced on them by persecution, and thus their journey was unanticipated. In other cases, they became strangers by choice, setting out on pilgrimage because of an inner compulsion or desire. *Pilgrim* and *pilgrimage* describe many of those who ventured forth and preached the gospel in new and strange places. Patrick and Columba self-describe as pilgrims and as being on pilgrimage. Pilgrim language is found in the writings of Eusebius, Muirchú, Adomanán, Jonas, and Bede, as they describe particular people and their activities. In *pilgrim* and *pilgrimage*, we find ancient language of movement, intersection, exile, and cause.

From the fourth century, Christian pilgrims established routes originating in various places in Europe and journeyed to Jerusalem and to sites related to Jesus' birth, life, and death.[37] The belief was that in these spots power to absolve a person of sins and to build faith could be found. Pilgrim destinations included sites in Rome, and shrines of the Archangel Michael at Monte Gargano in Italy and St. James at Compostella in Spain, but none of these rivaled journey to the sacred sites in the Holy Land. Thus, pilgrimage referred to the movement to sacred places, with Jerusalem being the holiest of all.

In addition to travel or movement, *pilgrim* became a term of identity for Christians moving through the world. *Pilgrim*, as a name for those who are sojourners or living in exile, can be found from the early church onward. Clement, bishop of Rome from 92 to 99, wrote his epistle to the Corinthians from "the Church of God which sojourns at Rome to the Church of God sojourning at Corinth."[38] The Epistle of Diognetus explains that Christians

---

[36]For a more complete discussion, see Andrew T. Lincoln, "Pilgrimage and the New Testament," in Bartholomew and Hughes, *Explorations in a Christian Theology of Pilgrimage*, 29-49.

[37]Diana Webb, *Medieval European Pilgrimage, c.700–c.1500*, European Culture and Society (New York: Palgrave, 2002), 1; Purkis, *Crusading Spirituality*, 59-61. For a history of the development of pilgrimage during the medieval period, see Webb, *Pilgrims and Pilgrimages*, 11-47. For the practice of pilgrimage prior to 1095, see Runciman, "Pilgrimages to Palestine," and James Muldoon, "Crusading and Canon Law," in *Palgrave Advances in the Crusades*, ed. Helen J. Nicholson (New York: Palgrave MacMillan, 2005), 45.

[38]Clement of Rome, "The First Epistle of Clement to the Corinthians," in *The Apostolic Fathers with Justin Martyr and Irenaeus*, ed. A. Cleveland Coxe, The Ante-Nicene Fathers 1 (Grand Rapids: Eerdmans, 1946), 5.

"reside in their respective countries, but only as aliens. They take part in everything as citizens and put up with everything as foreigners. Every foreign land is their home, and every home a foreign land."[39] Jerome (ca. 347–420) in a letter to Eustochium describes in detail the pilgrimage of Paula to Jerusalem, Bethlehem, Jericho, and other sites in the Holy Land. In this case, pilgrimage is used by Jerome to identify Paula as a person of piety and dedication.[40] Augustine, *The City of God*, distinguishes Christians as those who live as "pilgrims journeying toward the Lord," and as such they make "use of earthly and temporal things like a pilgrim in a foreign land." "This Heavenly City, therefore, is on pilgrimage in this world," and "calls out citizens from all nations and so collects a society of aliens, speaking all languages."[41] Pilgrim language gives identity that, in some ways, supersedes language, race, and ethnicity and gives the person a new name, identity, and cause.

Unique contributions to the Christian understanding of pilgrimage come via the Irish. Distinctive cultural understandings of pilgrimage among the pre-Christian Irish entered existing pilgrim practices for Catholic Europe, making pilgrimage more than a journey to a shrine or holy site, or a defining identity, but "a process of alienation."[42] The pilgrim separated himself from the familiar, home and family, and established himself as an alien in a foreign community. This kind of denial of self and relocation to a foreign place ostensibly turned into witness and the extension of the Christian faith.

Consensus exists among scholarly opinion that Urban adapted this long-standing tradition of *peregrinus* for a violent march on Jerusalem.[43] Marcus Bull characterizes Urban's message as a "co-option of pilgrimage."[44] Norman Housley judges "that most of those who went on the First Crusade saw

---

[39] James A. Kleist, trans., "The Epistle to Diognetus," in *The Didache: The Epistle of Barnabas, The Epistles and the Martyrdom of St. Polycarp, The Fragments of Papias, The Epistle to Diognetus,* Ancient Christian Writers 6 (Westminster, MD: Newman, 1948), 139.

[40] Jerome, "Letter 108: To Eustochium," in *Early Latin Theology,* ed. S. L. Greenslade, The Library of Christian Classics 5 (Philadelphia: Westminster, 1956), 345-82.

[41] Augustine, *Concerning the City of God Against the Pagans,* 19.17 (877, 878).

[42] Webb, *Medieval European Pilgrimage,* 7.

[43] Tyerman, *Fighting for Christendom,* 113, argues that the idea of armed pilgrimage predates Urban's sermon.

[44] Marcus Graham Bull, "Crusade and Conquest," in *Cambridge History of Christianity,* vol. 4, *Christianity in Western Europe c.1100–c.1500* (Cambridge: Cambridge University Press, 2009), 347.

themselves first and foremost as pilgrims to Jerusalem."[45] In his examination of the identity of Crusaders in medieval society, Giles Constable argues, "In addition to being sanctified soldiers and, in a certain sense, secular monks, crusaders were pilgrims, who were both called *peregrini* and regarded themselves as pilgrims and their expedition as pilgrimages."[46] "There is no doubt," according to Jonathan Riley-Smith, "that Urban preached the crusade at Clermont as a pilgrimage and many of the measures he took brought it into line with pilgrimage practices."[47] The undertaking of a pilgrimage and the identity as a pilgrim provide a holy mandate that connected men and women from every strata of society and vocation with a compelling vision of a journey to Jerusalem. Pilgrim language was holy language that propelled men and women to respond to Urban's call to holy war.

With Urban's summons, the ancient tradition of pilgrimage became an act of aggression. The transition from one to the other required beliefs and practices inherent in traditional pilgrimage to be repurposed to serve a cause deemed as holy and just. In connecting pilgrimage with the campaign to take the Holy Land, a number of elements within pilgrimage underwent a shift in meaning. And although meaning changed, the language of pilgrim and pilgrimage remained.

Taking up to being sent out. Pilgrimage, as expressed in Urban's summons, was an external charge to go to Jerusalem rather than an internal compulsion to retreat into exile or assume alienation. His charge was to a task rather than a way of being in the world. Jerusalem was a distance of more than two thousand miles from Clermont, and thus the necessity was to mobilize thousands for a hazardous journey to the point of encounter with the enemy. The aspect of movement, inherent in pilgrimage, assisted in mobilizing Latin Christians. Urban charged would-be pilgrims with a task and instructed them to pursue this task as a pilgrim. Pilgrimage was a command to go to Jerusalem.

With the Crusades, pilgrimage came to mean more than just taking up purse and staff to journey to a foreign place or to become a stranger—it became more than worshiping at a sacred destination. Instead, Latin

---

[45]Housley, *Fighting for the Cross*, 2.
[46]Constable, "Place of the Crusader in Medieval Society," 384.
[47]Riley-Smith, *Idea of Crusading*, 22. See also Runciman, "Pilgrimages to Palestine," 78.

Christians were summoned and dispatched. While still a form of movement, this was movement of another sort. It was mobilization on papal command. Rather than personally generated, Latin Christians were sent into holy warfare.

Devoted few to masses. The traditional practice of pilgrimage was seen as a special calling for a narrow group of the devoted, specifically those of the ascetic life with a monastic calling. This specific calling can be seen in individuals who journeyed into the desert to live as ascetics, retreated to a cave to seek God, or cloistered in an island community. It was the minority of Christians who went to the desert, cave, and island, not the majority. Even as journey to sacred sites became a more popular aspect of pilgrimage, it was still only a small number of individuals who elected to make pilgrimage. At the heart of pilgrimage was a monastic-like compulsion that the majority of Christians did not share.

Riley-Smith notes that before the Crusades the way of devotion and imitation of Christ "had been a withdrawal from the world, a renunciation of earthly things in a retreat into the cloister. Now laymen were given something to do that was almost equivalent to monasticism."[48] Guibert of Nogent, in *Dei gesta per Francos* (The deeds of God through the Franks), observes,

> In our time God has instituted holy warfare so that the knightly order (*ordo equestris*) and unsettled populace (*vulgus oberrans*) . . . might find a new way of deserving salvation. They are no longer to leave the world, as used to be the case, by choosing the monastic way of life or some religious profession, but in their accustomed freedom and habit, from their own office, they may obtain in some measure the grace of God.[49]

Applying the monastic ideals of crucifying self and taming mortal desires, the "unsettled populace" was able to take the cross as a means of imitating Christ.[50] Donning the cross and journeying to Jerusalem became, for the warring pilgrim, ways of conquering the world, the flesh, and the devil. They

---

[48]Riley-Smith, *Crusades: Short History*, 9. See also Duncalf, "Councils of Piacenza and Clermont," 245.

[49]Translated by Constable and cited in "Place of the Crusader in Medieval Society," 379-80.

[50]C. Matthew Phillips, "Crucified with Christ: The Imitation of the Crucified Christ and the Crusading Spirituality," in *Crusades—Medieval Worlds in Conflict*, ed. Thomas F. Madden, James L. Naus, and Vincent Ryan (Farnham, UK: Ashgate, 2010), 26, analyzes monastic and crusade sermons to demonstrate the element of the imitation of Christ in both.

lived a pilgrim existence as they abandoned wives, children, and work; fasted before major campaigns; made displays of public piety and devotion; and risked their lives through privation, exposure, and battle. Once in the Holy Land, they visited holy sites and venerated relics, all as acts of piety and in fulfillment of their vow. In these ways, the populace was able to mimic traditional pilgrim practices.

The whole company of Crusaders viewed themselves as "fighting pilgrims who set out to open the route to Jerusalem."[51] Jonathan Riley-Smith explains that if Urban's intent was to limit the campaign to "arm-bearing knights, to youngish, healthy men," and exclude monks, the infirmed, or elderly, then he failed.[52] In Urban's sermon and in letters and correspondence that followed, he commanded with threats for the old, weak, poor noncombatants to stay at home.[53] And yet, efforts to restrict the expedition to the fighting class of knights did little to stem the tide of noncombatant pilgrims. While knights and foot soldiers were part of the march to the East on the First Crusade, the bulk of those who responded were unorganized, undisciplined common folks wishing to become pilgrims. Because pilgrimage had traditionally been for the old, weak, and poor, these responded in mass. The First Crusade was not as much an army, but, as Riley-Smith describes, "waves of men and women" making their way as "a continual stream travelling East."[54] The number of common pilgrims vastly outnumbered the knights and seasoned soldiers. Those who marched were, according to Conor Kostick, "something of a slice of European society."[55] With fervor and expectation, farmers, mothers, clergy, knights, barons, and foot soldiers became pious pilgrims. The appeal of worship at holy shrines in Jerusalem combined with Urban's call to liberate the holy places captured the vision and emotion of people who had been schooled in the pilgrimage tradition, observed at a distance; they were now encouraged to take up the cross for themselves.

---

[51]Duncalf, "Councils of Piacenza and Clermont," 243.

[52]Riley-Smith, *Crusades: Short History*, 7-8.

[53]See Elizabeth Siberry, *Criticism of Crusading, 1095–1274* (Oxford: Clarendon, 1985), 25-32; Purkis, *Crusading Spirituality*, 12-14.

[54]Riley-Smith, *Crusades: Short History*, 18. According to Duncalf, "Clermont to Constantinople," "too many eager pilgrims, inspired by religious enthusiasm, and too few fighting men, had marched in these early bands" (266).

[55]Conor Kostick, *The Social Structure of the First Crusade*, The Medieval Mediterranean 76 (Leiden, The Netherlands: Brill, 2008), 290.

Holy war became a "way of the cross" that every person could potentially embrace. Pilgrimage became both a privilege and an obligation for the whole of Catholic Europe, rather than the choice of a few. Because it was an open invitation from the vicar of Christ, the whole of Europe was compelled to join the pilgrimage.

Pilgrim vow to crusader vow. The reasons for becoming a pilgrim were many, but for most, pilgrimage was a penitential exercise that demonstrated extreme contrition, and thus the hope of clearing one's sin. Traditionally, the pilgrim would take a vow to make a pilgrimage, and on fulfilling the vow, his or her sins would be absolved.[56] In a similar fashion, those who responded to the summons to capture Jerusalem took a pilgrim-type *votum*, a personal vow to journey to Jerusalem. As with the pilgrim vow, the principal aim of the Crusader was the remission of sins. So, the crusader vow was in effect the pilgrim vow.[57] Each was a spiritual exercise, with a spiritual outcome.[58] The crusader vow served the same purpose of the pilgrim vow, as both pilgrim and crusader journeyed to Jerusalem as an act of penance.[59] And yet, the crusader vow was more than a means of spiritual penance. It had a physical objective, a tangible goal. The vow was not fulfilled until the pilgrim fought for the liberation of Jerusalem, or died trying, and then worshiped at the Holy Sepulchre. Thus, warfare became an essential part of what was necessary to fulfill the vow.[60] The saving works of spiritual contrition and devotion became the work of war and assault. The connection between the two was pilgrimage.

---

[56]Sarah Hopper, *To Be a Pilgrim: The Medieval Pilgrimage Experience* (Gloucestershire, UK: Sutton, 2002), 9-10.

[57]See Constable, "Place of the Crusader in Medieval Society," 387-88.

[58]Bird, "Crusades," 142. According to Leclercq, Vandenbroucke, and Bouyer, *Spirituality of the Middle Ages*, "The crusader is by definition a man of abnegation," and thus he renounces the present life and its pleasures and serves the cause of Christ (132).

[59]Tyerman, *Fighting for Christendom*, reports that "the First Crusade drew excited praise as 'a new way of salvation' for the military classes. Apart from donations to monasteries so that monks could pray for their souls, increasingly laymen in the eleventh century found pilgrimages promoted by the clergy as a means to expiate sin, with Jerusalem prominent in practice and imagination" (112-13). Asbridge, *Crusades*, characterizes these pilgrimages as "salvific expeditions" (38).

[60]Joshua Prawer, *The World of the Crusaders* (New York: Quadrangle Books, 1973), concludes, "The concepts of pilgrimage and penitence joined forces with a new enterprise, a military with a religious aim. . . . The crusade became a penitential and martial pilgrimage" (15). According to Mayer, *Crusades*, "The crusade was a logical extension of the pilgrimage" (14).

Compelled to persuaded. Traditional pilgrimages were undertaken as part of the commitment of the devoted, usually among those who voluntarily took monastic vows. Or in some cases, the pilgrim was prompted to set out when there was a crisis in life, or the person was overwhelmed by guilt. In many cases, a pilgrimage was initiated because the person had been instructed to do so in a vision. Pilgrimage was not preached, nor were common folks summoned to take a pilgrimage. Urban's sermon marked a change in the manner in which pilgrimages were initiated. Whether he intended for pilgrimage to be proclaimed as an obligation for the whole of Catholic Europe, the wide and overwhelming response to his sermon suggests that it was heard as a universal call with a broad invitation.

Itinerant preachers had become popular during Gregory VII's papacy (1073–1085) and were an essential part of his reform initiatives.[61] These wandering preachers proclaimed personal piety and fidelity to Rome. Following Urban's sermon, similar preachers disseminated the pope's summons, spreading the crusade message into towns and hamlets and widening the appeal beyond the gentry and knightly classes. Propagandists, such as Peter the Hermit, traveled far and wide to "preach the cross," that is, to persuade people from all walks of life to make the vow, take the cross, and leave for the East. These appeals were in the form of crusade sermons that appealed to people's sense of need and to their emotions. Christoph Maier indicates that crusade sermons had wide appeal and good results. According to Maier, "It is probably no exaggeration to say that theoretically, the great majority of inhabitants of Europe would have had the opportunity of listening to several crusade sermons during their lifetime. Even those who never actually made it to a crusade sermon would probably have heard reports from other people."[62]

These sermons were the main source of popular understanding of the Crusades, and they were also the chief means by which people were persuaded to join the battle for Jerusalem.[63] Housley observes that crusade

---

[61]Tim Rayborn, *The Violent Pilgrimage: Christians, Muslims and Holy Conflicts, 850–1150* (Jefferson, NC: McFarland, 2013), 36. On the role of visionary preachers in the reform movement and the first crusade, see John France, "Two Types of Vision on the First Crusade: Stephen of Valence and Peter Bartholomew," in Kedar and Riley-Smith, *Crusades*, 1-5.

[62]Christoph T. Maier, *Crusade Propaganda and Ideology: Model Sermons for the Preaching of the Cross* (Cambridge: Cambridge University Press, 2006), 51.

[63]Cole, *Preaching of the Crusades*, ix.

sermons were not preached explicitly as a call to holy war. Rather, "crusading was preached as a redemptive process, a jubilee, and a trial set by God to test the faith of the new Israel that was Christendom."[64] While these ideals were expressed in a number of ways, pilgrimage was the rhetorical means to recruit, to raise money, to send Crusaders on their way, to encourage those at home, and to reassure Crusaders on the battlefield.

Peter the Hermit's crusade sermon came to him as a vision at the Holy Sepulchre while he was on a pilgrimage to Jerusalem. The vision foretold that infidels holding the Holy City could be driven out if pilgrims marched on the city. As he later preached this message, people from the common classes responded and formed an army of the poor, characterized as the Peasants' Crusade or People's Crusade. He personally guided this army across Hungary to Byzantium as the initial wave of the First Crusade.[65] This unruly and undisciplined mob, unable to wait for others or coordinate their actions with the Byzantines or any other force, pushed ahead in religious fervor, leaving mayhem in their path.

The foremost aim of the crusade sermon was to promote the holy cause and not to implement crusading itself. Preachers of the Crusades were mobilizers. Their preaching and promotion of pilgrimage was a new phenomenon that became something of an end in itself.

Staff to cross. The goal of the potential crusader-pilgrim was to become one marked with the cross or a cross bearer (*crucesignati*). The cross became powerful mobilizing imagery, as Urban and preachers of crusades linked pilgrimage with Christ's journey to Golgotha. The potency of the image increased even more as people were summoned to take and wear the cross themselves.[66] Traditionally, pilgrims had traveled with a wooden staff and scrip (purse) as identifying marks of their pilgrimage. While in some cases pilgrims carried a cross for all or part of their journey, Urban's innovation was to make the cross the primary symbol of this new kind of pilgrimage to Jerusalem, and thus they became known as crusade, *crozada*. Those vowing

---

[64]Housley, *Fighting for the Cross*, 37.
[65]Some believe Peter the Hermit and not Urban actually instigated the First Crusade. See the legacy of Peter's role as an instigator of the Crusades in Duncalf, "Clermont to Constantinople," 258.
[66]See Christopher Tyerman's discussions of the symbolism of the cross for the Crusades in *Invention of the Crusades*, 76-83, and the use of imagery and technique in crusade preaching in *Fighting for Christendom*, 126-34.

to liberate Jerusalem affixed a cross to their person in some manner. In some cases, a cross was branded into the flesh.[67]

Taking up the cross changed a person's status and disposition. He or she transitioned into a different mode of existence. No longer was the person simply part of the general Catholic populace, but he or she was a *crucesignatus* who wore the cause of Christ in a bodily form. This changed many aspects of life. As a matter of practicality, the cross-designated person was a pilgrim, and thus his changed status afforded him pilgrim privileges, such as protection and hospitality.[68] Along with privileges, taking the cross was the symbol of opposition to Muslims, the "enemies of the cross."[69] Thus, taking the cross made one a combatant. But taking the cross was about more than privilege, opposition to Muslims, or a willingness to fight an enemy. The vow was a person's stated intent to join the next expedition and to worship at the Church of the Holy Sepulchre, and thus the cross was a public confession of this vow. The traditional pilgrim vow was made to God and thus was private, but taking the cross turned the matter into a public event and made it binding. In many cases taking the cross was associated with receiving the elements of the mass. This turned the whole affair into a sacramental act of confession and commitment.[70] Once the cross bearer made a vow and took the cross, he had to depart for the East as promised, as soon as possible, or be excommunicated.[71]

Catholic Europeans signed with the cross at baptism, as they entered the church and became known as Christians. So taking the cross as a crusading pilgrim meant that they were in a sense doubly crossed and thus doubly Christian. Taking the cross a second time served a number of purposes. Besides being a way to address the consequence of their sinfulness, taking the cross was an act of Christ mimesis, or *imitatio Christi*.[72] By taking up the

---

[67]Duncalf, "Councils of Piacenza and Clermont," 239-40, attempts to reconcile the various reports of what transpired at Clermont.

[68]Riley-Smith, *Crusades: Short History*, xxix. According to Dass, *Deeds of the Franks and Other Jerusalem-Bound Pilgrims*, 85, 86, 98, the cross figures prominently in accounts of the First Crusade as a source of protection and strengthening power.

[69]Riley-Smith, *Idea of Crusading*, 24.

[70]Tyerman, *Invention of the Crusades*, 81.

[71]Riley-Smith, *Idea of Crusading*, 23. See also Duncalf, "Councils of Piacenza and Clermont," 247.

[72]William J. Purkis, "Religious Symbols and Practices: Monastic Spirituality, Pilgrimage and Crusade," in *European Religious Cultures* (London: Institute for Historical Research, 2008), 78-81. Imitation of Christ as a motivation for and image of the Crusades has been emphasized by a

cross, the pilgrim suffered hardships and privation and submitted to the point of death, and thus in a manner imitated the way of Christ. As Purkis explains, "The crusaders were understood by many contemporaries to be following 'the way of God' (*via Dei*), or, as the crusade was known to others, 'the way of the Lord' (*via Domini*) and 'the way of Christ' (*via Christi*)."[73] Hardship and suffering were means for the pilgrims to follow in the footsteps of Jesus, literally in the place where Jesus walked. As pilgrims on a particular errand, crusaders were on a Christlike quest. In the cross, crusading pilgrims found identity in Christ, and this transcended temporal identities, such as language and ethnicity. They bore a common identity and marched under a common symbol. Much of the imagery and language reserved for those in the monastic orders and the ascetic life now passed to those who took the cross.[74]

For many, taking the cross meant death. Those who died in the crusade effort were not just casualties of war but were understood to be martyrs for Christ.[75] The motivation to join the effort and then persevere through starvation, harsh conditions, and battle was bolstered by a legacy of martyrdom. The church was under threat by enemies of the cross, and thus to die in its defense was to be numbered among its martyrs. The difference was that this martyrdom was not passive or voluntary but achieved through fighting the enemy and thereby defending the faith.[76] Riley-Smith observes that whereas indulgence "was a gift from God, martyrdom is the martyr's gift of his own life. It was so great an act of merit that it justified the martyr immediately in God's sight."[77] A chronicler of the First Crusade names those of the initial wave of knights and pilgrims who were killed by Turks as "the first ones to

---

number of scholars. See, for example, Purkis, *Crusading Spirituality*, 30; Horst Ritcher, "Militia Dei: A Central Concept for the Religious Ideas of the Early Crusades and the German Rolandslied," in Sargent-Baur, *Journeys Toward God*, 118.

[73]Purkis, "Religious Symbols and Practices," 80.

[74]According to Riley-Smith, *Crusades: Short History*, "There was, in fact, an extraordinarily rapid transfer to crusading of phrases and images traditionally associated with monasticism: the knighthood of Christ, the way of the cross, the way to a heavenly Jerusalem, spiritual warfare" (37).

[75]On looking on the dead, Robert the Monk, "Historia Iherosolimitana," declares them as "Christian martyrs" (112).

[76]Housley, *Fighting for the Cross*, 188-90. See also Riley-Smith, *Idea of Crusading*, 115-18.

[77]Jonathan Riley-Smith, "Death on the First Crusade," in *End of Strife*, ed. David M. Loades (Edinburgh: T&T Clark, 1984), 19.

accept martyrdom in the name of the Lord Jesus."[78] Baldric reports the words of Urban's Clermont sermon: "And may you deem it a beautiful thing to die for Christ in that city in which He died for us. But if it befall you to die on this side of it, be sure that to have died on the way is of equal value, if Christ shall find you in his army."[79]

The suggestion that a martyr for the faith could be a "warrior martyr" helped to justify armed pilgrimage and make it a type of apostolic act.[80] Taking the cross was more than a symbolic gesture or opposition to an enemy. It meant the pilgrim imitated Christ, even in his death. In its association with cross bearing, pilgrimage became a way to actively pursue martyrdom.

Escape to activism. Urban's summons to pilgrimage was more than a call to prayer and fasting but to violent acts against enemies of the cross. With the call to violence, pilgrimage transitioned from a passive undertaking of self-mortification and worship to invasion and assault in the name of Christ.[81] Absolution of sins was often the motivation for undertaking a pilgrimage, and thus the ordeal of a long journey and its hardship were viewed as an atoning offering of self. But this self-sacrifice was mixed with the blood of others to create a perversion of the earlier idea of pilgrimage. With Urban's summons to an armed pilgrimage, the giving of one's life became the taking of another's life.[82]

Much like accounts in the Old Testament, crusading pilgrims saw themselves as God's army, tasked with the assignment of taking the Holy Land from God's enemies. The Old Testament provided examples of God's people at war and thus offered ample justification for violence. Old Testament ideas of God's war and God as warrior, as well as stories of the Israelites battling in the name of God, supplied language and illustrative material for those who defended the Crusades and propagandists who

---

[78]Dass, *Deeds of the Franks and Other Jerusalem-Bound Pilgrims*, 27, 62.
[79]Cited in Duncalf, "Councils of Piacenza and Clermont," 248.
[80]Riley-Smith, "Death on the First Crusade," 30-31.
[81]Rayborn, *Violent Pilgrimage*, 21-25, offers evidence that pilgrims were becoming more and more aggressive prior to Urban's sermon, and, in a manner, violence and pilgrimage was not a completely new idea.
[82]There is disagreement among interpreters of the Crusades as to whether pilgrims were armed. Constable, "Place of the Crusader in Medieval Society," summarizes this discussion and concludes that "crusaders can therefore be seen as armed pilgrims, and contemporaries drew no clear distinction between pilgrimage and crusade" (384-86n50).

recruited Crusaders.[83] Old Testament events and themes were translated directly into the struggles of the Latin church with its enemies. John Gilchrist makes the point that "while the Israelites of the Old Testament, the chosen people of God, became the Christian *populus Dei* or the crusading army, Muslims replaced Ishmaelites as the enemy. References to the Old Testament heroes, to Moses, Joshua, David, and Judas Maccabeus abound in the literature."[84] Old Testament justification for violence was clear and direct.

A vivid example of the curious mixture of pilgrimage and violence can be seen in the person of Raymond IV of Toulouse (Saint-Gilles). Following the siege and capture of Antioch, Raymond was selected to lead the march from Antioch to Jerusalem. As he set out in January 1099, the sixty-year-old commander-in-chief walked at the head of the troops, barefoot and dressed as a pilgrim.[85] Without doubt, his intent was to use force in order to breach the wall, and then kill those who controlled the city. And yet, he approached the city as a pious pilgrim, marching under the cross.[86] After several failed attempts to take Jerusalem, a priest by the name of Peter Desiderius was instructed in a vision by Bishop Adhémar, deceased papal legate taken by sickness, to have the Crusaders fast and make a procession around the walls of the city. Peter was told that, if done with sufficient piety, this procession would cause Jerusalem to fall within nine days. The Crusaders observed three days of ritual purification and a fast, and then bishops, clergy, princes, knights, and foot soldiers processed barefoot with palm fronds around the city.[87] Next they went to the Mount of Olives, where Peter the Hermit, along with others, exhorted them. Within seven days the city was taken, and a bloodbath ensued. In the words of Hans Mayer, "The crusaders hacked down everyone, irrespective of race or religion, who was unfortunate to

---

[83]Tyerman, *Fighting for Christendom*, 98-101, explores the use of crusading references within various Old Testament texts.

[84]Gilchrist, "Papacy and War," 188.

[85]The story of Count Raimond or Raymond is told in a number of ways, but the pilgrim element persists. See Mayer, *Crusades*, 58; Runciman, "Antioch to Ascalon," 327-28; Tyerman, *God's War*, 150. This account is also recorded in Dass, *Deeds of the Franks and Other Jerusalem-Bound Pilgrims*, 96.

[86]Runciman, "Antioch to Ascalon," 339, notes that after the city was taken and he refused to become king of Jerusalem, Raymond took his troops to Jericho and made pilgrimage to the Jordan River.

[87]Tyerman, *God's War*, 96; Runciman, "Antioch to Ascalon," 335-36.

come within reach of their swords."[88] *Gesta Francorum*, a chronicle of the First Crusade, reports, "There was so much slaughter that our men put down their feet in blood up to the ankle."[89] Catholic Europeans marched into Jerusalem as pious pilgrims, and their pilgrimage ended with the violent conquest of Jerusalem and the frenzied slaughter of people.[90]

In this strange distortion of pilgrimage, Catholic Europeans mixed pilgrim practices of prayer, procession, palm fronds, and prophetic visions with the destruction of life and property in the name of Jesus and under the cross. The paradox that Jesus taught peace and love for one's enemies and the cross as symbolic of his self-sacrifice, rather than the slaughter of others, did not seem contradictory. While the inconsistencies could not have been more obvious, being a pilgrim nonetheless gave the crusader permission to conquer and destroy in the name of Jesus. Above all, the violent liberation of Jerusalem was admissible because Urban, Christ's representative on earth, sanctioned holy pilgrimage as assault.[91]

Animosity toward Islam added to the justification for a pilgrimage of violence. Muslims were markedly different from heretics and Jews. Because Muslims occupied Christian territory in the East and the fringes of Europe, they ruled and subjugated Christians. In addition to this offense, they had defiled the holy places of Christ. They were a new and greater danger that warranted a shift from defensive to offensive war.[92] Without this clear enemy and the ensuing shift to an offensive posture, Urban's summons to send armed pilgrims to a place beyond Christendom to conquer in the name of the Roman church would have been of little effect. A clear enemy and a need for an offensive response to this

---

[88]Mayer, *Crusades*, 60. Runciman, "Antioch to Ascalon," reports, "When the carnage stopped, the streets were running with blood, and round the Temple area one stepped over corpses all the way. The horror of the massacre in the holy city was never forgotten nor forgiven by Islam" (337).

[89]Dass, *Deeds of the Franks and Other Jerusalem-Bound Pilgrims*, 103. Fulcher of Chartres, "Deeds of the Franks," reports, "If you had been there, your feet would have been stained up to the ankles with the blood of the slain" (77). Ralph of Caen, *Gesta Tancredi*, adds, "The sanctuary was covered with vast quantities of blood. . . . The doors, walls, seats, tables, columns, all were bloody. There was nothing without blood. The floor was completely covered by the slaughter. The walls were submerged knee high [in blood]" (148).

[90]On the siege of Jerusalem, see Runciman, "Antioch to Ascalon," 333-37.

[91]According to William Purkis, *Crusading Spirituality*, "The associations between pilgrimage, warfare, and penance" were known prior to Urban's sermon, and yet, "the idea of a penitential pilgrimage-in-arms was a revolutionary prospect for Christendom at large" (19).

[92]Erdmann, *Idea of Crusade*, concludes that the Crusades were the point of "passage from defensive war to offensive" and "a decisive moment for the idea of war on the heathens" (96).

enemy bound pilgrimage to violence. In this way, the offering of one's life became tied to expending one's life in violent assaults on enemies of the cross.

In time, crusading extended beyond Muslims in the East to enemies who threatened Christianity in Spain (Moors), those perceived to be antichrists (Jews), heretics, schismatics, rebels, and pagans within Europe (groups of people in the Baltics), and even secular leaders and antipopes.[93] Pilgrimage transitioned from liberating the Holy Land and safeguarding the church of the East to crusading against the church's enemies. It became the Catholic church's expansion of control and extension of Latin Christianity. Crusading was the church's response to those it opposed both within and beyond the borders of Christendom.

Heavenly reward to temporal triumph. Jerusalem was the objective, both in a temporal and heavenly sense.[94] The physical and idealized Jerusalem had been the focus of pilgrimages from the fourth century onward and thus easily provided necessary inspiration and motivation for those who heard Urban's summons to retake the city.[95] This hope was fueled by the eschatological vision of the heavenly city and the reign of God. The goal of attaining the heavenly Jerusalem was to be realized by way of the Crusaders' arrival at the earthly Jerusalem.[96] Once Jerusalem was taken, leaders of the crusading forces called on the pope "to come out and open for us the gates of both Jerusalems."[97] Entrance into one was, in effect, access to the other.

---

[93]See Siberry, *Criticism of Crusading*, 156-89. For crusades against non-Christians in the Baltic region, see Alan V. Murray, ed., *Crusade and Conversion on the Baltic Frontier, 1150–1500* (Aldershot, UK: Ashgate, 2001).

[94]Mayer, *Crusades*, defines *crusade* as having the narrow objective of Jerusalem or the Holy Land. Conflict with heathen, infidels, and Muslims in other areas can be defined as holy war but not a crusade (283-86). The "exclusivist" approach dates the Crusades from 1099 to the loss of Acre in 1291. On the other hand, the "inclusivist" approach labels crusades as all wars authorized by the pope against any enemy of the church. Christopher Tyerman presents the various sides of this debate in *The Debates on the Crusades*, Issues in Historiography (Manchester, UK: Manchester University Press, 2011), 219-28.

[95]For survey of the place of Jerusalem as a pilgrim destination prior, during, and after the First Crusade, see Bernard Hamilton, "The Impact of Crusader Jerusalem on Western Christendom," *The Catholic Historical Review* 80, no. 4 (October 1994): 695-713; Matthew Gabriele, *An Empire of Memory: The Legend of Charlemagne, the Franks, and Jerusalem Before the First Crusade* (Oxford: Oxford University Press, 2011), 73-93; Hopper, *To Be a Pilgrim*, 12-27.

[96]See Mayer, *Crusades*, 11-13; Riley-Smith, *Crusades: Short History*, 37; Housley, *Fighting for the Cross*, 26.

[97]As reported by Riley-Smith in *Idea of Crusading*, 119. Robert the Monk, "Historia Iherosolimitana," states, "Jerusalem is the navel of the Earth" (81).

Early critics of traditional pilgrimages, such as Augustine of Hippo and Gregory of Nyssa, pronounced them to be dangerous because the journey to the physical Jerusalem became the chief point and the journey to the heavenly Jerusalem was diminished or lost.[98] For them, a focus on the earthly Jerusalem was a distraction from the eternal Jerusalem. And yet, such warnings did not curb the desire to make pilgrimage to Jerusalem. From the beginning of the church, pilgrimages to Jerusalem were regularly made by small groups and occasionally by the lone ascetic. The popularity of pilgrimages to the Holy City began to increase in the eighth century through the influence of the Celtic church and the Irish. By the tenth century, conditions had improved for travel through Italy, allowing for larger and more frequent groups of pilgrims to set out for the Holy City. Another reason for the increased interest in pilgrimages was the millennium celebration of Christ's death and resurrection (1033), which drew a flood of pilgrims to Bethlehem and Jerusalem. A pilgrimage to Jerusalem in 1064–1065 led by German bishops consisted of approximately seven thousand men and women. This and other millennium pilgrimages were fueled by rumors and prophecies of an approaching Day of Judgment.[99]

Catholic Christians believed that because Jerusalem had been the place of Christianity's beginning, it would be the place of its culmination (parousia). It was from Jerusalem that Christ sent his disciples to make disciples of all nations, and naturally this mandate would find its fulfillment in the same physical spot. An eschatological vision of Jerusalem's ultimate purpose elevated the object of the Crusaders beyond mere conquest and liberation to a pilgrimage of a higher and more eternal end.[100] The crusading pilgrim was contributing to and participating in the return of Christ. Pilgrimage became a means of establishing the kingdom of God on earth.

---

[98]Runciman, "Pilgrimages to Palestine," 69-70.

[99]Riley-Smith, *Idea of Crusading*, 23; Runciman, "Pilgrimages to Palestine," 76. For historical accounts of the "Great German Pilgrimage," see Webb, *Pilgrims and Pilgrimages*, 41-43; Einar Joranson, "The Great German Pilgrimage of 1064-5," in *The Crusades, and Other Historical Essays, Presented to Dana C. Munro by His Former Students*, ed. Louis John Paetow (New York: F. S. Crofts, 1928), 3-43.

[100]Leclercq, Vandenbroucke, and Bouyer, *Spirituality of the Middle Ages*, 131-32. For the place of Jerusalem in Western thought during this period, see Adriaan Hendrik Bredero, *Christendom and Christianity in the Middle Ages: The Relations Between Religion, Church, and Society*, trans. Reinder Bruinsma (Grand Rapids: Eerdmans, 1994), 79-104.

INSTRUMENTAL LANGUAGE

Changes in the meaning of pilgrimage mirrored shifts in attitudes and assumptions of Latin Christians in the period leading up to the Crusades. Urban's sermon signaled the culmination of rising militancy within the Roman
church and the ascendancy of papal ambition. These tendencies were seen in
the two papacies prior to Urban, Alexander II (1061–1073) and Gregory VII
(1073–1085). Both popes offered inducements for knights and bestowed
special status on those who fought in military ventures sponsored by the
church. Alexander II was the first to grant indulgences to those who fought
for the church in Spain. This was the initial step in what became quite commonplace for popes as an inducement for crusading. In addition, Alexander
permitted fighters to march under the *vexillum sancti Petri*, the banner of
Peter.[101] The banner was the insignia of the papal blessing and thereby made
those who marched under it papal vassals. Like taking the cross, the banner
of Peter designated the pope as their leader and signified their armies as
standard bearers for Christ. Even before becoming pope, Alexander II was
instrumental in drawing the military into the sphere of the church. As Anselm
of Baggio, Alexander was one of the founders of the Pataria, a lay movement
of military service. Following him was Erlembald, who as a knight led this
popular movement for more than a decade. At Erlembald's death, he became
the first knight-saint, thus modeling what was to become the spiritual knight.[102]

Gregory VII extended and developed this growing relationship of the
papal office and military service. He enhanced the status of those who sol-
diered for Christ by bestowing on them the title of *militia sancti Petri,*
knights of St. Peter.[103] Whereas soldiers of Christ had been viewed as a defensive peacekeeping group, the militia of St. Peter took on more significance
and greater power and thus became an offensive force at the pope's command.

---

[101]Riley-Smith, *Idea of Crusading*, 5. See Carl Erdmann's chapter "Holy Banners" and the movement toward holy war in *Idea of Crusade* (35-56) and specifically his discussion of *Vexillum
Sancti Petri* in chapter 6 (182-200).

[102]Erdmann, *Idea of Crusade*, 140-43. Erdmann's assessment of Gregory is that "more than anyone before him, he overcame the inhibitions that had once restrained the church from being
warlike in preaching and warlike in action. For he was as much a warrior as a priest and
politician" (181).

[103]Mayer, *Crusades*, 20; Blake, "Formation of the 'Crusade Idea,' " 13-17; Tim Davis, "Miles Christi,"
Encyclopedia of Medieval Pilgrimage, 423; Tyerman, *Fighting for Christendom*, 111. See also
Erdmann's chapter on Hildebrand-Gregory VII, *Idea of Crusade*, 148-81.

In addition, the biblical idea of a soldier of Christ (2 Tim 2:3) began to be used more often to refer to monks, nobles, and saints.[104] This shift in terminology can certainly be seen in Gregory's time, as he exploits such language for church and papal authority. The causes of the church and those of military forces were merged to the point that it appeared "the contrast between *militia Christi* and *militia saecularis* was overcome."[105] From the time of Gregory to Urban, the knightly class was increasingly incorporated into the activities of the church and utilized as enforcement of papal decrees. Likewise, ideals of piety became associated with Christian knighthood. The language and ideal of knighthood of Christ and doing battle for the church were already in place prior to Urban's Clermont sermon, so the language of Christ's knight (*milites Christi*), soldier, or warrior naturally became common descriptors for the Crusader.[106] The key dimensions that Urban added to *militia sancta Petri* were Jerusalem as its goal and the link with pilgrimage and spiritual reward. Skills and training of ecclesiastical knighthood were united with religious and eternal aims. The Poor Fellow-Soldiers of Christ and of the Temple Solomon, or the Knights Templar, founded in the twelfth century, was the eventual, full incorporation of *milites Christi* into the work of the church.[107] Following the capture of Jerusalem, the assignment of this elite fighting force was to protect pilgrims and to guard the city and its sacred sites. In their oath to protect the earthly Jerusalem, they aimed to win the heavenly Jerusalem as well.

A milestone on the road to Urban's summons was Gregory VII's proposal of a military operation in 1074. The aim was to assist the Byzantine ruler in his struggle against the Seljuk Turks.[108] Though there was a positive response to his proposal, Gregory was unable to pursue it because of an ongoing

---

[104]Davis, "Miles Christi," gives a historical overview of the use of the term.

[105]Erdmann, *Idea of Crusade*, 57.

[106]See Dass, *Deeds of the Franks and Other Jerusalem-Bound Pilgrims*, 29, 34, 41, 47, 86, 90, 101, 102, 107.

[107]Christopher Dawson, *The Formation of Christendom* (New York: Sheed and Ward, 1967), indicates that the Order of the Temple was "a society of fighting monks living under a strict rule composed by St. Bernard." Its founding "marks the culmination of the reformer's attempt to introduce a Christian element into the barbaric traditions of Western feudalism" (207).

[108]H. E. J. Cowdrey, "Pope Gregory VII's 'Crusading' Plans of 1074," in *Outremer: Studies in the History of the Crusading Kingdom of Jerusalem*, ed. Benjamin Z. Kedar, Hans Eberhard Mayer, and R. C. Smail (Jerusalem: Yad Izhak Ben-Zvi Institute, 1982), 29-40. See also Riley-Smith, *Idea of Crusading*, 7-8; Duncalf, "Councils of Piacenza and Clermont," 222-23.

conflict with the French king, Philip I. Gregory continued to discuss holy war and prepared to fight against Muslims in the East, even proposing that he command the army himself. Though these plans went nowhere, they were a prelude to what Urban actually authorized and declared twenty-one years later.[109] Gregory's plans and Urban's call to arms were indicative of the ongoing struggle between altar and throne, papal power and secular authority. The First Crusade was the watermark event in this conflict, as dukes, counts, nobles, and kings were compelled to submit to the papal authority and participate in the crusading cause. The head of the Latin church commanded the allegiance and service of Europe's armies and, more importantly, its rulers.

Pilgrimage language was more than indicative of these changes. It was utility for papal assertion. On one hand, holy pilgrimage served papal aspirations and justified these aspirations not just in the eyes of knights and princes but everyone who took the cross. But on a much broader and more popular level, the actions of war became holy as they were linked with pilgrim intentions. If intentions were right, then violence was excusable and success in battle assured. When there was a military defeat or a reversal, the reason had to be the presence of sin among the Crusaders or because their intentions were less than noble.[110] Greed, fornication, adultery, excess, and vainglory were named as reasons for defeat. Whether the hope was for eternal salvation or the capture of a city, the Crusaders were continually reminded that the enemy was the "sinful Turks," and the battle against them must be with pure intentions.[111] So, pilgrim intentions—purity of heart, willingness to deprive oneself of luxury or excess, and devotion to Mary—purified motives and thereby ensured success for the Crusader. An inward, spiritual repentance, accomplished by way of a pilgrim's vow and physical demonstration of piety, had to accompany the war effort. If sufficiently pursued, these intentions assured successful conquest. In this way,

---

[109]Erdmann, *Idea of Crusade*, 165-69.

[110]In defeat, the chronicler of Dass, *Deeds of the Franks and Other Jerusalem-Bound Pilgrims*, proclaims, "such was the poverty and misery that God reserved for us because of our sins" (57).

[111]Ibid., 46. Prior to the battle for Antioch, the Crusaders prepared by undertaking a three-day fast and making procession to various churches. Then "everyone made confession of their sins, and once absolved, faithfully received in communion the Body and the Blood of Christ. And then they gave alms and had masses celebrated" (84-85).

destruction of the enemy of Christ was seen as tangible evidence of piety and repentance. Pilgrimage converted violence and aggression into virtue and piety.[112] Unsavory ends were justified by holy means. Pilgrim piety became the means by which Urban advanced papal dominance and compelled Europe to go to war.

As Crusade after Crusade was undertaken, the connection between pilgrimage and conquest became less prominent, but it never completely faded.[113] For example, what chroniclers describe as the Children's Crusade (1212 CE) was known as a "pilgrimage of lads" (*peregrinatio puerorum*).[114] Pilgrim language receded in Crusade accounts, and yet the changes to the concept of pilgrimage itself remained. Not only did it remain, but pilgrimage of holy conquest provided context and cause for mission language that was to come.

---

[112]According to Asbridge, *Crusades*, "Fusing the ideals of warfare and pilgrimage, [Urban] unveiled an expedition that would forge a path to the Holy Land itself, there to win back possession of Jerusalem, the most hallowed site in the Christian cosmos" (36). Christoph Maier, *Preaching the Crusades: Mendicant Friars and the Cross in the Thirteenth Century*, The Medieval Review (Cambridge: Cambridge University Press, 1994), suggests that no matter the outcome of a battle, "the crusader was a pilgrim for the good of his own soul, and a disastrous crusade was still able to provide the individual participant with a plenary indulgence" (1-2).

[113]Cecilia Gaposchkin, "From Pilgrimage to Crusade: The Liturgy of Departure, 1095–1300," *Speculum* 88, no. 1 (January 2013), disagrees and asserts that by the end of the fifteenth century "the concept of coming to the aid of the Holy Land no longer meant making a pilgrimage to Jerusalem. Taking the cross meant fighting to save Christendom" (79).

[114]See Gary Dickson, "Stephen of Cloyes, Philip Augustus, and the Children's Crusade of 1212," in Sargent-Baur, *Journeys Toward God*, 83.

6

Latin Occupation

Would that a great Prince might be found to lead a
new crusade, and to lay down his arms only when
no infidels are left to oppose the Catholic faith!

RAMON LLULL, IN *RAMON LULL: A BIOGRAPHY*

Whoever of them had the spirit of God and the eloquence
for preaching—cleric or lay—to him [Francis] would give
permission and an obedience to preach. They received
[Francis's] blessing with great happiness and joy in
the Lord Jesus Christ. They went through the world as
strangers and pilgrims, taking nothing for the journey,
except the books in which they could say their Hours.

JOHN OF PERUGIA, "THE BEGINNING OR FOUNDING OF THE ORDER"

The crusades were not missionary ventures but wars of
conquest and primitive experiments in colonization.

PAUL JOHNSON, *A HISTORY OF CHRISTIANITY*

HOLY PILGRIMAGE RESULTED in Latin colonies. Chief among the consequences of Urban's summons was the establishment of enclaves of Latin
Christianity in Syria and Palestine.[1] These were the spoils of hard-fought and

---

[1]For the history of Latin hierarchy in Syria and Palestine, the causes, structure, and lasting impact, see Bernard Hamilton, *The Latin Church in the Crusader States: The Secular Church*

costly campaigns. Unlike most traditional pilgrims, whose aim was to journey to the Holy Land, worship, and then return home, many of these later pilgrims stayed. Once Jerusalem, Antioch, and other cities were captured, the planting and sustaining of Latin colonies became the goal. Liberation and rescue may have been the pilgrims' original intentions, but the task shifted to the governance and security of Latin settlements.

In this new phase, existing struggles between the church and secular powers in Europe replicated themselves in the conquered territories. With the capture of Jerusalem, the stage was set for competing visions of church and state to clash. On one side, representatives of the church wanted Jerusalem to become a papal state similar to Rome.[2] On the other hand, lay Crusaders, such as Godfrey de Bouillon and Raymond de Saint-Gilles, vied among themselves and against the church for control and rule of Jerusalem as a secular kingdom, such as those found in Europe.[3]

Pope Urban's policy was to work in concert with Emperor Alexius I Comnenus and respect the historical place of the Eastern churches. The emperor's request for help represented for Urban an opportunity to unite the two churches, with the Roman pontiff as the supreme head and thus to consolidate and expand papal dominance. Urban's vision was that Alexius would remain in control of territories but submit to Rome. The task of the pope's legate, Adhémar de Monteuil, bishop of Le Puy, traveling with the main contingency of Crusaders, was to assure Emperor Alexius of the Latin church's honorable intentions and to coordinate their efforts. A requirement of the emperor in this arrangement was that the Crusaders take an oath of fidelity to him, which they did with Adhémar's coaching.

Once Jerusalem was captured, Urban's policy of cooperation, and thus the pope's vision of an expanded Christendom, was altered. Urban's policy and Crusaders' oaths of allegiance were set aside for several reasons. First, Adhémar, who worked hard to ensure coordination and cooperation, died

(London: Variorum, 1980); Malcolm Barber, *The Crusader States* (New Haven, CT: Yale University Press, 2012).

[2]Matthew Spinka, "Latin Church of the Early Crusades," *Church History* 8, no. 2 (June 1939): 115, 116.

[3]Ralph of Caen, *The Gesta Tancredi of Ralph of Caen: A History of the Normans on the First Crusade*, ed. Bernard S. Bachrach and David Stewart Bachrach, Crusade Texts in Translation 12 (Burlington, VT: Ashgate, 2005), 154.

of the plague soon after the capture of Antioch. Suddenly the official papal voice was gone, and no one was on the scene to encourage Crusaders to abide by their oaths. Second, the papal replacement, Daimbert, did not share the same understanding of Urban's vision and had ambitions of his own. His attitude was just the opposite of his predecessor. Daimbert encouraged the break with Alexius and campaigned for his own place and power. Third, when the Crusaders were in dire straits during the siege of Antioch and in need of reinforcements, Alexius failed to come to their aid. Byzantine troops were marching toward Antioch to aid the Crusaders, but the emperor's assessment was that all was lost, so he retreated and left the Crusaders to fend for themselves. Once Antioch and Jerusalem fell, Crusaders felt that these were their victories alone and thus they were not required to honor their oath.

Rather than an expansion of a united Christendom, captured territories became Latin ecclesial and political domains. On the ecclesial side, Arnulf, an Italian bishop among the conquering forces, was selected as the Latin patriarch of Jerusalem. The pope had not yet confirmed his election nor vested him with papal authority, yet Arnulf promptly established Latin ecclesial dominance in Jerusalem. His first act as patriarch was to expel Armenians, Copts, Jacobites, and Nestorians from the Holy Sepulchre and set up its administration under Latin clergy.[4] When the new papal legate, Daimbert, finally arrived, Arnulf was not affirmed as patriarch but removed from office. Instead, Daimbert was named the first Latin patriarch of Jerusalem. As the chief representative of the Latin church, he appointed Latin bishops to the sees at Edessa, Tarsus, Mamistra, and Artah, thus establishing a Latin hierarchy in the region.[5] In effect, Latin ecclesial authority turned Jerusalem, Antioch, and captured principalities into Catholic quarters, thereby displacing local Christians and their long-standing rites and traditions. The result—pilgrimage became the Latinization of Eastern Christendom.

On the political side, dukes, counts, and nobles envisioned the captured cities being administrated like states in Europe. How the church fit into this

---

[4]Hamilton, *Latin Church in the Crusader States*, 12-14.
[5]Ibid., 16. Harold S. Fink, "The Foundation of the Latin States, 1099–1118," in *A History of the Crusades*, vol. 1, *The First Hundred Years*, ed. Marshall W. Baldwin (Madison: The University of Wisconsin Press, 1969), 377-79, details Daimbert's arrival, his election as patriarch, and the unseating of Arnulf.

scheme was not at all clear. Latin political administration was established in four territories: Godfrey of Bouillon ruled the kingdom of Jerusalem, Bohemund of Taranto claimed Antioch, Baldwin of Boulogne ruled Edessa, and Raymond of St. Gilles created the state of Tripoli.[6] Daimbert, as patriarch of Jerusalem, assigned archbishoprics and bishoprics in these areas, thus creating an ecclesial hierarchy to mirror the political one. Left to be determined was whether Latin expansion and rule would be ecclesial or political, or a mixture of both.

LATIN EXPANSION

The struggle between ecclesial and secular dominance centered in Jerusalem. According to Thomas Asbridge, Daimbert viewed Jerusalem as "the physical embodiment of God's kingdom on Earth, capital of an ecclesiastical state with the patriarch at its head."[7] Jerusalem should become the Rome of the East, an independent, ecclesial state. And yet, political and military authority for Jerusalem and the surrounding area lay with Godfrey, and without his support, Jerusalem would not remain in Latin control for long. With Godfrey as the secular authority and Daimbert as the ecclesial ruler, the power relations in Jerusalem were unclear, and the city was unstable within, and so it became vulnerable to attacks from outside forces. Control and command needed to be clarified in order for the Latin settlement to succeed. When Godfrey suddenly became a fatality of an epidemic (July 18, 1100), Daimbert saw an opportunity to assert his claims and to act on his theocratic dream. However, oppositional parties invited Baldwin, ruler of Edessa and Godfrey's brother, to seize control of Jerusalem. Baldwin made his way to Jerusalem before Daimbert could consolidate support and entered the city with all the fanfare of a king. Baldwin was crowned as such on December 25, 1100, in the Church of the Virgin in Bethlehem. In an act of concession and in order to claim some role for himself, Daimbert anointed and crowned

---

[6]Christopher MacEvitt, *The Crusades and the Christian World of the East: Rough Tolerance*, The Middle Ages Series (Philadelphia: University of Pennsylvania Press, 2008), 5; Norman Housley, *Fighting for the Cross: Crusading to the Holy Land* (New Haven, CT: Yale University Press, 2008), 7.

[7]Thomas Asbridge, *The Crusades: The Authoritative History of the War for the Holy Land* (New York: HarperCollins, 2010), 118.

Baldwin of Boulogne as Baldwin I, the first Frankish king of Jerusalem.[8] With the crowning of Baldwin as king, Jerusalem became a secular state with a lay ruler. Any notion of the Holy Land or Jerusalem becoming a theocratic state or the new Rome was gone.

Even as Urban had altered the tradition of pilgrimage, the aims of his summons and the impulse that sent thousands of pilgrims on a holy errand had likewise drastically changed. Rather than a pilgrimage summoned by the vicar of Christ to liberate Christians of the East and retake holy sites, the cause became the establishment and maintenance of a Christian presence and hierarchy in the Holy Land. While the church and crown cooperated in the expansion of Christendom into the Levant, the church was relegated to an auxiliary partner in an occupied Holy Land. As Catholic Europe extended its presence in the centuries ahead, the church continually sought ways to reexert its influence and control.

The expansion of Christendom meant the establishment of Latin identity and extending the boundaries of Latin dominance. Agency of this expansion was through efforts to conquer and convert.

Identity and boundary. The majority of those on the First Crusade were French and Italian, but as pilgrims they found common identity in crusading.[9] The Crusades, according to Tyerman, "helped fashion for adherents a shared sense of belonging to a Christian society, *societas christiana,* Christendom, and contributed to setting its geographical frontiers. In these ways, the Crusades helped define the nature of Catholic Europe."[10] Through crusading the notion of Christian Europe was further realized, and the distinctions of race, tribe, and language became less important, and feudalism subsided.

Christendom, decreed earlier by Charlemagne as a territorial identity, was solidified as corporate identity through Urban's holy pilgrimage.[11]

---

[8]Ralph of Caen, *Gesta Tancredi,* 157. On Baldwin's selection, see Spinka, "Latin Church of the Early Crusades," 119; Asbridge, *Crusades,* 120. Godfrey had refused to be crowned king of Jerusalem but instead took the designation of "Advocate of the Holy Sepulchre."

[9]John France, *The Crusades and the Expansion of Catholic Christendom, 1000–1714* (London: Routledge, 2005), 5.

[10]Christopher Tyerman, *God's War: A New History of the Crusades* (Cambridge, MA: Harvard University Press, 2006), xiii; Christopher Dawson, *The Formation of Christendom* (New York: Sheed and Ward, 1967), 207.

[11]At the same time, the solidifying of Catholic Europe's identity weakened and eventually undermined Christianity. Dawson, *Formation of Christendom,* reports, "In the Fourth Crusade . . .

The enduring result of the vicar of Christ's summons for Catholic Europe to capture Jerusalem was the expansion and fortification of Latin identity. As Christopher Dawson explains, "It was the Crusade more than any other single factor which brought the unity of Christendom home to the lay society as a fact of daily experience."[12] Crusading was but another step in fortifying this identity at the center and incorporating peoples on the fringe. Christians worshiping in other languages and via other rites and those of other doctrinal positions were brought into Western Christendom as they submitted to the Latin Rite. The Latin Rite was not necessarily the means of expansion, but its adoption and enforcement were signs of the West's domination and control. Through liturgy, Latin identity "came to a have quasi-ethnic nuance, as in the phrase *gens latina*, 'the Latin people.'"[13] Entrance into European identity came via the ecclesial language of Latin.

Pilgrimage against a clearly defined enemy—"Turks, enemies of God and of holy Christianity"—further galvanized Catholic Europe into a people known as Latin Christendom.[14] The Crusades changed the way Latin Christians viewed themselves and those with whom they battled. Prior to the time of these encounters, "the peoples of the 'Catholic core,'" notes John France, "were cut off from the rest of the world by the Atlantic to the west, the pagan people of the steppe fringe to the north-east and Islam to the east."[15] France explains that as the fringe was threatened, the core responded with force in order to either incorporate or destroy the troubling elements at the fringe. Those on the fringe either identified with the Catholic core and thus submitted to the Latin rite, or they continued to resist. Continuing conflict, in time, broke the resistance of fringe groups, and Catholic Europe expanded and in the process became more defined.

Constantinople was captured for the first time in its history and a Latin emperor and patriarch were installed in the sacred city" (264).

[12]Ibid., 208.

[13]Robert Bartlett, *The Making of Europe: Conquest, Colonization and Cultural Change, 950–1350* (Princeton, NJ: Princeton University Press, 1993), 19, 251. Stephen Neill adds, "The languages of the barbarians were uncouth, unculturated, and unwritten, and were judged to be ill-adapted to the dignity of liturgy; Latin came with all the prestige of antiquity and of the civilizing power" (*HCM*, 73).

[14]Nirmal Dass, ed., *Deeds of the Franks and Other Jerusalem-Bound Pilgrims: The Earliest Chronicle of the First Crusades* (Lanham, MD: Rowman & Littlefield, 2011), 55.

[15]France, *Crusades and the Expansion*, 3.

Muslims, however, proved to be quite resistant, and the Holy Land was not on the immediate fringe but thousands of miles away. Rather than acculturating them into Latin Christianity, the best the Latin church could do was establish islands of Latin Christianity in Muslim-dominated regions. Hamilton's assessment is that the Latin church "remained alien to the culture of Syria despite being established there for two hundred years."[16] While pilgrimage was the bridge for Latin culture to enter into and inhabit the Levant, Latin identity, in the end, was transplanted into the region and perpetuated only through foreign clergy and military force. Latin identity was replicated in the Latin settlements, not transferred to indigenous peoples in the region.

For Christians in the East, the establishment of Latin political administration and an ecclesial hierarchy was the beginning of two hundred years of Latin domination. Any hope of healing the split of 1054 was dashed by the unilateral actions of the Catholic conquerors and was completely destroyed in subsequent Crusades. In a letter written to Urban following the defeat of Turkish forces at Antioch, Crusade leaders confess, "We have overcome the Turks and heathens; heretics, however, Greeks and Armenians, Syrians, and Jacobites, we have not been able to overcome." Then they project that Urban will "come to the place of your fatherhood; that you, who are the vicar of Saint Peter, sit on his throne; that you keep us, thy sons, obedient in doing all things rightly; and that you eradicate and destroy all heresies, of whatever nature they be, with your authority and with our strength."[17] Crusaders viewed non-Latin Christians as heretics and envisioned the head of Latin Christianity eventually sitting as head over a united Christendom. The varieties of ancient Christians of the region (Melkites, Jacobites, Armenians, Maronites, Nestorians, Nubians,

---

[16]Hamilton, *Latin Church in the Crusader States*, 367.

[17]Reported by Fulcher of Chartres, "Deeds of the Franks on Their Pilgrimage to Jerusalem," in *The First Crusade: The Chronicle of Fulcher of Chartres and Other Source Materials*, ed. Edward Peters (Philadelphia: University of Pennsylvania Press, 1971), 68. MacEvitt, *Crusades and the Christian World of the East*, suggests that this letter expresses the Crusaders' alarm at "the religious diversity of the Christian world of the Middle East. Turks and Muslims they were prepared for, but for Armenians, Greeks, and Jacobites they were not" (2). MacEvitt argues that rather than a "dichotomized understanding of interreligious relations" between Latin and Eastern Christians, there was "'rough tolerance,' which encompassed conflict and oppression yet allowed multiple religious communities to coexist in a religiously charged land" (2-3).

Copts, and Georgians) were not Latin in language or rite and were thus viewed as "abnormal." While they were needed as allies against the Muslim majority, they were still seen as deviant brands of Christianity.[18] Doctrine and traditions differed, but to Latin Catholics the barrier was ultimately linguistic. Rather than Latin, the liturgy of these groups was in Syriac, Arabic, and lesser-known languages.

For Muslims, who were not in direct contact with the margins of Catholic Europe but located at a distance, the Crusades served to solidify rather than weaken their identity. The physical and social margins were great, and thus the chance of being converted and acculturated into Catholic Europe was highly unlikely. The strength of position and firm religious conviction gave Muslims the resolve to resist and eventually repel the invading forces. The Crusades reinforced identity for both Latin Christians and Muslims and initiated new ways of viewing and relating to each other that have stretched into the modern era.[19] Just as Latin identity was strengthened by the Crusades, Muslim identity and cause were solidified.

The linguistic and communal identity for Catholic Europe became a territorial description known as Christendom. "The inhabitants of Christian Europe," according to Bartlett, "came increasingly to think of themselves as inhabiting a part of the world called Christendom, to picture an opposing and surrounding 'heathendom' and to regard as a praiseworthy and thinkable goal the expansion or extension of Christendom."[20] The Latin Rite signaled the the terms of this expansion—submission and obedience to a place, Rome, and incorporation into a realm, Christendom. As submission to the church expanded, so did Christendom. As rulers conquered in the name of the church, new subjects were incorporated into the Latin church. Latin became the signature of this identity and the bridge over

---

[18]For a succinct description of these religious communities and how they were viewed by Catholic Europe, see MacEvitt, *Crusades and the Christian World of the East*, 7-10; Barber, *Crusader States*, 40-44.

[19]According to Eleanor Harvey Tejirian and Reeva Spector Simon, *Conflict, Conquest, and Conversion: Two Thousand Years of Christian Missions in the Middle East* (New York: Columbia University Press, 2012), "The First Crusade established a paradigm for relations among Western Christendom, the Eastern Christian churches, and the Muslim Middle East for centuries to come" (28).

[20]Bartlett, *Making of Europe*, 254. Bartlett reports that "between 950 and 1350 Latin Christendom roughly doubled in area, and, while this religious expansion did not always involve either conquest or immigration, it often did" (292).

which new peoples found their way into Christendom, except for the Muslim.

Conversion and conquest. While there are reports of Crusaders persuading those they encountered to convert to Christianity, the expansion of Christendom's identity and boundary came chiefly by means of conquest. Conversion was the exception rather than the norm.[21] What we find is that Jews and Muslims were given an ultimatum to convert and be baptized or to be put to death. The vast majority of Crusaders did not evangelize Muslims and Jews, nor was conversion their aim.[22] In part this was because Latin Christians viewed them as opponents in a conflict. Jews and Muslims were enemies of the cross, and thus persons to conquer and kill rather than to evangelize. Occasionally Crusaders describe Muslims as worthy opponents and note their bravery in battle, but in general they are vilified as pagans, barbarians, enemies of God, "infernal Turks," "profane ones," and nonbelievers.[23]

The rare attempts to convert Muslims were usually mixed with coercion and penalty. The model of conversion for Crusaders was the widely popular *Chanson de Roland* (Song of Roland). It recounts the story of Charlemagne offering a Muslim the opportunity to convert during the heat of battle, but once defeating his foe, Charlemagne forcibly baptizes him.[24] Thus, according to Kedar, "forcible baptism of Saracens is extolled in a work that probably shaped the ethic of the crusading stratum par excellence—the knighthood—more decisively than many an encyclical or learned treatise."[25] Duty, rather than concern, was the motivator that permitted the use of force. The duty to subjugate the enemy included the possibility of forcible baptism.

---

[21]See Jonathan Riley-Smith, *The First Crusade and the Idea of Crusading*, The Middle Ages (Philadelphia: University of Pennsylvania Press, 1986), 109-11.

[22]See Benjamin Kedar, *Crusade and Mission: European Approaches Toward the Muslims* (Princeton, NJ: Princeton University Press, 1984), 57-74, for an extensive discussion on the absence of conversion as an explicit aim of the First Crusade. He offers limited evidence of some conversions from Islam to Christianity with subsequent Crusades. On the other hand, Allan Cutler, "First Crusade and the Idea of Conversion (First Installment)," *Muslim World* 58, no. 1 (January 1968): 57-71, argues the case that conversion was a significant aim of Urban II and various Crusaders.

[23]Dass, *Deeds of the Franks and Other Jerusalem-Bound Pilgrims*, 30, 43, 45, 46, 49, 51, 52, 58, 61, 71, 79, 81, 94, 97, 102, 107.

[24]See J. Hoeberichts, *Francis and Islam* (Quincy, IL: Franciscan, 1997), 26-27.

[25]Kedar, *Crusade and Mission*, 69.

And yet, according to Jonathan Riley-Smith, love was not absent. He argues that along with other rhetoric that stirred and mobilized Crusaders, love must be included. In papal encyclicals and sermons of apologists for the Crusades, words such as *caritas, charitei,* or "charity" are prevalent, and thus "the idea of the crusader expressing love through his participation in acts of armed force was an element in the thinking of senior churchmen in the central Middle Ages."[26] However fraught and contradictory in the modern mind, the picture of the Crusader Riley-Smith constructs is one of men and women who took up the cross and conquered others out of love for God and love of neighbor. The intent of using force as a means of love was to correct and to save the Muslim from error, and thus force had a benevolent intention. "To coerce one's neighbor," Riley-Smith explains, "could be to love him and the man who punished evil did not persecute but loved."[27] Violence was characterized as a necessary act of Christian charity.

Augustine provides the rationale for violence as love. His conviction was that force was necessary, and even commanded by God, in order to express true love to those who were heretics. Just as a parent disciplines a child, or a physician must take severe measures in order to heal a person's malady, so force must be applied by the Christian on those in error and even to the enemy.[28] For the Crusaders, Augustine's notion of charity extended to include not just heretics and schismatics but Muslims as well. Thus, as a double movement, conquering and converting went hand in hand. While uneven and inconsistent in the period leading up to the First Crusade, the sentiment of the Crusader toward the Muslim was that they convert or die.

---

[26]Jonathan Riley-Smith, "Crusading as an Act of Love," *History* 65 (1980): 177.

[27]Ibid., 188. This sentiment can be seen in Humbert's treatise (ca. 1272–1274) in defense of the Crusades: "It is possible that if the Saracens were well shaken they would not place so much trust in their Muhammad. In reply to the point made about sending them to hell, it should be said that it is not the Christians' intention to do this but to deal with them, as is just, like a judge dealing with a thief. May they see for themselves where they are going when they leave this world. Nevertheless divine providence threats them kindly, because it is better for them to die sooner rather than later on account of their sins which increase as long as they live" (reported by Louise Riley-Smith and Jonathan Riley-Smith, *The Crusades: Idea and Reality, 1095–1274*, Documents of Medieval History 4 [London: Edward Arnold, 1981], 114).

[28]Augustine, *Concerning the City of God Against the Pagans*, trans. Henry Bettenson (London: Penguin Books, 1984), 19.12 (866-70). See Riley-Smith's discuss of love and the Crusades in *Idea of Crusading*, 27, 113-15, and "Crusading as an Act of Love," 177-92.

The fate for Muslim and local Christian communities of the East living under Latin administration was to submit to regulations, pay taxes, and serve the needs of the colonies. Submission, not conversion, was the chief aim. When conversion occurred, the end goal was absorption into Latin identity. Whatever the means, preaching, charity, or other forms of persuasion, the aim was Latinization. Through this process, Latin identity solidified, Christendom's boundaries expanded, and cultural and religious enclosures of *gens latina* (Latin people) were established.

Christendom was not Christianity writ large but Latin Christianity. While marked by territorial limits, its ultimate designation was Latin. Adherence to the Latin liturgy and rite set the boundary of Christendom. Thus, to perform the Latin mass in Jerusalem was tantamount to extending the boundary of Christendom. Outposts of Latin expression created beachheads for expansion and the frontier for Western Christendom.[29] Greek Christianity was not Latin Christianity, and thus it too came under attack and was brought under Latin control for a period.

The language of colonization came into use at the close of the First Crusade with the establishment of Latin enclaves.[30] To conquer was as much an act of possession of places and people. These became colonies of Western Christendom, outposts of Catholic Europe. Both the extension of Christendom boundaries and the incorporation of people into the Latin sphere meant the exploitation of local resources in order to solidify Latin identity and to maintain the new boundaries.[31] Through Latin occupation, pilgrimage turned into the expansion of Christendom and the exploitation of local peoples and resources. Pilgrims became expatriates and masters.

---

[29]For a survey of scholarship on Latin settlements as "frontier societies," see Nora Berend, "Frontiers," in *Palgrave Advances in the Crusades*, ed. Helen J. Nicholson (New York: Palgrave MacMillan, 2005), 148-71.

[30]Colonization, some maintain, began at the close of the First Crusade and became the pattern for subsequent Crusades as Latin bishoprics were installed and Latin administration was established in territories (Cyprus, Constantinople, and cities in Spain and Greek islands). The enclaves or colonies in the Levant existed for two centuries, coming to an end in 1291, when the Mamluk sultanate reconquered Acre and other strongholds. For the history of this pattern, see Joshua Prawer, *The Latin Kingdom of Jerusalem: European Colonialism in the Middle Ages* (London: Weidenfeld and Nicolson, 1973), 469-82. Prawer regards "the Crusader kingdom as the first European colonial society" (foreword).

[31]Charles Verlinden, *The Beginnings of Modern Colonization: Eleven Essays with an Introduction*, trans. Yvonne Freccero (Ithaca, NY: Cornell University Press, 1970), xii, 79-80.

MISSION AND CRUSADE

In the occupation and colonization of the Levant by European Catholics, a connection between the Crusades and mission might seem reasonable and expected. But is there such a connection? What is the place of "mission" in Urban's holy pilgrimage and the ensuing Latin colonies? Were the Crusades "mission" efforts? Was the crusading pilgrim a "missionary" of sorts? Or, were there individuals and groups who refused to join the crusading effort and thus dissented or obstructed by means of "missionary" work? Did anyone attempt to both march against the Muslim and labor as a "missionary"?

From a literal or linguistic point of view, the answer to these questions is simple. Since mission language is not present in sermons, encyclicals, letters, or accounts of popes and Crusaders, the crusading pilgrim was not a missionary, the Crusades were not a missionary effort, no one was able to oppose the Crusades by way of mission, and the tasks of crusading and mission were not one and the same. Much like the preceding centuries in Christian history, the language of *mission* was simply nonexistent before and during the Crusades.[32] Because persons called *missionaries* did not exist and thus could not be sent, missionaries were not active among Muslims. Mission, as organized and concerted efforts of evangelization in the modern sense of the word, was not named by those inside or outside the church to describe the activities of Christians toward non-Christians. Instead, men and women from a variety of life situations, such as soldiers, knights, farmers, clergy, friars, and kings, took the cross, became pilgrims, and in so doing, encountered people of other faith traditions. They joined the crusading movement in hopes of treasures, out of the fear of damnation, to find political advantage, to extend the bounds of Christendom, to preach a gospel message, or to express a type of charity. Whatever the motive, they were not "missionaries" sent by the pope or a mission entity, nor were they sent under the banner of "mission."

From the vantage point of modern Christianity, the answer to these questions might initially seem equally cut and dried. What transpired because of Urban's summons, as tens of thousands of Latin Christians marched across

---

[32]While calling Columba and others missionaries, Paul Johnson, *A History of Christianity* (New York: Atheneum, 1976), on this point agrees.

Europe and into the Levant, defeated Muslims in battle, captured cities with extreme brutality, and then established islands of Western Christendom, is not what modern Christians mean by *mission*. To inject this modern term into an era and events a millennium away only increases the ambiguity and confusion regarding "mission" that already exists. And yet, modern interpreters of the medieval era and the Crusades find reason to liberally insert *mission* and *missionary* into the narrative of the Crusades. Once again, because of the elasticity of mission language, interpreters find reason to appropriate modern terminology to explain medieval activities and to identify their actors. However, in this appropriation, they ascribe nineteenth-century assumptions and aims to eleventh-century events and individuals. As with the early church, *mission* and *missionary* are supplied terms and thus are inappropriate language for persons and movements in the Crusade era.[33] When interpreters apply mission language to crusading efforts, they are attempting to portray either continuity, obstruction, or coexistence.

Continuity. Interpreters of the Crusades use mission language to describe what they construe as continuity between evangelizing and crusading efforts. For them crusading was the fundamental "mission" of Catholic Europe in response to Muslims in the East, as well as enemies on the Iberian Peninsula, and heretical groups in central Europe, the Baltic region, and North Africa.[34] Crusaders were accessory to mission activities that brought others into the Catholic sphere of influence. Because the aims of both are contiguous, the language of mission merges with that of crusade.

Some interpreters imply continuity between mission and crusade, and others explicitly state it. For example, Christopher Tyerman connects the two when he states that the Clermont decree to liberate Jerusalem "marked a new beginning in western Christianity's use of war to further its religious

---

[33]For example, *HCM*, 114; Dana Lee Robert, *Christian Mission: How Christianity Became a World Religion* (Chichester, UK: Wiley-Blackwell, 2009), 25; *HEC*, 2:400; Stephen B. Bevans and Roger Schroeder, *Constants in Context: A Theology of Mission for Today* (Maryknoll, NY: Orbis Books, 2004), 137.

[34]The Crusades are characterized by various historians and theologians as Western Christianity's religious mission or missions; see Christopher Tyerman, *Fighting for Christendom: Holy War and the Crusades* (Oxford: Oxford University Press, 2004), 27, 84, 174; Hans Wolter, "Elements of Crusade Spirituality in St. Ignatius," in *Ignatius of Loyola, His Personality and Spiritual Heritage, 1556–1956: Studies on the 400th Anniversary of His Death*, ed. Fredrich Wulf, trans. Louis W. Roberts, Modern Scholarly Studies About the Jesuits, in English Translations (St. Louis: The Institute of Jesuit Sources, 1977), 129.

mission."[35] With this particular use of *mission*, Tyerman either appears to imply that crusading is an extension of previous missionary kinds of activities of the Roman church, or his reference to mission is to general religious purpose. In a similar manner, Benjamin Kedar connects mission and crusade. He reasons that since the sentiment was that "God's vicar on earth has jurisdiction over Christians as well as infidels," the pope had a right to rule over all peoples. Thus, military crusades to open a way for Catholic preachers for "mission" were viewed as acceptable.[36] What Tyerman and Kedar suggest, Karen Armstrong declares. She asserts that "the Muslim world associates Western imperialism and Christian missionary work with the Crusades," and "they are not wrong to do so."[37] For her, the connection is more than one of an association of ideas; rather, mission and crusade are one and the same act.

Carl Erdmann goes as far as to cast the Crusades in terms of "missionary wars." He reasons that because the message of Christ is meant for all of humanity, Christianity is a missionary religion, and its adherents must spread the faith to every person. Thus, because the Crusades were "holy wars" of a "missionary religion" with a clear "missionary duty," force was used to subject people and bring them to faith. These were "wars against heretics within [Christendom], to preserve the purity of the church," as well as "missionary wars without [Christendom], to extend the faith."[38] The development of these "indirect and direct missionary wars" began with the Constantinian fusion of state and church powers. Erdmann explains the progression of this relationship.

> At a time when the authorities of state and church were closely bound together, missions could hardly avoid being under state leadership and availing

---

[35]Tyerman, *Fighting for Christendom*, 27. See also Diarmaid MacCulloch, *Christianity: The First Three Thousand Years* (New York: Viking, 2009), 384.

[36]Kedar, *Crusade and Mission*, 159. This linkage was made in a pronounced manner during the papacy of Innocent IV. Kedar observes that "by unequivocally rejecting forcible conversion while at the same time endorsing the forcible opening of an infidel country to Catholic preachers, Innocent largely reconciled the fundamental principle of free choice with the popularly evolved notion of Christianization as one of the goals of crusading" (161).

[37]Karen Armstrong, *Muhammad: A Biography of the Prophet* (San Francisco: HarperSanFrancisco, 1993), 40.

[38]Carl Erdmann, *The Origin of the Idea of Crusade*, trans. Marshall Baldwin and Walter Goffart (Princeton, NJ: Princeton University Press, 1977), 4, 10, 11.

themselves of the state means of enforcement. The early medieval theory of indirect missionary war had already bridged the contradiction between conquest and conversion: military subjection was to contribute to the peaceful mission that would follow.[39]

Thus, Urban's summons to a crusading pilgrimage was the culmination of a long and circuitous route of development from Augustine's doctrine of just war as a defensive act to Gregory's notion of war in service of the church's victory over the enemies of the cross. Alongside and woven into this development was "mission." In order for war and mission to coalesce and become partners, war had to be "transformed into a stark issue of belief, in which the opponent is peremptorily faced with the alternative of death or baptism, and in which the killing of a heathen is held to be a deed pleasing to God."[40] For Erdmann, mission and crusade are one and the same in the medieval mind. Therefore, mission language is permitted and can be generously applied to the Crusades and Crusaders, their aims and activities.

Obstruction. Other interpreters use mission language to describe individuals and groups who opposed crusading endeavors and sought to evangelize Muslims and Jews. These interpreters maintain that missionaries were actually present and active during the Crusades, but, rather than crusading or supporting the Crusades, they provided an alternative message and used different means. These interpreters identify individuals and organizations as "missionary" and contrast their attitude and activity as thoroughly different from those of the Crusaders. For these interpreters, mission language marks an alternative approach and opposition to the Crusades.

Blocher and Blandenier open their discussion of the Crusades with the qualification that they are "not to be confused in any way as missionary efforts."[41] By this, they imply the activities of missionaries were in opposition to the Crusades and Crusaders, and mission is other than crusading. Likewise, Robert Glover asserts, "The Crusades were not in any true sense

---

[39]Ibid., 105.

[40]Ibid., 12. Bosch, *TM*, 229-30, maintains that Erdmann does not see crusade and mission as contiguous. However, it appears that Erdmann is merely identifying the obvious contradiction but still views the contradiction between conquest and conversion as having been bridged in the medieval mind.

[41]Jacques A. Blocher and Jacques Blandenier, *The Evangelization of the World: A History of Christian Mission* (Pasadena, CA: William Carey Library, 2013), 103.

a missionary movement."[42] The examples often cited as exceptions to crusading activities are Frances of Assisi, Peter the Venerable, Thomas Aquinas, Ramon Llull, and other Franciscans and Dominicans.[43] These individuals and groups are named as dissenters and obstructionists, who opposed the Crusades and forged a distinct, missionary response to Muslims. Thus, "mission" means opposition to the Crusades.

Coexistence. Others acknowledge the existence of mission activities at the time of the Crusades, but rather than being accessory to or distinct from crusading efforts, missionaries and proponents for mission supported crusading against the Muslims. For them, mission and crusading, while distinct, coexisted and at times collaborated with crusading efforts. Though mission and crusade are not interchangeable, they stand alongside each other as cooperating partners.

G. F. Maclear is representative of those who view the Crusades and missionary work as different but coexisting. He believes that crusading eventually subsided as mission efforts grew. But before this time, "the fiery propagandism of the Crusades" was stronger than the "few instances of missionary zeal."[44] In their study of conversion during this era, Tejirian and Simon chronicle the existence of mission alongside diplomatic and crusading activities. Though they indicate that following the Fourth Lateran Council, what "had been distinct concepts, crusade and mission, were now merged," and though the distinction between missionaries and diplomats sent by the pope was not always clear, Tejirian and Simon use *mission* and *missionary* as descriptors of activities and agents different from *crusading* and *crusader.*[45] They maintain that a "missionary enterprise," consisting of "missionary work" and "missionary thrust," was in operation through "missionary orders" that established missions in Spain, Jerusalem, and the East.[46] Bevans and Schroeder note the role of military conquest in the spread of Christianity but identify missionaries, particularly of the mendicant

---

[42]Robert Hall Glover, *The Progress of World-Wide Missions* (New York: Harper & Row, 1960), 36.

[43]Mathias Braun, "Missionary Problems in the Thirteenth Century: A Study in Missionary Preparation," *The Catholic Historical Review* 25, no. 2 (July 1939): 147, cites St. Frances and St. Dominic as prime examples.

[44]G. F. Maclear, *A History of Christian Missions During the Middle Ages* (Cambridge: Macmillan, 1863), 351.

[45]Tejirian and Simon, *Conflict, Conquest, and Conversion,* 38, 40.

[46]Ibid., 34, 36, 37, 38, 39, 43.

orders, as "the ones who offer an alternative approach to Islam."[47] Baldwin, in his study of mission during the crusading era, concludes that medieval missionaries "shared the feelings of their contemporaries and accepted the war with Islam as an unavoidable necessity," and that this could not have been otherwise.[48] His contention is that missionary work existed alongside the crusading movement, either in a blatant or furtive manner, but not in opposition to the Crusades. Latourette notes that though the Crusades were an obstacle to the spread of Christianity, they also helped. In particular, he claims that from "the towns and fortresses in the hands of the Franks missionaries went forth."[49] Latourette neither names these missionaries nor cites examples of their mission activities, but only asserts their presence. For those who represent an alternative to the violent confrontation of the Muslim, Latourette names Thomas Aquinas, Roger Bacon, Pope Honorius IV, Francis of Assisi, and Ramon Llull. In his opinion, "the burden of the missions of the thirteenth, fourteenth, and fifteenth centuries" fell to the Franciscans and Dominicans.[50]

UNFORTUNATE LANGUAGE

Problems exist with all three portrayals of the relationship between "mission" and the Crusades. Again, the difficulty lies in language. Mission language, used to express either accessory, dissent, or coexistence, does not add clarity

---

[47]Bevans and Schroeder, *Constants in Context*, 142.

[48]Marshall W. Baldwin, "Missions to the East in the Thirteenth and Fourteenth Centuries," in *A History of the Crusades*, vol. 5, *The Impact of the Crusades on the Near East*, ed. Norman Zacour and Harry W. Hazard (Madison: The University of Wisconsin Press, 1985), 517. The coexistence of crusading and mission appears to be the position of Cutler, "First Crusade and the Idea of Conversion (First Installment)," and Robert I. Burns, "Christian-Islamic Confrontation in the West: The Thirteenth-Century Dream of Conversion," *The American Historical Review* 76, no. 5 (December 1971): 1386-1434.

[49]Latourette believes the specific or named intent of the Crusades was not to spread Christianity, but in the end they "proved both a help and an obstacle to the spread of Christianity" (*HEC*, 2:317, 318).

[50]Ibid., 2:320. Elizabeth Siberry, "Missionaries and Crusaders, 1095–1274: Opponents or Allies?," in *Church and War: Papers Read at the Twenty-First Summer Meeting and Twenty-Second Winter Meeting of the Ecclesiastical History Society*, ed. W. J. Sheils (Oxford: Basil Blackwell, 1983), takes issue with this claim and shows that those noted by Latourette and others for their missionary zeal did not oppose the crusading movement. In fact, "they seem to have regarded it as a stimulus to conversion and the new order of friars [Franciscans and Dominicans] became the foremost apologists of the crusades" (110). She demonstrates that figures such as Peter the Venerable, St. Francis, Roger Bacon, and other Dominicans and Franciscans did not condemn the Crusades and in many cases were its proponents.

or sharpen our view of the Crusades. Rather, mission language pollutes our understanding by injecting an unrecognized category of service and a profession that did not exist. Mission language is inexact and misleading language that disguises the actors and their motives, and thus it poisons our interpretation. Or to state the problem in another way, mission language subverts the history of the Crusades.

Charlemagne's legacy, Urban's summons, doctrinal controversies, social conventions, and political dynamics are obscured by the much more eminent, better-known nomenclature and experience of mission. To insist that mission language be used as a convenience, or because to not use it would be pedantic, disregards the potential of erroneous images and faulty impressions that comes with such language. What is known as mission in the modern era is foreign rhetoric for the Middle Ages, and what is known as crusading is ruinous for modern mission efforts. It is improper and wrong to position mission and crusade as opposing ideas, accessory to the other, or coexisting. When applied to the crusades, mission language confounds a proper understanding for both the Middle Ages and the modern era. The problem with all three portrayals is illustrated in the way interpreters have treated the motives and actions of Francis of Assisi and Ramon Llull. More than any others in the crusading era, mission language has been inserted into the lives and activities of these two figures.

Francis of Assisi (ca. 1181–1226) is often cited as the chief example of a medieval missionary who opposed the Crusades. The basis for these claims is his encounter with the sultan of Egypt. During the battle for the port of Damietta (1219) in the Fifth Crusade (1217–1221), Francis approached and tried to convert the ruler of Egypt, the successor of Saladin, Malik-al-Kâmil (ca. 1177–1238).[51] This incident is offered as a clear example of mission and a missionary approach as distinct from crusading. In some cases, the

---

[51]This encounter is explored by John Tolan, *Saint Francis and the Sultan: The Curious History of a Christian-Muslim Encounter* (Oxford: Oxford University Press, 2009); Steven J. McMichael, "Francis and the Encounter with the Sultan (1219)," in *The Cambridge Companion to Francis of Assisi*, Cambridge Companions to Religion (Cambridge: Cambridge University Press, 2012), 127-42; Paul Moses, *The Saint and the Sultan: The Crusades, Islam, and Francis of Assisi's Mission of Peace* (New York: Doubleday, 2009); Francis de Beer, "St. Francis and Islam," *Spirit and Life: A Journal of Contemporary Franciscanism* 6 (1994): 161-75; and Walbert Bühlmann, "Francis and Mission According to the Rule of 1221," *Spirit and Life: A Journal of Contemporary Franciscanism* 6 (1994): 89-96.

characterization of Francis as missionary and obstructionist is explicitly and intentionally stated. For example, while Dale Irvin and Scott Sunquist carefully report the historical fact of the Crusades, discussing the reasons for them and avoiding a characterization of them as "mission," they do portray Francis as "a missionary."[52] Hilarin Felder goes even further, labeling Francis a "missionary" who plans mission activities and goes on missionary journeys.[53] Stephen Neill writes of Francis's "missionary zeal," the "missionary methods" he instituted, and the "missionary enterprise" that resulted in the founding of the Franciscan order.[54] Marshall Baldwin contends that "effective promotion of oriental missions had to await the appearance of that *vir catholicus et totus apostolius*, Francis of Assisi." In fact, "Francis of Assisi was the first to state clearly the ideal of missions to Moslems."[55] For Baldwin, Francis is the fountainhead of medieval mission. Likewise, John Moorman, in his history of the Franciscan movement, has Francis "proposing to go off on a mission to a foreign and hostile country" and taking "missionary journeys."[56] According to Moorman, when Francis and his companion, Brother Illuminato, concluded their conversation with the sultan, Malik-al-Kâmil "was glad to give the two missionaries a safe-conduct back to their own camp."[57]

None of the early chroniclers describe Francis's encounter as "mission," nor do they name Francis a "missionary."[58] Francis is identified as a Christian,

---

[52]Dale T. Irvin and Scott W. Sunquist, *History of the World Christian Movement*, vol. 1, *Earliest Christianity to 1453* (Maryknoll, NY: Orbis Books, 2001), 416. See also Baldwin, "Missions to the East in the Thirteenth and Fourteenth Centuries," 455-56; Kenneth Scott Latourette, *Christianity Through the Ages* (New York: Harper & Row, 1965), 112-13; Maclear, *History of Christian Missions During the Middle Ages*, 353.

[53]Hilarin Felder, *The Ideals of St. Francis of Assisi*, trans. Berchmans Bittle (New York: Benziger Brothers, 1925), 303, 304, 305. Felder calls Francis "the father of the modern missionary movement" (316).

[54]*HCM*, 99.

[55]Baldwin, "Missions to the East in the Thirteenth and Fourteenth Centuries," 453, 455.

[56]John R. H. Moorman, *A History of the Franciscan Order from Its Origins to the Year 1517* (Oxford: Clarendon, 1968), 27, 28, 75.

[57]Ibid., 49.

[58]Tolan, *Saint Francis and the Sultan*, provides accounts from a variety of sources: a letter from Jacques de Vitry (1220), *Historia occidentalis* by Jacques de Vitry (1223–1225), an anonymous *Chronicle of the Crusades* (1227–1229), Thomas de Celano's life of St. Francis, *Vita prima* (1228), Henry of Avranches's poem *Versified Life of Saint Francis* (1232), Bonaventure's *Legenda maior* (1263), *Sermo de Sancto Francisco* (1267), *Collationes in Hexaemeron* (1273), Angelo Clareno's *Chronicle* (1326), and Ugolino da Montegiorgio's *Deeds of Blessed Francis and His Companions* (1327–1337). Christoph Maier offers the same assessment of sources in *Preaching the Crusades:*

messenger, cleric, holy man, "intrepid knight of Christ," "man of God," "the friend of Christ," shepherd, servant, and pilgrim, but not a missionary. When one looks to St. Francis's writings, mission language is absent, and it is not found in early Franciscan sources.[59] In fact, Francis's journey to Damietta is described as a "pilgrimage." Because he is delayed on the way to Jerusalem, and thus waiting at the Crusader encampment, he decides to cross the battle lines.[60] His encounter with the sultan is unanticipated and unplanned. Thus, his action is not against crusading, in protest of crusading, or in distinction from it. Rather, he seeks to proclaim the gospel and wants to become a martyr. Benjamin Kedar's appraisal is that "Francis's attitude to the armed struggle against the Muslims must remain a moot point, since none of his scanty writings bears on the issue."[61] Rather than an example of mission, chroniclers of the event use Francis's encounter as reason to argue for additional Crusades. The sultan's refusal to convert is evidence that the only way to deal with Muslims is through force.[62]

Francis was a child when Jerusalem fell to Saladin in 1187.[63] He grew up with ideals of knighthood and spent his early life in military pursuits. His dream of knighthood was interrupted when he was captured and imprisoned. Time in prison and sickness caused him to reflect on his life and prompted the radical changes that were to come. He determined to become

---

Mendicant Friars and the Cross in the Thirteenth Century, The Medieval Review (Cambridge: Cambridge University Press, 1994), 8-16.

[59]Charles V. Finnegan, "Franciscans and the 'New Evangelization,'" *Spirit and Life: A Journal of Contemporary Franciscanism* 6 (1994): 3.

[60]Tolan, *Saint Francis and the Sultan*, 148. E. Randolph Daniel, *The Franciscan Concept of Mission in the High Middle Ages* (Lexington: University Press of Kentucky, 1975), names St. Francis as "the first Franciscan missionary" (41).

[61]Kedar, *Crusade and Mission*, 129. Kedar conjectures that Francis "regarded his own attempts at preaching as supplementary rather than a contradictory alternative to the crusade, with options imbued with the values of chivalry and demanding a willingness to undergo martyrdom" (131). On the opposing side, Moses, *Saint and the Sultan*, 6, 11, 105-19, maintains that Francis was an active opponent to war. McMichael, "Francis and the Encounter with the Sultan," counters that no one can really be sure and argues that Francis "probably disapproved of the Crusades" (128). See also James M. Powell, "St. Francis of Assisi's Way of Peace," *Medieval Encounters* 13 (2007): 271-80.

[62]See Tolan's discussion of Jacques's *Historia occidentalis*, in *Saint Francis and the Sultan*, 35-39.

[63]For the details of the formative military influences of Francis's early life and his attitude toward the Crusades, see Michael Robson, *The Franciscans in the Middle Ages*, Monastic Orders (Woodbridge, UK: Boydell, 2006), 12-13; McMichael, "Francis and the Encounter with the Sultan," 129.

"a knight of Christ" and serve the cause of God with his whole being.[64] Three times between 1212 and 1219 Francis attempted pilgrimages to Jerusalem. His audience with al-Kâmil was on the second of these. The encounter took place while Francis was a pilgrim, not a missionary, and in the context of a pilgrimage to Jerusalem, not on a mission to Egypt. Francis's earliest biographer, Thomas of Celano (d. 1260), describes the motivation for this encounter as Francis's "desire to undergo martyrdom," but in the end "the Lord did not fulfill his desire."[65] Francis's chief aim in the daring encounter was to achieve martyrdom "for the sake of God."[66]

Crossing enemy lines and preaching the gospel to the sultan is an example of Francis's pursuit of *vita apostolica*, the life of the apostles. This pursuit is most clearly expressed in his *Regula prima*. In chapter sixteen, "Those Going Among the Saracens and Other Nonbelievers," he instructs brothers "to live spiritually" in two ways. First, they are not "to engage in arguments or disputes," and second, they are "to announce the Word of God, when they see it pleases the Lord, in order that [nonbelievers] may believe in almighty God, the Father, the Son and the Holy Spirit, the Creator of all, the Son, the Redeemer and Savior, and be baptized and become Christians."[67] Throughout this chapter, as well as the rest of *Regula prima*, those who go among Muslims are never referred to as missionaries but as "brothers," "ministers," "servants," or "preachers." The nature of this pursuit is the same whether they are among European Christians, Jews, or Muslims. Francis does not imbue these pursuits with "mission dimensions" but characterizes them as announcing the Word of God. The brothers are simply to call people to repentance and penance.[68]

While there is no evidence that Francis himself preached sermons in support of the Crusades, other Franciscans did.[69] Hugh of Turenne and Jacques of Virtry (1180–1240), both Franciscans, actively preached in support of the Crusades, participated in the recruitment, and even accompanied

---

[64]Felder, *Ideals of St. Francis of Assisi*, 300.
[65]Thomas of Celano, "The Life of Saint Francis," in *Francis of Assisi: Early Documents*, vol. 1, *The Saint*, ed. Regis J. Armstrong, J. A. Wayne Hellmann, and William J. Short (New York: New City, 1999), 229, 231.
[66]Beer, "St. Francis and Islam," 162-67.
[67]"*Regula prima*," in Armstrong et al., *Francis of Assisi: Early Documents*, 1:74.
[68]Daniel, *Franciscan Concept of Mission*, 37-39.
[69]Robson, *Franciscans in the Middle Ages*, 74.

Crusaders, as did Ramon of Penyaforte (c. 1175–1275) and Gullaume of Cordelle.[70] And in the case of friars who provoked Muslim reaction in Spain and Morocco, there is evidence that Francis's words and actions were used as justification "to preach and confess Christ's faith and assail the religion of Machomet."[71] As pilgrims, Franciscans provided care for Crusaders and participated in diplomatic efforts, but they were not obstructionists.[72]

When applied to Francis's life and actions, mission language contaminates the account. It is far better to let Francis be who he was—pilgrim, preacher, and pious martyr. To coat him with *mission* and *missionary* burdens his narrative with unnecessary and unfortunate language.

Ramon Llull (c. 1232–1316) of Majorca is likewise cited as a missionary obstructionist. It is claimed that rather than killing Muslims, Llull campaigned for their conversion to Christianity. Thus, in Robert Glover's estimation, "Raymond Llull [is] the first and still the greatest missionary to the Muslims."[73] The picture Glover paints is one in which the Crusades failed, and thus, Llull initiated an alternative method through which Christians fought "for the Cross with spiritual instead of carnal weapons, and approached the Saracens with the Word of Truth rather than with force of arms."[74] In a similar manner, Tejirian and Simon name the fall of Acre to the Mamluk in 1291 as "the end of Crusades and missionary work in Palestine." But this was not the complete end, as they insist that "instead of crusade, the church turned to mission, replacing military arms with sermons and public disputations. To that end, Raymond Llull, whose mission work took him to North Africa, worked to convert the Saracens."[75] Maclear maintains that in the midst of the crusading fervor "there was a Raymond Llull to protest

---

[70]Kedar, *Crusade and Mission*, 138-39; John M. Hull, *Towards the Prophetic Church: A Study of Christian Mission* (London: SCM Press, 2014), 73; Maier, *Preaching the Crusades*, 9, 144.

[71]As reported by Kedar, *Crusade and Mission*, 126.

[72]See Bevans and Schroeder, *Constants in Context*, 151; Robson, *Franciscans in the Middle Ages*, 74. According to Housley, *Fighting for the Cross*, "The bulk of the [Crusade] preaching was entrusted to the new orders of the friars, Franciscans and Dominicans" (32). Hoeberichts, *Francis and Islam*, offers considerable discussion on chapter 16, "the missionary chapter," of the Franciscan's *Regula non bullata*. Hoeberichts maintains that "traces of Francis' rejection of the crusade" can be found in his words and actions (58).

[73]Glover, *Progress of World-Wide Missions*, 36. Neill ranks Llull "as one of the greatest missionaries in the history of the Church" (*HCM*, 114).

[74]Glover, *Progress of World-Wide Missions*, 36.

[75]Tejirian and Simon, *Conflict, Conquest, and Conversion*, 42.

against propagandism by the sword, to develop 'a more excellent way' for winning over the Moslem."[76] In like manner, Samuel Zwemer gives Llull the title of "first missionary to the Moslems" and claims that he set out "to attack with new weapons of love and learning instead of the Crusaders' weapons of fanaticism and the sword."[77] To substantiate this claim, Zwemer lists Llull's founding of a "missionary training-school" that "included in its curriculum the geography of missions and the language of the Saracens," as well as his desire to have leaders of the church and Europe "become missionary enthusiasts like himself."[78] Zwemer chronicles Llull's multiple "missionary voyages" to North Africa on his "spiritual crusade"[79] along with his missionary zeal and missionary method, continually giving him the titles of "missionary" and "missionary knight" and naming Llull's aim as "world-wide missions."[80] While "popes clung to the crusade idea as the ideal of missions," Llull, according to Zwemer, "conceived the idea of founding an order of spiritual knights who should be ready to preach to the Saracens and so recover the tomb or Christ by a crusade of love."[81]

Contrary to the claims of Glover, Zwemer, Maclear, and others, Llull did not oppose the Crusades, and, in fact, he argued for additional ones, presented crusading plans, and advocated for campaigns in North Africa and Spain.[82] His crusading ideas appear not in one place and at one time but in several of his tracts and books.[83] Latourette's opinion is that Llull felt the

---

[76]Maclear, *History of Christian Missions During the Middle Ages*, 405.

[77]Samuel Marinus Zwemer, *Raymond Lull, First Missionary to the Moslems* (New York: Funk & Wagnalls, 1902), 49, 55. Or according to Zane G. Pratt, M. David Sills, and Jeff K. Walters, *Introduction to Global Missions* (Nashville: B&H, 2014), Llull was one of the few true missionaries of this period and "served as an example to later missionaries" (104).

[78]Zwemer, *Raymond Lull*, 67, 69. See similar language in Prawer, *World of the Crusaders*, 151.

[79]Zwemer, *Raymond Lull*, 80, 87.

[80]Ibid., 128, 133, 134. Latourette, *HEC*, 2:321-24, use the same kind of language of "missionary," "missionary methods," and "missionary interest" to describe Llull. See also Moorman, *History of the Franciscan Order*, 230-31.

[81]Zwemer, *Raymond Lull*, 74, 76. David Bosch, as well, claims in *Witness to the World: The Christian Mission in Theological Perspective* (Atlanta: John Knox, 1980), that Llull "condemned the Crusades in no uncertain terms" (113).

[82]Llull asserts, "Would that a great Prince might be found to lead a new crusade, and to lay down his arms only when no infidels are left to oppose the Catholic faith!" (Cited in E. Allison Peers, *Ramon Lull: A Biography* [New York: Burt Franklin, 1969], 200).

[83]For example, *Liber de Acquisitione Terrae Sanctae* (Book on the acquisition of the Holy Land), 1309. These works are mentioned and discussed in numerous sources, most notably Peers, *Ramon Lull*, 233, 253, 339-40, 352. See also Baldwin, "Missions to the East in the Thirteenth and Fourteenth Centuries," 465; Bevans and Schroeder, *Constants in Context*, 151.

Crusades "had failed, and the Holy Land was to be gained only by love, prayer, and tears." But Latourette also admits that Llull "believed that Crusades should be continued as an auxiliary to mission" and promoted the one that captured the island of Rhodes.[84] It appears that Llull may have had in his early writings designs for a crusade of love rather than force, but his sentiments changed with time to commending and arguing for new crusades.[85] In *Vita coaetanea*, Llull recounts his proposal to the people of Pisa that they establish "an order of Christian religious knights devoted to doing continual battle against the treacherous Saracens for the recovery of the Holy Land."[86] He was so persuasive that officials of the Pisa wrote to the pope, asking permission to pursue this project, and the city allocated funds for crusading efforts. In another instance, Llull purposed to attend a general council called by Pope Clement V in order to propose that all the Christian military religious orders be combined into a single order, "one that would maintain continual warfare overseas against the Saracens until the Holy Land had been reconquered."[87] Llull was not an obstructionist but emphasized a two-pronged or "two swords" approach.[88] Christians are to "do battle both with preaching and with arms against men that are unbelievers."[89]

In addition to these claims of obstruction, interpreters of Llull frequently use the rhetoric of mission to characterize him as the "ultimate missionary" in the crusading age. Irvin's and Sunquist's assessment is that Lull "formulated a comprehensive missionary alternative to crusading late in the thirteenth

---

[84]*HEC*, 2:322.

[85]Kedar, *Crusade and Mission*, 189-99.

[86]Ramon Llull, *Selected Works of Ramón Llull (1232–1316)*, trans. Anthony Bonner (Princeton, NJ: Princeton University Press, 1985), 1:45. See also Peers, *Ramon Lull*, 335-36.

[87]Llull, *Selected Works of Ramón Llull*, 1:46.

[88]Llull states this clearly in *Phantasticus*: "For the universal church of the catholics has two swords, as was said in the gospel; namely a corporate sword, that is, literally, a sword, and a spiritual [sword], that is knowledge and devotion. And with these two swords, the church has sufficient to lead all infidels to the path of truth" (trans. and cited by Pamela Beattie, "Evangelization, Reform and Eschatology: Mission and Crusade in the Thought of Ramon Llull" [PhD diss., University of Toronto, 1995], 106).

[89]Llull, cited by Peers, *Ramon Lull*, 317. Pamela Drost Beattie, "'Pro Exaltatione Sanctae Fidei Catholicae': Mission and Crusade in the Writings of Ramon Llull," in *Iberia and the Mediterranean World of the Middle East: Studies in Honor of Robert I. Burns* (Leiden: E. J. Brill, 1995), 128, 129, makes the assessment that both ideas are "intermeshed," and thus, "simultaneously endorse crusade and promote peaceful missions." In her PhD thesis, "Evangelization, Reform and Eschatology," Beattie argues, "Llull's crusade plans are always discussed in the context of his missionary goals. In fact, Llull never discusses crusade without also calling for evangelism" (75).

century." Therefore, Llull's "conception of missions as an alternative to the violence of the crusades and his advocacy of a comprehensive program that included language study and translation pointed in the direction that future generations of missionaries would follow."[90] Stephen Neill notes that Llull was "the first to develop a theory of missions," and thus Llull "must rank as one of the greatest missionaries in the history of the church."[91] E. Allison Peers writes of Llull's "missionary journeys," "missionary career," "zeal for missions," and his efforts on behalf the "missionary enterprise."[92]

Vita coaetanea, Llull's accounts of his life, tells of his vision of Christ and his call to "the task of converting to [Christ's] worship and service the Saracens who in such numbers surrounded the Christians on all sides."[93] In order to accomplish this, Llull sets three aims for his life: first, to write a book, "the best in the world, against the errors of unbelievers"; second, to set up monasteries "in which selected monks and others fit for the task would be brought together to learn the languages of the Saracens and other unbelievers"; and third, to die "for Christ in converting the unbelievers."[94] Llull wrote more than one book. In fact, during his lifetime, he wrote hundreds of books and pamphlets in multiple languages. He did set up a special *studia* for language learning and culture. He founded the first of these in 1245 and eventually established other schools in Tunis, Murcia, Valencia, Barcelona, and Játiva.[95] And, though the circumstances of his death are not clear, he seemingly died a martyr's death at age eighty-three or eighty-four in Tunis.[96] The rhetoric Llull uses to describe these acts and identities is varied: *pilgrim, friar, hermit, man of God*, and *servant of God*.[97] In *Ars demonstrativa*, *Ars brevia*, and *Ars generalis ultima*,[98] Llull portrays himself as an "artist" or

---

[90]Irvin and Sunquist, *History of the World Christian Movement*, 1:418.
[91]*HCM*, 114-15. Baldwin, "Missions to the East in the Thirteenth and Fourteenth Centuries," asserts that Lull "spent most of his life promoting missions" (488).
[92]Peers, *Ramon Lull*, 131, 144, 235, 246, 255.
[93]Llull, *Selected Works of Ramón Llull*, 1:15.
[94]Ibid., 1:15-16.
[95]Daniel, *Franciscan Concept of Mission*, 10.
[96]For details of Llull's life, see ibid., 66-74; Bonner, "Historical Background and Life," in Lull, *Selected Works of Ramón Llull*, 1:3-52; Peers, *Ramon Lull*.
[97]Llull, *Selected Works of Ramón Llull*, 1:17, 31, 40, 43, 44, 47.
[98]*Ars demonstrativa* is the fuller, longer work, and *Ars brevia* and *Ars generalis ultima* come later and are abbreviations of the *Ars demonstravia*. See introduction to *Ars Brevis* by Bonner in ibid., 1:571-72.

"artisan," one who uses figures and numbers, principles and diagrams invented as tools for a detailed and complex system to explain and answer questions regarding theology, science, philosophy, and law.[99] As tools, *Ars* explores the principles of philosophy, science, law, and theology, and thereby, he offers a rational, calculated account for God and Christian virtues, and thus the means for his encounters with Muslims, Jews, and those who hold heretical teachings. Llull's ultimate hope was that others would be trained in the methods of *Ars*, translate them into many languages, and use them to guide nonbelievers out of their error.

Llull lists guiding, preaching, interpreting, teaching, and disputing among the modes to be found in the *Ars*.[100] These best describe how Llull views the encounter between the artisan and the unbeliever. *Ars*, not mission, is his method or strategy. He is an artisan and not a missionary. *The Hundred Forms* is Llull's conceptual dictionary of essential "principles and rules," which is meant to guide intellectual investigation and practice.[101] In this dictionary, Llull lists rhetoric, preaching, and prayer as the essential forms of encounter with nonbelievers. During his lifetime, Llull wrote, lectured, preached, and debated, but nowhere does he describe his life work as mission. In these endeavors, Llull's aim is to expose the "false opinions and errors" of the Gentiles so that "those in error might be shown the path to glory without end and the means of avoiding infinite suffering."[102] And yet, he does not characterize these aims as mission or himself as a missionary.

Mission language does not serve to clarify Llull's life and actions, nor does it elevate his reputation. It obscures the disjointed story of his complicated life. Rather than mission illuminating Llull's story, interpreters use Llull's story to advance mission, its language and cause.[103] To inject mission

---

[99]*Ars demonstrativa* in ibid., 1:324, 333.

[100]*Ars demonstrativa* in ibid., 1:425-33. Llull explains "Guiding" as the following: "You who are in Y [Truth], by which you go to A [God], and who want to guide those who are in Z [Falsehood], by which they go to the torments of the everlasting fires of hell, you must learn various languages and teach your own language, and you must translate this Art into foreign languages so as to teach it joyfully, with the aim of destroying Z [Falsehood], to those whom you wish to convert, and toward whom you must be friendly and not frightening, proud, thoughtless, or unjust."

[101]*Ars brevis* in ibid., 1:616-25.

[102]Prologue to *The Book of the Gentiles*, in ibid., 1:110.

[103]There are certainly exceptions to this statement. While serious studies of Llull, such as those by Kedar, Hillgarth, and Beattie, employ mission language, their purpose is not promotion but a

language into Llull's story in this way is improper and even subverts an accurate assessment of his intentions with the *studia*, his publications, and his witness to Muslims.

SEEDBED FOR MISSION LANGUAGE

Rather than continuity between modern "mission" language and the Crusades, there is discontinuity. There is no evidence that those who obstructed crusading efforts engaged in activity called "mission" or self-identified as "missionary." Likewise mission language does not coexist with crusade language. Instead, those who responded to Urban's appeal saw themselves as pilgrims and their task as marching on Jerusalem, with the aim of subjugating the enemies of God. Their identity as God's chosen people produced a sense of divine purpose, inspired by the spirit of the age and accomplished through the means at hand. Rather than joining a mission or becoming missionaries, Pope Urban's summons was to take up the cross and become pilgrims. A consequence of this pilgrimage was the establishment of colonies, which extended the identity and boundary of Christendom. *Pilgrim* and *pilgrimage*, rather than *missionary* and *mission*, are the fundamental rhetoric that faithfully reconstructs the historical realities of these endeavors. There was oppositional activity, such as preaching, and attempts to convert others to the Catholic faith, but these are represented in language other than *mission*.

The altered version of pilgrimage emerging from the Crusades is a prelude to a linguistic innovation that is to come. The ancient tradition of pilgrimage, co-opted by the crusading endeavor, is, in the process, transformed. And yet, pilgrimage endured as a seminal vision from which the language of modern mission emerged. Pilgrimage, as movement, a means to penance, religious duty, an eschatological expectation, mobilization, taking up the cross, and triumphant occupation resembled what was to come in the spirit and practice of modern mission. Hints of this shift in the vision and purpose of pilgrimage were seen in the Dominicans, who in 1304 developed within their order the *Societas fratrum peregrinantium propter Christum*, from 1312 known as *fratres peregrinantes inter gentes* (Society of traveling friars). Franciscans formed a

---

scholarly examination of motives and actions. See Kedar, *Crusade and Mission*, 189-99; J. N. Hillgarth, *Ramon Lull and Lullism in Fourteenth-Century France*, Oxford-Warburg Studies (Oxford: Clarendon, 1971); Beattie, "Evangelization, Reform and Eschatology."

similar society at a later date called *Societas peregrinantium* (Society of pilgrims).[104] The focus of both societies was outward rather than inward, and for witness to the world at large. They preached and ministered to whomever they made contact with, and even made the occasional convert from Islam, paganism, and non-Latin forms of Christianity. At the same time, their activities were mixed with political aims, and conversion was not the only thrust of their presence or their task. Contrary to the tendency of advocates and interpreters to classify early Franciscans and Dominicans as mission organizations, with missionary intent, or their members as missionaries, mission language is applied only after the fact.[105] The most that can be said is that in both societies evidence of a shift under way can be seen.

The changes to pilgrimage created a climate in which identities were reshaped and differences reinforced, Christendom and its territorial boundaries were established, and new ways of encountering others were explored. Through these changes, monasticism was repurposed, and the church developed a distinct program of expansion. The stage was set for the entrance of mission language. With the birth of another order, the Society of Jesus, mission emerged as modern rhetoric. This new language made its debut

---

[104]See Baldwin, "Missions to the East in the Thirteenth and Fourteenth Centuries," 481, 492, 504; *HEC,* 2:324. According to John Moorman, *History of the Franciscan Order,* 434, the *Societas Peregrinantium* is mentioned in a papal bull dated 1398.

[105]See, for example, Daniel, *Franciscan Concept of Mission;* Burns, "Christian-Islamic Confrontation in the West," 1395; Johnson, *History of Christianity,* 244, 250; Katherine Jansen, "The Word and Its Diffusion," in *The Cambridge History of Christianity,* vol. 4, *Christianity in Western Europe c. 1100–c. 1500,* ed. Miri Rubin and Walter Simons (Cambridge: Cambridge University Press, 2009), 119, 123-25; Tejirian and Simon, *Conflict, Conquest, and Conversion,* 37; Baldwin, "Missions to the East in the Thirteenth and Fourteenth Centuries," 456, 481, 487, 491-92; Rosalind B. Brooke, *The Coming of the Friars,* Historical Problems: Studies and Documents 24 (London: G. Allen & Unwin, 1975), 22, 109; Moorman, *History of the Franciscan Order,* 20, 25, 27-28, 48-49, 52, 50, 65-66, 68, 72, 75, 166, 226-39, 429-38. Robson, *Franciscans in the Middle Ages,* 24, 25, 26, 73, 108-18, highlights exemplary Franciscans who labored in places such as Morocco, India, and China. He uncritically labels this kind of work as mission and these individuals as missionaries. In his assessment, "at the heart of the friar's vocation was a missionary impulse, which found recognition in the life of the founder and the twelfth chapter of his Rule" (80). Regarding the Dominicans, Robin Vose, *Dominicans, Muslims and Jews in the Medieval Crown of Aragon,* Cambridge Studies in Medieval Life and Thought (Cambridge: Cambridge University Press, 2009), does not deal with mission and missionary language per se but concludes, "Missionary activism" by Dominicans among Muslims and Jews "tended to be rare, marginal and short-lived" (22). Vose's opinion is "the myth of the medieval missionaries" emerged when "modern concepts of mission were projected back, and the specific circumstances of medieval relations between Jews, Muslims, and Christians were largely forgotten" (259). Neill simply states that these orders "lived a genuine missionary impulse" (*HCM,* 99).

with the Jesuits, in their letters, diaries, encyclicals, and conversations. As such, we must refrain from making the crusading era into something it was not. The repurposing of pilgrimage and the founding of colonies were a seedbed for what was to come. The seeds of mission germinated in the soil of medieval Christianity, and the language of mission appeared at the close of this age, 440 years after Urban's sermon.

7

Mission Vow

At this moment other lights came to me, namely, how the Son
first sent the Apostles to preach in poverty, and afterwards,
the Holy Spirit, giving His Spirit and the gift of tongues,
confirmed them, and thus the Father and the Son sending
the Holy Spirit, all Three Persons confirmed the mission.

IGNATIUS OF LOYOLA, *SPIRITUAL JOURNAL*

Since one's being sent on a mission of His Holiness will be
treated first, as being most important, it should be observed
that the vow which the Society made to obey him as the
supreme vicar of Christ without any excuse, meant that the
members were to go to any place whatsoever where he judges
it expedient to send them for the greater glory of God and
the good of souls, whether among the faithful or the infidels.

IGNATIUS OF LOYOLA, *THE CONSTITUTIONS OF THE SOCIETY OF JESUS*

MISSION, IN ITS MODERN MEANING AND USE, made its appearance
in the sixteenth century. Ignatius de Loyola (1491–1556) took existing
language and repurposed it.[1] He took "mission"—*misión* in Spanish and

---

[1]Born Iñigo López de Loyola in the Basque territory of northern Spain in 1491, Ignatius died at
the age of sixty-four in Rome as the Father General of the Jesuits. The present study examines
narrow aspects of Ignatius's thought and not the whole of his life. For biographical details of
Ignatius's life, see John W. O'Malley, *The First Jesuits* (Cambridge, MA: Harvard University Press,

missio in Latin—and extended its meaning and intent.[2] But Ignatius did more than co-opt an existing term and give it new meaning. Ignatius translated mission into his context and experience, thereby transforming mission into distinctively Ignatian or Jesuit nomenclature. Mission offered Ignatius a medium through which his ideals and commitments meshed with the notions and spirit of his age. Taken together, these prompted Ignatius and a small group of friends to make a unique vow of obedience to Christ's purposes in the world and then designate this as *mission*. More than a new kind of commitment of a nascent monastic order, mission was the translation of Ignatius's own life and commitments into activism. In mission, Ignatius, the penitent sinner, soldier of Christ, poor pilgrim, and mystic, innovated a vocation characterized by robust service, obedience, and mobility. Mission was a transformational marker for Ignatius and became a corporate one as well after being adopted by the Society; indeed, in a short time, mission language transformed established religious vocabulary for Catholics and eventually for Protestants. From Ignatius's introduction of mission into the speech of the Society, a major shift began that eventually reformed the way the church talked about and framed its encounter with the world. In Ignatius's innovation, the era of mission began and the modern mission movement has its roots. The genesis of this shift was a gathering of friends in a chapel and their common vow.

1993); Mary Purcell, *The First Jesuit, St. Ignatius Loyola (1491–1556)* (Chicago: Loyola University Press, 1981); Cándido de Dalmases, *Ignatius of Loyola, Founder of the Jesuits: His Life and Works*, trans. Jerome Aixalá (St. Louis: Institute of Jesuit Sources, 1985); Philip Caraman, *Ignatius Loyola* (London: HarperCollins, 1990); James Brodrick, *Saint Ignatius Loyola: The Pilgrim Years 1491–1538* (New York: Farrar, Straus and Cudahy, 1956); Javier Osuna, *Friends in the Lord: A Study in the Origins and Growth of Community in the Society of Jesus from St Ignatius' Conversion to the Earliest Texts of the Constitutions (1521–1541)*, trans. Nicholas King, The Way Series 3 (London: The Way, 1974); André Ravier, *Ignatius of Loyola and the Founding of the Society of Jesus* (San Francisco: Ignatius, 1987).

[2]Ignatius's repurposing of *mission* is attested by numerous interpreters: John W. O'Malley, "Mission and the Early Jesuits," *Ignatian Spirituality and Mission: The Way* supplement 79 (Spring 1994): 3; Paul Kollman, "At the Origins of Mission and Missiology: A Study in the Dynamics of Religious Language," *Journal of the American Academy of Religion* 79, no. 2 (June 2011): 425; L. Nemer, "Mission and Missions," in *New Catholic Encyclopedia* (Washington, DC: Catholic University of America Press, 2003), 683; Anne Fremantle, "Preface," in *Beyond All Horizons: Jesuits and the Missions*, ed. Thomas J. M. Burke (Garden City, NY: Hanover House, 1957), 5; Douglas Webster, "Missionary, The," in *Concise Dictionary of the Christian World Mission*, World Christian Books (London: Lutterworth, 1971).

THE MONTMARTRE VOW

On the Feast of the Assumption, 1534, Ignatius and six young men gathered to celebrate mass in the monastery chapel at Montmartre on the north side of Paris. Each was a student, but one was the center of gravity around which the others rallied. Ignatius had come to Paris alone, but in his service to others, a group of "friends in the Lord" emerged.[3] First Pierre-Antoine Favre (1506–1546) and then Francis Xavier (1506–1552) linked themselves with Ignatius by way of his guidance through his unique devotional practice, called the *Spiritual Exercises*.[4] Following Favre and Xavier, Simón Rodrigues (1510–1579), Diego Laynez (1512–1565), Alonso Salmerón (1515–1585), and Nicolás Bodadilla (1509–1590) joined Ignatius to complete the band of seven who gathered in the chapel.[5] Pierre Favre, the only priest among them, prayed and distributed bread and wine to the six. As each took Holy Communion, they made solemn vows to poverty, chastity, and the intent to journey to Jerusalem. In the last of these vows, they stated that if hindered in the journey to Jerusalem, they would place themselves at the disposal of the pope to be sent wherever he assigned them.[6] Following the mass and vow, they ate a simple meal and rejoiced in their common commitment.

The vow made by seven students was more than a burst of youthful fervor or a naive promise. It marked the spiritual beginning of an order of men that would eventually number in the thousands and span the globe. Only four years after their gathering at Montmartre, Pope Paul III (1468–1549) established the Society of Jesus. Their vows of poverty and chastity were not unique, as these could be found in other orders, such as Franciscans and Dominicans. But the *votum de missionibus* or the mission vow,

---

[3]Per the title of Javier Osuna's excellent study, *Friends in the Lord*.

[4]More than a book to be studied, O'Malley, *First Jesuits*, explains that *Exercises* were "a set of materials, directives, and suggestions for the person helping another through that course. They are in that regard more like a teacher's manual than a student's textbook" (37).

[5]For details of the lives of these companions, see Ravier, *Founding of the Society of Jesus*, 62-70; William V. Bangert, *A History of the Society of Jesus*, 2nd ed. (St. Louis: Institute of Jesuit Sources, 1986), 16.

[6]Dalmases, *Ignatius of Loyola*, 121. Similiar accounts of the Montmartre vow can be found in Pierre Favre, "The Memoriale," in *Spiritual Writings of Pierre Favre*, trans. Edmund C. Murphy, Jesuit Primary Sources in English Translations 16 (St. Louis: Institute of Jesuit Sources, 1996), 68; Ravier, *Founding of the Society of Jesus*, 70-73; Joseph F. Conwell, *Impelling Spirit: Revisiting a Founding Experience, 1539, Ignatius of Loyola and His Companions; An Exploration into the Spirit and Aims of the Society of Jesus as Revealed in the Founders' Proposed Papal Letter Approving the Society* (Chicago: Loyola Press, 1997), 106-17.

known specifically as the Fourth Vow, defined the new order and gave it the dynamism necessary to become one of the most powerful forces for the expansion of the Roman Catholic church.[7] Their vow to the sovereign pontiff declared that they would "go anywhere His Holiness will order, whether among the faithful or the infidels, without pleading an excuse and without requesting any expenses for the journey, for the sake of matters pertaining to the worship of God and the welfare of the Christian religion."[8] The vow made by seven students eventually mobilized thousands to serve in hospitals, schools, and universities, to travel to newly discovered lands, and to counter the Reformation. The Montmartre vow to be pilgrims became the mission vow that formed the Society into a frontline force for the Latin church.

CIRCA MISSIONES

Mission was an immediate and prominent feature in the papal bulls that established the Society, *Regimini militantis ecclesiae* (1540) and *Exposcit debitum* (1550), and its foundational documents, *The First Sketch of the Institute of the Society of Jesus* (1539), *The Formula of the Institute of the Society of Jesus* (1550), *The General Examen and Its Declaration* (1546), and *The Constitutions of the Society of Jesus* (1491–1556).[9] The second article of *The First Sketch of the Institute of the Society of Jesus* declares that the companions of the Society are "soldiers of God under faithful obedience" to the pope. This obedience is described as mission (*missionum, missione*) three times in

---

[7]Nemer, "Mission and Missions," 683; Thomas H. Clancy, *An Introduction to Jesuit Life: The Constitutions and History Through 435 Years* (St. Louis: Institute of Jesuit Sources, 1976), 99. This vow is included in the *Formula* of 1540 and was subsequently incorporated into the papal bulls that established the Society of Jesus.

[8]Ignatius Loyola, *The Constitutions of the Society of Jesus*, trans. George E. Ganss (St. Louis: Institute of Jesuit Sources, 1970), 79-80; hereafter cited as CSJ. See a similar description in a letter from Ignatius to James de Gouvea, November 23, 1538, in *Letters of St. Ignatius of Loyola*, trans. William J. Young (Chicago: Loyola University Press, 1959), 35.

[9]See the full text of *Regimini militantis ecclesiae* in John C. Olin, ed., *The Catholic Reformation: Savonarola to Ignatius Loyola*, Fordham ed. (New York: Fordham University Press, 1992), 205. See also *The Formula of the Institute* (68), *The General Examen and Its Declaration* (104), and *The Constitutions of the Society of Jesus* (238, 239, 253, 267-80) in CSJ. *The First Sketch* is the earliest declaration concerning the Society and eventually became *The Formula of the Institute*. The *Formula* was the basis for the bull *Exposcit debitum* (1550). *The General Examen* (1546) was to guide those considering entrance into the Society. *The Constitutions of the Society of Jesus* was composed between 1491 and 1556 and published two years after Ignatius's death.

the article.[10] As companions took the vow of obedience, the pope sent them "to the Turks or to the New World or to the Lutherans or to others be they infidel or faithful."[11] *The First Sketch* (1539) developed into *The Formula of the Institute* and eventually became the basis for the bull *Exposcit debtium* (1550), by which Pope Julius III reconfirmed the initial establishment of the Society. *The Formula* uses *missionibus* and *missiones* to express the same emphasis and meaning found in *The First Sketch*.[12] *Regimini militantis ecclesiae*, the bull establishing the Society of Jesus in 1540, reasserts the vow of the *First Sketch*: after taking "a special vow" the members of the Society are to go wherever the Roman pontiff might send them, "whether among the Turks or other heathen, and even to the Indies, or among whatsoever heretics and schismatics, or among any believers whomsoever." Each member is to leave the matter of these missions (*missionibus*) completely to the Roman pontiff and not "make solicitation of the Pope concerning [their] own mission (*missione*) in one way or the other."[13] *The General Examen* is a prospectus for those wishing to enter the Society. It instructs potential members to be "ready to travel about in various regions of the world, on all occasions when the supreme pontiff or our immediate superior orders us." The hope is that these superiors "proceed without error in such missions (*missiones*)."[14] Part seven, chapters one, two, and three of the *Constitutions* discuss at length "concerning mission" (*circa missiones*).[15] For members of the Society, mission means they are assigned by the Holy Father, sent "to any part of Christ's vineyard," either traveling or "by residing steadily and continually in certain places," all for "the great service of God and the good of

---

[10]Appendix 3 of Ignatius Loyola, *The Autobiography of St. Ignatius Loyola*, trans. Joseph F. O'Callaghan (New York: Fordham University Press, 1992), 107, 108. The Latin text of *Prima Societatis Jesu Instituti Summa* is found in Ignatius Loyola, *Monumenta Ignatiana, ex autographis vel ex antiquioribus exemplis collecta. Series tertia. Sancti Ignatii de Loyola Constitutiones Societatis Jesu*, Monumenta Historica Societatis Jesu 63 (Rome: Typis Pontificiae Universitatis Gregorianae, 1934), 14-21.

[11]Ibid.

[12]Loyola, *Monumenta Ignatiana*, 378.

[13]*Regimini militantis ecclesiae* from Olin, *Catholic Reformation*, 205. Latin is from "Prima Societatis Approbatio—1540," in Loyola, *Monumenta Ignatiana*, 28.

[14]"The General Examen and Its Declarations," in *CSJ*, 104. See "Examen Cum Declarationbus," in Loyola, *Monumenta Ignatiana*, 74.

[15]"Constitutiones de Missionibus," in Loyola, *Monumenta Ignatiana*, 159. In English, the titles of chapters 1 and 2 are "Missions from the Holy Father" and "The Missions Received from the Superior of the Society," *CSJ*, 267-81.

souls." The *Constitutions* delineates that the superior general, as well as the pope, can determine which members are suitable for a mission and where they are to go.[16] Mission in these bulls and documents introduces a new notion of obedience and mobility "for the greater glory of God and the good of souls."[17] It was, however, only in a brief period of time that Ignatius's rudimental notion of mission evolved into a specialized term to describe the sending of ecclesial agents to near as well as distant places, as well as the destination to which agents are sent.[18]

Prior to Ignatius, the words of choice for the expansion of the faith had been *evangelizatio, propagatio Christianae Fidei*, and *Fides propaganda*.[19] The common element in each of these is the spread of the faith—evangelizing non-Catholics and propagating its Catholic form. As we have observed in

---

[16]*CSJ*, 267-69.

[17]Ibid., 268.

[18]Jehu Hanciles, *Beyond Christendom: Globalization, African Migration, and the Transformation of the West* (Maryknoll, NY: Orbis Books, 2008), observes: "This arcane theological concept was first adopted by Ignatius Loyola (1491–1556), the extraordinary gifted founder of the Society of Jesus, to describe Jesuit efforts outside Europe. Founded in 1540, the Society incorporated a vow of 'special obedience to the Pope regarding the missions' and became the church's dominant missionary force, as active in winning back Protestant lands in Europe as it was extending the Catholic faith in Africa, Asia, and America" (91). Details of the Jesuit innovation of mission are noted also by John O'Malley, "Introduction," in *The Jesuits II: Cultures, Sciences, and the Arts, 1540–1773* (Toronto: University of Toronto Press, 2006), xxiv; Kollman, "At the Origins of Mission and Missiology," 426; *TM*, 1, 233; Luke Clossey, *Salvation and Globalization in the Early Jesuit Missions* (New York: Cambridge University Press, 2008), 14. Ignatius's innovation is mentioned in passing by Walter Kaiser, *Mission in the Old Testament: Israel as a Light to the Nations* (Grand Rapids: Baker Books, 2000), 11; Michael W. Goheen, "Bible and Mission: Missiology and Biblical Scholarship in Dialogue," in *Christian Mission: Old Testament Foundations and New Testament Developments*, ed. Stanley E. Porter and Cynthia Long Westfall, McMaster New Testament Studies Series (Eugene, OR: Pickwick, 2010), 211; F. Hahn, *Mission in the New Testament*, trans. Frank Clarke (London: SCM Press, 1965), 16n1; Thomas Ohm, *Machet zu Jüngern alle Völker: Theorie der Mission* (Freiburg im Breisgau: Erich Wewel Verlag, 1962), 37-38; John H. Yoder, "Reformation and Missions: A Literature Survey," in *Anabaptism and Mission*, ed. Wilbert R. Shenk, Missionary Studies 10 (Scottdale, PA: Herald, 1984), 44-45; Jan A. B. Jongeneel, *Philosophy, Science, and Theology of Mission in the 19th and 20th Centuries*, Studien Zur Interkulturellen Geschichte Des Christentums 92 (Frankfurt am Main: Peter Lang, 1995), 59; Howard Peskett and Vinoth Ramachandra, *The Message of Mission: The Glory of Christ in All Time and Space*, The Bible Speaks Today (Downers Grove, IL: InterVarsity Press, 2003), 29. Catherine Mooney, "Ignatian Spirituality, A Spirituality for Mission," *Mission Studies* 26 (2009): 201, takes issue with this being "mission ad extra," noting that it is somewhat misleading. According to Mooney, to characterize the Jesuits' use of mission as only evangelistic efforts outside Europe or the evangelization of Protestants is reductionistic. The scope of Jesuit mission, she maintains, must include a wider array of ministries and without restricting their endeavors to foreign locations.

[19]Clossey, *Salvation and Globalization in the Early Jesuit Missions*, 13.

previous chapters, a variety of terms and phrases paralleled these, such as *pilgrimage, journey,* and *to go to the infidel.* These terms of movement indicated that crossing distance or moving away from one's home territory was necessary. But no one term or an all-encompassing word or phrase dominated; instead, many terms and phrases were in use. More importantly, these previous categories lacked the professional and institutional status latent in Ignatius's vow. Abruptly, mission, as a way of describing the movement of people to assignments, in order to proclaim the Christian faith, made its debut. Interpreters of the Jesuits describe Ignatius's introduction of mission language as "a shift," "an innovation," "a crucial discursive breakthrough," and a "daring conception."[20] Ignatius's turn to mission language was more than an adjustment or tinkering with a side issue. Once introduced into the foundational documents and papal bulls, "mission" became the central tenet for Ignatius and the Society. Joseph de Guibert calls mission the principle "most originally Ignatian" and "the fundamental concept of Ignatius in the founding of the Society."[21] Ignatius himself describes mission as "an end eminently characteristic of our Institute" and "our starting point and principal foundation."[22]

Ignatius's innovation prompts two fundamental questions. From where does he appropriate mission language? Or, what are the sources of his use of the word? Second, with what does he associate this term? What precise meaning does he attach to mission language?

MISSIO, MISIÓN, MISSÃO, MISSION

Ignatius did not create *mission* but instead appropriated an existing word and filled it with fresh intent and meaning. As he does not offer an explanation for this refashioning of established language, we can only infer why he adopted mission.[23] In Ignatius's context, mission was in use in four languages and with multiple meaning: *missio* (Latin), *misión* (Spanish),

[20]Kollman, "At the Origins of Mission and Missiology," 426, 427, 429, 430; O'Malley, "Mission and the Early Jesuits," 4; Joseph de Guibert, *The Jesuits: Their Spiritual Doctrine and Practice; A Historical Study,* trans. William J. Young (Chicago: Institute of Jesuit Sources, 1964), 149.
[21]Guibert, *Jesuits,* 149, 150.
[22]*CSJ,* 267.
[23]Critical analysis of the source of Ignatius's use of *mission* is offered by a few interpreters. O'Malley is the first to analyze Ignatius's adoption of *mission* in his 1994 article, "Mission and the Early Jesuits." Clossey extends this analysis in his 2008 book, *Salvation and Globalization in the Early*

missão (Portuguese), and *mission* (Old French). These uses were active parts of Ignatius's world of language and thus easily employed. The meaning and influence of each were a possible source for Ignatius's innovation of a new kind of mission.

First, Latin *mitto* and *missio* were terms in use to explain the inner workings of the Trinity. While trinitarian expressions of Father, Son, and Spirit were part of the language of the early church from the beginning, Irenaeus, Tertullian, and Augustine developed fuller theological statements of the Trinity. In their theological writings, they used the verb *mitto* to describe the act of the Father in sending Christ and Holy Spirit. Augustine, for example, writes of the Father sending the Son as a unique divine act.

> As the Father, therefore, begot and the Son was begotten, so the Father sent [*ita pater misit*] and the Son was sent [*filius missus est*]. But as He who begot and He who was begotten are one, so He who sent and He who was sent [*ita et qui misit et qui missus est*] are one, because the Father and the Son are one.[24]

Mitto, as a common verb, designated the action of the Father, who sends the Son. As in the New Testament and early church writing, the common-sense meaning of *mitto* was "to throw, send, or dispatch." Augustine also uses the noun form to reference the mission of the Son of God (*missio filii dei*).[25]

Trinitarian thought continued to develop into the Middle Ages with various writers, most notably Thomas Aquinas (1225–1274). Thomas Aquinas writes extensively on the mission of the divine persons (*de missione divinarum personarum*). He asks whether the mission of the divine persons is eternal or temporal, invisible or visible, directed or undirected.[26] Throughout Aquinas's discussion he uses noun and verb forms of *mission*, as subject and predicate. He asserts that it is fitting to speak of mission as the

---

Jesuit Missions, and Kollman investigates the origins of Ignatius's use of *mission* in his article, "At the Origins of Mission and Missiology" (2011).

[24] Augustine, *The Trinity*, trans. Stephen McKenna, The Fathers of the Church 45 (Washington, DC: Catholic University of America Press, 1963), book 4, chapter 20.28 (p. 167). Latin text is from Augustine, *Sancti Aurelii Augustini, De Trinitate Libri XV*, Corpus Christianorum Series Latina 50 (Turnhout: Brepols, 1968), 4.10.29 (p. 199). Our interest is primarily in the language of *missio* and not Augustine's theology of the Trinity. For a treatment of Augustine and the Trinity, see Lewis Ayres, *Augustine and the Trinity* (Cambridge: Cambridge University Press, 2010).

[25] Augustine, *De Trinitate Libri XV*, 4.19 (p. 193).

[26] Thomas Aquinas, *The Summa Theologiæ of Saint Thomas Aquinas: Latin-English*, vol. 1 (Scotts Valley, CA: NovAntiqua, 2008), Q. 43 (p. 509).

way of divine personhood (*missio igitur divinae personae convenire potest*) and mission as eternal (*ergo et missio*). While the language of *missio* is liberally used in reference to the divine persons of the Son and the Holy Spirit, Aquinas does not extend its use to the church or human agency but restricts his use of the term to the Trinity.

Trinitarian language of *missio* was central to the theological language of Ignatius's day, and thus we can reasonably assume that this rich Latinate texture was known to him. In fact, while studying in Paris, Ignatius attended lectures on Aquinas at the Dominican convent of Saint-Jacques.[27] A study of Aquinas's *Summa Theologiae* would have included *considerandum de missione divinarum personarum*. Thus, it would have been natural for Ignatius to appropriate a term previously restricted for the sending of Christ in order to identify his and the actions of the Society with those of the triune God.[28] This seems highly likely, as we shall see, given the place of the Trinity in Ignatius's visions and devotion.

Second, *misión* and *missão* were terms in wide use to describe the diplomatic and military activities of Iberians in foreign lands. At least from the time of Charlemagne, imperial *missi* were appointed to visit other countries in a representative role, to investigate the actions of officials, and to certify that edicts and orders were being followed. In the ninth century, Charlemagne (742–814) created the post of *missi dominici* (messenger of the lord), whose task was to supervise and manage local leaders throughout the empire.[29] As agents of the emperor, they acted as personal envoys, reporting only to him and representing his wishes. These emissaries were selected

---

[27]Ignatius acquired a preference for Aquinas's doctrine during this time. See O'Malley, *First Jesuits*, 28; James Brodrick, *The Origin of the Jesuits* (Chicago: Loyola University Press, 1986), 44; Dalmases, *Ignatius of Loyola*, 122-23; Dauril Alden, *The Making of an Enterprise: The Society of Jesus in Portugal, Its Empire, and Beyond, 1540–1750* (Stanford, CA: Stanford University Press, 1996), 5.

[28]O'Malley, "Mission and the Early Jesuits," 3. See also Stephen B. Bevans and Roger Schroeder, *Constants in Context: A Theology of Mission for Today* (Maryknoll, NY: Orbis Books, 2004), 173; Ohm, *Machet zu Jüngern alle Völker*, 37.

[29]For a history of the rise and decline of *missi dominici* as an administrative device, see James Westfall Thompson, *The Decline of the Missi Dominici in Frankish Gaul* (Chicago: The University of Chicago Press, 1903); Rosmond McKitterick, *Charlemagne: The Formation of a European Identity* (Cambridge: Cambridge University Press, 2008), 213-14, 218-22, 256-66; Victor Krause, "Geschichte Des Institutes Der Missi Dominici," *Institut Für Österreichische Geschichtsforschung, Mitteilungen* 11 (January 1890): 193-300; C. H. Lawrence, *Medieval Monasticism: Forms of Religious Life in Western Europe in the Middle Ages*, 3rd ed. (Harlow, UK: Longman, 2001), 127-28.

from the circle of those at court, both clergy and laity, or were local land-
owners. As this administrative system developed, these envoys were further
classified as *missi minores* and *missi majores*.[30] Spain and Portugal adopted
a similar system and began using the terms *misión* and *missão* in the period
prior to Ignatius to designate political and military posts to which royal
agents were sent.[31] Both *misión* and *missão* carried the sense of a legate or
envoy that represented a ruler or government. Thus, by extension a representative entity, a *misión* or *missão* was dispatched to negotiate terms of
cooperation and trade with local chiefs and rulers and to maintain a presence
in a foreign place. Likewise, agents of *misión/missão*, such as diplomats, soldiers, and ecclesial representatives, were sent by the Spanish and Portuguese
crowns to administrate ecclesiastical as well as political affairs. In the case
of Portugal, *missão civilizadora* (civilizing mission) signified the multifaceted engagement of Portuguese powers in their interaction with local
peoples and entities in Brazil, Africa, India, and parts of Asia.[32]

Third, the Old French word *mission* (*mession, mecion, mision, mesion*)
was in wide use and was the etymological source for the Spanish word
misión. In Old French, *mission* meant "expense," "cost," "outlay," "dis-
bursement," or "charge," conveying a sense of obligation, and thus it was a
legal term of indebtedness between parties in a monetary agreement.[33] This
use is seen in medieval Spanish contractual agreements. In a text dated 1297
from a principal city in Navarra, the region of Ignatius's birth, Old French
mission is used to note the legal obligations of parties. The text is a letter to
the court regarding bail and expenses.[34]

---

[30]Thompson, *Decline of the Missi Dominici*, 17.

[31]Kollman, "At the Origins of Mission and Missiology," 432; Clancy, *Introduction to Jesuit Life*, 99.

[32]The use of *missão* as a term of the Portuguese crown and exploration can be seen in letters from
the digital archives of "Carte," *Arquivo Distrital de Portalegre*, September 30, 2008, http://adptg
.dglab.gov.pt, as well as in João de Barros and D. do Conto, *Decadas da Asia* (Lisbon: Na Regia
Officina Typografica, 1777).

[33]Alan Hindley, Frederick W. Langley, and Brian J. Levy, "Mission," in *Old French-English Dictionary* (Cambridge: Cambridge University Press, 2000); Randle Cotgrave, "Mission," in *A Dictionarie of the French and English Tongues (Reproduced from the First Edition, London, 1611)* (Columbia: University of South Carolina Press, 1950); Walter W. Skeat, "Mission," in *An
Etymological Dictionary of the English Language* (Oxford: Clarendon, 1953).

[34]"E si algun o alguns les volia far força o demas ad algun o ad alguns deuanditz, el o els donant
les fiança de dreit per tant quant la Cort General de Nauarra mandaria, e non li fus o non les fus
cabuda, que els li ajuden o les ajudien ben & leyalment a lur cost & a lur mission troa tant que
li faguen o les faguen (o les faguen) a calçar lur dreit." In D. J. Gifford and F. W. Hodcroft, eds.,

Though Ignatius does not indicate his source of *mission* or why he makes it the defining tenet of the Society, he seemingly draws on the existing theological and political concepts of mission and combines these with the Old French sense of obligation in order to create a unique vocation and calling for the Society of Jesus. What is obvious is that forms of "mission" were in wide use and thus easily adopted without explanation. Ignatius exploits the various uses of *mission*, but he also expands these meanings. To understand why he selects and repurposes mission, it is necessary to do more than acknowledge these words as source for his rhetorical innovation. With what does he associate mission? What meaning does he attach to mission language? The world surrounding his choice of words and the dynamics of Ignatius's personal faith, mystical experiences, and self-identification are the broader context for his use of the word. Taken together this contextual milieu provides clues regarding Ignatius's use of mission and, indeed, the origins of modern mission itself.

IGNATIUS'S WORLD

Ignatius's vow of mission and Pope Paul III's approval of the Society are part of the Latin church's response to the changing political and ecclesial landscape of the late medieval period. Two factors in particular characterize the context that contributes in a unique way to Ignatius's rhetorical innovation. The notions of *conquista* and *padroado* are sources that shaped the meaning and intention of Ignatius's mission language.

Conquista. In 1498 four ships from Portugal with red crosses aglow on white sailcloth arrived off the Indian coast. With their arrival, Vasco da Gama (1469–1524) opened the eastern sea route to India and thus moved Portugal into a position to dominate the lucrative trade of spices and silks. The ships and their passage were the culmination of a century of development of knowledge and technology necessary for the historic voyage.[35] While the

---

Textos Lingüísticos Del Medioevo Español, Preparados Con Introducciones Y Glosario (Oxford: Dolphin Book, 1959), 146.

[35]K. K. N. Kurup, "Contribution of Malabar Rulers in Delaying Dominance by Foreign Powers in Malabar Region," in *The Portuguese, Indian Ocean and European Bridgeheads 1500–1800* (Kerala, India: Institute for Research in Social Sciences and Humanities of MESHAR, 2001), 111. For an account of da Gama's voyage and landing, see Stephen Neill, *A History of Christianity in India: The Beginning to AD 1707* (Cambridge: Cambridge University Press, 1984), 87-93. For a summary of Portugal's ascendency and expansion, see Wolfgang Reinhard, "The Seaborne Empires," in

Portuguese were not the first Europeans to venture eastward or the first to establish settlements on the Indian coast, the appearance of da Gama and his crew initiated settlements in the East and thus a new period in history, one K. M. Panikkar designates as the "Vasco da Gama epoch."[36] For Panikkar and others, this event marked the beginning of Western dominance throughout Asia. The Portuguese, along with the Spanish, led the way, with the Dutch, French, Germans, and British to follow.

As Vasco da Gama set out from Lisbon, he received the Flag of the Order of Christ from King Manuel I (1469–1521), and the king charged him with these words: "Carry with this flag the honor of my country. Go and implant it on the Indian soil and protect it with the cross of your sword. Bring me the news of that land which is hidden for so long in the shadow of centuries. Make this dream come true."[37] When da Gama returned from this venture, King Manuel dispatched letters announcing the "discovery" of India. In a letter to Pope Alexander VI, the king identified himself as "Lord of Guinea and of the Conquests, Navigations and Commerce of Ethiopia, Arabia, Persia, and India."[38] Both da Gama and Manuel asserted Portugal's sovereign right and destiny to rule over lands and peoples located outside Europe. By the end of the sixteenth century, these assertions became reality, as Portuguese presence could be found in India, Brazil, the Azores, Greenland, Labrador, Newfoundland, Nova Scotia, New Guinea, Moluccas, Japan, Timbuktu, Mali, Ceylon, and Korea. From the Western rim of Christendom, Portugal ventured to all the major continents, with the exception of Antarctica and Australia.[39] As the ruling maritime people, the Portuguese carried goods and ideas to and from the world, and as they touched the far

---

Handbook of European History, 1400–1600: Late Middle Ages, Renaissance and Reformation, vol. 1, *Structures and Assertions*, ed. Henry Jansen, Thomas A. Brady, and Heiko A. Oberman (Leiden, The Netherlands: E. J. Brill, 1994), 644-45.

[36]K. M. Panikkar, *Asia and Western Dominance: A Survey of the Vasco Da Gama Epoch of Asian History, 1498-1945* (London: G. Allen & Unwin, 1959), 13, dates the da Gama epoch as beginning in 1498 and ending with the departure of British forces from India in 1947.

[37]Cited and translated by Joseph de Barros, "Discoveries and Martyrs of Missionary Expansion in the East," in *Discoveries, Missionary Expansion and Asian Cultures* (New Delhi: Concept, 1994), 85.

[38]According to Donald Lach, *Asia in the Making of Europe*, vol. 1, *The Century of Discovery* (Chicago: The University of Chicago Press, 1965), 97, this salutation was in a letter sent to the cardinal protector.

[39]A. J. R. Russell-Wood, *A World on the Move: The Portuguese in Africa, Asia, and America, 1415–1808* (New York: St. Martin's, 1993), 9-10.

corners of the globe, they established a political, military, mercantile, and eccelsial presence.

The Iberian expansion of the fifteenth and sixteenth centuries originated from the recently formed nations of Spain and Portugal.[40] From a small, landlocked kingdom, Portugal expanded its borders in 1095 southward to include Lisbon and the coastline. With victories against the Moors and Spanish, treaties and marriage alliances with England, and assistance from northern European Crusaders, the Portuguese crown grew from strength to strength, eventually establishing itself as a European power.[41] The eventual conquest of Muslim enclaves within its border in 1205 finalized Portugal's struggle and set boundaries similar to what is modern Portugal. Once its borders were secure and internal resistance settled, Portugal turned its sights toward expansion and trade in other regions. The golden age of Portuguese expansion and conquest began in 1415 with capture of Ceuta, a North African Muslim port.[42]

While Portugal's aspirations and capacity for maritime expansion developed gradually over time, the vision for this expansion can be traced to the reign of King John I (1385–1433). From his initiatives, the breadth and force of expansion increased with each subsequent ruler.[43] The principal architect of Portugal's exploration along the west coast of Africa and beyond was Henry the Navigator (1394–1460), the third son of King John. As a young man, Henry participated in Portugal's conquest of Ceuta. From a fortress at Sagres, the southernmost point of the Iberian Peninsula, Henry

[40]A fuller treatment of Iberian expansion would include much more regarding the development of Spanish or Castillian powers and their exploits in the Americas. However, since the first missionaries of the Society of Jesus departed from Lisbon and under the sponsorship of the Portuguese crown, the focus of this study is chiefly on Portugal. For treatments of the spirit and institutions of the Iberian powers of this era, see C. R. Boxer, *The Portuguese Seaborne Empire, 1415-1825* (New York: A. A. Knoft, 1969); Boxer, *The Church Militant and Iberian Expansion* (Baltimore: Johns Hopkins University Press, 1978); Ravier, *Founding of the Society of Jesus*, 36-54.

[41]Lach, *Asia in the Making of Europe*, 51. For details of Portugal's national story, see Sanjay Subrahmanyam, *The Portuguese Empire in Asia, 1500-1700: A Political and Economic History* (London: Longman, 1993), 30-54.

[42]For details of the capture of Ceuta, see Bailon de Sá, "The Genesis of Portuguese Discoveries and Their Influence on Indian Culture," in *Discoveries, Missionary Expansion and Asian Cultures*, 69; Malyn Newitt, *A History of Portuguese Overseas Expansion, 1400-1668* (London: Routledge, 2005), 19-21.

[43]Boxer, *Portuguese Seaborne Empire*, 15. Lyle McAlister provides a succinct summary of these developments in *Spain and Portugal in the New World, 1492-1700*, Europe and the World in the Age of Expansion 3 (Minneapolis: University of Minnesota Press, 1984), 46-49.

gathered information, planned, and launched expeditions that pushed the Portuguese presence down the African coast. By 1420 Henry was named the "apostolic administrator of the Order of Christ," the Portuguese version of the crusading Knight Templar, thus providing him with considerable funds and privileges from Rome.[44] Henry laid the groundwork for the rulers who followed him to extend Portuguese presence and solidify their hold on conquered lands and people by establishing ports and settlements along the African coast. Portugal's expansion and conquest gathered momentum as John II (d. 1495) began his reign in 1481. The first feat was to round the Cape of Good Hope, which Bartolomeu Dias accomplished in 1487. Ten years after Dias's return, Vasco da Gama made his historic journey beyond the Cape and onward to India. As their maritime skills and capacity increased, the Portuguese were able to extend their reach beyond the *Estado da Índia* and into the lands of Asia. The spirit of exploration building over nearly a century manifested itself in the establishment of commercial colonies throughout the East over the next century.

While no one motive dominated, the efforts of these kings and explorers were a mixture of economic, political, and religious aspirations, as well as a broader spirit of adventure and curiosity.[45] Commerce was a clear objective, as the promise of luxurious and profitable goods had become a proven reality. Early traders from Italy and Spain, as well as those from Islamic areas, had demonstrated that wealth was to be gained, and thus the objective was to capture a known market.

Running throughout these motives was an anti-Muslim sentiment, an extension of the crusade spirit of the previous era.[46] The Iberian reconquest

---

[44]Lach, *Asia in the Making of Europe*, 1:52n5. According to Scott Sunquist, *Understanding Christian Mission: Participation in Suffering and Glory* (Grand Rapids: Baker Academic, 2013), Henry's "first movement out from Portugal was actually called a Crusade against the Moors (1415), the Muslims of North Africa" (50).

[45]See Sá, "Genesis of Portuguese Discoveries," 68-70; A. J. R. Russell-Wood, "Patterns of Settlement in the Portuguese Empire, 1400–1800," in *Portuguese Oceanic Expansion, 1400–1800*, ed. Francisco Bethencourt and Diogo Ramada Curto (New York: Cambridge University Press, 2007), 162; C. R. Boxer, *Four Centuries of Portuguese Expansion, 1415–1825: A Succinct Survey* (Berkeley: University of California Press, 1969), 5-6.

[46]Werner Ustorf, "Vasco Da Gama and the Periodization of Christian History," in *Identity and Marginality: Rethinking Christianity in North East Asia* (Frankfurt am Main: Peter Lang, 2000), characterizes Portuguese expansion as "a movement of restoration, namely the restoration of a visionary, perhaps eschatological, imperium christianum" (90-91).

was, according to Mayer, a "proto-crusade" against Islam.[47] Muslims invaded
and captured large portions of the region in the eighth century, and thus
they were an ongoing threat at the doorstep of Europe. The desire to liberate
the Iberian Peninsula from Muslim control existed long before the First
Crusade and extended into the sixteenth century.[48] According to Christopher Tyerman, "The habit of crusading died hard; in the fifteenth century
crusading formulae were natural appendages for the expansion of European
power down the west coast of Africa and into the eastern Atlantic, as they
were in the religious wars in Bohemia as well as in defence against the
Turks."[49] Atlantic and African reconnaissance began in earnest, and bases of
operation were established along the African coast from Lago to Cape Bo-
jador for Portugal's "colonial, commercial, and crusading expansion."[50] In
Lyle McAlister's words, "Crusading zeal, geographical curiosity, and commercial enterprise" pushed the Portuguese farther and farther eastward.[51] As
Muslim powers and reach increased, European powers sought ways to check
the Muslim political and economic advance.

   The crucial turn came when King John III (1502–1557) moved against the
Muslims on the Indian subcontinent. Just as the Muslim-Christian conflict
in Europe spawned the Crusades of a previous period, the same spirit motivated and justified the aggressive intrusion and conversion of inhabitants

[47]Mayer, *Crusades*, 20. See also Subrahmanyam, *Portuguese Empire in Asia*, 37-38; Sanjay Subrahmanyam, *The Career and Legend of Vasco Da Gama* (Cambridge: Cambridge University Press,
1997), 54-57.

[48]Christopher Tyerman, *The Invention of the Crusades* (Toronto: University of Toronto Press, 1998),
89; J. Riley-Smith, *The Crusades: A Short History* (New Haven, CT: Yale University Press, 1987),
241-54.

[49]*Fighting for Christendom*, 123, 175. According to Isabel dos Guimarães Sá, "Ecclesiastical Structures and Religious Action," in Bethencourt and Curto, *Portuguese Oceanic Expansion*, "At the
beginning of the Portuguese expansion, with the conquest of Ceuta in 1415, the method used to
convert other people to the Christian religion was not unlike the method applied by the crusaders toward Muslims: It consisted basically of building churches on the ruins of destroyed
mosques" (255).

[50]C. Raymond Beazley, "Prince Henry of Portugal and the African Crusade of the Fifteenth Century," *The American Historical Review* 16, no. 1 (October 1910): 12. Beazley asserts, "It is Prince
Henry the Crusader, as much as Prince Henry the Navigator" (21).

[51]McAlister, *Spain and Portugal in the New World*, 48. According to Ogbu Kalu, "Globalization and
Mission in the Twenty-First Century," in *Mission After Christendom: Emergent Themes in Contemporary Mission*, ed. Obgu U. Kalu, Peter Vethanayagamony, and Edmund Kee-Fook Chia
(Louisville, KY: Westminster John Knox, 2010), the "crusades could not dislodge [Islam], but
the discovery of a sea route did and enabled Europe to regain the upper hand" (33).

in India.[52] Christians viewed Muslims as a threat to Europe, as well as the chief commercial rival for commercial interests outside Europe, and thus Spain and Portugal marshaled resources against them. The eventual establishment of Portugal's political and commercial rule in India meant the expansion of control over both Muslims and Hindu subjects.

Economic, political, and strategic motives did not exist solely to themselves, but were thoroughly imbued with religious aims. The Roman church played its part in expansion by providing sanction for the state's political and commercial aims, and in turn the church was able to advance its cause. For the Roman-centered church, the goal was Christianization, which meant Latinization. More than evangelizing, the aim was to make conquered peoples into Christians of the Catholic variety, loyal subjects of Rome.[53] What was generally acknowledged and virtually uncontested, according to Carlos Cipolla, was that "religion supplied the pretext and gold the motive" for European expansion.[54] The Roman church justified and supported the Iberian commercial and political reach, and the Iberian powers facilitated and protected the church's program of Christianization.[55] The symbiotic relationship between the church and crown became an evolving interplay of divergent interests, while their mutual dependence steadily deepened. Even as the reach of the Portuguese throne into Africa and India was enabled by newly developed technology and fueled by both the Muslim threat and the prospects of wealth, this reach required a rationale that in some way justified conquest and domination. Papal decrees provided justification for these ends. And at the same time, papal bulls obligated the Portuguese crown to act in the interest of the Latin church and in the name of God.

The Latin church needed the power of the state because of threats on two fronts. First, the long-standing threat of Muslim powers had to be addressed,

---

[52]Cf. Subrahmanyam, *Portuguese Empire in Asia*, 49-51.

[53]According to Joseph Schmidlin, *Catholic Mission History*, ed. Matthias Braun (Techny, IL: Mission Press, S. V. D, 1933), "Beginning with Columbus and Vasco da Gama, all the Spanish and Portuguese explorers regarded their expeditions as like-wise crusades and missionary voyages" (264). "The Portuguese expeditions of discovery and conquest were simultaneously missionary journeys" (290).

[54]Carlo M. Cipolla, *European Culture and Overseas Expansion* (Middlesex, UK: Penguin Books, 1970), 101.

[55]Ibid., 17. For factors that fueled Portuguese exploration, see M. N. Pearson, *The Portuguese in India*, New Cambridge History of India (New York: Cambridge University Press, 1988), 5-6.

and second, the new reality of a fractured and warring Christendom brought about by the Reformation required a realignment of power. Spanish and Portuguese ships and trade were just the right antidote for both Muslim and Protestant threats.

Among the words used to describe these activities was *conquista*. The notion of *conquista* paralleled that of *reconquista*, the term associated with the establishment of Christian rule throughout the Iberian Peninsula. The project to reestablish Christian rule in areas of Iberia conquered by Muslims in the eighth century was all but complete with the victory of Granada in 1492. The long and difficult task of displacing Muslim institutions, systems of governance, and cultural patterns of resistance and discrimination became an integral part of Spain and Portugal's identity and determination. Ventures into North Africa and the coastline of Africa were in part a continuation of this campaign to establish Portuguese identity and conquer regions of Iberia. João de Barros (c. 1496–1570), an early chronicler of Portuguese exploits in Asia, expressed the popular sentiment that "the Portuguese were entitled to act as both spiritual and temporal *conquistadores*."[56] In Barros's words, the role of these *conquistadores* was to wage war "against the infidels."[57] The Portuguese, according to C. R. Boxer, saw expansion as "a patriotic crusade, with Portugal as the standard-bearer of the Faith (*Alferes da Fé*)."[58] These campaigns were more than Portugal's self-assertion, but a defense of the Latin church and central to the church's expansion. In Portugal's *conquista* activities, the spirit of the medieval Crusades provided impetus for Portugal's program of discovery and exploitation.

Conversion tactics and forced expulsion of Muslims and Jews in the reconquest of the Iberian Peninsula continued as *conquista*, as crown and church pushed into North Africa and Asia.[59] In Stephen Neill's assessment,

---

[56]See C. R. Boxer's assessment of Barros's *Décadas da Ásia* in "A Note on Portuguese Missionary Methods in the East: Sixteenth to Eighteenth Centuries," in *Christianity and Missions, 1450–1800*, An Expanding World, The European Impact on World History 1450–1800, vol. 28 (Hampshire, UK: Ashgate, 1997), 162.

[57]João de Barros, cited by C. R. Boxer, *João de Barros, Portuguese Humanist and Historian of Asia*, XCHR Studies Series 1 (New Delhi: Concept, 1981), 116.

[58]Ibid. See also Newitt, *History of Portuguese Overseas Expansion*, 130.

[59]William R. Da Silva and Rowena Robinson, "Discover to Conquer: Towards a Sociology of Conversion," in *Discoveries, Missionary Expansion and Asian Cultures*, 56. Jennifer Price, "Alfonso I and the Memory of the First Crusade: Conquest and Crusade in the Kingdom of Aragon-Navarre," in *Crusades—Medieval Worlds in Conflict* (Farnham, UK: Ashgate, 2010), 75-94,

European expansion of the sixteenth century belongs under the headings of "Crusades, Curiosity, Commerce, Conversion, Conquest and Colonisation, in that order."[60] Where the Iberian empires traveled, the Latin church followed. "It was a matter of logistics," according to Jonathan Wright.[61] The church's intent to Christianize followed in the footsteps of the crown's aim to Latinize.[62] The two paralleled and served each other, and thus, for those who received Vasco da Gama, Latin Christianity arrived in his ships.

Padroado real. The crusading spirit remained a defining force for the church well into the sixteenth century, especially in its collaboration with the Spanish and Portuguese crowns.[63] Because the Crusades created common cause for church and state in the eleventh and twelfth centuries, the spirit and mentality of the Crusades provided an ongoing basis for cooperation. The need to defend Christendom from Muslim advances and the threat to unity from heretics within Christendom prolonged their dependent relationship. For the Catholic church in the late Middle Ages, this relationship became even more crucial as Spain and Portugal emerged as seafaring powers and dramatically extended their interests beyond the bounds of Europe and into places where the church did not have presence or jurisdiction. As both Spain and Portugal aligned their kingdoms solidly with the church, they looked to Rome for conceptual and legal framework to address the new conditions. A series of papal bulls beginning in the

---

examines the connection between Aflonso I's (1104–1134) use of imagery and language of the First Crusade for his purposes in Iberia. As Constantinople fell in 1453, igniting crusading sentiments, Pope Leo X (1475–1521) initiated plans for another Crusade against the Turks in 1513 and issued crusade indulgences in 1517, but the crusading forces never materialized. Cf. Reinhard, "Seaborne Empires," 639-40.

[60]Neill, *History of Christianity in India*, 87. Benjamin Z. Kedar, *Crusade and Mission: European Approaches Toward the Muslims* (Princeton, NJ: Princeton University Press, 1984), 159-69, 203, calls this the "Innocentian linkage," referring to policies and attitudes originating during the papacy of Innocent IV (1195–1254) that connected "Christian warfare and infidel conversion." See also Boxer, *Four Centuries of Portuguese Expansion*, 6.

[61]Jonathan Wright, *God's Soldiers: Adventure, Politics, Intrigue, and Power, A History of the Jesuits* (New York: Doubleday, 2004), 106.

[62]André Rétif, "Evolution of the Catholic Idea of Mission: A French Roman Catholic Bibliography," *Student World* 53, nos. 1–2 (January 1960): 265-66.

[63]Cf. James D. Tracy, "Introduction," in *The Political Economy of Merchant Empires*, ed. James D. Tracy, Studies in Comparative Early Modern History (New York: Cambridge University Press, 1991), 9-10.

fifteenth century created an arrangement of responsibilities for Spain and Portugal and strengthened their connection with the church.[64]

Regimini militantis Ecclesiae (1540), the founding papal bull for the Society of Jesus, was not unlike the bulls that preceded it. While dealing specifically with the establishment of the new Society, it was an ecclesial response to the changing conditions in which the church found itself. Seven bulls leading up to *Regimini* determined the church's direction and role in these changes, which in turn precipitated the founding of the Society: *Sane charissimus* (1418), *Rex regum* (1436), *Illius qui se* (1442), *Dum diversas* (1452), *Romanus Pontiflex* (1455), *Inter caetera* (1456), and *Inter caetera Divinae* (1493). These papal actions came about in response to the rising power of Spain and Portugal and new situations arising from their encounters with peoples and their occupation of lands outside Europe.

The first of these situations requiring papal jurisdiction arose when the Portuguese conquered Ceuta in 1415, which initiated their expeditions along the African coast. Portugal's expansion prompted Pope Martin V (1369–1431) to issue *Sane charissimus* (1418). Eugenius IV (1383–1447) reinforced *Sane charissimus* with his bull *Rex regum* (1436). In both bulls, the papacy called on all Christians to aid John I of Portugal in his war against the Moors.

Four bulls in the following forty years offered incentives for those who aided the rulers of Portugal and Spain, but they also provided warrant and means for exploration and exploitation. But just as much as these provided justification for state power, they also addressed the needs of the Latin church. These papal bulls reinforced a crusading spirit of a united Catholic Europe and reflected the church's power to call princes and emperors to common causes. In addition, the bulls projected a new kind of papal authorization with increasing clarity and specificity by sanctioning the subjugation of native peoples to the Latin church. The issues of Latin identity and boundaries crucial for the territories conquered in the First Crusade now extended into Africa and Asia.

---

[64]Claude Alvares and Norma Alvares, "The Christian and the Wild," in *Discoveries, Missionary Expansion and Asian Cultures*, 20.

Dum diversas (1452) marked the initiation of what became known as the Doctrine of Discovery.[65] Issued on June 18, 1452, the chief concern of Pope Nicholas V (1397–1455) in this bull was the Moors of Morocco. It gave King Alfonso V of Portugal "full and free permission to invade, search out, capture, and subjugate the Saracens and pagans and any other unbelievers and enemies of Christ wherever they may be, as well as their kingdoms, duchies, counties, principalities, and other property" and in doing so "to reduce their persons into perpetual servitude."[66] *Dum diversas* established the basis for state policy during this era and the foundation for subsequent papal pronouncements.

The fall of Constantinople in 1453 prompted Pope Nicholas V to call for yet another crusade. Because the king of Portugal, Alfonso V (1432–1481), responded positively to Nicholas's call to arms, Alfonso garnered favor from Rome for his claims against Castile.[67] The result was *Romanus Pontifex*, issued by Nicholas on January 8, 1455, and posted on the door of the Lisbon Cathedral in October of that same year. The bull arbitrated the claims of Portugal and Castile regarding territories along the African coast in favor of Portugal. In the text, Nicholas acknowledges the colonizing work of Prince Henry and King Alfonso V and commends their efforts to bring salvation to Saracens and other nonbelievers and to defend the faith against the same. *Romanus Pontifex* characterizes the pope as the one who

> rewards with deserved favors and special privileges those Catholic kings and princes, whom we know by clear evidence to be, as it were, athletes of the Christian Faith and fearless warriors (not only restraining the ferocity of the Saracens and other infidel foes to the Christian name, but also conquering them, their kingdoms and territories, even when situated in the most distant and unknown places, and subjecting them to their temporal dominion for the sake of the protection and increase of that same Faith, sparing no toils and expenses) in order that those kings and princes, relieved from any possible

---

[65]For context and circumstances leading to the bull, see A. J. R. Russell-Wood, "Iberian Expansion and the Issue of Black Slavery: Changing Portuguese Attitudes, 1440–1770," *The American Historical Review* 83, no. 1 (February 1978): 16-42.

[66]Cited in Diana Hayes, "Reflections on Slavery," in *Change in Official Catholic Moral Teaching*, ed. Charles E. Curran, Readings in Moral Theology 13 (New York: Paulist, 2003), 67.

[67]Sidney Z. Ehler and John B. Morrall, eds., *Church and State Through the Centuries: A Collection of Historic Documents with Commentaries* (Westminster, MD: Newman, 1954), 145.

obstacles, may be all the more encouraged to the undertaking of so eminently salutary and praiseworthy work.[68]

The bull goes on to note that Henry, Infante of Portugal, and his successor, Alfonso V, are "fired greatly with zeal for the salvation of souls and enthusiasm for the Faith, as . . . true soldier[s] of Christ."[69] What is striking is the political and commercial tenor of the papal instructions. In addition to the ecclesiastical language, the bull reads much like a contractual agreement regarding items of trade (arms, iron, wood for construction), territorial limits (provinces, islands, harbors, seas, and places), and colonializing activities (invade, search out, capture, vanquish, and subjugate). The bull gives

> full and free permission to King Alfonso to invade, search out, capture, conquer and subjugate all Saracens and pagans whatsoever and other enemies of Christ wherever they exist, together with their kingdoms, duchies, principalities, lordships, possessions and whatever goods, movable and immovable, which may be held and possessed by them, and to bring their persons into perpetual slavery and to apply, appropriate and turn to the use and profit of themselves and their successors the kingdoms, duchies, counties, principalities, lordships, possessions and goods (of these people).[70]

In *Romanus Pontifex,* Nicholas V granted King Alfonso and his successors more than maritime and commercial dominance but carte blanche to do whatever they wished in order to subjugate and profit from those encounters. Representatives of the Portuguese king in faraway places were charged to conquer and enslave people and generate commercial gain. They were to fulfill this charge with the permission of God and the church.

Included in Portugal's exclusive permit to explore, exploit, and colonize was the obligation to Christianize. *Romanus Pontifex* named Portuguese political authorities as representatives of the church and actors in founding and building "churches, monasteries and other holy places."[71] Within the terms of the "right of conquest," the pope tasked them with sending "ecclesiastical persons" to live in these territories, hear confessions, offer absolution, and

---

[68]Translation of *Romanus Pontifex* is from ibid., 146.
[69]Ibid.
[70]Ibid., 149.
[71]Ibid., 151.

administer sacraments. The bull designated the king and his representatives as the direct agents of ecclesial administration and expansion.

Romanus Pontifex mentions Saracens, but absent from the list of activity is their care or conversion. The chief concern was that Muslims not receive aid but be conquered and subjugated. Whereas *Dum diversas* (1452) reinforced previous prohibitions against European trade with Muslims, *Romanus Pontifex* (1455) granted an exception to the king of Portugal, as long as he did not trade in "iron instruments, wood for building purposes, ropes, ships or types of armour."[72] *Romanus Pontifex* repeats three times the general prohibition against assisting Muslims with material goods (iron, weapons, wood for building) and censures those who teach them the art of sailing with excommunication and interdiction. Even in regard to Indian Christians, *Romanus Pontifex* expressed the hope "to be able to negotiate with them and prevail upon them to provide aid to the [Latin] Christians against the Saracens and other similar enemies of the Faith, and might also be able to conquer certain Gentile and pagan peoples living between, who are not infected with the sect of the most infamous Mahomet."[73]

Territorial disputes settled by Nicholas V in *Romanus Pontifex* (1455) flared up again with Christopher Columbus's arrival in the New World in 1492 and Spain's subsequent claims in the Americas. When John II asserted Portugal's "right to conquer" in the whole of the world, including the Americas, Spain's Ferdinand and Isabella made an appeal to their friend, the Spanish-born Pope Alexander VI (1431–1503). This time papal confirmation favored Spain. With *Inter caetera Divinae* (1493), Alexander VI divided the interests of Portugal as defined by *Romanus Pontifex* by drawing a line on the map from the North Pole to the South Pole, west of the Azores islands and Cape Verde. Thus, everything west of this line belonged to Spain, and new lands east of the line remained with Portugal, with the proviso that "mainlands and islands found or to be found, discovered or to be discovered . . . be not possessed by some other Christian king or prince."[74] The Hispano-Portuguese Treaty of Tordesillas of 1494 modified this demarcation by moving the line more to the west and thus incorporated Brazil into the Portuguese realm.

---

[72]Ibid., 150.
[73]Ibid., 147. Pope Calixtus III issued *Inter caetera* (March 1456) to reinforce *Romanus Pontifex*.
[74]*Inter caetera Divinae* in Ehler and Morrall, *Church and State*, 157.

Inter caetera Divinae established several new arrangements. First, it did for Ferdinand and Isabella of Spain what *Romanus Pontifex* had done for Henry the Navigator and Alfonso V. The bull acclaimed Ferdinand and Isabella as Catholic rulers of "illustrious and well-known deeds," which are demonstrated in their "re-conquest of the kingdom of Granada from the tyranny of the Saracens."[75] The decree expressed hope that these Spanish rulers would bring the "inhabitants and natives" to the worship of Christ and "to the confession of the Catholic faith."[76] These hopes were punctuated by the gravity of "Apostolic benediction," "Apostolic orders," "Apostolic favour," and "Apostolic power," but no specific instructions were given to deploy ecclesiastical persons or offices to spread the Catholic faith in the discovered lands. The Spanish rulers and their representatives were simply instructed to undertake "the expansion of Christian rule."[77]

Second, both *Romanus Pontifex* and *Inter Caetera Divinae* portrayed the church as a full partner in state-initiated and state-sponsored colonial expansion. Popes Nicholas and Alexander understood that the church's place and dominance were at stake, and thus they placed its authority alongside that of the secular state. As the fortunes of these political entities rose or fell, so went the status of the church.

Third, the boundaries of Christendom were extended around the world. *Inter caetera Divinae* destroyed "the geographical compactness of Catholic Christendom (as limited to Europe only) which had been, during the ten centuries of the Middle Ages, a stable framework of its international organization."[78] Rather than extending the reach of Christendom only to Latin enclaves in the Holy Land, the boundaries of Christendom were redrawn to include the Americas, Asia, and Africa. By virtue of the papal claim to be sovereign over all of humanity, Alexander decreed all known peoples to be within the realm of church authority. *Romanus Pontifex* described the Roman pontiff as "looking with paternal interest upon all the regions of the world and the specific natures of all the people who dwell in them, seeking and desiring the salvation of every one of them."[79] In apportioning regions

---

[75]Ibid., 155-56.
[76]Ibid., 156.
[77]Ibid.
[78]Editorial comments by Enler and Morall in ibid., 100.
[79]*Romanus Pontifex* in ibid., 146.

to Spain and Portugal, Alexander in *Inter caetera Divinae* did so by "sure knowledge and plentitude of Apostolic power, by the Vicariate of Jesus Christ which we discharge on earth—all the islands and mainlands, found or to be found, discovered or to be discovered westwards or southwards."[80]

Fourth, these bulls were the beginning of the *padroado real* (*patronatus* in Spanish).[81] This system delegated political and ecclesial responsibility for regions of the world to Spain and Portugal, and thus ecclesial activities were included in the state's *misión* or *missão*. According to C. R. Boxer, the *padroado*, for the Portuguese crown, was "a combination of the rights, privileges and duties granted by the papacy to the crown of Portugal as patron of the Roman Catholic mission and ecclesiastical establishments in the vast regions of Africa, of Asia and in Brazil."[82] Thus, the *padroado* gave the king, or his assigned deputy, authority over churches where foreigners attended and authorized evangelizing efforts among non-Christians. The king's assignment included the creation of bishoprics, the construction of new churches, appointment of apostolic commissaries, and funding for the maintenance of priests and their work. Religious agents (priests and monks) who operated in Portuguese territories were funded by the crown and thus had to abide by Portuguese rules.[83] In fact, agents in Portuguese areas were only able to operate there by permission of the Portuguese crown, had to travel on Portuguese ships, and were subordinate to Portuguese control.[84] In this arrangement, the work of colonization and Christianization went hand in hand.

Along with the *padroado,* the king of Portugal was designated the "Grand Master of the Order of Christ," and was thus commissioned to conquer, evangelize, and administer territories with divine authority. The order, founded in 1319 by King Dom Dinis, aided in the conquest of Muslims and the establishment of Portugal but in time turned its emphasis toward territories beyond Portugal. Prince Henry, as administrator of the order, was able

---

[80]*Inter caetera Divinae* in ibid., 157.
[81]Newitt, *History of Portuguese Overseas Expansion*, 30.
[82]Boxer, *Portuguese Seaborne Empire*, 228-29. Stephen Neill, *History of Christianity in India*, explains, "The pope was glad to hand over the labours of conquest and evangelisaton to secular rulers who had access to resources far greater than he could himself supply. So from the start [the *padroado*] was an arrangement of convenience and advantage to both sides" (111).
[83]Sá, "Ecclesiastical Structures and Religious Action," 257.
[84]Boxer, *Portuguese Seaborne Empire*, 230.

to draw from the order's resources in order to finance Portugal's expanding exploration along the African coast.[85]

Because religious and military orders and institutions were under the control and at the direction of the king of Portugal, state action was religious action. This cooperative arrangement was the state of affairs at the time of Ignatius and remained so until the *padroado* began to wane with the establishment in 1622 of the *Congregation de Propaganda Fide*. The *Propaganda Fide* was the papal response to what was considered to be too much state influence, and in some cases state domination in ecclesial matters.[86] Added to these concerns were the rise of Dutch and British colonial aspirations and the decline of Spain and Portugal's ability to maintain their dominance in the Americas and Asia.

The mandate of the *padroado* to bring the lands discovered and their peoples into the Christian faith gave ecclesial sanction to and justification for the civilizing mission undertaken by Portugal. Through the *padroado* arrangement, Christendom conventions of medieval Europe continued to shape the state's approach to peoples outside Europe. The crown's *misión/ missão* was an ecclesial mission, as well as a political one.

The reach and power of the crown's *misión/missão* beckoned the Latin church to reach beyond Europe as well, and its response came in the form of Ignatius's mission vow. Whereas the rhetoric of "mission" was absent in the early crusades, it can be found in the crusading spirit of the *conquista* and *padroado*, and thus gives language for the emerging relationship between the church and new territories and peoples. Mission serves as utility for the church and impetus for the Jesuits, the ground force of Catholic expansion. And yet, mission language is more than the church's response to a changing political and ecclesial context but became a distinct ecclesial posture toward the world. Portugal and Spain, *conquista* and *padroado*, and existing language were the context in which Ignatius innovated "mission." These provided the impulse for what emerged as the Ignatian mission.

---

[85]Boxer, *Four Centuries of Portuguese Expansion*, 65.
[86]Sá, "Ecclesiastical Structures and Religious Action," 259.

8

Ignatian Mission

After the pilgrim realized that it was not God's
will that he remain in Jerusalem, he continually
pondered within himself what he ought to do.

IGNATIUS OF LOYOLA, *AUTOBIOGRAPHY*

I promise special obedience to the Supreme Pontiff
in regard to the missions as contained in the bull.

IGNATIUS OF LOYOLA, 1541

THE FOUNDING PAPAL BULL and constitutive documents of the Society of Jesus are a reflection of the changing context of church-state relationships and the ensuing adjustments. It is natural that the term the
Spanish and Portuguese used for exploration and expansion would be repurposed for the Latin church. *Misión* and *missio* appear in the Society's
founding documents, and thus "mission" became unique language for the
Society's way of proceeding in the world. And yet, mission was more than
the church's adjustment to the changing situation. It emerged from Ignatius's personality and life experience. As mission became for Ignatius personal principle and vocation, it was the same for those who entered the
Society. The Ignatian character of mission is evident in his "mission profession." On April 19, 1541, Ignatius was elected as the Society's General. He
celebrated mass and professed,

I, the undersigned [Ignatius of Loyola] promise to Almighty God and the Supreme Pontiff, his vicar on earth, in the presence of his Virgin Mother and the whole heavenly court, and of the Society, perpetual poverty, chastity, and obedience, according to the manner of living which is contained in the bull of the Society of our Lord Jesus and in its Constitutions adopted or to be adopted. Moreover, I promise special obedience to the Supreme Pontiff in regard to the missions as contained in the bull.[1]

FORMATIVE IDEALS

Mission was more than ideology or strategy; it was personal identity and purpose for Ignatius. And just as Ignatius's profession of mission was personal, so were the causes that shaped this new category. Spain, Portugal, and the Latin church provide context, but Ignatius's adoption of mission language was motivated by ideals of chivalry, mystical visions, and his desire to make pilgrimage. The political and ecclesial context warranted a rhetorical shift, and Ignatius's life provided the catalyst for this change.

Militant faith and vocation. Central to Loyola's self-understanding and thus to his interpretation of vocation was his vision of the church and his personal expression of faith.[2] These are fundamental to the spirit of the Society and key to his adoption of mission language. The nature and intensity of Ignatius's faith and vocation arose from his military background and temperament.

As a young man of Navarre, Ignatius was not a career soldier, but a courtier trained in the art of diplomacy and the use of weapons.[3] He describes himself as "a man given over to vanities of the world; with a great

---

[1]Ignatius Loyola, *The Autobiography of St. Ignatius Loyola*, trans. Joseph F. O'Callaghan (New York: Fordham University Press, 1992), 54. Hereafter cited as *AIL*. Pierre Favre's account of his profession, including the promise of "obedience to the Supreme Pontiff with regard to missions," can be found in "The Memoriale," in *Spiritual Writings of Pierre Favre*, trans. Edmund C. Murphy, Jesuit Primary Sources in English Translations 16 (St. Louis: Institute of Jesuit Sources, 1996), 77-78.

[2]The foundational sources of Ignatius's faith are not altogether clear, as there is little information regarding his childhood and the religious milieu of Navarre. Lu Ann Homza, "The Religious Milieu of the Young Ignatius," in *The Cambridge Companion to The Jesuits*, ed. Thomas Worcester, Cambridge Companions to Religion (Cambridge: Cambridge University Press, 2008), 13-31, provides a helpful sketch of the Catholicism in Spain during Ignatius's time.

[3]Philip Caraman, *Ignatius Loyola* (London: HarperCollins, 1990), 18.

and vain desire to win fame he delighted especially in the exercise of arms."[4] Contributing to this desire to "win fame" were the ideals of knighthood, the *reconquista*, and the glories of the Crusades.[5] All three of these were, for Ignatius, part of the lore of recent history and the spirit of the age. Norman Tanner notes Ignatius's intimate knowledge of these ideals was near to hand, since "one of his brothers met his death in the Spanish *Conquista* of America, another . . . on crusade against the Turks in Hungary."[6] Interpreters refer to these ideals as "crusade spirituality," in which pious, noble knights fought for the poor and weak and defended the faith, all as part of following Christ.[7] Christ is the king to follow, in whose name the knight is willing to fight and die. As his followers, Christ's knights are to take up arms against the enemies of the church and suffer for Christ's honor. These noble ideals prompt Ignatius to ready himself to take up arms for a noble cause.

Ignatius's desire to soldier became a reality when in 1517 the viceroy of Navarre, Antonio Manrique de Lara, called Loyola into military service. "For almost four years Ignatius filled his days with jousts, the chase, business of the duke, and the continued reading of romances," until the Navarrese finally marched for Charles V against the French at Pamplona.[8] The battle turned against the Navarrese, and their position seemed to be lost. While most of the soldiers thought it folly to defend the fortress of the city and felt it necessary to surrender, Ignatius stood firm. He rallied those present to make a stand. But their defense of the citadel was short-lived, as Ignatius was struck

---

[4]*AIL*, 21. For an account of Ignatius's early life, see William V. Bangert, *A History of the Society of Jesus*, 2nd ed. (St. Louis: Institute of Jesuit Sources, 1986), 3-22; Jonathan Wright, *The Jesuits: Missions, Myths, and Histories* (London: HarperCollins, 2004), 13-18; José Ignacio Tellechea Idígoras, *Ignatius of Loyola: The Pilgrim Saint* (Chicago: Loyola University Press, 1994); Mary Purcell, *The First Jesuit, St. Ignatius Loyola (1491-1556)* (Chicago: Loyola University Press, 1981).

[5]According to Hans Wolter, "Elements of Crusade Spirituality in St. Ignatius," "The crusade idea was very much alive during the youth and adulthood of St. Ignatius" (103).

[6]Norman Tanner, "Medieval Crusade Decrees and Ignatius's Meditation on the Kingdom," *Heythrop Journal* 31 (1990): 506.

[7]See Hans Wolter, "Elements of Crusade Spirituality in St. Ignatius," in *Ignatius of Loyola, His Personality and Spiritual Heritage, 1556-1956: Studies on the 400th Anniversary of His Death*, ed. Fredrich Wulf, trans. Louis W. Roberts, Modern Scholarly Studies About the Jesuits, in English Translations (St. Louis: Institute of Jesuit Sources, 1977), 97-134; C. Matthew Phillips, "Crucified with Christ: The Imitation of the Crucified Christ and the Crusading Spirituality," in *Crusades—Medieval Worlds in Conflict*, ed. Thomas F. Madden, James L. Naus, and Vincent Ryan (Farnham, UK: Ashgate, 2010), 25-33; William J. Purkis, *Crusading Spirituality in the Holy Land and Iberia, c.1095-c.1187* (Woodbridge, UK: Boydell, 2008).

[8]Bangert, *History of the Society of Jesus*, 4.

with a cannon shot that shattered his right leg.[9] Ignatius's days as a soldier
ended almost as quickly as they began.

Following the surrender, Ignatius was taken back to Loyola, where his
leg underwent surgery in order to correct the procedure performed on
the field at Pamplona. His condition worsened to the point that it was
thought he would not live. He made his confession and prepared for the
worst. He even received the sacraments, but by morning he had improved. A bone was protruding so much so that it caused his leg to look
deformed and ugly. So, he submitted himself to yet another surgery,
making himself "a martyr to his own pleasure."[10] Pain and the severity of
the situation initiated his turn toward faith and his life of service. While
convalescing from his second surgery, Loyola requested books about
"knight-errantry," but as there were no books on chivalry and "knightly
romance" at hand, he was forced to read books about the saints and their
devotion.[11] These books included *Vita Christi* (The life of Christ), by
either Juan de Padilla or the Carthusian monk Ludolph of Saxony, and
Legenda Aurea (Golden legend), by Jacobus de Voragine (1229–1298).[12]
Vita Christi challenged Ignatius to imagine the physical form and actions
of Christ and imitate them. In particular, *Vita Christi* presents Christ as
a medieval king who conquers and reigns.[13] And like one who follows an
earthly king, the followers of Christ are to obey and imitate the king for
his fame and honor.

---

[9]*AIL*, 21.

[10]Ibid., 22. Throughout his *Autobiography*, Ignatius refers to himself in the third person.

[11]James Brodrick, *Saint Ignatius Loyola: The Pilgrim Years 1491–1538* (New York: Farrar, Straus and
Cudahy, 1956), 38-45; Tellechea Idígoras, *Ignatius of Loyola*, 119. Among the materials Ignatius
read, *Amadís de Gaula*, a work of fiction, was a favorite. Originally composed in Spanish by an
unknown author(s), this work was revised and supplemented many times. The chief aim of the
novel was to extol the virtue of knighthood and note the dangers knights would face via the
story of Amadís.

[12]*AIL*, 23. See also Tellechea Idígoras, *Ignatius of Loyola*, 119-21; Caraman, *Ignatius Loyola*, 27-32;
Brodrick, *Loyola: The Pilgrim Years*, 63-68.

[13]For the influence of this small book on Ignatius's understanding of Christ and the way it shaped
Spiritual Exercises, see Paul J. Shore, *The Vita Christi of Ludolph of Saxony and Its Influence on the
Spiritual Exercises of Ignatius of Loyola*, Studies in the Spirituality of Jesuits (St. Louis: Seminar
on Jesuit Spirituality, 1998). Shore indicates that the word *Jesuit* may have come from Ludolph.
To substantiate this claim, Shore quotes from *Vita Christi*: "Likewise the name of Christ is a name
of grace, but the name of Jesus is a name of glory. Just as through the grace of baptism Christians
are called such by Christ, in heavenly glory it will be Jesus himself who will call us Jesuits, that
is, saved by the Savior" (15).

In *Legenda Aurea*, Ignatius read of the heroism and adventures of the church's saints, such as Augustine, Bernard, Dominic, Francis, and Humphrey. In Bernard of Clairvaux, Ignatius found a man whose father was a "knight valorous in worldly affairs," and brother "a stalwart knight," who provided inspiration for the Second Crusade.[14] St. Francis had knightly ambitions and, like Ignatius, suffered defeat in battle. Likewise, it was during Francis's time of convalescence from illness that "the Lord chastened him with the whip of ill health and quickly made a different man."[15] Ignatius read that Francis renounced his former life and pursued a life of poverty and service, had visions of Christ, followed a rule of life, established an order, and made a pilgrimage to Jerusalem. The depiction in *Legenda Aurea* of Francis encountering knights and confronting their skepticism and pride challenged Ignatius to consider his own life.[16] What's more, in *Legenda Aurea* St. James, the patron saint of Spain, appears to pilgrims in the image of "knightly array."[17] Over and over, *Legenda Aurea* portrays saints as "soldiers of Christ" battling with the "soldiers of the devil."[18] In much the same way, these "*cabelleros de Dios* or knights in service of the eternal Prince" challenged the young Ignatius and impressed on him an alternative vision of religious or spiritual valor.[19]

Ignatius put "his reading aside . . . to think about the things he had read and at other times about the things of the world that he used to think about before."[20] His thoughts alternated between doing valiant service to a certain unidentified lady of high nobility or living as St. Francis and St. Dominic had done. In the end, he found thinking about the ways of the world left him "dry and discontented," and that saintly deeds, such as a pilgrimage to Jerusalem or the rigors of a saint's life, would make him "content and happy."[21] His desire to imitate the life of the saints grew until he came to the conclusion

---

[14]Jacobus de Voragine, *The Golden Legend: Readings on the Saints*, trans. William Granger Ryan (Princeton, NJ: Princeton University Press, 1993), 2:98, 100.

[15]Ibid., 2:220.

[16]Jacobus de Voragine, *Golden Legend*, 2:226, 227, 229. For examples of the striking parallels between the early lives of Francis of Assisi and Ignatius, see Michael Robson, *The Franciscans in the Middle Ages*, Monastic Orders (Woodbridge, UK: Boydell, 2006), 12-13.

[17]Jacobus de Voragine, *Golden Legend*, 2:7.

[18]Ibid., 2:190.

[19]Quoted by Caraman, *Ignatius Loyola*, 27.

[20]*AIL*, 23.

[21]Ibid., 24.

that as soon as he recovered he would go to Jerusalem, "performing all the disciplines and abstinences which a generous soul, inflamed by God, usually wants to do."[22] His change of heart was complete following a night vision of Mary, standing before him with the holy child Jesus. The accumulative effect was that rather than chivalrous adoration and deeds toward a countess or duchess, Ignatius turned his worship and service toward Mary and Christ. This decision marked his turn from "vanity" and was when "the things of the flesh" left him.[23] As Jerusalem was not an immediate possibility, he considered doing penitence and living an obscure existence at the Carthusian house in Seville, but this idea did not seem to be enough. "He feared," as he says in his autobiography, "that he would not be able to give vent to the hatred that he had conceived against himself."[24] Thus, he felt something more than mere penitence or obscurity was required of him.

As soon as he recovered, he set out for Jerusalem. On his journey from home, he gradually stripped away, piece by piece, his former life and underwent external and internal change. At his first stop, Montserrat, he exchanged his fine clothes for those of a pilgrim, made his confession, and left his sword and dagger at the altar of a pilgrim church.[25] He entered as a nobleman and left as a pilgrim with staff in hand. Loyola's life transitioned from worldly ideals of duels and daring deeds, but he did not completely abandon the ideals of chivalry and glory. Instead, he transferred these to the spiritual realm. Rather than a soldier marching under the banner of the viceroy of Navarre, he was now a soldier of Christ at the service of the Holy Mother on pilgrimage to Jerusalem.

Ignatius's next stop was Manresa, where he spent almost a year. During this time, he began composing the *Spiritual Exercises*. His new vision of fervent faith and ardent vocation is evident throughout the *Exercises*. More than a book for inspiration or a treatise on devotional life, this little volume is "a manual to be translated into personal activity."[26] *Exercises* mirrors the

---

[22]Ibid.
[23]Ibid., 25.
[24]Ibid.
[25]Lynn Talbot, "Montserrat," in *Encyclopedia of Medieval Pilgrimage* (Leiden: Brill, 2010).
[26]Bangert, *History of the Society of Jesus*, 9. Ignatius began writing *Exercises* following his "mystical illumination" at Manresa in 1521. The original work developed and expanded over the next twenty-five years, and provided foundation and spirit for the Society, as it became the means by which men were trained and entered its ranks. According to John O'Malley, *The First Jesuits*

rigors of preparation for military service and thus is the means by which one is to train and discipline oneself as a new soldier of Christ.[27] The language and tenor of the *Exercises* is direct, active, and militant in tone.[28]

As Ignatius led those he encountered through the *Exercises*, a group of like-minded men became his companions. This group was the nucleus of what would become the Society of Jesus. The traditional term in Spanish for society, *compañía*, denoted either "military groups or pious associations of great variety."[29] And while Loyola employed the term to describe his companions' loyalty to one another and to a common cause, subsequent interpreters demonstrate that such virtues were secondary to the disciplined and organized nature of the *Compañía de Jesús* and their devotion to their papal commander. In structure, the new order was centralized in authority, more hierarchical than democratic, and thus military in tenor. The superior general was appointed for life rather than a limited term. The general governed the Society with broad powers to appoint, send, remove, and discipline. The line of command for the members ran from the lowest and most humble brother through a chain of authority to the superior general and ultimately to the vicar of Christ.[30] In the same manner that Spain and Portugal had formulated centralized systems for the governance in their emerging nations and for the administration of their new territories, the Society formed itself into a hierarchical structure. And just as such centralized structure was required for efficiency and discipline of colonial enlargement, the same was needed for the Society. During the time of the Society's formation, disunity characterized the general rank of the priesthood,

---

(Cambridge, MA: Harvard University Press, 1993), "There is no understanding of the Jesuits without reference to that book" (4).

[27] Ignatius Loyola, *The Spiritual Exercises of Saint Ignatius: A Translation and Commentary by George E. Ganss S.J.* (Chicago: Loyola University Press, 1992), 53-55. Hereafter cited as *SE*.

[28] Cf. O'Malley, *First Jesuits*, 45-46. See Sam Zeno Conedera's discussion of terms of fraternity and cooperation among military orders in Spain, "Brothers in Arms: Hermandades Among the Military Orders in Medieval Iberia," in *Crusades—Medieval Worlds in Conflict* (Farnham, UK: Ashgate, 2010), 35-44. Tanner, "Medieval Crusade Decrees," 505-15, explores parallels between Crusade decrees and Ignatius's thought, especially in his sections on the kingdom in *Spiritual Exercises*. While admitting that there is little to no material evidence to suggest that Ignatius had read these decrees, Tanner highlights similarities between Ignatius's writings and the medieval Crusader tradition.

[29] Supplementary notes, *CSJ*, 345-46.

[30] Dauril Alden, *The Making of an Enterprise: The Society of Jesus in Portugal, Its Empire, and Beyond, 1540–1750* (Stanford, CA: Stanford University Press, 1996), 10.

and abuse of privilege by priests plagued the church; thus those desiring reform and stability welcomed the authority and structure exemplified in the emerging Society.

The foundation of the strict, disciplined nature of the Society is evident in Ignatius's personal life as well. Cándido de Dalmases, for example, argues that the characteristic regimentation of the Society has its beginnings with the vow at Montmartre.[31] Just as members of a military unit would surrender all rights to their commander-in-chief and pledge to obey any order, the band of future Jesuits made a similar vow. Two distinct elements of the vow need to be noted. First, the vow was more than to journey to Jerusalem: Jesuits placed themselves at the service of the pope to go wherever he wished. It was a vow of absolute obedience to their supreme commander. Second, it was a vow of corporate allegiance. Even though there seemed to be no thought at this time of a Society or of others beyond this small company, their vow was to service together in a singular act of obedience.[32] This intent to obey no matter the cost established the pattern and ethos of the Society.

Ignatius submitted an initial draft of the constitution of the Society, also known as the *Summa institute* or *Formula instituti*, in June 1539. After minor changes, the constitution was incorporated into the bull *Regimini militantis Ecclesiae* (To the government of the church militant) and approved on September 27, 1540.[33] The wording in Pope Paul III's approval of the Society reflects an activist rather than a contemplative tone and in places is overtly militaristic. The *Formula* opens with language reminiscent of the Crusades: "Whoever desires to serve as a soldier of God beneath the banner of the cross in our Society." Throughout the *Formula*, the Society is referred to as a "militia of Jesus Christ."[34] Section 4 states, "Then, after they have enlisted through the inspiration of the Lord in this militia of Christ, they ought to be in carrying out this obligation which is so great, being clad for battle day

---

[31]Cándido de Dalmases, *Ignatius of Loyola, Founder of the Jesuits: His Life and Works*, trans. Jerome Aixalá (St. Louis: Institute of Jesuit Sources, 1985), 121-22.
[32]See Joseph F. Conwell, *Impelling Spirit: Revisiting a Founding Experience, 1539, Ignatius of Loyola and His Companions; An Exploration into the Spirit and Aims of the Society of Jesus as Revealed in the Founders' Proposed Papal Letter Approving the Society* (Chicago: Loyola Press, 1997), 112.
[33]*CSJ*, 63-73. The constitution was slightly revised again in 1550 by Julius III and reissued as *Exposcit debitum*.
[34]Ibid., 66, 68, 71.

and night."[35] According to Juan de Polanco, secretary of the Society during Loyola's lifetime, those who joined the order enlist in "the militia of Christ," and those who suffered in its cause are "a faithful soldier of Christ."[36]

Biographers and interpreters of Ignatius's early life highlight the influence of Loyola's soldier background and the military tone of the *Formula* and the *Constitution.*[37] Joseph Griffin portrays the Jesuits' formation as an effort "to imitate the old spirit of the Crusaders," and Hans Wolter insists, "For an understanding of the genesis and nature of Ignatian spirituality a study of crusade spirituality . . . is indispensable."[38] James Brodrick notes the aggressive reputation of the Society of Jesus, describing it as "built for action, a regiment on war-footing."[39] Others minimize the importance of these influences, citing the fact that military language and symbols were part of the church from its infancy and throughout its history right up to Loyola.[40] And yet, no matter what language preceded the Society, a military tone and hierarchical structure are present in its earliest documents, and this language distinguishes it from other orders, except for the military orders founded during the Crusades, such as the Templars and Hospitallers.

Another component of Loyola's vision of fervent faith and ardent vocation is his view of Christ. Rather than solely the Lord of heaven to be

---

[35]*CSJ*, 68.

[36]Juan de Polanco, *Year by Year with the Early Jesuits (1537–1556): Selections from the "Chronicon" of Juan de Polanco, S.J.*, Jesuit Primary Sources in English Translations 21 (St. Louis: Institute of Jesuit Sources, 2004), 1, 5, 8, 10, 37.

[37]Alden, *Making of an Enterprise*, 9; Jonathan Wright, *God's Soldiers: Adventure, Politics, Intrigue, and Power, A History of the Jesuits* (New York: Doubleday, 2004); René Fülöp-Miller, *The Jesuits: A History of the Society of Jesus*, trans. D. F. Tait (New York: Capricorn Books, 1963), 27.

[38]Joseph A. Griffin, "The Sacred Congregation de Propaganda Fide: Its Foundation and Historical Antecedents," in *Christianity and Missions, 1450–1800*, The Expanding World, The European Impact on World History 1450–1800 vol. 28 (Hampshire, UK: Ashgate, 1997), 71; Wolter, "Elements of Crusade Spirituality in St. Ignatius," 134.

[39]These comments come from James Brodrick, *Robert Bellarmine: Saint and Scholar* (Westminister, MD: The Newman Press, 1961), 42.

[40]Contrary to the military or the soldier elements of Ignatius's life, some indicate that he was first and foremost a mystic, responding out of love and the promptings of the Spirit. See Conwell, *Impelling Spirit*, xix; Harvey D. Egan, "Ignatius of Loyola: Mystic at the Heart of the Trinity, Mystic at the Heart of Jesus Christ," in *Spiritualities of the Heart* (Mahwah, NJ: Paulist, 1990), 97–113; Joseph de Guibert, *The Jesuits: Their Spiritual Doctrine and Practice; A Historical Study*, trans. William J. Young (Chicago: Institute of Jesuit Sources, 1964), 172–74. John W. O'Malley, "The Society of Jesus," in *Companion to the Reformation World* (Malden, MA: Blackwell, 2004), maintains that despite the military imagery, the Society was not "grounded on a military model" (224). Cf. Alden, *Making of an Enterprise*, 10.

worshiped and adored, Christ is seen as a king who strives against the forces of Satan to establish his kingdom. Thus, Christ's soldiers are to join in the struggle for victory over the powers that oppose the Savior. Ignatius's early expressions of Christ as king are present in *Spiritual Exercises*.[41] It is noteworthy that the one going through the *Exercises* is to contemplate or envision the reality of the kingdom of Jesus. They are to imagine how they might submit to a human, temporal king. The king says,

> My will is to conquer the whole land of the infidels. Hence, whoever wishes to come with me has to be content with the same food I eat, and the drink, and the clothing which I wear, and so forth. So too each one must labor with me during the day, and keep watch in the night, and so on, so that later each may have a part with me in the victory, just as each has shared in the toil.[42]

Loyola's point, and thus instruction, is that one's response is to be the same to Christ, whose "will is to conquer the whole world and all my enemies, and thus to enter into the glory of my Father."[43] In this imagery, one hears the crusading mentality of a recent age. The summons is to join Christ, the conquering king, in his labor, pain, and glory, as "an unworthy knight."[44] In another section of the *Exercises*, Loyola asks the exercitant to meditate on the two standards: one being "Christ, our Supreme Commander," and the other being "Lucifer, the mortal enemy of our human nature."[45] Under the standards of these two forces, people gather on opposing plains, Jerusalem and Babylon, under opposing commanders, Christ and Satan. Under the standard of Christ, "persons, apostles, disciples, and the like" are sent "throughout the whole world, to spread his doctrine among people of every state and condition."[46] The *Exercises* is Loyola's call to arms for "the Supreme and True Captain, Our Lord Christ" as the "church militant."[47]

The language of *kingdom* and *commander* has not gone unnoticed by those who chronicle the history of the church in this age. In an

---

[41]Introduction by George E. Ganss in *SE*, 3-4.
[42]*SE*, 53.
[43]Ibid., 54.
[44]Ibid.
[45]Ibid., 65.
[46]Ibid., 66.
[47]Ibid., 133.

examination of the church's mission originating from Portugal in the fifteenth and sixteenth centuries, C. R. Boxer characterizes the Jesuits as "the Guards Brigade of the Church Militant."[48] Boxer's assessment is that Jesuit missionaries were conscious of their "vital role in the overseas expansion of Europe which initiated the making of the modern world" and thus operated as the religious representation of Portugal's forward advance.[49] Bailon de Sá, historian of Portugal's early expansion, notes that there were only a few Indian conversions to Christianity until the Jesuits arrived as "the spearhead of the Church Militant."[50] Superior organization and strict discipline increased the level of evangelization and placed the Jesuits at the frontlines of the confrontation with local religions.

Fervent faith and ardent vocation merged with existing images and language to create Ignatian mission. The new mission rhetoric signaled the church's intent to advance alongside diplomatic, military, and economic endeavors already in operation. Loyola and his companions played their part in this advance as Christ's soldiers, enlisted in his mission to conquer the land of the infidel. Mission was the connection among Ignatius's aggressive personal faith, his militant vision for the church, and his understanding of Christ as supreme commander, and mission was the linguistic vehicle through which these found expression.

Mystical union and service. After renouncing his former life and going through his period of struggle at Manresa (1522–1523), Ignatius began thinking and writing about the Trinity. His devotion to the "Most Holy Trinity" expressed itself in the form of prayers to "the three Persons individually."[51] He reported that his prayer and thoughts caused him to talk

---

[48]C. R. Boxer, *The Church Militant and Iberian Expansion* (Baltimore: Johns Hopkins University Press, 1978), 71.

[49]Ibid., x.

[50]Bailon de Sá, "The Genesis of Portuguese Discoveries and Their Influence on Indian Culture," in *Discoveries, Missionary Expansion and Asian Cultures* (New Delhi: Concept, 1994), 71.

[51]*AIL*, 37. Concerning the "trinitarian character" of Ignatius's mysticism, see Hugo Rahner, *The Vision of St. Ignatius in the Chapel of La Storta*, 2nd ed. (Rome: Centrus Ignatianum Spiritualitatis, 1979). For his "trinitarian turn," see Adolf Haas, "The Mysticism of St. Ignatius According to His Spiritual Diary," in *Ignatius of Loyola, His Personality and Spiritual Heritage, 1556-1956: Studies on the 400th Anniversary of His Death*, ed. Fredrich Wulf, trans. G. Richard Dimler, Modern Scholarly Studies about the Jesuits, in English Translations (St. Louis: Institute of Jesuit Sources, 1977), 172-85.

constantly about the "Most Holy Trinity" and to weep uncontrollably.[52] His inward vision of the persons of the Trinity and the activities of God in creation and the incarnation began shaping his mystical illumination, as well as the way he identified his life and work in the world.

In 1537, while on his way to Rome to present himself to the pope, Ignatius, along with Peter Faber and Diego Laynez, stopped at the outskirts of the city at the settlement of La Storta. Ignatius entered a small chapel and prayed for divine favor. During his prayers, Ignatius saw in an illumination of Jesus carrying the cross and the Father at his side. Ignatius reports that Jesus said to him, "I wish you to serve us." God the Father added that he "will be propitious to [Ignatius] in Rome," and then placed Ignatius at the side of Jesus.[53] As Ignatius reports in his autobiography, he "experienced such a change in his soul and saw so clearly that God the Father had placed him with His Son Christ that his mind could not doubt that God the Father had indeed placed him with His Son."[54] Ignatius from this point forward began speaking of his life as joined together with the sending of the Son and of himself as part of the divine mission.

Loyola recounts that while in the midst of prayers at La Storta, "all Three Persons," the Father, Son, and Holy Spirit, "confirmed the mission" given to him to be the same that the Son first gave the apostles.[55] This vision recorded by Loyola in *Spiritual Journal* not only connects his activity with that of Jesus but also couches this connection in terms of mission. The connection of his actions and those of the Trinity gives Loyola's commission a divine nature and, more specifically, ties his mission to the trinitarian life of God. Concerning Ignatius's mystical union, Ulrich Lehner notes, "By serving Christ, one becomes one with him, and thus with the Trinity. Apostolic service and adoration of the Trinity coincide."[56] Ignatius's mystical union with the Trinity formed the basis of a new understanding as he moved toward Rome.

---

[52]In *SJ*, Ignatius refers repeatedly to his love and devotion to the Most Blessed Trinity and the Most Holy Trinity.

[53]As reported by O'Malley, *First Jesuits*, 34.

[54]*AIL*, 89. Ignatius references his La Storta vision and the Father placing him with the Son in *SJ*, 16.

[55]*SJ*, 4.

[56]Ulrich L. Lehner, "The Trinity in the Early Modern Era (c.1550–1770)," in *The Oxford Handbook of the Trinity*, ed. Gilles Emery and Matthew Levering (Oxford: Open University Press, 2011), 241.

He had been placed with Christ, and thus he shared the life of Jesus and was to imitate his service and suffering. The message for Ignatius in this vision was that he was to live in service with the Trinity. It was with this confidence and on this mandate that Ignatius and his companion arrived in Rome and established the Society of Jesus.

In both his Manresa and La Storta visions, Ignatius experienced a mystical union with the Holy Trinity that gave him a perspective on the course before him and his companions. More than an inner light or awareness of God as triune, Ignatius perceived the Trinity as the end of all things in history. Most poignantly, Ignatius viewed the essence of the Trinity as Jesus' suffering and crucifixion.[57] The invitation from God the Father to Ignatius was to join the Son in this suffering.

John O'Malley points to Ignatius's mystical union with the mission of Christ as the catalyst for "the transformation of the ideal of the 'apostolic life' (*via apostolica*)."[58] Whereas the "apostolic way" up to Loyola's day had been chiefly one of contemplation and perfection within one's self, Loyola conceives of it as movement toward others in service and suffering. Rather than merely an inward journey of holiness and purity, apostolic life joins Christ in service to humanity.

The tradition of the apostolic life since the early church had expressed itself in voluntary poverty, wandering preaching, and a hermit's existence or communal life and thus in the vocation of a monk.[59] As the aim was to imitate the apostles, there was an emphasis on the activities of the apostles, such as preaching, miracles, and prayer, but in the main there was "a powerful 'nostalgia for the early Church.'"[60] The ideal was the tradition of the infant church as described in Acts—a communal life with all things in common and renunciation of the world. Thus, the emphasis was on forming communities that valued fasting, modest clothing, penance, manual labor, charity, and prayer. In fact, according to M. H. Vicaire, the evangelizing of

---

[57]Rahner, *Vision of St. Ignatius*, 88-97.

[58]John W. O'Malley, "Mission and the Early Jesuits," *Ignatian Spirituality and Mission: The Way* supplement 79 (Spring 1994): 4. See also Joseph H. Lynch, *The Medieval Church: A Brief History* (London: Longman, 1992), 192-96.

[59]See M. H. Vicaire, *The Apostolic Life* (Chicago: Priory Press, 1966), 15-18; William J. Purkis, "Religious Symbols and Practices: Monastic Spirituality, Pilgrimage and Crusade," in *European Religious Cultures* (London: Institute for Historical Research, 2008), 70-72.

[60]Vicaire, *Apostolic Life*, 30-31.

pagans was not the chief aim of monasticism for the first twelve centuries of the church.[61] The apostolic life was a means of discipline and perfection and about one's own salvation. The chief desire was to return to a purer, more perfect life, which entailed a renunciation of the world, contemplation, and self-mortification in communal life.[62]

Contemplation and devotion were still present and formed a significant part of Ignatius's apostolic life, but for him spirituality was a means to an activist end. Ignatius insisted that members of the Society not observe the celebration of the canonical hours or Divine Offices in common, because this time would be better spent in preaching, caring for the sick, hearing confessions, and guiding others through the *Exercises*.[63] In a letter to John Peter Caraffa, the Theatine archbishop, Ignatius is critical of the Theatines as "they do not preach," and "they do not practice the corporal works of mercy, such as burying the dead, saying Mass for the dead, and so on."[64] In other words, because their apostolic life ends with them, they do not serve the divine cause of healing and service to souls. Jerónimo Nadel, assistant to Ignatius, characterizes this sentiment: "We are not monks. . . . The world is our house."[65]

The apostolic life, as expressed in monasticism of the Middle Ages, had most certainly offered witness to the Christian life by way of the example of holy men and women in communities of order and saintliness. Modern histories of the expansion of the church during the medieval period often point to monasticism as an outstanding example of witness and even characterize it as "mission." By their existence among nonbelieving pagans, they demonstrated an alternative vision of life. And yet, their witness was by means of a static example in the midst of heathens rather than a dynamic or aggressive engagement. A more complete transformation of the monastic

---

[61]Ibid., 14, 43.
[62]According to Brian Patrick McGuire, "Monastic and Religious Orders, C. 1100–C. 1350," in *The Cambridge History of Christianity*, vol. 4, *Christianity in Western Europe c. 1100–c. 1500*, ed. Miri Rubin and Walter Simons (Cambridge: Cambridge University Press, 2009), "Monastic or religious life in the Middle Ages meant living according to a rule of life based on community, prayer and obedience. Traditional monasticism required vows of stability, obedience and *conversio morum* (change in ways of life)" (54).
[63]O'Malley, "Society of Jesus," 225.
[64]Ignatius of Loyola, *Letters of St. Ignatius of Loyola*, trans. William J. Young (Chicago: Loyola University Press, 1959), 30.
[65]Cited in O'Malley, *First Jesuits*, 68.

idea occured as Ignatius reenvisioned the apostolic life in light of his mystical union with the Holy Trinity.

The Jesuits were not the first, nor were they alone, in this modification of the apostolic life. Orders established in the late Middle Ages, such as the Oratorians, Ursulines, and Capuchins, combined action along with contemplation, service with penance. In particular, Franciscans and Dominicans of the twelfth and thirteenth centuries focused on the needs of individuals and society.[66] They included the notion of mobility and preaching as part of the apostolic life.[67] And yet, these expressions of outwardly focused activity were secondary at best, and they were not identified as mission. The identification of these actions as "mission" is unique to the Society of Jesus.

At the heart of the *corpus Societatis* of the Jesuits was a unity founded in its "apostolic dynamism."[68] Unity and harmony of the Society were steadfastly maintained not for the sake of members or on principle but for an apostolic calling. In the words of Catherine Mooney, "For Ignatius, mission trumps asceticism."[69] While a practiced mystic and one who leaned on divine initiative and the action of God, Ignatius was "at the same time a practical apostolate aware of carnal realities: he knew from experience that grace passes through temperaments, situations and social conditioning: his apostolate was, in this sense, very human."[70] Mystical union and apostolic life underwent a change when combined with mission. Mission became for Ignatius language for union and service with Christ.

Pilgrim obedience and mobility. The notions of pilgrim and pilgrimage had gone through radical change with Pope Urban II's summons to march on Jerusalem. The narrow tradition of journeying to Jerusalem was co-opted

[66]Robert Bartlett outlines a fourfold development of Western monasticism from being cloistered and local to being mobile and reproducible in *The Making of Europe: Conquest, Colonization and Cultural Change, 950–1350* (Princeton, NJ: Princeton University Press, 1993), 255-60. See also Christopher Dawson, *The Formation of Christendom* (New York: Sheed and Ward, 1967), 213; Robert E. Scully, "The Society of Jesus: Its Early History, Spirituality, and Mission to England," in *Catholic Collecting: Catholic Reflection 1538–1850*, ed. Virginia Chieffo Raguin (Washington, DC: Catholic University of America Press, 2006), 129.

[67]Dominicans were trained to preach and even called themselves the "Order of Preachers." McGuire, "Monastic and Religious Orders," 65.

[68]André Ravier, *Ignatius of Loyola and the Founding of the Society of Jesus* (San Francisco: Ignatius Press, 1987), 444.

[69]Catherine Mooney, "Ignatian Spirituality, A Spirituality for Mission," *Mission Studies* 26 (2009): 195.

[70]Ravier, *Founding of the Society of Jesus*, 413.

and expanded for the purpose of mobilizing Catholic Europe to war against enemies. In the process, the ancient practice of self-mortification and penance of the few became the mode through which a wide range of people journeyed from familiar to foreign places to encounter others beyond the borders of Christendom. Thus, the number of pilgrimages increased, and pilgrimage was incorporated into a greater number of causes. Pilgrim language signified a range of virtues, such as piety, chivalry, courage, and sacrifice, and thereby became the language of knights and kings, not just of monks and ascetics. As these ideals and causes merged with the political and ecclesial expansion of the sixteenth century, pilgrim language turned into mission language. Mission became the idiom of another kind of pilgrimage taken with another kind of vow.

Ignatius embodied this new kind of pilgrimage. During his convalescence, Ignatius became convicted of his worldly ways and decided to follow the path of the saints. In his reading of *Vita Christi*, he glosses "pilgrimage" as perpetual state of journey with Christ: "Therefore we who are pilgrims in this world—if we have no permanent city, but we seek one that is to come—if we have within ourselves in a spiritual sense the things that those pilgrims had, the Lord will be a companion on our journey."[71] Ignatius reasons within himself, "What if I should do what St. Francis did, what St. Dominic did?" He resolves, that if "St. Dominic did this, therefore I have to do it. St. Francis did this, therefore, I have to do it."[72] The first act of imitation of St. Francis and St. Dominic was to set out on a pilgrimage to Jerusalem. Ignatius traveled from Loyola to the shrine of Our Lady at Aránzazu, then to the shrine at Montserrat. From Manresa, he made his way to Joppa and then onward to Jerusalem. Once he arrived, "his firm intention was to remain in Jerusalem continually visiting the holy places, and, in addition to this devotion, he also planned to help souls."[73] He petitioned the Franciscan guardians for permission to reside longer in the Holy Lands, but his request was denied. "He replied that he was very firm in his purpose and had resolved that he would not fail to carry it out for any

---

[71]This section of *Vita Christi* is translated and cited by Paul Shore, *Vita Christi of Ludolph of Saxony and Its Influence*, 11.
[72]*AIL*, 23.
[73]Ibid., 49.

reason," but in the end he was forced to leave.[74] Ignatius's pilgrim stay in the Holy Land was less than three weeks. Though he completed the physical pilgrimage and returned to Spain, this was not the end of his pilgrimage. Another permutation of the idea of pilgrimage would shape Ignatius's understanding of mission.[75]

While the physical journey to Jerusalem was the chief way Ignatius had conceived pilgrimage, it was not to be restricted to this dimension alone. Joseph Conwell describes three possible meanings for pilgrimage, all of which Ignatius and the Society used and embraced. Pilgrimage could mean to visit a shrine, to go into exile, and to preach.[76] Each of these can be seen in Ignatius's life, as he visited the holy places in Jerusalem, separated himself from home and his former identity, and led those he encountered through the *Exercises*. What began as pilgrimage to the Holy Sepulchre expanded to a variety of activities and the whole of his life.

Toward the end of his life, Ignatius dictated his life story to Luis Gonçalves da Câmara, a young Portuguese Jesuit. In Câmara's account, Ignatius refers to himself seventy-two times as "the pilgrim." The "pilgrim who sets out" is Ignatius's way of self-identifying in both his *Autobiography* and *Spiritual Exercises*.[77] Ignatius was a pilgrim as he set out for Jerusalem, as he traveled to Paris to study, went to Venice to meet his companions, and offered himself and the Society to Pope Paul. To the end of his life, Ignatius steadfastly identified as a pilgrim. Throughout his life, Ignatius signed his letters, "The poor pilgrim" (*El pobre peregrine*).[78] Though he was confined to Rome for the last sixteen years of his life, Ignatius continued his life as a pilgrim.[79]

Inherent in the idea of pilgrimage were commitments to mobility and obedience. Purkis points out that during the eleventh and twelfth centuries,

[74]Ibid., 50. Dalmases, *Ignatius of Loyola*, 80, surmises that when Ignatius insisted on staying, the Fransican guardian threatened him with excommunication if he disobeyed.
[75]Michael Sievernich, "Die Mission Und Die Missionen de Gesellschaft Jesu," in *Sendung, Eroberung, Begegnung: Franz Xaver, Die Gesellschaft Jesu Und Die Katholische Weltkirche Im Zeitalter Des Barock*, ed. Johannes Meier, Studien Zur Aussereuropäischen Christentumsgeschichte (Asien, Afrika, Lateinamerika), Studies in the History of Christianity in the Non-Western World 8 (Wiesbaden, Germany: Harrassowitz Verlag, 2005), 9.
[76]Conwell, *Impelling Spirit*, 166.
[77]*AIL*, 29.
[78]Conwell, *Impelling Spirit*, 481n32.
[79]"Die äußerliche Pilgerreise ist daher für Iñigo auch Ausdruck einer innerlichen Pilgerreise." Sievernich, "Die Mission und Die Missionen," 9.

pilgrimage, already an emphasis in monastic life, became even more prominent and linked to the apostolic life.[80] Thus, in a pilgrim existence the religiously devoted person was to itinerate and practice their spirituality on the
road. Rather than in cloistered ministries or institutions, Ignatius envisioned
an order whose members would itinerate in the same manner as the apostle
Paul. They were to serve the needs of people wherever they found them.

Among the requirements for those who desired to enter the Society, the
General Examen states that the candidate is to spend a month "in making
a pilgrimage without money and even in begging from door to door, at
appropriate times, for the love of God our Lord, in order to grow accus-
tomed to discomfort in food and lodging."[81] The set of guidelines for those
who had become Jesuits was known as the *Regulae peregrinatium*, or "Rules
of Pilgrimage."[82]

As a pilgrim, Ignatius's aim was to help other souls find their way to the
path of penance and devotion. *The First Sketch of the Institute of the Society
of Jesus* indicates that the Society's ministries, such as publicly preaching,
privately exhorting, hearing confessions, directing people in holy medita-
tions, and serving in hospitals were to be accomplished "by pilgrimaging"
(*peregrinando*) among those in need. According to John O'Malley, one
phrase, "to help souls," dominates Ignatius's language in the *Autobiography,
Constitutions*, and correspondence.[83] Besides caring for physical and spiritual needs, helping other souls meant that Ignatius was to make others into
what he had become—a pilgrim.[84]

---

[80]Purkis, "Religious Symbols and Practices," 75-76.

[81]"The General Examen and Its Declarations" in *CSJ*, 97.

[82]Luke Clossey, *Salvation and Globalization in the Early Jesuit Missions* (New York: Cambridge University Press, 2008), 28.

[83]O'Malley, *First Jesuits*, 18-19.

[84]Interpreters of Ignatius and Francis Xavier, as well as the activities of early Jesuits, liberally use the language of *pilgrim* and *pilgrimage*. Some referred to them as pilgrim priests (*preti peregrine*). For example, see Georg Schurhammer, *Francis Xavier; His Life, His Times*, vol. 1, *Europe 1506–41*, trans. M. Joseph Costelloe (Rome: Jesuit Historical Institute, 1973), 281, 282, 283, 292, 297, 316, 320, 323, 324, 326, 327, 330; Peter Du Brul, *Ignatius: Sharing the Pilgrim Story: A Reading of the Autobiography of St. Ignatius of Loyola* (Leominster, UK: Gracewing, 2003); Brodrick, *Loyola: The Pilgrim Years*; James Brodrick, *The Origin of the Jesuits* (Chicago: Loyola University Press, 1986), 47, 53, 68; Javier Osuna, *Friends in the Lord: A Study in the Origins and Growth of Community in the Society of Jesus from St Ignatius' Conversion to the Earliest Texts of the Constitutions (1521–1541)*, trans. Nicholas King, The Way Series 3 (London: The Way, 1974), 5, 8, 15, 27, 44, 55, 64, 67; Marjorie O'Rourke Boyle, *Loyola's Acts: The Rhetoric of the Self*, The New Historicism 36

The Society's fourth vow was "a vow of mobility."[85] It was a pilgrim vow.[86] In the vow at Montmartre, Ignatius extended the logic of pilgrimage to its next step—a mission vow. Ignatius converted pilgrimage to Jerusalem into mission as assigned by the pope. In the early years of the Jesuits, *mission* and *pilgrimage* shared similar meaning and frequency and were even interchangeable.[87] While Patrick, Columba, and Columban self-identify as pilgrims but do not rhetorically connect this identity with mission, Ignatius and the early company of Jesuits make the connection. Nicolás de Bobadilla, one of the original companions, comments to a friend, "My pilgrimages have not been undertaken in this spirit [of just wandering]; they are true missions from my superiors, held first in their hearts and their desires, communicated to me by a word, which I have obeyed and put into execution. My pilgrimaging is not mere running around, as some have thought."[88] Of Ignatius at his death, Jerome Nadal writes, "He died when he had accomplished his mission."[89] According to Jonathan Wright, "Mission was, in a sense, the culmination of the Ignatian apostolic ideal; to be a missionary was to be the finest kind of Ignatian pilgrim."[90] Pilgrim obedience converged with mission language to infuse the pilgrim vow with new meaning. The pilgrim vow became the mission vow. Pilgrimage, for Ignatius, was mission.

IGNATIAN MISSION

The beginnings of the modern use of *mission* lie within Ignatius's innovation, but "mission" as conceived by Ignatius nonetheless must remain in the

---

(Berkeley: University of California Press, 1997), 147-84; Purcell, *First Jesuits*, 50, 82, 84, 87, 88, 89, 93, 115, 123; Conwell, *Impelling Spirit*, 55, 174.

[85] O'Malley, "Society of Jesus," 224. See also Scully, "Society of Jesus," 129; Paul Kollman, "At the Origins of Mission and Missiology: A Study in the Dynamics of Religious Language," *Journal of the American Academy of Religion* 79, no. 2 (June 2011): 430.

[86] Regarding the fourth vow, O'Malley, *First Jesuits*, remarks, "Nadal provided the clearest and most eloquent explanation of what the vow symbolized. As we have seen, for him as for his confreres, 'missions' and 'journeying for ministry,' and sometimes even 'pilgrimage,' were synonymous" (300).

[87] Ibid.; Clossey, *Salvation and Globalization in the Early Jesuit Missions*, 14.

[88] From *Bobadillae Monumenta in Monumenta Historica Societatis Iesu*, 637-38, trans. and cited by Conwell, *Impelling Spirit*, 116.

[89] "Fontes narrativi de Sancto Ignatio" (1:770), cited in Dalmases, *Ignatius of Loyola*, 298.

[90] Wright, *God's Soldiers*, 77. According to O'Malley, *First Jesuits*, the vow "was the 'principal foundation' of the Society because it concerned what was utterly central to the Jesuit calling-ministry" (299).

sixteenth century and rest within Ignatius's personality and initiatives.[91] The concept of modern mission appears only after this innovation goes through further changes following its beginnings with the Society of Jesus. As we have seen, Ignatius's adoption of the rhetoric of mission arose from a particular set of political and ecclesial conditions, within a changing vision of the apostolic life, and from a notion of pilgrimage formed by the Crusades and knighthood. It was from this particular beginning that mission developed for the Society, then for Franciscans and Dominicans, eventually for others within the Catholic church, and finally for Protestants.

For Ignatius, *mission* was not a technically defined term, nor was it extensively qualified language. He used *mission* in a manner that left room geographically and included a range of activities. Because mission included any place to which the pope might send members of the order, this most often meant mission was to locales within Europe, and only occasionally to places beyond its borders. According to Guibert, while "not principally, or at least not exclusively, missions among infidels, . . . the meaning of the term 'mission' is much broader and includes every apostolic labor, every work either of reform or of evangelization which the pope can ask of a Jesuit in virtue of the vow by which the latter has placed himself at the free disposal of the pontiff."[92] Even before the Society received papal approval, members were sent on "missions" by the pope in Rome, throughout Europe, and beyond for the purpose of reform and teaching.[93] During one of their conversations with Paul III concerning their desire to go to Jerusalem, the pope responded to Ignatius and his companions, "Italy is a good and true Jerusalem, if you wish to yield fruit in the Church of God."[94] The first members sent on a mission, Paschase Broët and Simón Rodrigues, and Francisco de Estrada, a candidate for the Society, went to nearby Siena to reform a

---

[91]David Lonsdale, "Ignatian Mission," *Ignatian Spirituality and Mission: The Way* supplement 79 (Spring 1994), notes that even for contemporary Jesuits imitating Ignatius's approach is inadequate. "For one thing today's cultural, social and ecclesial conditions are very different from those of the mid-sixteenth century" (92).

[92]Guibert, *Jesuits*, 149.

[93]Thomas H. Clancy, *An Introduction to Jesuit Life: The Constitutions and History Through 435 Years* (St. Louis: Institute of Jesuit Sources, 1976), 51, 56; Osuna, *Friends in the Lord*, 98-99. The details of the group's deliberations about whether to stay together or split up for ministries are found in Schurhammer, *Francis Xavier*, 1:453-65.

[94]Cited in Osuna, *Friends in the Lord*, 90.

monastery in that city.[95] Their mission was the first but not the only one. About the same time, members were chosen and sent to Parma, Barnoregio, Naples, Siena, Trent, Germany, Spain, Ireland, and Portugal.[96] For these men, mission meant preaching, caring for those in hospitals, hearing confessions, and serving the poor. The scope of mission, for Ignatius, was defined in his phrase "Christ's vineyard."[97] The intent of the vow was to go, as commanded by the pope or general, to wherever Christ was at work in the world.[98]

Xavier, the Missionary

Xavier was the first Jesuit to venture beyond the bounds of Europe under the new designation of *mission*. Because of the terms of the *padroado*, King John III of Portugal sent a request via Don Pedro Mazcarenhas, his ambassador in Rome, to Pope Paul III for priests from the Society of Jesus to be deployed to India. The pope deferred by stating that such a risky undertaking could not be commanded, but only undertaken voluntarily. So, the ambassador took the request directly to Ignatius and asked that ten men be allocated for the Portuguese interests in the East. Ignatius replied, "Señor Ambassador, there are only ten of us Companions. If you take six for India and the East, only four remain in the rest of the world."[99] In the end, Ignatius agreed to send two of their members. Simón Rodrigues and Nicolás Bodadilla were selected to make the voyage onward to India. Because Bodadilla was ailing and unable to travel to Lisbon, much less make the hard, arduous journey to India, Ignatius turned to his companion and the Society's secretary, Francisco Xavier. Ignatius told Xavier, "The work is yours." To which Xavier replied, "Pues, sus! Heme aquí!"—Good [Splendid], I am your man![100] This

---

[95]Ibid., 99.

[96]Guibert, *Jesuits*, 150; Osuna, *Friends in the Lord*, 98-103.

[97]O'Malley, "Mission and the Early Jesuits," maintains that the "most pervasive metaphor for where their 'missions' were exercised was 'the vineyard of the Lord'" (9).

[98]In a short period of time, this early understanding of mission would shift from a charge of mobility to permanence and place. Such redefinition can be seen in the settlements (*missiones* or *reducciones*) in New Spain and with the Franciscans in America. See Adriano Prosperi, "The Missionary," in *Baroque Personae*, ed. Rosario Villari, trans. Lydia G. Cochrane (Chicago: The University of Chicago Press, 1995), 183; Bailey W. Diffie, *Latin-American Civilization: Colonial Period* (Harrisburg, PA: Stackpole Sons, 1945), 359.

[99]Cited in Purcell, *First Jesuits*, 221.

[100]Reported in Brodrick, *Origin of the Jesuits*, 85.

exchange occurred on March 14, 1540, and two days later, Xavier and Rodrigues left for Lisbon.

After a full year in Lisbon, King John III requested Rodrigues to stay in order to address needs in Lisbon, but the king allowed Xavier to travel onward to India as both apostolic nuncios (legate or envoy of the pope) and under commission from the king. In this dual capacity, Xavier was sent by the church and the crown and represented the interests of both. Following a thirteen-month voyage aboard the *Santiago*, Xavier, accompanied by a priest and a young boy, landed in Goa along with the Governor Martim Afonso de Sousa. For a decade, Xavier labored along the coast of India, Ceylon, Malacca, Japan, and on the fringes of China. In December 1552, he died on the island of Sancian off the mainland of China.

With Xavier and these meager undertakings, the mission era began. In a matter of years, Jesuits extended their presence beyond India, Japan, and Macao to reach around the world. The initial company of ten grew to a thousand by Ignatius's death in 1556, and 15,544 members by 1626. By 1700, the Jesuits were a force of more than twenty thousand dedicated to the prop-agation and defense of the Catholic faith.[101] What Ignatius initiated and grew into a worldwide organization was more than the beginning of an order or the extension of the Latin church. Such scale and level of organization marked the inauguration of *mission*.

The letters of Francis Xavier, written prior to his departure for India and immediately after his arrival, do not mention "mission." He chooses instead to write of "fields or spheres of labour," "our work," "service," "converting the heathen," "penetrate," "advancement of the gospel," "propagating the gospel," and "holy occupations." Xavier refers to himself and others as "apostolical labourers," preachers, and priests.[102] It was only years after his arrival in India that Xavier referred to those the Society sends out for the work of car-rying the gospel to the heathen as "missionaries" and their work being that

---

[101]See Wright, *Jesuits*, 44; Alden, *Making of an Enterprise*, 17; J. Carlos Coupeau, "Five Personae of Ignatius of Loyola," in *The Cambridge Companion of The Jesuits*, ed. Thomas Worcester (Cambridge: Cambridge University Press, 2008), 36; John Patrick Donnelly, "New Religious Orders for Men," in *The Cambridge History of Christianity*, vol. 6, *Reform and Expansion 1500–1660*, ed. R. Po-chia Hsia (Cambridge: Cambridge University Press, 2007), 171.

[102]Henry James Coleridge, *The Life and Letters of St. Francis Xavier* (London: Burns and Oates, 1912), 1:95, 101, 121, 122, 136, 194, 265, 300, 354.

of "mission."[103] Even the *Propaganda de Fide*, founded in 1622 by Pope Gregory XV, almost a century after the start of the Jesuits, generally favors the language of propaganda rather than mission, though *mission* is mentioned four times in the first congregational letter of the *Propaganda Fide*.[104] It was in the evangelization of the Americas, chiefly by Franciscans in the seventeenth century, that other designations became less prominent and *mission* became the word of choice. The Franciscans use the term not only to describe the activity of spreading the faith or moving beyond the border of Christendom, but in a strange twist, they turn *mission* into the designation for stationary, established ecclesial outposts, or "frontier institutions."[105] *Mission*, in due course, triumphed over all other terms and became the preferred way of describing the expansion of the faith.

THE MISSION ERA

The Jesuits were not the first to preach the Christian message or to venture beyond the bounds of Europe.[106] Witness to the risen Christ was central to the spirit and activities of the early church. Persecution drove the disciples out of Jerusalem to neighboring territories and beyond. Traders and sailors, bishops and monks, rulers and princesses, slaves and freemen told the story as they went. Groups of Christians, such as the Nestorians, embodied the faith in their community life and culture. Individuals, such as Cyril and

---

[103]Mentioned in letters to Francis, Mancias, Ignatius Loyola, Father Paul of Camerino and Simon Rodrigues in ibid., 1:188, 273, 385, 2:16, 145, 146, 376. Juan de Polanco, who took up the duties of secretary for the Society in 1547, describes Xavier's selection as the first Jesuit to be sent and his deployment to India as "mission." Generally, Polanco categorizes activities of the Society within countries under Catholic control as ministries (preaching, teaching, acts of charity) and those in foreign places or "of great distances" (Ireland, the Indies, Ethiopia, Brazil) as mission. See *Selections from the "Chronicon,"* 4, 5, 7, 13, 14, 41, 42, 51, 90.

[104]Clossey, *Salvation and Globalization in the Early Jesuit Missions*, states that though *mission* was in use by the Jesuits from 1539, "the modern meaning began to congeal in the 1620's, especially in the usage of Propaganda" (15). Jan A. B. Jongeneel, *Philosophy, Science, and Theology of Mission in the 19th and 20th Centuries*, Studien Zur Interkulturellen Geschichte Des Christentums 92 (Frankfurt am Main: Peter Lang, 1995), indicates that the *Propaganda* received the term *mission* "with thanks to the Jesuits" (59).

[105]Mission as institution is most visibly observed in the Franciscans among the Amerindians and the Jesuit reductions in Paraguay. See Boxer, *Church Militant*, 71; Clossey, *Salvation and Globalization in the Early Jesuit Missions*, 13-14.

[106]Isabel dos Guimarães Sá, "Ecclesiastical Structures and Religious Action," *Portuguese Oceanic Expansion, 1400–1800*, ed. Francisco Bethencourt and Diogo Ramada Curto (New York: Cambridge University Press, 2007), 256.

Methodius, proclaimed the gospel in frontier areas. And yet, none of these activities were represented as *mission*, nor were these representatives identified as *missionaries*.

In the medieval age, the monastic orders were the chief means of witness, especially at the fringe of Christendom. Rather than crossing language and cultural boundaries to give witness or plant churches, the central and guiding principle of monastic life was Christian purity and perfection. The monastic orders emerged from a desire to escape the world rather than confront it. As monastic groups established communities of faith in new territories, they brought a civilizing and Christianizing influence, and as such, they became the vanguard of the Latin church. Through personal purity and pious activities, they extended church influence into the places where the church did not have a presence. They did not set out to be "missionaries," or form a "missionary order," or go on "mission," but they evangelized peoples they encountered through their exemplary communities.[107]

The monastic ideal began to shift with Francis of Assisi and the order that formed around him. In the Franciscans, perfection combined with service to the poor radically refocused monastic aims.[108] Franciscan friars served as emissaries, legates, chaplains, and preachers in various locations, and were found in India as early as 1500. The Dominicans followed in 1503.[109] Over a hundred priests from the Franciscan and Dominican orders were already present in Goa when Xavier arrived in 1542.[110] These were performing the rites necessary for the regularization of the church in India. Even D. John d'Albuquerque, a Franciscan, had already been installed as the bishop (1537) in Goa.[111] The Catholic church was well on its way to becoming established in India and solidifying its presence with churches, priests, vicars, and a bishop. Franciscans led the way in ministries to Indians and those of mixed race, and a small number of Indians

---

[107]See Lynch, *Medieval Church*, 29-34.

[108]O'Malley, "Mission and the Early Jesuits," 4.

[109]Franciscans and Dominicans were particularly active in India; see Samuel H. Moffett, *A History of Christianity in Asia,* vol. 2, *1500–1900* (Maryknoll, NY: Orbis Books), 7-8; Wright, *Jesuits*, 2.

[110]Moffett, *History of Christianity in Asia,* 2:10.

[111]Stephen Neill, *A History of Christianity in India: The Beginning to AD 1707* (Cambridge: Cambridge University Press, 1984), 117-18.

converted to the church, often by way of forcible means and under questionable motives.[112]

Traveling to a location outside Christian Europe and ministering in a foreign place as a priest did not distinguish Xavier. Rather, the endeavor launched by Ignatius and the band of like-minded men differed in meaning and classification because of how they identified and structured the church's task. Mission, and all this uniquely Ignatian term entailed, was the difference. In the Jesuits' introduction and use of mission, a monumental shift occurred in the language and meaning of the church's reach beyond Christendom. Ignatius's innovation and Xavier's voyage signaled the beginnings of the modern mission era.[113]

---

[112]Sharon da Cruz, "Empire and Mission: Portuguese State and Franciscan Collaboration in Establishing the Goa Mission (1510–1534)," *Indian Church History Review* 44, no. 2 (2010): 111-23.

[113]Scott Sunquist, *Understanding Christian Mission: Participation in Suffering and Glory* (Grand Rapids: Baker Academic, 2013), agrees that the Jesuits should be considered the first modern missionaries. He lists their unique spirituality centered in the Ignatius's *Spiritual Exercises*, their activitic engagement, emphasis on education, and their "intentional incarnational awareness." In these innovations, "they laid the foundation for modern Christian mission, be it Catholic, Protestant, or Spiritual" (46-47).

III

Revising
mis·sion

Mission, prefigured in pilgrimage and colonial endeavors and then established with the founding of the Jesuit order, became, during the nineteenth century, the rhetoric of a modern tradition. Mission began as distinct Catholic language but in time became one of the signature characteristics of Protestantism. The period leading up to the early twentieth century witnessed mission garnering the status of a tradition as it expanded in meaning and increased in prominence. The rise and establishment of the mission tradition was evident at the 1910 Edinburgh Mission Conference, as delegates and speakers spoke of *mission* and *missionary* as both ancient and modern. In the decades following Edinburgh, the legitimacy of the mission tradition suffered serious setbacks and underwent critique and censorship. The Laymen's Inquiry (1932) recast the meaning and use of mission, and at the same time initiated a vigorous defense of the Edinburgh tradition. Much of the current confusion over the meaning and use of mission originates in the shift that took place between Edinburgh and the Laymen's Inquiry.

In this final section, I trace the journey of mission from its Catholic roots to its entrance into the Protestant lexicon and explore why it has become such contested language. I conclude with an examination of the Edinburgh Mission Conference and the Laymen's Inquiry and how these two events gave rise to Partisans, Apologists, and Revisionists.

9

Protestant Reception

The Lutheran Heretics have never crossed the sea,
nor seen Asia, Africa, Egypt or Greece. Wherein we
understand that what is found in the beginning of the
preface on the Concord of the Lutherans, published
in 1580, is a lie, where they say that the Augsburg
confession has spread throughout the whole world, and
has begun to be in the mouth and speech of all.

ROBERTO BELLARMINE, *ON THE MARKS OF THE CHURCH*

My brothers and sisters, today is the day of missions.

COUNT NICOLAUS LUDWIG VON ZINZENDORF

THE IGNATIAN INNOVATION of mission emerged from not one event or a single influence but a multitude of events and influences—papal patronage, Ignatius's militant faith and mystical union with the Trinity, reframing of the apostolic life, and pilgrimage. From these, mission specified for Catholics the particular activity of sending ecclesial agents to foreign lands. The new term began with the Jesuits, as they led in the church's expansion beyond Christendom, and in time, Dominicans, Franciscans, and the wider church adopted it as well, but the new term did not remain solely Catholic rhetoric. In time, Protestants embraced mission and developed it into a modern tradition—but only after considerable hesitation.[1]

---

[1] The focus of this chapter is the language of mission, its development, and role as a modern tradition. Many studies explore the overall course and various aspects of mission among Protestants in the modern era. Chief among these is Bosch's chapter "Mission in the Wake of the

REFORMERS' HESITATION

At the time Ignatius innovated mission, a schism was taking place in Western Christianity. Among the protests of the Reformers against the Catholic church was its "mission." In the Protestant lexicon, *mission* signified Catholic expansion and control, and thus it had to undergo a shift from language of papal authority and religious orders to a voluntary, societal, and organizational term. It had to change from a designation tied exclusively to monastic orders and Roman Catholicism to a term signifying a movement that included all types of people. In this shift, mission expanded in meaning to include more than Ignatius intended and the Catholic church could imagine. And yet, concepts and images inherent in the original innovation of mission endured and made the long journey from Ignatius to the Protestant tradition.

Many modern Protestants assume that the Reformers spoke and wrote about "mission" from the beginning. While the Catholic church may have been late in coming to mission language, surely the Reformers were quick to adopt *mission* and eager to declare their commitment to the cause. And yet, such assumptions would be wrong not just in terms of the Reformers' practice but also in their conceptual framework.

Critics of the Reformers' hesitancy toward mission are quite severe. Gustav Warneck asserts that Protestantism of the Reformation era lacked any missionary activity or sentiment. According to Warneck, "We miss in the Reformers not only missionary action, but even the idea of missions, in the sense in which we understand them today."[2] William Richey Hogg echoes Warneck and adds, "The Reformers evidenced no concern for overseas missions to non-Christians."[3] Johannes van den Berg concludes, "It is very difficult to find one real missionary venture at the Protestant side during the sixteenth century" and notes that the excuses some make for

---

Enlightenment," in *TM*, 268-353; Scott Sunquist, *Understanding Christian Mission: Participation in Suffering and Glory* (Grand Rapids: Baker Academic, 2013), 86-168; Dana Lee Robert, *Christian Mission: How Christianity Became a World Religion* (Chichester, UK: Wiley-Blackwell, 2009), 53-79; Stephen B. Bevans and Roger Schroeder, *Constants in Context: A Theology of Mission for Today* (Maryknoll, NY: Orbis Books, 2004), 239-80.

[2]Gustav Warneck, *Outline of a History of Protestant Missions from the Reformation to the Present Time* (New York: Fleming H. Revell, 1901), 9.

[3]William Richey Hogg, "The Rise of Protestant Missionary Concern, 1517-1914," in *The Theology of Christian Mission*, ed. Gerald H. Anderson (Nashville: Abingdon, 1961), 95.

the Reformers do not explain their lack of missionary work. The situation is such, according to van den Berg, that there was not "even a *latent* missionary zeal" present. Mission was absent in the Reformers' words, actions, and "*world of thought*."[4] The writings of the Reformers, according to Carl Braaten, "are totally devoid of any missionary consciousness."[5] Latourette measures the Protestant mission activity in light of robust Roman Catholic mission endeavors and finds Protestants lacking. Among the reasons for their delay, he mentions the Reformers' all-consuming task of redefining the faith and reforming the church. Doctrinal issues, ecclesial roles, and ritual practices were their first order of business. Also, they were preoccupied with internal conflicts, had no monastic system in place, and lacked contact with non-Christian peoples, and their sponsoring governments were indifferent to the spread of the Protestant faith.[6] Even with these excuses, Latourette considers the Reformers' commitment to mission unacceptable.

David Bosch's assessment is that "very little happened by way of a missionary outreach during the first two centuries after the Reformation" for many of the same reasons noted by Warneck, Neill, Latourette, and Hogg.[7] And yet, in defense of the Reformers, Bosch argues that it is unfair to expect them to subscribe "to a definition of mission which did not exist in their own time."[8] In other words, the absence of mission language and references to "missionaries" in sermons and treatises was not so much evidence of the Reformers' rejection of an idea but their ignorance of, or hesitation to use, mission language.

Bosch is correct. The level of the Reformers' proselytizing activity might be open to debate, but what is certain is that mission language was absent among Protestants during the early years of the Reformation.

---

[4]Johannes van den Berg, *Constrained by Jesus' Love: An Inquiry into the Motives of the Missionary Awakening in Great Britain in the Period Between 1698 and 1815* (Kampen: J. H. Kok, 1956), 4, 5. Van den Berg's emphasis.

[5]Carl Braaten, *The Flaming Center: A Theology of the Christian Mission* (Philadelphia: Fortress, 1977), 15.

[6]*HEC*, 2:25-27. See also William Richey Hogg, *Ecumenical Foundations: A History of the International Missionary Council and Its Nineteenth Century Background* (New York: Harper & Brothers, 1952), 2.

[7]*TM*, 250.

[8]Ibid., 249.

Mission and *missionary* were not adopted until the early eighteenth century and did not become established, common rhetoric until the nineteenth century. One looks in vain throughout the works of Luther, Calvin, and other early Protestants for the language of mission or missionaries. But more than not being literally present, the modern notion of mission is foreign to their thought.

Martin Luther (1483–1546) raises the question of the gospel going into all the world, but he does not prescribe particular actions or designate roles regarding the evangelization of those outside Europe.[9] Should a Christian find himself in a place where there are no Christians, "he needs no other call than to be a Christian, called and anointed by God from within. Here it is his duty to preach and to teach the gospel to erring heathen or non-Christians, because of the duty of brotherly love, even though no man calls him to do so."[10] The duty is to preach and teach; the role is that of a Christian. He does write of sending in such terms as *sendung, senden,* and *missio.* In the case of *sendung* and *senden,* Luther uses these as nonspecialized words to denote sending of various types. He does not employ these words in the modern sense of organizational and professionalized sending, or of a special vocation for those who travel abroad. In the case of *missio,* Luther identifies the provenance of such sending as *Dei, Patre,* and *Spiritus,* not human activity in general or the church in particular.[11] The most that can be said is that Luther emphasizes the reform of the church and the proclamation of the gospel, and thereby provides the foundation for the eventual reach of Protestants beyond Europe. But this can hardly be considered his justification for vast mission programs and institutional mission agencies. Indeed, Luther states that the gospel is universal and thus includes Jews, Turks, and those classified as

---

[9]See Paul D. L. Avis, *The Church in the Theology of the Reformers* (Atlanta: John Knox, 1980), 168-69, 177-79. Avis's judgment is that "it would be anachronistic to expect Luther to speak in terms of the missionary movement of the nineteenth century: he certainly had no clearly defined concept of the structure of missionary work" (178).

[10]Martin Luther, *Luther's Works,* vol. 39, *Church and Ministry I,* ed. Eric W. Gritsch (Philadelphia: Fortress, 1970), 310.

[11]Pekka Huhtinen and Gregory Lockwood, "Luther and World Missions: A Review," *Concordia Theological Quarterly* 65, no. 1 (January 2001): 16-17. Cf. James A. Scherer, *Gospel, Church & Kingdom: Comparative Studies in World Mission Theology* (Eugene, OR: Wipf & Stock, 2004), 55-57.

heathen, but he does not label the universal nature of the gospel as *mission* or those who preach to Jews and Turks as *missionaries*. The structures of thought we know as "modern mission" did not exist for Luther.[12]

Though John Calvin (1509–1564) does not write specifically of *mission* as a definite action of the church and *missionary* as a role for Christians, he does make reference to the mission of Christ, the mission of reconciliation, and the mission of the twelve apostles.[13] The world beyond Geneva is a concern for Calvin, and involvement in that world is evident in his writings, but this concern and call for the church's involvement are not expressed in mission language.[14] Yet Calvin is often cited in attempts to establish an early Protestant mission legacy. David Bosch reports that Calvin cooperated "in the selection of two of the twelve missionaries who Gaspar[d] de Coligny sent to Brazil to found a Christian colony—the first Protestant overseas missionary, which, however, soon failed."[15] The facts as reported are correct: Coligny (1519–1572), a French nobleman and admiral, solicited Calvin's assistance in establishing a Huguenot settlement in Brazil. But the request was for pastors rather than for missionaries. The need was for pastoral oversight and care of the Huguenot settlers. So, in 1557, two pastors, along with a dozen Swiss Calvinists, arrived in Brazil.[16] Though they traveled from

---

[12]While not always speaking of Jews in a positive manner, Luther sees them as needing and as worthy of the gospel. See "The Bondage of the Will," in *Martin Luther's Basic Theological Writings*, ed. William R. Russell and Timothy F. Lull, 3rd ed. (Minneapolis: Fortress, 2012), 141-47.

[13]Jean Calvin, *Institutes of the Christian Religion* (Philadelphia: Westminster, 1960), 279, 1035, 1058, 1152.

[14]R. Pierce Beaver, "The Genevan Mission to Brazil," in *The Heritage of John Calvin: Heritage Hall Lectures, 1960–1970*, ed. John H. Bratt (Grand Rapids: Eerdmans, 1973), 55-73. Beaver maintains that "while Calvin may not have explicitly exhorted the Reformed churches to undertake mission, he certainly was not hostile to worldwide evangelism. In fact, his theology logically calls for mission action, although he did not enunciate it" (56).

[15]David J. Bosch, *Witness to the World: The Christian Mission in Theological Perspective* (Atlanta: John Knox, 1980), 122. Samuel Zwemer, "Calvinism and the Missionary Enterprise," *Theology Today* 7 (1950), voices a similiar sentiment: "When we come to the pragmatic test in regard to foreign missions, Calvin was the only Reformer who actually planned and organized a foreign mission enterprise" (211).

[16]Michael A. G. Haykin and C. Jeffrey Robinson Sr., *To the Ends of the Earth: Calvin's Missional Vision and Legacy* (Wheaton, IL: Crossway, 2014), 71. Philip Hughes, "John Calvin: Director of Missions," in Bratt, *Heritage of John Calvin*, states that the two went "in the dual capacity of chaplains to the French Protestants and missionaries to the South American Indians" (47-48). However, such a claim is conjecture, since the letters of request to Calvin no longer exist. Beaver, "Genevan Mission to Brazil," 57-72, offers a careful explanation of the reasons and circumstances surrounding the establishment of this colony.

Europe to South America, and even though their intent was in part to preach the gospel to native Brazilians, *mission* and *missionary* are not terms Calvin applied to these endeavors and persons. To name the "heathen," Turks, and Jews as objects of the gospel message, to advocate for the extension of the kingdom of God, and even to send pastors or preachers to foreign locations speaks to Calvin's conviction regarding the universal nature of the gospel. But these facts do not represent a programmatic commitment to a mission or a mission strategy. The practice of many is to inject mission language into the accounts about and by Calvin as either a way to substantiate modern mission or in an attempt to establish a mission legacy within Calvinism.[17] Yet, *mission* as a description of the church and *missionary* as an agent of the church are not part of Calvin's language.

The writings of Luther and Calvin contain rich theological language that generates Protestant witness and service beyond Germany and Geneva, but the rhetoric of mission as utility of the church or missionaries as agents is foreign to their theological or ecclesical vocabulary.[18] In these Reformers we find theological foundations for the eventual launch of what became the missionary expansion of the Protestant faith, but this came a century later. Their lack of mission rhetoric has more to do with the absence of the conceptual framework of "mission" at their time than their understanding of the gospel as universal in scope.

EARLY ADOPTERS?

Interpreters of Protestant mission identify Adrianus Saravia, Justus Heurnius, and Justinian von Welz as mission pioneers and the Anabaptists as an early mission group. While these individuals and this group may have pointed Protestants beyond Christendom, and while they may have been courageous in their willingness to preach in distant places, they only hint at the rhetoric of mission. In pamphlets, letters, and sermons, they write about the apostolate, preaching, and the propagation of the gospel, but not about "mission." Adrianus Saravia (1532–1613), lauded often as an early champion of the Great Commission, advocated the preaching of the gospel among the

---

[17]See Zwemer, "Calvinism and the Missionary Enterprise," 206-16; Hughes, "John Calvin: Director of Missions," 9-54.

[18]See Berg, *Constrained by Jesus' Love*, 8-12; *TM*, 248-52.

nations, but he made this appeal in language other than *mission*.[19] In *De diversis ministrorum Evangelii gradibus, sicut a Domino fuerunt insituti* (1590), he argues that the Great Commission is still binding on the church. His argument is that certain ministerial offices continued from the New Testament era to his day, and thus succession of the office of bishop is to be observed. He claims that only through apostolic power vested in this office can church unity be maintained and schisms averted. His argument is built on the assertion that apostolic authority is found in the New Testament. While controversial, this was not a new idea. What was new was that along with the concern for apostolic succession was his belief that "the command of preaching the gospel and the sending to every nation are precepts to be understood of the apostles, but are also understood to oblige the church."[20] According to Willem Nijenhius, this belief was "striking as the Reformation in general paid scarcely any attention to mission in contrast to the Roman church which, in the Jesuit order, possessed a great missionary force."[21] Yet, Savaria did not state this striking belief in the rhetoric of mission. Though the conceptual beginnings of mission can be heard, nowhere in his 1590 treatise are *mission* and *missionary* found. It is easy to see why modern interpreters of Savaria characterize his novel belief and his emphasis as mission, even though mission is not his language.[22]

Many interpreters label Justus Heurnius (1587–1651) as an early Dutch pioneer in mission thought and identify him as a missionary. After petitioning the East India Company and the Dutch church to send him overseas, Heurnius prevailed and was sent to Jakarta, Indonesia, in 1624. He produced *Dictionarium Sinense*, a Dutch-Latin-Chinese glossary, in order to

---

[19]For the life and emphases of Saravia, see Warneck, *History of Protestant Missions*, 20-23; *TM*, 252-53; Willem Nijenhuis, *Adrianus Saravia (c. 1532–1613): Dutch Calvinist, First Reformed Defender of the English Episcopal Church Order on the Basis of the Ius Divinum* (Leiden: E. J. Brill, 1980).

[20]From *De Diversis Ministrorum Evangelii Gradibus, sicut a Domino fuerunt institui*, 64-67, cited in *Classic Texts in Mission and World Christianity*, ed. Norman E. Thomas, American Society of Missiology Series 20 (Maryknoll, NY: Orbis Books, 1995), 42.

[21]Nijenhuis, *Adrianus Saravia*, 240.

[22]See Jan A. B. Jongeneel, *Philosophy, Science, and Theology of Mission in the 19th and 20th Centuries*, Studien Zur Interkulturellen Geschichte Des Christentums 92 (Frankfurt am Main: Peter Lang, 1995), 51; Warneck, *History of Protestant Missions*, 21; Johannes Verkuyl, *Contemporary Missiology: An Introduction* (Grand Rapids: Eerdmans, 1978), 20-21; Carlos F. Cardoza-Orlandi and Justo L. González, *To All Nations from All Nations: A History of the Christian Missionary Movement* (Nashville: Abingdon, 2013), 183.

communicate the gospel with the large population of Chinese in Batavia.[23] The claim for his role as a mission pioneer is made for the most part on the basis of the title of his 1618 book, *An Exhortation, Worthy of Consideration, to Embark upon an Evangelical Mission Among the Indians*.[24] Though *mission* appears in the title of the English translation, *missio* or *missiones* is not in the Latin, *De legatione evangelica ad Indos capessenda admonitio*. The term *legatione* is most often rendered as "embassy" or "commission." Not only is mission language not patently expressed in Heurnius's title, he does not use *mission* in the book to describe the work of Christians or the church. Instead, he writes of the reign of Christ spreading, propagation and proclamation of the gospel, preaching and martyrdom.[25] And yet, Warneck characterizes Heurnius's book as "missionary writing," and Latourette indicates that through Heurnius's appeal "a missionary seminary was established at Leyden which in the succeeding ten years trained twelve youths who were sent as missionaries to the East."[26] It is because Heurnius's concern was about witness outside the Netherlands and because he worked in Indonesia that the language of *mission* and *missionary* is assumed and applied to him. Heurnius was an early and important sign of the rising tide of mission as a concept for Protestants, but he was not an early adopter of mission rhetoric.

Justinian von Welz (1621–1666), an Austrian nobleman, wrote a number of tracts in which he opposed dominant opinions within Lutheran orthodoxy and proposed the sending of witnesses by means of a society.[27] His contention was that the zeal and love of *Evangelische Christen* had grown cold

---

[23]Rint Sybesma, "A History of Chinese Linguists in the Netherlands," in *Chinese Studies in the Netherlands: Past, Present and Future*, ed. Wilt Idema (Leiden, The Netherlands: Koninklijke Brill, 2013), 127-28.

[24]See Bosch, *Witness to the World*, 126; Samuel H. Moffett, *A History of Christianity in Asia*, vol. 2, *1500–1900* (Maryknoll, NY: Orbis Books), 218. Verkuyl, *Contemporary Missiology*, goes as far as to say that Heurnius constructs in his book "a biblical foundation for mission" and discusses "the methodology of mission" (21).

[25]Justus Heurnius, *De legatione evangelica ad Indos capessenda admonitio* (Lugdunum Batavorum, 1618), 37, 48, 50, 66, 93, 173, 180, 198, 286. Heurnius reserves his use of mission language to divine activities (*qui divinæ missioni*, 58), or as simply the verb "to send" (70, 157, 168, 184, 248).

[26]Warneck, *History of Protestant Missions*, 43; *HEC*, 3:43. See also Verkuyl, *Contemporary Missiology Introduction*, 21.

[27]For details of Welz's life, see James A. Scherer, "Part 1: The Life and Significance of Welz," in *Justinian Welz: Essays by an Early Prophet of Mission* (Grand Rapids: Eerdmans, 1969), 9-46; *TM*, 257; Jacques A. Blocher and Jacques Blandenier, *The Evangelization of the World: A History of Christian Mission* (Pasadena, CA: William Carey Library, 2013), 240-43.

and thus admonished "all orthodox Christians" to "propagate the evangelical truth in foreign lands" through the formation of societies composed of those who seek a *rechtes Christliches Einsidler-Leben* (true Christian hermit life).[28] In an attempt to implement such a plan, he created the "Jesus-Loving Society."[29] Welz referred to his society as a *bekehrende Gesellschafft* (converting society)[30] and to the traveling agents of this society as *die ausgesendete* (the transmitted or sent ones).[31] Even though Welz does not use *Mission* or *Missionsgesellschaft*, English translations of Welz's treatises render his intent with mission language.[32] It is reasonable to apply *mission* and *missionary* to Welz's works, to interpret his treatises as "missionary documents," and to characterize him as "an early prophet of mission."[33] But it must also be acknowledged that for Welz, mission is what Roman Catholics do in the "propagation of their false teaching," and thus he associates the word with Catholic activities.[34] He praises the earnestness and resolve of the "Papists" in establishing their doctrine and church throughout the world and suggests that such should be an example to incite evangelical Christians to spread pure doctrine. He stresses a similar aim to that of Catholics but does not employ their rhetoric. Welz refers to the work of Rome's *Congregatio De Propaganda Fide* but proposes an entirely different kind of organization, a Jesus-Loving Society (*Jesusliebende Gesellschaft*).[35] The purpose of this new society in part was to counter the Catholic mission effort, so it was an anti-Catholic, and thus, an antimission initiative.[36] He acknowledges that there exists Catholic criticism of Protestants and their lack of effort in propagating their "religion" in foreign lands. And yet, he views the Catholic criticism as motivation for Protestants to carry their faith to distant people by unique

---

[28]Justinian Ernst von Welz, *Der Missionsweckruf des Baron Justinian von Welz in treuer Wiedergabe des Originaldruckes vom Jahre 1664* (Leipzig: Akademische Buchhandlung, 1890), 3.

[29]Welz, *Justinian Welz*, 75, 77.

[30]Welz, *Der Missionsweckruf des Baron Justinian von Welz*, 17.

[31]Ibid., 39, 46.

[32]See Welz, *Justinian Welz*, 63, 64, 66; W. Gröszel, *Justinian von Welz, der Vorkämpfer der lutherishcen Mission* (Leipzig: Akademische Buchhandlung, 1891), 78-79, cited in Harry R. Boer, *Pentecost and Missions* (Grand Rapids: Eerdmans, 1961), 21-22.

[33]See the title of Scherer's edited book of Welz's essays, *Justinian Welz: Essays by an Early Prophet of Mission*. Hogg, "Rise of Protestant Missionary Concern, 1517–1914," 101-2, claims that Welz formed a missionary society and died as a missionary.

[34]Ibid., 62.

[35]Welz, *Der Missionsweckruf des Baron Justinian von Welz*, 67.

[36]Welz, *Justinian Welz*, 62; *Der Missionsweckruf des Baron Justinian von Welz*, 15-16.

Protestant means. Criticism caused him to oppose Catholic mission rather than to adopt mission language. Though Welz pioneers conceptual and organizational components for modern missions, he does not step across the rhetorical line.

Savaria, Heurnius, and Welz push the boundaries of Protestant involvement in the world beyond Europe by taking Reformation theology to its conclusion. For this, they are true pioneers. To classify their pioneering efforts as "mission" helps to signal their role in developing what is to come, and thus, they are forerunners to the Protestant mission era. And yet, these harbingers of the "mission concept" do not employ mission language, nor do they simply mimic Catholic mission structures. It is important to draw these fine distinctions in order to demonstrate the Catholic roots of mission and to identify the points at which Protestants eventually differed from these. These distinctions are in part what caused Protestants to delay in adopting mission language.

Interpreters consider Anabaptists to be the singular group among the sixteenth-century Reformers, with the most developed missionary impulse, concern, and theology.[37] Jesus' command in Matthew 28:19-20 was central to Anabaptist theology and practice. Franklin Littell ably highlights the place of "the Great Commission" in Anabaptist confessions, rites, and testimony. While the commission may have been the emphasis of specialized groups prior to the Anabaptists, Littell notes, "Anabaptists were among the first to make the Commission binding upon all church members."[38] According to David Bosch, every Anabaptist "became a missionary and was allocated a specific missionary territory. Europe was once again a mission field."[39] Yet, while the Anabaptists may be noted for their "distinct concept of mission," mission language was not part of their confessions or the writings of early Anabaptists.[40] Rather, they viewed themselves most often as pilgrims and martyrs.

---

[37]See *HEC*, 2:779, 781, 786; Cornelius J. Dyck, "The Anabaptist Understanding of the Good News," in *Anabaptism and Mission*, ed. Wilbert R. Shenk, Missionary Studies 10 (Scottdale, PA: Herald, 1984), 24, 35, 39; Franklin H. Littell, "The Anabaptist Theology of Mission," in Shenk, *Anabaptism and Mission*, 21.

[38]Franklin H. Littell, *The Anabaptist View of the Church: A Study in the Origins of Sectarian Protestantism*, 2nd ed. (Boston: Starr King, 1958), 112.

[39]Bosch, *Witness to the World*, 128.

[40]Avis, *Church in the Theology of the Reformers*, 175.

Anabaptists had no use for creeds, but they wrote confessions of faith to explain their beliefs and to describe their communal life. These confessions affirm the universal nature of the gospel and the necessity of preaching this message to the whole world, but these were not expressed in mission language, and *missionary* was not an office or designation for the messenger of the gospel.[41] Instead, Anabaptist leaders, such as Balthasar Hübmaier (1480–1528) and Menno Simons (1496–1561), highlight the significance of Matthew 28:19-20, proclamation of the gospel, and baptism for every believing adult. Hübmaier, for example, specifies the tasks of proclaimers, prophets, preachers, workers, evangelists, and apostles as heralding, witnessing, preaching, and baptizing. Mission and missionary are absent among these descriptors and actors.[42] The Anabaptist emphasis on Matthew 28:19-20 provides a conceptual and biblical framework for widespread witness and proclamation but not for the rhetoric of mission.[43]

Early Anabaptists did not use mission rhetoric for several reasons. First, mission carried with it territorial implications. Unlike Catholics who saw mission as the extension of the church into territories beyond Christendom, the Anabaptist aim was to establish the true churches within the realm of Christendom. Their focus was on the errors within Catholic Europe, and thus specialized language to differentiate between Europe and the rest of the world was unnecessary. A distinct territorial designation for witness and proclamation, such as mission, made little sense to Anabaptists since witness happened everywhere. Because church for them was contrary to notions of land and sacrament, the gospel was to be preached wherever Anabaptists found themselves. Second, their evangelizing activities were more spontaneous and informal than organized and concerted endeavors of the church

---

[41]See Balthasar Hübmaier's "Eighteen Dissertations" (1524), "The Schleithem Confession" (1527), and "The Waterland Confession" (1580) in William L. Lumpkin, *Baptist Confessions of Faith*, 4th ed. (Valley Forge, PA: Judson Press, 1980), 19-78.

[42]Balthasar Hübmaier, *Balthsar Hübmaier: Theologian of Anabaptism*, Classics of the Radical Reformation, ed. and trans. H. Wayne Pipkin and John H. Yoder (Scottdale, PA: Herald, 1989), 64, 68, 114-27, 143, 337, 512.

[43]See, for example, Menno Simons, *The Complete Writings of Menno Simons, C. 1496–1561*, ed. John Christian Wenger, trans. Leonard Verduin (Scottdale, PA: Herald, 1956), 120, 394, 682. "We desire with ardent hearts even at the cost of life and blood that the holy Gospel of Jesus Christ and His apostles, which only is the true doctrine and will remain so until Jesus Christ comes again upon the clouds, may be taught and preached through all the world as the Lord Jesus Christ commanded His disciples as a last word to them while He was on earth" (303).

or a specialized group sanctioned by the church.[44] John Yoder suggests that the Anabaptist evangelizing tactic should be classified as sedition rather than sending.[45] Severe persecution dictated that Anabaptists operated "on the run," as people under threat from both religious and secular authorities. Thus, these seditious dissenters had no established base of operation, nor were they able to mount an organized effort. When they eventually sent their members in a systematic manner, they designated them not as missionaries but "apostles."[46] While Anabaptists focused on Matthew 28:19-20 and contributed to the eventual adoption of mission language, *mission* and *missionary* are absent among their descriptions of their undertakings and roles.

Some argue that the absence of mission rhetoric among Luther, Calvin, Heurnius, Welz, and early Anabaptists was because they had more immediate concerns, such as doctrinal purity of the church and their own survival.[47] Stephen Neill notes that for Protestants "there was little time for thought of missions," as they were fighting for their lives and warring with each other.[48] Their attention was on the reform of the church located in Europe rather than in places where the church was not. Plus, interpreters note that the structures and means present within the Catholic church, such as monastic orders and a developed church hierarchy, were not present for the Protestants, and thus they did not have the organizational framework or resources at hand to initiate mission structure or activity.[49] Others observe that while early Protestants did not overtly propose definitive plans to evangelize the world, their theology had "missionary potential."[50] And yet, our question is not whether they viewed the gospel as universal or actively sought to engage Turks and Jews, but why mission language was absent among early Protestants. Impulse and activity were present; mission language was lacking.

---

[44]Hans Kasdorf, "The Anabaptist Approach to Mission," in Shenk, *Anabaptism and Mission*, 55-58, describes Anabaptists' methods as this way prior to August 1527.

[45]Yoder, "Reformation and Missions," 49.

[46]Kasdorf, "Anabaptist Approach to Mission," 59.

[47]*TM*, 248-50; Robert Hall Glover, *The Progress of World-Wide Missions* (New York: Harper & Row, 1960), 40.

[48]*HCM*, 187.

[49]*TM*, 250.

[50]Jan A. B. Jongeneel, "The Protestant Missionary Movement up to 1789," in *Missiology: An Ecumenical Introduction, Texts and Contexts of Global Christianity*, ed. F. J. Verstraelen (Grand Rapids: Eerdmans, 1995), 223.

First, Protestant hesitation to use mission language stems from the fact that it was a programmatic Catholic concern.[51] Activities of the Catholic church in places such as India and Brazil under the sponsorship of Portuguese rulers were known as mission, and thus were known as distinct Catholic undertakings. In other words, mission as ecclesial language was known to be a distinctly Catholic innovation tied to the Roman church and Catholic political powers. In many places, this arrangement meant Protestants were the recipients of Catholic mission effort, some of which included forced reconversion.[52] It is understandable why Protestants did not have a positive view of mission and thus no place for the term. Protestants had to make their own start with mission, in practice and rhetoric, but theirs would be from another starting point and via a different route.[53]

Second, Protestants hesitated to use *mission* on theological grounds. They saw mission as an endeavor that interfered with God's activity. Justification by faith rather than works placed not only the initiative but also the work of salvation squarely in the realm of the divine. Thus, the use of temporal means to accomplish eternal divine work was theologically untenable to Lutherans and Calvinists. Mission meant human means and thus was another work-based Catholic heresy.[54]

Third, at the heart of the Protestants' hesitation to adopt the language of mission was their understanding of church. John Yoder explains that Protestants' provincialism was more than "a simple geographic narrowness," but it was due to the location of the church's focus on the "*Land* or *Volk*" under the rule of a particular prince.[55] Unlike the Catholics, whose reach followed that of expanding European powers, *Volk* narrowed the range of proclamation

---

[51]Berg, *Constrained by Jesus' Love*, 6.
[52]Interpreters characterize Jesuit activity among Protestants as *mission*. See Robert, *Christian Mission*, 37; David J. Bosch, *Believing in the Future: Toward a Missiology of Western Culture* (Valley Forge, PA: Trinity Press International, 1995), 29; Paul M. Collins, "Ecclesiology and World Mission/Missio Dei," in *Routledge Companion to the Christian Church* (London: Routledge, 2008), 627; Verkuyl, *Contemporary Missiology*, 2.
[53]Yoder, "Reformation and Missions," 44-45.
[54]The association of mission with the pope and Catholic church continued into the eighteenth century. In a pamphlet written in 1700, Daniel Defoe contends that among reasons to forbid priests from marrying is that "they could not so easily be sent on Missions, and encompass Sea and Land to make Proselytes." Daniel Defoe, *Reasons Humbly Offer'd for a Law to Enact the Castration or Gelding of Popish Ecclesiastics, &c.: As the Best Way to Prevent the Growth of Popery in England* (London: A. Baldwin, 1700), 7.
[55]See Yoder, "Reformation and Missions," 46-47.

of the Protestants to local identity and territory. Witness took place in their locale, and therefore mission as a foreign type of witness was irrelevant language. Not until Protestant countries began their own expansion of commerce and rule did the church of the Reformers adopt language necessary to describe the church's geographic expansion.

Fourth, *mission* for Protestants was an extraecclesial term. At a time when massive and thorough reform of the church was under way and various forms of church were being examined, why should Reformers burden their understanding of church with non-church language? Ecclesial reform meant excising the church of unnecessary, nonbiblical forms and offices and returning to a pristine understanding of church.

THE RHETORICAL TURN

In spite of these barriers, *mission* gradually made its way into Protestant language and eventually became part of its vocabulary as forces and circumstances enabled a rhetorical turn. Among the forces that moved Protestants toward mission language were Catholic accusations and the rise of colonial interests among Protestant powers. At the same time, the innovation of extraecclesial entities known as *societies* provided the occasion for the turn.

Forces. The most serious indictment against Protestantism's lack of mission practice and language came from Robert Bellarmine (1542–1621), a cardinal and Jesuit theologian. Bellarmine, the chief architect of the Catholic response to the Protestant Reformation, addressed problems posed by the Reformers and mounted counterattacks against their positions and in defense of Catholic doctrine. In *Inquiries into Controverted Points of the Christian Faith,* Bellarmine dismisses Protestants as not being the true church. While the Catholic church "has many marks, or testimonies, or signs, which discern her from every false religion of the Pagans, of Jews, and Heretics," Protestants demonstrate none of these.[56] The fourth of these marks or signs of the true church is "The Multitude of Believers." "Indeed," Bellarmine claims, "a Church that is truly Catholic ought not only to embrace all time but all places, all nations and all races of men." As a result, Bellarmine concludes,

---

[56]Roberto Francesco Romolo Bellarmine, *De Notis Ecclesia/On the Marks of the Church*, trans. Ryan Grant (n.p.: Mediatrix, 2015), 13.

In our time, the Roman Church apart from Italy and all of Spain, apart from nearly all of France, Germany, England, Poland, Bohemia, Hungary, Greece, Syria, Ethiopia and Egypt, in which many Catholics are found, in the new world itself, we have Churches without the mingling of heretics, in all four parts of world; to the east, in the Indies, to the west, in America; to the north in Japan; to the south in Brazil, and in the further part of Africa. But the sects of the heretics have never occupied the new world, or at least, only a scanty part of it.[57]

"The heretics," according to Bellarmine, "are never read to have converted any heathens or Jews to the faith, but only to have perverted Christians."[58] While thousands of Jews and Turks have converted to the Catholic faith, "the Lutherans have scarcely converted one or the other, although they compare themselves with the apostles and evangelists, and they have many Jews in Germany, and in Poland and in Hungary there are many Turks nearby."[59] In Bellarmine's estimation, because preaching to Jews and Turks and converting them to Christianity are essential marks of the church, Protestants cannot claim to be the true church.

A critique similar to that of Bellarmine existed inside Protestantism as well. If the church of Protestantism is the true church, then Protestants should be propagating right doctrine to the heathen in order to counter the Catholics. John Amos Comenius (1592–1670), philosopher, educator, and bishop of the Unitas Fratrum (United brethren), challenged fellow Protestants to match the Catholic effort. "Look here, you Zealous Protestants, look with shame," he exhorts, "from hated Jesuites learn to spread Christ's name, and Heathens from their idols to reclaim."[60] Protestants, according to Comenius, should halt the diffusion of false Catholic teachings by the spread of the true gospel. Similarly, in his argument for a Protestant society to match the work of the Catholic *Propaganda Fide*, Justinian von Welz complains that "evangelicals should also take it to heart

---

[57]Ibid., 36.
[58]Ibid., 89.
[59]Ibid., 93. Bellarmine cites Francis Xavier as example of one "famous in India for every kind of miracle" and who thereby converted many to the Catholic faith (111).
[60]Johann Amos Comenius, *A Generall Table of Europe, Representing the Present and Future State Thereof Viz. the Present Governments, Languages, Religions, Foundations, and Revolutions Both of Governments and Religions, the Future Mutations, Revolutions, Government, and Religion of Christendom and of the World &c*, Microform (London: Benjamin Billingsley, 1670), 13.

that the papists have so often reproached us for calling ourselves true-
believing and good Christians, and yet not once attempting to propagate
our religion in distant lands."[61] While Bellarmine, Comenius, and Welz
make their accusations in language other than that of mission, the force
of their critique is still there—Protestants should do what Catholics, and
especially Jesuits, do.

Another force that pushed Protestants toward mission language was their
colonial aspirations. Their adoption of mission rhetoric coincided with the
entrance of Protestant countries into the quest for colonies, and the ensuing
need for organizational means and methods for the church to accompany
the state to its colonies.[62] Just as Spanish and Portugese colonizing efforts
facilitated the expansion of the European Catholic church, initiatives by
Dutch and British commercial and political entities, such as the East India
Company, did the same for Protestants. According to Scott Sunquist, Dutch
political forces supplanted the Portuguese Catholic presence in places such
as India, paving the way for Protestants to extend their influence.[63] Soon
after Protestant countries expanded their political and commercial reach,
mission language appeared in the titles, charters, and sermons of societies.
As with the Catholic church of the late medieval period, Protestants in the
early modern era adopted mission, and with it came its political and diplomatic connotations. Rather than arising solely from theological conviction,
mission emerged with Protestant colonial aspirations and the need to
organize and operationalize religious interests abroad.[64]

Mission entered Protestant rhetoric as a matter of convention and convenience. Another way of expressing this is to say its adoption was not solely
a principled decision or due to overwhelming convictions. Mission already
existed as a descriptive term for the Catholic church's expansion, and

---

[61]Welz, *Justinian Welz*, 62; *Der Missionsweckruf des Baron Justinian von Welz*, 15-16.
[62]See Jeffrey Cox, "Master Narratives of Imperial Missions," in *Mixed Messages: Materiality,
Textuality, Missions*, ed. Jamie S. Scott and Gareth Griffiths (New York: Palgrave Macmillan,
2005), 5; Bosch, *Witness to the World*, 123; Orlando E. Costas, *Christ Outside the Gate: Mission
Beyond Christendom* (Maryknoll, NY: Orbis Books, 1982), 59.
[63]Sunquist, *Understanding Christian Mission*, 78.
[64]The East India Company provided a model and encouragement for William Carey as he initiated
the Baptist effort. See Bevans and Schroeder, *Constants in Context*, 211; Robert, *Christian Mission*,
45; Wilbert R. Shenk, "New Wineskins for New Wine: Toward a Post-Christendom Ecclesiology,"
International Bulletin of Missionary Research 29, no. 2 (April 2005): 74.

Protestants found it convenient to adopt it as their own. Protestants began using mission in the early eighteenth century, just as Protestant powers took control of the seas and entered the race for colonies.[65]

Occasion. The occasion for the entrance of mission language into the Protestant vocabulary was the rise of voluntary societies. Modeled after independent commercial enterprises already operating in colonies, societies expedited the entrance of Protestants into these same areas. Societies did what Protestant churches were ill-fitted and incapable of doing, and thus societies provided a convenient way for mission to become Protestant language without becoming ecclesial language. The Protestant view of church as an autonomous, local body, loosely affiliated around doctrinal convictions, meant its churches were provincial and locally focused. When convictions about the universal nature of the gospel emerged and forces from outside pressed for overseas involvement, these churches did not have structures, means, or outlook to make a response. So while Protestants did not create the language of mission, they innovated the mission society as their unique response to the world.

Protestant societies did not start out explicitly as "mission" societies. Early societies used the language of *propagation, foreign,* and *heathen* in their charters and titles. The earliest of these, Society for the Propagation of the Gospel in New England (1649) and the Church of England's Society for the Propagation of the Gospel in Foreign Parts (1701), opted for words other than *mission* and *missionary.* The charters of these early Protestant societies listed a wide range of activities, such as "to promote Christian Knowledge,"[66] but mission as a description of the society's work was absent. The chief aim of these societies was the care for white settlers from England rather than preaching for the conversion of the native population.[67] They sent chaplains rather than missionaries. In many cases, the evangelization of local inhabitants was incidental and even prohibited.

---

[65]See Berg, *Constrained by Jesus' Love,* 15, 21.

[66]From the charter of 1699 for the Society for Promoting Christian Knowledge as recorded in H. Thompson, *Into All Lands: The History of the Society for the Propagation of the Gospel in Foreign Parts, 1701–1950* (London: SPCK, 1951), 12.

[67]Norman Etherington, "Missions and Empire," in *The Oxford History of the British Empire,* vol. 5, *Historiography,* ed. Robin W. Winks (Oxford: Oxford University Press, 1999), 303; Andrew Porter, "Religion, Missionary Enthusiasm, and Empire," in *The Oxford History of the British Empire,* vol. 3, *The Nineteenth Century,* ed. Andrew Porter (Oxford: Oxford University Press, 1999), 228.

When the Society for the Propagation of the Gospel in New England was established in 1649, one of its initial undertakings was to raise funds for the work of John Eliot (1604–1690). Eliot, celebrated today as one of the first Protestant missionaries and named as the "Apostle of the Indians," migrated from England to the Massachusetts Bay Colony in 1632.[68] While pastoring a church, he became concerned for Indians in the surrounding area. He learned their language, evangelized a number of them, established Christian Indian towns, and translated the catechism and the Old and New Testaments into the Algonquin language. The new society viewed Eliot as a way to fulfill its charter, and thus brought him under their sponsorship. Though in every way representative of modern mission activity, the charter of the society and Eliot's work were not described as "mission."

The Society for Promoting Christian Knowledge (SPCK), founded in 1698 by John Bray (1656–1730), began for the purpose of printing and distributing educational materials for schools in British colonies. Bray modified the society's name and charter in 1701 to reflect its widening interests. In its new form, King William the Third granted corporation to the Society for the Propagation of the Gospel in Foreign Parts with the charge to minister to "loving subjects" in British colonies and to combat "Romish Priest and Jesuits [who] are the more encouraged to pervert and draw over our said loving subjects to Popish superstition and idolatry."[69] The society's original charter does not use the word *mission*, nor does it refer to those who carry out the duties of the society as missionaries but as "officers, ministers and servants."[70] Yet, in a pamphlet of the society published in 1700, *A Memorial Representing the Present State of Religion, on the Continent of North America*, mission language is evident and frequent. Bray argues for "a sufficient numbers of proper missionaries" to counteract the efforts of "Papists" among the colonists.[71] Following his survey of each of the colonies, he concludes that forty Protestant missionaries are needed. An early history of the society

---

[68]Neville B. Cryer, "Biography of John Eliot," in *Five Pioneer Missionaries* (London: The Banner of Truth Trust, 1965), 218, 231; *HEC*, 3:218-20; Bosch, *Witness to the World*, 141.

[69]David Humphreys, *An Historical Account of the Incorporated Society for the Propagation of the Gospel in Foreign Parts* (New York: Arno, 1969), xxvi.

[70]Ibid., xxv.

[71]Thomas Bray, *A Memorial, Representing the Present State of Religion, on the Continent of North America* (London: William Downing, 1700).

published in 1730 by David Humphreys, secretary of the society, names throughout his accounts the agents of the society as missionaries, but refers in general to "the Work" or "the Trust" of the society.[72] He uses *mission* sparingly as a means to describe the activities of traveling preachers, as well as the overall work of the society.[73] With Bray and the SPCK, *mission* was introduced into societal language, but not as a central statement of the society's purpose.

The growing concern among Protestants for non-Christians in foreign lands and the desire to send people to preach the Christian faith solidified and became explicit mission language with the Danish-Halle Mission and the Moravians. The Royal Danish-Halle Mission, founded in 1704, later known as the Tranquebar Mission, was the first society with *mission* in its title and thus signals the institutionalization of Protestant mission rhetoric. The founding of the Danish-Halle Mission and its connection with the Germany Lutheran church came by way of unique circumstances. The Danish Crown established a presence in India nearly a century prior (1616) under King Christian IV (1588–1648) in the form of a trading company, the Danish East India Company, and a colony of Danish citizens. Both the trading company and the colony were situated in the village of Tranquebar on the east coast of India.[74] What prompted King Frederick IV (1671–1731) to charter the Royal Danish Mission is not entirely clear.[75] In all likelihood, this initiative originated from the Danish crown, rather than from urgings of the Danish Lutheran church. The Danish church maintained that the gospel was sufficiently preached by the apostles throughout the world and believed the Danish church had no right to place uninvited ministers, except in areas where the Danish king ruled. The king's action to charter the mission was

---

[72]See for example, Humphreys, *Historical Account of the Incorporated Society*, 16, 18, 20, 22, 353.
[73]For examples of Humphreys's use of *mission*, see ibid., 45, 57, 66, 68, 74.
[74]See Daniel Jeyaraj, *Bartholomäus Ziegenbalg, the Father of Modern Protestant Mission: An Indian Assessment* (Delhi: Indian Society for Promoting Christian Knowledge, 2006), 11.
[75]Daniel Jeyaraj, "Mission Reports from South India and Their Impact on the Western Mind: The Tranquebar Mission of the Eighteenth Century," in *Converting Colonialism: Visions and Realities in Mission History, 1706–1914*, ed. Dana Lee Robert, Studies in the History of Christian Missions (Grand Rapids: Eerdmans, 2008), 21-42, suggests that the founding of two societies in Britain, the Society for Promoting Christian Knowledge and the Society for the Propagation of the Gospel in Foreign Parts, "exerted indirect influence on the formation of the Royal Danish Mission in 1704" (23). Cf. Stephen Neill, *A History of Christianity in India: The Beginning to AD 1707* (Cambridge: Cambridge University Press, 1984), 28-40.

more of a political move to counteract and eventually supplant Portuguese Jesuits in Tranquebar.[76] The royal charter placed the mission under sponsorship of the Danish crown, and thus its support came from the Danish government and not the church. Because the Danish crown administrated the affairs of the Danish citizens in the colony, as well as the Indians in Tanquebar, the mission operated under the principle of *cujus region ejus religio*, the religion of the ruler is the religion of the ruler's subjects. Thus, the first explicit Protestant mission society followed a pattern already established in Portuguese and Spanish Catholic efforts.

A collection of letters from the first "Danish missionaries," Bartholomäus Ziegenbalg (1682–1719) and Heinrich Plütschau (1677–1752), published in 1708, provides an account of their journey to India and the difficulties they encountered. These were translated from German into English by Anton Wilhelm Böhme (1673–1722), the court chaplain at the chapel at St. James in London, and published in 1709.[77] Mission language is used throughout both German and English versions. Böhme prefaces the letters with "A Preliminary Discourse Concerning the Character of a Missionary," in which he equates missionaries with New Testament apostles and contrasts these "True Apostles" or "rightful Missionaries" with "Roman-Catholick Missionaries" who travel to distant parts of the world to proselytize people to their particular religion and thus make them "twofold more the Child of Hell than themselves."[78] Böhme distinguishes *missionary* as used in the letters to describe Ziegenbalg and Plütschau from its use for Roman Catholic missionaries. Ziegenbalg writes of the dangers the two Danish missionaries encountered "on account of the Roman Catholicks" (Jesuits) who were already at work in Tranquebar.[79] Along with Hindus and Muslims, they found a considerable number of Roman Catholic Christians in Tranquebar and the surrounding district and view all three groups as objects of their work.[80] The Danish-Halle

---

[76]Jeyaraj, *Bartholomäus Ziegenbalg, the Father of Modern Protestant Mission*, 30-35. See also Sunquist, *Understanding Christian Mission*, 79.

[77]Anton Wilhelm Böhme, *Propagation of the Gospel in the East: Being an Account of the Success of Two Danish Missionaries, Lately Sent to the East-Indies for the Conversion of the Heathens in Malabar* (London: J. Downing, 1709).

[78]Ibid., v, vii, xi, xii.

[79]Ibid., xii, 26-31.

[80]Jeyaraj, *Bartholomäus Ziegenbalg, Father of Modern Protestant Mission*, 15, 27.

Mission, the first extraecclesial entity to identify its purpose as "mission," contrasts its activities from what Catholics do under the same name. The introduction of mission language by the Danish-Halle Mission had a ripple effect throughout Protestantism, chiefly through the publication of its missionary reports.[81] The first to feel this effect were the Moravians.

The Moravians, or Herrenhuter, went throughout the world with the aim "to win souls for the Lamb."[82] As heirs of the legacy of the Unitas Fratrum and their last bishop, John Amos Comenius, these refugees were well acquainted with suffering and a nomadic lifestyle.[83] The combination of their exilic outlook and Pietism, mediated to them by way of Augustus Francke (1663–1727) and Nicolaus Ludwig von Zinzendorf (1700–1760), produced an unusual outlook on the world and a zeal for Christ. As a result, they sent members from their community to places around the world in order to suffer for the Lamb and bear witness to Christ's wounds. Moravians sent Brethren from Herrnhut as early as 1732 to work among African slaves in the West Indies and with Eskimos in Greenland. Leonhard Dober and Christian David, the first Moravians deployed, did not go as religious professionals or missionaries but as a potter and carpenter. By 1740 eighty-six of their community had been sent, and at the time of Zinzendorf's death twenty years later over three hundred had left Herrnhut for places such as Greenland, Georgia, Labrador, West Indies, and Africa.[84] The number of those sent from Herrnhut and the places where they landed had an astonishing affect on the whole of Protestantism. Their exploits influenced both John Wesley and William Carey, and inspired Protestants throughout Europe.[85] Paulus Pham notes that there were "no significant activities in missionary theory and praxis" in the first two centuries of Protestantism, and it was "only with Nicolaus Ludwig von Zinzendorf and his Moravians that the Protestant mission became organized and carried on systematically in the Pietist spirit."[86]

---

[81]Daniel Jeyaraj details the impact of these reports in "Mission Reports from South India," 28-42.

[82]See Hogg, *Ecumenical Foundations*, 2-3.

[83]See Michael W. Stroope, "The Legacy of John Amos Comenius," *International Bulletin of Missionary Research* 29, no. 4 (October 2005): 204-8.

[84]Heinz Motel, "Zinzendorf, Nikolaus Ludwig von," in *Concise Dictionary of the Christian World Mission*, ed. Stephen Neill, Gerald H. Anderson, and John Goodwin (Nashville: Abingdon, 1971).

[85]For example, *HCM*, 201-3; Bosch, *Witness to the World*, 131-32; Moffett, *History of Christianity in Asia*, 2:241-43.

[86]Paulus Y. Pham, *Towards an Ecumenical Paradigm for Christian Mission: David Bosch's Missionary Vision*, Documenta Missionalia 35 (Roma: Gregorian Biblical, 2010), 77, 78. See assessments of

As a youth, Zinzendorf attended Augustus Francke's Paedagogium at
Halle, where he witnessed the formation of the Danish-Halle Mission and
interacted with Ziegenbalg.[87] Zinzendorf left Halle, but as he attended university, worked in Dresden, and eventually established Herrnhut, he followed the Danish-Halle Mission via the *Halle Reports*.[88] Through Francke's
involvement with the Danish effort and ongoing reports of their endeavor,
Zinzendorf became familiar with the language of *mission* and *missionary*.

From the beginning, Zinzendorf's theological outlook certainly included
"all humanity," "all souls," the "whole world," and the "nations and peoples of
the earth," and he highlighted Matthew 28:19-20 and Mark 16:15 as universal
appeals for the true church.[89] Yet, the early Zinzendorf did not frame these
as mission. He describes early Moravians sent from Herrnhut as witnesses,
servants, disciples, and Jesus Christ's fighters (*Streiter*), and names their
exploits as witnessing and preaching.[90] The stated aim of their service was
not mission but service to "the bleeding Lamb." They did not depart Herrnhut with the designation of *missionary*. Instead, they went via their trade
and craft, and thus they were known as weavers, brewers, and carpenters. It
was only after the initial period of sending that Zinzendorf switched to the
language of mission.

---

the Moravian place in the emergence of modern mission in *TM*, 259-60; Bosch, *Witness to the
World*, 131-32; *HCM*, 201-3; *HEC*, 3:47; Moffett, *History of Christianity in Asia*, 2:241-43; Glover,
Progress of World-Wide Missions, 52.

[87]Erich Beyreuther, *Studien zur Theologie Zinzendorfs: Gesammelte Aufsätze* (Germany: Neukirchener Verlag, 1962), 140-41; Jeyaraj, "Mission Reports from South India," 33; David A. Schattschneider, "The Missionary Theologies of Zinzendorf and Spangenberg," *Transactions of the
Moravian Historical Society* 22, no. 3 (January 1975): 216.

[88]Jeyaraj, "Mission Reports from South India," 33.

[89]Nicolaus Ludwig Zinzendorf, *Christian Life and Witness: Count Zinzendorf's 1738 Berlin Speeches*,
ed. Gary Steven Kinkel, Princeton Theological Monograph Series 140 (Eugene, OR: Pickwick,
2010), 12, 23-24, 49, 55, 67, 117; Zinzendorf, *Nine Public Lectures on Important Subjects in Religion:
Preached in Fetter Lane Chapel in London in the Year 1746*, ed. George W. Forell (Iowa City: University of Iowa Press, 1973), 14, 16, 23, 32, 73.

[90]For example, Zinzendorf, *Nine Public Lectures*, 26; Zinzendorf, *Christian Life and Witness*, 3, 73,
91, 109, 127; Zinzendorf, "Des Ordinarii Fratrum Berlinische Reden (1738)," in *Hauptschriften*,
ed. Erich Beyreuther and Gerhard Meyer (Darmstadt, Germany: Hildesheim, G. Olms Verlagsbuchhandlung, 1962), 1:13, 110, 137, 161, 162, 187; Zinzendorf, *Die Wichtigsten Missionsinstruktionen Zinzendorfs*, ed. O. Uttendörfer, Hefte Zur Missionskunde 12 (Herrnhut, Germany: Verlag
der Missionsbuchhandlung, 1913), 24. A. J. Lewis, "Count Zinzendorf," *London Quarterly and
Holborn Review* 185 (April 1960), translates Zinzendorf's words to George Schmidt, an early
Moravian sent to the Hottentots, "Die Streitersache ist das Geschaft Jesu Christi auf seinem
Erdbodem" as "the missionary cause is Jesus Christ's affair in His world" (128). *Streitersache* is
literally "fighter thing" rather than *missionary*.

Mission and *missionary* do not appear in the first two volumes of Zinzendorf's *Hauptschriften*, but both entered his writings and addresses by volume three. His 1746 discourse titled *Vom Grund-Plane Unserer Heiden-Missionen* opens with the declaration, "My brothers and sisters, today is the day of missions."[91] Activities described by a variety of terms to this point coalesce in mission, and thereby Zinzendorf brings the Moravian efforts abroad in line with the Danish-Halle Mission. For Zinzendorf, the difference between the Danish-Halle Mission and the Moravians had been that activity for one was initiated from the state and for the other from the community of faith. Whereas the Danish Mission was founded for the specific purpose of mission, the Community of the Brethren existed to "help individuals love the Savior and meditate on his merits."[92] Thus, the blood and wounds of Christ were central and not mission. They won "souls for the Lamb" as the brethren embraced Christ and his suffering. Zinzendorf's preference for community language of *Gemeine* underlines the importance of intimate relationship and intense discipline in pursuit of Christ and the heavenly nature of the community.[93] He refers to the worldwide community of the faithful church as *Brüdergemeine* (Community of the Brethren), and he calls scattered communities *Pilgergemeinen* (Pilgrim congregations).[94] For Zinzendorf, *Gemeine* rather than mission is the ideal.

Just as Ignatius innovated mission language for the Roman Catholic orders, Zinzendorf and the Moravians introduced mission as ecclesial language for Protestants. Yet, this use of mission as church language is tempered.

---

[91]"Meine Geschwister! heute ist der tag der Missionen." Nicolaus Ludwig Zinzendorf, "Die an Den Synodum Der Brüder in Zeyst, Vom 11. May Bis Den 21. Junii 1746, Gehaltene Reden," in *Hauptschriften*, ed. Erich Beyreuther and Gerhard Meyer (Hildesheim, Germany: Georg Olms Verlagsbuchhandlung, 1963), 3:186. See also his use of *mission* at the same synod in Nicolaus Ludwig Zinzendorf, *Texte zur Mission* (Hamburg: Wittig Verlag, 1979), 91. In *Die Wichtigsten Missionsinstruktionen*, (1732), 8, Zinzendorf uses *missionary* in reference to instructions given him from Ziegenbalg of the Danish-Halle Mission.

[92]Craig D. Atwood, *Community of the Cross: Moravian Piety in Colonial Bethlehem* (University Park: The Pennsylvania State University Press, 2004), 109.

[93]Ibid., 62-63.

[94]Zinzendorf, *Die Wichtigsten Missionsinstruktionen*, 33; Zinzendorf, *Texte zur Mission*, 63. See John R. Weinlick, *Count Zinzendorf: The Story of His Life and Leadership in the Renewed Moravian Church* (Bethlehem, PA: Moravian Church in America, 1989), 129-35; Jacob John Sessler, *Communal Pietism Among Early American Moravians* (New York: AMS, 1971), 14-15. Atwood, *Community of the Cross: Moravian Piety in Colonial Bethlehem*, mentions that "there was no one type of *Gemeine*, but each was an expression of local needs." Thus, scattered congregations went by a variety of designations besides *Pilgergemeinen* (61).

David Schattschneider's characterization of the Moravians as "the whole church as mission" and "every member a missionary" overstates the connection between church and mission.[95] Zinzendorf does not equate the two. He differentiates between the Community of Brethren on one hand and state-initiated and -sponsored mission on the other. While Moravians subsequently linked the language of mission with the church, Zinzendorf continued in his understanding of the church as a disestablished pilgrim community that supersedes mission.

Oblique references to mission in Zinzendorf's writings and the Moravians' early foundational documents became full-blown expressions of mission and missionary in the second generation of Moravians. Zinzendorf's successor, August Gottlieb Spangenberg (1704–1792), summarizes the work of the Moravians in *Von der Arbeit der evangelische Brüder unter den Heiden* (1782).[96] Spangenberg uses the language of mission to refer to the places where the Moravians labor, such as Greenland and St. Thomas, and names those sent as missionaries.[97] In the back of this publication are rules and articles for a Moravian society for mission under the title "The Brethren's Society for the Furtherance of the Gospel Among the Heathen" (*Der Brüdersocietät zur Förderung des Evangeliums unter den Heiden*). Mission language appears throughout these articles.[98] For example, article four states, "The design of this society being to assist those missionaries [*Mißonarien*] and their helpers, whom the directors of the missions [*Mißionen*] of the Brethren's church may send to the heathen in different parts of the world, we

---

[95]Schattschneider, "Missionary Theologies of Zinzendorf and Spangenberg," 214, 229. See also Costas, *Christ Outside the Gate*, 60-61; William J. Danker, "Mammon for Moravian Missions," *Concordia Theological Monthly*, no. 36 (April 1965): 251, 259; Kenneth B. Mulholland, "Moravians, Puritans, and the Modern Missionary Movement (paper presented as the Missions and Evangelism Lectureship, Dallas Theological Seminary, N 2–5, 1997)," *Bibliotheca Sacra*, no. 156 (June 1999): 222.

[96]August Gottlieb Spangenberg, *Von der Arbeit der evangelischen Brüder unter den Heiden* (Barby: Bey Christian Friedrich Laux, 1782). English translation of this work was published in 1788 as *An Account of the Manner in Which the Protestant Church of the Unitas Fratrum, or United Brethren, Preach the Gospel and Carry on Their Missions Among the Heathen* (London: H. Trapp, 1788).

[97]For example, among Spangenberg's many usages of mission language in the English translation (1788), one finds "mission" (39, 53, 84), "heathen mission" (54, 56, 57), and "missionary" (75, 76, 80, 81). Mission language can also be seen as early as 1777 in a Moravian history by Christian Georg Andreas Meier Oldendorp, *Historie der caribischen Inseln Sanct Thomas, Sanct Crux und Sanct Jan, inbesondere der dasigen Neger und der Mission der evangelischen Brüder unter denselben*, vol. 51 (Berlin: Verlag für Wissenschaft und Bildung, 2000), 33, 85.

[98]Spangenberg, *Account*, 121-27.

will not confine our assistance of those missionaries to gifts and contributions only."[99] The incorporation of mission language into the Moravian vocabulary reflects a shift already realized with the Danish-Halle Mission,
under way with British societies, and indicative of Spangenberg's effort to
make the *Brüdergemeine* look and sound more normal in the wake of severe
criticism. Though he signals a definite shift to mission language for the
Moravian church and society, Spangenberg does not use *mission* or *missionary* to describe endeavors and people in the Old and New Testaments.
Instead, Jesus, the disciples, Peter, and Paul preached, served, and labored
in the gospel among the Gentiles as laborers, elders, bishops, overseers,
watchmen, and apostles.[100] Thus, Spangenberg uses mission language to
refer to contemporary endeavors and as a recent role or specialized vocation.

Moravians made the ecclesial to societal shift soon after they adopted the
language of mission. By the second generation (1782), British Moravians
established a society, and with it *mission* became for Moravians a societal
term. The Brethren's Society for the Furtherance of the Gospel Among the
Heathen held once-a-month meetings for its members and conducted
business related to the promotion of its missions and support of Moravian
missionaries. The society employed deputies and corresponding agents to
collect and manage funds. As mentioned above, Zinzendorf's reasons for
initiating a change in language are not altogether clear, but the shift marked
a change in language and a new day for the Moravians.

Eighty-seven years after the founding of the Danish-Halle Mission and
sixty years after the sending of the first Moravians, British Baptists formed
the Particular Baptist Society for the Propagation of the Gospel Amongst
the Heathen (1792). The name of the society was shortened almost
immediately to the Baptist Missionary Society. Following the Baptists, other
societies soon followed: the London Missionary Society (1795), the Edinburgh and Glasgow Missionary Societies (1796), the Anglican Society for
Missions to Africa and the East, later known as the Church Missionary
Society (1799), and the Wesleyan Missionary Society (1813).[101]

---

[99] Ibid., 122.
[100] Ibid., 12, 13, 14, 22, 25, 26, 29, 30.
[101] For the relationship of these societies in formation and development, see Andrew Porter, *Religion Versus Empire? British Protestant Missionaries and Overseas Expansion, 1700–1914*
(Manchester, UK: Manchester University Press, 2004), 40–45.

As with Catholics, the rise of mission among Protestants began not within the life of the *corpus Ecclesiae* but in the dynamism of the *corpus Societatis*. In its fundamental nature, Protestant mission emulated Catholic mission. Via these extraecclesial entities, *corpus Societatum*, mission made its way into the mainstream of Protestant speech.

The rhetorical turn toward mission for Protestants came via forces outside the church and in entities on the margin of Protestantism. Because of its outsider status, *mission* had to contend for its place in Protestant language from the start. However, in the course of two centuries, mission moved from questionable language to an established tradition. The Danish-Halle Mission, Zinzendorf, and the Moravians played catalyzing roles in enabling this transition.

10

Missionary Problems

The end of the conference is the beginning of the Conquest.
The end of the planning is the beginning of the Doing.

JOHN R. MOTT, EDINBURGH MISSIONARY CONFERENCE OF 1910

The aim of Christian missions today in our conception
would take this form: To seek with people of other lands
a true knowledge and love of God, expressing in life and
word what we have learned through Jesus Christ, and
endeavoring to give effect to his spirit in the life of the world.

RE-THINKING MISSIONS: A LAYMEN'S INQUIRY AFTER ONE HUNDRED YEARS

THE EARLIEST RECORDED use of *mission* in the English language referring to persons sent by religious groups or churches to proselytize others
is by Francis Bacon in *An Advertisement Touching on Holy War* (1629). In this
pamphlet, Bacon poses a fictitious debate between five persons concerning
whether it is lawful for Christendom to engage in holy war for the expansion
of Christianity. In contrast to the acts of war by the state, "the Church (indeed)
maketh her Missions, into the extream [*sic*] parts of the Nations, and Isles;
And it is well: But this is, *Ecce Vnus Gladius hic* [Behold a single sword here]."[1]
The church's sword is in contrast to but exists alongside the sword of the state.
Bacon's assertion is that both are necessary. In Bacon's use, mission operates
alongside the state in the expansion of the church. Just as the state has its

---

[1]Francis Bacon, "An Advertisement Touching a Holy War," in *Certain Miscellany Work* (London:
William Rawley, 1629), 34.

forces for expansion, the church has its sword. Over the course of two centuries, Bacon's singular notion of church expansion took shape in societies
and grew in dimensions and usages, until it developed into a tradition—the
modern mission movement. From a single word expressing the action of the
church, a tradition denoting a modern movement emerged.

A Modern Movement

The modern mission movement—definite article, two adjectives, and a
noun—represents a set of historical occurrences imbued with religious,
social, national, and emotional connotations. *Movement*, the noun, denotes
a common ideology, belief, or system. An array of religious, political, and
social movements, either from the past or in the present, provides examples
of what movements might look like and what they do. These movements
have been social (women's suffrage movement), religious (the Jesus
movement), and political (the civil rights movement); or they can designate
a type or period of art (Impressionism). Just as adjectives qualify other
movements (the environmental movement, the suffragist movement, or the
Occupy Wall Street movement), *modern* and *mission* likewise qualify this
particular nineteenth-century movement with particular meaning and tone
and give it definition. The first adjective, *modern*, places the movement in a
particular period of history, beginning at some point in the sixteenth century,
and characterizes it as shaped by the Enlightenment ideals. *Mission*, on the
other hand, gives the movement a purpose that can be general and un-
determined, but in this case points to the expansion of the Christian religion.
The definite article identifies movement as known and distinguishable, and
thus particular and historical.

As a whole, *the modern mission movement* functions as rhetorical device—
slogan or motto—of a tradition. More than a historical period or ideological
category, the modern mission movement identifies means and intent as
Christians relate to the world. The modern mission movement functions
like any other identity, motto, or slogan, as "an instrument of continuity and
of change, of tradition and of revolution," and thus it is a reminder of the
recent past and a call for a response.[2] In this way, the modern mission

---

[2]Richard McKeon, *Rhetoric: Essays in Invention and Discovery* (Woodbridge, CT: Ox Bow,
1987), 2.

movement structures reality, and maintains and advances specific percep-
tions and values for individuals and the church. While significance can be
found in each of the three words (*modern, mission, movement*), taken
together they offer a distinct concept that frames identity and cause.

At some point early in the nineteenth century, the modern mission
movement appeared, or one might more accurately say the rhetoric of "the
modern mission movement" came into use. The use of the four words
brought into being the idea of a constituted set of characteristics that designated a particular cause. Who first joined these words together or what
events gave rise to their use is difficult to determine. The first appearance
of the phrase in print coincides with the centenary celebration of the
founding of the Baptist Missionary Society. Louis A. Banks in an article
published in 1889 for *Zion's Herald* describes the modern mission movement
as "a century plant" and locates its origins in the "agitation" of William
Carey.[3] The following year, Oswald Dykes, in an article titled "The Modern
Mission Movement," celebrates the force and labor of the movement begun
with Carey and notes that the idea is still progressing with "sobriety" and
"improved position." He explains that the "century of toil has been worthily
spent, is plainly sub-structural work, valuable mainly for the use of it, a
laying of deep foundations on which Providence must mean us and ours
sons to build strongly."[4] In other words, a century of modern mission labor
laid a firm foundation for the movement, on which progress could then
build and grow. Two years later, in 1892, the phrase appeared once again in
reference to the mission efforts of modern Baptists.[5] In all three instances,
the phrase refers to a movement one hundred years old, initiated with the
founding of the Baptist Missionary Society, and marked by the departure
of William Carey from England for the distant shores of India.

By 1927, Baptist historian Henry C. Vedder regarded "the real beginning
of the modern missionary movement" with English Baptists.[6] In similar
fashion, British Baptist historian Ernest A. Payne characterizes the history

---

[3]Louis Albert Banks, "Carey's Missionary World and Ours," *Zion's Herald (1868–1910)*, October 16,
1889, 330.
[4]J. Oswald Dykes, "The Modern Missionary Movement," *Baptist Missionary Magazine (1873–1909)*,
February 1890, 38.
[5]"Baptist Foreign Mission Centenary," *Berrow's Worcester Journal*, September 24, 1892, 3.
[6]Henry C. Vedder, *A Short History of Baptist Missions* (Philadelphia: Judson, 1927), 28.

of British Baptist mission effort as "the story of the modern missionary movement." While Payne admits that there were forerunners to the movement in the persons of Frances Xavier, John Eliot, David Brainerd, Moravians, and John Wesley, these were only foreshadows of what was to come in the Baptist Missionary Society. He makes clear that it was with Carey and the formation of the Baptist Society for Propagating the Gospel Among the Heathens that the modern mission movement began.[7] Leon McBeth identifies Carey's booklet, *An Enquiry into the Obligations of Christians to use means for the Conversion of the Heathen* (1792), as "the charter of the modern missionary movement."[8] Another modern Baptist historian, William R. Estep, notes while others may have contributed to a growing missionary awareness and progenitors certainly exist, such as the Moravians, the modern mission movement commenced with Carey, specifically on October 2, 1792, at the formation of a society with the intent of sending Baptist missionaries.[9] While Baptist historians locate the inauguration of the modern mission movement narrowly with British Baptists, others have made the same assessment.[10]

Not only were Baptists placed at the head of the modern mission movement, but William Carey was named as its father. Carey was certainly not the first to make an appeal for "mission" in sermons and writings, nor was he the first to call for the formation of a missionary society, nor was he the first Protestant to actually be sent on a mission endeavor, and yet, Carey is almost universally recognized as the "Father of the Modern Mission

---

[7]Title page, Ernest A. Payne, *The Church Awakes: The Story of the Modern Missionary Movement* (London: Carey, 1942).

[8]Leon McBeth, *The Baptist Heritage* (Nashville: Broadman, 1987), 185.

[9]William R. Estep, *Whole Gospel—Whole World: The Foreign Mission Board of the Southern Baptist Convention, 1845–1995* (Nashville: Broadman & Holman, 1994), notes, "The year 1792 marks the birth of the modern mission movement, a movement whose time had come" (9). Ernest A. Payne, "Introduction," in *An Enquiry into the Obligations of Christians to Use Means* (London: Carey Kingsgate, 1961), claims that "the modern era of the missionary expansion of the Christian Church may be conveniently dated from 1792" (i).

[10]Lucius E. Smith (1822–1900), early biographer and historian of Christian missions, agrees. See *Heroes and Martyrs of the Modern Missionary Enterprise: A Record of Their Lives and Labors* (Providence, RI: Potter, 1856), 26. See also *HCM*, 222; William Richey Hogg, *Ecumenical Foundations: A History of the International Missionary Council and Its Nineteenth Century Background* (New York: Harper & Brothers, 1952), 8.

Movement."[11] Those who give Carey this designation are usually English speakers and Protestants, and thus want to identify Carey and the Baptist Society as the genesis of the mission movement with which they are associated.[12] Some claim that lesser-known, non-English-speaking individuals rather than Carey should be placed at the head of the modern mission movement.[13] For example, Daniel Jeyaraj names Bartholomaus Ziegenbalg (1683–1719) and Heinrich Plütschau (1677–1746), who arrived in India in 1706, as the first Protestant missionaries and thus the originators of the modern mission movement.[14] He goes as far as to say that it is a historical error to name Carey as the father of modern Protestant missions, and that Ziegenbalg, "the true father of modern Protestant missionary movement," should bear this title.[15] Arno Lehmann in particular takes issue with the dating of Protestant missions to the arrival of William Carey and John Thomas in India in 1793. In a slim volume commemorating the 250th anniversary of Danish-Halle Mission, Lehmann chronicles the repeated omission of Ziegenbalg and Plütschau in mission accounts and histories, and seeks to rectify this

---

[11]Jeffrey Cox, *The British Missionary Enterprise Since 1700*, Christianity and Society in the Modern World (New York: Routledge, 2008), maintains, "The arguments Carey used were by the 1790s familiar ones, designed to combat the entrenched opinion that missionary enterprises were not timely, that God had yet to open the appropriate providential doors, and that much more work should be done to Christianize Great Britain before wasting scarce resources overseas" (70).

[12]William A. Smalley, *Translation as Mission: Bible Translation in the Modern Missionary Movement* (Macon, GA: Mercer University Press, 1991), 41. A. Christopher Smith, "William Carey, 1761–1834: Protestant Pioneer of the Modern Mission Era," in *Mission Legacies: Biographical Studies of Leaders of the Modern Missionary Movement*, American Society of Missiology Series 19 (Maryknoll, NY: Orbis Books, 1994), judges that poserity has saluted Carey "rather inaccurately as 'the father of modern missions' " because of the need "to co-opt him as a heroic figurehead for the revitalization of missions in the 'modern era' " (245). Andrew F. Walls, "The Eighteenth-Century Protestant Missionary Awakening in Its European Context," in *Christian Missions and the Enlightenment*, ed. Brian Stanley, Studies in the History of Christian Missions (Grand Rapids: Eerdmans, 2001), states that "the Protestant missionary awakening did not begin in 1792 or anywhere near that date. What happened in that period was British entry into a well-established continental tradition. This was, indeed, no insignificant event" (34).

[13]See *HCM*, 222; J. Herbert Kane, *A Global View of Christian Missions from Pentecost to the Present*, (Grand Rapids: Baker Book House, 1985), 109; Andrew Porter, *Religion Versus Empire? British Protestant Missionaries and Overseas Expansion, 1700–1914* (Manchester, UK: Manchester University Press, 2004), 15-28.

[14]Samuel H. Moffett, *A History of Christianity in Asia*, vol. 2, *1500–1900* (Maryknoll, NY: Orbis Books), 238.

[15]Daniel Jeyaraj, *Bartholomäus Ziegenbalg, the Father of Modern Protestant Mission: An Indian Assessment* (Delhi: Indian Society for Promoting Christian Knowledge, 2006), 1-2, 9.

historical inaccuracy.[16] Likewise, the Moravians, based at Herrnhut on the estate of Count Zinzendorf, who began sending members of their community in the 1730s, sixty years before Carey, would seem to qualify for the distinction of initiating the "modern world-wide Missionary Movement."[17] And the title is not just contested among Protestants but Catholics as well. Catholic historian Hilarin Felder asserts that St. Francis is "the father of the modern missionary movement."[18] Catholic historian Joseph Schmidlin marks the founding of the mendicant orders as the beginning of the modern mission movement.[19]

If the question of the beginning of the modern mission movement is a matter of rhetoric, then none of these early pioneers, including William Carey, are its father, as none claimed this distinction for themselves or used the phrase.[20] The modern mission movement is an invented tradition, a rhetorical construction. It represents a metaphorical retrospective on Protestant mission endeavors of the eighteenth and nineteenth century. At some point in the later part of the nineteenth century, ideas and activities coalesced into the notion of a movement that was both missionary and modern, and thus, the modern mission movement came to designate the way in which modern Christians described the encounter with the world beyond Europe and America. The phrase has stretched into present-day use in such a manner that it has become a modern Protestant tradition.

A MODERN TRADITION

Historian Eric Hobsbawm defines "invented tradition" as "a set of practices, normally governed by overtly or tacitly accepted rules and of a ritual or symbolic nature, which seek to inculcate certain values and norms of

---

[16]E. Arno Lehmann, *It Began at Tranquebar: The Story of the Tranquebar Mission and the Beginnings of Protestant Christianity in India Published to Celebrate the 250th Anniversary of the Landing of the First Protestant Missionaries at Tranquebar in 1706* (Madras, India: Christian Literature Society on behalf of the Federation of Evangelical Lutheran Churches in India, 1956), 15-16.

[17]A. J. Lewis, "Count Zinzendorf," *London Quarterly and Holborn Review* 185 (April 1960): 128; Jacob John Sessler, *Communal Pietism Among Early American Moravians* (New York: AMS, 1971), 225.

[18]Hilarin Felder, *The Ideals of St. Francis of Assisi*, trans. Berchmans Bittle (New York: Benziger Brothers, 1925), 316.

[19]Joseph Schmidlin, *Catholic Mission History*, ed. Matthias Braun (Techny, IL: Mission Press, S. V. D, 1933), 254-56.

[20]Moffett, *History of Christianity in Asia*, 2:253.

behaviour by repetition, which automatically implies continuity with the past."[21] What might appear to be an ancient or primal tradition is, in fact, recent in origin and oftentimes invented. Hobsbawm notes constructed traditions in architecture, festivals, ceremonies, and institutions, each invented and then solemnly or joyously acknowledged over and over in order to establish continuity with the past. His primary interest is with the invented tradition or innovation of "nation," with its accompanying nationalism represented in symbols, rituals, and history. Despite his emphasis on the creation of national symbols and imagery, Hobsbawm's notion of an invented tradition could easily include the modern mission movement.[22]

The modern mission movement as metaphorical language aptly describes a modern tradition—a shorthand symbol for a host of events, people, ideas, and emotions. Through shared experience and the communication of the phrase, the modern mission movement has become the ground of understanding that serves as a way of organizing reality and translates aims into specific actions. Thus, while the modern mission movement refers to historical events, it is less than a historical occurrence or an actual movement. It includes specific people and groups of people who travel to faraway places and perform certain activities, and yet, the phrase does not refer to a specific place or actual event and has no originator or founder. The modern mission movement functions somewhat like a belief. As a belief, it sustains convictions that cause thousands of individuals to structure reality in a particular manner and to such an extent that they expend finances, leave home and family to take up residence in another culture, and give their lives for the cause. As a metaphor, "the modern mission movement" provides modern organizations with imagery and ethos for programs of work, as well as a means to recruit personnel and raise funds. The modern mission movement connects people and organizations to a defining ideology that forms the basis for collective belief and action.

---

[21]Eric Hobsbawm, "Introduction: Inventing Traditions," in *The Invention of Traditions*, ed. Eric Hobsbawm and Terence Ranger, Past and Present Publications (Cambridge: Cambridge University Press, 1983), 1.

[22]Among the chapters in Eric Hobsbawm and Terence Ranger's anthology, *Invention of Tradition*, are "The Invention of Tradition: The Highland Tradition of Scotland," "Representing Authority in Victorian India," and "The Invention of Tradition in Colonial Africa."

Hobsbawm delineates the characteristics of three overlapping types of invented traditions: "a) those establishing or symbolizing social cohesion or the membership of groups, real or artificial communities, b) those establishing or legitimizing institutions, status or relations of authority, and c) those whose main purpose was socialization, the inculcating of beliefs, value systems and conventions of behaviour."[23] While these types can express ritualized and repeated behaviors or practices, invented traditions are chiefly ideological. For example, Hobsbawm cites American patriotism and school spirit as examples of ideas surrounded by and ritualized in an array of symbols, music, and practices. In a similar manner, the modern mission movement is an ideology that offers "social cohesion," has established "institutions," and inculcates "beliefs, value systems and conventions of behaviour."

Social cohesion occurs as the symbols, music, and practices of mission reinforce its institutions and prescribe beliefs, values, and behaviors. Key ideas and devices contribute to the invention of the modern mission tradition. First and foremost, the modern mission tradition finds justification in ideas from Scripture. More than just the notion of mission as the Great Commission, the apparatus, techniques, institutions, and organizations of the modern mission movement are justified by reference to biblical figures and Scripture passages and themes. As demonstrated in chapter two, interpreters from a range of denominational and confessional perspectives construct justifications for the modern mission movement by way of biblical foundations and themes.

Second, among the symbols of the modern mission movement are exemplary persons. Such heroic individuals as William Carey, Henry Martyn, Hudson Taylor, and Lottie Moon embody the values and spirit of the movement. The founding acts of the movement can be found in the imagery of young William Carey at his cobbler's bench with leather maps of the world on the walls and at the meeting of ministers at Kettering where Carey delivered his sermon. These lives and their actions have grown to mythological proportions, providing a powerful narrative for many of the beliefs of the tradition. The founding of mission societies, mission schools, mission stations,

---

[23]Hobsbawm, "Introduction: Inventing Traditions," 9.

and the legacy of missionary clergy and priests serve to bolster the tradition. In order to justify the place of these components in the tradition, each has continuity in some measure with the biblical narrative and evidence of their practice in the New Testament era. Central to the support and strength of the tradition is the construction and maintenance of a founding narrative based in Scripture but connected to modern figures and institutions.

Third, the invented tradition is more than its modern heroic figures, such as Zinzendorf and Carey. It is built on a line of progenitors, represented in individuals and groups, that can be traced back through the medieval period and Constantine to the early church and Paul. Thus, as noted in chapter three, Patrick, Boniface, and the Nestorians are presented as precursors of the modern mission movement. This historical lineage is meant to parallel and validate the professional, full-time, career missionary in the modern tradition, as well as their methods. Nineteenth-century mission literature chronicles their lives and substantiates the portrayal of "missionary" as an established tradition.[24] The effect, as with any invented tradition, is to create an identity and rally support for the modern movement.

Fourth, mission magazines and journals, mission biographies, and popular mission histories are public monuments to the movement's founders, exemplars, and heroes. The study of these publications by women and children's groups, in churches and societies, as well as by families at home, reinforces themes and ideas and advances the narrative of the movement. In addition, these impart the tradition to potential supporters and practitioners.[25]

Fifth, funding mission through pledges and offerings provides opportunity for wide voluntary participation and thus a low threshold for "joining" the movement. No matter how small the amount or infrequent the contribution, participation in the cause can occur for anyone. One of the functions of the growing number of societies in the modern era was to provide forums for wide participation in the modern mission movement via small,

---

[24]Jeffrey Cox and Shelton Stromquist list what they considers to be key mission texts that contribute to this professionalization for English readers: Jeffrey Cox and Shelton Stromquist, "Introduction: Master Narratives and Social History," in *Contesting the Master Narrative: Essays in Social History*, ed. Jeffrey Cox and Shelton Stromquist (Iowa City: University of Iowa Press, 1998), 6.

[25]For the role of "missionary magazines" in fomenting public sentiment, see Andrew F. Walls, *The Missionary Movement in Christian History: Studies in the Transmission of Faith* (Maryknoll, NY: Orbis Books, 1996), 251-52.

incremental giving. The act of giving reinforces the educational process of instilling the tenets and history of the tradition.

Sixth, mission conferences are platforms to recite the progress and triumphs of the modern mission movement and thus reinforce the tradition's narrative. The mission enthuses those present, flags of nations line the walls and stage, and tales of exploits and victories are recounted. In this manner, speakers and organizers promote tenets of the movement and reinforce solidarity with its participants. Toward the end of the nineteenth century, a host of student or general mission conferences were held with increasing regularity.[26]

Seventh, the modern mission tradition establishes an alternative narrative. The modern mission movement is read by most as "modern Protestant missions." The narrative of modern mission tradition highlights the expansion of Protestantism in the modern era, and thereby the modern mission movement is glossed as a Protestant movement over against that of Catholics and Orthodox. The article on the modern era of mission in *The Encyclopedia of Missions: Descriptive, Historical, Biographical, Statistical* (1904) is titled "Modern Protestant Missions." There are no articles on modern Catholic or Orthodox missions, as modern mission is considered to be distinctively Protestant. Thus, the modern mission tradition is established as a distinct Protestant version of mission whose legacy stretches back to the New Testament era.[27] This gives a reasonable and vibrant defense for Protestant mission over against that of Catholic mission.

Finally, watchwords and slogans encapsulate the spirit of the mission tradition in compact, pithy statements. Somewhat like flags that symbolize new states and republics, these watchwords and slogans represent and continually reinforce the ideals of the mission tradition. They are images that need

---

[26]For example, Conference on Mission, Liverpool, 1860; Student Volunteer Movement for Foreign Missions 1886, 1888, 1891; Ecumenical Conference on Mission, New York, 1900; International Conference of the Student Volunteer Missionary Union, London, 1900; Convention for the Laymen's Missionary Movement, Birmingham, AL, 1909. See H. C. Ostrom, ed., *The Modern Crusade: Addresses and Proceedings of the First General Convention of the Laymen's Missionary Movement, Presbyterian Church in the U.S., Birmingham, Ala., Feb. 16–18, 1909* (Athens: Laymen's Missionary Movement, 1909); *Students and the Missionary Problem: Addresses Delivered at the International Student Missionary Conference, London, January 2–6, 1900* (London: Student Volunteer Missionary Union, 1900).

[27]*The Encyclopedia of Missions: Descriptive, Historical, Biographical, Statistical*, 2nd edition (New York: Funk & Wagnalls, 1904).

no explanation and easily evoke an emotional response for the tradition. They remind participants of the history of the movement, and they also project a future narrative of progress and ultimate success. The watchwords of the Student Volunteer Movement, "The Evangelization of the World in This Generation," and of the World Missionary Conference, Edinburgh, "World Evangelization in our Generation," communicated that the fulfillment of the tradition was possible and even imminent.

Mission as a modern tradition, expressed in the language of the modern mission movement, was a retrospective creation, solidified by the end of the nineteenth century through the work of a growing number of mission societies for men, women, and children, propagated in mission conferences, and disseminated through printed mission materials. By the opening of the twentieth century, the modern mission movement was firmly fixed as a Protestant tradition and represented the new orthodoxy. Justification of "mission" is a modern phenomenon motivated by the need to substantiate this modern tradition. Through the constructed narrative of mission history, the modern mission movement is both established and sustained. In reading Scripture through the "missional lens," the modern mission movement is made into sacred language. In the face of Catholic accusations, the modern Protestant mission movement establishes a legacy rooted in the early church and the Bible. As a sustained and promoted tradition, the modern mission movement offers Protestant identity and purpose as they encounter the world.

Robert Speer, secretary of the American Presbyterian Mission, spoke directly to the significance of the modern mission movement at the International Conference of the Student Volunteer Missionary Union in 1900. In his address, "What the Movement Means," he explains that the movement and its watchword means "nothing hasty, immature, or ill-judged." For Speer, it meant that he turned "from law to the missionary life." Speer reassured the student mission volunteers that the movement to which they were committing themselves was "the calmest, quietest, deepest, most purposeful, spiritual blessing of our lives."[28] Speer believed the movement to be an idea whose day had arrived. It symbolized the struggle of Christianity over other religions and against world forces and signaled its eventual victory. Speer's

---

[28]Robert E. Speer, "What This Movement Means," in *Students and the Missionary Problem*, 187, 188.

sentiments regarding the power and vitality of symbols, rituals, and tradition of the modern mission movement reached their zenith ten years later
at the World Missionary Conference at Edinburgh, Scotland. By the time
the conference convened in 1910, *mission* was thoroughly entrenched
rhetoric for Protestants and heralded by the conferees as the answer to the
world situation.

THE MISSIONARY PROBLEM

More than twelve hundred delegates from church traditions and societies
across Western Protestantism gathered at Edinburgh, Scotland, in 1910 for
what was the latest and the most substantial of conferences, dating back to
1854.[29] Other conferences were larger and even broader in scope, but they
were prelude to the grand gathering at Edinburgh. Though ecumenical in
spirit, the conference was predominantly male and Euro-American with only
a handful of representatives from Asia, Africa, and Latin America. Absent
were delegates from the Catholic and Greek churches and the Catholic missionary orders. From across the broad spectrum of Protestant doctrine,
worship, and polity, pastors, church leaders, and missionaries came to Edinburgh to talk about one matter—mission.[30] Mission was not only the subject
for the twelve hundred delegates but the central concern of ministers and
missionaries from across the world and hundreds of correspondents whose
contributions formed the reports of the conference's eight commissions.

The Edinburgh Conference is often noted as a turning point in Christian
history for a number of reasons. Chief among these is that it was the high
point of the modern mission movement and a benchmark for mission
rhetoric in the twentieth century.[31] In the opening address to the conference,

---

[29]Brian Stanley, "The World Missionary Conference, Edinburgh 1910: Sifting History from Myth,"
in *Walk Humbly with the Lord: Church and Mission Engaging Plurality*, ed. Viggo Mortensen and
Andreas Østerlund Nielsen (Grand Rapids: Eerdmans, 2010), 17; Porter, *Religion Versus Empire?*,
300-306.

[30]In the opening address of the conference, Lord Balfour states, "It is not to be forgotten that as a
Conference we express no opinion, we enter into no debate on any matter of doctrine or of
Church government on which we differ." "Opening Address," in *World Missionary Conference,
1910: The History and Records of the Conference Together with Addresses Delivered at the Evening
Meetings* (Edinburgh: Oliphant, Anderson, & Ferrier, 1910), 9:143. Hereafter cited as *WMC*.

[31]For assessment of the significance of the Edinburgh Conference, see *HCM*, 332-34; Hogg, *Ecumenical Foundations*, 98-142; W. H. T. Gairdner, *Echoes from Edinburgh, 1910: An Account and
Interpretation of the World Missionary Conference* (New York: Fleming H. Revell, 1910); Brian

Lord Balfour of Burleigh (1849–1921), former secretary of state for Scotland, signaled the theme and tone of the gathering. In his estimation, the conference was "no small and unimportant gathering," as people from all over the world "drawing together now as perhaps we have never been drawn together, in the persecution of the great enterprise in which we are all interested."[32] He pled for unity in the midst of obvious diversity in order that they might undertake one central obligation in response to the opportunities before them. The archbishop of Canterbury, Randall Davidson (1848–1930), followed Lord Balfour and emphasized the necessity of obedience in the presence of such an unparalleled event in human history. Just as Balfour pled for unity in face of obligation and opportunity, the archbishop insisted that "among the duties and privileges which are ours in the Church of Christ, the place which belongs of right to missionary work is the central place of all."[33] The reports and addresses that followed Balfour and Davidson named mission as the obligation above all other obligations, and missionary work as the ultimate task. In Davidson's words, the missionary work of the modern mission movement stood above all other matters and "ought to loom largest" among the many convictions one might have. "The place of missions in the life of the Church must be the central place, and none other. That is what matters."[34] John R. Mott (1865–1955), the chief organizer and chair of the conference, proclaimed to the delegates that mission was a modern enterprise whose time had come.

The chief agenda of Edinburgh was to buttress the validity and place of mission. Addresses and reports were forceful partisan pronouncements of and arguments for mission. Speaker after speaker justified and historicized mission as more than just right or proper but as a mandated obligation. Presenters declared Paul, Barnabas, and Jesus as missionaries, involved in

---

Stanley, *The World Missionary Conference, Edinburgh 1910*, Studies in the History of Christian Missions (Grand Rapids: Eerdmans, 2009), 303-24; Stephen B. Bevans, "From Edinburgh to Edinburgh: Toward a Missiology for a World Church," in *Mission After Christendom: Emergent Themes in Contemporary Mission*, ed. Obgu U. Kalu, Peter Vethanayagamony, and Edmund Kee-Fook Chia (Louisville: Westminster John Knox, 2010), 1-11; Scott Sunquist, *Understanding Christian Mission: Participation in Suffering and Glory* (Grand Rapids: Baker Academic, 2013), 116-23. George Robson, "History of the Conference," in *WMC*, goes as far to say that "never has there been such a gathering in the history of the Kingdom of God on earth" (9:18).

[32]Balfour, "Opening Address," in *WMC*, 9:142.

[33]Randall Davidson, "The Central Place of Missions in the Life of the Church," in *WMC*, 9:147.

[34]Ibid., 147, 150.

missionary labor, work, and preaching. According to W. H. Frere, Augustine was a missionary, monastic institutions were part of "Mediæval Missions," Boniface was a "missionary hero," and St. Francis's approach to the sultan was an example of missionary method.[35] Speakers characterized the New Testament as a missionary document and historicized mission as an early church and medieval reality.[36] More than justified or historicized, mission was theologized. "God is the great Missioner," and thus mission is a divine enterprise.[37] Edinburgh was certainly the high point for mission rhetoric and established the pattern for how Partisans in the years following would mobilize personnel and resources for the mission endeavor.

Mission defined every aspect of Christian life and work, and thus mission saturated the language of Edinburgh. From beginning to end, mission language dominated the addresses, reports, and correspondence of the conference. *Mission* and *missionary* modified ideas and concepts, qualified activities and actors, and quantified aims and objectives. The answer to the "modern missionary situation" was mission or missionary work (endeavor, effort, service, or labor) undergirded by a wide and varied list of actors, entities, actions, and arenas, all qualified by the *missionary* adjective.[38] Persons, activities, and organizations were to be viewed from the "missionary

---

[35]W. H. Frere, "Mediæval Missions in the Bearing on Modern Missions," in *WMC*, 9:187, 190, 192.

[36]See H. A. A. Kennedy, "The Missions of the Early Church in Their Bearing on Modern Missions," in *WMC*, 9:174, 175, 178.

[37]*WMC*, 1:351.

[38]The list of persons, entities, actions, and arenas qualified by *missionary* in the addresses and reports seems to be endless: missionary force, missionary leaders, special missionary training, missionary physicians, missionary evangelists, missionary preachers and teachers, missionary staff, missionary correspondents, missionary heroes, missionary advocates, mission doctors, missionary specialists, missionary vocations, missionary calls, missionary institutions, missionary property, missionary organizations, missionary schools and colleges, missionary churches, mission centers, mission stations, missionary propaganda, mission history, missionary census, missionary investigations, missionary writings, missionary opinions, missionary efforts, missionary knowledge, missionary answers, missionary influence, missionary provisions, missionary equipment, missionary expansion, missionary methods, missionary strategy, missionary approaches, missionary instruments, missionary testimony, missionary sermons, missionary ministrations, missionary auspices, missionary development, mission presses, missionary boards and societies, missionary agencies, missionary bodies, missionary counsels, missionary circles, missionary devotion, missionary spirit, missionary zeal, missionary enthusiasm, missionary impulse, missionary-hearted men, missionary study circles, missionary instinct, missionary duties, missionary care, missionary resources, missionary polity, missionary comity, missionary programs, missionary contributions, missionary purposes, missionary operations, missionary campaigns, missionary occupation, mission territories, missionary outposts, mission areas, mission fields, and the missionary enterprise.

point of view" or the "missionary position," in the hope that their labor might not be hindered by "missionary apathy" or "missionary neglect." The ultimate hope was for "missionary progress," "missionary successes," "missionary results," and "missionary movements." For the Edinburgh delegates, mission language fit every situation, countered each question, and framed every response. As adjectives, *mission* and *missionary* modified everything imaginable: "missionary money," "missionary standards," "missionary intelligence," "missionary direction," "missionary buildings," "missionary exhibitions," "missionary questions," and "missionary litany." Mission language filled the conference hall—the foreign missionary was the agent, the mission field was the context, and the missionary message was the means. For the delegates at Edinburgh, mission was the idea whose time had come, the emblem of right belief, and the language of the faithful— the Christian tradition.

Central to the concerns of the addresses and reports from the eight commissions was the "missionary problem." This curious phrase was not unique to Edinburgh but appeared both before and after the conference. The phrase is found in the title of publications leading up to the Edinburgh Conference and the years following: *The Missionary Problem* (1883), *The Missionary Problem—Home and Foreign—and Its Solution* (1896), *Students and the Missionary Problem* (1900), *The Key to the Missionary Problem* (1901), *The Missionary Problem and the Denial of Christ in Christendom* (1911), *The Real Heart of the Missionary Problem* (1915), and *Islam in India as Modern Mission Problem* (1917).[39]

Reports, addresses, and discussions at Edinburgh refer continually to the missionary problem.[40] The subtitle to the nine-volume report of the

---

[39]James Croil, *The Missionary Problem: Containing a History of Protestant Missions in Some of the Principal Fields of Missionary Enterprise, Together with a Historical and Statistical Account of the Rise and Progress of Missionary Societies in the Nineteenth Century* (Toronto: William Briggs, 1883); William Crosbie, *The Missionary Problem—Home and Foreign—and Its Solution. Thoughts on an Ancient Missionary Prayer* (Nottingham, UK: E. H. Lee, 1896); *Students and the Missionary Problem*; Andrew Murray, *Key to the Missionary Problem*, ed. Leona F. Choy (Fort Washington, PA: Christian Literature Crusade, 1979); R. H. Glover, *The Real Heart of the Missionary Problem* (New York: Christian and Missionary Alliance, 1915). See also Peter Beyerhaus, *Die Selbständigkeit der jungen Kirchen als missionarisches Problem*, Studia missionalia Upsaliensia (Barmen: Wuppertal, 1956).

[40]See *WMC*, 1:3, 47, 114-16, 137, 204; 3:2, 135; 4:27, 71, 72, 250; 8:120. There are variations on this phrase: "problems of missions" (2:37), "missionary problem of the church" (1:47), "the whole

conference commissions and addresses states Edinburgh's aim was "to consider Missionary Problems in relation to the Non-Christian World."
Volume four states the intent of the conference was "to study the problems
involved in the presentation of Christianity to the minds of the non-
Christian peoples."[41] The language of *missionary problem* points to two
beliefs of the delegates at the conference. First, the missionary problem did
not mean *mission* and *missionary* were problems. In fact, mission was seen
as separate or beyond the problems of the world. The missionary represented the progress and advancement of Christendom, and practitioners
of non-Christian religions and natives were the problems because of their
backward and pagan ways. Missionaries were mildly criticized for flaws in
character and incompetence, but mission was beyond critique. While
mission was steadfastly justified, lukewarm churches and unrepentant
Western representatives of corporations and governments were cited as
among the impediments that hindered mission.

Second, the missionary problem was the way of talking about the task.
Problems hindered the progress of world evangelization, and thus the key
was to remedy these through missionary endeavors. Competing religions,
societal ills, and unbelief were the missionary problems to be confronted
with mission answers (activities, resources, strategies, devotion, zeal, and
spirit). The solution was missionary in scope and nature rather than ecclesial
or theological. In the spirit of the Enlightenment, all problems were solvable
through the missionary enterprise.[42] And yet, in distinction to the Enlightenment, the solution did not lie in science, education, and technology alone
but had to be accompanied by missionaries utilizing these modern means.

The missionary problem explains the intent of Edinburgh. Whatever hindered the mission movement and its progress was the problem, and thus the
concern of Edinburgh was to name and counter these with the missionary
unfettered, supported, and empowered. The missionary problem defined
pockets of resistance that needed to be solved before there could be

---

missionary problem" (5:4), and "the great world missionary problem" (6:19). The reports, discussions, and addresses are full of the language of "obstacles" (1:265), "hindrances" (4:12, 42), and
"world problems" (3:303).
[41]Ibid., 4:1.
[42]The aim of the recommendations was to consider "the problem before us" (*WMC*, 5:12) and solve
it (1:287).

missionary advance. As mission was certain, and world evangelization was assumed, the goal of Edinburgh was to identify the problems and advance the mission endeavor through more missionaries, more resources, and more devotion. These problems could be overcome by missionary conquest, occupation, and triumph.

Missionary conquest. The missionary problem was to be solved by missionary work, described in language that was militaristic in tone and actual words. The archbishop of Canterbury opened the conference with language reminiscent of early Jesuits. He addressed the delegates as "Fellow-workers in the Church Militant, the Society of Christ on earth."[43] Robert Speer of the American Presbyterian Mission spoke of "foes who are to be vanquished" and the victory to come.[44] Professor H. A. A. Kennedy of Edinburgh University characterized the missionary task as "a campaign among heathen peoples."[45] Reports and addresses were full of language of missionary forces, foes being vanquished, occupying territories, and conquering enemies: battle, victory, campaign, operations, missionary forces, army, reinforcements, invasion, weapons, and conquest.[46] The mission endeavor as a military campaign was not merely implied; the connection was direct and explicit. Missionaries were compared to "infantry, artillery, the engineer corps."[47] The problem of world evangelization was described as "'the far-flung battle line' of the army of God" that was "at many points a perilously slender line."[48] Though R. F. Horton, Congregationalist minister at Hampstead, spoke on "the sufficiency of God," the "insufficiency of man," and the inability of the church, he concluded his address with the assertion that the delegates "were called together in Edinburgh to take steps to move on the Army of Christ for the Conquest of the World."[49] The conference, Brian Stanley observes, was heralded as "an evangelical crusade . . . evoking the distant memory of the Medieval Crusades."[50] The delegates were addressed repeatedly as "representatives

---

[43]Davidson, "The Central Place of Missions in the Life of the Church," in *WMC*, 9:146. In these words, one hears the papal bull establishing the Jesuits.
[44]Robert E. Speer, "Christ the Leader of the Missionary Work of the Church," in *WMC*, 9:154.
[45]Kennedy, "Missions of the Early Church," 173.
[46]*WMC*, 1:11, 42, 80, 128, 420; 2:198, 214; 4:214; 5:97, 170; 6:121.
[47]Ibid., 1:299.
[48]Ibid., 1:288.
[49]R. F. Horton, "The Sufficiency of God," in *WMC*, 9:339, 341.
[50]Stanley, *World Missionary Conference, Edinburgh 1910*, 5-6.

of the Church Militant," and personnel on various fields were referred to as "missionary forces."[51] David Bosch describes Edinburgh's use of mission as "undisputed power. Mission stood in the sign of world conquest. Missionaries were referred to as 'soldiers,' as Christian 'forces.' . . . Military metaphors such as 'army,' 'crusade,' 'council of war,' 'conquest,' 'advance,' 'resources,' and 'marching order' abounded."[52] Victory in the battle was assured as long as the missionary problems were addressed with sufficient force.

In the language of conquest, the modern mission movement carried with it the legacy of Western expansion. This expansion was the history and spirit that formed mission and continued to inform the delegates at Edinburgh.[53] W. A. Visser 't Hooft, first general secretary of the World Council of Churches, observed, "The 'Vasco da Gama era' of Western expansion was still going strong" at Edinburgh.[54] John R. Mott summarized this sentiment clearly in the conference's final address. He closed with the pronouncement, "The end of the conference is the beginning of the Conquest. The end of the planning is the beginning of the Doing."[55] In the rhetoric of Edinburgh, one hears vestiges of Urban's summons to march on the Holy Land and Ignatius's militia for Christ that conquered for the glory of God. The legacies of aggression and conquest inherent in mission are on public display in the language of Edinburgh.

Mission as conquest continued following the conference, as Mott and others promoted the vision and hope of Edinburgh. Sherwood Eddy, a participant at Edinburgh, offered a retrospective look thirty-five years after the conference from "the far-flung battle line of missions" and characterized the

---

[51]Gairdner, *Echoes from Edinburgh*, 16.

[52]*TM*, 346.

[53]Lesslie Newbigin, *A Word in Season*, observes that "the pattern of the modern missionary movement, its attitudes and methods, were shaped by the fact that missionaries of the modern era . . . were also representatives of the expanding and colonizing races of the West. In this respect the modern missionary movement has been totally different from what we find in the New Testament" (12).

[54]W. A. Visser 't Hooft, "The Asian Churches in the Ecumenical Movement," in *A Decisive Hour for the Christian Mission: The East Asia Christian Conference 1959 and the John R. Mott Memorial Lectures* (London: SCM Press, 1960), 50. David J. Bosch, *Witness to the World: The Christian Mission in Theological Perspective* (Atlanta: John Knox, 1980), indicates that for many "the gradual termination of Western dominance started in the nineteenth century" (5).

[55]Mott, "Closing Address," in *WMC*, 9:347. See also John R. Mott, *Strategic Points in the World's Conquest: The Universities and Colleges as Related to the Progress of Christianity* (New York: Fleming H. Revell, 1897).

task as "nothing less than a missionary crusade." He acknowledged that the Crusades of the eleventh and twelfth centuries were "sordid affairs of slaughter and lust," "a strange mixture of good and evil," but persisted in his depiction of missionaries throughout the ages and pioneers of the mission movement as crusaders and in his call to the present world missionary crusade.[56] Mission for Edinburgh meant the world situation and its problems required the marshaling of the army of God for the conquest of the world.

Missionary occupation. Those at Edinburgh viewed the world as divided into two spheres, Christendom and heathendom.[57] On one side was Christendom, expressed as Western Christian civilization. Europe and America were named as Christendom, from which missionary forces were to be deployed.[58] On the other side was heathendom, represented as backwardness, barbarism, primitiveness, and that which was "ignorant, uncivilized, and warlike."[59] The task of the "missionary societies of Christendom" was to "turn heathendom into Christendom."[60] Entrance into heathendom was spoken of in terms of invasion or a campaign with the ultimate goal of entering these places and occupying them. Addresses and reports classified various parts of heathendom as either occupied or unoccupied. The "unoccupied fields" were the main focus of concern. These places were "sections untouched and not included in any existing scheme of missionary operation," and thus the chief missionary problem.[61] The conference reports listed which places were occupied and which were not. The expressed aim was the occupation of more and more of the unoccupied fields.[62] As in a military campaign, "the efficient occupation of every field must be continually kept in view and striven for until it is accomplished. The disposition of the present available forces should be determined in view of the expected realisation of this ideal."[63]

---

[56]Sherwood Eddy, *Pathfinders of the World Missionary Crusade* (New York: Abingdon-Cokesbury, 1945), 5-7, 11.
[57]For Christendom, see *WMC* 1:11, 25, 242, 286; 2:268; 4:223, 228-29; 5:5, 6, 14, 106; 6:1; 8:10; and for heathendom, see 1:41, 80, 114; 2:211, 234, 235, 254, 261; 4:30.
[58]Ibid., 1:78, 242.
[59]Ibid., 2:241, 244, 260; 4:36; 7:93, 96.
[60]Ibid., 1:297, 424.
[61]Ibid., 1:279.
[62]Ibid., 1:21, 55, 58, 90, 99, 100, 104, 110, 112, 157, 158-60, 177, 181, 184, 196, 227, 229, 232; 2:240; 8:17.
[63]Ibid., 1:295.

Once occupied, the missionary aim was Christianization. Through various aspects of mission activities, the lifeways of the occupied territories and countries would become Christian ways. This meant "the full Christianization of the life of the nation" through education, medicine, improved social conditions, better political systems, and rescue from non-Christian religions. The missionary was "to assist in building up a Christian civilization among backward and half-barbarous races."[64] Proclaiming and civilizing were closely related intentions and actions. Mission thus became part and parcel of disseminating the norms of Western society rather than just the good news announced by a first-century rabbi. Or as stated more directly in the conclusions of one of the conference's commissions, "The evangelization of nations, the Christianizing of empires and kingdoms, is the object before us."[65]

The language of occupation and Christianization is akin to the Latinization of the Levant following the First Crusade and the subjugation of peoples in Spanish and Portuguese colonizing efforts. Outposts of Christian presence meant the establishment of Christendom in the midst of heathendom. National identity and the religion of Christendom were seen as opposing each other. One had to supplant the other. According to Ashley Carus-Wilson of the Church Missionary Society, "We must expect nothing less from God than such an expansion of Christianity as shall result in an expansion of Christendom which will mean Christendom will be nothing less than the whole world."[66] One of the threats to missionary progress identified at Edinburgh was rising nationalism among colonialized people. It was feared that national identity and the revival of ancient religious traditions would harm the progress of the gospel. The answer to this threat was mission, which translated into the occupation and civilization of non-Christian lands and peoples.

Missionary triumph. Hope for world evangelization and boundless optimism were the overwhelming sentiments of Edinburgh. Speakers listed reason after reason for "unparalleled openness" to the gospel and "dazzling

---

[64]Ibid., 5:131.
[65]Ibid., 8:132.
[66]Ibid., 1:425.

opportunities" that were within reach.[67] Fifty years after the fact, Visser 't Hooft notes that

> in 1910 we find therefore the fathers at Edinburgh looking out on a world in which there seemed to be almost unlimited possibilities for the spread of the Gospel. The prestige of Western Christian civilization was high. Christianity did not seem to have any adversaries which could seriously challenge it. All other religions or ideologies appeared to be merely localised forces without missionary perspective. Only Christianity seemed to be a spiritual world-force in the true sense of the term.[68]

The spirit of Edinburgh was one of anticipation and expectation. There was a sense that the mission movement came into existence at a time in history when anything was possible. Confidence ran high in the "triumphant power of the gospel" and the time for the "greatest progress."[69] And yet, delegates were warned that the time to act was at hand as "the present opportunities will pass."[70]

The optimism of Edinburgh was based on what mission societies were doing and could do. When the church was mentioned, it was usually in regard to its laxness and unwillingness to shoulder the mission cause. The church's role was to provide the resources for mission, education for mission, and a context conducive for mission. Mission meant societies and boards, as these entities sent and supported missionaries. *Mission* entered the Protestant vocabulary as an endeavor outside the church, and at the opening of the twentieth century it remained at the margins of the church. This modern arrangement was not new, as the encounter with the world prior to the modern era was governed many times by forces either outside the church or those that gave shape to the church. In the fourth century, the church's encounter with the world shifted from a pilgrim church that existed as minority and martyr to an imperial church located at the center of power, representing the politically sanctioned culture. With Urban's summons to march on Jerusalem, the imperial church became the militant church doing battle with the world. The

---

[67] Ibid., 1:10; 21:186.
[68] Visser 't Hooft, "Asian Churches in the Ecumenical Movement," 51.
[69] *WMC*, 1:40, 41. See also 1:24, 369. Caution against an overly optimistic and triumphant attitude was expressed, especially in regard to the training of missionaries (*WMC*, 5:96-97, 101-4, 216-18, 323-24), but this was definitely a minority voice.
[70] Ibid., 1:23, 403.

church shifted yet again following the First Crusade and the ensuing Age of Discovery and turned into an occupying church. Cultural forces in the early modern period sidelined the Protestant church and located the world encounter in societies. In the modern era, *mission* entered the Protestant vocabulary as a movement alongside and in competition with the church, in many ways dependent on the church and yet separated from it.

Since the modern mission movement proclaimed at Edinburgh was chiefly an encounter between societies and the world located outside the church, *mission* oriented its initiative, operation, and possibilities elsewhere.[71] Colonial aspirations and models of political and commercial endeavors framed how Christianity interacted with the world. In the modern expression of mission, church was auxiliary. Thus, missionary hope and triumph resided in societies, not the church. Mission at Edinburgh meant the triumph of Christianity through societies.

Mission, as expressed at Edinburgh, held vestiges of Urban's summons and Ignatius's vow. Its notions of conquest, occupation, and triumph were from previous eras, dressed in modern garb but motivated by similar aims. Mission was the link between the two eras, and through this language Christendom assumptions of one era are conveyed to the other.[72] In this manner, Ignatius's rhetorical innovation found full expression and reached its logical conclusion at the Edinburgh Mission Conference.

THE PROBLEM OF MISSION

Within two decades of the Edinburgh Mission Conference, the problems *for* mission became the problem *of* mission. While the Edinburgh focus had been on the removal of all barriers that hindered the mission task, a host of factors, including a world war and worldwide financial collapse, soured

---

[71]Andrew Walls, "Eighteenth-Century Protestant Missionary Awakening," notes that the structural changes within Protestantism resulted from "a highly successful form of Christian adaptation to the European Enlightenment. It reconciled the developed consciousness of individual responsibility, so characteristic of Enlightenment thought, with Christian faith, while the development of close fellowship that it fostered among the like-minded provided an antidote to the societal and ecclesial atomization that individualism could produce" (29-30).

[72]Lesslie Newbigin, *The Household of God: Lectures on the Nature of the Church* (London: SCM Press, 1957), observes that "a study of the beginnings of the modern missionary movement shows how strongly this movement was still controlled by the old Christendom idea. Missions were conceived of as the extension of the frontiers of Christendom and the conveyance of the blessings of Christian civilisation to those who had hitherto been without them" (12).

Edinburgh's optimism and called mission into question. Uncertainties regarding mission emerged at the Jerusalem meeting of the International Missionary Council in 1928 and persisted into the next decade. With the financial backing of John D. Rockefeller and at the initiation of a group of prominent laymen, a commission representing seven American denominations formed in 1930 to make "a new and thorough study of the basis and purport of missions and of their operations."[73] William E. Hocking (1873–1966), Harvard philosophy professor, served as chairman of the commission and edited its report, *Re-thinking Mission* (also known as the Laymen's Inquiry). The aim of the commission was no longer to address the problems facing the mission situation but to rethink "mission" itself.

The report of the inquiry cites declining funds and growing indifference as reasons for the need to reappraise mission. Yet, within the pages of the report, other reasons are obvious. The report criticizes various aspects of mission, such as types of tasks undertaken, how these were done, and the competency of personnel and the quality of their work. Rather than promoting mission activity and announcing the imminent triumph of the mission enterprise, the commission reviewed mission's presuppositions and probed the "widest possible consideration of the meaning of the mission enterprise."[74] What delegates at Edinburgh assumed regarding the facts of mission, the commissioners of the Laymen's Inquiry questioned. The problem was no longer the obstacles that stood in the path of the mission enterprise, but "whether these missions ought any longer to go on. And if they were to continue, whether it should be with great change, or little change, or none."[75] The chief question pursued by the commissioners was not about best methods, or a better use of resources, or the eventual triumph of the Christian religion, but the foundation and meaning of mission.

---

[73]*RM*, ix. *Re-thinking Missions*, the summary version of the full report, appeared in 1932, and the complete seven-volume report was published in 1933. For background on the Laymen's Inquiry and assessment of its influence on subsequent mission thinking, see Kenneth Scott Latourette, "Reassessment of W E Hocking's Rethinking Missions After Twenty-Five Years," *International Review of Mission* 46, no. 182 (April 1957): 164-70; Latourette, *A History of the Expansion of Christianity* (Grand Rapids: Zondervan, 1970), 7:51-53. Latourette points out that several of those who had backed the Laymen's Missionary Movement in 1914 were now part of the Laymen's Missionary Inquiry (51). Support for a movement had turned into an inquiry.

[74]*RM*, x.

[75]Ibid., 3.

In their appraisal of mission, the commissioners looked beyond piety and good works to the motives and quality of the missionary. They judged the motives of missionaries to be "not alone legitimate, but in an eminent sense noble."[76] The commissioners observed the character and quality of those serving in mission settings and found many missionaries "of the finest spirit" with "traits of greatness and originality," but others they classified "as misfits, unable to cooperate, running more or less individual ventures, more often than not a discredit to the name of Christianity."[77] Yet, these critiques were peripheral, for something more than an evaluation of the efficacy of particular missionaries was at the heart of the report. Rather than missionaries changing world problems, the totality of mission was evaluated in light of changes in the world situation.

Of the "sweeping changes" across the globe, the commissioners focused on three: "an altered theological outlook, the emergence of a basic world-culture, the rise of nationalism in the East."[78] Mission, the report asserts, must account for the ongoing theological adjustments due to progress in scientific truth and philosophical concepts. Also, mission must accept that many of its services, such as education and health care, were no longer needed, and that mission was no longer the sole provider of these services. And mission must recognize that Western culture and institutions were viewed as defective in light of the Great War and rising nationalism. Common to these changes was the need to uncouple the Christian religion from its alliance with the power and prestige of Western culture. The report indicated that such an uncoupling would occur when missionaries noted Christianity's claims of superiority and its language of conquest and occupation as deficient or misguided.

From their appraisal, the commissioners concluded that the continuance of mission was not "beyond serious question," but they qualified their affirmation with the suggestion that a change in the meaning of

---

[76]Ibid., 12. Of the motives of previous eras, the commissioners reported, "The expansion of Christendom between the fifth and the tenth centuries into the Germanic world was on the whole a semi-political and more than semi-forcible conversion of tribes and peoples: it was the original mass movement. The Catholic missionary orders of the sixteenth century accompanied the explorer-conqueror or preceded him. The Protestant missionary of the eighteenth and nineteenth centuries followed in the wake of trade" (10).

[77]Ibid., 13.

[78]Ibid., 18-23.

mission was needed.[79] First, they redefined mission as the communication of the high spiritual values of Christianity, motivated by the "preparation for the world unity in civilization."[80] The new emphasis would be on world unity, mutual understanding, and a shared civilization rather than merely conversion to the Christian religion. Second, while the tendency of mission organizations and churches was "self-preserving and self-developing in its view of its future functions," the commissioners suggested that mission in its nature should be temporary. Thus, they proposed that mission should transition from a permanent and perpetual occupation to one that is temporary.[81] Thus the call to mission should issue from "the spiritual unity of men and races, the coming of the life of God into the lives of men, and the maturity and full measure of development of individuals and social groups," and not the perpetuation of organizations and their presence in countries.[82] In these changes to the basic understanding of mission, Edinburgh's ideals of conquest, occupation, and triumph were on trial and judged as problematic.

As was the case with the Edinburgh conference, the report of the inquiry and the supplement series are full of mission language. Such language is affirmed at every turn. Yet the difference is that the meaning and sense of *mission* is more than being challenged; this language is being infused with ideas and concepts contrary to addresses and reports at Edinburgh. The Laymen's Inquiry claimed that traditional practices and concepts of Edinburgh belonged to a different time and that new attitudes and ideas were needed for the new era. *Mission* could be retained but must be infused with modern meaning. In some cases, this call for a shift is subtle, and in other cases, it is rather abrupt. The commissioners promoted mission, but as a qualified, more matured mission. The report goes as far to hint that a shift in rhetoric could be forthcoming. "Whether this change in conception of mission should involve a change of name, as to one suggesting the foreign

---

[79]Ibid., 4, 325.
[80]Ibid., 8.
[81]Ibid., 24-26. "We would define this transition, not in terms of retirement nor primarily in terms of 'devolution,' but as a *change from the temporary to the permanent functions* of these representatives of Christianity in foreign lands" (25).
[82]Rufus M. Jones, "The Background and the Objective of Protestant Foreign Missions," in *Laymen's Foreign Missions Inquiry, Regional Reports of the Commission of Appraisal, China* vol. 2 (New York: Harper & Brothers, 1933), xxii.

service of the Church, we need not advise: words will acquire their own connotations."[83] So, while the language of mission remained, its meaning and intent were assessed as inadequate and in need of redefining, putting the whole enterprise in question.

The view of many was that the inquiry was a direct and brazen assault on mission, and thus reaction came from several directions.[84] It was thought that theological liberalism promoted cultural understanding and religious cooperation over a historic understanding of mission, and thus the report undermined the biblical mandate for the mission endeavor. Immediately after its publication, Robert Speer, a participant at Edinburgh, offered a respectful and comprehensive response to the report. He criticized its lack of historical background, absence of biblical treatment, narrow perspective of the world, and theological bias. Speer argued that the report proposed an administrative model that was impossible and a definition of *mission* based in "old Protestant liberalism."[85] In response, Hocking insisted that the report did not have "a theology" but was the result of "a working union of fifteen theologies, conservative and liberal together."[86] He maintained that the

---

[83]*RM*, 27.

[84]See Carl Braaten, *The Flaming Center: A Theology of the Christian Mission* (Philadelphia: Fortress, 1977), 9. It is noteworthy that the same year of *Re-thinking Missions* was published, Karl Barth addressed the Brandenburg Missionary Conference on the topic "Theology and Mission in the Present Time." Barth's new orthodoxy was used to counter aspects of the theology of the Laymen's Inquiry in Hendrik Kraemer's contribution to the 1938 Tambaram Ecumenical Conference, *The Christian Message in a Non-Christian World* (Grand Rapids: Kregel, 1938). Rather than confidence, Kraemer says the church is in crisis (24-25). Rather than continuity with the world of religions, the revelation of God in Jesus Christ is distinct and unique (142-47).

[85]Robert E. Speer, *"Re-thinking Missions" Examined: An Attempt at a Just Review of the Report of the Appraisal Commission of the Laymen's Foreign Mission Inquiry* (New York: Fleming H. Revell, 1933), 29. Speer takes up his theological concerns on 27-36.

[86]William Ernest Hocking, "Introduction," in *Laymen's Foreign Missions Inquiry, Regional Reports of the Commission of Appraisal*, vol. 1, *India-Burma*, ed. Orville A. Perry (New York: Harper & Brothers, 1933), xv, xvi. "The position of the Report toward theology is not the liberalism of the past; it is the Catholicity of the future. It appeals to the conservative to remain conservative in the true sense of the conserving, not of excluding; of holding fast that which is good, not as rejecting spiritual comradeship with those who as yet hold fewer articles of faith. It appeals to the Catholic to broaden and strengthen his catholicity, until it can reunite the shattered fragments of the church of Christ" (xvii). In later works, Hocking argues that mutual understanding and cooperation among the various religious traditions should be promoted in preparation for the coming world society. See Hocking, *Living Religions and a World Faith* (New York: Macmillan, 1940); Hocking, *The Coming World Civilization* (New York: Harper, 1956). Speer, *"Re-thinking Missions" Examined*, 20-21, counters that the report is not a laymen's report but the report mainly of two philosophers.

report merely presented obvious facts concerning the church and the world and called for obvious action.

The commissioners' attempt to reconcile modernist trends with realities in the world set in motion a redefinition of mission in keeping with these trends. They did not discard the language but updated it to include much more. The report declared rather pointedly, "The preliminary stage of Protestant missions . . . is past: a new stage is opening."[87] Practices of the past, such as political involvement, conquest, and church enlargement, were noted and appraised as inadequate. These practices were judged as abuses, and thus mission needed to be rehabilitated. The commissioners insisted that if mission was to survive in the modern era, it must adapt to the transitions under way in society and the church. In retrospect, the Laymen's Inquiry was more than an attempt to modernize mission—it set in motion three responses to mission rhetoric that are current today.

The Edinburgh version of mission represents the Partisan mode of mission rhetoric. The Partisan calls for more and more missionaries and funding in order to address the world problems. These calls are positive and at times triumphant. Mission as "the Evangelization of the World in This Generation" is no longer in vogue, but similar slogans have come and gone in the intervening years that represent a partisan maintenance and promotion of the modern mission tradition.

In contrast to Edinburgh, the commissioners of the Laymen's Inquiry are Revisionists. Revisionists retain the language of mission but create alternative narratives or new foundations on which mission is justified. *Re-thinking Missions* began what has become a perpetual revising of mission. These revisions have spawned a multitude of mission definitions and expressions from a variety of perspectives. Soon after the publication of *Re-thinking Missions*, Kenneth S. Latourette, professor at Yale University, responded to the report in *Missions Tomorrow* (1936). He claims that if Christian mission is to survive, it "must be adjusted to the conditions of the day which is dawning." It will do this by making "alternations," and "if rightly modified and faithfully supported, have an even greater function in the decades immediately ahead than

---

[87]Hocking, "Introduction," xii.

they have had in the century just closing."[88] Latourette likewise points to the
loss of interest among younger Christians and declining income and
expresses the fear that the postwar focus on world peace and social reorga-
nization had made mission "irrelevant." And yet, he proposes a revision of
mission that is more optimistic than the Laymen's Inquiry. He declares, "Re-
trenchment must cease." Rather, there must be "thorough reconsideration
and, where necessary, drastic revision."[89] Latourette was only the first of what
has become a long line of Revisionists. From the 1930s until today, Revisionists have continued to redraw, reformulate, rehabilitate, refresh, reorient,
rediscover, repossess, and reenvision mission.[90] Revisionists from every
spectrum of Christianity have sought to reform mission into their agenda,
retell the mission story as their narrative, and recreate the missionary in
another image. Because of Revisionists, mission now can mean almost anything, and its meaning is diffused and muddled.

The inquiry had little effect on those who continued in the partisan affirmation of an Edinburgh version of mission. However, for those in ecumenical circles and involved in discussions associated with the International
Missionary Council and the World Council of Churches, the question of
mission persisted.[91] Partisans were active prior to the Laymen's Inquiry and
continued afterward. Nonetheless, the visibility of Hocking's position as a
Harvard professor, Rockefeller's support of the inquiry, and the substantive
arguments in the report raised the stakes and initiated the rise of mission
Apologists. As the title of the report states, "After One Hundred Years," the
inquiry appraises the condition of the modern mission movement from its
beginning at the end of the eighteenth century to the early twentieth century.[92] The commissioners framed the inquiry as an appraisal of the modern
mission tradition and thus viewed it as separate from the endeavors of the

---

[88]Kenneth Scott Latourette, *Missions Tomorrow* (New York: Harper & Brothers, 1936), xi, xii.

[89]Ibid., 125-27, 155.

[90]Orlando E. Costas, *Christ Outside the Gate: Mission Beyond Christendom* (Maryknoll, NY: Orbis
   Books, 1982), 69; Lesslie Newbigin, *A Word in Season: Perspectives on Christian World Missions*
   (Grand Rapids: Eerdmans, 1994), 12; *TM*, 8; Scott A. Bessenecker, *Overturning Tables: Freeing
   Missions from the Christian-Industrial Complex* (Downers Grove, IL: InterVarsity Press, 2014), 37,
   41, 43, 66, 113, 185.

[91]D. T. Niles, "A Church and Its 'Selfhood,'" in *A Decisive Hour for the Christian Mission: The East
   Asia Christian Conference 1959 and the John R. Mott Memorial Lectures* (London: SCM Press,
   1960), 89-92.

[92]*RM*, 60.

church prior to that time. Whereas Edinburgh attempted to draw lines of continuity between current mission endeavors with activities of the Jesus, Paul, and the early and medieval churches, the inquiry only assessed the modern era. The report hardly mentions New Testament or medieval mission endeavors.[93] This omission suggests that the Laymen's Inquiry viewed mission as a modern undertaking, and thus it questioned the biblical and historical legitimacy of mission.

In the wake of the report, Apologists mounted arguments for continuity between the modern mission enterprise and the biblical and historical narratives. Partisans-turned-Apologists shifted from promotion and mobilization to justifying and historicizing mission. Prior to 1932, there had not been much need for such arguments, and thus works on the Bible and mission were sparse and rather thin in content. One of the few exceptions was W. O. Carver's *Missions in the Plan of the Ages* (1909).[94] His objective in these printed lectures to students at Southern Baptist Theological Seminary was to counter the effects of higher biblical criticism and "speculative theology," which he viewed as discounting the Bible as the "textbook of missions."[95] After the publication of *Re-thinking Missions*, books and pamphlets detailing the biblical basis of mission appeared from every direction.[96]

---

[93]This is Speer's main critique of the report. See*"Re-thinking Missions" Examined*, 16.

[94]Carver, *Missions in the Plan of the Ages: Bible Studies in Missions* (New York: Fleming H. Revell, 1909), asserts, "The historical origin of missions is found in the work, the life, the command of Jesus Christ projected in the lives of His followers" (15).

[95]Ibid., 20.

[96]A host of books and studies arguing the biblical basis for missions appeared in the decades following the report: William Owen Carver, *The Course of Christian Missions: A History and an Interpretation* (New York: Fleming H. Revell, 1939); Carver, *God and Man in Missions* (Nashville: Broadman, 1944); Julian Price Love, *The Missionary Message of the Bible* (New York: Macmillan, 1941); Robert Hall Glover, *The Bible Basis of Missions* (Chicago: Moody, 1946); Inter-Varsity Christian Fellowship, *Therefore Go: The Bible Basis of Missions* (Chicago: Inter-Varsity Press, 1949); Lewis H. Kreuzer, "The Biblical Basis for the Missionary Obligation of the Church" (BD thesis, Andover Newton Theological School, 1953); Charles W. Ranson, *The Biblical Basis of the Christian Mission*, Austin Seminary Bulletin, vol. 71, no. 10 (Austin: Austin Presbyterian Theological Seminary, 1956); *The Biblical Basis of the Church's Mission: Addresses of the Niagara Falls Conference on Missionary Education, 3–4–5 May, 1960* (Toronto: Committee on Missionary Education, Canadian Council of Churches, 1960); Edwin Cyril Blackman, *The Biblical Basis of the Church's Missionary Enterprise*, Essays on Mission (London: London Missionary Society, 1961); Donald Orrin Teachout, "The Biblical Basis of Missions" (ThB thesis, Baptist Bible Seminary, 1961); Ronald Bocking, *Has the Day of the Missionary Passed?*, Essays on Mission 5 (London: London Missionary Society, 1961); John M. L. Young, *Missions: The Biblical Motive and Aim* (Pittsburgh: Crown & Covenant, 1964); Robert Edward Harlow, *Drawn unto Death: The Bible Basis of Missions* (Kansas City, KS: Walterick, 1966);

Cleland McAfee of the Board of Foreign Missions, Presbyterian Church, USA, attempted to answer questions emerging from the International Missionary Council at Jerusalem in 1928 and to anticipate the questions raised by the Laymen's Inquiry in *The Uncut Nerve of Missions: An Inquiry and an Answer* (1932). He acknowledged the "reduced interest and support" in the mission endeavor but credited this to conditions or opinions that "'cuts the nerve of missions,' that is, checks or destroys the impulse toward missions."[97] McAfee took up some of the same issues addressed by the inquiry but vindicated rather than criticized mission. McAfee was a Partisan who believed the nerve of mission had not been cut by wrong motives, rising nationalism, inadequate missionary methods, and the poor condition of mission work. Rather, "if the nerve of missions has been cut anywhere, it is here in the heart of the home Church."[98] For McAfee, the crisis in mission was not with mission itself but with the lack of support and enthusiasm in the home church, and thus he sounded much like the delegates at Edinburgh.

However, the tone of other books and pamphlets in years following the report was quite different. For example, Julian Love's concern in *The Missionary Message of the Bible* (1941) was with "stemming the tide of retreat" and criticized the Laymen's Report as a source of this ebbing support. While attacks on mission had always existed, he saw the report as "a much deeper and more trenchant criticism, cutting at the theology behind missions and at the basic purposes of the churches, and resulting in a confusion of the whole idea and program in the minds of leaders as well as followers." Cyril Blackman did not name the Laymen's Inquiry in *The Biblical Basis of the Church's Missionary Enterprise* (1961), but he referenced "new pressures and opportunities" that called for other terms to "be substituted for the time-honoured 'mission' and 'missionary.'" Such revision of terminology and call

---

Don W. Hills, *The Biblical Basis of Missions* (Chicago: Moody Press Institute, 1977). Others defended the report and developed its criticisms of mission even further, most notably Archibald G. Baker, *Christian Missions and a New World Culture* (Chicago: Willett, Clark, 1934); Hugh Vernon White, *A Theology for Christian Missions* (New York: Willett, Clark, 1937). Chapter four of White's book, "The Basis for a New Apolgetic" (94-121), contrasts the old apologetic of a narrow missionary belief system with a "sound modern apologetic for missionary Christianity" (110).

[97]Cleland Boyd McAfee, *The Uncut Nerve of Missions: An Inquiry and an Answer* (New York: Fleming H. Revell, 1932), 5.

[98]Ibid., 153.

for new nomenclature, Blackman asserted, were not insignificant matters, as "this re-thinking means a re-thinking not of methods but foundations."[99] In the years following the report, the theology of *Re-thinking Mission* was most often cited as the chief concern of Apologists, but rather than a theological counteroffense, the approach most often was to construct a bridge from the Bible to the modern mission enterprise.

As a modern tradition seen as the remedy for the world problems, the mission tradition itself became the problem. Because of the place of mission in Protestant rhetoric, the commissioners and the report could not be ignored or dismissed but demanded response.

THE SHIFT UNDER WAY

Partisans, Apologists, and Revisionists have honed their response to the crisis in mission. Partisans promote mission with vigor. Apologists seek to defend mission via a host of means. Revisionists work to rehabilitate mission per current religious and cultural shifts. The result is that mission is widely contested, and the word creates a confusing conceptual terrain. Difficulty exists for all three approaches to mission rhetoric. Partisans and Apologists are anachronistic in their use of mission, and Revisionists relativize mission to such an extent that the term has become diffused in meaning and semantically unanchored. Partisans and Apologists totalize the term, and Revisionists make it so elastic that it can mean anything. The shared problem for all three approaches is the persistent use of mission language itself. Rather than preserving or rescuing or revising mission as sacred language or a biblical concept, and rather than attempting to reformulate the legacy of mission to suit modern sensibilities, it is time for a shift of another kind—a transition to more appropriate, more useful language. Such a shift is necessary because the heart of the "missionary problem" is the problem of mission language.

Not only is the shift a necessity, but the shift away from mission language is under way. What Ignatius innovated and Protestants made into a modern tradition is ebbing in its usefulness and vitality—but more importantly, contemporary Christians have begun to recognize the conceptual dissonance

---

[99]Blackman, *Biblical Basis of the Church's Missionary Enterprise*, 9, 11.

with mission language and its tradition. A number of factors should signal that rather than redoubling efforts to defend mission, or to promote the latest revision of mission, or to anticipate what mission should be in light of the newest trend or the next conference, it is time to recover ancient language that will enable a more vibrant and appropriate encounter between the church and world.

Waning Christendom signals that mission language should be abandoned. As Christendom recedes, Christianity as a centerless religion becomes more and more apparent. Europe is no longer the home or geographical bastion of the faith. America is not—and very well may never have been—a Christian nation. Christendom, both as a territorial entity and an ideological frame of reference, is passing into oblivion. Christendom was fundamental to the mission impulse, as it narrated two contrasting realms, one Christian and the other non-Christian, and the necessity of crossing from one to the other. Mission was the language of Europe crossing into Asia—Christians being sent from Christendom to heathendom. The disappearance of Christendom dispels the notion of sending to another realm, confronting and overcoming geographical barriers, and crossing the boundaries of Christendom into heathendom inherent in mission language.

The colonial legacy of mission is difficult to overcome and cannot be casually dismissed. As demonstrated in chapters five and six, the roots of this legacy are much deeper than the colonies of Protestant powers, but include the right of patronage of Spain and Portugal, Latin colonies in the Holy Lands, and the Crusades. Mission language is firmly rooted in the spirit of conquest and colonialization. Modernity does not inoculate mission from these problems but is instead inclined toward them with a spirit of its own.[100] An attempt to reframe, redesign, or reform mission does not erase these memories, nor does it rescue mission from its legacy. While *mission* may hold warm and positive historic meaning for some Christians in the West, the remembrance for many in the rest of the world is anything but virtuous

---

[100]For a careful, documented study of the complex relationship between British missionaries and modern overseas expansion, see Porter, *Religion Versus Empire*; Peter van der Veer, *Imperial Encounters: Religion and Modernity in India and Britain* (Princeton, NJ: Princeton University Press, 2001). See also Wilbert R. Shenk, "The 'Great Century' Reconsidered," in *Anabaptism and Mission*, ed. Wilbert R. Shenk, Institute of Mennonite Studies, Missionary Studies 10 (Scottdale, PA: Herald, 1984), 158-77.

or noble.[101] Rather than helpful language that facilitates, mission is a liability that distorts. Rather than creating possibilities and opening doors, mission limits and restricts. Rather than clarifying Scripture and Christian tradition, mission infuses both with disturbing noise.

Pluralism ends the rationale for mission language. The missionary as an ecclesial agent sent from the place where Christianity *is* to another place where Christianity *is not*—such an idea is no longer intelligible. In common vernacular, *mission* is usually foreign or international mission, and it includes travels or a trip. And yet, "over there" is no longer just over there. Neighborhoods in the West are a highly diverse mixture of ethnicities, languages, and religions. One does not have to travel (or be sent) from Dallas to India to meet a Hindu or to Japan to talk to a Buddhist. Hindus and Buddhists, as well as Muslims, Sikhs, and animists, shop in local stores, go to school, and live alongside Western men and women—are, in fact, Western men and women themselves. Social and religious homogeneity is still a possibility but chiefly as a choice reserved for those with the means to live in gated communities and suburban enclaves. Modern European and American cities, such as London, Hamburg, Chicago, and Houston, are patchworks of different peoples created by migration, war, employment, and displacement. Pluralism is the new reality that makes mission language redundant.

As modernity declines so will mission. Mission is modern. Introduced at the outset of the modern era, mission grew alongside modernity and embodied its ideas and sensibilities.[102] It is not that modernity came along after the fact and captured mission—mission was and is modern. Mission and modernity grew up together as siblings in the same household and thus learned from each other and mimicked the language and ways of the other. Each has family resemblance to and traits of the other, because they share the same Enlightenment birthright. How they became linked and the implications of this linkage have become a matter of much discussion and

---

[101]See Desmond Van der Water, ed., *Postcolonial Mission: Power and Partnership in World Christianity* (Upland, CA: Sopher, 2011); Arun Shourie, *Missionaries in India: Continuities, Changes, Dilemmas* (New Delhi, India: HarperCollins, 1997).

[102]See Bert Hoedemaker, "Mission Beyond Modernity," in *Christian Mission in Western Society: Precedents, Perspectives, Prospects*, ed. Simon Barrow and Graeme Smith (London: CBTI, 2001), 212-33.

debate.[103] What is certain is that the two are connected in origin and dependent one on the other. According to Werner Ustorf, "Mission is inhibiting its own progress because of its fixation with modernist conceptions of its task—that is to say, with memories and ideas that have their origin not simply in the Bible, but, more specifically, in Western dreams of control and knowledge."[104] The mission fixation with modernity has subverted the narrative of the ancient tradition, and the place of the local church and the power of divine disclosure have receded behind modern ideals. As the modern narrative and its ideals decline, so will modern mission.

The existence of Christianities also challenges the notion of mission. The concept of mission presupposes that Christian faith must move from a center where it is firmly and correctly established to the periphery where it is not. Most of what sustains the modern mission movement is the idea that faith has one true center in the West. The faith, it is assumed, must move from this center to places where it does not exist or is not fully established. The mobilization of personnel and resources must move from us to them, from our church to the world. Central to mission justification and promotion is the illusion that faith does not exist at the margins, and everything must be done to transport it from here to there. And yet, the new reality, well documented and visibly evident, is that Christian faith exists in almost every country and is making its way from people to people. In some cases, what were once frontiers are now vibrant centers of Christian faith.[105]

Mission language perpetuates the belief that one form of Christianity is meant to dominate all others. Some counter that the Christianities that exist at the margins are not real or are less than orthodox Christian faith. Mission, they maintain, is needed in order to replicate a denominational brand or a narrow notion of Christianity. When used in this way, *mission*

---

[103]See Brian Stanley, "Christian Missions and the Enlightenment: A Reevaluation," in *Christian Missions and the Enlightenment*, ed. Brian Stanley, Studies in the History of Christian Missions (Grand Rapids: Eerdmans, 2001), 1.

[104]Werner Ustorf, "1910–2010: From Foreign Mission to the Home Policies of a World Religion," in *Walk Humbly with the Lord: Church and Mission Engaging Plurality*, ed. Viggo Mortensen and Andreas Østerlund Nielsen (Grand Rapids: Eerdmans, 2010), 36.

[105]Philip Jenkins, *The Next Christendom: The Coming of Global Christianity* (Oxford: Oxford University Press, 2002); Felix Wilfred, "From World Mission to Global Christianities: A Perspective from the South," in *From World Mission to Inter-Religious Witness*, Concilium 2011/1 (London: SCM Press, 2011), 13-26; Mark A. Noll, *The New Shape of World Christianity: How American Experience Reflects Global Faith* (Downers Grove, IL: IVP Academic, 2009).

is another word for church extension, the spread of our version of orthodoxy, or proselytization.

Others point to the use of mission language among Christian communities around the work as proof of the need to continue using such vocabulary. And yet, *mission* appears outside the West most often in places where there is a long and deep history of Western mission. For example, mission language is quite prominent in Korea and India, because they have been schooled in its use and legacy. In contrast to this persistent use, mission language is under scrutiny in far more places throughout the world as a vestige of the colonial era.

The modern mission movement, an invented tradition, birthed in the modern era and sustained by various means, is falling out of use. It is dated and thus no longer has the ring of a present reality. Rather, it looks, feels, and sounds like a worn project of the nineteenth and early twentieth centuries. With the passing of modernity, this modern movement is losing currency. In its place a new tradition, the missional movement, has emerged. As with the modern mission movement, the missional "conversation," "under-standing," or "movement" offers language and belief that serve as defining ideology for church, the world, and God—missional church, missional identity, missional engagement, missional God, and so on.[106] As in the case of the modern mission movement, the missional movement is promoted and sustained by biblical, theological, and programmatic arguments and justifications.[107] As indicated in chapter one, missional is but the latest re-vision of mission. And while this movement has reinvigorated the use of mission language, at the same time it has added to the ambiguity and murk-iness surrounding mission. Missional is still mission language, and thus, it shares the same legacy and carries with it many of the same problems and liabilities of the modern mission tradition. Lesslie Newbigin, referring to movements in general, observes that any movement that must mobilize re-sources and justify its existence "runs the risk of becoming chiefly interested

---

[106]Craig Van Gelder and Dwight J. Zscheile, *The Missional Church in Perspective: Mapping Trends and Shaping the Conversation*, The Missional Network (Grand Rapids: Baker Academic, 2011), 3, 5, 8, 15, 97, 154.

[107]See Darrell L. Guder et al., *Missional Church: A Vision for the Sending of the Church in North America* (Grand Rapids: Eerdmans, 1998); Guder, *Called to Witness*; Van Gelder and Zscheile, *Missional Church in Perspective*; Reggie McNeal, *Missional Renaissnace: Changing the Scorecard for the Church* (San Francisco: Jossey-Bass, 2009); Ross Hastings, *Missional God, Missional Church: Hope for the Re-evangelizing the West* (Downers Grove, IL: IVP Academic, 2012).

in its own existence and development."[108] In other words, the danger for any movement, but the missional movement in this case, is that movement as a means becomes movement as the end—the promotion and defense of *missional this* or *missional that*, and thus a diversion that could consume time and resources and ultimately undermine faithful witness. As present-day followers of Christ look to invest their lives in sacrificial love and service, they want the assurance that whatever movement or tradition they give themselves to is ancient and ultimate, rather than recent and ancillary.

The desire for empathy and mutual exchange creates space for language other than mission. Rather than being laden with a foreign political agenda or replicating a Western pattern of Christianity, the exigencies of the present moment demand that we live in solidarity with believers around the world and in humility with brothers and sisters. Too often mission has been the unidirectional exporting and franchising of particular forms of Christian faith rather than the mutuality of people being transformed by people who are themselves being transformed. Instead of merely delivering the Christian religion, the sentiment must be one of reciprocity in which we come to listen and learn from each other, to be transformed by others. Solidarity and mutuality, either with those who live nearby or those faraway, enriches and enlivens transformative exchange. The shift is away from mission as one-way deliverables to an authentic faith exchange that converts and transforms in both directions.

Future Shift

Mission emerged in the modern era and eventually became a modern tradition. And yet, at the outset of the twenty-first century, both mission and the modern mission movement seem to be antiquated language retroactively applied to the preceding sixteen centuries of Christian history—an anachronistic conceptual framework ill-suited for the challenges of the twenty-first century. Confusion regarding the origin and meaning of mission language has compounded over the last one hundred years, and such uncertainty offers little help for the church's current encounter with the world. We find ourselves in "the new post-foreign mission situation," requiring us to

---

[108]Newbigin, *Word in Season*, 4.

reconceive the church and world encounter, not redefine or reform mission.[109] More than ever, mission, its past and future, is in question. More than ever, our pioneering task is to discover fresh impulse and renewed witness for vision to the gospel of Jesus Christ.

When we defend and promote mission, we may find that we are championing the wrong cause. Worthy aims and good results may be associated with mission, but these same aims and results existed prior to the rhetoric of mission and will continue well beyond mission. In fact, not only might we be championing the wrong cause, we may find ourselves hindering the right cause. As modern rhetoric, mission can obscure the calling and witness of historical figures, hinder a clear reading of the biblical texts, and totalize a single aspect of church and ministry to the point that the gospel and its implications are muffled or obscured. We may find ourselves defending a tradition and its language rather than defending the good news of the gospel.

The necessity of transcending the rhetoric of the modern mission movement is critical, given its past associations and its present implications. The historical legacy and modernization of mission call into question the future of the whole enterprise. To return both conceptually and rhetorically to more biblical language will be an unnerving venture for some. However, through such a risk we acknowledge and embrace the enduring work of God in the past and point toward God's future. Through its long sojourn from the death and resurrection of Jesus to the present day, the gospel has survived all manner of shifts, movements, and traditions. The original impulse of the gospel endures and awaits new expressions. To discover and participate in these fresh manifestations of the gospel will require that we acknowledge our weakness before the powers and principalities of the present age and seek the Holy Spirit's work in and through our lives. Transcending mission is more than a shift in rhetoric; it is witness to our continual conversion to the gospel story.

---

[109]Ustorf, "1910–2010," 36.

Epilogue

Toward Pilgrim Witness

For He rescued us from the domain of darkness, and
transferred us to the kingdom of His beloved Son, in
whom we have redemption, the forgiveness of sins.

Colossians 1:13-14

But He said to him, "Allow the dead to bury
their own dead; but as for you, go and proclaim
everywhere the kingdom of God."

Luke 9:60

IMAGINE A YOUNG MOTHER in Kolkata, India. Having suffered the loss of her husband and ensuing destitution for herself and an infant child, she lives on the streets without shelter and with only scraps of food. Those who should have been there for her are unable to help, and some have even turned against her. With each passing day, she and her child fall deeper and deeper into despair. She is lost and without hope. As her situation worsens, she cries aloud to the gods for rescue. And yet, rather than getting better, her situation becomes even more grave and hopeless. One night as she sits on the pavement with her listless child in her lap, she looks up to see a man kneeling beside her. Rather than disgust and bother, his eyes are full of compassion and love, and his words are kind and soothing. He says to her, "The Lord, your God, has heard your cries. Your liberation is at hand. The reign of God is in the midst of this city. Find people of peace, and find hope for you and your child."

As day breaks, she sits on the pavement wondering whether someone actually spoke to her in the night or whether she was dreaming. She hears melodious chants coming from an open door beyond the iron fence on which she is leaning. She gathers her child, rises to her feet, and follows the sounds through the door. Once inside, she finds a group of white-clad devotees seated in a circle on the floor singing along with tabla drum and cymbals. At one side of the circle of devotees, she sees a figure of an Indian man in a painting. His arms are extended, and in his face she recognizes compassion and love. As the singing stops, one of the devotees says, "Come to me, you who are weak and heavy laden, and I will give you rest." She softly mutters, "I need to rest. I want rest." As the chant continues, she weeps.

Conversations with devotees in the group eventually lead to her declaration of Jesus Christ as the true God. From these Christ devotees, she receives food, medicine, and love. She begins meeting with some in their homes and in public spaces. When they gather, they sing songs of devotion, pray to God the Father, Son, and Spirit, and listen to the Holy Scriptures. From the Scriptures, she learns that the one true God as revealed in Jesus Christ desires to establish his reign throughout the earth. She hears that this rule is not far off but near, not just in the future but now, and not dormant but powerful and growing. In the sayings and parables of Jesus, she learns that the rule of God is like a small, obscure seed that is growing in the soil of her city and one day will be as large as a banyan tree. So the certainty of God's reign and the expectation of its increase and eventual arrival grow stronger and stronger in her. She talks with devotees about how the reign of God will look when it arrives and prays for its increase in her life, as well as the lives of her relatives and friends.

What the young mother comes to realize is that the kingdom of God is unlike any political, military, or governmental rule she has ever known. Rather, the reign of God begins in the mind and heart, works its way into speech and actions, and eventually changes everything about life. As God's reign becomes more prominent, peace, joy, goodness, and patience will characterize her interactions with other devotees as well as friends and neighbors she encounters in the course of her day. Her growing anticipation is that the reign of God will change her neighborhood and city as it becomes a transforming force in her own life. More and more she realizes that hope does not rest in her position in society, the power of the group of devotees, or even their collective moral force. She remembers how destitute she was before Jesus encountered her, and now she longs for the coming reign of God to transform her life and the life of her daughter. For this young mother, the reign of God is *the* reality for which she lives, *the* source of her hope, and *the* cause to which she gives herself. As a devotee of Jesus, she lives by the words that came to her at the point of deepest need—"The Lord, your God, has heard your cries. Your liberation is at hand."

Whether one is a young mother in Kolkata, a businessman in Hong Kong, a student in The Gambia, a waitress in London, or an engineer in Houston, the story is the same. The reign of God brings transformation and offers hope. Education, privilege, and religion make the promise of liberation, but these do not have the power to transform life and instill hope. True liberation does not come by way of human ingenuity or power, much less through a religious tradition. Instead, God declares his power to liberate and transform creation *by his words* and demonstrates this power *through his deeds*. As mothers, students, and engineers encounter the words and deeds of Jesus, they come to believe the speech and action of God are more powerful than any other speech and action. God's mighty deeds establish his kingdom, and by his words God gives witness to his coming reign. The promise is that the kingdoms of this world will give way to "the kingdom of our Lord and of His Christ; and He will reign forever and ever" (Rev 11:15).

The reign of God is the central narrative, the message of Jesus, and hope for humanity. The coming reign of God is what the Bible is all about, the heart and core of God's plan, and the reason we exist. For those outside the modern mission tradition with only Scripture and their experience to guide them, this is clear and evident. And yet, this is not as obvious to those formed to think that they exist for mission or that they must sell all and suffer great loss for the sake of mission. Mission is not the answer to the problems of young mothers, businessmen, students, and engineers, for those living in India, Africa, or America. At best, mission represents a tradition that grew up around the proclamation of God as Creator and Lord—a means to an end. But inherent beliefs and assumptions become glaring difficulties when justification and promotion of "mission" becomes the goal. Mission is contested language that requires continual promotion, defense, and revision, as this vocabulary is supplied language to the Christian tradition. When mission ascends to the status of sacred language, it can eclipse the kingdom and thus limit our view of God's reign and muddle our ability to participate in his kingdom. The language of the reign of God, on the other hand, expresses an abiding theme throughout the Bible that culminates in the message of Jesus. When discovered and embraced, God's reign forms us into pilgrim witnesses, who, though weak and afflicted, are liberated to live alongside and love those we encounter along the way.

THE KINGDOM OF GOD

From beginning to end, Scripture narrates the day of the Lord, the kingdom of God, or the reign of God.[1] The overarching theme from Genesis to the Psalms and in the Prophets is the coming reign of God. At the heart of Jesus' teaching and central to his identity and ministry is the kingdom of God.[2] The apostle Paul proclaims the coming kingdom of God, and John writes of the victory of God's reign. Kingdom language permeates Scripture (*basileia* occurs 162 times in the New Testament alone).[3] Scholars from a variety of traditions and perspectives identify the kingdom as the theme from which God and history, Christ and the church, and the Spirit and witness are to be interpreted. According to John Bright, "To grasp what is meant by the Kingdom of God is to come very close to the heart of the Bible's gospel of salvation."[4] George Ladd asserts that the kingdom of God is "the central message of Jesus."[5] Jesus' earthly ministry, according to N. T. Wright, was

---

[1] For variations in terminology and Old Testament antecedents, see Leonhard Goppelt, *Theology of the New Testament*, ed. Jürgen Roloff, trans. John E. Alsup (Grand Rapids: Eerdmans, 1981), 1:44-51.

[2] Alan Richardson, "Kingdom of God," in *A Theological Word Book of the Bible*, ed. Alan Richardson (London: SCM Press, 1957), 119; G. R. Beasley-Murray, *Jesus and the Kingdom of God* (Grand Rapids: Eerdmans, 1986), 338.

[3] N. T. Wright, *Jesus and the Victory of God*, Christian Origins and the Question of God 2 (Minneapolis: Fortress, 1996), 663-70, provides a helpful catalog of kingdom of God passages in early Christian literature.

[4] John Bright, *The Kingdom of God: The Biblical Concept and Its Meaning for the Church* (Nashville: Abingdon-Cokesbury, 1953), 7.

[5] George Eldon Ladd, *A Theology of the New Testament*, rev. ed. (Grand Rapids: Eerdmans, 1993), 54.

the "prophetic proclamation" of the continuing story and praxis of God's kingdom—a challenge within Judaism and "the presupposition for the church."[6] The kingdom of God is vibrant biblical language, chief among the themes of Scripture, and thus a worthy hermeneutical lens.

The signature expression of the coming of the kingdom is the incarnation of the Son of God.[7] In humility and weakness, Jesus enters the human predicament (Phil 2:5-8), and in power the kingdom of God arrives as well. God's reign comes as a defenseless child, birthed in suspicion and in the lowest of circumstances. Jesus summarizes his coming and his teachings, saying, "The time is fulfilled, and the kingdom of God is at hand; repent and believe in the gospel" (Mk 1:15). Throughout Judea, he preaches the kingdom of God, for he is "sent for this purpose" (Lk 4:43). As Jesus proclaims the kingdom, he confronts evil in all its forms, initiates a way of believing and acting, and eventually gives his life for all humanity. While the resurrection points to complete and ultimate victory, the life of Jesus signals a different way of power and another type of rule. Jesus' announcement of the kingdom initiates change that permeates like leaven throughout every aspect of life (Mt 13:33; Lk 13:21). Jesus' miracles are signs of the kingdom, as he confronts demons and all kinds of evil (Mt 12:26-29; Mk 9:1), but these spectacular signs are not ultimate marks of the kingdom. "The kingdom of God is not coming with signs to be observed," Jesus proclaims, "nor will they say, 'Look, here it is!' or, 'There it is!' For behold, the kingdom of God is in your midst" (Lk 17:20-21). According to Jesus, the arrival of the kingdom of God is most visible among those who are childlike, as well as those who are poor in spirit, those who persevere under persecution, and those who hunger for God's

---

[6] Wright, *Jesus and the Victory of God*, 2:11, 226.

[7] While kingdom of God language is absent in the Old Testament, the coming of Yahweh, the day of the Lord, and the rule of God are pervasive themes. According to Beasley-Murray, *Jesus and the Kingdom of God*, "In the Old Testament, the ultimate purpose of the future coming of the Lord and the Day of the Lord is the establishment of the kingdom of God" (17). For discussions on the idea of the kingdom prior to Jesus and the influence of prophetic and apocalyptic literature on Jesus and the disciples' view and use of "kingdom of God," see John Fuellenbach, *The Kingdom of God: The Message of Jesus Today* (Maryknoll, NY: Orbis Books, 1995), 25-78; Bright, *Kingdom of God*, 17-186; Rudolf Schnackenburg, *God's Rule and Kingdom* (New York: Herder and Herder, 1963), 11-75; Leonhard Goppelt, *Theology of the New Testament*, ed. Jürgen Roloff, trans. John E. Alsup (Grand Rapids: Eerdmans, 1981), 1:67-76; George Eldon Ladd, *Jesus and the Kingdom: The Eschatology of Biblical Realism* (New York: Harper & Row, 1964), 41-97; Wright, *Jesus and the Victory of God*, 2:198-226.

reign and righteousness (Mt 5:3, 10, 20; 6:33). Those who enter into the kingdom must come to God as children, or they cannot receive it at all (Mk 10:15). The paradoxical reign of God provokes a crisis in what power looks like, how it is to be used, and from where it originates. The kingdom of God is not the obscene power of brutal conquest and forced occupation. Rather, the power of the kingdom of God is a child who becomes the sacrificial Lamb and thereby liberates the world from sin and death.

Though the promised reign of God arrives in Jesus, his announcement of the kingdom is not the end but its beginning. The kingdom is both present and future, has arrived and is still to come.[8] The people of God are to pray for the kingdom to come (Mt 6:10), seek first the kingdom of God (Mt 6:33; Lk 12:31), and preach the gospel of the kingdom (Mt 9:35; 24:14; Mk 1:14; Lk 4:43; 8:1; 9:60; Acts 8:12; 20:25). Jesus gives his disciples "power and authority over all the demons and to heal diseases." And he sends them out "to proclaim the kingdom of God and to perform healing" (Lk 9:1-2). The ultimate end is not the sending of messengers but the message of the kingdom of God. Sending is ordinary means to an unusual end—the kingdom of God. Jesus calls those who would follow him to leave house, wife, brother, parents, and children "for the sake of the kingdom of God" (Lk 18:29). The supreme goal is for all people to encounter Christ and receive the kingdom of God (Mk 10:15), to enter into the kingdom of God (Mt 19:24; Mk 9:47; Jn 3:5; Lk 18:23, 24), and to proclaim the kingdom (Lk 9:60; 16:16).

Paul writes of the kingdom of God as the aim of life. Christ's victory over death and resurrection are but "the first fruits," or signs of the liberation to come. In the end, "all rule and all authority and power" will be abolished, and the kingdoms of this world will be delivered to God (1 Cor 15:24). Thus, the people of God are to live worthy of the kingdom of God (1 Cor 6:9; Gal 5:21; Eph 5:5), labor for the kingdom of God (Col 4:11), and suffer for the kingdom of God (1 Thess 1:5). Luke concludes Acts with Paul in Rome under house arrest but still able to testify and preach to all who come to him concerning the kingdom of God (Acts 28:23, 30-31). Paul's words and life declare

---

[8]The debate regarding the future or present tense of Jesus' pronouncements of the kingdom of God, particularly in Mk 1:15, is discussed by Beasley-Murray, *Jesus and the Kingdom of God*, 71-83; Ladd, *Jesus and the Kingdom*, 3-38; Ladd, *Theology of the New Testament*, 54-67.

that the people of God are to orient their lives to the kingdom, long for the kingdom, and proclaim the kingdom.

Because it is the kingdom *of* God, and not of men and women, God establishes this reign in his way and by his means. Human agents proclaim the kingdom of God, and natural objects (mustard seed, leaven, a merchant, drag net) illustrate the nature of the kingdom, but people and objects can only point to the kingdom and never build, control, create, or manipulate it.[9] For those who know power only as force or coercion, the kingdom of God is a bewildering paradox and a confusing mystery (Mt 13:11; Mk 4:11; Lk 8:10; 17:20-21; Jn 18:36). In contrast to human conquest and occupation, the kingdom of God comes in weakness and humility (Mt 5:19; Lk 6:20), and is hidden and obscure (Mt 13:33; Lk 13:18-21). Rather than a power for the advantaged and authoritative, only those who humble themselves can enter into the kingdom of God (Mt 18:3-4; Mk 10:14). Thus, the powerful and the wealthy are the least likely to gain it. Abundance and power (Lk 18:24-25) are liabilities, for it is the poor and gentle who are assured to inherit the kingdom (Mt 5:3, 5). The kingdom is and remains God's kingdom and is not relinquished to the church or any other human agency. God establishes his kingdom in his way, by his means, and in his time.

The language of Scripture refers to the already-and-coming kingdom of God rather than the mission of God. Jesus' instruction to his disciples, their speech to one another, and Jesus' prayer to the Father center on the coming reign of God rather than mission. Rather than preaching mission, advocating for mission, mobilizing for mission, or revising mission, the biblical injunction is to proclaim, promote, and live the kingdom of God. Jesus does not proclaim the arrival of mission but the coming of the kingdom. Jesus shows the disciples his pierced hands and feet and then says to them: "Peace be with you; as the Father has sent Me, I also send you" (Jn 20:21). Going and sentness are incidental; wounds and sacrifice are essential. Jesus' meaning is clear—in the same manner and for the same purpose I was sent, I am sending you. But when sending becomes the overwhelming focus, the reconciling deeds of the kingdom are diminished or lost. The central meaning of Jesus' words is that he is sent in order to proclaim and establish

---

[9]George Eldon Ladd, *The Presence of the Future* (Grand Rapids: Eerdmans, 1996), 193.

the coming reign of God, and not that the kingdom of God provides the foundation or rationale for sending. Thus, kingdom must not be co-opted in order to justify mission.[10] To elevate mission language to the status of sacred language places extrabiblical assumptions and beliefs and a foreign narrative onto Scripture that compete with the kingdom of God. The result is that mission, a modern means, obscures the kingdom of God, the essential reality. The coming reign of God throughout the whole of creation is Jesus' message, and it is to be the message of his followers. The kingdom of God should be read for what it is—words and deeds evidenced in the life of Jesus Christ and God's rule enacted by the power of the Spirit—not as a prelude to or justification for something else. The kingdom of God is distinct in its language and manifestation, distinguishable from all other action and speech, because it is language of revelation and hope.

Language of revelation. God's reign over the whole of his creation is more than a theme to be explored; it is a reality of the first order. More than a tradition or strategy, the reign of God exists from the beginning of time and precedes all traditions, schemes, and plans. The biblical expression of God's dominion is primordial, revealed language and as such is *sui generis* (in a class of its own). It stands apart from any concept, idea, or metaphor, because it is original impulse and intent.

Scripture records disclosures of God creating, covenanting, liberating, and judging. These demonstrate that God is the one who speaks into human history to reveal who he is and what he does. In these disclosures, we witness God establishing his reign by his grace and in his love. The kingdom of God is the language of divine disclosure in that it reveals that God is not just any god acting in any manner, but God who establishes his reign in his particular

---

[10]Arthur Glasser, *Announcing the Kingdom: The Story of God's Mission in the Bible* (Grand Rapids: Baker Academic, 2003), combines the kingdom of God and mission in order to argue that "the whole Bible, both Old and New Testaments, is a missionary book." Through his "missional reading of the Bible," he blurs the lines between the kingdom of God and mission (11, 17). The result is that mission and kingdom of God are joined together as "God's Kingdom mission" (68, 201, 227, 228). Ross Langmead, *The Word Made Flesh: Towards an Incarnational Missiology* (Lanham, MD: University Press of America, 2004), uses the kingdom of God to arrive at his incarnational missiology. In a similar manner, Alex Luc, "The Kingdom of God and His Mission," in *Discovering the Mission of God: Best Missional Practices of the 21st Century*, ed. Mike Barnett and Robin Martin (Downers Grove, IL: IVP Academic, 2012), 85-98, links the Old Testament idea of the reign of God with mission. He does this by merging the language of God's mission, our mission, and the kingdom of God.

ways. Because he is before all time and thus like none other, the words and deeds that distinguish him are not just any words and deeds. We know God because of words he speaks to Abraham, Jacob, Joseph, Moses, and Daniel. We know what God does because of his actions among the Egyptians, in the wilderness, and at Mount Horeb. Within these words and actions, God tells us who he is and what he does—how God reigns.

God reveals himself in flesh and blood, as Christ enters human history. Indirect speech becomes direct speech, whispered words become spoken, and the promised covenant takes on the fleshly of acts of healing, feeding, forgiving, and dying in the midst of humanity. We know who God is and what he does most definitely because of the words and deeds of Jesus. The sayings of Jesus are those of the Father. Jesus says, "The things I speak, I speak just as the Father has told Me" (Jn 12:50). In the speech of Jesus, the words of God from eternity are revealed. In the acts of Jesus, we see what the Father is doing among humanity (Jn 5:19-20). Jesus' words and deeds are manifestations of God's work within his creation.

God's speech and actions reveal God as Creator, Redeemer, Liberator, Savior, and Lord; and as such, these do not restrict the nature of God but distinguish him as the one true God. In our effort to explain or expand, we tend to say too much about God or try to explain what must remain mystery. Though the particular words and deeds of Scripture only go so far and leave much unsaid and unexplained, in these the mystery of God's work and intent are revealed. To cloak disclosure of God's person and intent in temporal causes or a modern tradition does not always help but can often hinder the proclamation of the reign of God.

The young mother in Kolkata knows the Creator because of the revealed speech and action of God and the witness to these in Scripture. In these words and deeds, she recognizes the one true God as different from Ganesh, Shiva, and Kali. For an engineer in Houston, God, as revealed through the Bible, is unlike the gods of consumption, hedonism, and nation. For the young mother and the engineer, the language of Scripture contradicts and, at times, opposes the speech of the modern world. Whenever the language of revelation is diminished or ignored, there is the risk of making God into the champion of an ordinary cause, the god of a religious way, or into a movement that serves the assumptions and beliefs of a certain period of history or a nation's aspirations. Kingdom language precedes talk about temporal causes, national aspirations, and religious ways, and thus it is distinguishable from all other speech.

Language of hope. Contrary to modern aversions to apocalyptic images that perplex and terrify, apocalypticism and apocalyptic language were part of the fabric of first-century Judaism.[11] Messianic expectations and the reign of God framed the general understanding of world events and the hope of liberation from evil and suffering.[12] The prophet Daniel voiced this hope:

> One like a Son of Man was coming. . . .
> And to Him was given dominion,
> Glory and a kingdom,
> That all the peoples, nations, and men of every language
> Might serve Him. (Dan 7:13-14)

In the same expectation and hope, people in Jesus' day looked for the future to intrude on present existence to effect God's triumph in the here and now. The Davidic throne was still vacant, and the Messiah had not come, so expectations of the coming reign of God were on the minds of the Jewish people.

The term *apocalyptic* comes from *apokalypto* or *apokalypsis*, meaning "to uncover" or "to unveil."[13] In its simplest, most straightforward rendering, it

---

[11]The cultural, political, economic, and religious reasons for current apocalyptic interest are explored by J. Christiaan Beker, *Paul's Apocalyptic Gospel: The Coming Triumph of God* (Philadelphia: Fortress, 1982), 21-28.

[12]As a genre, Jewish apocalypticism rose to prominence in the period prior to Jesus' birth. The more noteworthy among apocalyptic writings are the books of Daniel, Enoch, Jubilees, 2 Esdras, 4 Ezra, and the Apocalypse of Abraham. This literature is characterized by a dualism in which two worlds and two ages stand over against or in opposition to each other. Also, there is usually promise of a messianic age to come in which Israel will be vindicated. For discussions on the literature classified as apocalyptic, see D. S. Russell, *Divine Disclosure: An Introduction to Jewish Apocalyptic* (London: SCM Press, 1992), 35-59; Klaus Koch, *The Rediscovery of Apocalyptic: A Polemical Work on a Neglected Area of Biblical Studies and Its Damaging Effects on Theology and Philosophy*, Studies in Biblical Theology (Second Series) 22 (London: SCM Press, 1972), 19-20, 34-35.

[13]On the variations and difficulties of defining *apocalyptic*, see Richard E. Sturm, "Defining the Word 'Apocalyptic': A Problem in Biblical Criticism," in *Apocalyptic and the New Testament: Essays in Honor of J. Louis Martyn*, ed. Joel Marcus and Marion L. Soards, Journal for the Study of the New Testament 24 (Sheffield, UK: Sheffield Academic, 1989), 17-48. Some maintain that however one uses *apocalyptic*, it should be linked with known "apolclyptic texts" such as Daniel, Ezekiel, and Revelation in order that its meaning be maintained.

means "to make known what has been veiled or hidden." The term is found throughout the New Testament and is usually translated as "revelation" or "disclosure." Revelation, John's account of his vision on the Isle of Patmos, is literally "the *apokalypsis* of Jesus Christ." The angel of the Lord gives John a vision of "the things which must soon take place" (Rev 1:1). John sees the coming defeat of evil and the victory of God over the forces of this world, and thus he finds reason to hope. The works of evil and the reign of Satan are destroyed by the Lamb, and a new heaven and a new earth are established (Rev 21–22). John's "*apokalypsis* of Jesus Christ" is a glimpse of the coming victory of God.

Likewise, in Jesus' words and deeds, the kingdom of God arrives as anticipated victory and reign.[14] Apocalyptic media, found throughout the Gospels and the Epistles in words, symbols, and events, indicate that more is under way than what appears on the surface as conventional events and activities or normal words and symbols. While it may look as though evil and suffering, in all their forms, rule human existence, the reign of God is a reality present within and coming to the human predicament. The apocalyptic is a grander, more constructive view of reality, and thus it provides a more complete and hopeful interpretation of history. When this grander possibility intersects with the limited, more restrictive reality, something has to give, and the seams of experience and understanding come apart. In the breach, God manifests himself. This disruption, according to Jesus, is akin to putting new wine into old wineskins. "The wineskins burst," Jesus explains, "and the wine pours out" (Mt 9:17). In Jesus, the reign of God invades human reality and changes everything.

Jesus' discourses are full of apocalyptic references. The inauguration of the kingdom in the incarnation of Jesus is portrayed as the fullness or completion of time and the demonstration of divine victory over the power of evil forces. The Gospel writers couple Jesus' activities of miraculous healing

---

[14]The narrative of Jesus' birth, for example, is full of apocalyptic words and images. Through the events surrounding the announcement and birth of Jesus Christ, God disrupts common history: the angel Gabriel appears to Zacharias (Lk 1:11-20), Gabriel confers with Mary (Lk 1:26-38), angels appear to Joseph (Mt 1:20, 24; 2:13, 19, 22), Mary conceives by way of the Holy Spirit (Mt 1:18), a multitude of angels suddenly appear to shepherds watching their flocks (Lk 2:8-14), the magis dream (Mt 2:12), and Simeon and Anna foretell Jesus' life and death (Lk 2:25-38). Luke records Simeon's pronouncement of the infant Jesus "as a light of revelation to the Gentiles" (Lk 2:32).

(Mt 4:25; 9:35; Lk 8:1-2; 9:11) and casting out demons (Mt 12:28) with the proclamation of the kingdom. Jesus arrives in Galilee, saying, "The time is fulfilled, and the kingdom of God is at hand; repent and believe in the gospel" (Mk 1:15). And Jesus instructs his disciples to do the same. They are to heal the sick, raise the dead, cleanse lepers, and cast out demons and proclaim the kingdom of God (Mt 10:8). In Luke 10:9, Jesus instructs the seventy to heal the sick and then tells them, "The kingdom of God has come near to [them]." The incursion of the miraculous and confrontations with evil are signs and proofs of the kingdom of God has come with power (Mk 9:1). In these proclamations and events, more than information about God is revealed. Through dreams, angels, and healing, God speaks, confronts evil, and establishes his reign.

Not only does Jesus reflect existing Jewish apocalyptic themes and patterns, but he gives new meaning to them.[15] He is more than a prophet of an apocalyptic vision; he is its fulfillment. In Jesus, the kingdom arrives, and through him the apocalyptic vision is realized. However, in his teachings concerning the kingdom, Jesus makes plain that it is far more important to identify the kingdom in the midst of history than to anticipate national liberation or to calculate the end of time. The kingdom is to be found not through prognostications or in some climactic historical event but in Jesus' words and deeds.[16] As Jesus proclaims the kingdom, he announces its arrival as his words and deeds.

Paul's language signals a similar reorientation of apocalyptic themes. After an encounter with Christ and induction into his Way, Paul radically reorients his received Jewish apocalyptic vision around the person of Christ.[17] The apostle refers to the preaching of Jesus Christ as "the revelation of the mystery which has been kept secret for long ages past" (Rom 16:25). Paul reshapes the Jewish apocalyptic vision by reinterpreting Israel's history and emphasizing the powerful incursion of the Christ event in the present age. This change is described by J. Christiaan Beker as a proclamation of the

---

[15]Cf. Russell, *Divine Disclosure*, 129-31; Wright, *Jesus and the Victory of God*, 2:172.
[16]Russell, *Divine Disclosure*, 131.
[17]The discussion regarding the apocalyptic and Paul is long and complicated. For a critique of the various schools of interpretation, see N. T. Wright, *Paul and His Recent Interpreters: Some Contemporary Debates* (Minneapolis: Fortress, 2015), 135-220.

triumph of God in Jesus Christ.[18] In this triumph, God brings about his universal cosmic rule and thus hope. When defending the authority of his message and his call to preach to the Gentiles, Paul says both are received through "a revelation [apocalypse] of Jesus Christ" (Gal 1:12; cf. Eph 1:17). He also asserts that his message is based on his "visions and revelations of the Lord" (2 Cor 12:1). Thus, the impulse for Paul's life and witness is rooted in more than some temporal concern or organizational structure but flows from a heavenly vision, and to this apocalyptic vision he is compelled to be faithful (Acts 26:19).

This vision of God's victory represents the future but also has present effect. As well as being a book of "apocalyptic prophecy," Richard Bauckham emphasizes that the book of Revelation is a letter written to encourage specific churches in their day and for their context.[19] Those who received John's Revelation are able to see beyond the power of Rome and view "the world from the heavenly perspective."[20] According to Bauckham, "It is not that the here-and-now are left behind in an escape into heaven or the eschatological future, but that the here-and-now look quite different when they are opened to transcendence."[21] The disclosure of God's triumph changes the view of present circumstances for the reign of God is the *current* and the *coming* reality that offers *present* and *future* hope.

The kingdom of God refers to more than events at the margins of common history, as if they are breaking the boundaries of history only here and there. Rather, it reveals something about the center of history. The kingdom of God

---

[18]Major works appeared in the last half-century that both highlight the apocalyptic element in the writings of Paul and characterize his emphasis as "this worldly." For example, J. Christiaan Beker, *Paul's Apocalyptic Gospel,* offers a vigorous defense of the apocalyptic in Paul's letters and attempts to distance Paul from modern-day varieties of apocalyptic (see 11-17). Beker claims apocalyptic does not lie at the margins or is a disposable adornment of Paul's gospel or just a specialized doctrine of the end times. Rather, it is at the center, and thus "the substance of the gospel is for him unthinkable apart from its future apocalyptic mooring" (106). See also Beverly Roberts Gaventa, *Our Mother Saint Paul* (Louisville: Westminister John Knox, 2007).

[19]Richard Bauckham, *The Theology of the Book of Revelation,* New Testament Theology (Cambridge: Cambridge University Press, 1993), 6-7, 12-17.

[20]Ibid., 7.

[21]Ibid., 7-8. Bosch contends that for twentieth-century mainline Christianity, "Christian history after the Christ-event was regarded as little more than the working out of God's once-for-all action in Christ. The expectation of a 'new heaven and a new earth' was spiritualized away." Thus, the apocalyptic was neutralized or silenced. The events of history were void of real meaning, and thus "all salvation lies only in the future" (*TM,* 140, 141).

describes the presence of God in history and anticipates his continuing presence and his rule. Instead of canceling the significance of the here and now of history, the kingdom intersects and fills history with ultimate meaning. Common events are not empty, but the coming kingdom of God imbues them with hope.

As language of revelation, the kingdom of God originates before contemporary time, and thus brings eternal, eschatological meaning and hope to time. As language of hope, the kingdom of God points to the power of God to intervene in history to make himself present and known. Kingdom language is distinguishable from all other speech, causes, traditions, and movements; as such, the kingdom of God reveals God as the one who heals, liberates, and transforms.

TRANSFORMED LIVES

The kingdom of God, made known in Jesus' words and deeds, continues to be made manifest through the church and realized in transformed lives. A young mother encounters God through revealed language, and this is enough to change her existence. The kingdom of God is the biblical witness, hermeneutical lens, and the paradigm or theme through which she discovers God's activity in the world and discerns how she is to participate in the Spirit's work. This discovery and discernment lead to a life of devotion to Christ and give witness to what she has seen and heard.

The language of the kingdom of God surpasses mission language because of its transformative power. Kingdom language is revelatory and hopeful, and thus it transcends routine speech and programmatic agendas. The gospel of the kingdom is the message of transformative events, as evidenced in the incarnation, cross, and resurrection. Because these originate from eternity, they are more than common events. Because their intent is to interrupt and change the course of peoples' histories, their proclamation is more than normal speech. This transformative power of the kingdom can be seen in its effect on the apostles and the early church, and their unrelenting proclamation of the reign of God as an alternative view of reality.

Jesus' inauguration of the kingdom confounds everyone, because it shatters conventional notions of power and change. The kingdom of God caused consternation for John the Baptist (Lk 7:20), the Sadducees and

Pharisees (Mt 12:24-25), and even the disciples, for it was unlike the kingdoms around them and was radically different from the kingdom they were expecting. After two to three years of hearing the words of Jesus and seeing his deeds, the disciples asked, "Lord, is it at this time You are restoring the kingdom to Israel?" (Acts 1:6). They were anticipating the Davidic kingdom of former glory by means of "militaristic nationalism."[22] The change promised in the gospel of the kingdom originated in humility and displacement, rather than in the conquest of armies, or the power of occupying forces, and thus Jesus' language of the kingdom of God contradicted the disciples' assumptions and beliefs and confounded their messianic expectations. In the kingdom of God, Jesus recalibrated power and reoriented change.

Mission, on the other hand, is synthetic, modern language that is an attempt to represent eternal matters. Because it is modern, mission language must stress human roles and actions to be fulfilled and results to be realized and measured. Indeed, even when used of God (i.e., the mission of God), mission language tends to present God's words and deeds as temporal realities and modern activities. On the other hand, the revealed, apocalyptic language of the kingdom of God signifies that past realities and future possibilities are charged with supernatural means and results. The difference between mission and the kingdom of God is that kingdom language bears the stamp of divine origin, means, and outcomes. Because God is the actor, the results are supernatural. Rather than qualifying divine activity with the language of *missio* or mission, kingdom language indicates that divine power is unqualified and prior to any human action, and the changes that ensue are beyond what ordinary means might affect.

Likewise, kingdom language creates the possibility of a different orientation for the church's life and witness. Rather than the execution of strategies based on the cause and effect of a business or military model, the church's existence and activities point to a reality that is beyond history and yet present and active. The church's involvement is more than a stylized, existential, or cultural idea of religious life, program, and methodology, with faint promises of cosmic import and meaning. Instead, the life and activity of the church are rooted in ancient language, and its story is of God making

---

[22]Wright, *Jesus and the Victory of God*, 450.

himself known in time and history. The resulting orientation transforms men and women into holy people, and common events into divine encounters. The revealed, apocalyptic language of the kingdom reorients the mind to perceive God at work and to affirm divine initiative.

Embracing the kingdom of God does not remove us from the world but transforms our encounters within the world. Orientation to and formation in the kingdom of God readies us for engagement with the world by transforming us into *witnesses to* the kingdom and *pilgrims of* the kingdom. As *pilgrim witnesses we participate in the coming reign of God.*

Witnesses to the Kingdom

Kingdom language contradicts modern speech, disputes history as a closed continuum, and acknowledges forces beyond human understanding. As a result, the kingdom of God prompts witness to divine realities and possibilities. Most moderns believe that medicine and education have moved us beyond primal notions, such as demons, evil forces, and Satan, and have provided us with a more sophisticated understanding of human existence. Prayer and fasting as sacred practices may be of use for human stress or as a desperate, last-ditch remedy for cancer, but in the modern perspective these are only means of escape or diversion rather than active engagement with the real forces of power. Modernity has replaced these "superstitions" with more reliable scientific therapy and management, and sophisticated programs full of best practices that offer predictable success. In the end, modernity manufactures its own version of awe and promotes these as spectacular vision. Religion and its programs have difficulty competing with the modern spectacle, so we abandon talk about God and his reign.

The biblical witness counters and contradicts the modern spectacle. The kingdom of God posits that God confronts demonic forces, heals disease, liberates the oppressed, and destroys the works of Satan.[23] Time and again, Scripture points to men and women who encounter the power of the kingdom, and as a result they are healed, liberated, and forgiven. Walking away from these encounters, they are not quiet but give witness to God's

---

[23] According to N. T. Wright, the real enemy for Jesus and thus the point of the "kingdom story" is Satan. Ibid., 2:451-74.

power and dominion.[24] They acknowledge more than change by way of organizational prowess or the well-conceived strategies of a superior religion. Rather, they exclaim, "Great is the Lord, mighty to save." The Samaritan leper, blind Bartimeaus, and Gerasene demoniac experience the power of God over sickness, blindness, and demons, and they tell their neighbors and friends what Jesus has done (Mk 1:40-45; 2:1-12; 5:20). What "the Bible presents us," according to Suzanne de Dietrich, is "a *body of witnesses*."[25] More than a peripheral or minor word, witness to the power of God's reign dominates the biblical record.

While *witness* may have baggage for some moderns because of the misuse of the term and exploitative practices associated with it, it is scriptural language and thus deserving of vindication. *Witness* is not a synonym for *persuasion, argument,* or *coercion.* Witness runs in two directions, each compounding the other. Witness is both beholding and telling. To *behold* is to witness something that changes one's existence. *Beholding* is more than seeing with physical eyes; it is to be captured by a vision of that which is revealed (apocalyptic), and thus hopeful and transformative. To *tell* is to do more than recount events with a line of argument or in a dispassionate manner; rather, *telling* is to convey with one's words and life what has been seen and experienced. This means that witness is more than a task or presentation, skill, or technique. Because it originates from one's encounter with God and his reign, witness encompasses all of life, and as such becomes our identity.[26] Rather than doing or performing witness, we *are* witnesses (Mt 28:19; 1 Jn 1:1-3) of what we have beheld of the reign of God.

Witness cannot happen without an encounter with the reign of God. Unless one understands one's desperate state without the power of God and has beheld the power of God to forgive, transform, and redeem one's broken life, one has little to say and not much to show. One may speak words of apologetics, doctrine, and mission, but these are not necessarily words of

---

[24]"Bearing witness" to the kingdom is the emphasis of DeYoung and Gilbert's section on the kingdom of God in Kevin DeYoung and Greg Gilbert, *What Is the Mission of the Church? Making Sense of Social Justice, Shalom, and the Great Commission* (Wheaton, IL: Crossway, 2011), 115-39.

[25]Suzanne de Dietrich, *The Witnessing Community: The Biblical Record of God's Purpose* (Philadelphia: Westminster, 1958), 14. Dietrich's emphasis.

[26]See James Wm. McClendon Jr., *Systematic Theology*, vol. 3, *Witness* (Waco, TX: Baylor University Press, 2012), 353-63.

witness. As the young mother from the streets of Kolkata speaks of what she has seen of the power of God and the miracle of transformation in her life, she is a witness.

While witness includes the details of the human story, it is not self-generated. Witness is the human echo of divine words and deeds. The language of witness indicates the telling and retelling of what has been seen, heard, or experienced of the coming kingdom of God. The teller gives witness to that which is beyond her creation and control, and thus her words are of transcendent realities. God, according to Karl Barth, makes people "witnesses of the fact that He is, or of who and what He is in and for Himself in His hidden Godhead. . . . They are witnesses of the God who was who He was, is who He is and will be who He will be in these acts of His."[27] The rhetoric of witness specifics that the teller's words echo that which is revealed of God by God, and has been made known in revelation that is not of the teller's contrivance or control.

In a dynamic sense, witness collapses human speech and actions within the time and space of divine words and deeds. As such, witness is the Spirit's work in and through human words and deeds, for "it is the Spirit who testifies, because the Spirit is the truth" (1 Jn 5:6; see also Jn 5:30-39; 1 Jn 5:10; Heb 10:15). The weight and uniqueness of human words and deeds become secondary to the Spirit's witness. Witness to the divine alters the importance of temporalities such as nationality, language, and culture. While these historical and cultural markers have significance, they are not ultimate or sacred. Rather, a vision of the coming kingdom opens the possibility for all men and women, to can give witness to eternal words and deeds.

Modern conceptions of cause and effect have taught us to flatten divine words and deeds into one-dimensional ideas and events. And while flattened words may communicate effectively and can even be inspiring, in the end they remain temporal words. They may give witness to the power of the speaker's skill and technique but do not always echo the divine. What often passes as witness is too flat and one-dimensional, and thus too human and inept. This anemic version of witness consists solely of words with little power and pathos, and often as staged, artificial performance of rehearsed

---

[27]Karl Barth, *Church Dogmatics*, trans. Geoffrey William Bromiley (Edinburgh: T&T Clark, 1961) IV/3, 575. For Barth's discussion of witness and weakness, see 673-74, 742-51.

sound bites by reluctant witnesses or polished professionals. Witness, on the other hand, happens as one movement—*beholding* and *retelling* of divine words and deeds.

PILGRIMS OF THE KINGDOM

A vision of the kingdom of God dislocates men and women from temporal hopes and transforms them into people who journey toward a greater vision. This vision, and thus pilgrimage, means we join those who live with displacement, expulsion, and separation. The language of *pilgrim* offers an image of a homeless wanderer exposed to the elements who must rely on others for basic needs, such as a beggar on the streets of Kolkata, exposed to rain, heat, and mosquitoes, in borrowed spaces and at risk of abuse. A beggar has little to no assurance of medical care, food, or security. Asleep at the curb and in alleyways, she may be mistaken for a heap of trash rather than a human being. She is without home, begging for her existence, and outside the structures of power and privilege. Those with power, privilege, money, and means may think that God has preferred them over those sleeping on the street, when the opposite may be the case.

The point is not to be without food or shelter but to be a pilgrim of the kingdom of God. Poverty and homelessness are not virtues in themselves except as they dislodge us from privilege and create dependence on God. Whether in a home or on the street, with plenty of food or in great hunger, mother or engineer, the ultimate aim of the pilgrim is to be defined by Christ's reign and his way. Pride of possession, place of birth, ample means, and religious ways keep us from seeing ourselves as we actually are— desperate exiles in need of rescue.

Modern-day pilgrims, sojourners, aliens, and strangers are not alone, for these same words describe the people of God in the Old and New Testaments. Abraham, Jacob, Moses, and Israel sojourned in foreign places and among strangers.[28] The writer of the book of Hebrews describes Jesus as suffering outside the gate and suggests his readers should "go out to Him outside the camp, bearing His reproach" (Heb 13:12-13). Peter names the believers "scattered throughout Pontus, Galatia, Cappadocia, Asia, and

---

[28]See Walter Brueggemann, *Genesis: A Bible Commentary for Teaching and Preaching*, Interpretation (Atlanta: John Knox, 1982), 121-25.

Bithynia" as those who reside as aliens (1 Pet 1:1). Followers of Christ are meant to wander, as his people have done from the beginning.

Even if displacement is not an actual, physical state, a pilgrim existence is possible. Though one may stay within their country of birth, on a familiar street, and in their ancestral home, pilgrimage is their calling and commitment. Augustine observes that pilgrimage is the recognition that one is "by grace a pilgrim below, and by grace a citizen above."[29] Pilgrimage is the admission that the present is transitory and unstable, and that hope must be for another place of home. Thus, Christendom is not home, and occupation is not the aim. Whether in a territorial or political reality or Christian nation, or some other kind of realized sacred place, one must refuse to homestead any place as the ultimate place of arrival. Pilgrims, passing through alien countries, foreign lands, are never truly at home.

The trauma of physical and sexual abuse, broken relationships, devastating wars, racial injustice, economic woes, and personal loss has destroyed for many the illusion of sanctuary and wholeness in the here and now. Christendom assumptions regarding place and privilege that exist throughout the Western world, and its refrains of God and country, triumphant Christianity, and naive optimism, ring hollow in the face of such severe personal and societal afflictions. When no longer culturally privileged or politically courted, Western Christians will have to choose whether or not they will sojourn as aliens and pilgrims in the wasteland of what was once Christendom. To think otherwise is a delusion.

The counternarrative of pilgrimage is the gospel of privilege and power. While territorial and political Christendom may have disappeared, enclaves of cultural Christendom still exist, where Christians maintain a vision of a kingdom on earth in which they are entitled to the best life possible, political advantage, and freedom from suffering or inconvenience. Within ghettoized Christendom, religious personalities and superstars function as exemplars of success. The not-so-subtle message goes something like this: "If you follow Christ, you can have it all, right now. Like me, you can live large, be

---

[29]Augustine, *Concerning the City of God Against the Pagans*, trans. Henry Bettenson (London: Penguin Books, 1984), 15.1 (p. 596). For more on Augustine's use of *pilgrim* and *pilgrimage* as identifying markers of the Christian, see M. A. Claussen, "'Peregrinatio' and 'Peregrini' in Augustine's 'City of God,'" *Traditio* 46 (January 1991): 33-75.

known, and have the benefits of all kingdoms." Yet, the biblical account of Jesus sending out the seventy with no provision and as lambs among wolves contradicts these narratives of success and grandeur, human ingenuity, and power. These narratives are contrary to Jesus' words of the kingdom of God being small and hidden. They are in conflict with the lived experience of the early church and the conditions of contemporary Christians in places of war, displacement, and imprisonment.

Obsession with organization and power evidences our loss of pilgrimage. Faith and witness become reified as systems and objectives, plans and roles, methods and strategies. Rather than means to a pilgrim existence, schemes and institutions become ends that consume the church, with their operation and maintenance. Instead of pilgrims, men and women become managers of programs, employees of organizations, professionals, and power brokers. Sojourning in the Christ Way is displaced by religious events, mission trips, and thirdhand involvement in social causes.

As was the case in the Crusades and colonialism, modern mission often perverts pilgrimage. Christendom assumptions and beliefs inherent in "mission" convert pilgrim existence into missionary conquest, missionary occupation, and missionary triumph. Rather than pilgrimage being the state for every believer in whatever vocation and in each locale, modern mission emphasizes the specialized employment of professional pilgrims deployed to mission fields. Mission becomes a perversion of pilgrimage when missionaries are viewed as the only true pilgrims, while everyone else observes their journey and vicariously participates.

As in the case of "the kingdom of God," the language of *pilgrim* and *sojourner* is prior to "mission," sourced from Scripture, and spoken by the ancient church. Pilgrim language has provided the early church and Christians throughout the centuries with a safeguard against claiming a posture of power and the aggrandizement of institutions and traditions.[30] And yet, as we have seen, pilgrimage can be co-opted and perverted. While pilgrimage has been used for violence and personal gain, Jesus instructs his followers to make disciples *as they go*, without purse or position. The concern for salvation and liberation that characterized Patrick, Columba, and

---

[30]Martin Robinson, "Pilgrimage and Mission," in *Explorations in a Christian Theology of Pilgrimage*, ed. Craig Bartholomew and Fred Hughes (Aldershot, UK: Ashgate, 2004), 174-75.

Columban was tempered by their displacement and suffering. Their pilgrim existence kept them on the move and without power. In the same way, modern disciples are called to be ceaseless pilgrims in God's kingdom, seeing Christ outside the gate and constantly moving toward him.

BETTER LANGUAGE

As language enters vocabulary, integrates with thought, and becomes the content of communication, it changes the way one sees God, it shapes identity, and it determines actions. Kingdom language prompts those who follow Christ to live as pilgrims who give witness to the coming reign of God. They are not called *missionaries*, and their life purpose is not named as *mission*. To supplant the structures of thought expressed in Scripture with the language of a modern tradition is to underestimate the power of God's kingdom to change the world through witnesses and pilgrims. The modern framework of mission language blunts the effects of the biblical language by offering a narrow representation of God and the world and by tempering expectations of what could happen. Attempts to couch mission in kingdom language may provide substance and validity to mission but diminish the place and power of the kingdom.[31] Conversely, kingdom language frees the modern believer from ordinary expectations and expands the range of possibilities. Kingdom language is the better choice of language, because it is rooted in revelation, includes all types of believers, prioritizes formation of life, expands possibilities, underscores the place of the church, liberates from Christendom assumptions, and points to the Spirit's work.

Rooted in revelation. Causes, ideas, and movements come and go, ebb and flow, but the kingdom of God endures as ancient language. Its pedigree is long, sustained, and biblical. *Kingdom, witness,* and *pilgrim* orients the mind, emotions, and person in ultimate rather than penultimate matters. The desire of every man and woman is to focus life on what is meaningful and ultimate. To give oneself to mission is to root one's identity and life in disputed language and a modern tradition, and thus in a foundation that is constructed and temporal. The kingdom of God is an eternal and sure

---

[31]Glasser, *Announcing the Kingdom,* proposes a "Kingdom missiology" that gives priority to participation in and responsibility to modern mission with the kingdom of God as accessory or proof.

foundation. Witness and pilgrim are biblical identities that are transformative, because they are firmly rooted in what is ancient and revealed, not recent and modern.

Includes all believers. The qualification for a witness and pilgrim is submission to the reign of God. *Witness* and *pilgrim* are not exclusive or narrow occupations that require a special calling or commission. Rather, both terms include anyone who has seen the coming of the kingdom of God, and thus is compelled to tell others about it and then journey with others to where the reign of God leads. The reign of God, rather than location (mission field) and title (missionary), determines whether one is a witness and pilgrim. If someone is excluded or disqualified, it is for the right reasons; either they refuse to be a pilgrim (they want to homestead or occupy), or they do not know the reign of God personally (and thus have little to say). For some, kingdom language is too inclusive and not professional enough, and so they preference language that creates levels of participation—missionary and nonmissionary. On the other hand, the kingdom of God is an open invitation to be transformed by the reign of God into witnesses and pilgrims.

Prioritizes formation of life. The aim of Christ following is the manifestation of the reign of God in individual lives and corporate bodies. The ultimate goal is for people to be transformed into witnesses and pilgrims who speak of God and embody the Spirit's fruits of patience, gentleness, humility, love, and unity (Eph 4:1-3). This in turn results in more witnesses and pilgrims; formation begets transformation. The antithesis of formation is mobilization. Mission mobilizers exist because people must be convinced to do something they are incapable of or don't want to do. Without formation, believers must be forced from outside themselves rather than from within their character and from conviction. They must be convinced to get up from where they are and go to somewhere they are not. The mobilizer's task is to justify mission to churches and individuals with the result that some will surrender to the mission call and others will fund the mission endeavor. *The net effect is an overemphasis on the deployment of unformed people.* While many are mobilized to travel to foreign places, they may not be able to give witness in word and deed to their own life transformation. The language of mobilization fits with the imagery of amassing forces for an assault in order to subdue and occupy enemy territory. While the marshaling of forces implies mobilization, submission to the kingdom points to the formation of people. Some will argue that mission mobilization is necessary because of the urgency of the task—"God is not known, the need is great, and thus there is an urgent responsibility to mobilize." Formation, on the other hand, is not urgent but deliberate, does not fight against enemies but journeys alongside fellow human beings, and does not marshal forces for an assault but cultivates witnesses and pilgrims. The aim of mission is scale and force, and the objective of the kingdom is formation that begets transformation. Cultivating pilgrim witness focuses the task of pastors, teachers, and parents on the formation of parents, students, and children toward becoming witnesses who embody the power of the resurrected Christ in word and deed.

Expands possibilities. Kingdom language places the end results with what God does, by the means he chooses, and according to his timetable. Formational practices are meant to equip people to recognize and speak of the reign of God, not create a prescribed result. Schooling within a kingdom mindset and pilgrim practices readies God's people to give faithful witness to what God could do within the course of their daily work, among friends and family, and in the face of opposition and pressures. Rather than a focus on specific places and times, through certain people, the possibility of the arrival of the reign of God is unlimited and unpredictable.

Mission language, on the other hand, often communicates that particular tasks are to be achieved in a certain way and measured by a specific matrix. This is most clearly seen in the tendency to couple mission efforts with the language of business (markets, objectives, enterprise) and warfare (strategy, operations, targets, assault). While mission rhetoric projects a more defined role for individuals and promotes personal involvement, in the end, what is accomplished may be limited to their abilities and within the realm of what they think is possible. The language of kingdom moves beyond the prescriptions of what *should* happen and opens the possibilities of what *could* happen.

Underscores the place of the church. Kingdom language recognizes the place of the community of faith in the activity of God. Some view the church as the problem or an impediment, so they advocate a "kingdom orientation" rather than a "church orientation," as if we must choose between the two.[32] For sure, the church is not the kingdom of God, but the church, as the body of Christ, exists in the world to speak and embody kingdom values. As a community of people being transformed into the likeness of Christ, the church is able to witness to Christ's teaching, life, and death. By the very fact that people surrender personal desires and their agenda to live alongside others, they offer a counterwitness to the pervasive individualism of modern life.

In the early church, communities of faith emerged in cities and regions and became centers of witness of Christ to those living around them. As Lesslie Newbigin notes, Paul did not establish "in Philippi or in Derbe or in Lystra two organizations, one called the church and the other called the Antioch mission, Lystra branch."[33] Rather, ancient churches formed by an encounter with God existed in particular locales as expressions of the Spirit's witness in their corner of the world. As the Spirit speaks to the church (Acts 13:1), the witness of the Spirit is extended into adjoining as well as faraway regions. But when another entity becomes the primary mode of witness, the church becomes secondary and is even perceived as a problem. The example from Scripture is that witness spreads from local communities of faith, as believers move through their neighborhoods, across the city, and into the world.[34]

Mission, on the other hand, tends to extract individuals from churches and divert them into mission organizations to give witness as missionaries. Through the transfer of its witness, the place and purpose of these churches are subverted. The obvious conclusion is that mission organizations must exist, because the church is inadequate or unwilling. While the church is far from perfect and often too modern, its calling is to be a witnessing, pilgriming community, as it continually reorients its life toward the reign of

---

[32]Dave Tomlinson, *Re-enchanting Christianity: Faith in an Emerging Culture* (Norwich, UK: Canterbury, 2008), 132.

[33]Lesslie Newbigin, *A Word in Season: Perspectives on Christian World Missions* (Grand Rapids: Eerdmans, 1994), 25-26.

[34]Harry R. Boer, *Pentecost and Missions* (Grand Rapids: Eerdmans, 1961), maintains, "Societies have done the work that the Church in her totality should have performed. The missionary society is, scripturally speaking, an abnormality. But it has been a blessed abnormality" (214). See also Andrew Walls's chapter "Missionary Societies and the Fortunate Subversion of the Church," in *The Missionary Movement in Christian History: Studies in the Transmission of Faith* (Maryknoll, NY: Orbis Books, 1996), 241-54.

God. If the church is deficient, the antidote is surrender to and formation in the reign of God, not mission.

The answer for some is to combine church and mission. If the church is inadequate, it is because it lacks mission in its essence or substance. The corrective is to define the church *as* mission.[35] In this solution, mission makes the church truly church, and without mission the church is less than authentic church. Emil Brunner is often quoted in this regard: "The Church exists by mission, just as a fire exists by burning. Where there is no mission, there is no Church; and where there is neither Church nor mission, there is no faith."[36] However, such a formula becomes a zero-sum proposition insofar as it is based entirely on an ambiguous term. The church existed prior to modern mission and will continue beyond it. Those who quote Brunner's words fail to acknowledge his nuanced use of *mission* and that his ultimate emphasis is on the proclamation of the gospel. Rather than mission, it seems more appropriate to say the church exists through its proclamation of Christ by the power of the Spirit and its witness to the coming reign of God.

Liberates from Christendom. The kingdom of God serves as a constant reminder that the church is not a privileged society or club, and it is certainly not in charge. Rather, the church is a sojourning people who give witness to God, who controls and sustains all things. The kingdom is God's kingdom; the kingdom is not just in Christendom, but everywhere. It is like scattered seed that takes roots and grows in the far corners of humanity.

At the height of Christendom, mission meant the crossing of geographical, linguistic, religious, cultural, and civilizational boundaries to confront heathendom. Emissaries of the church crossed vast bodies of water in order to extend the reach of the Latin and then Protestant church. The extension of the church was the extension of Christendom. Today the church exists on all continents, speaks almost every language, and has made itself at home in nearly every culture. Residual ideas of boundaries and extensions are just

---

[35]See Newbigin's discussion of church and mission in *One Body, One Gospel, One World: The Christian Mission Today* (London: Wm. Carling, 1958), 15-17, 25-27.

[36]Emil Brunner, *The Word and the World* (London: SCM Press, 1931), 108. The sentences that follow are seldom quoted: "It is a secondary question whether by that we mean Foreign Missions, or simply the preaching of the Gospel in the home Church. Mission, Gospel preaching, is the spreading out of the fire which Christ has thrown upon the earth." Rather than a justification of mission as the essence of the church, Brunner emphasizes the inflammatory nature of Christ's gospel.

that—ideas and not reality. These inherent Christendom assumptions in mission language are wrong and destructive. In the current era, communities of witnesses and pilgrims exist all over the world and move in every direction. Acknowledging the pervasive reach of its kingdom of God liberates the Western church from the burden of its Christendom past and the illusion of control and transforms it into a serving, humble partner. The Christendom mindset of mission views the gospel trafficking in one direction—from the West to the rest. Kingdom language automatically reframes the reach of the gospel as witnesses from all nations and with its direction from every region.

Points to the Spirit's work. Kingdom language moves beyond a discussion regarding what is relevant or irrelevant, what will work or not work, or what is efficient and effective; instead, kingdom language gravitates toward who God is and what God is doing. Rather than adopting business or military techniques and strategies, and rather than outsourcing witness to experts or professionals, assemblies of pilgrims look to the Spirit's direction and power for witness. The language of the kingdom of God directs attention from the next, best strategy to the powerful advent of the Spirit.

Following Jesus' ascension, the disciples waited in Jerusalem for the Spirit. On the day of Pentecost, the disciples experienced wind and noise and then "tongues as of fire distributing themselves" and resting on them (Acts 2:3). The Spirit set the disciples' tongues loose so that those gathered heard of the mighty deeds of God in their own language. Peter told those gathered that what they were witnessing was not the antics of drunken men but an apocalyptic event that had been predicted by the prophet Joel. Joel's prophecy is vivid and bold: dreams, visions, wonders in the sky above, signs on the earth, blood, fire, vapor of smoke, the sun turned into darkness, and the moon into blood (Joel 2:28-32). The Spirit gave powerful witness in an apocalyptic display of God's mighty work.

The coming of the Spirit at Pentecost set in motion the witness of the early church. Jesus instructed the disciples "to wait for what the Father had promised" (Acts 1:4). Only as the Spirit came on them did they receive power and become witnesses "in Jerusalem, and in all Judea and Samaria, and even to the remotest part of the earth" (Acts 1:8). The empowerment of the Spirit initiated the expansion of the church from Jerusalem to the corners of the world. This promised power of the Spirit became witness as the reign of God arrived in the apostles' lives.

Postmission Encounters

Imagine a man named Jack, in his early forties, who works for an engineering firm in Houston. Jack and his wife, Sarah, have two children and live in a middle-class, surburban neighborhood. Their lives are busy with work, weekend activities, and civic responsibilities. Although Jack's life is full of activity, he is numbed by it all. He feels that life is going nowhere and that there must surely be something more to life. He gets up, goes to work, comes home, mows the yard, goes to soccer practice with the kids, and takes his annual vacation. The routine and grind seem to be pointless. It is not that life is hard or that they are destitute, but it is all so empty. His numbness grows into anxiety and personal crisis. The internal struggle reaches such a point that one afternoon he blurts out to his wife that he is quitting his job and changing his life. Both are standing in the kitchen, she at the sink and he at the table. She immediately turns off the tap and looks at him in disbelief. "I want more out of life, too," she says, "but throwing away all that we have worked for and putting our family and home at risk is not the answer. Is all you can do think of yourself?" Their exchange becomes heated, and accusations are made in both direction. Finally, Jack storms out of the house, gets in his car, and drives out of the city. After an hour of aimless driving, he stops at a small roadside diner. As he sits at the counter, shoulders hunched and eyes trained on the worn surface of a coffee cup, he thinks to himself, "I am trapped in this job—in this life. I need to know that life is about more than money, a mortgage, and work. Isn't there more to all of this?"

An older, graying man behind the counter can't help but notice Jack, and asks, "What's up? Everything okay?" Jack does not hestitate but tells him everything—his feelings of being trapped, the emptiness of the routine, the encounter with Sarah, and his desperation to know life is more than an endless, meaningless rut. He cannot stop talking as he unloads all of this on a complete stranger. Once Jack has said everything he can, he looks at the waiter confused and embarrassed.

The man behind the counter gives Jack a slight smile and says, "I was right where you are four years ago—trying to make sense of everything. I gave up a good job at an investment firm, moved to a smaller house, and in the process nearly ruined my marriage. For me, it was about destitute people on the streets of Houston and the feeling that I had to do something about it. I tried to solve the injustice and inequality, but in no time at all, I found myself spent and wondering if I was making any difference. After working for a nonprofit for a year, I left disillusioned, because of a conflict with a fellow worker, and confused by the politics of it all." He pauses for a moment and then continues. "I thought maybe religion might be the answer. I had grown up in the church and knew the lingo but was not sure what all of it meant. I had heard people talk about being a missionary as the ultimate form of sacrifice and doing mission work as the ultimate way of service. So, I talked my wife into going down that road. We considered becoming missionaries and moving to Brazil, but once I started making inquiries and even began the application process with a mission agency, I knew being a missionary was not me and mission was not the answer I was looking for."

He stops, looks toward the street for moment, and then at Jack. "I became so desperate to know why I existed and what I was to do that I started questioning if there was any meaning to life and if I should go on living. I came to the end of myself and my way of putting it all together. I had never really read the Bible. Oh, I heard it read in church and heard plenty of sermons from the Bible, but I had not read it for myself. So, I decided I would give it a try. I began reading from the beginning of the New Testament searching for an answer—some kind of answer. I noticed immediately Jesus talking a lot about the kingdom of God. It jumped off the page and grabbed me. I had read of the kingdom of God before but had not really *seen* it. The kingdom of God and kingdom of heaven were everywhere, and I began to connect with kingdom words. Over a period of time and after loads of discussion with friends, I began to understand that the kingdom was Jesus' thing. I discovered that the point of Christianity is not church attendance, or me being a moral person, or about me getting something from God or doing for God. It is about God's reign coming to my life and spreading throughout my family, my city, and the world. Once I understood this, I started on a journey that has taken me in a direction I could have never imagined. The details of my life are still not settled; in fact, they may be a bit more messy, but I am sure of the direction."

The waiter pauses again for a long time, looks down at his hands on the counter, and then back up at Jack. "I believe that God is up to something in and around me, in this town—in the world. My life is meant to coincide with what he is doing to establish his reign in the systems, situations, and lives around me. I don't have to make sense of how this will happen. In fact, I can't make sense of it. What I must do is believe that he is at work and yield myself to him. Life now is like a trip into the new world of God and his activities. I exist for the ride and to tell those I meet along the way what I am seeing and experiencing. It is like this: God wants to bring sense to this crazy, dysfunctional world, and he wants to do it as he makes sense of my crazy, dysfunctional life." Jack has heard everything the man behind the counter has said. But more than hearing or even fully understanding, he can see that the man has found an answer—a life-altering answer.

Jack's story of anxiety and emptiness is more than an imagined narrative. Many caught in the shift of the landscape of modern life know a similar loss of meaning and are looking for hope. Their questions demand more than a pat answer or a static, one-dimensional response. They need to take a journey—a pilgrimage—that is dynamic and expansive. The reign of God offers men and women meaning and hope and beckons them to travel new pathways in the changing landscape.

Kingdom language allows a waiter to speak to an engineer of more than church talk and also of matters that encompass the whole of creation—the social, economic, ecological, and political dimensions of life. By its nature, the kingdom of God encompasses the whole of creation—all of the cosmos— and thus provides the intersection that touches every corner of life. The kingdom of God redeems the crises that exist within modern men and women by pointing them to the transformative power of the Spirit.

The role of the pilgrim witness is to watch what God does in and around him or her and to continually ask, What could God do in my life, through my presence in this place? This kind of expectation is more probable when the language of the kingdom is front and center. With such language, men and women are primed to move at the Spirit's prompting, though with possibly fewer people and far less fanfare. Formation is slower than mobilization, and formation runs deeper than mission orientation; however, pilgrimage offers the possibility of participation with the Spirit in witness to the world.

The transformation of a young mother and an engineer begins with an encounter but continues throughout their lives. The process of transformation for both does not center in a religion that conquers, ideas that originate in the West, or through civilizational uplift. Rather, their encounter with the kingdom of God as revealed in Jesus Christ transforms who they are and how they will act throughout the course of their lives. The reign of God means they live as pilgrims in the way of the kingdom, and they give witness to family and friends of the kingdom's power to confront and transform. The reign of God will manifest itself in their conversations and choices. As pilgrims, they give witness as they go. Their going may or may not be of their choice, as they may go as migrants, or because of employment, displacement, political partition, or ethnic cleansing. Historically these have caused pilgrims to move from place to place. Opportunities in work may open the option of going to a new city or a different country. The need for work may mandate a move to a new place. A community of faith in Kolkata or Houston may hear the Spirit say, "Send a young mother in your midst to the other side of the city," or, "Support an engineer who is being transferred by his company to Afghanistan." Or *going* may be of another sort, as the majority within society comes to detest what followers of Christ preach and represent and thus pushes them to the margins of place and power, or even sends them into exile. The crux of the matter lies not in the sending or the going but in the reign of God that converts men and women into pilgrim witnesses. The testimony of Scripture and the story of the church declare that the kingdom of God that has come and keeps coming as people are transformed by people who are continually being transformed by the power of God's reign.

Works Cited

Addison, James Thayer. *The Medieval Missionary: A Study of the Conversion of Northern Europe, A.D. 500–1300*. Studies in the World Mission of Christianity 2. New York: International Missionary Council, 1936.

Adewuya, J. Ayodeji. "The Sacrificial-Missiological Function of Paul's Sufferings in the Context of 2 Corinthians." In *Paul as Missionary: Identity, Activity, Theology, and Practice*, edited by Trevor J. Burke and Brian S. Rosner, 88-98. Library of New Testament Studies 420. London: T&T Clark, 2011.

Adomanán. *Life of St Columba*. Translated by Richard Sharpe. Middlesex, UK: Penguin Books, 1995.

Agnew, Francis H. "The Origin of the NT Apostle-Concept: A Review of Research." *Journal of Biblical Literature* 105, no. 1 (March 1986): 75-96.

Alden, Dauril. *The Making of an Enterprise: The Society of Jesus in Portugal, Its Empire, and Beyond, 1540–1750*. Stanford, CA: Stanford University Press, 1996.

Allen, Roland. *Missionary Methods: St. Paul's or Ours?* Grand Rapids: Eerdmans, 1983.

Alvares, Claude, and Norma Alvares. "The Christian and the Wild." In *Discoveries, Missionary Expansion and Asian Cultures*, edited by Teotonio R. de Souza, 19-31. New Delhi: Concept, 1994.

Anderson, Rufus. *Foreign Missions: Their Relations and Claims*. New York: Charles Scribner, 1869.

Aquinas, Thomas. *The Summa Theologiæ of Saint Thomas Aquinas: Latin-English*. Vol. 1. Scotts Valley, CA: NovAntiqua, 2008.

Arias, Mortimer. "Mission and Liberation, The Jubilee: A Paradigm for Mission Today." *International Review of Mission* 73 (January 1984): 33-48.

Armstrong, Karen. *Muhammad: A Biography of the Prophet*. San Francisco: HarperSanFrancisco, 1993.

Asbridge, Thomas. *The Crusades: The Authoritative History of the War for the Holy Land*. New York: HarperCollins, 2010.

Atwood, Craig D. *Community of the Cross: Moravian Piety in Colonial Bethlehem*. University Park: The Pennsylvania State University Press, 2004.

Augustine. *Concerning the City of God Against the Pagans.* Translated by Henry Bettenson. London: Penguin Books, 1984.

———. *Sancti Aurelii Augustini, De Trinitate Libri XV.* Corpus Christianorum. Series Latina 50. Turnhout: Brepols, 1968.

———. *The Trinity.* Translated by Stephen McKenna. The Fathers of the Church 45. Washington, DC: Catholic University of America Press, 1963.

Avis, Paul D. L. *The Church in the Theology of the Reformers.* Atlanta: John Knox, 1980.

Ayres, Lewis. *Augustine and the Trinity.* Cambridge: Cambridge University Press, 2010.

Bacon, Francis. "An Advertisement Touching a Holy War." In *Certain Miscellany Work.* London: William Rawley, 1629.

Bainton, Roland H. *Early and Medieval Christianity.* The Collected Papers in Church History. Boston: Beacon, 1962.

Baker, Archibald G. *Christian Missions and a New World Culture.* Chicago: Willett, Clark, 1934.

Baldwin, Marshall W. "Missions to the East in the Thirteenth and Fourteenth Centuries." In *A History of the Crusades.* Vol. 5, *The Impact of the Crusades on the Near East,* edited by Norman P. Zacour and Harry W. Hazard, 452-518. Madison: The University of Wisconsin Press, 1985.

Balfour, Lord. "Opening Address." In *World Missionary Conference, 1910: The History and Records of the Conference Together with Addresses Delivered at the Evening Meetings,* 9:141-45. Edinburgh: Oliphant, Anderson, & Ferrier, 1910.

Bangert, William V. *A History of the Society of Jesus.* St. Louis: Institute of Jesuit Sources, 1986.

Banks, Louis Albert. "Carey's Missionary World and Ours." *Zion's Herald (1868–1910),* October 16, 1889.

"Baptist Foreign Mission Centenary." *Berrow's Worcester Journal,* September 24, 1892.

Barber, Malcolm. *The Crusader States.* New Haven, CT: Yale University Press, 2012.

Barlow, Frank. "The English Background." In *The Greatest Englishman: Essays on St. Boniface and the Church at Crediton,* edited by Timothy Reuter, 13-29. Exeter, UK: Paternoster, 1980.

Barnett, Mike, and Robin Martin, eds. *Discovering the Mission of God: Best Missional Practices for the 21st Century.* Downers Grove, IL: InterVarsity Press, 2012.

Barnett, Paul. *Jesus & the Rise of Early Christianity: A History of New Testament Times*. Downers Grove, IL: InterVarsity Press, 1999.

———. *Paul: Missionary of Jesus*. Vol. 2 of *After Jesus*. Grand Rapids: Eerdmans, 2008.

Barram, Michael D. "The Bible, Mission, and Social Location: Toward a Missional Hermeneutic." *Interpretation* 61, no. 1 (January 2007): 42-58.

———. *Mission and Moral Reflection in Paul*. Studies in Biblical Literature 75. New York: Peter Lang, 2006.

Barr, James. *Biblical Words for Time*. Studies in Biblical Theology 33. London: SCM Press, 1962.

———. *The Semantics of Biblical Languages*. Oxford: Oxford University Press, 1961.

Barrett, C. K. *Acts: A Shorter Commentary*. London: T&T Clark, 2002.

Barros, João de, and D. do Conto. *Decadas da Asia*. Lisbon: Na Regia Officina Typografica, 1777.

Barros, Joseph de. "Discoveries and Martyrs of Missionary Expansion in the East." In *Discoveries, Missionary Expansion and Asian Cultures*, edited by Teotonio R. de Souza, 85-90. New Delhi: Concept, 1994.

Barth, Karl. *Church Dogmatics*. Vol. 4, part 3. Translated by Geoffrey William Bromiley. Edinburgh: T&T Clark, 1961.

Bartholomew, Craig G. *Introducing Biblical Hermeneutics: A Comprehensive Framework for Hearing God in Scripture*. Grand Rapids: Baker Academic, 2015.

Bartlett, Robert. *The Making of Europe: Conquest, Colonization and Cultural Change, 950–1350*. Princeton, NJ: Princeton University Press, 1993.

Bauckham, Richard. *Bible and Mission: Christian Witness in a Postmodern World*. Grand Rapids: Baker Academic, 2003.

———. *The Theology of the Book of Revelation*. New Testament Theology. Cambridge: Cambridge University Press, 1993.

Baus, Karl. *From the Apostolic Community to Constantine*. Handbook of Church History 1. Freiburg, West Germany: Herder, 1965.

Bavinck, J. H. *An Introduction to the Science of Missions*. Translated by David Hugh Freeman. Philadelphia: Presbyterian and Reformed, 1960.

Beasley-Murray, G. R. *Jesus and the Kingdom of God*. Grand Rapids: Eerdmans, 1986.

Beattie, Pamela. "Evangelization, Reform and Eschatology: Mission and Crusade in the Thought of Ramon Llull." PhD dissertation, University of Toronto, 1995.

———. "'Pro Exaltatione Sanctae Fidei Catholicae': Mission and Crusade in the Writings of Ramon Llull." In *Iberia and the Mediterranean World of the Middle East: Studies in Honor of Robert I. Burns*, 113-29. Leiden: E. J. Brill, 1995.

Beaver, R. Pierce. *From Missions to Mission: Protestant World Mission Today and Tomorrow*. New York: Association Press, 1964.

———. "The Genevan Mission to Brazil." In *The Heritage of John Calvin: Heritage Hall Lectures, 1960–1970*, edited by John H. Bratt, 55-73. Grand Rapids: Eerdmans, 1973.

Beazley, C. Raymond. "Prince Henry of Portugal and the African Crusade of the Fifteenth Century." *The American Historical Review* 16, no. 1 (October 1910): 11-23.

Bede. *Bede's Ecclesiastical History of England*. Translated by J. A. Giles and John Stevens. Bohn's Antiquarian Library. London: Bell & Sons, 1907.

———. *Ecclesiastical History of the English People*. Oxford Medieval Texts. Oxford: Clarendon, 1969.

———. *The Ecclesiastical History of the English People*. Translated by A. M. Sellar. Mineola, NY: Dover, 2011.

———. *The History of the Church of Englande (1565)*. Translated by Thomas Stapleton. Amsterdam: Theatrum Orbis Terratum, 1970.

Bediako, Kwame. *Jesus and the Gospel in Africa: History and Experience*. Maryknoll, NY: Orbis Books, 2004.

Beeby, H. D. *Canon and Mission*. Harrisburg, PA: Trinity Press International, 1999.

Beer, Francis de. "St. Francis and Islam." *Spirit and Life: A Journal of Contemporary Franciscanism* 6 (1994): 161-75.

Beker, J. Christiaan. *Paul's Apocalyptic Gospel: The Coming Triumph of God*. Philadelphia: Fortress, 1982.

Bellarmine, Roberto Francesco Romolo. *De Notis Ecclesia / On the Marks of the Church*. Translated by Ryan Grant. N.p.: Mediatrix, 2015.

Bentley, Jerry H. *Old World Encounters: Cross-Cultural Contacts and Exchanges in Pre-modern Times*. New York: Oxford University Press, 1993.

Berend, Nora. "Frontiers." In *Palgrave Advances in the Crusades*, edited by Helen J. Nicholson, 148-71. New York: Palgrave MacMillan, 2005.

Berg, Johannes van den. *Constrained by Jesus' Love: An Inquiry into the Motives of the Missionary Awakening in Great Britain in the Period Between 1698 and 1815*. Kampen: J. H. Kok, 1956.

Bergren, Theodore A. *A Latin-Greek Index of the Vulgate New Testament: Based on Alfred Schmoller's Handkonkordanz Zum Griechishen Neuen Testament with an Index of Latin Equivalences Characteristic of "African" and "European"*

Old Latin Versions of the New Testament. Resources for Biblical Study 26. Atlanta: Scholars Press, 1991.

Berkwitz, Stephen C. "Hybridity, Parody, and Contempt: Buddhist Responses to Christian Missions in Sri Lanka." In *Cultural Conversions: Unexpected Consequences of Christian Missonary Encounters in the Middle East, Africa, and South Asia,* ed. Heather J. Sharkey, 99-120. New York: Syracuse University Press, 2013.

Bessenecker, Scott A. *Overturning Tables: Freeing Missions from the Christian-Industrial Complex.* Downers Grove, IL: InterVarsity Press, 2014.

Best, Ernest. "The Revelation to Evangelize the Gentiles." *Journal of Theological Studies* 35, no. 1 (April 1984): 1-30.

Betz, Hans Dieter. *Galatians: A Commentary on Paul's Letter to the Churches in Galatia.* Hermeneia—A Critical and Historical Commentary on the Bible. Philadelphia: Fortress, 1979.

Bevans, Stephen B. "From Edinburgh to Edinburgh: Toward a Missiology for a World Church." In *Mission After Christendom: Emergent Themes in Contemporary Mission,* edited by Obgu U. Kalu, Peter Vethanayagamony, and Edmund Kee-Fook Chia, 1-11. Louisville: Westminster John Knox, 2010.

Bevans, Stephen B., and Roger Schroeder. *Constants in Context: A Theology of Mission for Today.* Maryknoll, NY: Orbis Books, 2004.

Beyer, Bryan E. "Jesus Christ—The Living Word—and the Mission of God." In *Discovering the Mission of God: Best Missional Practices of the 21st Century,* edited by Mike Barnett and Robin Martin, 114-29. Downers Grove, IL: InterVarsity Press, 2012.

Beyerhaus, Peter. *Die Selbständigkeit der jungen Kirchen als missionarisches Problem.* Studia missionalia Upsaliensia. Barmen: Wuppertal, 1956.

———. "Mission, Humanization, and the Kingdom." In *Crucial Issues in Missions Tomorrow,* edited by Donald A. McGavran, 54-76. Chicago: Moody Press, 1972.

Beyreuther, Erich. *Studien zur Theologie Zinzendorfs: Gesammelte Aufsätze.* Germany: Neukirchener Verlag, 1962.

The Biblical Basis of the Church's Mission: Addresses of the Niagara Falls Conference on Missionary Education, 3–4–5 May, 1960. Toronto: Committee on Missionary Education, Canadian Council of Churches, 1960.

Bieler, Ludwig. "Muirchú's Life of St. Patrick as a Work of Literature." In *Studies on the Life and Legend of St. Patrick,* edited by Richard Sharpe, 9:219-33. Variorum Reprint CS244. London: Variorum Reprints, 1986.

Bird, Jessalynn. "Crusades." In *Encyclopedia of Medieval Pilgrimage*, edited by Larissa Taylor, Leigh Ann Craig, John B. Friedman, Kathy Gower, Thomas Izbicki, and Rita Tekippe. Leiden: Brill, 2010.

Bird, Michael F. *Jesus and the Origins of the Gentile Mission*. Library of Historical Jesus Studies. London: T&T Clark, 2006.

Blackman, Edwin Cyril. *The Biblical Basis of the Church's Missionary Enterprise*. Essays on Mission. London: London Missionary Society, 1961.

Blake, E. O. "The Formation of the 'Crusade Idea.'" *Journal of Ecclesiastical History* 21, no. 1 (January 1970): 11-31.

Blauw, Johannes. *The Missionary Nature of the Church: A Survey of Biblical Theology of Mission*. New York: McGraw-Hill, 1962.

Blocher, Jacques A., and Jacques Blandenier. *The Evangelization of the World: A History of Christian Mission*. Pasadena, CA: William Carey Library, 2013.

Bocking, Ronald. *Has the Day of the Missionary Passed?* Vol. 5, *Essays on Mission*. London: London Missionary Society, 1961.

Bockmühl, Klaus. *Evangelicals and Social Ethics: A Commentary on Article 5 of the Lausanne Covenant*. Translated by David T. Priestley. Outreach and Identity: Evangelical Theological Monographs 4. Downers Grove, IL: InterVarsity Press, 1979.

Boda, Mark J. "'Declare His Glory Among the Nations': The Psalter as Missional Collection." In *Christian Mission: Old Testament Foundations and New Testament Developments*, edited by Stanley E. Porter and Cynthia Long Westfall, 13-41. McMaster New Testament Studies Series. Eugene, OR: Pickwick, 2010.

Boer, Harry R. *Pentecost and Missions*. Grand Rapids: Eerdmans, 1961.

Böhme, Anton Wilhelm, trans. *Propagation of the Gospel in the East: Being an Account of the Success of Two Danish Missionaries, Lately Sent to the East-Indies for the Conversion of the Heathens in Malabar*. London: J. Downing, 1709.

Boniface. *Die Briefe Des Heiligen Bonifatius Und Lullus*. Monumenta Germaniae Historica. Berlin: Weidmannsche Verlagsbuchhandlung, 1955.

———. *The English Correspondence of Saint Boniface: Being for the Most Part Letters Exchanged Between the Apostle of the Germans and His English Friends*. Translated by Edward Kylie. The Medieval Library. New York: Cooper Square, 1966.

———. *The Letters of Saint Boniface*. Translated by Ephraim Emerton. Records of Civilization 31. New York: Columbia University Press, 1940.

Bonner, Anthony. "Historical Background and Life." In *Selected Works of Ramón Llull (1232–1316)*, 1:3-52. Translated by Anthony Bonner. Princeton, NJ: Princeton University Press, 1985.

Bosch, David J. *Believing in the Future: Toward a Missiology of Western Culture.* Valley Forge, PA: Trinity Press International, 1995.

———. "Reflections on Biblical Models of Mission." In *Landmark Essays in Mission and World Christianity*, 3-16. American Society of Missiology Series 43. Maryknoll, NY: Orbis Books, 2009.

———. "Theological Education in Missionary Perspective." *Missiology* 10, no. 1 (January 1982): 13-34.

———. *Transforming Mission: Paradigm Shifts in Theology of Mission.* Maryknoll, NY: Orbis Books, 2011.

———. "The Why and How of a True Biblical Foundation for Mission." In *Zending Op Weg Naar de Toekomst*, edited by J. Verkuyl, 33-45. Kampen: J. H. Kok, 1978.

———. *Witness to the World: The Christian Mission in Theological Perspective.* Atlanta: John Knox, 1980.

Bowen, Roger. *So I Send You: A Study Guide to Mission.* London: SPCK, 1996.

Bowers, W. Paul. "Paul and Religious Propaganda in the First Century." *Novum Testamentum* 22, no. 4 (October 1980): 316-23.

Boxer, C. R. *The Church Militant and Iberian Expansion.* Baltimore: Johns Hopkins University Press, 1978.

———. *Four Centuries of Portuguese Expansion, 1415–1825: A Succinct Survey.* Berkeley: University of California Press, 1969.

———. *João de Barros, Portuguese Humanist and Historian of Asia.* XCHR Studies Series 1. New Delhi: Concept, 1981.

———. "A Note on Portuguese Missionary Methods in the East: Sixteenth to Eighteenth Centuries." In *Christianity and Missions, 1450–1800*, 161-74. An Expanding World, The European Impact on World History 1450–1800, vol. 28. Hampshire, UK: Ashgate, 1997.

———. *The Portuguese Seaborne Empire, 1415–1825.* New York: A. A. Knoft, 1969.

Boyle, Marjorie O'Rourke. *Loyola's Acts: The Rhetoric of the Self.* The New Historicism 36. Berkeley: University of California Press, 1997.

Braaten, Carl E. *The Flaming Center: A Theology of the Christian Mission.* Philadelphia: Fortress, 1977.

Braun, Mathias. "Missionary Problems in the Thirteenth Century: A Study in Missionary Preparation." *The Catholic Historical Review* 25, no. 2 (July 1939): 146-59.

Bray, Thomas. *A Memorial, Representing the Present State of Religion, on the Continent of North America.* London: William Downing, 1700.

Bredero, Adriaan Hendrik. *Christendom and Christianity in the Middle Ages: The Relations Between Religion, Church, and Society.* Translated by Reinder Bruinsma. Grand Rapids: Eerdmans, 1994.

Bright, John. *The Kingdom of God: The Biblical Concept and Its Meaning for the Church.* Nashville: Abingdon-Cokesbury, 1953.

Brodrick, James. *The Origin of the Jesuits.* Chicago: Loyola University Press, 1986.

———. *Robert Bellarmine: Saint and Scholar.* Westminister, MD: Newman, 1961.

———. *Saint Ignatius Loyola: The Pilgrim Years 1491-1538.* New York: Farrar, Straus and Cudahy, 1956.

Brooke, Rosalind B. *The Coming of the Friars.* Historical Problems: Studies and Documents 24. London: G. Allen & Unwin, 1975.

Brotherton, Dennis Othel. "An Examination of Selected Pauline Passages Concerning the Vocational Missionary: An Interpretative Basis for Critiquing Contemporary Missiological Thoughts." PhD diss., Southwestern Baptist Theological Seminary, 1986.

Brown, Peter Robert Lamont. *The Rise of Western Christendom: Triumph and Diversity, AD 200-1000.* Cambridge, MA: Blackwell, 1996.

Brown, Schuyler. "Apostleship in the New Testament as an Historical and Theological Problem." *New Testament Studies* 30, no. 3 (July 1984): 474-80.

Brownson, James V. "Speaking the Truth in Love: Elements of a Missional Hermeneutic." In *The Church Between Gospel and Culture: The Emerging Mission in North America*, edited by George R. Hunsberger and Craig Van Gelder, 228-59. Grand Rapids: Eerdmans, 1996.

———. *Speaking the Truth in Love: New Testament Resources for a Missional Hermeneutic.* Christian Mission and Modern Culture. Harrisburg, PA: Trinity Press International, 1998.

Bruce, F. F. *The Spreading Flame: The Rise and Progress of Christianity from Its First Beginnings to the Conversion of the English.* Grand Rapids: Eerdmans, 1958.

Brueggemann, Walter. *Genesis: A Bible Commentary for Teaching and Preaching.* Interpretation. Atlanta: John Knox, 1982.

———. *Hope for the World.* Louisville: Westminster John Knox, 2001.

Brul, Peter Du. *Ignatius: Sharing the Pilgrim Story; A Reading of the Autobiography of St. Ignatius of Loyola*. Leominster, UK: Gracewing, 2003.

Brunner, Emil. *The Word and the World*. London: SCM Press, 1931.

Bühlmann, Walbert. "Francis and Mission According to the Rule of 1221." *Spirit and Life: A Journal of Contemporary Franciscanism* 6 (1994): 87-107.

Bull, Marcus Graham. "Crusade and Conquest." In *Cambridge History of Christianity*. Vol. 4, *Christianity in Western Europe c.1100–c.1500*, 340-52. Cambridge: Cambridge University Press, 2009.

Burke, Trevor J. "The Holy Spirit as the Controlling Dynamic in Paul's Role as Missionary to the Thessalonians." In *Paul as Missionary: Identity, Activity, Theology, and Practice*, edited by Trevor J. Burke and Brian S. Rosner, 142-57. Library of New Testament Studies 420. London: T&T Clark, 2011.

Burke, Trevor J., and Brian S. Rosner. "Introduction." In *Paul as Missionary: Identity, Activity, Theology, and Practice*, 1-8. Library of New Testament Studies 420. London: T&T Clark, 2011.

Burns, Robert I. "Christian-Islamic Confrontation in the West: The Thirteenth-Century Dream of Conversion." *The American Historical Review* 76, no. 5 (December 1971): 1386-1434.

Byrd, Jessalynn. "Crusades." In *Encyclopedia of Medieval Pilgrimage*, edited by Larissa Taylor, Leigh Ann Craig, John B. Friedman, Kathy Gower, Thomas Izbicki, and Rita Tekippe. Leiden: Brill, 2010.

Calvin, Jean. *Institutes of the Christian Religion*. 2 vols. Philadelphia: Westminster, 1960.

Caraman, Philip. *Ignatius Loyola*. London: HarperCollins, 1990.

Cardoza-Orlandi, Carlos F. *Mission: An Essential Guide*. Nashville: Abingdon, 2002.

Cardoza-Orlandi, Carlos F., and Justo L. González. *To All Nations from All Nations: A History of the Christian Missionary Movement*. Nashville: Abingdon, 2013.

Carey, William. *An Enquiry into the Obligations of Christians to Use Means for the Conversion of the Heathens*. London: Carey Kingsgate, 1961.

"Carte." *Arquivo Distrital de Portalegre*, September 30, 2008. http://adptg.dglab.gov.pt.

Carver, William Owen. *The Course of Christian Missions: A History and an Interpretation*. New York: Fleming H. Revell, 1939.

———. *God and Man in Missions*. Nashville: Broadman, 1944.

———. *Missions in the Plan of the Ages: Bible Studies in Missions*. New York: Fleming H. Revell, 1909.

Cerfaux, Lucien. *Apostle and Apostolate According to the Gospel of St. Matthew.* Translated by Donald D. Duggan. New York: Desclee, 1960.

Chadwick, Henry. *The Early Church.* The Pelican History of the Church 1. Harmondsworth, UK: Penguin Books, 1967.

Charles-Edwards, T. M. "Palladius, Prosper, and Leo the Great: Mission and Primatial Authority." In *Saint Patrick, A.D. 493–1993,* edited by David N. Dumville, 1-12. Studies in Celtic History 13. Woodbridge, UK: Boydell, 1993.

Chidester, David. *Christianity: A Global History.* San Francisco: HarperSanFrancisco, 2000.

Cipolla, Carlo M. *European Culture and Overseas Expansion.* Middlesex, UK: Penguin Books, 1970.

Clancy, Thomas H. *An Introduction to Jesuit Life: The Constitutions and History Through 435 Years.* St. Louis: Institute of Jesuit Sources, 1976.

Claussen, M. A. "'Peregrinatio' and 'Peregrini' in Augustine's 'City of God.'" *Traditio* 46 (January 1991): 33-75.

Clement of Rome. "The First Epistle of Clement to the Corinthians." In *The Apostolic Fathers with Justin Martyr and Irenaeus,* edited by A. Cleveland Coxe, 1:5-21. The Ante-Nicene Fathers. Grand Rapids: Eerdmans, 1946.

Clossey, Luke. *Salvation and Globalization in the Early Jesuit Missions.* New York: Cambridge University Press, 2008.

Cole, Penny J. *The Preaching of the Crusades to the Holy Land, 1095–1270.* Medieval Academy Books 98. Cambridge, MA: The Medieval Academy of America, 1991.

Coleridge, Henry James. *The Life and Letters of St. Francis Xavier.* 2 vols. London: Burns and Oates, 1912.

Collins, Paul M. "Ecclesiology and World Mission/Missio Dei." In *Routledge Companion to the Christian Church,* 623-36. London: Routledge, 2008.

Comenius, Johann Amos. *A Generall Table of Europe, Representing the Present and Future State Thereof Viz. the Present Governments, Languages, Religions, Foundations, and Revolutions Both of Governments and Religions, the Future Mutations, Revolutions, Government, and Religion of Christendom and of the World &c.* Microform. London: Benjamin Billingsley, 1670.

Conedera, Sam Zeno. "Brothers in Arms: Hermandades Among the Military Orders in Medieval Iberia." In *Crusades—Medieval Worlds in Conflict,* 35-44. Farnham, UK: Ashgate, 2010.

Constable, Giles. "The Place of the Crusader in Medieval Society." *Viator* 29 (January 1998): 377-403.

Conwell, Joseph F. *Impelling Spirit: Revisiting a Founding Experience, 1539, Ignatius of Loyola and His Companions; An Exploration into the Spirit and Aims of the Society of Jesus as Revealed in the Founders' Proposed Papal Letter Approving the Society.* Chicago: Loyola Press, 1997.

Costambeys, Marios, Matthew Innes, and Simon MacLean. *The Carolingian World.* Cambridge: Cambridge University Press, 2011.

Costas, Orlando E. *Christ Outside the Gate: Mission Beyond Christendom.* Maryknoll, NY: Orbis Books, 1982.

Cotgrave, Randle. "Mission." In *A Dictionarie of the French and English Tongues (Reproduced from the First Edition, London, 1611).* Columbia: University of South Carolina Press, 1950.

Coupeau, J. Carlos. "Five Personae of Ignatius of Loyola." In *The Cambridge Companion of The Jesuits,* edited by Thomas Worcester, 32-51. Cambridge: Cambridge University Press, 2008.

Covey, Stephen R. *The Seven Habits of Highly Effective People: Restoring the Character Ethic.* New York: Simon and Schuster, 1989.

Cowdrey, H. E. J. "Pope Gregory VII's 'Crusading' Plans of 1074." In *Outremer: Studies in the History of the Crusading Kingdom of Jerusalem,* edited by Benjamin Z. Kedar, Hans Eberhard Mayer, and R. C. Smail, 27-40. Jerusalem: Yad Izhak Ben-Zvi Institute, 1982.

Cox, Jeffrey. *The British Missionary Enterprise Since 1700.* Christianity and Society in the Modern World. New York: Routledge, 2008.

———. "Master Narratives of Imperial Missions." In *Mixed Messages: Materiality, Textuality, Missions,* edited by Jamie S. Scott and Gareth Griffiths, 3-18. New York: Palgrave Macmillan, 2005.

Cox, Jeffrey, and Shelton Stromquist. "Introduction: Master Narratives and Social History." In *Contesting the Master Narrative: Essays in Social History,* edited by Jeffrey Cox and Shelton Stromquist, 1-15. Iowa City: University of Iowa Press, 1998.

Crawley, Winston. *Biblical Light for the Global Task: The Bible and Mission Strategy.* Nashville: Convention, 1989.

Croil, James. *The Missionary Problem: Containing a History of Protestant Missions in Some of the Principal Fields of Missionary Enterprise, Together with a Historical and Statistical Account of the Rise and Progress of Missionary Societies in the Nineteenth Century.* Toronto: William Briggs, 1883.

Crosbie, William. *The Missionary Problem—Home and Foreign—and Its Solution. Thoughts on an Ancient Missionary Prayer.* Nottingham, UK: E. H. Lee, 1896.

Crossley, James G. "Defining History." In *Writing History, Constructing Religion,* edited by James G. Crossley and Christian Karner, 9-29. Aldershot, UK: Ashgate, 2005.

Cruz, Sharon da. "Empire and Mission: Portuguese State and Franciscan Collaboration in Establishing the Goa Mission (1510–1534)." *Indian Church History Review* 44, no. 2 (2010): 109-29.

Cryer, Neville B. "Biography of John Eliot." In *Five Pioneer Missionaries,* 171-231. London: The Banner of Truth Trust, 1965.

Cutler, Allan. "First Crusade and the Idea of Conversion (First Installment)." *Muslim World* 58, no. 1 (January 1968): 57-71.

Da Silva, William R., and Rowena Robinson. "Discover to Conquer: Towards a Sociology of Conversion." In *Discoveries, Missionary Expansion and Asian Cultures,* 55-64. New Delhi: Concept, 1994.

Dalmases, Cándido de. *Ignatius of Loyola, Founder of the Jesuits: His Life and Works.* Translated by Jerome Aixalá. St. Louis: Institute of Jesuit Sources, 1985.

Dames, G. E. "New Frontiers for Mission in a Post-Modern Era: Creating Missional Communities." *Missionalia* 35, no. 1 (April 2007): 34-53.

Daniel, E. Randolph. *The Franciscan Concept of Mission in the High Middle Ages.* Lexington: University Press of Kentucky, 1975.

Daniélou, Jean, and Henri Marrou. *The Christian Centuries: A New History of the Catholic Church.* Vol. 1, *The First Six Hundred Years.* Translated by Vincent Cronin. New York: McGraw-Hill, 1964.

Danker, William J. "Mammon for Moravian Missions." *Concordia Theological Monthly* 36 (April 1965): 251-60.

Dass, Nirmal, ed. *The Deeds of the Franks and Other Jerusalem-Bound Pilgrims: The Earliest Chronicle of the First Crusades.* Lanham, MD: Rowman & Littlefield, 2011.

Daube, David. *The New Testament and Rabbinic Judaism.* Jordan Lectures 1952. London: Athlone, 1956.

Davidson, Linda Kay, and Maryjane Dunn-Wood. *Pilgrimage in the Middle Ages: A Research Guide.* Garland Medieval Bibliographies 16. New York: Garland, 1993.

Davidson, Randall. "The Central Place of Missions in the Life of the Church." In *World Missionary Conference, 1910: The History and Records of the Conference*

Together with Addresses Delivered at the Evening Meetings, 9:146-50. Edinburgh: Oliphant, Anderson, & Ferrier, 1910.

Davies, J. G. *The Early Christian Church.* History of Religion Series. New York: Holt, Rinehart and Winston, 1965.

———. "Pilgrimage and Crusade Literature." In *Journeys Toward God: Pilgrimage and Crusade,* 1-30. Studies in Medieval Culture. Kalamazoo, MI: Medieval Institute Publications, 1992.

Davis, Tim. "Miles Christi." *Encyclopedia of Medieval Pilgrimage,* edited by Larissa Taylor, Leigh Ann Craig, John B. Friedman, Kathy Gower, Thomas Izbicki, and Rita Tekippe. Leiden: Brill, 2010.

Dawson, Christopher. *The Formation of Christendom.* New York: Sheed and Ward, 1967.

———. *The Making of Europe: An Introduction to the History of European Unity.* New York: Sheed & Ward, 1932.

———. *Religion and the Rise of Western Culture.* New York: Sheed & Ward, 1950.

Deanesly, Margaret. *A History of the Medieval Church, 590–1500.* London: Methuen, 1951.

Defoe, Daniel. *Reasons Humbly Offer'd for a Law to Enact the Castration or Gelding of Popish Ecclesiastics, &c.: As the Best Way to Prevent the Growth of Popery in England.* London: A. Baldwin, 1700.

Dent, Don. "Apostles Even Now." In *Discovering the Mission of God: Best Missional Practices of the 21st Century,* edited by Mike Barnett and Robin Martin, 355-69. Downers Grove, IL: InterVarsity Press, 2012.

DeYoung, Kevin, and Greg Gilbert. *What Is the Mission of the Church? Making Sense of Social Justice, Shalom, and the Great Commission.* Wheaton, IL: Crossway, 2011.

Dickson, Gary. "Stephen of Cloyes, Philip Augustus, and the Children's Crusade of 1212." In *Journeys Toward God: Pilgrimage and Crusade,* 83-105. Studies in Medieval Culture 30. Kalamazoo, MI: Medieval Institute Publications, 1992.

Dickson, John P. *Mission-Commitment in Ancient Judaism and in the Pauline Communities: The Shape, Extent and Background of Early Christian Mission.* Wissenschaftliche Untersuchungen Zum Neuen Testament. Tübingen: Mohr Siebeck, 2003.

Dietrich, Suzanne de. *The Witnessing Community: The Biblical Record of God's Purpose.* Philadelphia: Westminster, 1958.

Diffie, Bailey W. *Latin-American Civilization: Colonial Period.* Harrisburg, PA: Stackpole Sons, 1945.

Donnelly, John Patrick. "New Religious Orders for Men." In *The Cambridge History of Christianity*, vol. 6, *Reform and Expansion 1500–1660*, edited by R. Po-chia Hsia, 162-79. Cambridge: Cambridge University Press, 2007.

Donovan, Vincent J. *Christianity Rediscovered: An Epistle from the Masai*. 3rd ed. London: SCM Press, 2001.

Douglas, J. D. "Patrick." In *Evangelical Dictionary of World Missions*, ed. A. Scott Moreau. Grand Rapids: Eerdmans, 2000.

DuBose, Francis M. *God Who Sends: A Fresh Quest for Biblical Mission*. Nashville: Broadman, 1983.

Dudden, F. Homes. *Gregory the Great: His Place in History and Thought*. 2 vols. New York: Longmans, Green, 1905.

Dujardin, Carine, and Claude Prudhomme, eds. *Mission & Science, Missiology Revised, 1850–1940*. Leuven, Belgium: Leuven University Press, 2015.

Dumville, David N. *Saint Patrick, A.D. 493–1993*. Studies in Celtic History 13. Woodbridge, Suffolk, UK: Boydell, 1993.

Duncalf, Frederic. "The Councils of Piacenza and Clermont." In *A History of the Crusades*, vol. 1, *The First Hundred Years*, edited by Marshall W. Baldwin, 220-52. Madison: The University of Wisconsin Press, 1969.

———. "The First Crusade: Clermont to Constantinople." In *A History of the Crusades*, vol. 1, *The First Hundred Years*, edited by Marshall W. Baldwin, 253-79. Madison: The University of Wisconsin Press, 1969.

Durant, Will, and Ariel Durant. *The Lessons of History*. New York: Simon and Schuster, 1968.

Dussel, Enrique. "Toward a History of the Church in the World Periphery." In *Towards a History of the Church in the Third World*, edited by Lukas Vischer, 3:110-30. Geneva, Switzerland: Evangelische Arbeitsstelle Oekumene Schweiz, 1983.

Dyas, Dee. "Medieval Patterns of Pilgrimage: A Mirror for Today?" In *Explorations in a Christian Theology of Pilgrimage*, edited by Craig Bartholomew and Fred Hughes, 92-109. Aldershot, UK: Ashgate, 2004.

Dyck, Cornelius J. "The Anabaptist Understanding of the Good News." In *Anabaptism and Mission*, edited by Wilbert R. Shenk, 24-39. Missionary Studies 10. Scottdale, PA: Herald, 1984.

Dykes, J. Oswald. "The Modern Missionary Movement." *Baptist Missionary Magazine (1873–1909)*, February 1890.

Dyrness, William A. "Listening for Fresh Voices in the History of the Church." In *Teaching Global Theologies: Power & Praxis*, edited by Kwok Pui-Lan,

Cecilia González-Andrieu, and Dwight N. Hopkins, 29-43. Waco, TX: Baylor University Press, 2015.

Eddy, Sherwood. *Pathfinders of the World Missionary Crusade*. New York: Abingdon-Cokesbury, 1945.

Edwards, David Lawrence. *Christianity: The First Two Thousand Years*. Maryknoll, NY: Orbis Books, 1999.

Egan, Harvey D. "Ignatius of Loyola: Mystic at the Heart of the Trinity, Mystic at the Heart of Jesus Christ." In *Spiritualities of the Heart*, 97-113. Mahwah, NJ: Paulist, 1990.

Ehler, Sidney Z., and John B. Morrall, eds. *Church and State Through the Centuries: A Collection of Historic Documents with Commentaries*. Westminster, MD: Newman, 1954.

The Encyclopedia of Missions: Descriptive, Historical, Biographical, Statistical. 2nd ed. New York: Funk & Wagnalls, 1904.

Erdmann, Carl. *The Origin of the Idea of Crusade*. Translated by Marshall Baldwin and Walter Goffart. Princeton, NJ: Princeton University Press, 1977.

Escobar, Samuel. "Evangelical Missiology: Peering into the Future at the Turn of the Century." In *Global Missiology for the 21st Century: The Iguassu Dialogue*, edited by William D. Taylor, 101-22. Grand Rapids: Baker Academic, 2000.

Estep, William Roscoe. *Whole Gospel—Whole World: The Foreign Mission Board of the Southern Baptist Convention, 1845–1995*. Nashville: Broadman & Holman, 1994.

Etherington, Norman. "Missions and Empire." In *The Oxford History of the British Empire*, vol. 5, *Historiography*, edited by Robin W. Winks, 303-14. Oxford: Oxford University Press, 1999.

Eusebius. *Ecclesiastical History*. Translated by Christian Frederick Cruse. Grand Rapids: Baker Book House, 1955.

———. *Ecclesiastical History*. Translated by Roy J. Deferrari. The Fathers of the Church 19. New York: Fathers of the Church, 1953.

———. *The Ecclesiastical History*. Translated by Kirsopp Lake. The Loeb Classical Library. Cambridge, MA: Harvard University Press, 1926.

———. *The Ecclesiastical History and the Martyrs of Palestine*. Translated by Hugh Jackson Lawlor and John Ernest Leonard Oulton. 2 vols. London: SPCK, 1927.

———. *The History of the Church from Christ to Constantine*. Translated by G. A. Williamson. Minneapolis: Augsburg, 1975.

Evans, Craig A. "A Light to the Nations: Isaiah and Mission in Luke." In *Christian Mission: Old Testament Foundations and New Testament Developments*, edited by Stanley E. Porter and Cynthia Long Westfall, 93-107. McMaster New Testament Studies Series. Eugene, OR: Pickwick, 2010.

Favre, Pierre. "The Memoriale." In *Spiritual Writings of Pierre Favre*, translated by Edmund C. Murphy, 57-315. Jesuit Primary Sources in English Translations 16. St. Louis: Institute of Jesuit Sources, 1996.

Felder, Hilarin. *The Ideals of St. Francis of Assisi*. Translated by Berchmans Bittle. New York: Benziger Brothers, 1925.

Filbeck, David. *Yes, God of the Gentiles, Too: The Missionary Message of the Old Testament*. A BGC Monograph. Wheaton, IL: Billy Graham Center, Wheaton College, 1994.

Fink, Harold S. "The Foundation of the Latin States, 1099–1118." In *A History of the Crusades*, vol. 1, *The First Hundred Years*, edited by Marshall W. Baldwin, 368-409. Madison: The University of Wisconsin Press, 1969.

Finnegan, Charles V. "Franciscans and the 'New Evangelization.'" *Spirit and Life: A Journal of Contemporary Franciscanism* 6 (1994): 1-6.

Finney, John. *Recovering the Past: Celtic and Roman Mission*. London: Darton, Longman & Todd, 1996.

Fiorenza, Elisabeth Schüssler. "Miracles, Mission, and Apologetics: An Intro-duction." In *Aspects of Religious Propaganda in Judaism and Early Christianity*, 1-25. South Bend, IN: University of Notre Dame Press, 1976.

Flemming, Dean. *Recovering the Full Mission of God: A Biblical Perspective on Being, Doing and Telling*. Downers Grove, IL: IVP Academic, 2013.

———. "Revelation and the *Missio Dei*: Toward a Missional Reading of the Apocalypse." *Journal of Theological Interpretation* 6, no. 2 (2012): 161-78.

———. *Why Mission?* Reframing New Testament Theology. Nashville: Abingdon, 2015.

Fletcher, R. A. *The Barbarian Conversion: From Paganism to Christianity*. New York: Henry Holt, 1998.

Flett, John G. *The Witness of God: The Trinity, Missio Dei, Karl Barth, and the Nature of Christian Community*. Grand Rapids: Eerdmans, 2010.

Foster, John. *The Church of the T'ang Dynasty*. London: Society for Promoting Christian Knowledge, 1939.

———, ed. *The Nestorian Tablet and Hymn: Translations of Chinese Texts from the First Period of the Church in China, 635–C. 900*. Texts for Students 49. London: Society for Promoting Christian Knowledge, 1939.

Fox, Robin Lane. *Pagans and Christians*. San Francisco: Harper & Row, 1995.

France, John. *The Crusades and the Expansion of Catholic Christendom, 1000–1714*. London: Routledge, 2005.

———. "Two Types of Vision on the First Crusade: Stephen of Valence and Peter Bartholomew." In *Crusades*, edited by Benjamin Z. Kedar and Jonathan Riley-Smith, 5:11-20. Society for the Study of the Crusades and the Latin East. Hampshire, UK: Ashgate, 2006.

Francis of Assisi. *Francis of Assisi: Early Documents*. Vol. 1, *The Saint*. Edited by Regis J. Armstrong, J. A. Wayne Hellmann, and William J. Short. New York: New City, 1999.

Frankopan, Peter. *The First Crusade: The Call from the East*. Cambridge, MA: Belknap Press of Harvard University Press, 2012.

Freeman, Philip. *The World of Saint Patrick*. Oxford: Oxford University Press, 2014.

Fremantle, Anne. "Preface." In *Beyond All Horizons: Jesuits and the Missions*, edited by Thomas J. M. Burke, 5-9. Garden City, NY: Hanover House, 1957.

Frend, W. H. C. "The Missions of the Early Church, 180–700 A. D." In *Religion Popular and Unpopular in the Early Christian Centuries*, edited by W. H. C. Frend, 3-23. London: Variorum Reprints, 1976.

———. *The Rise of Christianity*. Philadelphia: Fortress, 1984.

Frere, W. H. "Mediæval Missions in the Bearing on Modern Missions." In *World Missionary Conference, 1910: The History and Records of the Conference Together with Addresses Delivered at the Evening Meetings*, 9:186-94. Edinburgh: Oliphant, Anderson, & Ferrier, 1910.

Freytag, Walter. "Strukturwandel der Weslichen Missionen." In *Reden und Aufsätze*. Theologische Bücherei 13:1, 111-20, 1961.

Fuellenbach, John. *The Kingdom of God; The Message of Jesus Today*. Maryknoll, NY: Orbis Books, 1995.

Fulcher of Chartres. "Deeds of the Franks on Their Pilgrimage to Jerusalem." In *The First Crusade: The Chronicle of Fulcher of Chartres and Other Source Materials*, edited by Edward Peters, 24-90. Philadelphia: University of Pennsylvania Press, 1971.

Fülöp-Miller, René. *The Jesuits: A History of the Society of Jesus*. Translated by D. F. Tait. New York: Capricorn Books, 1963.

Gabriele, Matthew. *An Empire of Memory: The Legend of Charlemagne, the Franks, and Jerusalem Before the First Crusade*. Oxford: Oxford University Press, 2011.

Gairdner, W. H. T. *Echoes from Edinburgh, 1910: An Account and Interpretation of the World Missionary Conference.* New York: Fleming H. Revell, 1910.

Gaposchkin, M. Cecilia. "From Pilgrimage to Crusade: The Liturgy of Departure, 1095–1300." *Speculum* 88, no. 1 (January 2013): 44-91.

Garland, David E. *Luke.* Zondervan Exegetical Commentary Series on the New Testament 3. Grand Rapids: Zondervan, 2011.

Gaventa, Beverly Roberts. "The Mission of God in Paul's Letter to the Romans." In *Paul as Missionary: Identity, Activity, Theology, and Practice*, edited by Trevor J. Burke and Brian S. Rosner, 65-75. Library of New Testament Studies 420. London: T&T Clark, 2011.

———. *Our Mother Saint Paul.* Louisville: Westminister John Knox, 2007.

Gibbon, Edward. *The Triumph of Christendom in the Roman Empire.* Edited by J. B. Bury. New York: Harper & Row, 1958.

Gibson, Richard J. "Paul the Missionary, in Priestly Service of the Servant-Christ (Romans 15.16)." In *Paul as Missionary: Identity, Activity, Theology, and Practice*, 51-62. Library of New Testament Studies 420. London: T&T Clark, 2011.

Gifford, D. J., and F. W. Hodcroft, eds. *Textos Lingüísticos Del Medioevo Español, Preparados Con Introducciones Y Glosario.* Oxford: Dolphin Book Company, 1959.

Gilchrist, John. "The Papacy and War Against the 'Saracens,' 795–1216." *The International History Review* 10, no. 2 (May 1988): 174-97.

Gilliland, Dean S. *Pauline Theology & Mission Practice.* Eugene, OR: Wipf and Stock, 1998.

Giustozzi, Antonio, and Artemy Kalinovsky. *Missionaries of Modernity: Advisory Missions and the Struggle for Hegemony, from the 1940s to Afghanistan.* London: Hurst, 2016.

Glasser, Arthur F. *Announcing the Kingdom: The Story of God's Mission in the Bible.* Grand Rapids: Baker Academic, 2003.

Glover, Robert Hall. *The Bible Basis of Missions.* Chicago: Moody Press, 1946.

———. *The Progress of World-Wide Missions.* New York: Harper & Row, 1960.

———. *The Real Heart of the Missionary Problem.* New York: Christian and Missionary Alliance, 1915.

Goerner, Henry Cornell. *All Nations in God's Purpose: What the Bible Teaches About Missions.* Nashville: Broadman, 1979.

———. *Thus It Is Written: The Missionary Motif in the Scriptures.* Nashville: Broadman, 1944.

Goheen, Michael W. "Bible and Mission: Missiology and Biblical Scholarship in Dialogue." In *Christian Mission: Old Testament Foundations and New Testament Developments*, edited by Stanley E. Porter and Cynthia Long Westfall, 208-35. McMaster New Testament Studies Series. Eugene, OR: Pickwick, 2010.

———. *Introducing Christian Mission Today: Scripture, History, and Issues*. Downers Grove, IL: InterVarsity Press, 2014.

Goldman, Seth, Barry Nalebuff, and Choi Soonyoon. *Mission in a Bottle: The Story of Honest Tea*. New York: Crown Business, 2013.

Goodman, Martin. *Mission and Conversion: Proselytizing in the Religious History of the Roman Empire*. Oxford: Clarendon, 1994.

Goppelt, Leonhard. *Theology of the New Testament*. Edited by Jürgen Roloff. Translated by John E. Alsup. 2 vols. Grand Rapids: Eerdmans, 1981.

Gorman, Michael J. *Becoming the Gospel: Paul, Participation, and Mission*. Grand Rapids: Eerdmans, 2015.

Gougaud, Louis. *Christianity in Celtic Lands: A History of the Churches of the Celts, Their Origin, Their Development, Influence, and Mutual Relations*. Translated by Maud Joynt. London: Sheed & Ward, 1932.

Grant, Robert M. *Augustus to Constantine: The Rise and Triumph of Christianity in the Roman World*. San Francisco: Harper & Row, 1970.

Gregory the Great. *The Letters of Gregory the Great*. Translated by John R. C. Martyn. 3 vols. Mediaeval Sources in Translation 40. Toronto: Pontifical Institute of Mediaeval Studies, 2004.

Grenz, Stanley J. *Theology for the Community of God*. Grand Rapids: Eerdmans, 1994.

Griffin, Joseph A. "The Sacred Congregation de Propaganda Fide: Its Foundation and Historical Antecedents." In *Christianity and Missions, 1450–1800*, 57-95. The Expanding World, The European Impact on World History 1450-1800, vol. 28. Hampshire, UK: Ashgate, 1997.

Griffths, Michael C. "Today's Missionary, Yesterday's Apostle." *Evangelical Missions Quarterly* 21, no. 2 (April 1985): 154-65.

Gröszel, W. *Justinian von Welz, der Vorkämpfer der lutherishcen Mission*. Leipzig: Akademische Buchhandlung, 1891.

Guder, Darrell L. *Called to Witness: Doing Missional Theology*. Grand Rapids: Eerdmans, 2015.

———. "Theological Formation for Missional Practice." In *Walk Humbly with the Lord: Church and Mission Engaging Plurality*, edited by Viggo Mortensen and Andreas Østerlund Nielsen, 307-12. Grand Rapids: Eerdmans, 2010.

Guder, Darrell L., Lois Barrett, Inagrace T. Dietterich, George R. Hunsberger, Alan J. Roxburgh, and Craig Van Gelder. *Missional Church: A Vision for the Sending of the Church in North America*. Grand Rapids: Eerdmans, 1998.

Guibert, Joseph de. *The Jesuits: Their Spiritual Doctrine and Practice: A Historical Study*. Translated by William J. Young. Chicago: Institute of Jesuit Sources, 1964.

Haas, Adolf. "The Mysticism of St. Ignatius According to His Spiritual Diary." In *Ignatius of Loyola, His Personality and Spiritual Heritage, 1556–1956: Studies on the 400th Anniversary of His Death*, edited by Fredrich Wulf, translated by G. Richard Dimler, 164-99. Modern Scholarly Studies About the Jesuits, in English Translations 2. St. Louis: Institute of Jesuit Sources, 1977.

Hahn, Ferdinand. *Mission in the New Testament*. Translated by Frank Clarke. London: SCM Press, 1965.

Hallett, Garth L. *Theology Within the Bounds of Language: A Methodological Tour*. Albany: State University of New York Press, 2011.

Hamilton, Bernard. "The Impact of Crusader Jerusalem on Western Christendom." *The Catholic Historical Review* 80, no. 4 (October 1994): 695-713.

———. *The Latin Church in the Crusader States: The Secular Church*. London: Variorum, 1980.

Hammond, David M. "Hayden White: Meaning and Truth in History." *Philosophy & Theology* 8, no. 4 (June 1994): 291-307.

Hanciles, Jehu. *Beyond Christendom: Globalization, African Migration, and the Transformation of the West*. Maryknoll, NY: Orbis Books, 2008.

Harlow, Robert Edward. *Drawn unto Death: The Bible Basis of Missions*. Kansas City, KS: Walterick, 1966.

Harnack, Adolf. *The Mission and Expansion of Christianity in the First Three Centuries*. New York: Harper, 1962.

Harris, R. Geoffrey. *Mission in the Gospels*. London: Epworth, 2004.

Hastings, Adrian. "150–500." In *A World History of Christianity*, edited by Adrian Hastings, 25-65. Grand Rapids: Eerdmans, 1999.

———, ed. *A World History of Christianity*. Grand Rapids: Eerdmans, 1999.

Hastings, Ross. *Missional God, Missional Church: Hope for Re-evangelizing the West*. Downers Grove, IL: IVP Academic, 2012.

Hayes, Diana. "Reflections on Slavery." In *Change in Official Catholic Moral Teaching*, edited by Charles E. Curran, 63-75. Readings in Moral Theology 13. New York: Paulist, 2003.

Haykin, Michael A. G., and C. Jeffrey Robinson Sr. *To the Ends of the Earth: Calvin's Missional Vision and Legacy*. Wheaton, IL: Crossway, 2014.

Hebst, Michael. "Plural Mission and Missionary Plural in a Post-Socialist Context: Using the Example of a Post-'Volkskirche,' East German Region." In *Mission and Postmodernities*, edited by Rolv Olsen, 39-56. Regnum Edinburgh 2010 Series. Eugene, OR: Wipf & Stock, 2012.

Helland, Roger. *Missional Spirituality: Embodying God's Love from the Inside Out.* Downers Grove, IL: InterVarsity Press, 2011.

Hengel, Martin. "The Origins of the Christian Mission." In *Between Jesus and Paul: Studies in the Earliest History of the Christianity*, translated by John Bowden, 48-64. Waco, TX: Baylor University Press, 2013.

Heurnius, Justus. *De legatione evangelica ad Indos capessenda admonitio.* Lugdunum Batavorum, 1618.

Hillgarth, J. N. *Ramon Lull and Lullism in Fourteenth-Century France.* Oxford-Warburg Studies. Oxford: Clarendon, 1971.

Hills, Don W. *The Biblical Basis of Missions.* Chicago: Moody Press Institute, 1977.

Hindley, Alan, Frederick W. Langley, and Brian J. Levy. "Mission." *Old French-English Dictionary.* Cambridge: Cambridge University Press, 2000.

Hindley, Geoffrey. *The Crusades: A History of Armed Pilgrimage and Holy War.* London: Constable & Robinson, 2003.

Hobsbawm, Eric. "Introduction: Inventing Traditions." In *The Invention of Traditions*, edited by Eric Hobsbawm and Terence Ranger, 1-14. Past and Present Publications. Cambridge: Cambridge University Press, 1983.

Hobsbawm, Eric, and Terence Ranger, eds. *The Invention of Tradition.* Past and Present Publications. Cambridge: Cambridge University Press, 1983.

Hocking, William Ernest. *The Coming World Civilization.* New York: Harper, 1956.

——. "Introduction." In *Laymen's Foreign Missions Inquiry, Regional Reports of the Commission of Appraisal*, vol. 1, *India-Burma*, edited by Orville A. Perry, xi-xvii. New York: Harper & Brothers, 1933.

——. *Living Religions and a World Faith.* New York: Macmillan, 1940.

——, ed. *Re-thinking Missions: A Laymen's Inquiry After One Hundred Years.* New York: Harper & Brothers, 1932.

Hoeberichts, J. *Francis and Islam.* Quincy, IL: Franciscan Press, 1997.

Hoedemaker, Bert. "Mission Beyond Modernity." In *Christian Mission in Western Society: Precedents, Perspectives, Prospects*, edited by Simon Barrow and Graeme Smith, 212-33. London: CBTI, 2001.

——. *Secularization and Mission: A Theological Essay.* Harrisburg, PA: Trinity Press International, 1998.

Hoedemaker, L. A. "The People of God and the Ends of the Earth." In *Missiology: An Ecumenical Introduction, Texts and Contexts of Global Christianity*, edited by A. Camps, L. A. Hoedemaker, M. R. Spindler, and F. J. Verstraelen, 157-71. Grand Rapids: Eerdmans, 1995.

Hogg, William Richey. *Ecumenical Foundations: A History of the International Missionary Council and Its Nineteenth Century Background*. New York: Harper & Brothers, 1952.

———. "The Rise of Protestant Missionary Concern, 1517–1914." In *The Theology of the Christian Mission*, edited by Gerald H. Anderson, 95-111. Nashville: Abingdon, 1961.

The Holy Bible Translated from the Latin Vulgate: Diligently Compared with the Hebrew, Greek, and Other Editions in Diverse Languages. And First Published by the English College at Douay, Anno 1609. Newly Revised and Corrected, according to the Clementin Edition of the Scriptures. With Annotations for Clearing up the Principal Difficulties of Holy Writ. 4 vols. Edinburgh: J. Moir, 1796.

Homza, Lu Ann. "The Religious Milieu of the Young Ignatius." In *The Cambridge Companion to The Jesuits*, edited by Thomas Worcester, 13-31. Cambridge Companions to Religion. Cambridge: Cambridge University Press, 2008.

Hopkins, Bob, and Freddy Hedley. *Coaching for Missional Leadership*. ACPI, 2008.

Hopper, Sarah. *To Be a Pilgrim: The Medieval Pilgrimage Experience*. Gloucestershire, UK: Sutton, 2002.

Horton, R. F. "The Sufficiency of God." In *World Missionary Conference, 1910: The History and Records of the Conference Together with Addresses Delivered at the Evening Meetings*, 9:336-41. Edinburgh: Oliphant, Anderson, & Ferrier, 1910.

Housley, Norman. *Fighting for the Cross: Crusading to the Holy Land*. New Haven, CT: Yale University Press, 2008.

Howell, Don N., Jr. "Mission in Paul's Epistles: Genesis, Pattern, and Dynamics." In *Mission in the New Testament: An Evangelical Approach*, edited by William J. Larkin Jr. and Joel F. Williams, 63-91. American Society of Missiology Series 27. Maryknoll, NY: Orbis Books, 1998.

———. "Mission in Paul's Epistles: Theological Bearings." In *Mission in the New Testament: An Evangelical Approach*, edited by William J. Larkin Jr. and Joel F. Williams, 92-116. American Society of Missiology Series 27. Maryknoll, NY: Orbis Books, 1998.

Hübmaier, Balthasar. *Balthsar Hübmaier: Theologian of Anabaptism*. Edited and translated by H. Wayne Pipkin and John H. Yoder. Classics of the Radical Reformation. Scottdale, PA: Herald, 1989.

Hughes, E. Philip. "John Calvin: Director of Missions." In *The Heritage of John Calvin: Heritage Hall Lectures, 1960–1970*, edited by John H. Bratt, 40-54. Grand Rapids: Eerdmans, 1973.

Huhtinen, Pekka, and Gregory Lockwood. "Luther and World Missions: A Review." *Concordia Theological Quarterly* 65, no. 1 (January 2001): 15-29.

Hull, John M. *Towards the Prophetic Church: A Study of Christian Mission.* London: SCM Press, 2014.

Humphreys, David. *An Historical Account of the Incorporated Society for the Propagation of the Gospel in Foreign Parts.* New York: Arno, 1969.

Hunsberger, George R. "Proposals for a Missional Hermeneutic: Mapping a Conversation." *Missiology* 39, no. 3 (July 2011): 309-21.

Hunter Blair, Peter. *The World of Bede.* New York: St. Martin's, 1971.

Ignatius Loyola. *The Autobiography of St. Ignatius Loyola.* Translated by Joseph F. O'Callaghan. New York: Fordham University Press, 1992.

———. *The Constitutions of the Society of Jesus.* Translated by George E. Ganss. St. Louis: Institute of Jesuit Sources, 1970.

———. *Letters of St. Ignatius of Loyola.* Translated by William J. Young. Chicago: Loyola University Press, 1959.

———. *Monumenta Ignatiana, ex autographis vel ex antiquioribus exemplis collecta. Series tertia. Sancti Ignatii de Loyola Constitutiones Societatis Jesu.* Vols. 63–64. Monumenta Historica Societatis Jesu. Rome: Typis Pontificiae Universitatis Gregorianae, 1934, 1936.

———. *The Spiritual Exercises of Saint Ignatius: A Translation and Commentary by George E. Ganss, S.J.* Chicago: Loyola University Press, 1992.

———. *The Spiritual Journal of St. Ignatius Loyola, 1544–45.* Translated by William J. Young. Woodstock, MA: Woodstock College Press, 1958.

Inter-Varsity Christian Fellowship. *Therefore Go: The Bible Basis of Missions.* Chicago: Inter-Varsity Press, 1949.

Irvin, Dale T. *Christian Histories, Christian Traditioning: Rendering Accounts.* Maryknoll, NY: Orbis Books, 1998.

Irvin, Dale T., and Scott W. Sunquist. *History of the World Christian Movement.* Vol. 1, *Earliest Christianity to 1453.* Maryknoll, NY: Orbis Books, 2001.

Jacobus de Voragine. *The Golden Legend: Readings on the Saints.* Translated by William Granger Ryan. 2 vols. Princeton, NJ: Princeton University Press, 1993.

Jansen, Katherine. "The Word and Its Diffusion." In *The Cambridge History of Christianity*, vol. 4, *Christianity in Western Europe c. 1100–c. 1500*, edited by

Miri Rubin and Walter Simons, 114-32. Cambridge: Cambridge University Press, 2009.

Jedin, Hubert. "General Introduction to Church History." In *From the Apostolic Community to Constantine*, 1-56. Handbook of Church History 1. Freiburg, West Germany: Herder, 1965.

Jenkins, Philip. *The Lost History of Christianity: The Thousand-Year Golden Age of the Church in the Middle East, Africa, and Asia—and How It Died*. New York: HarperOne, 2008.

———. *The Next Christendom: The Coming of Global Christianity*. Oxford: Oxford University Press, 2002.

Jensen, Janus M. "Peregrinatio Sive Expedito: Why the First Crusade Was Not a Pilgrimage." *Al-Masaq: Islam and the Medieval Mediterranean* 15, no. 2 (September 2003): 119-37.

Jerome. "Letter 108: To Eustochium." In *Early Latin Theology*, edited by S. L. Greenslade, 5:345-82. The Library of Christian Classics. Philadelphia: Westminster, 1956.

Jesuits. *The Constitutions of the Society of Jesus*. St. Louis: Institute of Jesuit Sources, 1970.

Jewett, Robert. *Romans: A Commentary*. Hermeneia—A Critical and Historical Commentary on the Bible. Minneapolis: Fortress, 2007.

Jeyaraj, Daniel. *Bartholomäus Ziegenbalg, the Father of Modern Protestant Mission: An Indian Assessment*. Delhi: Indian Society for Promoting Christian Knowledge, 2006.

———. "Mission Reports from South India and Their Impact on the Western Mind: The Tranquebar Mission of the Eighteenth Century." In *Converting Colonialism: Visions and Realities in Mission History, 1706–1914*, edited by Dana Lee Robert, 21-42. Studies in the History of Christian Missions. Grand Rapids: Eerdmans, 2008.

John of Perugia. "The Beginning or Founding of the Order and the Deeds of Those Lesser Brothers Who Were the First Companions of Blessed Francis in Religion." In *Francis of Assisi: Early Documents*, edited by Regis J Armstrong, J. Wayne Hellmann, and William J. Short, 2:29-58. New York: New City, 1999.

Johnson, Paul. *A History of Christianity*. New York: Atheneum, 1976.

Johnston, Arthur. *The Battle for World Evangelism*. Wheaton, IL: Tyndale House, 1978.

Jonas. *Life of St. Columban.* Translations and Reprints from the Original Sources of European History, vol. 2, no. 7. Felinfach: Llanerch, 1895.

Jones, Rufus M. "The Background and the Objective of Protestant Foreign Missions." In *Laymen's Foreign Missions Inquiry, Regional Reports of the Commission of Appraisal*, vol. 2, *China*, xi-xxiii. New York: Harper & Brothers, 1933.

Jongeneel, Jan A. B. *Philosophy, Science, and Theology of Mission in the 19th and 20th Centuries.* Studien Zur Interkulturellen Geschichte Des Christentums 92. Frankfurt am Main: Peter Lang, 1995.

———. "The Protestant Missionary Movement up to 1789." In *Missiology: An Ecumenical Introduction, Texts and Contexts of Global Christianity*, edited by F. J. Verstraelen, 222-28. Grand Rapids: Eerdmans, 1995.

Joranson, Einar. "The Great German Pilgrimage of 1064–5." In *The Crusades, and Other Historical Essays, Presented to Dana C. Munro by His Former Students*, edited by Louis John Paetow, 3-43. New York: F. S. Crofts, 1928.

Kaiser, Walter. *Mission in the Old Testament: Israel as a Light to the Nations.* Grand Rapids: Baker Books, 2000.

Kalu, Obgu U. "Globalization and Mission in the Twenty-First Century." In *Mission After Christendom: Emergent Themes in Contemporary Mission*, edited by Obgu U. Kalu, Peter Vethanayagamony, and Edmund Kee-Fook Chia, 25-42. Louisville: Westminster John Knox, 2010.

Kane, J. Herbert. *A Global View of Christian Missions from Pentecost to the Present.* Grand Rapids: Baker Book House, 1971. Rev. ed., 1985.

Kasdorf, Hans. "The Anabaptist Approach to Mission." In *Anabaptism and Mission*, edited by Wilbert R. Shenk, 51-69. Scottdale, PA: Herald, 1984.

Kedar, Benjamin Z. *Crusade and Mission: European Approaches Toward the Muslims.* Princeton, NJ: Princeton University Press, 1984.

Kelly, J. N. D. *The Oxford Dictionary of Popes.* 2nd ed. New York: Oxford University Press, 2010.

Kennedy, H. A. A. "The Missions of the Early Church in Their Bearing on Modern Missions." In *World Missionary Conference, 1910: The History and Records of the Conference Together with Addresses Delivered at the Evening Meetings*, 9:173-85. Edinburgh: Oliphant, Anderson, & Ferrier, 1910.

Kim, Seyoon. "Paul as an Eschatological Herald." In *Paul as Missionary: Identity, Activity, Theology, and Practice*, edited by Trevor J. Burke and Brian S. Rosner, 9-24. Library of New Testament Studies 420. London: T&T Clark, 2011.

Kingsolver, Barbara. *The Poisonwood Bible.* New York: HarperCollins, 1998.

Kirk, Brian. *Missional Youth Ministry: Moving from Gathering Teenagers to Scattering Disciples*. Grand Rapids: Zondervan, 2011.

Kirk, J. Andrew. *What Is Mission? Theological Explorations*. London: Darton, Longman & Todd, 1999.

Kleist, James A., trans. "The Epistle to Diognetus." In *The Didache: The Epistle of Barnabas, The Epistles and the Martyrdom of St. Polycarp, The Fragments of Papias, The Epistle to Diognetus*, 135-47. Ancient Christian Writers 6. Westminster, MD: Newman, 1948.

Knowles, Michael P. "Mark, Matthew, and Mission: Faith, Failure, and the Fidelity of Jesus." In *Christian Mission: Old Testament Foundations and New Testament Developments*, edited by Stanley E. Porter and Cynthia Long Westfall, 64-92. McMaster New Testament Studies Series. Eugene, OR: Pickwick, 2010.

Koch, Klaus. *The Rediscovery of Apocalyptic: A Polemical Work on a Neglected Area of Biblical Studies and Its Damaging Effects on Theology and Philosophy*. Studies in Biblical Theology (Second Series) 22. London: SCM Press, 1972.

Kollman, Paul. "After Church History? Writing the History of Christianity from a Global Perspective." *Horizons* 31, no. 2 (2004): 322-42.

———. "At the Origins of Mission and Missiology: A Study in the Dynamics of Religious Language." *Journal of the American Academy of Religion* 79, no. 2 (June 2011): 425-58.

Köstenberger, Andreas J. *The Missions of Jesus and the Disciples According to the Fourth Gospel: With Implications for the Fourth Gospel's Purpose and the Mission of the Contemporary Church*. Grand Rapids: Eerdmans, 1998.

———. "The Two Johannine Verbs for Sending: A Study of John's Use of Words with Reference to General Linguistic Theory." In *Linguistics and the New Testament*, 125-43. Sheffield, UK: Sheffield Academic, 1999.

Köstenberger, Andreas J., and Peter Thomas O'Brien. *Salvation to the Ends of the Earth: A Biblical Theology of Mission*. New Studies in Biblical Theology 11. Downers Grove, IL: InterVarsity Press, 2001.

Kostick, Conor. *The Social Structure of the First Crusade*. The Medieval Mediterranean 76. Leiden, The Netherlands: Brill, 2008.

Kraemer, Heindrik. *The Christian Message in a Non-Christian World*. Grand Rapids: Kregel, 1938.

Krause, Victor. "Geschichte Des Institutes Der Missi Dominici." *Institut Für Österreichische Geschichtsforschung, Mitteilungen* 11 (January 1890): 193-300.

Kreider, Alan. *The Patient Ferment of the Early Church: The Improbable Rise of Christianity in the Roman Empire*. Grand Rapids: Baker Academic, 2016.

Kreuzer, Lewis H. "The Biblical Basis for the Missionary Obligation of the Church." BD thesis, Andover Newton Theological School, 1953.

Kruger, Michael J. *The Question of Canon: Challenging the Status Quo in the New Testament Debate*. Downers Grove, IL: IVP Academic, 2013.

Küng, Hans. *Christianity: Essence, History, and Future*. Translated by John Bowden. New York: Continuum, 2003.

Kurup, K. K. N. "Contribution of Malabar Rulers in Delaying Dominance by Foreign Powers in Malabar Region." In *The Portuguese, Indian Ocean and European Bridgeheads 1500–1800*, 111-18. Kerala, India: Institute for Research in Social Sciences and Humanities of MESHAR, 2001.

Lach, Donald F. *Asia in the Making of Europe*. Vol. 1, *The Century of Discovery*. Chicago: The University of Chicago Press, 1965.

Ladd, George Eldon. *Jesus and the Kingdom: The Eschatology of Biblical Realism*. New York: Harper & Row, 1964.

———. *The Presence of the Future*. Grand Rapids: Eerdmans, 1996.

———. *A Theology of the New Testament*. Rev. ed. Grand Rapids: Eerdmans, 1993.

Laing, Mark T. B. "Missio Dei: Some Implications for the Church." *Missiology* 37, no. 1 (January 2009): 89-99.

Lambert, Malcolm. *Christians and Pagans: The Conversion of Britain from Alban to Bede*. New Haven, CT: Yale University Press, 2010.

Langmead, Ross. *The Word Made Flesh: Towards an Incarnational Missiology*. Lanham, MD: University Press of America, 2004.

Larkin, William J., Jr. "The First Decades of the Mission of God." In *Discovering the Mission of God: Best Missional Practices of the 21st Century*, edited by Mike Barnett and Robin Martin, 189-204. Downers Grove, IL: InterVarsity Press, 2012.

———. "Introduction." In *Mission in the New Testament: An Evangelical Approach*, edited by William J. Larkin Jr. and Joel F. Williams, 1-7. American Society of Missiology Series 27. Maryknoll, NY: Orbis Books, 1988.

———. "Mission in Acts." In *Mission in the New Testament: An Evangelical Approach*, edited by William J. Larkin Jr. and Joel F. Williams, 170-86. American Society of Missiology Series 27. Maryknoll, NY: Orbis Books, 1998.

———. "Mission in Luke." In *Mission in the New Testament: An Evangelical Approach*, edited by William J. Larkin Jr. and Joel F. Williams, 152-69. American Society of Missiology Series 27. Maryknoll, NY: Orbis Books, 1998.

Latourette, Kenneth Scott. *Christianity Through the Ages*. New York: Harper & Row, 1965.

———. *A History of the Expansion of Christianity*. 7 vols. Grand Rapids: Zondervan, 1970.

———. *Missions Tomorrow*. New York: Harper & Brothers, 1936.

———. "Reassessment of W E Hocking's Rethinking Missions After Twenty-Five Years." *International Review of Mission* 46, no. 182 (April 1957): 164-70.

Lawrence, C. H. *Medieval Monasticism: Forms of Religious Life in Western Europe in the Middle Ages*. 3rd ed. Harlow, UK: Longman, 2001.

Leclercq, Jean, Dom Francois Vandenbroucke, and Louis Bouyer. *The Spirituality of the Middle Ages*. A History of Christian Spirituality. New York: Desclee, 1968.

Lee, Helen. *The Missional Mom: Living with Purpose at Home and in the World*. Chicago: Moody, 2011.

Lehmann, E. Arno. *It Began at Tranquebar: The Story of the Tranquebar Mission and the Beginnings of Protestant Christianity in India Published to Celebrate the 250th Anniversary of the Landing of the First Protestant Missionaries at Tranquebar in 1706*. Madras, India: Christian Literature Society on Behalf of the Federation of Evangelical Lutheran Churches in India, 1956.

Lehner, Ulrich L. "The Trinity in the Early Modern Era (c.1550–1770)." In *The Oxford Handbook of the Trinity*, edited by Gilles Emery and Matthew Levering, 240-53. Oxford: Open University Press, 2011.

Letter, P. de. "Introduction." In *The Call of All Nations*, by Prosper. Ancient Christian Writers: The Works of the Fathers in Translation 14. Westminster, MD: Newman, 1952.

Lewis, A. J. "Count Zinzendorf." *London Quarterly and Holborn Review* 185 (April 1960): 125-32.

Lincoln, Andrew T. "Pilgrimage and the New Testament." In *Explorations in a Christian Theology of Pilgrimage*, edited by Craig Bartholomew and Fred Hughes, 29-49. Burlington, VT: Ashgate, 2004.

Littell, Franklin H. "The Anabaptist Theology of Mission." In *Anabaptism and Mission*, edited by Wilbert R. Shenk, 13-23. Missionary Studies 10. Scottdale, PA: Herald Press, 1984.

———. *The Anabaptist View of the Church: A Study in the Origins of Sectarian Protestantism*. 2nd ed. Boston: Starr King, 1958.

Little, Christopher R. *Mission in the Way of Paul: Biblical Mission for the Church in the Twenty-First Century*. Studies in Biblical Literature 80. New York: Peter Lang, 2005.

Llull, Ramon. *Selected Works of Ramón Llull (1232–1316)*. Translated by Anthony Bonner. 2 vols. Princeton, NJ: Princeton University Press, 1985.

Lonsdale, David. "Ignatian Mission." *Ignatian Spirituality and Mission: The Way Supplement* 79 (Spring 1994): 92-100.

Louw, Johannes P., and Eugene Nida, eds. *Greek-English Lexicon of the New Testament, Based on Semantic Domains*. 2nd ed. New York: United Bible Societies, 1989.

Love, Julian Price. *The Missionary Message of the Bible*. New York: Macmillan, 1941.

Luc, Alex. "The Kingdom of God and His Mission." In *Discovering the Mission of God: Best Missional Practices of the 21st Century*, edited by Mike Barnett and Robin Martin, 85-98. Downers Grove, IL: IVP Academic, 2012.

Lumpkin, William L. *Baptist Confessions of Faith*. 4th ed. Valley Forge, PA: Judson, 1980.

Luther, Martin. *Church and Ministry I*. Luther's Works 39. Edited by Eric W. Gritsch. Philadelphia: Fortress, 1970.

———. *A Commentary upon the Epistle of Paul to the Galatians*. Connecticut: Salmon S. Miles, 1837.

———. *Martin Luther's Basic Theological Writings*. Edited by William R. Russell and Timothy F. Lull. 3rd ed. Minneapolis: Fortress, 2012.

Luzbetak, Louis J. *The Church and Cultures: New Perspectives in Missiological Anthropology*. American Society of Missiology Series 12. Maryknoll, NY: Orbis Books, 1988.

Lynch, Joseph H. *Early Christianity: A Brief History*. New York: Oxford University Press, 2010.

———. *The Medieval Church: A Brief History*. London: Longman, 1992.

MacCraith, Michael. "The Legacy of Columba." In *Christian Mission in Western Society: Precedents, Perspectives, Prospects*, 65-91. Edited by Simon Barrow and Graeme Smith. London: CTBI, 2001.

MacCulloch, Diarmaid. *Christianity: The First Three Thousand Years*. New York: Viking, 2009.

MacEvitt, Christopher. *The Crusades and the Christian World of the East: Rough Tolerance*. The Middle Ages Series. Philadelphia: University of Pennsylvania Press, 2008.

Maclear, G. F. *A History of Christian Missions During the Middle Ages*. Cambridge: Macmillan, 1863.

MacMullen, Ramsay. *Christianizing the Roman Empire: (A.D. 100–400)*. New Haven, CT: Yale University Press, 1984.

Maier, Christoph T., ed. *Crusade Propaganda and Ideology: Model Sermons for the Preaching of the Cross*. Cambridge: Cambridge University Press, 2006.

———. *Preaching the Crusades: Mendicant Friars and the Cross in the Thirteenth Century*. The Medieval Review. Cambridge: Cambridge University Press, 1994.

Márkus, Gilbert. "Iona: Monks, Pastors and Missionaries." In *Spes Scotorum, Hope of the Scots: Saint Columba, Iona and Scotland*, edited by Dauvit Broun and Thomas Owen Clancy, 115-38. Edinburgh: T&T Clark, 1999.

Markus, Robert A. "Gregory the Great and a Papal Missionary Strategy." In *The Mission of the Church and the Propagation of the Faith: Papers Read at the Seventh Summer Meeting and the Eight Winter Meeting of the Ecclesiastical History Society*, edited by G. J. Cuming, 29-38. Studies in Church History 6. Cambridge: Cambridge University Press, 1970.

———. "The Papacy, Missions and the Gentes." In *Integration Und Herrschaft: Ethnische Identitäten Und Soziale Organisation Im Frühmittelalter*, edited by Walter Pohl and Max Diesenberger, 37-42. Forschungen Zur Geschicte Des Mittelalters 3. Wien: Verlag der Österreichischen Akademie der Wissenschaften, 2002.

Marshall, I. Howard. *Beyond the Bible: Moving from Scripture to Theology*. Acadia Studies in Bible and Theology. Grand Rapids: Baker Academic, 2004.

———. "Luke's Portrait of the Pauline Mission." In *The Gospel to the Nations: Perspectives on Paul's Mission*, edited by Peter Bolt and Mark Thompson, 99-113. Downers Grove, IL: InterVarsity Press, 2000.

Mayer, Hans Eberhard. *The Crusades*. Translated by John Gillingham. London: Oxford University Press, 1972.

Mayr-Harting, Henry. *The Coming of Christianity to Anglo-Saxon England*. 3rd ed. University Park: Pennsylvania State University Press, 1991.

McAfee, Cleland Boyd. *The Uncut Nerve of Missions: An Inquiry and an Answer*. New York: Fleming H. Revell, 1932.

McAlister, Lyle N. *Spain and Portugal in the New World, 1492-1700*. Europe and the World in the Age of Expansion 3. Minneapolis: University of Minnesota Press, 1984.

McBeth, Leon. *The Baptist Heritage*. Nashville: Broadman, 1987.

McClendon, James Wm., Jr. *Systematic Theology.* Vol. 3, *Witness.* Waco, TX: Baylor University Press, 2012.

McDaniel, Ferris L. "Mission in the Old Testament." In *Mission in the New Testament: An Evangelical Approach,* edited by William J. Larkin Jr. and Joel F. Williams, 11-20. American Society of Missiology Series 27. Maryknoll, NY: Orbis Books, 1998.

McDonald, Lee Martin. *Formation of the Bible: The Story of the Church's Canon.* Peabody, MA: Hendrickson, 2012.

McGavran, Donald A. "Crisis of Identity for Some Missionary Societies." In *Crucial Issues in Missions Tomorrow,* edited by Donald A. McGavran, 188-201. Chicago: Moody, 1972.

McGrath, Alister. *Christian Theology: An Introduction.* 3rd ed. Oxford: Blackwell, 2001.

McGuire, Brian Patrick. "Monastic and Religious Orders, C. 1100–C. 1350." In *The Cambridge History of Christianity,* vol. 4, *Christianity in Western Europe c. 1100–c. 1500,* edited by Miri Rubin and Walter Simons, 54-72. Cambridge: Cambridge University Press, 2009.

McKeon, Richard. *Rhetoric: Essays in Invention and Discovery.* Woodbridge, CT: Ox Bow, 1987.

McKitterick, Rosamond. *Charlemagne: The Formation of a European Identity.* Cambridge: Cambridge University Press, 2008.

McKnight, Scot. *A Light Among the Gentiles: Jewish Missionary Activity in the Second Temple Period.* Minneapolis: Fortress, 1991.

McMichael, Steven J. "Francis and the Encounter with the Sultan (1219)." In *The Cambridge Companion to Francis of Assisi,* 127-42. Cambridge Companions to Religion. Cambridge: Cambridge University Press, 2012.

McNeal, Reggie. *Missional Renaissnace: Changing the Scorecard for the Church.* San Francisco: Jossey Bass, 2009.

Megill, Allan. "Grand Narrative and the Discipline of History." In *A New Philosophy of History,* edited by Frank Ankersmit and Hans Kellner, 151-73. Chicago: University of Chicago Press, 1995.

Mendels, Doron. *The Media Revolution of Early Christianity: An Essay on Eusebius's Ecclesiastical History.* Grand Rapids: Eerdmans, 1999.

Messer, Donald E. *A Conspiracy of Goodness: Contemporary Images of Christian Mission.* Nashville: Abingdon, 1992.

Metzger, Bruce M. *The Canon of the New Testament: Its Origin, Development, and Significance.* Oxford: Clarendon, 1987.

Miller, James C. "Paul and His Ethnicity: Reframing the Categories." In *Paul as Missionary: Identity, Activity, Theology, and Practice*, edited by Trevor J. Burke and Brian S. Rosner, 37-50. Library of New Testament Studies 420. London: T&T Clark, 2011.

Moffett, Samuel H. *A History of Christianity in Asia*. Vol. 1, *Beginnings to 1500*. Maryknoll, NY: Orbis Books, 1998.

———. *A History of Christianity in Asia*. Vol. 2, *1500–1900*. Maryknoll, NY: Orbis Books, 2005.

Mooney, Catherine M. "Ignatian Spirituality, A Spirituality for Mission." *Mission Studies* 26 (2009): 192-213.

Moorhead, John. *Gregory the Great*. The Early Church Fathers. London: Routledge, 2005.

Moorman, John R. H. *A History of the Franciscan Order from Its Origins to the Year 1517*. Oxford: Clarendon, 1968.

Moreau, A. Scott. "Mission and Missions." Edited by A. Scott Moreau. *Evangelical Dictionary of World Missions*. Grand Rapids: Baker Books, 2000.

Moses, Paul. *The Saint and the Sultan: The Crusades, Islam, and Francis of Assisi's Mission of Peace*. New York: Doubleday, 2009.

Motel, Heinz. "Zinzendorf, Nikolaus Ludwig von." In *Concise Dictionary of the Christian World Mission*. Edited by Stephen Neill, Gerald H. Anderson, and John Goodwin. Nashville: Abingdon, 1971.

Mott, John R. "Closing Address." In *World Missionary Conference, 1910: The History and Records of the Conference Together with Addresses Delivered at the Evening Meetings*, 9:347-51. Edinburgh: Oliphant, Anderson, & Ferrier, 1910.

———. *Strategic Points in the World's Conquest: The Universities and Colleges as Related to the Progress of Christianity*. New York: Fleming H. Revell, 1897.

Muirchú. "The Vita Patricii by Muirchú." In *Discovering Saint Patrick*, translated by Thomas O'Loughlin, 192-229. London: Darton, Longman & Todd, 2005.

Muldoon, James. "Crusading and Canon Law." In *Palgrave Advances in the Crusades*, edited by Helen J. Nicholson, 37-57. New York: Palgrave MacMillan, 2005.

Mulholland, Kenneth B. "Moravians, Puritans, and the Modern Missionary Movement (Paper Presented as the Missions and Evangelism Lectureship, Dallas Theological Seminary, N 2–5, 1997)." *Bibliotheca Sacra* 156 (June 1999): 221-32.

Mundadan, A. Mathias. "The Changing Task of Christian History: A View at the Onset of the Third Millennium." In *Enlarging the Story: Perspectives on*

Writing World Christian History, edited by Wilbert R. Shenk, 22-53. Maryknoll, NY: Orbis Books, 2002.

Murray, Alan V., ed. *Crusade and Conversion on the Baltic Frontier, 1150–1500.* Aldershot, UK: Ashgate, 2001.

Murray, Andrew. *Key to the Missionary Problem.* Edited by Leona F. Choy. Fort Washington, PA: Christian Literature Crusade, 1979.

Murray, John. *The Epistle to the Romans: The English Text with Introduction, Exposition and Notes.* Grand Rapids: Eerdmans, 1968.

"NASA—Missions." Accessed February 21, 2012. www.nasa.gov/missions/index .html.

Neill, Stephen. *Creative Tension.* London: Edinburgh House, 1959.

———. *A History of Christian Missions.* 2nd ed. London: Penguin Books, 1986.

———. *A History of Christianity in India: The Beginning to AD 1707.* Cambridge: Cambridge University Press, 1984.

———. "The History of Missions: An Academic Discipline." In *The Mission of the Church and the Propagation of the Faith: Papers Read at the Seventh Summer Meeting and the Eight Winter Meeting of the Ecclesiastical History Society*, edited by G. J. Cuming, 149-70. Studies in Church History 6. Cambridge: Cambridge University Press, 1970.

Nemer, L. "Mission and Missions." In *New Catholic Encyclopedia.* Washington, DC: Catholic University of America Press, 2003.

Newbigin, Lesslie. "The Future of Missions and Missionaries." *Review & Expositor* 74, no. 2 (March 1977): 209-18.

———. *The Household of God: Lectures on the Nature of the Church.* London: SCM Press, 1957.

———. *One Body, One Gospel, One World: The Christian Mission Today.* London: Wm. Carling, 1958.

———. *The Open Secret: An Introduction to the Theology of Mission.* Rev. ed. Grand Rapids: Eerdmans, 1995.

———. "Recent Thinking on Christian Beliefs, 8: Mission and Missions." *The Expository Times* 88, no. 9 (1977): 260-64.

———. *A Word in Season: Perspectives on Christian World Missions.* Grand Rapids: Eerdmans, 1994.

Newitt, Malyn. *A History of Portuguese Overseas Expansion, 1400–1668.* London: Routledge, 2005.

Newman, Barclay M., and Eugene A. Nida. *A Translator's Handbook on the Acts of the Apostles.* New York: United Bible Societies, 1966.

Nida, Eugene A., and Charles Taber. *The Theory and Practice of Translation.* Leiden: E. J. Brill, 1982.

Nijenhuis, Willem. *Adrianus Saravia (c. 1532–1613): Dutch Calvinist, First Reformed Defender of the English Episcopal Church Order on the Basis of the Ius Divinum.* Leiden: E. J. Brill, 1980.

Niles, D. T. "A Church and Its 'Selfhood.'" In *A Decisive Hour for the Christian Mission: The East Asia Christian Conference 1959 and the John R. Mott Memorial Lectures,* 72-96. London: SCM Press, 1960.

———. *Upon the Earth: The Mission of God and the Missionary Enterprise of the Churches.* New York: McGraw-Hill, 1962.

Nissen, Johannes. *New Testament and Mission: Historical and Hermeneutical Perspectives.* 2nd ed. Frankfurt am Main: P. Lang, 2002.

Noll, Mark A. *The New Shape of World Christianity: How American Experience Reflects Global Faith.* Downers Grove, IL: IVP Academic, 2009.

Ohm, Thomas. *Machet zu Jüngern alle Völker: Theorie der Mission.* Freiburg im Breisgau: Erich Wewel Verlag, 1962.

Okoye, James Chukwuma. *Israel and the Nations: A Mission Theology of the Old Testament.* American Society of Missiology Series 39. Maryknoll, NY: Orbis Books, 2006.

Oldendorp, Christian Georg Andreas Meier. *Historie der caribischen Inseln Sanct Thomas, Sanct Crux und Sanct Jan, inbesondere der dasigen Neger und der Mission der evangelischen Brüder unter denselben.* Vol. 51. Berlin: Verlag für Wissenschaft und Bildung, 2000.

Olin, John C., ed. *The Catholic Reformation: Savonarola to Ignatius Loyola.* Fordham ed. New York: Fordham University Press, 1992.

O'Loughlin, Thomas. *Discovering Saint Patrick.* London: Darton, Longman & Todd, 2005.

O'Malley, John. "Introduction." In *The Jesuits II: Cultures, Sciences, and the Arts, 1540–1773,* xxiii-xxxvi. Toronto: University of Toronto Press, 2006.

O'Malley, John W. *The First Jesuits.* Cambridge, MA: Harvard University Press, 1993.

———. "Mission and the Early Jesuits." *Ignatian Spirituality and Mission: The Way Supplement* 79 (Spring 1994): 3-10.

———. "The Society of Jesus." In *Companion to the Reformation World,* 223-36. Malden, MA: Blackwell, 2004.

Orchard, R. K. *Missions in a Time of Testing: Thought and Practice in Contemporary Missions.* Philadelphia: Westminster, 1964.

Osborne, Grant R. *The Hermeneutical Spiral: A Comprehensive Introduction to Biblical Interpretation*. Downers Grove, IL: InterVarsity Press, 1991.

Ostrom, H. C., ed. *The Modern Crusade: Addresses and Proceedings of the First General Convention of the Laymen's Missionary Movement, Presbyterian Church in the U.S., Birmingham, Ala., Feb. 16–18, 1909*. Athens: Laymen's Missionary Movement, 1909.

Osuna, Javier. *Friends in the Lord: A Study in the Origins and Growth of Community in the Society of Jesus from St Ignatius' Conversion to the Earliest Texts of the Constitutions (1521–1541)*. Translated by Nicholas King. The Way Series 3. London: The Way, 1974.

"P&G Worldwide Site: The Power of Purpose." www.pg.com/en_US/company /purpose_people/index.shtml.

Panikkar, K. M. *Asia and Western Dominance: A Survey of the Vasco Da Gama Epoch of Asian History, 1498–1945*. London: G. Allen & Unwin, 1959.

Patrick. "Confessio: Text and Translation." In *The Book of Letters of Saint Patrick the Bishop*, edited and translated by D. R. Howlett, 51-134. Liber Epistolarum Sancti Patricii Episcopi. Dublin: Four Courts, 1994.

———. "Epistola Ad Milites Corotici: Text and Translation." In *The Book of Letters of Saint Patrick the Bishop*, translated by D. R. Howlett, 25-46. Liber Epistolarum Sancti Patricii Episcopi. Dublin: Four Courts, 1994.

Payne, Ernest A. *The Church Awakes: The Story of the Modern Missionary Movement*. London: Carey, 1942.

———. "Introduction." In *An Enquiry into the Obligations of Christians to Use Means for the Conversion of the Heathens*, i-xx. London: Carey Kingsgate, 1961.

Pearson, M. N. *The Portuguese in India*. New Cambridge History of India. New York: Cambridge University Press, 1988.

Peers, E. Allison. *Ramon Lull: A Biography*. New York: Burt Franklin, 1969.

Peskett, Howard, and Vinoth Ramachandra. *The Message of Mission: The Glory of Christ in All Time and Space*. The Bible Speaks Today. Downers Grove, IL: InterVarsity Press, 2003.

Peters, George W. *A Biblical Theology of Missions*. Chicago: Moody, 1972.

Peterson, David G. "Maturity: The Goal of Mission." In *The Gospel to the Nations: Perspectives on Paul's Mission*, edited by Peter Bolt and Mark Thompson, 185-204. Downers Grove, IL: InterVarsity Press, 2000.

Pham, Paulus Y. *Towards an Ecumenical Paradigm for Christian Mission: David Bosch's Missionary Vision*. Documenta Missionalia 35. Roma: Gregorian Biblical, 2010.

Phillips, C. Matthew. "Crucified with Christ: The Imitation of the Crucified Christ and the Crusading Spirituality." In *Crusades—Medieval Worlds in Conflict*, edited by Thomas F. Madden, James L. Naus, and Vincent Ryan, 25-33. Farnham, UK: Ashgate, 2010.

Plummer, Robert L. *Paul's Understanding of the Church's Mission: Did the Apostle Paul Expect the Early Christian Community to Evangelize?* Paternoster Biblical Monographs. Exeter, UK: Paternoster, 2006.

Polanco, Juan de. *Year by Year with the Early Jesuits (1537–1556): Selections from the "Chronicon" of Juan de Polanco, S.J.* Jesuit Primary Sources in English Translations 21. St. Louis: Institute of Jesuit Sources, 2004.

Porter, Andrew. "Religion, Missionary Enthusiasm, and Empire." In *The Oxford History of the British Empire*, vol. 3, *The Nineteenth Century*, edited by Andrew Porter, 222-46. Oxford: Oxford University Press, 1999.

———. *Religion Versus Empire? British Protestant Missionaries and Overseas Expansion, 1700–1914*. Manchester: Manchester University Press, 2004.

Porter, Stanley E. "The Content and Message of Paul's Missionary Teaching." In *Christian Mission: Old Testament Foundations and New Testament Developments*, edited by Stanley E. Porter and Cynthia Long Westfall, 135-54. McMaster New Testament Studies Series. Eugene, OR: Pickwick, 2010.

———. "Reconciliation as the Heart of Paul's Missionary Theology." In *Paul as Missionary: Identity, Activity, Theology, and Practice*, edited by Trevor J. Burke and Brian S. Rosner, 169-79. Library of New Testament Studies 420. London: T&T Clark, 2011.

Porter, Stanley E., and Cynthia Long Westfall. "A Cord of Three Strands: Mission in Acts." In *Christian Mission: Old Testament Foundations and New Testament Developments*, edited by Stanley E. Porter and Cynthia Long Westfall, 108-34. McMaster New Testament Studies Series. Eugene, OR: Pickwick, 2010.

Powell, James M. "St. Francis of Assisi's Way of Peace." *Medieval Encounters* 13 (2007): 271-80.

Pratt, Zane. "The Heart of the Task." In *Discovering the Mission of God: Best Missional Practices of the 21st Century*, edited by Mike Barnett and Robin Martin, 130-43. Downers Grove, IL: InterVarsity Press, 2012.

Pratt, Zane G., M. David Sills, and Jeff K. Walters. *Introduction to Global Missions*. Nashville: B&H, 2014.

Prawer, Joshua. *The Latin Kingdom of Jerusalem: European Colonialism in the Middle Ages*. London: Weidenfeld and Nicolson, 1973.

———. *The World of the Crusaders*. New York: Quadrangle Books, 1973.

Price, Jennifer. "Alfonso I and the Memory of the First Crusade: Conquest and Crusade in the Kingdom of Aragon-Navarre." In *Crusades—Medieval Worlds in Conflict*, 75-94. Farnham, UK: Ashgate, 2010.

Prosper. *The Call of All Nations.* Translated by P. de Letter. Ancient Christian Writers: The Works of the Fathers in Translation 14. Westminster, MD: Newman, 1952.

———. *De Vocatione Omnium Gentium.* Edited by Roland J. Teske and Dorothea Weber. Corpus Scriptorum Ecclesiasticorum Latinorum 97. Wien: Verlag der Österreichischen Akademie der Wissenschaften, 2009.

Prosperi, Adriano. "The Missionary." In *Baroque Personae*, edited by Rosario Villari, translated by Lydia G. Cochrane, 160-94. Chicago: The University of Chicago Press, 1995.

Purcell, Mary. *The First Jesuit, St. Ignatius Loyola (1491-1556).* Chicago: Loyola University Press, 1981.

Purkis, William J. *Crusading Spirituality in the Holy Land and Iberia, c.1095-c.1187.* Woodbridge, UK: Boydell, 2008.

———. "Religious Symbols and Practices: Monastic Spirituality, Pilgrimage and Crusade." In *European Religious Cultures*, 69-88. London: Institute for Historical Research, 2008.

Quinlan, John. "A Missionary Reflection From St. John." In *A New Missionary Era*, edited by Padraig Flanagan, 119-26. Maryknoll, NY: Orbis Books, 1979.

Rae, George Milne. *The Syrian Church in India.* Edinburgh: W. Blackwood, 1892.

Rahner, Hugo. *The Vision of St. Ignatius in the Chapel of La Storta.* 2nd ed. Rome: Centrus Ignatianum Spiritualitatis, 1979.

Ralph of Caen. *The Gesta Tancredi of Ralph of Caen: A History of the Normans on the First Crusade.* Edited by Bernard S. Bachrach and David Stewart Bachrach. Crusade Texts in Translation 12. Burlington, VT: Ashgate, 2005.

Ranger, Terence. "New Approaches to the History of Mission Christianity." In *African Historiography: Essays in Honour of Jacob Ade Ajayi*, edited by Toyin Falola, 180-94. Ikeja, Nigeria: Longman Nigeria, 1993.

Ranson, Charles W. *The Biblical Basis of the Christian Mission.* Austin Seminary Bulletin, vol. 71, no. 10. Austin: Austin Presbyterian Theological Seminary, 1956.

Ravier, André. *Ignatius of Loyola and the Founding of the Society of Jesus.* San Francisco: Ignatius, 1987.

Rayborn, Tim. *The Violent Pilgrimage: Christians, Muslims and Holy Conflicts, 850-1150.* Jefferson, NC: McFarland, 2013.

Redford, Shawn Barrett. *Missiological Hermeneutics: Biblical Interpretation for the Global Church*. American Society of Missiology Monograph Series 2. Eugene, OR: Pickwick, 2012.

Reinhard, Wolfgang. "The Seaborne Empires." In *Handbook of European History, 1400–1600: Late Middle Ages, Renaissance and Reformation*, vol. 1: *Structures and Assertions*, edited by Henry Jansen, Thomas A. Brady, and Heiko A. Oberman, 637-59. Leiden, The Netherlands: E. J. Brill, 1994.

Rengstorf, Karl Heinrich. "ἀποστέλλω." In *Theological Dictionary of the New Testament*, edited by Gerhard Kittel. Grand Rapids: Eerdmans, 1964.

Report of Commission I: Carrying the Gospel to All the Non-Christian World. Edinburgh: Oliphant, Anderson, & Ferrier, 1910.

Rétif, André. "Evolution of the Catholic Idea of Mission: A French Roman Catholic Bibliography." *Student World* 53, nos. 1–2 (January 1960): 262-71.

Reuter, Timothy. "Saint Boniface and Europe." In *The Greatest Englishman: Essays on St. Boniface and the Church at Crediton*, edited by Timothy Reuter, 69-94. Exeter, UK: Paternoster, 1980.

Richardson, Alan. "Kingdom of God." In *A Theological Word Book of the Bible*, edited by Alan Richardson. London: SCM Press, 1957.

Riley-Smith, Jonathan. *The Crusades: A Short History*. New Haven, CT: Yale University Press, 1987.

———. "Crusading as an Act of Love." *History* 65 (1980): 177-92.

———. "Death on the First Crusade." In *End of Strife*, edited by David M. Loades, 14-31. Edinburgh: T&T Clark, 1984.

———. *The First Crusade and the Idea of Crusading*. The Middle Ages. Philadelphia: University of Pennsylvania Press, 1986.

———. *The First Crusaders, 1095–1131*. Cambridge: Cambridge University Press, 1997.

———, ed. *The Oxford History of the Crusades*. Oxford: Oxford University Press, 1999.

Riley-Smith, Louise, and Jonathan Riley-Smith. *The Crusades: Idea and Reality, 1095–1274*. Documents of Medieval History 4. London: Edward Arnold, 1981.

Ritcher, Horst. "Militia Dei: A Central Concept for the Religious Ideas of the Early Crusades and the German Rolandslied." In *Journeys Toward God: Pilgrimage and Crusade*, edited by Barbara N. Sargent-Baur, 107-26. Kalamazoo, MI: Medieval Institute Publications, 1992.

Robert, Dana Lee. *Christian Mission: How Christianity Became a World Religion*. Chichester, UK: Wiley-Blackwell, 2009.

Robert the Monk. "Historia Iherosolimitana." In *Robert the Monk's History of the First Crusade*, translated by Carol Sweetenham, 73-214. Crusade Texts in Translation. Aldershot, Hants, UK: Ashgate, 2005.

Robinson, Charles Henry. *History of Christian Missions*. International Theological Library. New York: Charles Scribner's Sons, 1915.

Robinson, Martin. "Pilgrimage and Mission." In *Explorations in a Christian Theology of Pilgrimage*, edited by Craig Bartholomew and Fred Hughes, 170-83. Aldershot, UK: Ashgate, 2004.

Robson, George. "History of the Conference." In *World Missionary Conference, 1910: The History and Records of the Conference Together with Addresses Delivered at the Evening Meetings*, 9:3-31. Edinburgh: Oliphant, Anderson, & Ferrier, 1910.

Robson, Michael. *The Franciscans in the Middle Ages*. Monastic Orders. Woodbridge, UK: Boydell, 2006.

Rosenberg, Emily S. *Financial Missionaries to the World: The Politics and Culture of Dollar Diplomacy (1900–1930)*. American Encounters / Global Interactions. Durham, NC: Duke University Press, 2004.

Rosner, Brian S. "The Glory of God in Paul's Missionary Theology and Practice." In *Paul as Missionary: Identity, Activity, Theology, and Practice*, edited by Trevor J. Burke and Brian S. Rosner, 158-68. Library of New Testament Studies 420. London: T&T Clark, 2011.

Rowley, H. H. *The Missionary Message of the Old Testament*. London: Carey, 1945.

Roxburgh, Alan J. *Joining God, Remaking Church, Changing the World: The New Shape of the Church in Our Time*. New York: Morehouse, 2015.

Roxburgh, Alan J., and Fred Romanuk. *The Missional Leader: Equipping Your Church to Reach a Changing World*. San Francisco: Jossey-Bass, 2006.

Rufinus. *The Church History of Rufinus of Aquileia, Books 10 and 11*. Translated by Philip R. Amidon. New York: Oxford University Press, 1997.

Runciman, Steven. "The First Crusade: Antioch to Ascalon." In *A History of the Crusades*, vol. 1, *The First Hundred Years*, edited by Marshall W. Baldwin, 308-41. Madison: The University of Wisconsin Press, 1969.

———. "The First Crusade: Constantinople to Antioch." In *A History of the Crusades*, vol. 1, *The First Hundred Years*, edited by Marshall W. Baldwin, 280-307. Madison: The University of Wisconsin Press, 1969.

———. "The Pilgrimages to Palestine Before 1095." In *A History of the Crusades*, vol. 1, *The First Hundred Years*, edited by Marshall W. Baldwin, 68-78. Madison: The University of Wisconsin Press, 1969.

Russell, D. S. *Divine Disclosure: An Introduction to Jewish Apocalyptic*. London: SCM Press, 1992.

Russell, Mark. *The Missional Entrepreneur: Principles and Practices for Business as Mission*. Birmingham, AL: New Hope, 2010.

Russell-Wood, A. J. R. "Iberian Expansion and the Issue of Black Slavery: Changing Portuguese Attitudes, 1440–1770." *The American Historical Review* 83, no. 1 (February 1978): 16-42.

———. "Patterns of Settlement in the Portuguese Empire, 1400–1800." In *Portuguese Oceanic Expansion, 1400–1800*, edited by Francisco Bethencourt and Diogo Ramada Curto, 161-96. New York: Cambridge University Press, 2007.

———. *A World on the Move: The Portuguese in Africa, Asia, and America, 1415–1808*. New York: St. Martin's, 1993.

Ryan, James D. "Conversion or the Crown of Martyrdom: Conflicting Goals for Fourteenth-Century Missionaries in Central Asia?" In *Medieval Cultures in Contact*, edited by Richard F. Gyug, 19-38. Fordham Series in Medieval Studies. New York: Fordham University Press, 2003.

Sá, Bailon de. "The Genesis of Portuguese Discoveries and Their Influence on Indian Culture." In *Discoveries, Missionary Expansion and Asian Cultures*, 65-75. New Delhi: Concept, 1994.

Sá, Isabel dos Guimarães. "Ecclesiastical Structures and Religious Action." In *Portuguese Oceanic Expansion, 1400–1800*, edited by Francisco Bethencourt and Diogo Ramada Curto, 255-82. New York: Cambridge University Press, 2007.

Safian, Robert. "Find Your Mission." *Fast Company Magazine*, November 2014.

Sandnes, Karl Olav. "A Missionary Strategy in 1 Corinthians 9:9-23?" In *Paul as Missionary: Identity, Activity, Theology, and Practice*, edited by Trevor J. Burke and Brian S. Rosner, 128-41. Library of New Testament Studies 420. London: T&T Clark, 2011.

Sanneh, Lamin. "World Christianity and the New Historiography: History and Global Interconnections." In *Enlarging the Story: Perspectives on Writing World Christian History*, edited by Wilbert R. Shenk, 94-114. Maryknoll, NY: Orbis Books, 2002.

Saussure, Ferdinand de. *Course in General Linguistics*. London: Duckworth, 1983.

Schattschneider, David A. "The Missionary Theologies of Zinzendorf and Spangenberg." *Transactions of the Moravian Historical Society* 22, no. 3 (January 1975): 213-33.

Scherer, James A. *Gospel, Church & Kingdom: Comparative Studies in World Mission Theology.* Eugene, OR: Wipf & Stock, 2004.

———. "Part 1: The Life and Significance of Welz." In *Justinian Welz: Essays by an Early Prophet of Mission*, 13-46. Grand Rapids: Eerdmans, 1969.

Schlatter, Adolf von. *The Theology of the Apostles: The Development of New Testament Theology.* Translated by Andreas J. Köstenberger. Grand Rapids: Baker Book House, 1999.

Schmidlin, Joseph. *Catholic Mission History.* Edited by Matthias Braun. Techny, IL: Mission Press, S. V. D, 1933.

Schnabel, Eckhard J. "'As the Father Has Sent Me, So I Send You' (John 20:21): The Mission of Jesus and the Mission of the Church." *Missionalia* 33, no. 2 (August 2005): 263-86.

———. *Early Christian Mission.* 2 vols. Downers Grove, IL: InterVarsity Press, 2004.

———. "Evangelism and the Mission of the Church." In *God and the Faithfulness of Paul: A Critical Examination of the Pauline Theology of N. T. Wright*, edited by Christoph Heilig, J. Thomas Hewitt, and Michael F. Bird, 683-707. Tübingen, Germany: Mohr Siebeck, 2016.

———. "Mission, Early Non-Pauline." In *Dictionary of the Later New Testament & Its Development*, edited by Ralph P. Martin and Peter H. Davids. Downers Grove, IL: IVP Academic, 1997.

———. *Paul the Missionary: Realities, Strategies and Methods.* Downers Grove, IL: IVP Academic, 2008.

Schnackenburg, Rudolf. *God's Rule and Kingdom.* New York: Herder and Herder, 1963.

Schurhammer, Georg. *Francis Xavier; His Life, His Times.* Vol. 1, *Europe 1506–41.* Translated by M. Joseph Costelloe. Rome: Jesuit Historical Institute, 1973.

Scott, Florence R. "Columba of Iona." In *Evangelical Dictionary of World Missions*, edited by A. Scott Moreau. Grand Rapids: Baker Books, 2000.

Scully, Robert E. "The Society of Jesus: Its Early History, Spirituality, and Mission to England." In *Catholic Collecting: Catholic Reflection 1538–1850*, edited by Virginia Chieffo Raguin, 127-38. Washington, DC: Catholic University of America Press, 2006.

Sebastian, J. Jayakiran. "Interrogating Missio Dei: From the Mission of God Towards Appreciating Our Mission to God in India Today." In *Mission and Postmodernities*, edited by Rolv Olsen, 204-21. Regnum Edinburgh 2010 Series. Eugene, OR: Wipf & Stock, 2012.

Seccombe, David. "The Story of Jesus and the Missionary Strategy of Paul." In *The Gospel to the Nations: Perspectives on Paul's Mission*, edited by Peter Bolt and Mark Thompson, 115-29. Downers Grove, IL: InterVarsity Press, 2000.

Senior, Donald, and Carroll Stuhlmueller. *The Biblical Foundations for Mission*. Maryknoll, NY: Orbis Books, 1983.

Sessler, Jacob John. *Communal Pietism Among Early American Moravians*. New York: AMS, 1971.

Seumois, Andrew V. "The Evolution of Mission Theology Among Roman Catholics." In *The Theology of the Christian Mission*, edited by Gerald H. Anderson, 122-34. Nashville: Abingdon, 1961.

Sharpe, Eric J. "Reflections on Missionary Historiography." *International Bulletin of Missionary Research* 13, no. 2 (April 1989): 76-81.

Shenk, David W. *God's Call to Mission*. Scottdale, PA: Herald, 1994.

Shenk, Wilbert R. *Changing Frontiers of Mission*. Maryknoll, NY: Orbis Books, 1999.

———. "A Global Church Requires a Global History." *Conrad Grebel Review* 15, nos. 1–2 (December 1997): 3-18.

———. "The 'Great Century' Reconsidered." In *Anabaptism and Mission*, edited by Wilbert R. Shenk, 158-77. Institute of Mennonite Studies, Missionary Studies 10. Scottdale, PA: Herald, 1984.

———. "New Wineskins for New Wine: Toward a Post-Christendom Ecclesiology." *International Bulletin of Missionary Research* 29, no. 2 (April 2005): 73-79.

———. "The Relevance of a Messianic Missiology for Mission Today." In *The Transfiguration of Mission: Biblical, Theological & Historical Foundations*, edited by Wilbert R. Shenk, 17-36. Institute of Mennonite Studies, Missionary Studies 12. Scottdale, PA: Herald, 1993.

———. *Write the Vision: The Church Renewed*. Valley Forge, PA: Trinity Press International, 1995.

Shore, Paul J. *The Vita Christi of Ludolph of Saxony and Its Influence on the Spiritual Exercises of Ignatius of Loyola*. Studies in the Spirituality of Jesuits. St. Louis: Seminar on Jesuit Spirituality, 1998.

Shourie, Arun. *Missionaries in India: Continuities, Changes, Dilemmas.* New Delhi: HarperCollins, 1997.

Siberry, Elizabeth. *Criticism of Crusading, 1095–1274.* Oxford: Clarendon, 1985.

———. "Missionaries and Crusaders, 1095–1274: Opponents or Allies?" In *Church and War: Papers Read at the Twenty-First Summer Meeting and Twenty-Second Winter Meeting of the Ecclesiastical History Society*, edited by W. J. Sheils, 103-10. Oxford: Basil Blackwell, 1983.

Sievernich, Michael. "Die Mission Und Die Missionen de Gesellschaft Jesu." In *Sendung, Eroberung, Begegnung: Franz Xaver, Die Gesellschaft Jesu Und Die Katholische Weltkirche Im Zeitalter Des Barock*, edited by Johannes Meier, 8:7-30. Studien Zur Aussereuropäischen Christentumsgeschichte (Asien, Afrika, Lateinamerika) / Studies in the History of Christianity in the Non-Western World. Wiesbaden, Germany: Harrassowitz Verlag, 2005.

Sills, M. David. *Changing World, Unchanging Mission: Responding to Global Challenges.* Downers Grove, IL: InterVarsity Press, 2015.

Simons, Menno. *The Complete Writings of Menno Simons, C. 1496–1561.* Edited by John Christian Wenger. Translated by Leonard Verduin. Scottdale, PA: Herald, 1956.

Skeat, Walter W. "Mission." In *An Etymological Dictionary of the English Language.* Oxford: Clarendon, 1953.

Skreslet, Stanley H. *Comprehending Mission: The Questions, Methods, Themes, Problems, and Prospects of Missiology.* American Society of Missiology Series 49. Maryknoll, NY: Orbis Books, 2012.

Smalley, William A. *Translation as Mission: Bible Translation in the Modern Missionary Movement.* Macon, GA: Mercer University Press, 1991.

Smith, A. Christopher. "William Carey, 1761–1834: Protestant Pioneer of the Modern Mission Era." In *Mission Legacies: Biographical Studies of Leaders of the Modern Missionary Movement*, 245-54. American Society of Missiology Series 19. Maryknoll, NY: Orbis Books, 1994.

Smith, David. *Mission After Christendom.* London: Darton, Longman and Todd, 2003.

Smith, George. *The Conversion of India: From Pantaenus to the Present Time, A.D. 193–1893.* New York: Fleming H. Revell, 1894.

Smith, John. *The Life of St. Columba, the Apostle and Patron Saint of the Ancient Scots and Picts, and Joint Patron of the Irish.* Edinburgh: Mundell & Son, 1798.

Smith, Lucius E. *Heroes and Martyrs of the Modern Missionary Enterprise: A Record of Their Lives and Labors.* Providence, RI: Potter, 1856.

Sovik, Arne. *Salvation Today*. Minneapolis: Augsburg, 1973.

Spangenberg, August Gottlieb. *An Account of the Manner in Which the Protestant Church of the Unitas Fratrum, or United Brethren, Preach the Gospel and Carry on Their Missions Among the Heathen*. London: H. Trapp, 1788.

———. *Von der Arbeit der evangelischen Brüder unter den Heiden*. Barby: Bey Christian Friedrich Laux, 1782.

Speer, Robert E. "Christ the Leader of the Missionary Work of the Church." In *World Missionary Conference, 1910: The History and Records of the Conference Together with Addresses Delivered at the Evening Meetings*, 9:151-55. Edinburgh: Oliphant, Anderson, & Ferrier, 1910.

———. *"Re-thinking Missions" Examined: An Attempt at a Just Review of the Report of the Appraisal Commission of the Laymen's Foreign Mission Inquiry*. New York: Fleming H. Revell, 1933.

———. "What This Movement Means." In *Students and the Missionary Problem: Addresses Delivered at the International Student Missionary Conference, January 2-6, 1900*, 187-93. London: Student Volunteer Missionary Union, 1900.

Spindler, Marc R. "The Biblical Grounding and Orientation of Mission." In *Missiology: An Ecumenical Introduction, Texts and Contexts of Global Christianity*, edited by A. Camps, L. A. Hoedemaker, M. R. Spindler, and F. J. Verstraelen, 123-43. Grand Rapids: Eerdmans, 1995.

———. "The Protestant Mission Study: Emergence and Features." In *Mission & Science, Missiology Revised, 1850–1940*, edited by Carine Dujardin and Claude Prudhomme, 39-52. Leuven, Belgium: Leuven University Press, 2015.

Spinka, Matthew. "Latin Church of the Early Crusades." *Church History* 8, no. 2 (June 1939): 113-31.

Stanley, Brian. "Christian Missions and the Enlightenment: A Reevaluation." In *Christian Missions and the Enlightenment*, edited by Brian Stanley, 1-21. Studies in the History of Christian Missions. Grand Rapids: Eerdmans, 2001.

———. *The World Missionary Conference, Edinburgh 1910*. Studies in the History of Christian Missions. Grand Rapids: Eerdmans, 2009.

———. "The World Missionary Conference, Edinburgh 1910: Sifting History from Myth." In *Walk Humbly with the Lord: Church and Mission Engaging Plurality*, edited by Viggo Mortensen and Andreas Østerlund Nielsen, 15-26. Grand Rapids: Eerdmans, 2010.

Stanton, Graham N. "Presuppositions in New Testament Criticism." In *New Testament Interpretation: Essays on Principles and Methods*, edited by I. Howard Marshall, 60-72. Exeter, UK: Paternoster, 1985.

Stark, Rodney. *God's Battalions: The Case for the Crusades.* New York: HarperOne, 2009.

———. *The Rise of Christianity: How the Obscure, Marginal Jesus Movement Became the Dominant Religious Force in the Western World in a Few Centuries.* San Francisco: HarperSanFrancisco, 1997.

Starkes, M. Thomas. *The Foundation for Missions.* Nashville: Broadman, 1981.

Stokes, George Thomas. *Ireland and the Celtic Church: A History of Ireland from St. Patrick to the English Conquest in 1172.* London: Hodder & Stoughton, 1892.

Stott, John R. W. *Christian Mission in the Modern World.* Downers Grove, IL: InterVarsity Press, 1975.

Stroope, Michael W. "Eschatological Mission: Its Reality and Possibility in the Theology of Karl Barth and Its Influence on Contemporary Mission Theology." PhD thesis, Southwestern Baptist Theological Seminary, 1986.

———. "The Legacy of John Amos Comenius." *International Bulletin of Missionary Research* 29, no. 4 (October 2005): 204-8.

Students and the Missionary Problem: Addresses Delivered at the International Student Missionary Conference, London, January 2–6, 1900. London: Student Volunteer Missionary Union, 1900.

Sturm, Richard E. "Defining the Word 'Apocalyptic': A Problem in Biblical Criticism." In *Apocalyptic and the New Testament: Essays in Honor of J. Louis Martyn*, edited by Joel Marcus and Marion L. Soards, 17-48. Journal for the Study of the New Testament 24. Sheffield, UK: Sheffield Academic, 1989.

Subrahmanyam, Sanjay. *The Career and Legend of Vasco Da Gama.* Cambridge: Cambridge University Press, 1997.

———. *The Portuguese Empire in Asia, 1500–1700: A Political and Economic History.* London: Longman, 1993.

Sullivan, Richard E. *Christian Missionary Activity in the Early Middle Ages.* Variorum Collected Studies Series. Aldershot, UK: Variorum, 1994.

Sunquist, Scott. *Understanding Christian Mission: Participation in Suffering and Glory.* Grand Rapids: Baker Academic, 2013.

Sybesma, Rint. "A History of Chinese Linguists in the Netherlands." In *Chinese Studies in the Netherlands: Past, Present and Future*, edited by Wilt Idema, 127-58. Leiden, The Netherlands: Koninklijke Brill, 2013.

Talbot, C. H. *The Anglo-Saxon Missionaries in Germany: Being the Lives of SS. Willibrord, Boniface, Sturm, Leoba, and Lebuin, Together with the*

Hodoeporicon of St. Willibald and a Selection from the Correspondence of St. Boniface. Makers of Christendom. New York: Sheed and Ward, 1954.

———. "St. Boniface and the German Mission." In *The Mission of the Church and the Propagation of the Faith: Papers Read at the Seventh Summer Meeting and the Eight Winter Meeting of the Ecclesiastical History Society*, edited by G. J. Cuming, 45-57. Studies in Church History 6. Cambridge: Cambridge University Press, 1970.

Talbot, Lynn. "Montserrat." In *Encyclopedia of Medieval Pilgrimage*, edited by Larissa Taylor, Leigh Ann Craig, John B. Friedman, Kathy Gower, Thomas Izbicki, and Rita Tekippe. Leiden: Brill, 2010.

Tanner, Norman P. "Medieval Crusade Decrees and Ignatius's Meditation on the Kingdom." *Heythrop Journal* 31 (1990): 505-15.

Taylor, William David, ed. *Global Missiology for the 21st Century: The Iguassu Dialogue.* Grand Rapids: Baker Academic, 2000.

Teachout, Donald Orrin. "The Biblical Basis of Missions." ThB thesis, Baptist Bible Seminary, 1961.

Tejirian, Eleanor Harvey, and Reeva Spector Simon. *Conflict, Conquest, and Conversion: Two Thousand Years of Christian Missions in the Middle East.* New York: Columbia University Press, 2012.

Tellechea Idígoras, José Ignacio. *Ignatius of Loyola: The Pilgrim Saint.* Chicago: Loyola University Press, 1994.

Tellenbach, Gerd. *The Church in Western Europe from the Tenth to the Early Twelfth Century.* Translated by Timothy Reuter. Cambridge Medieval Textbooks. Cambridge: Cambridge University Press, 1993.

Terry, John Mark. "The Ante-Nicene Church on Mission." In *Discovering the Mission of God: Best Missional Practices of the 21st Century*, edited by Mike Barnett and Robin Martin, 205-19. Downers Grove, IL: InterVarsity Press, 2012.

Teske, Roland J., and Dorothea Weber. "Introduction." In *Prosper of Aquitane: De Vocatione Omnium Gentium.* Corpus Scriptorum Ecclesiasticorum Latinorum 97. Wien: Verlag der Österreichischen Akademie der Wissenschaften, 2009.

Thomas of Celano. "The Life of Saint Francis." In *Francis of Assisi: Early Documents*, vol. 1, The Saint, edited by Regis J. Armstrong, J. A. Wayne Hellmann, and William J. Short. New York: New City, 1999.

Thomas, Norman E., ed. *Classic Texts in Mission and World Christianity.* American Society of Missiology Series 20. Maryknoll, NY: Orbis Books, 1995.

Thompson, H. P. *Into All Lands: The History of the Society for the Propagation of the Gospel in Foreign Parts, 1701–1950*. London: SPCK, 1951.

Thompson, James W. "Paul as Missionary Pastor." In *Paul as Missionary: Identity, Activity, Theology, and Practice*, edited by Trevor J. Burke and Brian S. Rosner, 25-36. Library of New Testament Studies 420. London: T&T Clark, 2011.

Thompson, James Westfall. *The Decline of the Missi Dominici in Frankish Gaul.* Chicago: The University of Chicago Press, 1903.

Thompson, Mark D. "The Missionary Apostle and Modern Systematic Affirmation." In *The Gospel to the Nations: Perspectives on Paul's Mission*, edited by Peter Bolt and Mark Thompson, 365-82. Downers Grove, IL: InterVarsity Press, 2000.

Throop, Susanna. "Vengeance and the Crusades." In *Crusades*, edited by Benjamin Z. Kedar and Jonathan Riley-Smith, 5:21-38. Society for the Study of the Crusades and the Latin East. Hampshire, UK: Ashgate, 2006.

Tiedemann, R. G. "China and Its Neighbours." In *A World History of Christianity*, edited by Adrian Hastings, 369-415. Grand Rapids: Eerdmans, 1999.

Tolan, John. *Saint Francis and the Sultan: The Curious History of a Christian-Muslim Encounter*. Oxford: Oxford University Press, 2009.

Tomlinson, Dave. *Re-enchanting Christianity: Faith in an Emerging Culture.* Norwich: Canterbury, 2008.

Townsend, John T. "Missionary Journeys in Acts and European Missionary Societies." *Anglican Theological Review* 68, no. 2 (April 1986): 99-104.

Tracy, James D. "Introduction." In *The Political Economy of Merchant Empires*, edited by James D. Tracy, 1-21. Studies in Comparative Early Modern History. New York: Cambridge University Press, 1991.

Translation of the New Testament . . . from the Latin Vulgate. London, 1823.

Twain, Mark. *The Adventures of Tom Sawyer.* The Mark Twain Library. Berkeley: University of California Press, 1982.

Tyerman, Christopher. *The Debates on the Crusades.* Issues in Historiography. Manchester, UK: Manchester University Press, 2011.

———. *Fighting for Christendom: Holy War and the Crusades.* Oxford: Oxford University Press, 2004.

———. *God's War: A New History of the Crusades.* Cambridge, MA: Harvard University Press, 2006.

———. *The Invention of the Crusades.* Toronto: University of Toronto Press, 1998.

Ustorf, Werner. "1910–2010: From Foreign Mission to the Home Policies of a World Religion." In *Walk Humbly with the Lord: Church and Mission Engaging*

Plurality, edited by Viggo Mortensen and Andreas Østerlund Nielsen, 35-42. Grand Rapids: Eerdmans, 2010.

——. "Vasco Da Gama and the Periodization of Christian History." In *Identity and Marginality: Rethinking Christianity in North East Asia*, 89-97. Frankfurt am Main: Peter Lang, 2000.

Van Dam, Raymond. "Hagiography and History: The Life of Gregory Thaumaturgus." *Classical Antiquity* 1, no. 2 (October 1982): 273-308.

Van der Water, Desmond, ed. *Postcolonial Mission: Power and Partnership in World Christianity*. Upland, CA: Sopher, 2011.

Van Gelder, Craig, and Dwight J. Zscheile. *The Missional Church in Perspective: Mapping Trends and Shaping the Conversation*. The Missional Network. Grand Rapids: Baker Academic, 2011.

Van Rheenen, Gailyn. *Missions: Biblical Foundations & Contemporary Strategies*. Grand Rapids: Zondervan, 1996.

Vedder, Henry C. *A Short History of Baptist Missions*. Philadelphia: Judson, 1927.

Veer, Peter van der. *Imperial Encounters: Religion and Modernity in India and Britain*. Princeton, NJ: Princeton University Press, 2001.

Verkuyl, Johannes. *Contemporary Missiology: An Introduction*. Grand Rapids: Eerdmans, 1978.

Verlinden, Charles. *The Beginnings of Modern Colonization: Eleven Essays with an Introduction*. Translated by Yvonne Freccero. Ithaca, NY: Cornell University Press, 1970.

Vicaire, M. H. *The Apostolic Life*. Chicago: Priory, 1966.

Vicedom, Georg F. *Missio Dei: Einführung in Eine Theologie Der Mission*. München: Chr. Kaiser Verlag, 1958.

Visser 't Hooft, W. A. "The Asian Churches in the Ecumenical Movement." In *A Decisive Hour for the Christian Mission: The East Asia Christian Conference 1959 and the John R. Mott Memorial Lectures*, 46-58. London: SCM Press, 1960.

Vose, Robin J. E. *Dominicans, Muslims and Jews in the Medieval Crown of Aragon*. Cambridge Studies in Medieval Life and Thought. Cambridge: Cambridge University Press, 2009.

Wagner, C. Peter. *Acts of the Holy Spirit: A Modern Commentary on the Book of Acts*. Ventura, CA: Regal Books, 2000.

Waitley, Denis. *Empires of the Mind: Lessons to Lead and Succeed in a Knowledge-Based World*. London: N. Brealey, 1995.

Walker, G. S. M. "St. Columban: Monk or Missionary?" In *The Mission of the Church and the Propagation of the Faith: Papers Read at the Seventh Summer Meeting and the Eight Winter Meeting of the Ecclesiastical History Society,* edited by G. J. Cuming, 39-44. Studies in Church History 6. Cambridge: Cambridge University Press, 1970.

Walls, Andrew F. "The Eighteenth-Century Protestant Missionary Awakening in Its European Context." In *Christian Missions and the Enlightenment,* edited by Brian Stanley, 22-44. Studies in the History of Christian Missions. Grand Rapids: Eerdmans, 2001.

―――. "Eusebius Tries Again: The Task of Reconceiving and Re-visioning the Study of Christian History." In *Enlarging the Story: Perspectives on Writing World Christian History,* edited by Wilbert R. Shenk, 1-21. Maryknoll, NY: Orbis Books, 2002.

―――. *The Missionary Movement in Christian History: Studies in Transmission of Faith.* Maryknoll, NY: Orbis Books, 1996.

―――. "Structural Problems in Mission Studies." *International Bulletin of Missionary Research* 15, no. 4 (October 1991): 146-55.

Ward, Benedicta, and G. R. Evans. "The Medieval West." In *A World History of Christianity,* edited by Adrian Hastings, 110-46. Grand Rapids: Eerdmans, 1999.

Ware, James P. *The Mission of the Church in Paul's Letter to the Philippians in the Context of Ancient Judaism.* Supplements to Novum Testamentum 120. Leiden, The Netherlands: Brill, 2005.

Warneck, Gustav. *Outline of a History of Protestant Missions from the Reformation to the Present Time.* New York: Fleming H. Revell, 1901.

―――. *Outline of a History of Protestant Missions from the Reformation to the Present Time. A Contribution to Modern Church History.* New York: Fleming H. Revell, 1902.

Webb, Diana. *Medieval European Pilgrimage, c.700–c.1500.* European Culture and Society. New York: Palgrave, 2002.

―――. *Pilgrims and Pilgrimages in the Medieval West.* London: I. B. Tauris, 1999.

Webster, Douglas. "Missionary, The." In *Concise Dictionary of the Christian World Mission.* World Christian Books. London: Lutterworth, 1971.

―――. *Yes to Mission.* New York: Seabury, 1966.

Weiner, E. "Mission." In *The Oxford English Dictionary.* Oxford: Oxford University Press, 2004.

Weinlick, John R. *Count Zinzendorf: The Story of His Life and Leadership in the Renewed Moravian Church.* Bethlehem, PA: Moravian Church in America, 1989.

Welsh, R. E. *Challenge to Christian Missions: Missionary Questions and the Modern Mind.* New York: Young People's Missionary Movement, 1908.

Welz, Justinian von. *Justinian Welz: Essays by an Early Prophet of Missions.* Edited by James A. Scherer. Christian World Mission Books. Grand Rapids: Eerdmans, 1969.

———. *Der Missionsweckruf des Baron Justinian von Welz in treuer Wiedergabe des Originaldruckes vom Jahre 1664.* Leipzig: Akademische Buchhandlung, 1890.

White, Hayden V. *The Content of the Form: Narrative Discourse and Historical Representation.* Baltimore: Johns Hopkins University Press, 1990.

———. *Metahistory: The Historical Imagination in Nineteenth-Century Europe.* Baltimore: Johns Hopkins University Press, 1973.

———. *Tropics of Discourse: Essays in Cultural Criticism.* Baltimore: Johns Hopkins University Press, 1978.

White, Hugh Vernon. *A Theology for Christian Missions.* New York: Willett, Clark, 1937.

White, Newport J. D. "St. Patrick: Introduction." In *St. Patrick, His Writings and Life*, translated by Newport J. D. White, 1-28. Translations of Christian Literature, Series V: Lives of the Celtic Saints. London: Society for Promoting Christian Knowledge, 1920.

Wilfred, Felix. "From World Mission to Global Christianities: A Perspective from the South." In *From World Mission to Inter-Religious Witness*, 13-26. Concilium 2011/1. London: SCM Press, 2011.

Williams, Joel F. "Conclusion." In *Mission in the New Testament: An Evangelical Approach*, edited by William J. Larkin Jr. and Joel F. Williams, 239-47. American Society of Missiology Series 27. Maryknoll, NY: Orbis Books, 1998.

———. "The Missionary Message of the New Testament." In *Discovering the Mission of God: Best Missional Practices of the 21st Century*, edited by Mike Barnett and Robin Martin, 49-67. Downers Grove, IL: InterVarsity Press, 2012.

Willibald. *The Life of Saint Boniface.* Translated by George W. Robinson. Harvard Translations. Cambridge, MA: Harvard University Press, 1916.

Willis, Avery. *The Biblical Basis of Missions.* Nashville: Convention, 1986.

Wilson, Stephen G. *The Gentiles and the Gentile Mission in Luke–Acts.* Cambridge: Cambridge University Press, 1973.

Wolter, Hans. "Elements of Crusade Spirituality in St. Ignatius." In *Ignatius of Loyola, His Personality and Spiritual Heritage, 1556–1956: Studies on the 400th Anniversary of His Death*, edited by Fredrich Wulf, translated by Louis W. Roberts, 97-134. Modern Scholarly Studies about the Jesuits, in English Translations 2. St. Louis: Institute of Jesuit Sources, 1977.

Wood, Ian. "The Mission of Augustine of Canterbury to the English." *Speculum* 69, no. 1 (January 1994): 1-17.

———. *The Missionary Life: Saints and the Evangelisation of Europe, 400–1050*. Harlow, UK: Longman, 2001.

World Council of Churches. *Statements of the World Council of Churches on Social Questions*. 2nd ed. Geneva: Department on Church and Society, Division of Studies, 1956.

World Council of Churches, and World Conference on Mission and Evangelism. *"You Are the Light of the World": Statements on Mission by the World Council of Churches 1980–2005*. Geneva: WCC Publications, 2005.

World Missionary Conference, 1910. 9 vols. Edinburgh: Oliphant, Anderson & Ferrier, 1910.

Wright, Christopher J. H. *The Mission of God: Unlocking the Bible's Grand Narrative*. Downers Grove, IL: IVP Academic, 2006.

Wright, Jonathan. *God's Soldiers: Adventure, Politics, Intrigue, and Power; A History of the Jesuits*. New York: Doubleday, 2004.

———. *The Jesuits: Missions, Myths, and Histories*. London: HarperCollins, 2004.

Wright, N. T. *Jesus and the Victory of God*. Christian Origins and the Question of God 2. Minneapolis: Fortress, 1996.

———. *Paul and His Recent Interpreters: Some Contemporary Debates*. Minneapolis: Fortress, 2015.

———. *Paul and the Faithfulness of God*. Vol. 2. Minneapolis: Fortress, 2013.

Yoder, John H. "Reformation and Missions: A Literature Survey." In *Anabaptism and Mission*, edited by Wilbert R. Shenk, 40-50. Scottdale, PA: Herald, 1984.

Young, John M. L. *Missions: The Biblical Motive and Aim*. Pittsburgh: Crown & Covenant, 1964.

Youngman, Bernard R. *Into All the World: The Story of Christianity to 1066 A.D.* New York: St. Martin's, 1965.

Zinzendorf, Nicolaus Ludwig. *Christian Life and Witness: Count Zinzendorf's 1738 Berlin Speeches*. Edited by Gary Steven Kinkel. Princeton Theological Monograph Series 140. Eugene, OR: Pickwick, 2010.

———. "Des Ordinarii Fratrum Berlinische Reden (1738)." In *Hauptschriften*, edited by Erich Beyreuther and Gerhard Meyer, vol. 1. Darmstadt, Germany: Hildesheim, G. Olms Verlagsbuchhandlung, 1962.

———. "Die an Den Synodum Der Brüder in Zeyst, Vom 11. May Bis Den 21. Junii 1746, Gehaltene Reden." In *Hauptschriften*, edited by Erich Beyreuther and Gerhard Meyer, vol. 3. Hildesheim, Germany: Georg Olms Verlagsbuchhandlung, 1963.

———. *Die Wichtigsten Missionsinstruktionen Zinzendorfs*. Edited by O. Uttendörfer. Hefte Zur Missionskunde 12. Herrnhut, Germany: Verlag der Missionsbuchhandlung, 1913.

———. *Nine Public Lectures on Important Subjects in Religion: Preached in Fetter Lane Chapel in London in the Year 1746*. Edited by George W. Forell. Iowa City: University of Iowa Press, 1973.

———. *Texte zur Mission*. Hamburg: Wittig Verlag, 1979.

Zwemer, Samuel M. "Calvinism and the Missionary Enterprise." *Theology Today* 7 (1950): 206-16.

———. *Raymond Lull, First Missionary to the Moslems*. New York: Funk & Wagnalls, 1902.

Author Index

Subject Index

Scripture Index

Finding the Textbook You Need

The IVP Academic Textbook Selector
is an online tool for instantly finding the IVP books
suitable for over 250 courses across 24 disciplines.

ivpacademic.com